WRITTEN BY

RUBÉN MAESTRE

Data Science for SMEs and Freelancers

and Freelancers

What nobody tells you about how data can transform your business

"Success is no accident. It is hard work, perseverance, learning, studying, sacrifice and, above all, love for what you are doing or learning to do."

-- Pelé --

Table of Contents

Introduction

Haven't you heard that data is the new gold? If you haven't taken advantage of it yet, your business might be missing a unique opportunity. Until recently, only large companies had the power to transform data into accurate decisions, competitive advantages, and higher profits. Access to advanced tools, data analysis specialists, and cutting-edge technologies was a luxury few could afford. The rest of us watched from the sidelines, facing the daily challenge of running our SMEs, freelance businesses, or personal brands.

But that has changed. Technology has been democratized, and artificial intelligence has opened the door for anyone, regardless of their size, to use powerful analytics tools, many of them free. Data science is no longer a luxury; it's an accessible necessity that can make a difference for your business. If you have data, you have a goldmine to exploit. Now, the real question is: are you willing to take advantage of it?

This book is not just for tech experts. It's for you, whether you run an SME, are self-employed or a freelancer, and want to make smarter decisions, be more competitive, and transform your business with the power of data. If you've already taken your first steps into the world of data science, you probably remember how in Introduction to Data Science for SMEs and Freelancers I guided you so that, regardless of your previous experience, you could understand and apply the essential foundations of data science. My goal then was clear: to bring you closer to data analysis and use in a simple way, using accessible tools like Python and Excel, without getting lost in technicalities or intimidating formulas.

Then, with The Power of Data in Politics, I brought data science to a specific field, showing how its application can transform communication, strategy, and political management. You might not be passionate about politics, but that book also demonstrated how, through practical examples, the advanced tools, techniques, and libraries we explore have a direct and measurable impact on the reality of any sector.

Now, it's time to take it a step further. This book is designed to delve deeper into data science with an advanced approach, while keeping our feet on the ground: SMEs, freelancers, and independent professionals are our main focus. Here you'll find more complex concepts and practical applications that will help you make the most of your data, optimizing processes, improving your marketing, personalizing your offer, and predicting customer behavior. Yes, we'll talk more about Python, but with examples you can visualize in your daily work, always with a pragmatic and results-oriented approach.

And this doesn't stop here. I want to tell you that the next step in this series will focus on the world of sports, applying data science to sports management and performance, to show that from the field to the office, data can make a difference. But for now, let's focus on taking your business to a new level. Are you ready?

Data science is no longer a technical concept reserved for labs and large tech departments. Today, it is an indispensable tool in decision-making for any business, from the local corner shop to the freelancer looking to maximize time and resources. You don't need to be a programming expert to understand its value. Data science allows you to turn information chaos into concrete opportunities, make evidence-based decisions, and anticipate what's coming. In a market where every move counts, data is your best ally for minimizing risks and seizing every opportunity that arises.

Much of this transformation is due to artificial intelligence, which has democratized access to tools that were once unimaginable for small businesses and entrepreneurs. Today, any SME or freelancer can access technologies that allow them to segment their customers, personalize campaigns, automate processes, and predict trends with a level of precision that was once only available to large companies. With AI-based solutions, from simple analytics platforms to intelligent assistants, the path to optimization and growth is more open than ever. The challenge is no longer whether you can access these tools, but whether you're willing to make the most of them.

This democratization of technology has broken down the barriers that once separated small businesses from large corporations. Today, free or low-cost tools like Python, Google Data Studio, or interactive dashboards are within reach for any business, no matter how modest. These solutions allow SMEs and freelancers to compete on equal footing with market giants, extracting maximum value from their data and optimizing every aspect of their management.

The best part is that you don't need to be a data scientist to benefit from data analysis. With basic knowledge and a clear vision of your goals, you can start transforming your business. The key is to leverage these tools strategically, adapting them to your needs. It's not about becoming a technical expert, but about integrating data science into your daily routine to make more informed decisions, connect better with your customers, and discover new opportunities. The power is literally at your fingertips; now it's a matter of knowing how to use it to take your business to the next level.

With all these tools at your fingertips, it's time to move from theory to practice. Throughout this book, we'll explore concrete examples that you can apply directly to your business. We'll see how sales forecasting can help you anticipate your customers' needs, how to optimize inventory to reduce costs and maximize product availability, and how to segment your customers to personalize your offers and marketing campaigns. Data science isn't about abstract numbers; it's about solving real problems. Think about the last time you wondered why a customer stopped buying from you or how you could improve your stock flow. With a data-driven approach, these questions have practical answers that can make a difference in your day-to-day.

Adopting this approach not only involves using new tools, but also embracing a shift in mindset towards a 'data-driven' culture. This means that every decision you make, no matter how small, should be guided by data, not assumptions. Integrating data analysis into the DNA of your business will allow you to be more precise, minimize risks, and detect opportunities that others overlook. It's not about discarding intuition, but reinforcing it with real and valuable information. For your business to grow and prosper, you must be willing to rethink how you make decisions and how you use the data you already have at your disposal. This data culture is the foundation that will make every tool, every analysis, and every strategy truly work and generate results.

My journey into the world of data wasn't a planned path, but a natural process born from experience. For many years, I worked as a freelancer in digital marketing, immersed in campaigns that required constant analysis and precision to achieve results. It was this need to understand the data behind every click, every sale, and every campaign that led me to specialize as a data scientist. But my connection with analysis goes beyond marketing; I've always been surrounded by numbers, patterns, and statistics. In sports, every competition was a challenge that demanded analyzing metrics, performance, and behaviors. In politics and communication, I also found myself surrounded by data that could mean the difference between success and failure.

This experience has made me a cross-functional profile, with the ability to understand the dynamics of different businesses and sectors. But above all, it has taught me to be practical. It's not just about analyzing data; it's about solving problems, moving forward, and achieving concrete goals:

transforming sales, winning elections, or even leading a team to win a league championship.

Furthermore, I have the experience of being self-employed in my blood. I grew up watching my grandparents, parents, and uncles fight every day in their businesses, opening the shutters every morning and dealing with the daily challenges any small business faces. I know well those endless hours, the worries that don't stay at work when the shutters close, and the constant effort to improve, solve problems, or balance numbers on an Excel sheet. Yes, I've had moments when I thought about leaving it all behind and seeking the stability of a fixed salary. But those of us with an entrepreneurial spirit know that's impossible. As we say in my region, the goat always goes back to the mountain. My goal with this book is to help you make the most of your effort, using data so that every decision and every hour spent counts. Because, in the end, that's what it's all about: turning effort into results.

So here we are, you and I, ready to embark on this journey. The data is there, waiting for you to take it and turn it into your advantage. This is not an empty promise or an unattainable ideal; it is a real change within your reach. This book is your map, and each chapter is a tool to transform what seemed complicated into something powerful and useful for your business.

Remember, it's not about big leaps, but about consistent steps. You don't need to be perfect or know everything, just be willing to learn and apply what I share with you here. Your business, your daily effort, and your passion are the fuel; data is the spark that can ignite it all.

Now is your moment. Dare to take the first step, because every piece of data counts, every decision matters, and every small advance could be the one that makes the difference. Welcome to this transformation. Together, we will make every drop of sweat, every sacrifice, and every hour invested turn into the results you've always sought. Let's make it happen.

*"Some people want it to happen,
some wish it had happened,
others make it happen."*

■ Michael Jordan

Chapter 1 - Digital Transformation and Data in SMEs and Freelancers

1.1. The New Oil: How to Leverage Data to Boost Your Business

If there's one thing I've learned over the years working with businesses, in sports, digital marketing, communication, or politics, it's that data is everything. It's not an exaggeration or a cliché. We live in a world that moves faster and faster, and those who don't know how to adapt to the speed of change risk being left behind. But it's not just about surviving; it's about being competitive, leading, and staying ahead. In this context, data is the most powerful tool any business can have at its disposal.

We have reached what many call the era of 'Data-driven business,' a time when data is no longer a simple passive record of transactions or interactions. Today, data has become the main driver of the most accurate business decisions, and the companies that have understood this are making a difference. Those still guided by intuition, empirical experience, or worse, instinct, are at a clear disadvantage compared to those that have adopted a data-driven approach.

Why is it so crucial? Because data allows every decision to be grounded, reducing risks and increasing the chances of success. When I think about the impact of a decision made with evidence versus one based on assumptions, I see a huge difference. It's not just about having a rough idea of what might happen, but knowing precisely what could occur and how we can prepare for it. And this is where a big difference arises between traditional companies and those that have already understood the value of data.

The most successful companies I see today are those that have stopped relying on 'what has always worked' or gut feelings. They have transitioned to an approach where every decision, every strategic move, and every small operation is informed by real data. The clearest example of this transformation is giants like Amazon, Netflix, or Google. If we think about how they got to where they are, we find one constant: the intensive use of data. They don't rely on what their experience dictates or the intuition of their executives. Every new feature, every change in the interface, every personalized recommendation is the result of a deep analysis of millions of data points.

But not only these large companies can benefit from this approach. The interesting thing is that this model is entirely within reach of small and medium-sized enterprises. Today, any SME or freelancer with access to data, even if limited, holds a goldmine that, if well exploited, can provide them with an unprecedented competitive advantage. The key difference is not the amount of data, but how it is used. And this is where the key to success lies in the era of the 'Data-driven business.

One example I always like to highlight is how a data-driven decision can optimize marketing campaigns. Imagine you run an online store and have data on your customers' purchases: when they buy, which products they prefer, how many times they visit your site before making a purchase. With this information, you can not only personalize your promotions or adjust discounts, but also predict when a customer is most likely to make a purchase and which product generates the most interest. In other words, you can anticipate their needs.

Now, let's think about decisions based solely on intuition. When you base a marketing campaign or an advertising investment on your gut feeling, you're taking a huge risk. You might get it right, but you could also fail spectacularly. And in a world where the competition is using data to optimize every step they take, those mistakes can be very costly. Companies that have embraced the data-driven approach don't face that kind of uncertainty. For them, data is a continuous feedback mechanism, adjusting their strategies on the fly and allowing them to improve every action they take.

Moreover, data not only adds value when making strategic decisions but also in the day-to-day operations of a business. Operational decisions that often seem minor, such as adjusting stock, changing work shifts, or choosing which supplier to place an order with, can also greatly benefit from a data-driven approach. By having accurate information on customer behavior or market trends, companies can optimize their supply chain, adjust delivery times, or reduce operational costs.

And we can't forget a key factor: the difference between real-time data and historical data. Often, when we talk about the importance of data, we think of historical data, the kind we accumulate over time that allows us to see past patterns and behaviors. They are undoubtedly a valuable source of information for understanding what has happened and making decisions based on previous trends. But real-time data has changed the rules of the game. It's no longer just about looking to the past, but reacting to the present the moment it happens.

Let's take another practical example. An ecommerce company that monitors data in real time can identify a sudden increase in demand for a particular product due to an emerging trend on social media. With this information, they can quickly adjust their inventory, launch a promotion, or increase ad spending for that specific product. Meanwhile, companies that rely solely on historical data might not catch that trend until it's too late to capitalize on it.

Another advantage of the data-driven approach is the ability to monetize that data. The data economy is booming, and today data is not only an asset to improve your own operations but has also become a marketable product in itself. Large and small companies are beginning to sell, trade, or lease their data to other companies that can benefit from that information. If a small company has managed to obtain valuable data on consumer behavior in a specific niche, that data can be extremely valuable to larger companies looking to access the same market.

It's no longer just about obtaining data to improve your own business, but about knowing that this data can also generate additional revenue, even becoming an asset more valuable than many of the products or services being marketed. In this context, it's not an exaggeration to say that data is the new oil. Companies that have understood this are positioning themselves as leaders in their sectors, while those that have yet to embrace a data-driven culture are doomed to fall behind.

It is easy to see how this approach is transforming not only the way companies are managed but also the market as a whole. As more companies adopt the use of data in all areas—from marketing to logistics and finance—those that do not will become obsolete. Data not only allows companies to be more competitive but also more efficient and resilient in a world where change is the only constant.

In short, advancing in the use of data is not just business advice. It's a necessity. It's the path that will allow you to grow, adapt, and thrive in an increasingly unpredictable environment.

1.2. From looking at data to making it work for you

When we talk about data science and its application in the business world, we usually start with the basics: the data is there, and the first step is to understand it. This process of basic exploration, or what we technically know as Exploratory Data Analysis (EDA), is the beginning of any data science project, but it cannot stop there. The true value of data doesn't arise just from looking at it or understanding it, but from taking it one step further towards strategic implementation. This is where data begins to generate tangible value for companies, from the largest to the smallest.

In the early stages of any data science project, we usually work with a large amount of raw data. This data doesn't tell us anything at first, and our job is to explore it, understand its structure, and extract some initial insights. This exploration helps us identify patterns, detect outliers, find correlations, and ultimately get a clearer idea of what's happening within the company. This is the first step every SME should take when starting to work with data: understand what information they have and how it can be used.

The lifecycle of a data science project is based on this initial exploration step, but quickly extends to much more strategic phases. After exploring the data and gaining a basic understanding of what is happening, the next step is to design models that allow us to predict future behaviors or automate critical processes. A good example of this cycle is how a small business can move from asking, "Why are sales dropping this month?" to "How can I anticipate these sales declines and what measures should I take to prevent them in the future?

In this sense, I like to think of data science as an iterative process. It's not a linear path, but rather a series of cycles where initial exploration leads to deeper questions, and these, in turn, lead us to implement solutions based on models that we continuously improve and adjust. This is where the importance of iteration comes into play. We cannot simply apply a predictive model once and expect it to work forever. Companies and their markets are constantly changing, and models that work well today can become obsolete tomorrow. That's why, in any data science project, we must be willing to constantly review and adjust our strategies.

But what does 'implementing' data really mean? Often, when I talk to business owners, I notice a common confusion between exploring data and implementing it. Exploring data is a fairly passive activity: it's about looking at the past and understanding what has happened. It's a discovery phase, where the company gains insights that allow it to better understand its current situation. However, the strategic implementation of that data goes much further. Implementing means transforming those insights into concrete actions that impact the day-to-day operations of the business.

For example, let's imagine a small retail business that, after a data analysis, has identified that their sales drop during the first two weeks of every month, right after the monthly promotions. Exploring the data allows them to understand this pattern, but implementing that data means using the information to predict when those drops will happen again and taking measures to mitigate the impact. They could, for instance, automate the launch of specific promotions or discounts during those key weeks, ensuring that sales remain stable.

Implementing data can also involve developing more complex systems that not only help us predict future behavior but also automate real-time decisions. This is something that, until a few years ago, was only within the reach of large corporations, but today it is increasingly accessible for SMEs thanks to the growing availability of technological tools. From product recommendation systems based on customer purchasing habits to automated chatbots that offer personalized and efficient customer service, data science allows companies to optimize their processes and provide better experiences for their customers.

Let's take another example that illustrates this cycle from exploration to implementation: a small online store that, after analyzing user behavior data, discovers that a high percentage of customers abandon their carts right at the last stage of the purchasing process. This is a valuable insight that emerges in the data exploration phase, but to maximize its impact, it must be put into practice through strategic implementation. In this case, the company could choose to automate messages that remind the customer that they have products in their cart or, better yet, create a system that offers a personalized discount right at the moment of abandonment, incentivizing the final purchase.

This is how data is not only explored but integrated directly into business processes, creating a continuous cycle of improvement. By using predictive models and automation, the company no longer just responds to what has happened but can anticipate and make proactive decisions.

It's important to emphasize that this implementation doesn't have to be complex. In many SMEs, I see that the biggest obstacle is the perception that data science requires a complicated technological infrastructure or a specialized team to manage predictive models. Nothing could be further from the truth. There are increasingly accessible tools that allow data-driven solutions to be implemented without huge investments. Platforms like Google Cloud, Amazon Web Services (AWS), or Microsoft Azure offer solutions that allow predictive models and automated workflows to be implemented in a scalable way, tailored to each company's needs and capabilities.

Moreover, the project doesn't need to be ambitious from the start. In fact, it's preferable for SMEs to begin with small projects, focused on solving specific problems or improving particular processes. For example, a company could start by optimizing its inventory management, using historical data to predict demand and adjusting its orders accordingly. As the company becomes more familiar with the technology and sees the results of these implementations, it can start to scale its efforts and apply data science to other aspects of its operation.

A practical case I like to share is that of a small fashion store that, after conducting an exploratory analysis of its sales and customer data, identified that their stock of products regularly ran out in certain very popular sizes and colors. The exploratory analysis was a crucial first step: it allowed them to understand what was happening, but to solve this problem, they had to implement a predictive inventory system. This system not only adjusted their orders more precisely but also allowed them to automate stock management, avoiding both excess and shortages in their warehouse. The result was a significant improvement in customer satisfaction and an increase in sales, as they could always guarantee the availability of the most in-demand products.

Another typical case of data science implementation in SMEs is the use of predictive models for customer behavior. Imagine a service company that notices a drop in customer retention after the first year. After data analysis, they identify certain patterns in customer interactions that are directly correlated with their decision to continue using the service or not. Instead of just recording these patterns, the company implements a model that predicts when a customer is at risk of leaving the service and automates the offer of promotions or service improvements before that happens. Here, data science not only serves to explore what's happening but also to prevent future problems.

Ultimately, the transition from basic exploration to strategic implementation in data science is what makes the difference between understanding what has happened and taking control of what's to come. The SMEs that manage to move from the exploration phase to implementation are the ones that truly start to extract tangible value from the data, applying solutions that not only optimize their processes but also allow them to grow more efficiently and competitively. In this sense, it's not just about having data, but about making the data work for you, turning insights into concrete actions that improve every aspect of the business.

1.3. Data Science vs. Data Analysis

One of the most common mistakes I've seen among entrepreneurs who are starting to explore the world of data is the confusion between data science and data analysis. Although at first glance they might seem synonymous, they are very different concepts, and understanding the distinction between them is key to fully leveraging their potential in business. While data analysis is a fundamental part of the process, data science is a much broader and more complex field that encompasses various disciplines, from basic statistics to advanced techniques like machine learning and artificial intelligence.

I'm going to explain it from the simplest to the most advanced, because it's essential to understand this difference if we want to apply these concepts correctly in our SME or freelance business. Without this clear understanding, we risk staying on the surface, missing out on the full potential that data can offer us.

- **Data analysis: The starting point**

Data analysis is, without a doubt, the first step in any data-related process. It's the phase where we take available information and break it down to gain insights or conclusions about what is happening in our business. In simpler terms, data analysis focuses on describing what has happened or what is happening, using tools like basic statistics, graphs, and descriptive summaries.

For example, if you have an online store and analyze last month's sales, you're doing data analysis. The goal is to understand, from the numbers, which products sold the most, which were less successful, or on which days there was more web traffic. This is useful, no doubt, because it allows you to make more informed decisions about what worked and what didn't, but it's important to be clear that this approach is limited to looking at the past. Traditional data analysis, therefore, has a descriptive focus: it tells us what has happened and how the data is distributed, but it doesn't give us more answers.

Descriptive data analysis is usually based on basic statistical tools. In this sense, statistics are the natural starting point when working with data, as they allow you to synthesize large volumes of information into understandable metrics. Simple things like the mean, median, or standard deviations are part of this analysis. It also includes graphs, frequency tables, or scatter plots that help us visualize the data to find specific patterns or behaviors. But we don't stop there. This is where data science comes into play as a much deeper and more powerful discipline.

- **Data Science: A Comprehensive Approach**

Data science goes beyond descriptive analysis. While data analysis helps us look at the past and understand what has happened, data science takes a more comprehensive and predictive approach. It's about using advanced techniques that allow us not only to understand current data but also to predict what will happen in the future and automate decisions to improve outcomes.

While data analysis is part of the process, data science includes many more elements. It incorporates more advanced statistical techniques and also relies on disciplines like computer science, mathematics, and especially machine learning. Data science is more proactive than data analysis; it doesn't just settle for describing what has already happened, but aims to predict future behaviors, optimize processes, and generate value from the data.

Let's think about how this translates to the day-to-day operations of a company. While data analysis might indicate that a particular product was more successful in sales last month, data science would allow you, for example, to build a predictive model that anticipates the demand for that product in the coming months. Or even go further, developing an automated system that adjusts prices in real-time according to demand, market trends, or external conditions, thus optimizing sales without human intervention.

It's important to understand that data science integrates data analysis into its process but is not limited to it. This is just the starting point. Data science includes stages such as data collection, preprocessing (cleaning and preparation), developing predictive models, and implementing algorithms that enable automatic decision-making or real-time recommendations. It's a much more robust process that, over time, feeds on new data, creating a cycle of continuous improvement.

- **From basic statistics to machine learning**

One of the great pillars of data science is, without a doubt, statistics, but applied in a much more complex way than in conventional data analysis. Statistics remain at the core of much of the work we do in data science, as it allows us to model relationships between variables, make inferences, and validate hypotheses. However, as we work with more data and aim to answer more sophisticated questions, artificial intelligence and, in particular, machine learning become the key tools.

Traditional statistics focus on techniques like linear regression or analysis of variance (ANOVA), which are very useful when working with small amounts of data and wanting to find relationships between specific variables. But when we talk about large volumes of data (what is known as big data), classical statistics can fall short. This is where machine learning comes into play to help us process and analyze large amounts of information automatically and efficiently.

Machine learning, as an integral part of data science, allows us to create algorithms that learn from data, identify patterns, and make predictions without constant human intervention. For example, think of an online store that wants to predict which products will interest each customer on their next visit. By using machine learning, we can train a recommendation model that analyzes users' purchasing behavior and, based on that data, suggests products they are likely interested in, thus generating additional sales. These types of systems are very common on platforms like Amazon or Netflix, but today they are within reach of any SME looking to optimize its sales strategy.

The interesting thing about machine learning is that, unlike traditional statistics, it doesn't rely as much on prior assumptions. While in statistics it's essential to make hypotheses about the relationship between variables, machine learning algorithms can find patterns without us having to define those relationships beforehand. This makes machine learning especially useful when working with unstructured data (like text or images) or when the number of variables is too large to be handled by traditional statistical methods.

As a company evolves in its use of data, it usually goes through these different phases. Descriptive analysis is where it all begins: first, we look at the data to understand what has happened. Then, as we advance in the use of data science, we start applying machine learning techniques that allow us to predict and automate. Finally, when we have integrated data into business processes, we can develop complex artificial intelligence models that not only optimize decisions but also learn and improve continuously.

- ## Data Science Applied in Practice

Let's see how this translates into a practical example within the environment of an SME. Imagine you manage an online clothing store and, until now, you've been using basic data analysis to see which products sell the most each season. This has helped you adjust inventory, and it's a good start, but you know you can go further.

With data science, you could start analyzing not only what has been sold, but why it has been sold. Using machine learning techniques, you can train a model that analyzes your customers' behavior (their searches, the products they add to their cart, their purchase history) and, based on that data, predict what type of products they will prefer in the future. Not only that, you could also automate marketing campaigns that dynamically adjust promotions and discounts according to the likelihood that each customer will make a purchase.

This difference between data analysis and data science is the key to moving from observation to proactive action. With data analysis, you simply observe what has happened, but with data science, you prepare for what will happen and can optimize every aspect of your business to anticipate your customers' needs.

In summary, data science is a natural evolution of data analysis. While data analysis focuses on describing and understanding what has happened, data science is a much broader field that uses advanced tools like machine learning and artificial intelligence to predict, automate, and continuously improve business processes. By understanding this difference, you can ensure that your company doesn't just scratch the surface, but truly leverages the full potential that data has to offer.

1.4. Why data science is fundamental today

Today, it's hard to talk about business success without mentioning the impact of data. Digital transformation has radically changed the way companies operate, creating an environment where every interaction, every transaction, every action leaves a trail of valuable information. This explosion of data is both an opportunity and a challenge. Companies, regardless of their size, face the same reality: they must learn to manage and leverage this data strategically or risk being left behind. In this context, data science has become an essential tool, not just for large corporations, but also for small and medium-sized enterprises (SMEs) that want to stay competitive in a globalized and increasingly demanding market.

Digitalization has been one of the biggest drivers of growth and data accumulation in companies. Everything is digitized: from customer interactions through ecommerce platforms to internal operations like inventory management, finance, or human resources control. Every business process that was once manual is now carried out through digital systems, generating massive amounts of data. In the past, SMEs might have overlooked this asset, perhaps because they saw data as something reserved for large companies with enormous technological resources. But the reality is that all businesses, no matter how small, now have access to a volume of data that was previously unimaginable.

The problem is not so much the lack of data but the lack of strategy to manage it properly. This is where data science comes into play, providing the tools necessary for companies to organize, analyze, and extract value from the data they accumulate. And it's not just about creating reports or reviewing metrics; it's about leveraging data to improve decision-making, anticipate customer behavior, optimize operations, and automate processes. In an environment where competition is global and customer expectations are constantly changing, data is the competitive advantage that an SME needs to differentiate itself and grow.

Beyond digitalization, technological trends like the Internet of Things (IoT), Big Data, and machine learning are transforming industries at an unprecedented pace. Sometimes, when these terms are mentioned, small businesses see them as abstract concepts or something beyond their reach, but the reality is that many of these technologies are increasingly accessible and don't require large investments to start using them. The interesting thing about data science is that it offers scalable solutions: you can start with simple tools that meet immediate needs, and as your business grows, you can integrate more advanced technologies without a major technical leap.

The Internet of Things (IoT) is one of the biggest data generators in today's business environment. IoT connects physical devices with digital systems, allowing them to collect and transmit data in real time. From sensors in warehouses that monitor product storage conditions to devices that track the energy efficiency of a production plant, IoT is generating massive amounts of data that, if managed properly, can optimize a company's operations. For an SME, this can translate into better inventory management, greater resource efficiency, or the ability to identify problems before they become major costs. The most attractive aspect of IoT is that many solutions are already designed to be accessible and easy to implement, allowing small businesses to benefit from the technology without large resources.

Big Data, on the other hand, doesn't just refer to the massive accumulation of information, but also to the techniques and tools needed to process and analyze large volumes of data. For an SME, this might sound daunting at first, but with technological advances, it's no longer necessary to have huge infrastructures to take advantage of Big Data. There are cloud solutions like Google Cloud, AWS, or Microsoft Azure that allow you to process and analyze data on a large scale without needing your own servers or specialized technical teams. What's important here is to understand that Big Data is not just for large companies: an SME can use these tools to analyze the data it generates in its day-to-day operations and make more informed decisions, whether by adjusting its marketing strategy, better managing its supply chain, or personalizing the customer experience.

Machine learning is another technological trend that is revolutionizing the way companies use data. Through machine learning algorithms, a company can train models that learn from data and make predictions or recommendations automatically. Although the idea of machine learning may sound sophisticated, applications for SMEs are becoming increasingly simple and practical. A classic example is recommendation systems like those we see on platforms like Netflix or Amazon. But you don't have to be a large multinational to take advantage of this type of technology. A small online store can implement a recommendation system that analyzes customer purchasing behavior and suggests products they are more likely to be interested in. These personalized recommendations not only increase sales but also improve the customer experience, creating greater loyalty.

Machine learning also allows for the automation of processes that previously required constant supervision. For example, a company managing a large number of leads can use machine learning models to predict which customers are most likely to convert into actual sales. In this way, resources are allocated to the leads with the highest probability of success, improving efficiency and reducing sales effort.

Another key advantage of data science in today's context is that it's no longer necessary to have a team of data scientists to start reaping its benefits. Technology has been democratized, and nowadays any SME can access tools that were previously only available to large corporations. Open-source software has played a crucial role in this democratization, and languages like Python, with its libraries for data analysis and machine learning, have made it much more accessible to start working with data without a large budget. Tools like Google Colab or Jupyter Notebooks allow you to run machine learning models in the cloud without requiring complex infrastructure.

We cannot underestimate the impact these advances are having on how SMEs position themselves in the market. Those that adopt a data-driven approach are not only better prepared to respond to market changes, but they can also anticipate their customers' needs, optimize their operations, and find new business opportunities that would otherwise go unnoticed. Companies that do not take advantage of these trends risk becoming obsolete in an increasingly competitive and fast-paced environment.

The message here is clear: data science is not a luxury; it is a necessity to compete in today's world. It's not just about having access to data but knowing how to manage and leverage it strategically. In a world where digitalization is everywhere and technologies like IoT, Big Data, and machine learning are transforming industries, SMEs have an unprecedented opportunity to get ahead, optimize their resources, and offer more personalized experiences to their customers. The key is to take the first step, starting with accessible tools and growing from there.

1.5. What do you need before starting? Technical requirements and skills

When we decide to take the step towards data science in a small or medium-sized business, there is a fundamental point we cannot overlook: what do we need before we start? It's not just about having a clear idea of the potential that data can offer or understanding the value it brings to business decisions. It's crucial to have the right tools, the necessary technical infrastructure, and most importantly, the skills that allow us to turn that data into real and actionable results. Starting to work with data doesn't mean jumping into the void without preparation; on the contrary, it means creating a solid foundation upon which we can build effective analyses and well-founded strategies.

For an SME or freelancer looking to delve into the world of data science without facing insurmountable technical barriers, the first step is to have clarity about the essential tools and skills. This is where Python comes into play, the essential tool that serves as the foundation for much of the analysis and implementation in data science.

- **Python: the essential tool**

If you're already familiar with Python, you'll know it's not a new language, but its popularity has grown exponentially in the world of data science. And for good reason. Python offers a unique versatility that has made it one of the most used tools by both large corporations and small businesses looking to leverage the power of data. Its simplicity is one of its greatest strengths. You don't need to be an experienced programmer to start working with it, making it an excellent option for freelancers and SMEs that don't have large technical teams.

Python has a gentle learning curve, which means you can start writing code and see results without facing unnecessary complexities. But make no mistake: its simplicity is not a limitation. On the contrary, Python is supported by a massive community and an ecosystem of specialized libraries that make it extremely powerful when it comes to data analysis and machine learning.

Among the key libraries for data science in Python are Pandas and NumPy, which allow you to perform data manipulations and analysis efficiently. These libraries provide all the tools you need to work with large datasets, structure them, clean them, and extract the insights your business needs. Pandas, for example, is perfect for working with tabular data (like Excel), while NumPy specializes in more advanced numerical calculations. If you want to work with predictive models or implement machine learning algorithms, Scikit-learn is the library that will allow you to do so without complications.

Having covered Python in depth in a previous book, I just want to briefly remind you that if you already have some knowledge of this language, you'll be in a privileged position to advance more quickly. If you haven't delved deep yet, I recommend reviewing those fundamentals, as they will be the technical foundation on which we build all the analysis to come. Python is just the gateway, but it offers a wealth of resources that will facilitate the leap to more advanced data analysis.

- **Visual Studio Code and Jupyter Notebook**

Visual Studio Code (VSCode) and Jupyter Notebook are two of the most powerful and accessible tools for working in data science, especially if you're just starting out or if your goal is to integrate data analysis into the daily operations of your SME or freelance business. Both offer complementary approaches that, depending on the context and your level of experience, can be ideal for different phases of the project.

Starting with Visual Studio Code, the first thing to highlight is its versatility. Although VSCode has become one of the most popular tools among developers in general, its specific plugins and extensions for Python make it particularly valuable in data science. If you're working on more complex projects involving multiple Python scripts, database interactions, or integration with version control like Git, VSCode offers you a very comprehensive development environment.

The advantage of using VSCode in data science projects lies in its ability to handle large projects and offer you a space where you can have everything integrated: from data analysis to connecting with external systems, including process automation. Additionally, with its specific extensions for data science and machine learning, you can turn it into a tool customized to your needs.

Another key advantage of VSCode is its integration with Git, which makes collaborative work easier, especially if you have a small team managing different parts of the project. Version control is essential when working with data, as it allows you to test new approaches or modify models without fear of losing previous work, and it also provides a clear track of changes.

On the other hand, Jupyter Notebook is a particularly useful platform if you're just starting or if you prefer a more intuitive and visual approach to working with data. Unlike VSCode, Jupyter Notebook allows you to write code and see the results immediately, which is extremely useful when you're first exploring data or building simple models. The interesting thing about Jupyter is that you can not only see the results of your code immediately, but you can also document the entire process as you go, making it much easier to communicate your results to other team members or even to yourself in the future.

Jupyter Notebook is ideal for rapid prototyping and initial data exploration. You can run code snippets step by step, visualize charts and tables on the spot, and adjust calculations without restarting the entire process. This makes it an excellent tool for exploratory analysis and documenting your progress in real-time. Additionally, it allows you to easily share your analyses with others who may not be as familiar with programming, as they can read your notes alongside the code and results.

- ## Working with Data: Essential Skills

Data science, as the name suggests, revolves around data. And one of the most important skills anyone must develop to make the most of this field is data management. When we talk about data management, we mean the ability to manipulate, transform, and structure data efficiently. No matter how advanced the machine learning algorithms you choose to use; if you don't know how to properly handle your data, you won't be able to take advantage of it.

In this context, tools like Pandas and NumPy become fundamental once again. Both libraries allow you to manipulate large amounts of data efficiently, filter them, group them, and extract the insights that really matter. But it's not just a matter of tools; it's about developing a structured and methodical mindset for working with data. You'll need to know how to clean them, how to deal with missing or incorrect values, and how to structure the data so you can feed your predictive models efficiently.

Database knowledge is also an essential skill. Whether you're working with SQL, the most commonly used language for managing relational databases, or with NoSQL technologies to handle large volumes of unstructured data, such as document-oriented databases, you'll need to be familiar with how to access and extract data from these sources. After all, databases are where many companies store the bulk of their information, and knowing how to interact with them will give you invaluable access to that data.

- **Mental and Organizational Preparation**

Finally, and perhaps as important as the technical aspects, is the mental and organizational preparation. Data science is not just a technical discipline; it also requires an analytical mindset, curiosity, and openness to experimentation. I often encounter entrepreneurs who want quick and clear answers from data, but the reality is that working with data involves an iterative process. You must be willing to explore, test different approaches, adjust your hypotheses, and fail before reaching the right solution.

Success in data science is not about applying a magic formula, but about developing an inquisitive mindset, always questioning the results, looking for hidden patterns, and adjusting models. Patience and the ability to work in continuous improvement cycles are essential qualities.

In addition, the business organization must be aligned with this approach. Companies that make the most of their data not only have the right tools and skills, but they have also adopted a data-driven culture where all areas of the business are willing to make evidence-based decisions, and where collaboration between departments is encouraged. Make sure everyone in the organization understands the value of data and is willing to join this journey towards a more informed and efficient business.

With the right tools, the right mindset, and an organizational structure that supports data use, you'll be ready to make the most of data science in your SME or freelance business.

1.6. How the Cloud Transforms Data Access for Small Businesses

In the past, just thinking about working with large volumes of data, developing machine learning models, or carrying out advanced analyses required costly infrastructures, robust data centers, and dedicated IT teams. This was obviously out of reach for most SMEs or freelancers. However, this scenario has radically changed thanks to cloud solutions. Nowadays, cloud data infrastructure offers an accessible, flexible, and scalable alternative that allows small and medium-sized businesses to do all this without the need to invest in expensive hardware.

We've already discussed in depth the use of Python, machine learning, and other key tools like Pandas, NumPy, or Scikit-learn for working with data. What comes into play now is where and how we can do all this efficiently. It's not necessary for an SME to build and manage its own server or data center. Cloud solutions, such as Google Colab, Amazon Web Services (AWS), Microsoft Azure, or Google Cloud Platform (GCP), allow any company to access powerful computing and storage capabilities on demand, paying only for what they actually use.

The most immediate advantage of the cloud is its economic accessibility. A company no longer needs to buy expensive servers or worry about their maintenance. With platforms like Google Colab, which is free, any freelancer or small business can start working with Python and develop their own machine learning models without worrying about computing resources. Google Colab, for example, allows you to run code in the cloud without requiring major investments, and it also offers direct integration with libraries and tools we've mentioned earlier like Pandas, NumPy, and Scikit-learn, all without needing to install anything locally.

Another advantage of working in the cloud is automatic scalability. As a company grows and its data science projects become more complex, the cloud can automatically adjust to its needs. If you need more processing power or additional storage, cloud platforms provide it instantly and flexibly, allowing you to focus on your business rather than the technical infrastructure. This is especially useful when working with big data projects or machine learning models that require large amounts of data and computational capacity that couldn't be handled on a local computer.

Flexibility also plays a key role. Working in the cloud allows teams to access data and perform analyses from anywhere, facilitating collaboration among different team members, regardless of their location. Tools like Google Colab or Jupyter Notebooks, when used in a cloud environment, allow multiple users to work collaboratively in real-time, sharing code, results, and documentation without worrying about software compatibility or local installations.

Moreover, the cloud offers you the possibility to integrate advanced analytics tools without having to worry about technical configuration. On platforms like Google Cloud or AWS, you have access to a range of additional services that take your data science projects to the next level. For example, on Google Cloud, you can use BigQuery for analyzing large volumes of data, or even train and deploy machine learning models with AI Platform without the need for an advanced technical team.

Another important aspect is security. Although some companies are still hesitant to use the cloud due to security concerns, the main cloud computing platforms invest millions of dollars to ensure that your data is secure, encrypted, and accessible only to authorized users. This allows SMEs to have secure infrastructures without having to manage complex cybersecurity systems themselves.

In summary, cloud data infrastructure allows small businesses to access advanced technology without large initial investments. It's the perfect gateway to implementing data analytics, machine learning, and other solutions that until recently seemed reserved only for large corporations. The cloud democratizes access to technology, and if you're already familiar with the tools we've discussed, it allows you to move to the next level quickly and without major barriers.

Chapter 2 - Detect and Correct Critical Values in SME Data

2.1. Advanced data cleaning: detect and correct critical values

In the context of data science applied to SMEs, advanced data cleaning is a crucial step to ensure that analyses and predictive models are accurate and useful. One of the most complex aspects of this cleaning is the identification and handling of outliers. These values, which deviate significantly from the norm, can distort conclusions and lead to erroneous decisions if not managed correctly. In small and medium-sized enterprises, where every piece of data counts, detecting and dealing with outliers appropriately is essential to maximize the value of data analysis.

When we talk about small and medium datasets, the presence of outliers can have a disproportionate impact, as these anomalous points can skew the results of an analysis or model, severely affecting decision-making. For example, in the case of an SME managing a moderate volume of transactions or inventory, an outlier in sales figures could lead to incorrect predictions about future product demand or customer behavior.

- **Distance-based methods: Mahalanobis and its application in SMEs**

One of the most powerful techniques for detecting outliers in multidimensional datasets is the Mahalanobis method, which is based on the statistical distance between data points. Unlike traditional Euclidean distance, which measures the straight-line distance between two points, Mahalanobis distance takes into account the correlation between different variables in the dataset. This is especially useful in datasets with multiple interrelated variables, such as those containing customer, inventory, or sales data.

For an SME that collects data from various sources, such as sales records, customer profiles, and purchase preferences, the Mahalanobis method allows for the detection of anomalies in those data by considering how each variable relates to the others. For example, if a customer makes an unusually large purchase but does not have a consistent purchase history with that type of spending, Mahalanobis would detect this transaction as an outlier based on the correlation between purchase frequency, average transaction value, and other factors.

The use of this method in a company that manages data across multiple dimensions, such as sales, inventories, and customers, can help identify anomalous patterns that would otherwise go unnoticed if the variables were considered in isolation. Additionally, by taking into account the relationships between variables, the Mahalanobis distance is particularly useful for avoiding false positives, meaning situations where an observation might appear to be an outlier when it is not, considering the complete context.

- **Techniques based on clustering: Using k-means for outlier detection**

Another useful technique for detecting outliers in more complex datasets is clustering, particularly with the k-means algorithm. The goal of k-means is to divide the data into groups or clusters of observations that are similar to each other, based on the proximity between observations. Outliers, in this case, would be those points that do not clearly belong to any of the clusters or fall outside the formed groups.

For an SME, using k-means can be extremely beneficial in analyzing customer data. For example, by applying this algorithm to a dataset containing information about purchase preferences, visit frequency, and transaction value, you can identify natural clusters of customers with similar behavior patterns. Customers whose characteristics don't clearly fit into any of these groups could be considered outliers.

This approach is particularly useful when outliers are not necessarily extreme in a single dimension, but behave differently when considering multiple variables simultaneously. For example, a customer might have a normal purchase frequency but an exceptionally high or low transaction value, making them an outlier in the context of their group.

The use of k-means can also be applied to inventory management. In this case, we could group products based on their sales frequency, popularity at certain times of the year, and profit margins. Products that don't fit into any of the formed clusters could represent exceptions, such as items that sell unexpectedly or have atypical demand behavior. Detecting these outliers can help make more informed inventory decisions, adjusting demand forecasts or identifying possible issues in the supply chain.

• Predictive models for outlier detection: Linear regression and decision trees

In addition to distance-based methods and clustering, a third effective technique for detecting outliers is the use of predictive models, both simple and advanced. In its most basic form, a linear regression model can be used to predict the expected value of a variable based on other variables in the dataset. If the observed value deviates significantly from what the model predicts, we can consider this observation an outlier.

In an SME, linear regression could be applied to predict a product's sales volume based on variables such as price, active promotions, and historical sales trends. If in a given month the sales volume deviates significantly from what the model predicts, this could indicate an outlier. This approach is useful when the relationships between variables are clear and linear, and the model can fit the data well.

However, when the relationships between variables are more complex, we may need to resort to more advanced models, such as decision trees. These models are particularly useful because they not only detect outliers but also provide a clear visualization of how different variables contribute to the final outcome. Additionally, decision trees are robust against outliers as they divide the dataset into smaller branches, allowing outliers to be isolated without affecting the rest of the analysis.

In an e-commerce store, for example, we could use a decision tree to predict customer behavior based on variables such as visit frequency, purchase history, and average transaction value. If we find customers whose behavior does not fit any of the tree's branches, this could indicate the presence of an outlier that might require further analysis. Additionally, by using decision trees, we can better understand the interactions between different variables, allowing us to adjust business strategies more effectively.

A key advantage of predictive models is that they not only identify outliers, but they can also help predict future atypical behaviors. For example, if a customer is about to end their relationship with a company (known as churn), a predictive model based on their historical behavior can detect early signs of this situation and allow the company to take preventive measures, such as offering personalized promotions or improving customer service.

- **Outliers: when to remove them and when to harness their hidden potential**

Once outliers have been identified, the next step is to decide how to handle them. In some cases, it may be appropriate to remove outliers if we are sure they represent data errors. For example, if we find a sales value that is clearly an input error (such as a product sold at a ridiculously low or high price), removing this outlier may be the best option.

In other cases, outliers can represent exceptional behaviors that deserve more attention. For example, a customer making an unusually large purchase could be a key client requiring special treatment, or a product showing atypically high demand might represent a business opportunity not previously detected. Instead of removing these outliers, we might want to investigate them further to understand their cause and potentially adjust our strategies accordingly.

It is also important to note that not all outliers are problematic. In many cases, outliers can provide valuable insights into customer behavior or market conditions. Therefore, the treatment of outliers must be done carefully, ensuring that we are not removing useful information along with the anomalous data.

In summary, advanced outlier treatment in small and medium datasets is essential to ensure the quality of analysis and predictions in an SME. From using the Mahalanobis distance and k-means to linear regression and decision trees, there are multiple approaches to detect and manage these outliers. The most important thing is that, regardless of the method we choose, properly handling outliers allows us to make better business decisions, optimizing both data analysis and the commercial strategies based on them.

- **Transform your incomplete data into precise decisions**

When we talk about handling inconsistent or missing data in an SME, we're addressing a problem that's much more common than you might think. Any business owner who's managed a customer database or an inventory system knows that data quality is rarely perfect. Data entry errors, incomplete records, or inconsistencies in system updates are frequent issues, and if not handled correctly, they can lead to errors in analysis and business decisions based on faulty data.

One of the main challenges small and medium-sized enterprises face is how to handle missing values. These can appear as missing data in critical fields, such as a customer's purchase history, the date of their last interaction, or even the type of product they bought. Instead of ignoring or removing this incomplete data, which could lead to losing valuable information, there are imputation techniques that allow you to estimate these missing values, maintaining the integrity of the dataset and improving the accuracy of any subsequent analysis.

One technique that has proven particularly effective in small or medium datasets is imputation using the K-Nearest Neighbors (KNN) algorithm. The principle behind KNN is relatively simple yet powerful: when a data point is missing in a record, it looks for the closest or most similar records and uses the value from these 'neighbors' to fill the missing field. This proximity is measured based on the available features, so the closest neighbors in the data space are the most similar to the incomplete record.

For example, if you have a customer for whom you lack data on their purchase frequency, you could use information from other customers who share similar characteristics (such as average purchase value, geographic location, or preferred product types) to estimate what their purchase frequency might be. This approach is particularly useful when the volume of data is limited and every observation counts, as it not only allows you to keep the dataset complete, but also enhances the robustness of any subsequent analysis.

The advantage of using KNN for imputation is that it considers the similarities between observations, allowing for more accurate estimates compared to simpler methods like mean or median imputation. These more rudimentary methods can introduce biases by assuming that all records are the same, whereas KNN takes into account the specific characteristics of each customer or transaction, enabling a more personalized and precise approach.

However, as the volume of data grows, KNN may not always be the best option. Calculating distances between each point can become computationally expensive when the dataset reaches a certain size, leading to longer processing times and higher resource demands. For SMEs handling a moderate but growing volume of data, a more efficient alternative might be using predictive models like decision trees or neural networks, which can be trained to predict missing values based on the other available variables.

For example, in an online store, we might have a decision tree model trained to predict customers' monthly spending based on their purchase history, how often they visit the store, and the products they usually buy. If a customer has missing data regarding their monthly spending, the model could predict this value based on the characteristics of similar customers. The great advantage of decision trees is their ability to handle non-linear relationships between variables, making them a flexible and powerful tool for imputing missing data.

Another robust option for imputation is the use of multiple regression models, which allow you to predict the missing value of a variable based on several other predictor variables. This approach is particularly useful when the data follows a predictable pattern or when there is a clear relationship between the different variables in the dataset. For example, in a food distribution business, we could use a regression model to predict the sales volume in a store, using predictor variables such as geographic location, the number of regular customers, and active promotions. If sales data for a particular store is missing for a given month, the model can generate a prediction based on the values of the other variables.

In addition to methods based on KNN and regression, for SMEs that handle a larger volume of data, there's another very effective technique known as multiple imputation. This technique not only imputes a single value for each missing data point but generates several possible imputations, creating multiple complete datasets. Subsequently, the analysis is performed on each of these imputed datasets, and the results are combined to obtain a final estimate that better reflects the uncertainty generated by the missing data. This technique is especially useful when there is a large amount of missing data, and we want to avoid overconfidence in the results.

In any case, it's important to remember that there isn't a single perfect solution for all cases of missing values. The choice of method will depend on the volume of data, the business context, and the available resources. In SMEs, where technical and human resources are often limited, the key is to find a balance between precision and efficiency. Correctly imputing missing data is essential to ensure that subsequent analysis is reliable, as ignoring or systematically removing missing data can lead to a loss of crucial information.

Finally, we can't discuss handling inconsistent data without addressing automatic error correction. Often, errors in data aren't just missing values but stem from inconsistencies or entry errors, such as incorrect formats, duplicates, or clearly erroneous values. Cross-validation during data entry is a fundamental technique to minimize these types of errors. Establishing quality controls in the data collection and entry process, such as restricting the types of values that can be entered in a specific field or using validation rules that compare the new data with existing ones, can significantly reduce the occurrence of errors in databases.

In summary, handling inconsistent or missing data is a crucial aspect for any SME that wants to get the most out of its data. From KNN imputation for small datasets to more advanced techniques like multiple regression or multiple imputation for larger volumes of data, the goal is always to preserve the integrity of the dataset and avoid losing valuable information. Implementing validation systems during data entry, along with a clear strategy for managing missing values, ensures that any subsequent analysis is based on complete and accurate data, which ultimately translates into better business decisions.

- **Eliminate errors and improve your decisions with advanced data control**

When working with data, especially in the context of an SME, data quality is a critical factor that can determine the success or failure of any analysis-based initiative. Data entry, whether through sales systems, inventories, or CRMs, is prone to errors that, if not corrected, can spread and severely affect the conclusions drawn from subsequent analysis. This is where advanced error correction techniques come into play, aiming not only to detect inconsistencies but also to establish preventive and corrective mechanisms to ensure that the data is as accurate as possible.

One of the most useful tools in this regard is the automatic correction of input errors through cross-validation. When we talk about cross-validation, we mean establishing rules and controls that ensure the data entering the system meets the established consistency criteria. In an SME, where data can come from various sources, such as sales systems, e-commerce platforms, or inventory management tools, it's essential that all this data aligns correctly and doesn't contain errors that could affect operations.

For example, in an inventory system, it's common for errors to occur when manually entering product codes or available quantities. Cross-validation could implement rules that check whether the product code already exists in the database before allowing the quantity to be entered. This way, any typographical or formatting errors can be detected and corrected before the incorrect data is stored in the system. This type of validation can also be applied in CRMs to ensure that customer data, such as emails or phone numbers, follow a correct and consistent format.

Beyond cross-validation during data entry, SMEs can benefit from implementing automatic controls that verify consistency between different databases or information sources. Imagine a store managing its inventory both online and in physical locations. The online and in-store sales management systems might not be fully synchronized, leading to inconsistencies in available stock on each platform. By setting up cross-validations between the different systems, discrepancies in inventory can be detected, such as products shown as available online but not in-store, and vice versa. This automatic control not only reduces human error but also improves operational efficiency by preventing sales of products that are no longer available.

Another powerful technique in automatic error correction is the automated analysis of recurring error patterns. Often, data errors don't occur in isolation but follow certain patterns or trends that, if detected early, can be corrected before causing bigger issues. This is where using Python scripts becomes invaluable. With Python, we can write custom scripts that analyze large volumes of data and detect common error patterns, such as duplicates, incorrect formats, or inconsistencies between different fields.

For example, if an SME detects frequent duplications in its customer database (multiple entries for the same customer), a Python script can be written to analyze the database for matches between names, email addresses, or phone numbers that are repeated. This script could use techniques like fuzzy matching, which not only looks for exact matches but also for similarities, to detect possible duplicates entered with slight variations in spelling or format. Once the duplicate records are identified, the script can automatically merge them or flag suspicious cases for manual review, saving time and reducing the risk of losing valuable information.

The use of Python scripts also allows for automating the detection of formatting errors in large datasets. For example, if a company collects customer data that includes phone numbers, email addresses, or postal codes, some of these data may not follow the proper format. A script can automatically review all records, checking that email addresses contain the

"@" symbol or that phone numbers have the correct length. Moreover, we can extend this automated analysis to detect anomalies in numerical fields, such as prices or quantities, that are outside an expected range.

Let's take the case of a wholesale company. If the inventory management system receives an entry indicating that there are 100,000 units of a product available, when the average stock is usually 1,000 units, this type of anomaly may indicate an input error. An automated Python script could detect these outliers by comparing new entries with the historical range of values and alert the operations team before the error affects purchasing or sales decisions.

Automated error analysis can also be applied to improve the quality of data coming from external sources or multiple systems. If an SME uses different platforms to manage its inventory and sales, it's common for the data between these systems not to align perfectly. For example, one platform might report sales in one currency and another in a different one, or the product codes might slightly vary between systems. A Python script can review all these details and ensure that the data is integrated coherently, unifying formats and detecting discrepancies before they affect the overall analysis.

In summary, using advanced techniques for error correction in data is essential for any SME looking to maintain data quality in an environment where data comes from multiple sources and systems. From cross-validation at data entry to automated error pattern analysis using Python scripts, these tools not only improve data accuracy but also save time and resources by preventing costly errors before they spread throughout the company. Applying these controls ensures that data-driven business decisions are reliable and that operations remain efficient, allowing the company to focus on growth and continuous improvement.

2.2. Unifying Data for a Complete Business View

The combination and merging of datasets is an essential step in any data analysis process, especially in the SME environment, where data often comes from multiple sources that are not perfectly aligned. In many small and medium-sized enterprises, it's common to use different systems to manage operations. For example, billing systems, CRM, or online sales

DATA SCIENCE FOR SMES AND FREELANCERS

platforms can generate datasets that don't share the same keys or identifiers. This lack of alignment is a major challenge, as it makes it difficult to consolidate the data into a single, coherent, and accurate set.

- ### Overcome the challenge of imperfect keys in data merging

The challenge of merging datasets with imperfect keys arises when companies try to combine data from different sources that aren't fully synchronized. In an SME, for example, you might have a sales system that records customer information with a unique identifier and a CRM that stores additional data about those same customers, but with slight differences in the way the information is recorded. In these cases, traditional join methods or simple combinations based on exact keys fail, as a small error in the name, address, or any other field can cause records not to match correctly. This is where imperfect matching techniques, like fuzzy matching, come into play.

Fuzzy matching is a flexible approach to data merging when exact matches are not possible. Instead of looking for a perfect match between key values, fuzzy matching uses algorithms that measure the similarity between text strings, allowing you to match records that are similar but not identical. This is especially useful when working with customer names, addresses, or products that may have been entered with slight variations or typos. A customer registered as 'José Pérez' in the sales system might appear as 'Jose Perez' in the CRM, and while these two names don't match exactly, they are similar enough to be considered the same customer. The goal of fuzzy matching is to identify these close matches and treat them as a single entity, facilitating the merging of datasets.

To effectively implement fuzzy matching in an SME, one of the most useful tools is FuzzyWuzzy, a Python library that specializes in comparing text strings using similarity ratios. This tool is based on the Levenshtein algorithm, which measures the distance between two sequences of characters by calculating the minimum number of operations needed to transform one string into another. FuzzyWuzzy allows you to define a similarity threshold, so that only matches exceeding a certain percentage are considered valid. For example, if we set a similarity threshold of 90%, only those records that are at least 90% similar will be combined.

In practice, implementing FuzzyWuzzy in an SME can be key to consolidating customer databases from different platforms. Imagine you have a customer database from an invoicing system and another from a CRM. Although both systems contain information about the same customers, there are likely differences in how their names or addresses were recorded. By using FuzzyWuzzy, we can compare these records and find those that, while not exact matches, are similar enough to be treated as the same customer. This way, we can merge the databases and obtain a unique and complete set of customers, without unnecessary duplications and with greater data accuracy.

The use of fuzzy matching also extends to merging data from suppliers or products from different sources. In an SME that works with several suppliers, product names or supplier identifiers may not be perfectly aligned across different platforms. For example, the same supplier might be registered as "Distribuidora XYZ" in the purchasing system, but as "Dist XYZ" in the inventory system. These small discrepancies can cause problems when trying to perform a comprehensive data analysis, such as evaluating supplier performance or tracking inventory. By applying fuzzy matching, we can match these similar records and consolidate supplier or product information into a single, coherent dataset.

Another common challenge in merging datasets in SMEs is managing data quality after the merge. Even after applying fuzzy matching techniques, it's crucial to verify that the combined data is consistent and accurate. This involves performing quality checks to ensure that no unnecessary duplicates have been created or that the close matches are indeed correct. For instance, if records of two customers that are very similar but actually different people, like "Juan García" and "Juana García", are merged, this could cause problems in subsequent analysis. Therefore, it's advisable to conduct a manual review of the closest matches to avoid merging errors.

In addition to FuzzyWuzzy, there are other tools and approaches that can improve the process of merging datasets in SME environments. For example, you can use pandas, a widely used Python library for data analysis, to perform a merge between datasets by applying specific matching conditions on the keys. Pandas allows you to combine datasets not only based on exact matches but also on value ranges or logical conditions, providing greater flexibility when managing data from different sources that aren't always perfectly aligned.

For SMEs that handle large amounts of data from multiple sources, the ability to effectively combine and merge datasets is essential to gain a complete view of the business. Whether we're talking about consolidating data from customers, suppliers, inventory, or sales, using techniques like fuzzy matching allows companies to overcome the challenges posed by imperfect keys and achieve a unified dataset that more accurately reflects the reality of the business. This not only facilitates data analysis but also improves decision-making by providing a cleaner and more consistent database.

In conclusion, merging datasets with imperfect keys is a challenge that many SMEs face when working with data from different systems. Using advanced techniques like fuzzy matching with tools such as FuzzyWuzzy in Python allows you to overcome this obstacle, providing an efficient way to combine similar records and improve the overall quality of the data. Implementing these techniques is key to ensuring that data analysis is based on accurate and complete information, which in turn enhances the company's ability to make informed and strategic decisions.

- ## Advanced join for integrating heterogeneous data sources

Managing large volumes of data in SMEs requires careful execution of joins between different datasets, especially when working with various data sources such as transactional databases and social media data. These joins are essential to obtain a more complete and enriched view of the information handled by the company, enabling the connection of data that would otherwise remain siloed. However, one of the biggest challenges companies face when performing these joins is avoiding duplicate records and properly managing primary keys in heterogeneous datasets.

When we talk about advanced joins, we refer to the combination of datasets that do not share an identical structure and may have different schemas or primary keys that are not perfectly aligned. For example, a business may have a transactional database that stores each sale or customer interaction, while also obtaining social media data that contains information about the behavior of those same customers on platforms like Instagram, Facebook, or Twitter. These two data sources may not have a common primary key directly. The challenge lies in finding an effective way to join these datasets without generating duplicates and ensuring that each record is unique and correct.

A first step for performing advanced combinations is to ensure that each dataset has a clear and well-defined primary key. The primary key is the unique identifier that distinguishes each record within a dataset. In transactional databases, this could be the transaction number or a unique customer ID, while in social media, it could be an ID generated by the social platform itself or an email address associated with the profile. In many cases, these keys do not match exactly between datasets, complicating the merging process. One solution to this problem is to create composite keys, meaning keys that are built from multiple fields that together generate a unique identifier for each record. For example, you could use a combination of the customer's name, their email address, and the transaction date to create a unique key that allows you to correctly identify each record without duplications.

When working with heterogeneous databases, it's also important to select the right type of join for each situation. In many cases, you'll need inner joins, which only include records that have an exact match in both datasets, or left joins, which allow you to combine all records from one table, even if they don't have a match in the other. For example, if you want to analyze customer behavior on social media in relation to their purchases, you could perform a left join between sales data and social media data. This allows you to keep all the information about customer transactions, even if not all customers have an active presence on social media or if you've not obtained all their data from that platform.

One of the most common problems that arise when performing advanced joins is the duplication of records. This happens when the join generates more than one match for a given record, leading to multiple duplicated rows in the final result. To avoid this, it's crucial to carefully manage primary keys and ensure that each key is unique. This may involve removing duplicates before executing the join or normalizing the data to reduce the likelihood of duplications. Normalization involves reorganizing the data so that each table has only one specific function, avoiding redundancies and ensuring that each piece of data is stored only once.

Another useful technique to avoid duplicating records is using subqueries or joins with conditions that limit the join results to those absolutely necessary for the analysis. This may involve creating filters that ensure only unique records are included or that combinations are made under specific conditions to prevent multiple matches for a single record. For example, in the case of combining social media data with a customer database, you could set a condition that limits combinations to records where emails match exactly, but only select the latest post from each customer on social media, thus reducing the risk of duplicating information.

In situations where combinations involve heterogeneous data sources, such as transactional databases and social networks, one of the additional challenges is the difference in the update frequency of these systems. Transactional databases are usually updated in real-time or daily, while social media data may not be available as regularly. This means that when performing a join between both sources, it's important to consider the temporality of the data and adjust the combinations based on the most recent updates available in each dataset.

Finally, a good practice when performing advanced joins on large datasets is to verify the combination afterwards to ensure that no duplications have occurred and that no relevant records have been omitted. This can involve creating control reports that show how many records from each dataset have been successfully combined and how many were left out. It's also advisable to perform an analysis of duplicate keys after executing the join to identify potential issues in the combination.

SMEs that handle multiple data sources, such as sales databases and social media, can greatly benefit from these advanced join techniques, allowing them to consolidate information efficiently and gain more complete insights into customer behavior and business operations.

- **How to Add Context to Your Data for More Accurate Decisions**

Data enrichment has become a strategic tool for SMEs looking to gain a competitive edge in increasingly complex markets. When we talk about data enrichment, we refer to the integration of external data sources with a company's internal datasets to increase the value and analytical capacity of the existing information. This practice not only helps provide a broader and more complete view of the business, but also facilitates more informed decision-making, especially in dynamic environments where changes in the market, economy, or consumer behavior are constant.

One of the most effective ways to enrich internal data is by integrating external data obtained through public APIs or by purchasing specialized databases that provide valuable information. In the context of SMEs, using these external data sources can be particularly relevant when trying to better understand market trends, anticipate changes in demand, or proactively adapt business strategies. While large companies have access to teams and resources dedicated to the constant collection and analysis of data, SMEs can take advantage of more accessible and effective tools to obtain additional information without requiring massive investments.

The first step in data enrichment is identifying what type of external information can complement internal datasets. Market trends are one of the most common sources of external data that can be integrated with the sales data of an SME. For example, if an online clothing store is already collecting data on customer behavior (sales, product preferences, purchase patterns), it can enrich this data by integrating current fashion trends that help predict which products will be in higher demand in the future. This information can come from specialized databases in the sector or through public APIs that track changes in consumer preferences in real time.

One of the most widely used methods to obtain this type of external data is through public APIs. An API, or Application Programming Interface, is a set of protocols and tools that allow different systems to communicate with each other. There are multiple APIs that provide access to a variety of data sources, from social media trends to economic forecasts or weather analysis, depending on the needs of each company. For example, an SME dedicated to selling seasonal products could benefit from integrating weather data into its sales analysis. With this information, it would be possible to adjust the product offering based on weather forecasts and improve the accuracy of promotions.

The advantage of using public APIs is that they allow SMEs to access a large amount of information without the need to develop their own complex data collection systems. Many APIs provide real-time data or are regularly updated, enabling companies to make decisions based on the most up-to-date information available. A clear example is the use of APIs that provide financial data or economic forecasts. For a company operating in a market sensitive to economic fluctuations, such as selling imported products, integrating data on exchange rates, interest rates, or macroeconomic indicators can be crucial for adjusting prices or anticipating changes in demand.

In addition to public APIs, external databases also play an important role in data enrichment. These databases, which can often be purchased or subscribed to, offer detailed information on industry trends, consumer behavior, or competitive analysis. An example of this would be an SME that wants to expand into new geographic markets. By acquiring databases on consumption trends in different regions, the company can adjust its product offerings or marketing strategy to better align with local preferences. This type of information not only enhances the company's ability to make data-driven decisions but also allows it to adapt its operations to new business opportunities.

The use of social media data is also an important area of growth in the context of data enrichment. SMEs that already collect internal information about their customers and purchasing preferences can greatly benefit from integrating data from platforms like Facebook, Twitter, or Instagram. By using APIs that allow access to social media data such as comments, likes, interactions, or mentions, a company can gain a much more complete view of how its brand is perceived online and adjust its digital marketing strategies accordingly. For example, an online store that notices an increase in mentions of a specific product on social media can anticipate higher demand for that product and adjust its inventory before a shortage occurs.

A key aspect of data enrichment is the ability to use a company's internal transactional data and combine it with external information. Transactional data, such as sales history or customer behavior, is valuable on its own, but its value expands when integrated with external data that provides context. For example, if a distribution company notices that sales of a specific product have decreased, but by combining this data with external market trends they discover that the demand for that type of product has fallen globally, they can adjust their strategy to focus on products with higher demand. This integration of data sources allows companies to make more informed decisions aligned with market realities.

Predicting economic trends is another area where data enrichment can significantly impact SME operations. Integrating macroeconomic data, such as GDP growth projections, inflation rates, or employment levels, with the company's sales and customer behavior data allows businesses to anticipate changes in consumer purchasing power or the stability of key markets. A company that distributes consumer goods, for example, could benefit from integrating economic predictions to adjust stock levels based on growth or contraction expectations in certain markets. This is particularly relevant in international markets, where economic fluctuations can have an immediate impact on consumption patterns.

In addition to integrating market data and economic forecasts, using geospatial data can also be a powerful enrichment tool for SMEs. By integrating geographic data with customer or sales data, companies can gain a more detailed understanding of how the geographic context influences consumer behavior. For example, a retail store with multiple physical locations can combine data on the geographic distribution of its customers with online purchase heat maps to identify which locations have higher growth potential or which areas could benefit from increased investment in local marketing. APIs like Google Maps allow companies to integrate these geographic data with their own systems, providing a more comprehensive and detailed view of how local factors affect operations.

AI-based predictions are another factor that can enhance data enrichment. Integrating predictive models that leverage the company's internal data, such as historical sales, and combining those models with external data, like market growth projections, allows for much more precise and effective planning. Machine learning models can learn from historical patterns and make predictions about future customer behavior, which, when combined with external data on consumer trends or economic changes, can help companies optimize their operations and maximize their performance.

Data enrichment is not limited to using external sources of information. It also involves improving the quality of internal data by integrating fragmented data sources within the company itself. For many SMEs, data may be scattered across different systems, such as billing systems, CRM, or online sales platforms. Integrating these internal sources, combined with external data, provides a more complete and accurate view of the business. For example, by combining physical store sales data with online customer interaction data, an SME can gain a better understanding of how digital marketing campaigns are affecting purchasing behavior in their physical sales points.

Data enrichment also allows companies to personalize the customer experience more effectively. By integrating external data on consumer preferences or market behavior, a company can adjust its offers and promotions to better align with customer expectations. For example, if an online store discovers that its customers' preferences have changed due to an emerging fashion trend, it can adapt its marketing campaigns and adjust its inventory to capitalize on that trend before competitors do. Personalization based on data enrichment enables companies to create more relevant campaigns tailored to current consumer needs, which in turn can increase customer loyalty and improve conversion rates.

Finally, the use of external data can also improve the operational efficiency of SMEs. By integrating data on logistics and distribution, a company can optimize its delivery processes and reduce response times.

For example, an SME that relies on international shipping can combine data on the most efficient transport routes with weather data and economic forecasts to improve its supply chain planning. In this way, the company can anticipate possible delays or fluctuations in transport costs and adjust its logistics planning accordingly.

In short, data enrichment through the integration of external sources like public APIs, specialized databases, or predictive models provides SMEs with an effective way to increase the accuracy of their analysis and improve their ability to anticipate market changes.

2.3. Advanced analysis of text, images, and transactional data for SMEs

Handling unstructured data is one of the most challenging yet richest areas in data science. While structured data, like that from transactional databases, has a predefined and easy-to-interpret format, unstructured data requires advanced techniques to extract valuable information. For SMEs, managing unstructured data is becoming increasingly important, as many businesses accumulate large volumes of information from various sources such as social media comments, product reviews, or catalog images, which, if leveraged correctly, can provide key insights into customer behavior and market dynamics.

- **Applying NLP Techniques in SMEs for Sentiment Analysis and Keyword Extraction**

The processing of text data is a key component for SMEs looking to extract value from the interactions customers have with their products or services. In a world where much of the communication occurs online, whether through social media, reviews, or comments on platforms like Google, businesses need tools that allow them to analyze this data and turn it into actionable information. Natural Language Processing (NLP) is a technique that helps automate the analysis of large volumes of text, transforming that unstructured material into usable data that can influence decision-making in marketing, sales, and customer service.

One of the most important applications of NLP for SMEs is sentiment analysis. This technique allows businesses to measure whether the overall tone of opinions or comments is positive, negative, or neutral, helping them better understand how customers perceive the brand, products, or services. By analyzing the comments users leave on social media or review platforms, a company can quickly detect whether a launch has been well received or if there are recurring issues that need to be addressed. This is crucial for SMEs, which often don't have access to dedicated manual analysis resources and need automated solutions that can handle large volumes of textual data efficiently.

To perform sentiment analysis, one of the most accessible tools for SMEs is TextBlob, a Python library that simplifies text processing. TextBlob allows you to quickly analyze customer comments by assigning them a polarity score, ranging from -1 to 1, where negative values indicate negative sentiments, positive values reflect positive sentiments, and values close to zero are usually neutral. This tool is especially useful for small businesses because it's easy to use and doesn't require advanced technical knowledge in natural language processing. For example, if an SME launches a new product and wants to know how customers are reacting on social media, they can use TextBlob to automatically analyze hundreds of comments and get a clear view of whether customers are satisfied or not.

Another example of using TextBlob in SMEs is analyzing product reviews on Google or Amazon. Instead of manually reviewing each comment, which can be an overwhelming task, a company can automate the process using this library. TextBlob analyzes the text, detects the overall tone of each review, and assigns a polarity score that allows the company to see which products have more positive or negative opinions. From this, the company can identify patterns that might not have been evident through a manual reading, such as recurring issues with a specific product or the popularity of certain attributes that customers value positively.

In addition to TextBlob, another useful library for sentiment analysis in SMEs is NLTK (Natural Language Toolkit). Although it's more complex than TextBlob, NLTK provides a wider range of tools and greater control over text processing, making it a suitable option for businesses that require more detailed analysis. NLTK allows for more sophisticated analysis by breaking down sentences into grammatical components, analyzing the syntactic relationships between words, and offering a more accurate analysis of the context in which certain terms are used. This can be particularly useful when customer comments are more ambiguous or when the business needs to identify constructive criticism that could be mistakenly classified as negative in a superficial analysis.

For example, in the case of a review that expresses both positive and negative elements, NLTK can help break down the comment into sentences to identify the specific parts that are positive and those that are negative. Suppose a restaurant customer leaves a review saying: 'The service was excellent, but the food arrived cold.' A basic analysis might identify this as a neutral review, but NLTK allows you to separate the sentiments and provide a more nuanced view: positive for the service, negative for the quality of the food. This is key for SMEs that want to get a detailed analysis and focus on improving specific aspects of their business while keeping an eye on what is already working well.

Sentiment analysis is just one of the many ways SMEs can benefit from NLP. Another essential technique is keyword extraction, which allows businesses to identify the most important and recurring terms in customer comments. This technique is extremely useful when companies need to quickly detect the main topics in customer opinions without having to read each comment individually. The keyword extraction approach enables businesses to discover which aspects of their products or services are most mentioned, which in turn can help guide marketing strategies or product improvement efforts.

One of the most used tools for keyword extraction is TF-IDF (Term Frequency-Inverse Document Frequency). This technique measures the relevance of a word in a particular document compared to the entire set of documents. TF-IDF assigns a weight to each word based on how often it appears in an individual document and how many documents in the corpus contain that same word. The result is that words appearing frequently in a single document, but not in many others, stand out as particularly relevant. In the context of SMEs, this helps identify the most important topics for customers when they leave comments about a product or service.

For example, if an electronics store collects thousands of comments on a new model of headphones, it can use TF-IDF to quickly identify which keywords customers mention most frequently in their reviews. If words like "battery," "sound," or "comfort" have a high weight, this indicates that these are the aspects that most influence customer satisfaction. This not only provides valuable information to improve the product but can also influence marketing campaigns, allowing the company to highlight the most valued features in its ads and promotional materials.

Another complementary technique for keyword extraction is the approach known as Bag of Words. Unlike TF-IDF, which weighs the importance of words based on their appearance across multiple documents, the Bag of Words approach simply counts the frequency of each word in a set of documents. Although this technique does not take into account the context in which words appear, it is still very useful for quickly identifying the most common topics in a dataset. For a SME that wants a quick overview of customer comments without needing a deep analysis, Bag of Words is an effective and straightforward solution.

For example, a clothing store that collects feedback on its website can use Bag of Words to quickly identify which terms are mentioned most often. If the terms "size," "shipping," and "quality" are the most frequent words, the company will know that these are the aspects customers value the most or have issues with. This allows the company to adjust its customer service processes or improve product information on its website to address the topics most mentioned by consumers.

NLP also allows SMEs to adapt their marketing campaigns more efficiently. By analyzing customer comments and extracting important keywords, a company can adjust its communication strategy to highlight the aspects of its products or services that resonate most with its target audience. If, for example, an analysis of product reviews reveals that customers particularly value the durability of a product, the company can focus its marketing efforts on promoting this key feature. This makes advertising messages more relevant to customers and ultimately improves conversion rates.

Text data processing using TF-IDF or Bag of Words is not only useful for identifying common themes, but also for analyzing the competition. SMEs can apply these techniques not only to their own customer comments but also to those of their competitors. This allows them to identify which attributes or features other companies are highlighting the most and compare how customers perceive those aspects compared to their own products. If, for example, an SME discovers that comments about a competitor's products consistently highlight 'fast delivery' or 'customer service,' it could be a signal that these are areas they should also improve or highlight in their own marketing strategy to compete more effectively.

Text analysis is not limited to product reviews. Many SMEs receive large volumes of comments and inquiries through social media. Customers interact with brands on platforms like Facebook, Twitter, and Instagram, leaving opinions, questions, or even criticism that, if properly analyzed, can provide valuable insights on how to improve interaction with the public. By using TF-IDF and Bag of Words, companies can analyze these social media comments and discover common patterns that allow them to adjust their communication strategies and online reputation management.

An example would be a company analyzing mentions of its brand on Twitter. By using TF-IDF to analyze the tweets mentioning the brand, the company could identify that the most common keywords are related to customer service issues or delivery times. This not only allows the company to resolve specific problems but also to adjust its message on social media to proactively address these concerns and improve brand perception. Additionally, by automating the analysis of large volumes of text, the company can react more quickly to customer concerns, enhancing its ability to provide more efficient customer service.

Natural Language Processing (NLP) offers SMEs a range of powerful tools that allow them to transform unstructured data, such as comments and reviews, into insights that can directly influence their business operations and marketing strategies. Both sentiment analysis and keyword extraction using techniques like TF-IDF and Bag of Words provide companies with a fast and efficient way to analyze large volumes of text and make data-driven decisions.

- **Accessible solutions for image analysis and management in small businesses**

Image processing is a technology that has advanced significantly in recent years and is now accessible to businesses of all sizes, including SMEs. Thanks to tools like OpenCV and PIL (Python Imaging Library), even small and medium-sized enterprises can implement image processing solutions to improve their daily operations. These tools allow efficient image analysis, which can be useful in various contexts, from managing visual product catalogs to monitoring security cameras.

One area where SMEs can benefit from image processing is in managing visual catalogs. For an online store that relies on product images to attract customers, it is crucial that these images are high-quality and accurately represent what customers will receive. Using OpenCV or PIL, businesses can automate image reviews to ensure they meet certain quality standards. For example, a company could use these tools to detect defects in images, such as lighting issues, blurring, or misalignment of the product.

OpenCV is a powerful open-source library that offers a wide range of functions for image and video processing. One of its basic features is the ability to detect edges and anomalies in images. This is useful for SMEs that need to ensure the products in their catalogs are properly photographed and free of visual defects that could distort the customer's perception. For example, an online clothing store could use OpenCV to analyze images of garments and detect excessive shadows, wrinkles in the fabric, or focus issues, all in an automated manner.

In addition, image processing with OpenCV can also be used to perform more advanced tasks like detecting objects within images. If an SME managing a product inventory is photographing multiple items at the same time, OpenCV can identify and segment each of these items, ensuring they are captured clearly and separately. For example, an accessory company that takes photos of several products in the same space can use this functionality to identify each item individually and ensure they are properly highlighted in the catalog.

Another popular tool is PIL, which is ideal for performing simpler but equally important image processing tasks, such as resizing, rotating, and format conversion. In the context of an SME working with visual catalogs, PIL allows you to adjust images to specific sizes or change the format to ensure compatibility with the platform where they will be published. Suppose an online store needs all its product images in JPEG format and a resolution of 800x600 pixels. With PIL, this task can be automated, saving time and ensuring that all images meet the website's standards.

In addition to quality analysis in product catalogs, OpenCV and PIL can also be useful in security and monitoring applications. Many SMEs rely on security camera systems to monitor work areas or physical stores. Instead of relying solely on manual supervision, companies can implement automated solutions using OpenCV to analyze customer flow in stores or detect unusual behavior.

For example, with OpenCV, it is possible to implement a motion detection system that analyzes video from security cameras in real-time. If movement is detected in an area where there should be no activity, the system can generate an automatic alert, allowing security personnel to take quick action without the need to constantly monitor all cameras. This is particularly useful in situations where the company cannot afford constant surveillance or needs to optimize the use of security resources.

Another interesting application of OpenCV for SMEs is analyzing customer flow within a physical store. Using facial detection or object tracking techniques, businesses can analyze how customers move within the store and which areas receive the most attention. This not only allows companies to adjust product placement to optimize sales, but also provides valuable insights into customer preferences. For example, if the analysis reveals that customers spend more time in a specific section of the store, the company can reorganize the inventory to highlight popular products or place promotions in those areas.

In addition to analyzing customer flow, OpenCV can also be used to improve workplace safety. Imagine a company that needs to monitor a high-risk area, such as a warehouse with heavy machinery. By using OpenCV, a system can be set up to detect if a person is in a restricted area or if someone is not wearing the appropriate safety gear. This not only enhances the safety of the environment but also reduces legal risks for the company, as it can demonstrate that proactive measures have been taken to prevent accidents.

In the context of basic recognition, OpenCV offers simple yet effective solutions that can be applied in physical stores. SMEs can implement systems that track customer entry and exit patterns to analyze traffic peaks at certain times of the day or on specific days of the week. This not only helps optimize staffing and customer service but can also influence the planning of promotions and marketing campaigns. For example, if a store detects that Saturday mornings are the busiest time, they can plan special offers for that time to maximize sales.

In addition to real-time analysis, OpenCV allows for the analysis of stored videos to extract retrospective information. An SME can record customer behavior in the store over several weeks and then use video analysis tools to identify behavior patterns, such as areas of the store that customers tend to avoid or sections that generate more interest. This type of analysis can be invaluable for a store looking to optimize product placement or improve the overall customer experience.

On the other hand, PIL also has applications in automating tasks related to image management. For an SME that deals with large volumes of product images, manually adjusting each image to meet certain requirements can be tedious. PIL allows you to automate processes like brightness and contrast adjustments, background removal, or adding watermarks to images. This is especially useful for online stores that want to protect their product images with watermarks without having to edit them one by one.

Another application of PIL is image compression to optimize website performance. SMEs managing online stores must ensure that their pages load quickly to provide a good customer experience and improve their search engine ranking. PIL allows you to reduce the size of image files without losing too much quality, which improves website loading times. By automating this process, businesses can ensure that all images uploaded to the site meet performance requirements without sacrificing visual quality.

In summary, the use of OpenCV and PIL allows SMEs to improve their ability to manage and analyze images efficiently. Whether it's ensuring the quality of product images in a catalog, enhancing security through video analysis, or optimizing customer experience by analyzing foot traffic in a physical store, these tools offer accessible and customizable solutions that can make a significant difference in a company's operational performance and competitiveness. With the right implementation, even the smallest SMEs can leverage the benefits of image processing to improve efficiency and increase the value of their business offering.

- **Advantages of integrating transactional data in SMEs for strategic decision-making**

The integration of transactional data is one of the most valuable practices for SMEs looking to make the most of the information they already have at their disposal. Transactional data, such as purchase history, inventory, or customer interactions, is a rich and fundamental source for understanding consumer behavior, detecting patterns, and ultimately optimizing business strategies. However, the true value of this data lies not only in its collection but in its ability to be analyzed and used effectively. The main goal is to find the signals or indicators in this data that can anticipate future behaviors, such as the possibility of a customer stopping purchases or the likelihood that another will be receptive to a new sales campaign.

Transactional data provides a clear view of past customer interactions with the company. Each transaction, whether a purchase, a return, or contact with customer service, contains details that help build a profile of consumer behavior over time. One of the most valuable applications of integrating this data is the ability to detect behavior patterns, which can facilitate decision-making on how to manage inventories, personalize marketing campaigns, or even improve customer service.

When it comes to detecting behavioral patterns in transactional data, one of the first techniques that can be implemented is purchase frequency analysis. This analysis allows SMEs to identify how many times a customer makes a purchase within a given period, which in turn helps to segment customers according to their level of activity. For example, a customer who makes purchases regularly could be considered a loyal customer, while another who decreases their purchase frequency might be on the verge of leaving. This frequency analysis can reveal trends that are not immediately obvious, such as seasonality in purchases or the influence of external factors like promotions or discounts on customers' buying decisions.

A critical aspect of transactional data analysis is using these signals to identify customers who might be on the verge of leaving. In marketing, this phenomenon is known as churn or customer attrition. Detecting these customers in time is essential, as retaining an existing customer is much more profitable than acquiring a new one. Transactional data allows companies to analyze their customers' historical behavior and look for signals that indicate a risk of leaving. These signals can include a decrease in purchase frequency, a reduction in the average value of transactions, or an increase in product returns.

For example, an online store may notice that a customer who used to shop once a month hasn't made any purchases in the last three months. This change in behavior could be a sign that the customer is considering leaving the store or switching to a competitor. By using transaction history, the company can detect this anomaly and take proactive measures to retain the customer, such as offering a personalized discount or sending them a product recommendation based on their past purchases. This early intervention capability is key to reducing churn and maintaining a loyal customer base.

Another valuable use of transactional data is the ability to segment customers for personalized marketing campaigns. By analyzing purchase patterns, businesses can identify those customers who are good candidates for new sales campaigns. For example, if a customer has regularly purchased fitness-related products, they're likely interested in receiving information about new product launches in that category. Instead of sending generic campaigns to all customers, SMEs can use transactional data to segment their customer base and send more relevant messages, increasing the likelihood of conversion.

An effective technique for identifying customers receptive to new campaigns is the use of predictive models based on transactional data. These models allow you to predict which customers are most likely to make a new purchase based on their past behavior. One of the simplest approaches is RFM analysis (Recency, Frequency, Monetary), which classifies customers based on three key factors: the recency of their last purchase, how often they make purchases, and the total monetary value they've spent. This analysis allows SMEs to segment customers into different groups, such as high-value customers who buy frequently but whose last purchase was a long time ago, or recent customers who have made a single large purchase.

A fashion company, for example, can use RFM analysis to identify which customers should be prioritized in a sales campaign. If the company is launching a new line of sportswear, it can focus on those customers who have previously purchased sports products and have high recency and frequency of purchase. By targeting customers who have already shown interest in that category, the company increases the chances of the campaign being successful and maximizes the return on investment in marketing.

In addition to RFM analysis, another technique that can be used to leverage transactional data is logistic regression. This predictive model allows you to identify which customers are most likely to respond to a campaign or make an additional purchase. By analyzing the characteristics of previous transactions, such as the type of products purchased, the purchase channel used, or even the time of day when purchases were made, SMEs can develop models that predict future customer behavior. For example, an electronics store could analyze whether customers who regularly buy high-end products are more likely to take advantage of a premium accessories promotion.

Machine learning also plays a key role in integrating transactional data for pattern detection and customer behavior prediction. Classification and clustering algorithms allow companies to analyze large volumes of data and discover correlations between different transactional variables that might not be evident with simpler analyses. For example, a clustering algorithm could identify groups of customers with similar buying behaviors that have not yet been segmented by the company. This enables better personalization of offers and more precise targeting of specific segments.

Another application of machine learning in transaction data analysis is anomaly detection. Anomaly detection algorithms can identify unusual behaviors that might indicate fraud or errors in the inventory system. For example, if a company detects a sudden increase in product returns or an unexpected drop in stock levels, they can use anomaly detection models to identify the underlying causes and correct the issue before it negatively impacts operations. This type of analysis is particularly useful for SMEs handling large volumes of products or transactions, as it allows them to quickly identify and address problems before they become crises.

The integration of transactional data also has key applications in inventory management. By analyzing historical sales data and combining it with future demand forecasts, businesses can optimize their inventory levels and reduce the risk of overstock or stockouts. Transactional data analysis allows companies to identify products that sell faster during certain times of the year or are subject to seasonal fluctuations. With this information, SMEs can adjust their orders to suppliers to ensure they always have enough stock of the most in-demand products without incurring unnecessary costs by storing unsold items.

Moreover, analyzing inventory patterns based on transactional data allows SMEs to identify products that are not selling well and make informed decisions on how to manage them. For example, a home goods store might notice that a product has been in stock for several months without moving. By integrating this information with sales and return data, the company can decide whether to offer discounts on those products, move them to a more visible location in the store, or even remove them from inventory if they aren't generating enough interest.

The use of transactional signals to improve marketing strategies is also crucial in the realm of retention campaigns. SMEs can use past purchase data to identify patterns indicating if a customer is at risk of not returning. If a customer has been loyal for a long period but their purchasing activity has recently declined, this may indicate a problem the company needs to address, such as dissatisfaction with a product or competition from other brands. By identifying these customers before they leave entirely, SMEs can offer them personalized incentives, such as discounts or recommended products based on previous purchases, to win them back and restore their loyalty.

The ability of SMEs to detect behavior patterns in their transactional data is a strategic asset that can transform how they manage operations and engage with customers. From identifying customers at risk of leaving to precise segmentation for marketing campaigns, the effective use of transactional data allows companies to make informed and proactive decisions that improve customer satisfaction and maximize business performance.

2.4. Advantages of relational and non-relational databases for SMEs and freelancers (SQL vs NoSQL)

The use of databases is essential for the efficient operation of any modern business, and in the case of SMEs, the choice between relational and non-relational databases can have a significant impact on how data is managed and the flexibility the system offers to adapt to business needs. As small and medium-sized enterprises collect larger volumes of information, from transactional data to system logs or social media data, the need arises to choose the type of database that best suits the types of data being handled and how they will be used.

• **How to Choose Between SQL and NoSQL Databases According to Your Business Needs**

The concept of SQL databases has been a cornerstone in information management for decades. SQL, which stands for Structured Query Language, is based on a relational structure that organizes data into tables with rows and columns, making it ideal for structured and highly organized data. This type of database allows companies to ensure data integrity and perform complex queries using a standardized query language, facilitating the extraction of specific information quickly and efficiently. In the context of an SME, SQL databases are especially useful when transactional data is at the core of daily operations. For example, in a company that manages sales, inventories, or a customer relationship management (CRM) system, data consistency and accuracy are crucial aspects. SQL offers the advantage of efficiently managing these relationships, allowing complex queries to be executed quickly.

For an online store or a distribution business, where every sale or transaction involves multiple relationships between products, customers, and billing, SQL databases provide an organized structure that ensures all these relationships are maintained coherently. A good example is tracking an order: from the moment a customer makes a purchase, the information must be linked to the inventory to reduce the available stock, and then connected to the CRM database to update the customer's history. All of this needs to be managed in real-time and with precision to avoid errors in product availability or billing. SQL databases, such as MySQL, PostgreSQL, or Microsoft SQL Server, are best suited for managing this type of operation, as they allow for referential integrity and ensure that all processes are correctly aligned.

One of the most important aspects of SQL databases is their ability to ensure ACID transactions, which means Atomicity, Consistency, Isolation, and Durability. These properties ensure that transactions are completed safely and that, in the event of a system failure, the data remains in a consistent state. For SMEs that handle critical operations where data loss or corruption could have serious financial consequences, such as in sales or accounting, SQL databases provide the assurance that transactions will always be reliable and secure.

As SMEs begin to manage more complex and unstructured types of data, such as server logs, social media interactions, or large volumes of real-time information, relational databases can fall short in terms of flexibility and scalability. This is where NoSQL databases come into play, offering a viable alternative when data doesn't fit neatly into the rigid table structure used by SQL. NoSQL stands for Not Only SQL, indicating that these databases can handle data that isn't traditionally structured. NoSQL is designed to manage large volumes of data that don't necessarily need to be organized in tables, such as semi-structured or unstructured data.

For an SME that handles large volumes of unstructured or rapidly evolving information, such as data generated by sensors, system activity logs, or customer comments on social media, NoSQL databases offer the necessary flexibility to store and access this information without the need to define strict relationships between data in advance. For example, MongoDB, one of the most popular NoSQL databases, allows data to be stored in a document format (based on JSON), meaning each record can have a different structure, adapting to the changing nature of the data. This is particularly useful for companies that manage information that changes frequently or has different attributes in each record, such as customer data where not all fields are applicable for every person.

A typical example of the need for NoSQL in an SME is a company that manages system logs. Logs are files continuously generated by computer systems that record every event or change in an application or server. These records are often volatile, grow quickly, and vary in structure depending on the event. Trying to manage these logs with a traditional SQL database can be complicated and inefficient, as the data structure is not consistent and would require constant redefinition of tables and columns. In this context, NoSQL is a much more suitable solution, allowing logs to be stored as they come in, without worrying about adjusting the data to a fixed schema.

Another situation where NoSQL databases are useful for SMEs is in managing real-time data from multiple sources. An example of this would be a company that monitors social media interactions to assess customer behavior or measure the impact of a marketing campaign. The data from social media, such as tweets, comments, or likes, are not only highly dynamic but also structured in a non-uniform way. Some posts may have multiple replies or mentions, while others may contain images, links, or just text. Trying to manage this variety of data in an SQL database would result in a complicated and inefficient structure. Instead, with a NoSQL database like Couchbase, the company can store this data smoothly without needing to establish a rigid structure upfront.

Scalability is another key factor when choosing between SQL and NoSQL. In an SQL database, horizontal scalability (i.e., adding more servers to handle larger workloads) is difficult to achieve due to the nature of relationships and transactions between tables. NoSQL, on the other hand, is designed from the ground up to scale horizontally, allowing SMEs to handle increasing amounts of data without compromising performance. This is particularly important for growing businesses that don't want to be limited by their database's capacity as the number of users or transactions increases.

On a technical level, one of the most obvious differences between SQL and NoSQL is data querying. In SQL, the use of complex queries is one of its strengths, as it allows for detailed searches, table joins, and the creation of robust reports with relative ease thanks to a standardized language. In

NoSQL, the approach is different. Queries in NoSQL tend to be simpler and focus on speed and efficiency in data retrieval rather than query complexity. This means that NoSQL databases are ideal for tasks like fast data searches or retrieving large volumes of information, but they may not be as suitable when complex query operations involving multiple data relationships are required.

An example of the speed advantage of NoSQL could be an e-commerce application handling thousands of transactions per minute. Instead of managing the load on a traditional relational database, a NoSQL solution like Cassandra or DynamoDB would allow handling large volumes of traffic and retrieving information quickly, ensuring that users do not experience delays when searching for products or making purchases.

However, SQL remains the preferred option for SMBs that need to manage well-structured data and ensure the integrity of relationships between them. For example, in a CRM where customer, product, invoice, and supplier data is managed, maintaining consistency and avoiding data duplication is essential. SQL databases ensure that any change in the data is correctly reflected across all related tables. If a customer updates their address, this change will automatically be updated in all relevant areas of the database, thanks to the referential integrity that SQL provides.

Furthermore, in situations where data integrity is paramount, such as in accounting or financial management, relational databases are essential due to their transaction control and auditing capabilities. Financial transactions require extreme precision, and SQL databases ensure that operations are carried out correctly and that data is always synchronized.

For SMEs considering implementing NoSQL databases, one of the first questions they should ask is what type of data they are managing and how this data changes over time. If the company mainly handles unstructured or semi-structured data, such as customer records with different attributes or social media interactions that vary in format and length, NoSQL can provide the flexibility needed to manage these data more efficiently.

Ultimately, the choice between SQL and NoSQL is not just about the technical features of each type of database, but also about the specific use case and the needs of each SME.

- ## Strategies and advantages of migrating from SQL to NoSQL in small businesses

The migration from relational databases to NoSQL is an increasingly common process in the business world, especially for SMEs that start with a relational model but, over time, experience an increase in the amount or complexity of data, making a traditional relational database insufficient. Relational databases like MySQL are very suitable for managing well-structured data, transactions with multiple relationships, and strict consistency needs. However, when scalability needs increase, or when the company begins to handle unstructured or semi-structured data, a NoSQL database like MongoDB can provide the necessary flexibility and scalability.

Migrating from a relational database to NoSQL is not a simple process, as it involves significant changes in how data is stored, accessed, and structured. However, many SMEs handling growing volumes of data find that the effort is worth it, especially if the data is becoming increasingly heterogeneous or if the traditional relational system starts having performance issues as demand rises.

One of the most common reasons for migrating from MySQL to MongoDB is the need for horizontal scalability. While MySQL and other relational databases are designed for vertical scaling (increasing the capacity of a single server to handle more load), MongoDB and other NoSQL databases are designed for horizontal scaling, which means they can distribute data across multiple servers or nodes. This allows you to handle large volumes of information and growing workloads without needing to continuously upgrade server hardware. For an SME facing rapid growth, this horizontal scaling capability can be crucial for maintaining performance and avoiding downtime or service outages.

A practical example of migration could be an online store that initially started using MySQL to manage its products, customers, and transactions. As the business grew, it began collecting a large amount of unstructured data, such as customer reviews, website activity logs, and social media data. This data didn't fit well into the traditional relational model, as its structure was variable and didn't always follow a predefined schema. Additionally, the store started experiencing performance issues as the number of simultaneous queries increased with more customers accessing the website. This created a significant load on the servers, and the relational database could no longer scale fast enough to handle the growing traffic.

In this scenario, the company decided to migrate part of its database from MySQL to MongoDB. MongoDB, with its document model, allows data to be stored in a flexible and adaptable format, which meant the store could start storing product reviews and activity logs without worrying about defining a rigid schema in advance. Additionally, MongoDB's sharding capability allowed data to be distributed across multiple servers, significantly reducing the workload on a single server and improving the overall performance of the website.

The migration process began by identifying which parts of the relational database would benefit from being moved to MongoDB. Not all MySQL tables needed to be migrated, as some data were still better structured and organized in a relational model. For example, data related to sales transactions, inventories, and customer management remained in MySQL, as the nature of these operations requires consistency and well-defined relationships. However, the more dynamic and unstructured data, such as product reviews, were migrated to MongoDB, as they did not follow a predictable schema and grew rapidly over time.

The process of migrating product review data began with the creation of a model in MongoDB that allowed for efficient storage of these documents. Instead of storing reviews as rows in a table with fixed columns, as would be done in MySQL, the reviews were stored as JSON documents in MongoDB, where each review could have a different structure depending on its content. For example, some reviews included text, while others also had images or video links, and MongoDB could handle this variety without any issues. Additionally, the store was able to perform efficient queries on these reviews using specific indexes in MongoDB, which allowed searches and filtering to be done quickly, even as the data volume grew significantly.

One of the advantages of MongoDB is that, unlike MySQL, it doesn't require a rigid structure of tables and columns, which allowed the online store to add new features to the reviews without having to modify the database schema. For example, later on, a feature was added that allowed users to vote on whether a review was helpful or not. Instead of having to modify the database to add a new column for each vote, in MongoDB, these votes were simply added to each review document as needed, without having to modify the entire schema. This flexibility is one of the main reasons why many SMEs choose to migrate to NoSQL when their data becomes more diverse and difficult to structure.

Once the migration to MongoDB was underway, the store began to see improvements in scalability and performance. The ability to store and retrieve large volumes of product reviews without affecting performance was a key change that allowed the company to continue growing without worrying about bottlenecks in their database. MongoDB enabled unstructured data to be stored efficiently, and the store was able to start performing advanced analyses on the reviews, such as identifying patterns in the keywords used by customers to describe their experiences or analyzing the sentiment behind the reviews to improve their products and services.

However, not all SMEs migrating from SQL to NoSQL opt for a complete migration. In many cases, it makes more sense to adopt a hybrid model, where some parts of the database remain in SQL and others are migrated to NoSQL. This allows companies to take advantage of the best of both worlds: the consistency and well-defined relationships of SQL for data that requires a clear structure, and the flexibility and scalability of NoSQL for data that is more dynamic or unstructured.

A hybrid model can be particularly useful in companies that handle different types of data requiring different storage approaches. For example, a company managing both a CRM and an e-commerce platform can keep customer and transaction tables in MySQL to ensure that all relationships between these data are well-defined and controlled. At the same time, they can use MongoDB to store user activity logs, product reviews, or even temporary shopping carts, where the data structure may vary from one customer to another and where scalability is more important than relational consistency.

Implementing a hybrid system also requires a clear strategy to ensure both systems work harmoniously. This may involve using tools to synchronize data between the two databases or developing an abstraction layer to facilitate queries between them. For example, an online store using both MySQL and MongoDB could develop an API that allows searches in both the relational and non-relational databases, returning a unified result to the end user without them noticing the difference between the two systems.

An additional challenge in migrating from SQL to NoSQL is redefining queries and how data is accessed. In SQL, queries are highly structured and follow a standardized language (SQL) that allows for complex data joining and filtering operations. In NoSQL, queries tend to be simpler and optimized for speed and scalability, meaning companies must rethink how they interact with their data. This may involve a shift in how developers build their applications, as they will now need to adapt their queries and operations to the document or key-value structure used by NoSQL.

Finally, it's important to keep in mind that although NoSQL offers significant advantages in terms of scalability and flexibility, it also requires careful planning. Migrating to a NoSQL database like MongoDB involves not only changing how data is stored but also how queries, security, and access control are managed. For an SME considering this transition, it's crucial to conduct a thorough assessment of current and future needs and develop a migration strategy that minimizes disruptions and maximizes long-term benefits.

• How SMEs Apply SQL and NoSQL Databases to Maximize Their Efficiency and Scalability

The use of relational and non-relational databases has allowed many SMEs to optimize their performance, better manage their operations, and leverage large volumes of data to make more informed decisions. In this context, many small companies have adopted hybrid approaches, using SQL for structured and transactional data management, and NoSQL to handle large volumes of unstructured or real-time data. This type of mixed implementation allows businesses to benefit from the best of both worlds, taking advantage of SQL's structure, consistency, and transactionality, along with NoSQL's flexibility and scalability.

A practical example of an online store that uses both SQL and NoSQL can illustrate how these two types of databases can work together to improve performance. In this store, the inventory system and sales transactions are managed through a relational database (SQL), such as MySQL or PostgreSQL, because these data require a clear, organized structure and strict referential integrity. The products in the inventory are organized into tables, with clear relationships between them and other data, such as suppliers and product categories. Each time a sale is made, the SQL database updates the inventory in real-time, reducing the available stock quantities and ensuring there are no inconsistencies or duplicates in the records.

This SQL-based system is ideal for the store because sales transactions and inventory management require high precision and consistency. Any error in these operations can directly impact customer service, causing issues like displaying out-of-stock products as available or sending incorrect invoices. SQL, with its ACID transactions (atomicity, consistency, isolation, and durability), ensures these errors don't occur. Each transaction is atomic, meaning it either completes fully or doesn't happen at all, and data remains consistent over time.

However, when it comes to managing less structured data, like frequently changing product information or customer interactions, the store decides to use a NoSQL database like MongoDB. MongoDB is ideal for storing information that varies in structure, such as product descriptions that may include different attributes depending on the item. For example, some products may have detailed technical specifications, while others may only require a general description. MongoDB allows each product to be stored in a JSON document, with the flexibility for each document to have its own set of attributes. This means there is no need to modify the database schema every time new products with different features are added.

In addition, the store also uses MongoDB to store and manage customer comments and reviews. This data is highly dynamic and can contain various elements like text, images, or video links. By using a NoSQL database, the store can handle this type of data efficiently, allowing customers to interact smoothly with the system. MongoDB also facilitates scalability, which is key for an online store that is growing rapidly and needs to handle an increasing number of reviews and comments without compromising performance.

Another practical implementation case in an SME is a mobile app development company that uses a NoSQL database to manage large volumes of real-time data. This company, which offers a fitness app with live activity tracking, has chosen Cassandra, a NoSQL database known for its horizontal scaling capability and efficient management of large volumes of distributed data. The app constantly collects data on user performance, such as distance traveled, calories burned, and heart rate, which vary in real-time and need to be processed quickly.

In this context, a relational database wouldn't be the most suitable option, as the data model isn't rigidly structured and the volume of information arriving at the database at any given time is immense. Cassandra allows for handling this type of data by distributing the workload across multiple nodes, ensuring the database can scale smoothly as the number of active users grows. Additionally, Cassandra's high availability ensures that user data is always accessible, which is crucial for an application where response time must be minimal to guarantee a good user experience.

Behavioral analysis on websites is another scenario where NoSQL databases have proven to be very useful for SMEs. An example could be a small company managing an e-commerce site that wants to better understand how customers interact with the site by analyzing clicks, searches, and page views. By using Elasticsearch, a NoSQL database optimized for real-time search and analysis, the company can collect, index, and analyze all the events occurring on the site in real time, allowing them to understand which products receive the most attention, which navigation paths are most used, or where customers are abandoning their shopping carts.

This type of analysis is essential for optimizing the user experience on the website and improving conversion rates. Elasticsearch allows you to search among billions of records almost instantly, something that wouldn't be possible with a traditional relational database without a negative impact on performance. The company can use this information to improve site design, adjust product placement, or implement personalized marketing strategies based on user behavior.

Another interesting case is that of a logistics company that uses a combination of SQL and NoSQL databases to manage both structured data related to shipment management and unstructured data from sensors installed in their transport vehicles. The SQL part manages critical operations, such as shipment records, driver data, and established routes, where maintaining information consistency is crucial to avoid logistical errors. In parallel, the company uses Couchbase, a NoSQL database, to store data generated by vehicle sensors, such as temperature, real-time location, and engine status—data that varies constantly and requires a database capable of handling large volumes of information without losing performance.

By integrating SQL and NoSQL, the logistics company can efficiently manage both structured and unstructured data, ensuring consistency in critical operations while handling large volumes of real-time data that don't require a rigid structure. This allows for informed decision-making, such as adjusting routes based on traffic or vehicle status, thereby optimizing delivery times and reducing operational costs.

Finally, another practical example can be seen in a digital marketing company that uses NoSQL to analyze and manage large amounts of social media data in real time. This company manages advertising campaigns for different clients and uses Redis, an in-memory NoSQL database, to handle the constant flow of data from social networks, such as mentions, interactions, and impact metrics. Redis allows this data to be stored and processed quickly, which is crucial for a company that needs to respond in real time to user interactions with advertising campaigns.

The use of Redis provides the company with the ability to manage large volumes of data instantly and make quick decisions on adjustments to advertising campaigns, such as modifying targeting or ad distribution. By combining Redis for real-time data management with a relational database that stores historical campaign information, the company can analyze both live and historical data to adjust strategies and maximize clients' return on investment.

In summary, these examples show how SMEs are using SQL and NoSQL databases together to improve performance and adapt to their operational needs. Relational databases remain essential for operations requiring consistency and clear structures, while NoSQL databases offer the flexibility and scalability needed to manage large volumes of unstructured or real-time data.

2.5. ETL for SMEs: Data Automation with Apache NiFi and Airflow

The use of ETL (Extract, Transform, Load) tools has become indispensable for SMEs that handle data from multiple sources and need to consolidate, transform, and store it efficiently for further analysis. ETL tools allow you to automate the processes of extracting, transforming, and loading data, saving time, reducing errors, and improving the accuracy of information management. Traditionally, these processes were done manually, involving repetitive tasks and the risks associated with incorrect data handling. With the evolution of ETL technologies, SMEs can now access powerful and scalable solutions that were previously only available to large companies.

ETL tools handle three essential functions in data management. First, they extract data from various sources such as relational databases, files, APIs, or even social networks. Second, they transform this data to ensure it is consistent and ready for use. This may include data cleansing, normalization, aggregation, or format conversion. Finally, they load the transformed data into a specific destination, which could be a database, a data warehouse, or an analytics system, where it can be used for reports, visualizations, or to feed business intelligence systems.

One of the most useful tools for SMEs in this area is Apache NiFi, a system that facilitates the automation of data flows efficiently. NiFi is an open-source platform designed to move and manage large volumes of data between different systems. This tool stands out for its ability to automate the extraction of data from multiple sources and transform it according to business needs before loading it into a final destination. What makes NiFi especially suitable for SMEs is its intuitive graphical interface, which allows workflows to be designed without the need to write complex code.

In the context of a SME that needs to consolidate sales data from various platforms, such as a point of sale (POS) system, an online store, and a CRM, Apache NiFi allows you to extract data from each system, transform it so that everything follows the same format (for example, converting all dates to a single format or adjusting product names to match), and then load it into a centralized database. This database can be used to generate detailed sales reports or to conduct predictive analysis that helps the company make more informed decisions.

One of the great advantages of Apache NiFi is its ability to handle real-time data. This means that as new data is generated on the company's platforms, NiFi automatically extracts it, transforms it if necessary, and loads it into the target system without manual intervention. This is especially useful for SMEs that need to monitor their data in real-time to quickly adjust their operations or marketing campaigns. For example, an online store can use NiFi to continuously extract transaction data and analyze customer behavior at the time of purchase, allowing them to quickly identify emerging trends or performance issues on their website.

Another widely used ETL tool is Apache Airflow, which is also open-source and designed to orchestrate complex workflows. While NiFi is more focused on managing real-time data flow, Airflow excels at scheduling and executing workflows at specific times or on a regular basis. This makes it an ideal choice for SMEs that need to automate batch data loading processes or want to perform detailed analyses regularly, such as daily, weekly, or monthly reports.

Airflow allows companies to define ETL tasks in a detailed and structured way, establishing dependencies between them. In the context of an SME, Airflow can be used to extract data from various sources, such as SQL databases, external APIs, or even CSV files stored in local or cloud-based file systems. Once the data is extracted, Airflow facilitates its transformation, ensuring it follows the necessary format and business rules. For example, in a distribution company that receives data from multiple suppliers, Airflow can automate the task of extracting this data, unifying it into a single format, and then loading it into a centralized database where inventory is stored. This automation not only reduces manual workload but also minimizes errors that could arise from processing data manually.

One of Airflow's main features is its flexibility to schedule complex tasks. Companies can define when different phases of the ETL process should run, ensuring that data is loaded in a timely manner. For example, an e-commerce company that needs to generate sales reports at the end of each day can use Airflow to schedule the extraction of sales data at midnight, transform it to clean and normalize the information, and then load the data into a data warehouse or business intelligence system. These reports can be ready for review every morning without anyone having to intervene in the process.

Additionally, Airflow is highly scalable, which means it can handle large volumes of data as the company grows. This makes it a suitable tool for SMEs that experience a steady increase in the amount of data they need to manage. For example, a digital marketing company running campaigns on multiple platforms can use Airflow to extract data from each platform, transform it according to the requirements of each campaign, and load it into an analysis system. This allows the company to consolidate all campaign metrics and generate detailed reports without having to rely on manual data collection.

Another advantage of Airflow is its ability to handle dependent tasks and complex workflows. In an SME that performs inventory and sales analysis, for example, Airflow can ensure that inventory data is updated before generating sales reports. This way, if one of the steps in the process fails, the system can identify it and halt the workflow until the problem is resolved, ensuring that the reports generated are always based on accurate and up-to-date data. This guarantees greater reliability in the ETL process and avoids costly errors that could occur if tasks were not executed in the correct order.

An additional feature of Airflow is its ability to integrate with other tools and platforms. For SMEs working with cloud systems like Amazon Web Services (AWS) or Google Cloud Platform (GCP), Airflow offers direct integration with services like Amazon S3 or Google BigQuery, making it easier to extract and load data between different environments. For example, a company that stores data in Google Cloud Storage can use Airflow to extract that data, transform it according to business rules, and then load the results into BigQuery for advanced analysis. This is especially useful for companies that have adopted a multi-cloud strategy or rely on different cloud services for their daily operations.

Both tools, Apache NiFi and Apache Airflow, enable SMEs to improve operational efficiency by automating data management processes. Automation not only saves time but also enhances data quality by reducing human errors, ensuring that data is always up-to-date and ready for use in reports or analysis. This ability to manage and transform large volumes of data automatically allows companies to make faster, data-driven decisions, which is crucial in an increasingly competitive business environment.

In particular, for SMEs that do not have large teams dedicated exclusively to data management, these tools offer a cost-effective and efficient solution. NiFi allows for real-time management, which is useful for companies that require continuous data flows, such as e-commerce or online service platforms, while Airflow is ideal for companies that need to manage large scheduled workloads, such as financial services, inventory analysis, or international trade, where data accuracy and timeliness are critical for success.

In summary, both Apache NiFi and Apache Airflow are powerful and flexible ETL tools that can be implemented by SMEs to automate data management and optimize their business processes. The choice between one or the other will depend on the specific needs of the company, the type of data they handle, and whether they require a continuous data flow or more task-oriented scheduled processing. These tools not only allow for efficient management of large volumes of data, but also provide the scalability and flexibility needed to adapt to future data demands.

2.6. Data Optimization for SMEs with Automation in Cleaning and Transformation

Automating data cleaning and transformation is a crucial step for SMEs looking to manage their data efficiently, reducing errors and saving time and resources in the process. With the growing amount of information companies collect from various sources, such as transactional databases, social media, e-commerce platforms, or CRM systems, the challenge of cleaning and transforming that data before analyzing it or integrating it into decision-making systems becomes increasingly complex. This is where automation solutions come into play, allowing companies to eliminate much of the manual work associated with these tasks.

One of the most effective methods for automating data cleaning and transformation is through the use of Python scripts. Python has become the preferred programming language for data analysts due to its simplicity, flexibility, and the wide availability of specialized libraries that make data handling easier. For an SME, using Python can transform the way data is processed, allowing tasks that previously required hours or days of manual work to be completed in minutes or seconds.

One of the most useful tools for automating data cleaning in Python is the Pandas library, which allows you to manipulate, clean, and transform large datasets efficiently. Pandas provides a data structure called DataFrame that makes it easy to handle tables and matrices, enabling you to filter data, remove duplicates, manage missing values, and transform columns into more suitable formats for analysis. A SME that collects sales data from various sources, for example, can use Pandas to automatically clean those tables, unifying date formats, removing duplicate rows, or filling in missing values with median data or the average of other columns.

Let's say a small online store collects sales data from different platforms: the website, a point-of-sale (POS) system in their physical stores, and a sales API from an external marketplace. Each source might generate data with slightly different structures, such as different date formats, variations in product names, or missing values in fields like shipping addresses. With a Python script using Pandas, the store can automate the task of transforming this data into a consistent format. The script can convert all dates to a uniform format, normalize product names, and apply imputation methods to fill in missing values. All of this can be programmed to occur automatically every time new data is loaded, saving time and reducing the chance of human error.

In addition to Pandas, there are other Python libraries that are also useful for automating data transformation. NumPy is another key library that allows you to work with data arrays quickly and efficiently, facilitating the execution of mathematical and statistical operations on large volumes of data. For a company that needs to perform complex calculations or apply specific formulas to its data, NumPy allows these processes to be automated, ensuring that transformations are consistent and accurate every time.

Another practical example of how SMEs can benefit from automation is through the use of RPA (Robotic Process Automation). While Python scripts are more suited for tasks related to data manipulation, RPA offers a broader solution that allows the automation of repetitive processes involving multiple applications and systems. RPA tools are designed to mimic human behavior in interacting with software applications, enabling companies to automate tasks such as data entry, information extraction from documents, or data integration between different platforms.

For an SME facing the task of processing hundreds of emails, PDF invoices, and purchase orders daily, an RPA can automate much of this process. For example, an RPA bot can automatically extract data from invoices, convert the values into a suitable format for the company's accounting system, and then load this data into a spreadsheet or database without manual employee intervention. This not only saves time but also reduces errors associated with manual data entry, improving the overall accuracy and efficiency of operations.

In addition to automating the extraction and transformation of data from emails or PDF files, RPA can also be integrated with other software tools that an SME is already using. For example, a sales company that uses both a CRM and an ERP system can automate the transfer of data between these systems. Instead of employees having to manually export information from one system and then import it into another, RPA can perform this task automatically, ensuring that all systems are synchronized in real-time. This significantly improves the data flow within the company and minimizes bottlenecks in operational processes.

Another key advantage of RPA is that it doesn't require deep integration or restructuring of existing systems within the company. Unlike Python scripts, which require some level of programming and technical knowledge, RPA robots are designed to be implemented quickly without the need for coding, making the technology accessible to SMEs that don't have a specialized technical team. Modern RPA platforms typically have easy-to-use graphical interfaces where users can configure and program workflows by simply dragging and dropping components, allowing employees without technical knowledge to automate key processes.

A practical example of how an SME could use RPA for data transformation is in the context of a logistics company that needs to process shipping orders from different platforms and convert that information into a format compatible with its inventory management system. Every day, the company receives orders from various clients through multiple channels, such as their online store, phone calls, or emails. The orders may have different formats, and the data might be structured in various ways. With an RPA bot, the company can automate the process of extracting relevant data from each order, transforming it into a standard format, and then loading it into the inventory system automatically.

The automation of data cleaning and transformation also has a significant impact on data quality. One of the main reasons why data is inaccurate or unreliable is human error, either when entering data or manually manipulating it during the transformation process. With automation, SMEs can ensure that data is cleaned and transformed in a consistent and coherent manner, which improves the overall quality of the information available for analysis. Additionally, clean and correctly transformed data allows companies to gain more accurate insights from their analyses, enhancing decision-making.

For example, a company analyzing its customers' purchasing behavior to adjust its marketing strategy depends on the quality of the data being analyzed. If the data is poorly structured, contains errors, or hasn't been properly transformed, the conclusions drawn from the analysis will be unreliable. Automation ensures that data is processed consistently, eliminating these issues before analysts or business intelligence systems use it.

The use of Python and RPA to automate data cleaning and transformation is particularly valuable for SMEs, as it allows them to better manage their limited resources, reduce time spent on repetitive tasks, and ensure that the data used in analysis is accurate and reliable. These technologies not only enhance operational efficiency but also enable companies to adapt more quickly to market demands, optimizing internal processes and improving their ability to compete in an ever-evolving business environment.

Chapter 3 - Advanced Data Analysis and Visualization for SMEs

3.1. Advanced libraries for SMEs: SciPy, PySpark, and Dask in data optimization and analysis

In the world of data science, the use of advanced libraries is essential to efficiently handle large volumes of information and perform complex analyses. As SMEs start to collect and work with more data, the need for tools that facilitate this process becomes crucial. Python has been a popular choice due to its versatility and ease of use, and within its ecosystem, there are numerous libraries that can help take data analysis to the next level.

Among the most notable are SciPy, PySpark, and Dask. Each of these libraries offers specific solutions for different problems and data volumes. SciPy is widely used for advanced mathematical calculations and working with optimization, integration, and statistical algorithms, being a natural extension of NumPy. For SMEs that need to perform more sophisticated scientific analysis, SciPy is an essential tool.

On the other hand, PySpark, which is an interface to Apache Spark for Python, allows for efficient processing of large volumes of distributed data. It's especially useful for companies that need to work with Big Data, as it can manage millions of records quickly and in parallel. Finally, Dask is another Python library designed to scale data analysis processes across multiple cores or even machine clusters, allowing operations performed locally with Pandas or NumPy to be extended to much larger datasets without significantly changing the code.

In this chapter, we will introduce how each of these libraries can be used in the context of SMEs to improve data processing efficiency, optimize complex calculations, and enable the analysis of large volumes of information.

- **Advanced Analysis and Optimization with SciPy in SMEs**

SciPy is a Python library that offers a wide range of functionalities for advanced numerical data analysis and processing, serving as an extension of NumPy. While NumPy focuses on basic array operations and numerical data manipulation, SciPy expands these capabilities by providing more sophisticated tools, especially useful for problems that require advanced scientific, mathematical, or statistical calculations. For SMEs, SciPy can be a key tool in data-driven decision-making, as it facilitates solving complex problems like optimizing delivery routes, minimizing costs, or conducting advanced statistical analysis to better understand market behavior.

One of SciPy's strengths is its ability to perform advanced optimization. In the context of SMEs, optimizing resources and improving operational efficiency can make the difference between keeping costs under control or incurring unnecessary expenses. SciPy provides a series of optimization algorithms that can be applied to real business problems, such as delivery route planning, resource allocation, or inventory management.

Let's imagine a small distribution company that delivers products to its customers across a wide geographical region. The challenge is to plan delivery routes efficiently to minimize costs associated with fuel and transport time, while ensuring that all customers receive their products on time. By using SciPy's optimization functions, the company can find the shortest or least expensive routes for its delivery vehicles. The library includes functions like scipy.optimize.minimize, which allows solving optimization problems based on minimizing an objective function, which in this case could be the total delivery cost, defined in terms of kilometers traveled or time spent.

Let's say the distribution company wants to minimize the cost of delivery routes by considering variables like the distance between delivery points and time constraints for each customer. The minimize function can take these variables into account and find the optimal solution. This automation not only saves time in route planning but also reduces operating costs by identifying the most efficient routes. Using SciPy allows these complex calculations to be done quickly and accurately, something that would be very difficult to do manually or with more basic tools.

In addition to route optimization, SciPy can also be useful for manufacturing SMEs looking to minimize production costs. Imagine a company that manufactures different products and uses a variety of raw materials. The company wants to find the optimal combination of raw materials that minimizes the total production cost without compromising the quality of the final product. Using SciPy's optimization functions, the company can define an objective function that represents the total production cost and apply constraints based on product quality or raw material availability. SciPy's optimization algorithm can find the optimal combination of inputs, allowing the company to reduce costs while maintaining quality standards.

Another important aspect of SciPy is its ability to perform advanced statistical analysis. In particular, the scipy.stats module offers a robust set of tools for conducting statistical analyses that are essential for better understanding business data and making informed decisions. This type of analysis is especially useful for SMEs looking to understand market trends, validate business strategies, or improve operational efficiency through historical data analysis.

For example, an SME in the retail sector might be interested in analyzing historical sales data to identify patterns and seasonal trends. Using scipy.stats, the company can calculate basic descriptive statistics, such as the mean, median, and standard deviation, to get a general idea of sales behavior during different periods of the year. However, scipy.stats goes far beyond these basic analyses, allowing businesses to perform hypothesis testing that can help validate business assumptions or identify factors impacting performance.

Let's say an online store is considering implementing a new pricing strategy based on discounts during the summer months. Before launching the strategy, the company wants to ensure that the discounts will have a significant impact on increasing sales. To validate this hypothesis, hypothesis testing provided by SciPy can be used, such as the Student's t-test (scipy.stats.ttest_ind). This test allows you to compare two groups of data, in this case, sales with and without discounts, to determine if the difference in sales is statistically significant.

Let's imagine the company tests the new discount scheme for a month on a subset of its products and then compares the sales data with the same month in previous years when no discounts were applied. With the Student's t-test, they can analyze whether the increase in sales is significant enough to justify implementing the strategy across the entire store. If the results indicate that the difference is significant, the company can make the decision with confidence, knowing that their new pricing strategy is likely to be effective.

In addition to hypothesis testing, scipy.stats includes tools for performing linear regressions, which are useful for predicting future trends based on historical data. For an SME looking to project sales for the next quarter, linear regression can be a powerful technique. By modeling sales based on variables such as seasonality, customer behavior, or the effects of previous promotions, the company can obtain more accurate predictions to guide its future business decisions.

For example, if a SME in the food and beverage sector is evaluating the impact of a recent advertising campaign on sales, it can use a linear regression model to analyze the relationship between advertising spend and sales increase. Using scipy.stats.linregress, the company can identify if there is a significant correlation between the two variables and, if so, project how future changes in the marketing budget could affect sales. This ability to link different variables is especially useful for small and medium-sized enterprises, as it allows them to assess the return on investment in their campaigns and adjust their strategies in a more informed way.

Another valuable function provided by SciPy for statistical analysis is correlation, which allows you to measure the strength of the relationship between two or more variables. For a marketing company, for example, it could be interesting to understand how different factors are correlated, such as advertising spend, social media interactions, and sales. Using functions like scipy.stats.pearsonr, the company can calculate the Pearson correlation coefficient, which measures the linear relationship between two datasets. If the coefficient is high, this would indicate a strong correlation, and the company could focus more resources on the factors that are most related to sales growth.

In addition to Pearson correlation, SciPy offers other types of correlation analysis, such as Spearman correlation (scipy.stats.spearmanr), which is useful when the relationships between data are not linear. For an SME managing social media, it might be more useful to use Spearman correlation to analyze how social media interactions change in relation to sales, since the relationships between these factors may not always be linear. With these tools, SciPy allows businesses to explore different types of relationships in their data, gaining a deeper and more accurate understanding of the factors driving their performance.

In addition to statistical analysis, SciPy also includes a range of tools for performing advanced scientific calculations that can be useful for SMEs operating in sectors such as engineering, manufacturing, or biotechnology. For example, SciPy allows you to solve differential equations, perform Fourier transforms to analyze signals and periodic data, and compute numerical integrals of complex functions. These tools can be especially useful for SMEs that need to carry out precise and efficient calculations in the context of their operational activities.

For example, a small business working on optimizing manufacturing processes can use SciPy to model energy production in a manufacturing plant or to calculate energy conversion efficiency in a system. By modeling the plant's data using SciPy's calculation tools, the company can identify weaknesses in its production process and make adjustments to improve efficiency. These tools give SMEs capabilities that were previously only available to large companies with dedicated research teams.

Another example of using SciPy in manufacturing is the optimization of product design. Imagine an SME that produces parts for the automotive industry and needs to find a design that minimizes the weight of a part without compromising its strength. With SciPy's optimization functions, the company can model different geometries of the part and perform calculations to find the optimal combination of materials and design that maximizes strength while minimizing weight. This not only improves product quality but also reduces production costs by minimizing material use.

In summary, SciPy complements NumPy by providing a series of advanced tools for optimization and statistical analysis, allowing SMEs to tackle complex problems with data-driven solutions. From optimizing delivery routes to analyzing correlations and conducting hypothesis testing, SciPy facilitates informed decision-making and improves operational efficiency across multiple sectors. The capabilities offered by SciPy not only allow companies to gain deeper insights into their data but also provide them with tools to solve practical problems that have a direct impact on their daily operations.

- **Leverage the power of PySpark in the analysis of large volumes of data in SMEs**

PySpark is the interface of Apache Spark for Python, and it provides a powerful and accessible solution for distributed processing of large data volumes. In a business environment where data is growing at an accelerated pace, even SMEs face the need to manage massive amounts of information. PySpark emerges as a key tool to facilitate this process, enabling large-scale data handling quickly and efficiently. For small and medium-sized enterprises that are beginning to deal with large volumes of data, such as transactions, customer records, or social media data, PySpark offers a flexible and scalable option to tackle these challenges.

One of the fundamental features that make PySpark so attractive is its ability to process data in parallel across multiple nodes, allowing large datasets to be split and computations to be performed simultaneously, leveraging the power of multiple processors. This means that tasks that would normally take hours or even days to complete on a traditional processing system can be done in a fraction of the time when using PySpark. For SMEs, where resources are limited, the ability to handle large volumes of data without the need for expensive IT infrastructure is a major benefit.

One of the first things to understand when working with PySpark is the concept of RDDs (Resilient Distributed Datasets). RDDs are the core component of PySpark, representing a distributed collection of objects that can be processed in parallel. RDDs allow developers to work with distributed data efficiently, as Spark handles data distribution across different nodes and manages faults in case of errors during processing. For an SME handling large volumes of data, such as transaction or sales records, RDDs enable distributed data processing without worrying about the underlying infrastructure.

For example, a company that collects large amounts of server logs can use RDDs in PySpark to analyze these logs and extract useful information, such as the frequency of server errors or the identification of unusual patterns in network traffic. By splitting the logs into small parts and processing them in parallel, the company can analyze large volumes of data in real-time, something that would be impossible to achieve with traditional tools not designed to handle distributed data. PySpark allows for this type of analysis efficiently, enhancing the company's ability to identify problems before they severely impact operations.

However, for SMEs that are more familiar with traditional data management tools, working with RDDs can be complex and require a deeper understanding of how distributed processing works. This is where PySpark DataFrames come into play. A DataFrame is a distributed data structure that closely resembles a table in a relational database or a Pandas DataFrame in Python. DataFrames allow developers to work with distributed data using a simpler and more familiar API, making it easier to analyze large volumes of information without having to deal with the complexity of RDDs.

For an SME, the ability to work with DataFrames in PySpark is a significant advantage, as it allows analysts and data scientists who are used to working with tools like Pandas to quickly adapt to PySpark and start analyzing large-scale data without a deep learning curve in RDDs. For example, if an e-commerce company wants to analyze customer transactions to identify buying patterns or predict product demand, they can load that data into a PySpark DataFrame and perform the same operations they would with Pandas, but with the capacity to process millions of records in a distributed and efficient manner.

One of the most powerful features of DataFrames in PySpark is their ability to execute SQL queries over distributed data. This means that an SME already familiar with using SQL for queries and analysis of traditional databases can continue using that knowledge in a distributed environment without having to learn a new programming language or completely restructure their workflow. PySpark allows companies to combine the familiarity of SQL with the power of parallel processing, making it easier to transition to managing large volumes of data.

For example, a digital marketing company could use PySpark to analyze user behavior data on their web platform. This data may include metrics such as the number of page visits, session durations, ad interactions, or user journeys on the site. By loading this data into PySpark DataFrames, the company can run SQL queries on millions of records to identify trends or behavior patterns, such as the time of day when users are more likely to interact with certain types of content or which sections of the site generate the most traffic. This type of analysis is essential for optimizing advertising campaigns and improving user experience, and PySpark allows it to be done efficiently even with large volumes of data.

In addition to facilitating the analysis of large volumes of data, PySpark also offers support for real-time processing, which is essential for SMEs that need to analyze data as it is generated. This is especially relevant for companies handling real-time data, such as an e-commerce platform that needs to monitor live transactions to detect potential fraud or dynamically adjust prices based on demand. With PySpark, companies can process large data streams in real time using Spark Streaming, an extension of Spark designed to handle continuous data transmission. This allows real-time data to be divided into small batches, processed in parallel, and stored or analyzed almost instantly.

A practical case of using PySpark in an SME is a cloud services company that handles large volumes of server logs generated by clients. These logs contain information about server performance, resource usage, and any errors that occur during operation. Processing these logs manually or with traditional tools can be overwhelming due to the amount of data generated every second. However, by using PySpark, the company can distribute the logs across multiple processing nodes and analyze them in parallel, allowing them to quickly identify performance issues or potential server failures. This not only improves operational efficiency but also enables the company to offer better customer service by responding more quickly to problems.

What's more, PySpark is extremely useful for SMEs that rely on social media data analysis. Social networks generate huge amounts of unstructured data, and companies that want to leverage this data to improve their marketing strategies or better understand customer behavior need a tool that can handle this type of information at scale. With PySpark, a marketing company can collect, store, and analyze data from multiple social media platforms in real-time, allowing them to identify emerging trends, measure the impact of advertising campaigns, and adjust content strategies based on user reactions.

For example, a small fashion business trying to expand its presence on social media could use PySpark to analyze tweets and comments related to its products. By loading this data into DataFrames and applying natural language processing techniques, the company can identify which products are being talked about the most, which generate more positive or negative interactions, and how the audience responds to different promotional campaigns. This large-scale analysis provides the company with a clearer view of the impact of its brand on social media, allowing it to adjust its marketing approach more effectively and timely.

Another key aspect of PySpark is its ability to integrate with other distributed data systems and tools that are common in companies handling large volumes of data. For example, PySpark can easily integrate with Hadoop, a distributed file system that allows for efficient storage and management of large data volumes. For an SME already using Hadoop as its data storage infrastructure, adding PySpark as a distributed processing layer provides a complete solution that allows both storage and scalable processing of large amounts of data.

Let's imagine a logistics company that collects millions of data points every day related to the location of its vehicles, the status of shipments, and delivery routes. This company can store all this data in Hadoop and then use PySpark to process and analyze it in a distributed manner. The company could, for example, use PySpark to identify patterns in delivery delays or to optimize vehicle routes based on historical traffic data. This ability to handle large volumes of data and process them in a distributed way allows the company to be more efficient in its daily operations and reduce operational costs related to logistics.

Another example of integration with PySpark is its ability to work alongside machine learning tools like MLlib, which is the machine learning library for Apache Spark. This allows SMEs to apply machine learning algorithms to large datasets without having to transfer the data to another system or use additional tools. For instance, a company that wants to predict the churn rate can use PySpark to load historical customer behavior data, apply classification or regression algorithms from MLlib, and obtain predictions about which customers are most likely to leave the service. This allows the company to take preventive measures, such as offering personalized incentives or discounts to retain at-risk customers.

In summary, PySpark offers an accessible and scalable solution for SMEs to efficiently process large volumes of data. From optimizing logistics routes to real-time analysis of social media data or processing server logs, PySpark provides companies with the ability to leverage the power of distributed processing without the need for costly or complex infrastructure. Key features of PySpark, such as RDDs and DataFrames, allow working with large amounts of data in a flexible and familiar way, making it easier for SMEs to adopt this tool.

- **Dask for handling large volumes of data in small businesses**

Dask is a parallel computing tool that has gained popularity among SMEs for its ability to handle large volumes of data without the need to invest in costly infrastructure. Unlike other more complex distributed processing tools like PySpark, Dask integrates very easily into workflows that already use Pandas, NumPy, or scikit-learn, making it easy for companies that need to scale their analyses and optimize their resources. For small and medium-sized businesses working with data that exceeds available memory or wanting to parallelize tasks to improve efficiency, Dask offers an efficient and accessible solution.

One of the most notable features of Dask is its ability to work with DataFrames that don't fit in memory. SMEs that handle large amounts of data, such as daily sales transactions on e-commerce platforms or customer databases, often find that their datasets grow quickly and start to exceed the memory capacity of a single machine. This is where Dask comes into play, allowing companies to manage these large volumes of data in a way that wouldn't be possible using tools like Pandas alone.

Let's imagine an online store that handles hundreds of thousands of customer transactions every month. If the company is using Pandas to analyze the data, it will encounter limitations as the volume of information grows, since Pandas loads the entire dataset into memory, causing the system to slow down or even crash when the available memory is saturated. In contrast, Dask allows DataFrames to be split into smaller chunks called partitions, which can be processed separately and in parallel. This means that Dask DataFrames can handle much larger amounts of data without being limited by the amount of memory available on a single machine.

For an e-commerce SME, this means they can now perform more detailed and complex analyses on customer behavior without worrying that the data will exceed their system's capacity. For example, the company can use Dask DataFrames to analyze purchasing patterns during different times of the year, perform customer segmentation based on purchase history, or calculate the average transaction value efficiently, even if the customer database is very large. With Dask, businesses can load and analyze much larger datasets without the need to invest in expensive servers or complex distributed processing systems.

Another key advantage of Dask is its ability to facilitate parallel computing in Python. Unlike other tools that require complex setup to parallelize tasks, Dask is designed to easily integrate with the Python functions that businesses are already using. This allows SMEs to parallelize tasks that were previously executed sequentially, significantly improving performance and reducing processing times. For companies managing large volumes of historical data, such as sales transactions or inventory records, parallel computing with Dask offers a simple way to process that data efficiently.

Let's suppose a distribution company has several years of inventory data stored and needs to conduct a detailed analysis to identify long-term trends or forecast future demand. With Python, sequential analysis of this data can take a long time, especially if the data volume is large and the analysis requires complex calculations, such as demand forecasting based on seasonality or market behavior. However, with Dask, the company can parallelize the analysis, breaking the data into multiple tasks that run simultaneously. This allows the company to process the data in a fraction of the time it would take with a sequential approach.

Dask allows tasks to be distributed across different CPU cores on the same machine or, if necessary, on a cluster of machines. This means that companies can easily scale their data analysis as they grow, without having to significantly change their code or workflow. For an SME analyzing inventories, this can be crucial for making quicker decisions about product restocking, optimizing distribution routes, or adjusting production planning to reduce costs and avoid overstock or stockout issues.

Another important application of Dask in SMEs is its ability to work with large volumes of historical transaction data. Many companies collect sales data over several years, allowing them to identify patterns and trends that can help adjust their business strategies and optimize operations. However, working with these large volumes of data can be challenging when using traditional tools not designed to handle large datasets. With Dask, SMEs can parallelize the processing of this data, allowing analyses that previously took days to be completed in a matter of hours or minutes.

For example, a retail company that collects sales data over several seasons can use Dask to analyze the performance of specific products during different times of the year and discover what factors drive sales. Instead of processing all the data sequentially, Dask allows tasks to be divided and executed in parallel, speeding up the analysis and enabling the company to obtain results more quickly and efficiently. With this ability to process large volumes of historical data, the company can adjust its inventory strategies, optimize its marketing campaigns, and better predict future demand.

Another significant advantage of Dask is that it is highly scalable, meaning it can easily adapt to a company's growing needs as it handles more data or requires more complex analysis. SMEs can start using Dask on a single machine and, as their processing needs increase, they can scale their analyses by distributing tasks across a cluster of machines without changing the code. This scalability is especially useful for small businesses that are growing and need to increase their data processing capacity without making significant investments in infrastructure.

For a data analytics SME that provides consulting services to other companies, the ability to scale its analysis processes is essential to serve more clients without sacrificing performance or accuracy. Dask allows the company to handle large amounts of data for multiple clients simultaneously by distributing processing tasks across several cores or machines, ensuring that all analyses are performed efficiently and without delays. This flexibility is crucial for a company looking to expand its operations and increase its service capacity without incurring significant operating costs.

In addition to its scalability, Dask also offers the advantage of being compatible with many of the most used libraries in the Python ecosystem, such as Pandas, NumPy, and scikit-learn. This means that companies already using these tools can expand their capacity to handle large volumes of data without needing to learn new technologies or significantly change their workflow. Dask integrates seamlessly into existing workflows, allowing SMEs to leverage its distributed processing power without having to abandon the tools they are already familiar with.

For example, a fintech company using Pandas to analyze financial data can migrate to Dask DataFrames to handle larger datasets without needing to completely rewrite their code. By using Dask, the company can process and analyze large volumes of financial transactions in parallel, allowing them to identify patterns and anomalies in the data more quickly and respond more agilely to market demands. Dask's ability to scale and work with familiar tools like Pandas makes it a natural choice for SMEs looking to optimize their workflow without a steep learning curve.

Another key advantage of Dask is its ability to handle both memory-intensive calculations and disk-dependent computations, making it ideal for companies that need to work with large volumes of data that don't fit in memory. Many SMEs collect large amounts of data that may not be needed all at once but still need to be processed and analyzed to extract useful insights. With Dask, companies can work with these large datasets efficiently, as the system allows for calculations on disk when available memory is insufficient, providing a flexible solution for managing large-scale data.

An example of this would be a logistics company that collects location data from thousands of vehicles in real time. The location data may be too large to be handled in the memory of a single machine, but with Dask, the company can process this data in partitions and perform disk-based analysis without compromising performance. This allows the company to track the status of its vehicles in real time, optimize delivery routes, and improve operational efficiency without the need to invest in costly infrastructure or more complex processing solutions.

For SMEs that need to optimize their resources and improve their data analysis capabilities, Dask offers an accessible and scalable solution for handling large volumes of data and performing parallel computing efficiently. Its integration with the Python ecosystem and its ability to work with data that doesn't fit in memory make it a valuable tool for any company looking to make the most of their data without incurring the high costs associated with other distributed processing infrastructures.

3.2. Process optimization with Pandas and NumPy for large volumes of data

Pandas and NumPy are two of the most widely used libraries in Python for data analysis and manipulation. Although they are well-known for their ease of use and efficiency when working with moderately sized datasets, their true power can also be leveraged to optimize processes involving large volumes of data. For SMEs that are beginning to manage growing datasets, such as sales records, inventories, or customer transactions, it's essential to find ways to improve performance and efficiency in their workflows.

NumPy, with its ability to perform mathematical operations on arrays very efficiently, is the foundation upon which Pandas builds its data structures, like DataFrames. However, when data volumes start to grow, it's necessary to adopt techniques and best practices to ensure operations remain fast and system resources are used optimally.

In this context, Pandas offers several tools that allow for transformations and analysis on large datasets without compromising performance, from efficient column and row manipulation to reducing the amount of data in memory. At the same time, NumPy allows for vectorized numerical calculations, avoiding loops and making operations on large arrays significantly faster.

For an SME that needs to optimize its data analysis processes, whether in inventory management or sales analysis, the proper use of Pandas and NumPy not only improves performance but also facilitates real-time data-driven decision-making. In this section, we will explore how advanced techniques in these libraries can help companies work more efficiently with large volumes of data, maintaining scalability and reducing processing time.

- ### Maximize Pandas performance for large volumes of data

Code optimization with Pandas is essential when working with large volumes of data. For SMEs handling large datasets such as sales records, transactions, inventories, or customer data, using Pandas efficiently can make a big difference in processing speed and capacity. Pandas is an incredibly powerful tool for data manipulation, but its performance can suffer as data volumes grow if certain optimizations aren't applied. With the right techniques, like efficient data type management, vectorizing operations, and smart use of the apply function, companies can process more data in less time with fewer resources.

One of the first steps to optimizing the use of Pandas with large datasets is to ensure that the data types used in DataFrames are as efficient as possible. A common mistake when working with Pandas is to let the library automatically assign data types when loading large datasets, which often leads to unnecessary memory usage. By default, Pandas assigns data types like float64 or int64, which, although suitable for many operations, can be excessive if that precision or range of values is not needed. This is especially important when dealing with numerical or categorical data.

For example, if an SME is working with sales data where decimal precision isn't critical, reducing the data type from float64 to float32 can cut memory usage in half without compromising analysis accuracy. Changing data types may seem like a minor optimization, but when dealing with millions of records, the impact can be significant. A simple data type conversion can free up enormous amounts of memory, allowing the system to process data faster without resorting to disk usage or slowing down other operations. This type of optimization not only helps improve data processing efficiency but also reduces operational costs by decreasing the need for more powerful or expensive infrastructure to handle large data volumes.

Another example is when a company works with categorical data, such as product names or customer categories. When loading text data into a DataFrame, Pandas tends to assign the data type 'object', which can be quite inefficient in terms of memory. However, converting those columns to categories can drastically reduce memory usage. Categories allow Pandas to store unique values as a dictionary and assign an index to each of those values instead of repeatedly storing text strings. For a company managing thousands of products, this can reduce the DataFrame size by a factor of 10 or more, leading to a significant improvement in operational speed and a reduction in memory consumption.

A clear example would be an online store with a catalog of thousands of products, where each recorded transaction includes the product name, category, and other related data. If each record contains text strings describing these products, operations on this dataset can become extremely slow. By converting text columns into categories, not only is memory usage reduced, but operations like filtering or grouping by categories also become much faster, as Pandas only needs to handle indices instead of comparing text strings in each operation.

Another key technique for improving performance when working with large datasets is the vectorization of operations. Vectorization is a technique that allows operations on entire arrays instead of processing each element individually. Pandas and NumPy, on which Pandas is built, are designed to make the most of this technique. When vectorized operations are performed, processing is much faster because it avoids the use of loops in Python, which tend to be slow when handling large volumes of data.

Instead of processing a column or row of a DataFrame using a for loop, you can apply a vectorized operation to the entire column, which drastically reduces processing time. For example, if a SME needs to adjust the prices of its products based on a percentage increase or discount, instead of iterating over each row to calculate the new price, you can simply apply a vectorized mathematical operation to the entire price column. This not only reduces the code required but also significantly improves speed.

Let's say a retail company wants to increase all prices by 10% to adjust for inflationary costs. Instead of using a loop to update each price, you can apply the following vectorized operation in Pandas: df['price'] *= 1.10. This simple line of code allows you to adjust the prices of hundreds of thousands of products in seconds, whereas a loop-based approach might take much longer to complete. The efficiency gained by using vectorized operations is essential when handling large volumes of real-time data or when complex analysis needs to be performed in a short period of time.

In addition, vectorization is also crucial for more advanced operations, such as calculating statistics or applying complex functions to entire columns of data. For an SME analyzing sales data, for example, vectorization can speed up the execution of common operations like calculating averages, sums, or standard deviations over large datasets, allowing insights to be obtained much faster and more efficiently.

A frequently used tool in Pandas is the `apply` function. `apply` allows you to apply a custom function across the rows or columns of a DataFrame, and it's incredibly useful when you need to perform complex transformations that can't be easily achieved with standard vectorized operations. However, the `apply` function can also be a significant bottleneck in terms of performance if not used correctly. While it's flexible, `apply` is not optimized for working with large volumes of data, as it performs the operation row by row or column by column, meaning you lose the advantage of vectorization.

For SMEs working with large datasets, it's crucial to understand when to avoid using apply and switch to more efficient alternatives. While apply is useful in specific situations, whenever possible, it's better to use vectorized operations or functions that are already optimized in Pandas or NumPy. For example, if a company needs to calculate the total price of each transaction by multiplying the number of products by the unit price, instead of using apply to iterate over each row and perform the calculation, you can perform a vectorized operation directly: df['total'] = df['cantidad'] * df['precio_unitario']. This approach is not only simpler but also much faster, especially when handling millions of transactions.

However, there are situations where using apply is unavoidable, such as when you need to apply very specific or custom functions that can't be vectorized. In those cases, it is advisable to minimize its use by applying it only to specific columns rather than the entire DataFrame. You can also use optimizations like Numba, a library that allows you to compile functions at runtime to make apply faster. Numba optimizes functions written in Python and significantly speeds up operations, which can be useful when working with complex functions that can't be easily vectorized.

Another alternative to optimize the use of apply is to explore other tools that offer task parallelization. For example, libraries like Dask allow you to parallelize Pandas operations, including apply, by dividing the dataset into smaller chunks that are processed simultaneously across multiple CPU cores. This allows you to maintain the flexibility of apply without sacrificing performance in cases where the data volumes are too large to be efficiently handled by a single core.

Finally, another aspect to consider when optimizing code in Pandas is the use of built-in and specific Pandas functions instead of relying on general Python functions. Pandas native functions like groupby, merge, join, and agg are optimized to work with DataFrames and perform operations much faster than generic functions that are not specifically designed for table data processing. For an SME that frequently performs data grouping or merging operations, ensuring these operations are carried out using Pandas' optimized functions can drastically improve data analysis performance.

For example, a retail company that needs to combine multiple databases of products and transactions can use Pandas' merge function to efficiently join these datasets, instead of using Python's generic join functions. This not only reduces runtime but also allows handling large datasets more consistently without losing key information.

In summary, optimizing the use of Pandas for large volumes of data involves applying a series of techniques that improve code efficiency, reduce resource consumption, and speed up processing. By using efficient data types, taking advantage of vectorization, and optimizing the use of apply, SMEs can handle large data volumes without the need to invest in costly infrastructure or worry about performance bottlenecks.

- ### Optimization in managing massive data for SMEs

Handling large volumes of data has become a common challenge for SMEs as the business grows and data begins to accumulate continuously. In companies managing thousands of daily transactions, expanding customer databases, or detailed sales records, efficient handling of these data volumes is crucial for making informed decisions. However, many SMEs may find limitations in their usual tools when datasets start to exceed available memory, leading to performance issues and greater complexity in information processing.

One of the most effective techniques for working with large datasets in Pandas is reading by chunks. When trying to load a large file into memory, like a CSV with millions of sales or transaction records, the system may run out of memory, causing the process to slow down or even the program to crash. To avoid these issues, Pandas offers the option to read files in smaller pieces, known as chunks, which allows you to process portions of the dataset sequentially without overloading the memory.

Let's assume an e-commerce SME is working with a transaction data file containing several years of information, with millions of records documenting every purchase made on its platform. Trying to load this entire file in one go can be unfeasible if memory resources are limited. This is where the chunk reading technique comes into play. Instead of loading the whole file at once, Pandas allows you to load the file in smaller fragments using the chunksize parameter. This enables the file to be processed in more manageable data blocks.

For example, if the CSV file contains 10 million rows, it can be split into chunks of 100,000 rows using the following command in Pandas: pd.read_csv('transactions.csv', chunksize=100000). This way, the file will be loaded in blocks of 100,000 rows at a time, allowing you to work with each data fragment without overloading the memory. This approach is especially useful when you need to perform analysis or calculations on large datasets that don't fit in the available memory.

An additional advantage of reading in chunks is that it allows SMEs to process large volumes of data in a data pipeline efficiently. For example, if a company is analyzing daily sales to identify patterns or perform aggregations, it can read each chunk, perform the necessary operations, and then discard the data fragment once the analysis is complete. This ensures that only relevant and necessary information is kept in memory at any given time, optimizing resource usage.

Let's say the e-commerce company wants to calculate the total sales for each month over a five-year period. Instead of loading all the sales data into memory, they can process the data month by month using chunks, sum the sales for each month, and then move on to the next chunk. In the end, the company will have the desired results without having to load all the data into memory at once.

Another important technique for handling large volumes of data is the integration of NumPy to speed up intensive numerical calculations. NumPy is a fundamental library in the Python ecosystem, specifically designed to perform mathematical calculations and numerical operations efficiently, thanks to its ability to work directly with arrays and matrices. Since NumPy uses vectorized operations and is optimized at a low level, it can process large volumes of data much faster than traditional list-based or loop-based operations in Python.

For SMEs that handle large amounts of numerical data, such as financial analysis, sales margin calculations, or inventory forecasts, NumPy can be a key ally in large-scale data processing. A practical example would be a manufacturing company that needs to calculate the total production cost of thousands of products based on several factors, such as the cost of raw materials, labor costs, and indirect production costs. Instead of processing each row of data individually in a loop, NumPy allows these operations to be performed in a vectorized manner, applying calculations to an entire column of data at once, which significantly speeds up the process.

One of the most notable advantages of NumPy is that it's designed to operate directly on multidimensional arrays, allowing complex operations on large datasets with minimal memory and processing time. When combined with Pandas, NumPy can be integrated into the workflow to optimize calculations and improve the performance of operations. For example, if a retail company is analyzing prices and profit margins on millions of sales records, it can use NumPy to quickly calculate the differences between purchase and sale prices, instead of processing each record individually.

Let's imagine that the company needs to calculate the profit margin for each sale in a database containing millions of transactions. By using NumPy, this calculation can be vectorized as follows: profit_margin = np.subtract(df['sale_price'], df['purchase_price']), which subtracts the purchase prices from the sale prices across all records simultaneously. This approach allows the calculation to be performed in a fraction of the time it would take using loops or non-optimized functions. Moreover, NumPy can handle large volumes of data efficiently since it is optimized for numerical operations on arrays.

Another important aspect is that NumPy integrates perfectly into data pipelines, allowing SMEs to automate and optimize calculations within their processing flows. For example, a logistics company that needs to calculate delivery times for thousands of orders based on distance, traffic, and other factors can use NumPy to perform these calculations in parallel rather than sequentially. This ability to perform parallel computing and optimize calculations within a pipeline allows the company's operations to be more agile and executed in real time, improving both operational efficiency and the ability to make quick decisions.

A practical case of this integration would be a financial analysis company that handles large amounts of transaction data and historical prices. When processing financial data, it's crucial that operations are performed efficiently, as the analysis may include millions of data points that need to be calculated quickly to generate reports or recommendations for clients. By using NumPy within the data analysis pipeline, the company can calculate statistics such as standard deviations, moving averages, or regression analysis much faster than with traditional methods. This allows the company to offer a more efficient service to its clients while optimizing its own operational resources.

An additional advantage of NumPy is that it also allows logical and comparison operations to be performed in a vectorized way, which can be useful for filtering or classifying large volumes of data. For example, if a retail SME wants to identify all transactions where discounts of more than 20% were applied, they can use NumPy to quickly filter all records that meet this criterion. By performing these types of operations on entire arrays instead of using loops, NumPy allows these tasks to be carried out quickly and efficiently, even when working with millions of records.

A combined approach of reading by chunks with Pandas and using NumPy for intensive calculations is especially useful for SMEs that are in the process of scaling their operations and need to improve efficiency in data management without investing in expensive hardware or advanced IT infrastructures. These techniques allow for the optimization of both reading large volumes of data and performing intensive calculations that may arise in the day-to-day operations of businesses, from inventory and pricing management to sales forecasting or financial analysis.

For example, a distribution SME that tracks thousands of daily deliveries can use Pandas to process delivery data in chunks and then apply NumPy to calculate the efficiency of each delivery route based on distances traveled and delivery times. This approach not only allows the company to analyze large volumes of data efficiently but also optimizes its logistics operations by identifying areas where costs can be reduced or punctuality improved.

Moreover, the use of Pandas and NumPy is not limited to large companies. These tools are accessible to SMEs as they easily integrate into existing workflows and do not require significant investments in infrastructure. Techniques like reading in chunks and vectorized calculations with NumPy allow businesses to work with data that might have been too large or complex to handle before, enabling them to compete more effectively in markets where data-driven decision-making is increasingly important.

In the context of digital transformation, these techniques allow SMEs to leverage data more strategically. By using Pandas to handle large volumes of data in chunks and NumPy for intensive calculations, companies can not only optimize their internal processes but also gain valuable insights from their data that can directly influence profitability and growth. In an environment where the ability to handle large volumes of data is key to survival and success, mastering these techniques allows SMEs to remain competitive and adapt to the ever-changing market demands.

3.3. Creating efficient data pipelines with advanced functions in Python

Creating efficient data pipelines is a key aspect for SMEs that handle large volumes of information or need to automate their data workflows. A data pipeline is a sequence of steps that transform, clean, and process data in a structured way to achieve specific results, whether for analysis, reporting, or integration with other systems. As business data grows in volume and complexity, the need to optimize these pipelines becomes crucial to maintain efficiency and avoid bottlenecks in analysis processes.

Advanced functions in Python allow you to build pipelines that are not only efficient but also scalable and flexible. Python, with its rich ecosystem of libraries like Pandas, NumPy, and Dask, provides tools that make creating these workflows easier. By using techniques such as operation vectorization, reading in chunks, and integrating libraries for handling large volumes of data, it's possible to design pipelines that manage data smoothly and efficiently, even when hardware resources are limited.

For SMEs, creating efficient data pipelines offers multiple benefits, such as reducing processing times, saving operational costs, and enabling real-time data-driven decision-making. Additionally, with the use of advanced

Python functions, it's possible to integrate various data sources, automate repetitive processes, and optimize tasks that would otherwise require continuous manual intervention. For example, a company that collects daily sales data from multiple platforms can use an automated pipeline to integrate this data, clean it, and generate real-time reports that help identify trends or adjust business strategies.

In this section, we will explore how to leverage advanced functions in Python to create fast and efficient data pipelines, covering topics such as automating data cleaning processes, optimizing complex calculations, and integrating multiple streams of information into a single pipeline.

- ### How to Structure Data Pipelines for Effective Automation

Process automation with pipelines is essential for SMEs that want to optimize their workflows and reduce the time needed to process large volumes of data, from initial acquisition to actionable insights. Instead of relying on manual or fragmented processes, a well-designed pipeline allows data to flow continuously and structured through various processing stages, minimizing errors and maximizing efficiency. Automated pipelines not only speed up response times but also enable companies to handle real-time data, providing a solid foundation for data-driven decision-making.

One of the key elements in creating efficient pipelines is the use of lambda functions and higher-order functions. Lambda functions, also known as anonymous functions, are small, fast functions that don't need to be declared with a name and can be defined in a single line of code. These functions are particularly useful in process automation, as they allow for more concise and readable code, making it easier to integrate them into a pipeline without sacrificing functionality.

For example, let's imagine that a SME wants to process a dataset of daily sales for its products. To calculate the sales tax for each transaction, instead of creating a full function to perform the calculation, a lambda function can be used within the data pipeline. If the tax rate is 21%, the lambda function could be defined like this: lambda x: x * 0.21. This allows you to calculate the tax for each value in a price column of a Pandas DataFrame quickly and efficiently, integrating it into the pipeline flow without the need to write long functions that would later be difficult to reuse or maintain.

The use of lambda functions is especially beneficial in repetitive tasks or when it's necessary to apply a transformation to data in a simple yet effective way. Instead of writing multiple lines of code for basic mathematical operations, lambda functions allow these calculations to be applied more smoothly within the pipeline, optimizing development speed and reducing overall code complexity. This is particularly useful when working with simple transformations on large volumes of data, such as scaling values, adjusting prices, calculating discounts, or performing unit conversions. These small transformations can be applied at various stages of the pipeline without adding overhead to the code.

In addition to lambda functions, higher-order functions also play a crucial role in automating pipelines in Python. Higher-order functions are those that can take other functions as arguments or return functions as results. These functions allow pipelines to be modular and reusable, making it easier to create flexible and scalable workflows. For an SME that needs to continuously process different types of data, higher-order functions enable the application of common processing patterns consistently, without having to rewrite code for each new data set or situation.

An example of a higher-order function is the map() function, which applies a function to all elements of an iterable (like a list or a DataFrame) and returns a new iterable with the results. In a data pipeline, map() can be used to apply a transformation to each element of a dataset efficiently. Suppose a company has a list of product prices in dollars and wants to convert them to euros. Instead of writing a loop to perform the conversion for each individual price, you can use map() with a lambda function: map(lambda x: x * 0.85, price_list). This quickly applies the conversion to all prices and allows the pipeline to continue to the next stage of processing without interruption.

By using higher-order functions like map(), filter(), and reduce(), SMEs can create more modular pipelines that allow for data transformation, filtering, and aggregation in a single line of code. These functions not only make the code cleaner and more efficient but also enable more scalable pipelines, as the same functions can be applied to different datasets without needing to rewrite processing logic.

Another way to improve the efficiency of pipelines in Python is by using the itertools and functools libraries. These libraries provide a set of tools that allow you to create efficient pipelines by facilitating the handling of iterations and the composition of functions, which simplifies the processing of large volumes of data and improves code reusability. itertools is a library that provides functions to create complex iterators that can process data lazily, meaning they evaluate only when needed. This is particularly useful when working with large datasets or when handling continuous data streams, as it minimizes memory usage and optimizes processing time.

For example, if a logistics company wants to analyze the delivery times of thousands of orders and calculate the average only for those that exceeded a certain time threshold, itertools can facilitate the process. By using itertools.filterfalse(), orders that do not meet the threshold can be removed, while the pipeline continues processing only the relevant data. This efficiency in iteration allows the pipeline to run quickly, even when working with large volumes of data, and ensures that only the necessary data is included in the later stages of analysis.

Another useful function from itertools is itertools.groupby(), which allows you to group elements based on a criterion, which can be very valuable when working with data that needs to be aggregated or categorized before being processed. In a retail SME, for example, it may be necessary to group sales by product categories or specific time periods. By using groupby(), the pipeline can handle these grouping operations efficiently, allowing for aggregate calculations like sums, averages, or counts on large datasets without sacrificing performance.

Functools, on the other hand, offers additional tools for creating more modular and efficient pipelines, making it easier to create more powerful functions by combining and modifying other functions. One of the most useful tools in functools is functools.reduce(), which allows you to reduce a list or iterable to a single value by applying an accumulative function. For example, a company that needs to calculate the total sales for a day from a list of transactions can use reduce() to sum the sales values in an accumulative way, optimizing the process within the pipeline.

Another interesting function of functools is functools.partial(), which allows you to create partial functions by pre-configuring some of the arguments of a function. This is especially useful in a data pipeline where some functions need to be applied repeatedly with certain fixed parameters. For example, if a company needs to calculate the value-added tax (VAT) for multiple products with a fixed rate of 21%, instead of passing that value each time, you can use partial() to create a function that always applies that VAT rate, simplifying the code and reducing the potential for errors.

The combination of itertools and functools allows for the creation of reusable and highly efficient pipelines, where repetitive processes are simplified through the use of iterative and cumulative functions, and custom transformations can be encapsulated in partial functions. This is crucial for SMEs that need to handle constantly growing data and don't have large technical teams, as automation through pipelines enables faster data processing with less human intervention, freeing up time and resources to focus on other critical areas of the business.

Let's imagine a digital marketing company that collects and processes data from multiple social media platforms. Every day, the company receives hundreds of thousands of records that need to be analyzed to extract insights about user behavior, campaign effectiveness, and emerging trends. By using itertools to process this data in batches and functools to apply custom transformations, the company can create an automated pipeline that processes this data efficiently, performing aggregate calculations like counting mentions or identifying the most popular keywords, all without compromising performance or processing time.

The use of itertools and functools also allows for handling continuous data streams, which is essential for SMEs working with real-time data. Instead of processing the entire dataset at once, these libraries allow you to handle data as it arrives, applying transformations and calculations to each fragment without needing to load the entire dataset into memory. This is especially useful for companies that monitor financial transactions, online sales, or social media interactions in real-time, where the ability to process data quickly can make the difference between responding on time or missing a critical business opportunity.

In summary, lambda functions, higher-order functions, and the tools provided by itertools and functools enable SMEs to create more automated, efficient, and scalable data pipelines. These pipelines not only speed up data processing but also make it easier to manage complex workflows that range from initial data acquisition to obtaining strategic insights, optimizing real-time decision-making and reducing the manual workload of the technical team.

- **Luigi and Airflow for effective data pipeline management**

The integration of tasks and data pipeline management has become essential for SMEs that need to automate repetitive processes, such as the generation of daily reports, periodic data collection, or the execution of scheduled tasks in multiple stages. Tools like Luigi and Apache Airflow play a key role in this context, providing small and medium-sized businesses with the ability to create, manage, and monitor data pipelines efficiently. These tools allow for the complete automation of workflows, reducing manual intervention and ensuring that critical processes are executed consistently and on time. They also offer advanced monitoring and error handling features, ensuring that any issues that arise in the pipelines are detected and addressed quickly.

The first approach to task automation with Luigi focuses on managing data pipelines involving multiple interdependent stages. Luigi, developed by Spotify, is a workflow orchestration tool designed to automate long processes that depend on the completion of others. For example, an SME that needs to collect data daily from different sources (such as CRM systems, sales databases, or social media platforms) can build a pipeline with Luigi to ensure that each of these tasks is completed in the correct order before proceeding to the next step in the workflow. Luigi manages task dependencies, ensuring that subsequent tasks do not run until the previous ones have successfully finished.

For example, an e-commerce company could use Luigi to automate a data pipeline that starts by extracting transaction data from the day, cleaning it, transforming it into a suitable format, and finally loading that data into a business intelligence system or reporting database. Each of these tasks (extraction, transformation, loading) is interdependent, and Luigi ensures that the pipeline runs in the correct order and that any errors in a stage are handled appropriately. If a task fails, Luigi detects it and can retry the task or notify the responsible team to intervene, ensuring that data is always available for analysis without interruptions.

One of the main advantages of Luigi is its ability to handle complex tasks with multiple dependencies. Instead of executing all tasks simultaneously, Luigi allows SMEs to structure their workflows in a hierarchical manner, where tasks are executed based on others, and dependencies are strictly respected. This is especially useful for companies handling sensitive or critical data, as it ensures that the final results are consistent and accurate. Additionally, Luigi supports the use of checkpoints, where each completed task can be marked as successful and doesn't need to be repeated if a later task fails, saving time and resources.

Another useful feature of Luigi is its ability to easily integrate with a variety of data systems and tools. For example, Luigi can extract data from SQL databases, external APIs, or file systems, transform it using Python or Pandas, and then load the processed data into storage systems like Amazon S3 or Google Cloud Storage. This makes Luigi a very flexible tool for SMEs, as it can adapt to different workflows without the need to radically modify existing data infrastructures.

In addition, Luigi simplifies real-time pipeline monitoring. With Luigi, SMEs can see the current status of each task within the pipeline, identify potential bottlenecks, and take preventive measures to avoid failures. The clear visualization of workflows and detailed error logging allow companies to manage their processes more efficiently and make informed decisions about when to intervene manually. For businesses that handle large amounts of data and need to ensure that reports and analyses are available in a timely manner, Luigi offers a level of control and reliability that is hard to match with manual methods.

On the other hand, Apache Airflow is another powerful tool for managing data pipelines that has become a preferred option for many SMEs that need a more robust solution to manage and automate complex workflows. Airflow is a workflow orchestration system developed by Airbnb that allows for the scheduling, execution, and monitoring of tasks and processes. Airflow is highly scalable and designed to handle high-volume, complex workflows, making it an ideal tool for growing SMEs looking to automate their data processing.

One of the most notable aspects of Apache Airflow is its Directed Acyclic Graph (DAG) approach, which allows you to visually structure task dependencies and define how they should be executed in the pipeline. Each task in the pipeline is hierarchically connected, and Airflow ensures that tasks are executed in the correct order according to the dependencies defined in the DAG. This not only simplifies the management of complex processes but also provides a level of flexibility that allows SMEs to add or modify tasks without affecting the overall workflow.

For example, an SME that makes online sales might need a daily pipeline that collects sales data, processes that data, generates reports, and sends them via email to the marketing and finance teams. With Airflow, the company can define a DAG that includes all these tasks, from data extraction to report delivery, ensuring they are executed sequentially and that any errors are captured and managed in a timely manner. Moreover,

Airflow allows retrying failed tasks and applying automatic retry policies, which is essential to prevent small errors or temporary failures from completely interrupting the pipeline.

Another key advantage of Airflow is its ability to manage tasks through an intuitive web interface, which makes it easy to monitor and administer pipelines in real-time. SMEs can view the current status of all tasks, reschedule workflows, stop or pause pipelines, and analyze the detailed logs of each task directly from the Airflow control panel. This visual interface allows for a better understanding of the data flow and provides companies with a clear overview of their processes, enabling them to identify potential issues before they impact overall performance.

A fundamental feature of Airflow is its ability to scale horizontally, meaning it can handle an increasing number of tasks and data without compromising performance. This is crucial for SMEs that are growing rapidly and need to ensure that their data pipelines can scale with the increase in data volume and transactions. Airflow allows pipelines to be distributed across multiple nodes, improving processing speed and ensuring that critical data is available on time.

Like Luigi, Airflow also facilitates integration with multiple systems and tools. SMEs that already use cloud services like AWS, Google Cloud, or Azure can easily integrate Airflow to orchestrate tasks that interact with these services. For example, a company storing large volumes of data in Amazon S3 can use Airflow to schedule the extraction, transformation, and loading of that data into an analytics database or reporting system. Additionally, Airflow offers a wide range of operators that allow interaction with databases, APIs, file systems, and other services, making it easier to create complex pipelines without the need to write code from scratch.

Another area where Airflow excels is its ability to manage real-time data pipelines. SMEs that need to process large volumes of data continuously, such as monitoring transactions on e-commerce platforms or collecting data from social media, can use Airflow to define pipelines that run periodically or based on specific events. This allows companies to perform real-time analysis and make quick decisions based on up-to-date data, improving their ability to react to market changes or operational issues.

Let's imagine a marketing company that needs to constantly monitor user interactions on social media to evaluate the effectiveness of campaigns in real time. Airflow allows you to define pipelines that continuously extract this data from social media platforms, process it, and generate reports that are constantly updated. This real-time approach enables the company to adjust its campaigns proactively, based on up-to-date and accurate data.

Another significant advantage of Airflow is its ability to define and manage SLAs (Service Level Agreements) within a pipeline's tasks. This allows SMEs to set specific time limits for task completion. If a task exceeds the defined time, Airflow will send automatic alerts, enabling responsible teams to take corrective action immediately. For companies that rely on the timely completion of reports or daily processes, this functionality ensures that critical deadlines are met without interruptions.

In the context of SMEs, the ability of tools like Luigi and Airflow to manage and monitor complex workflows not only improves operational efficiency but also offers full visibility of processes, ensuring that critical data is processed in a timely and reliable manner. These tools allow companies to automate repetitive tasks, optimize periodic data collection, and ensure that reports and analyses are available when needed, freeing up resources so teams can focus on growth and innovation instead of manual or error-prone tasks.

- ## Task parallelism within a pipeline

Parallelizing tasks within a pipeline is an essential approach for SMEs that handle multiple data streams simultaneously and seek to optimize processing time. When a company manages large volumes of information or data that requires intensive processing, such as sales databases, transactions, or user flows on a platform, executing all tasks sequentially can be slow and inefficient. Parallelization allows several tasks to run simultaneously, distributing the workload across multiple CPU cores or machines, which significantly speeds up the pipeline execution time and optimizes available resources.

In the context of an SME, the ability to parallelize tasks is key to maintaining operational efficiency. Instead of waiting for each stage of the pipeline to complete before starting the next, parallelization allows multiple stages to run simultaneously, making the most of the hardware's processing power. This is particularly useful when managing several data streams that can be processed independently, such as collecting data from different sources, cleaning that data, and aggregating results in real-time. With a well-designed and parallelized pipeline, businesses can gain faster insights and make more informed decisions in less time.

One of the most used tools for task parallelization in Python is the concurrent.futures library, which offers a simple interface for executing tasks in parallel. concurrent.futures allows businesses to run functions in multiple threads or processes, which is especially useful when intensive calculations or simultaneous I/O tasks are needed. For an SME managing multiple data streams, such as collecting data from various APIs, parallelization with concurrent.futures can significantly improve pipeline performance.

For example, let's imagine a marketing company that collects social media data to analyze user behavior and brand mentions. This company may need to extract data from different platforms like Twitter, Facebook, and Instagram, and doing it sequentially would be inefficient and slow. With concurrent.futures, the company can set up a pipeline that makes requests to these platforms' APIs in parallel, allowing it to extract data from all platforms simultaneously, reduce wait times, and process the information faster. This is achieved using the following basic approach with ThreadPoolExecutor:

```python
from concurrent.futures import ThreadPoolExecutor
import requests

def fetch_data_from_api(api_url):
    response = requests.get(api_url)
    return response.json()

api_urls = ["https://api.twitter.com/...", "https://graph.facebook.com/...", "https://api.instagram.com/..."]

with ThreadPoolExecutor(max_workers=3) as executor:
    results = list(executor.map(fetch_data_from_api, api_urls))
```

In this example, requests to the APIs of different platforms are made in parallel using a ThreadPoolExecutor with three worker threads. Each thread handles a request and returns the results, allowing all the APIs to be queried simultaneously, reducing the total execution time of the pipeline.

Another advantage of using concurrent.futures is its ability to efficiently handle both threads and processes. While threads are useful for tasks that involve a lot of I/O, like API requests or file reading, processes are more suitable for computation-intensive tasks that require heavy CPU usage, such as complex mathematical calculations or analysis of large data volumes. For an SME conducting statistical analysis on large datasets,

ProcessPoolExecutor from concurrent.futures can distribute the workload across multiple processes, maximizing CPU resources and reducing the time needed to complete the analysis.

For example, a sales company that needs to calculate the total daily transactions across multiple databases can parallelize this calculation using ProcessPoolExecutor. Instead of calculating the transactions for each database sequentially, which could take hours, they can distribute the task among several processes and calculate them simultaneously.

```python
from concurrent.futures import ProcessPoolExecutor

def calculate_total_sales(db_connection):
    # Función para calcular el total de ventas de una base de datos
    query = "SELECT SUM(total) FROM ventas_diarias"
    result = db_connection.execute(query)
    return result.fetchone()[0]

databases = [db_conn1, db_conn2, db_conn3]

with ProcessPoolExecutor(max_workers=3) as executor:
    total_sales = list(executor.map(calculate_total_sales, databases))
```

In this case, each database is processed by a separate process, allowing the daily sales calculations to be performed simultaneously. This not only improves the pipeline's performance but also reduces the total time needed to obtain results, enabling the company to make data-driven decisions much faster.

Another powerful tool for task parallelization in Python is Dask, a library specifically designed to handle distributed computing and parallel processing for large volumes of data. While concurrent.futures is ideal for parallelizing relatively simple tasks, Dask is more suitable for workflows involving large datasets or complex calculations that need to be executed on machine clusters. For SMEs that are growing and starting to face data volumes that exceed the capacity of a single machine, Dask offers a flexible and scalable solution to run data pipelines in parallel.

Unlike other distributed processing tools, Dask integrates easily with Pandas, NumPy, and other popular Python libraries, making it an ideal choice for SMEs already using these tools for data analysis. Dask DataFrames, for example, allow you to work with datasets that don't fit in the memory of a single machine, by splitting the dataset into partitions that are processed in parallel and then combined to generate aggregated results. This allows companies to handle much larger data volumes without having to rewrite all the code or invest in expensive infrastructure.

For example, a logistics company that needs to analyze large volumes of daily delivery data can use Dask DataFrames to parallelize the analysis of delivery times, distances traveled, and transportation costs. Instead of loading all the data into a Pandas DataFrame, which could exceed available memory, Dask allows the dataset to be split into smaller chunks that are processed in parallel.

```
import dask.dataframe as dd

# Cargar el DataFrame de Dask desde un CSV grande
df = dd.read_csv('datos_entregas.csv')

# Calcular el promedio de tiempo de entrega en paralelo
average_delivery_time = df['tiempo_entrega'].mean().compute()
[ ]
```

In this example, Dask processes delivery data in parallel, allowing the company to get faster results and handle much larger datasets than would be possible with Pandas on a single machine. Additionally, Dask automatically distributes tasks across multiple CPU cores, optimizing resource usage and ensuring that the data pipeline runs efficiently.

Another key feature of Dask is its ability to handle complex data pipelines involving multiple processing stages. For example, an SME in financial services that needs to perform complex analyses on historical transaction data can use Dask to break down the tasks of cleaning, transforming, and analyzing into several stages that run in parallel. Each stage of the pipeline can process data independently, making the overall workflow much faster and more efficient. Dask also provides tools to visualize the pipeline and monitor its progress, allowing businesses to identify bottlenecks and optimize their pipeline in real-time.

Dask is especially useful when working with continuous or real-time data streams. For example, an e-commerce company that needs to analyze user behavior on its website in real time can use Dask to process large volumes of click, search, and transaction data as they are generated. By parallelizing these tasks, the company can quickly identify trends in user behavior and adjust its marketing campaigns or product recommendations in real time, improving customer experience and boosting sales.

In the context of parallelizing tasks in a pipeline, one of the major advantages of Dask is its ability to scale horizontally. SMEs that are starting to handle large volumes of data can begin by running their pipelines on a single machine and, as they grow, scale their infrastructure to run Dask on a cluster of machines, allowing them to handle even larger amounts of data without rewriting code. This scalability makes Dask an ideal solution for growing businesses that need to ensure their data pipeline can grow alongside their business.

In addition to concurrent.futures and Dask, other tools like joblib also offer options for task parallelization within a Python pipeline. joblib is particularly useful when repetitive tasks need to be performed in parallel, such as training multiple machine learning models or evaluating different parameter combinations in a prediction algorithm. joblib allows these tasks to run in parallel, distributing the work across multiple CPU cores, which significantly improves the speed of experiments and reduces the total time needed to train and evaluate models.

For a SME building a recommendation system based on machine learning, for example, joblib can be used to train several models simultaneously, exploring different parameters and algorithms without having to wait for each one to run sequentially. This speeds up the development process and allows the company to reach an optimal solution for its customers faster.

In summary, parallelizing tasks within a pipeline is an essential technique for SMEs that need to improve the efficiency of their workflows and handle large volumes of data simultaneously. With tools like concurrent.futures and Dask, companies can optimize data processing, reduce execution times, and scale their pipelines to handle more data as they grow, all while maintaining flexibility and control over their infrastructure and data processes.

3.4. Advanced Visualization with Matplotlib, Plotly, and Seaborn: Telling Stories with Data

In the previous chapter of my book 'Introduction to Data Science for SMEs and Freelancers,' we already discussed the basic concepts of data visualization and how these tools can help us better interpret the information at our disposal. Data visualization is not just about graphically representing numbers or statistics; it's about telling a story that allows companies to make informed and strategic decisions. In this new section, we will delve into the use of advanced visualization tools like Matplotlib,

Plotly, and Seaborn, which enable us not only to create more complex and attractive graphics but also to explore and communicate the hidden insights within the data.

Matplotlib is a classic library in the Python ecosystem, widely used to create static and highly customizable charts. Although we've already seen some basic uses in previous chapters, here we'll learn how to get more out of it to create more sophisticated visualizations tailored to the specific needs of SMEs. With Matplotlib, it's possible to customize every detail of a chart, from the axes to the colors, allowing data to be presented in the clearest and most effective way.

On the other hand, Seaborn, which is built on Matplotlib, makes it easier to create more complex statistical visualizations with less code. Seaborn is ideal for exploratory data analysis, as it allows you to visualize relationships between multiple variables quickly and effectively. With Seaborn, we can represent correlations, distributions, and trends in large data volumes, which is essential for companies looking to understand patterns in their sales, customer behavior, or product performance.

Finally, Plotly offers us the ability to create interactive charts, which are especially useful when we want to involve other departments or our clients in data interpretation. Interactive charts allow for exploration of different aspects of the data by zooming, selecting variables, or interacting directly with the visualization, adding an extra level of dynamism and understanding.

If you've already worked with the basic visualizations described in the previous book, this chapter will be another step in mastering data visualization tools. If you feel a bit lost or want to review concepts, you can always go back to the first book, where we covered the fundamentals of Matplotlib and the basics of visualization in Python. From here, we'll dive into more advanced techniques so you can tell impactful stories with your data and make the most of them.

• Advanced customization with Matplotlib and Seaborn

Advanced customization with Matplotlib and Seaborn allows SMEs to create data visualizations that are not only aesthetically pleasing but also communicate valuable information clearly and effectively. In a business environment, the ability to tell a compelling story through charts is essential for decision-making, as it allows the visualization of patterns, trends, and anomalies in the data. As companies progress in the use of data science, the demand for more sophisticated and personalized graphs becomes more important. This is especially true for those who want to integrate their visualizations into executive reports, presentations, or internal dashboards.

One of the most powerful aspects of Matplotlib and Seaborn is their ability to create complex and fully customized plots. While at basic levels you can generate simple line, bar, or scatter plots, at this advanced level it's essential to learn how to combine multiple types of charts and organize them coherently into subplots that can display different aspects of the data simultaneously. This ability to combine several plots in a single space allows SMEs to create simple dashboards, which are crucial for conducting deeper analysis and understanding the interaction between different variables.

For example, imagine a company wants to analyze daily sales, the number of website visits, and the number of returns. Instead of creating separate charts that show each metric individually, you can build a dashboard that combines a line chart for sales, a bar chart for visits, and a scatter plot for returns. This allows decision-makers to see the relationships between these variables at a glance and answer key questions, such as whether an increase in visits is correlated with an increase in sales or if returns have any relation to a specific change in website traffic.

To create a dashboard with subplots in Matplotlib, you can use several functions, such as plt.subplots() to define the layout of the plots in the grid. This function allows you to organize the plots in rows and columns, specifying how many plots should be displayed and in which position within the grid each one should appear. A basic example of how to combine plots in a subplot could be:

```
import matplotlib.pyplot as plt
import seaborn as sns
import numpy as np

# Datos de ejemplo
dias = np.arange(1, 11)
ventas = np.random.randint(100, 200, size=10)
visitas = np.random.randint(500, 1000, size=10)
devoluciones = np.random.randint(5, 15, size=10)

# Crear un subplot de 2x2
fig, ax = plt.subplots(2, 2, figsize=(10, 8))

# Gráfico de líneas para las ventas
ax[0, 0].plot(dias, ventas, marker='o', color='b')
ax[0, 0].set_title('Ventas diarias')

# Gráfico de barras para las visitas
ax[0, 1].bar(dias, visitas, color='g')
ax[0, 1].set_title('Visitas al sitio web')

# Gráfico de dispersión para las devoluciones
ax[1, 0].scatter(dias, devoluciones, color='r')
ax[1, 0].set_title('Devoluciones de productos')

# Ocultar el subplot vacío
ax[1, 1].axis('off')

# Ajustar el espaciado entre subplots
plt.tight_layout()
plt.show()
```

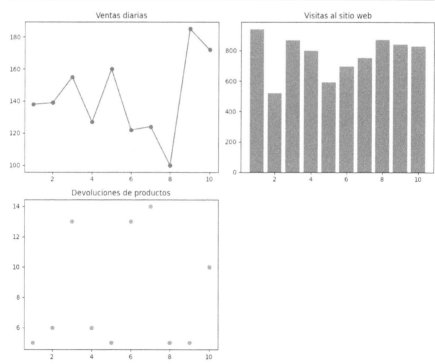

In this example, three charts are organized in a two-row by two-column dashboard, leaving a blank space in the last cell to avoid overloading the design. Each chart is customized to display different business variables (sales, visits, returns), and the use of plt.tight_layout() ensures that the charts do not overlap and that the spacing between them is adequate. This type of visualization can be easily extended and adapted to display more charts or additional information.

The customization of subplots is not limited to the arrangement of charts. Matplotlib allows you to personalize every aspect of the graph, from colors and lines to titles and legends. This is especially useful for companies that want to tailor their visualizations to a corporate aesthetic or maintain visual consistency in their reports. For example, the colors of lines and bars can be adjusted to match brand colors, line styles can be modified to highlight certain trends, and labels and legends can be customized to make the information clearer and more accessible.

Furthermore, Seaborn offers an even more intuitive way to work with complex graphs and perform exploratory data analysis. Seaborn is ideal when you need to visualize relationships between multiple variables or display data distributions in more detail. One of Seaborn's most useful features is its ability to work with multivariate graphs, such as correlation plots and scatter matrices, which allow you to see how multiple variables relate simultaneously. These graphs are essential when you want to understand hidden patterns or correlations in large volumes of data.

A typical example in a company would be creating a correlation matrix that shows how different business metrics are related, such as sales, returns, and website visits. Using Seaborn, you can easily generate a heatmap that displays the correlations between these variables and helps identify which ones are more closely related.

```
import seaborn as sns
import pandas as pd
import numpy as np

# Crear un DataFrame con datos de ejemplo
data = {
    'Ventas': np.random.randint(100, 200, size=10),
    'Visitas': np.random.randint(500, 1000, size=10),
    'Devoluciones': np.random.randint(5, 15, size=10)
}

df = pd.DataFrame(data)

# Calcular la correlación entre las variables
correlation_matrix = df.corr()

# Crear el heatmap de correlación
sns.heatmap(correlation_matrix, annot=True, cmap='coolwarm')
plt.title('Matriz de correlación entre métricas de negocio')
plt.show()
```

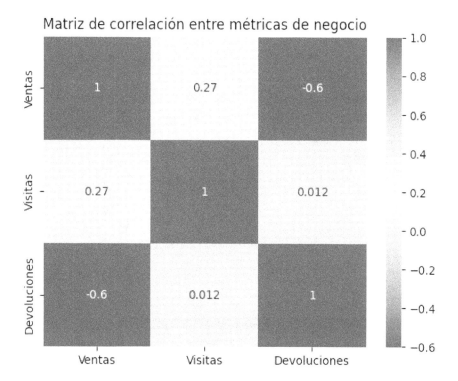

This code creates a heatmap where the correlations between different business metrics are represented on a color scale. Values close to 1 indicate a strong positive correlation, while values close to -1 indicate a negative correlation. This type of visualization is extremely useful for SMEs that want to identify which variables most affect their business performance and adjust their strategies accordingly.

In addition to creating subplots and complex charts, another key aspect of advanced customization with Matplotlib and Seaborn is the use of custom styles and themes. Companies may want to adapt their charts to match their brand identity or create a consistent set of visualizations that follow a specific design. Both Matplotlib and Seaborn allow you to apply predefined styles or fully customize the charts to achieve the desired visual effect.

In Matplotlib, predefined styles allow you to quickly change the appearance of your charts with a single command. For example, you can apply a dark style for a presentation or use a minimalist style for formal reports. By using plt.style.use(), you can choose from a variety of themes like 'ggplot', 'fivethirtyeight', 'seaborn-dark', among others.

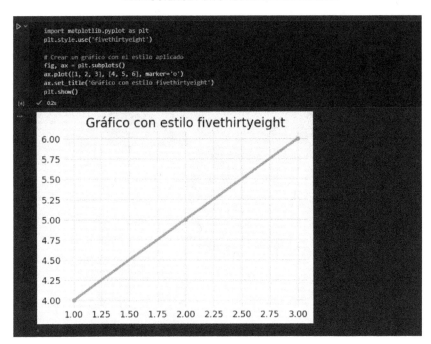

```
import matplotlib.pyplot as plt
plt.style.use('fivethirtyeight')

# Crear un gráfico con el estilo aplicado
fig, ax = plt.subplots()
ax.plot([1, 2, 3], [4, 5, 6], marker='o')
ax.set_title('Gráfico con estilo fivethirtyeight')
plt.show()
```

Moreover, for companies that want greater control over the aesthetics of their charts, Seaborn provides tools to modify visual themes in more detail. With Seaborn, you can adjust color palettes, font sizes, margins, and other key visual aspects to create charts that are both informative and visually appealing. Color palettes are particularly useful when you want to highlight certain aspects of the chart or use colors that match the company's corporate image.

For example, a company can customize Seaborn's style using sns.set_theme() to adjust the colors and sizes of the figures according to their preferences.

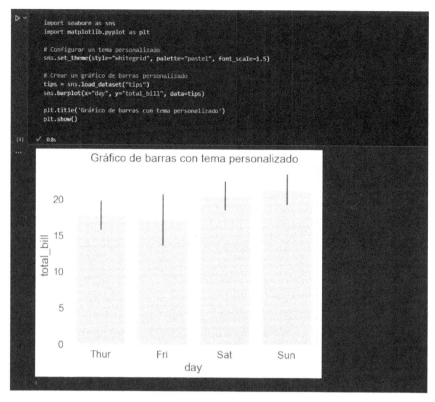

```
import seaborn as sns
import matplotlib.pyplot as plt

# Configurar un tema personalizado
sns.set_theme(style="whitegrid", palette="pastel", font_scale=1.5)

# Crear un gráfico de barras personalizado
tips = sns.load_dataset("tips")
sns.barplot(x="day", y="total_bill", data=tips)

plt.title('Gráfico de barras con tema personalizado')
plt.show()
```

In this case, the bar chart uses a pastel color palette and a whitegrid theme, which gives the chart a cleaner and more professional look. The ability to adjust the font_scale also makes the charts more readable in different formats, whether on large screens or printed presentations.

Personalizing charts at an advanced level allows SMEs to create visualizations that are not only useful from an analytical standpoint, but also tailored to the company's internal and external communication needs. Whether for executive presentations, client reports, or interactive dashboards, the advanced use of Matplotlib and Seaborn provides the flexibility needed to adapt visualizations to any context and audience, thus enhancing the company's ability to tell powerful, data-driven stories.

- **Interactivity and depth in data analysis with Plotly**

Interactive visualization has become an essential tool for SMEs looking not only to analyze their data statically but also to explore and delve into it dynamically. Plotly is one of the best solutions available for generating interactive charts that allow users to engage with their data in real-time, offering a much richer and more flexible analysis experience. Unlike other libraries such as Matplotlib, which focus on creating static charts, Plotly specializes in interactivity, enabling users to zoom, pan, select specific elements, and customize how they view their data without needing to modify the underlying code. For SMEs that handle large volumes of data and need to monitor various business metrics, the ability to use interactive visualizations is key to identifying trends, discovering patterns, and making more informed decisions.

Plotly offers a wide range of chart types, from the simplest like line and bar charts to more advanced options like 3D and animated charts. However, one of Plotly's most powerful features is its ability to integrate these charts into interactive dashboards. Dashboards not only present a complete view of the data but also allow users to filter, modify, and explore different aspects of the information directly on the chart. This is especially useful for SMEs that need to track key metrics such as sales, website visits, or marketing campaign performance, as it allows them to see the data in real-time and adjust their strategies based on what they discover by interacting with the charts.

A basic example of how SMEs can use Plotly Dash to create interactive dashboards is to build a panel that displays daily sales, marketing campaign performance, and customer behavior all in one place. With Plotly Dash, users can interact directly with the data by selecting specific dates, zooming in on certain areas, or filtering by categories. This is especially useful for managers or analysts who want to dive deeper into specific areas of the data without having to constantly switch views or generate new charts. The ability to manipulate graphs in real-time enhances data comprehension and allows for faster decision-making.

To start creating an interactive dashboard with Plotly Dash, the first thing you need to do is install Dash, which is the framework based on Plotly for building interactive web applications for data visualization. Dash makes it easy to create complex user interfaces where interactive charts are integrated into a single web application, allowing end users to interact with the charts directly through a browser.

The following example shows how to build a basic dashboard that visualizes sales data and website visits, allowing users to interact with the charts by selecting different dates and filtering the results.

```python
import dash
from dash import dcc, html
import plotly.express as px
import pandas as pd

# Crear una aplicación Dash
app = dash.Dash(__name__)

# Datos de ejemplo para el dashboard
df = pd.DataFrame({
    'Fecha': pd.date_range(start='2022-01-01', periods=30),
    'Ventas': [100 + i * 2 for i in range(30)],
    'Visitas': [500 + i * 10 for i in range(30)]
})

# Gráfico de líneas para las ventas
fig_ventas = px.line(df, x='Fecha', y='Ventas', title='Ventas diarias')

# Gráfico de líneas para las visitas
fig_visitas = px.line(df, x='Fecha', y='Visitas', title='Visitas al sitio web')

# Layout del dashboard con dos gráficos interactivos
app.layout = html.Div(children=[
    html.H1('Dashboard interactivo de ventas y visitas'),

    dcc.Graph(id='graph-ventas', figure=fig_ventas),

    dcc.Graph(id='graph-visitas', figure=fig_visitas)
])

# Ejecutar la aplicación
if __name__ == '__main__':
    app.run_server(debug=True)
```

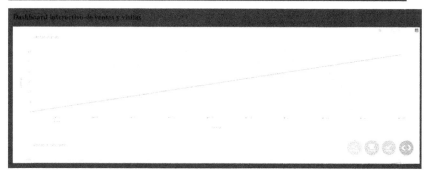

In this example, an interactive dashboard is created with two line charts: one to visualize daily sales and another for website visits. The Dash application allows users to interact with the charts, zoom in, select a date range, or click on specific points in the chart to get more details. Running in a browser, this interface is accessible to any employee in the company without requiring technical programming knowledge. This type of dashboard is ideal for monitoring business performance in real-time, as it can be automatically updated as new data is received.

In addition to simple dashboards like this one, Plotly Dash offers more advanced features that allow for the addition of filters, sliders, and dropdown menus to further customize data interaction. For example, users can filter graphs by different product categories, geographic regions, or time periods, making it easier to conduct in-depth analysis without the need to create multiple static graphs. These capabilities make Plotly Dash an extremely powerful tool for SMEs that need to perform detailed analysis of their sales performance, marketing, or any other aspect of the business.

Another notable advantage of Plotly is its ability to create 3D and animated charts, which adds a new dimension to data visualization. 3D charts are especially useful when working with data that has multiple variables and needs to be represented in a three-dimensional space to clearly see the relationships between variables. For example, a tech company that wants to analyze the relationship between server response time, the number of concurrent users, and system performance can greatly benefit from 3D charts, as they allow them to visualize these three variables simultaneously and easily detect stress points or areas for improvement.

A basic 3D plot in Plotly can be created as follows:

```python
import plotly.graph_objects as go
import numpy as np

# Crear datos para el gráfico 3D
x = np.linspace(-5, 5, 50)
y = np.linspace(-5, 5, 50)
x, y = np.meshgrid(x, y)
z = np.sin(np.sqrt(x**2 + y**2))

fig = go.Figure(data=[go.Surface(z=z, x=x, y=y)])
fig.update_layout(title='Superficie 3D de ejemplo', autosize=True,
                  scene = dict(
                      xaxis_title='Eje X',
                      yaxis_title='Eje Y',
                      zaxis_title='Eje Z'))
fig.show()
```

This code generates a surface based on the function $\sin(\sqrt{x^2 + y^2})$, which creates an interesting wavy shape to illustrate a 3D plot.

This example generates a 3D surface plot that is interactive and allows users to rotate, zoom in and out of the visualization, making it easier to understand the data in three dimensions. This capability is very useful for analyzing complex data, such as simulation results, sales trends across different geographic regions, or any other dataset involving multiple interrelated dimensions.

In addition to 3D charts, Plotly also offers the ability to create animated charts, which are especially useful for showing how data evolves over time. Animated charts allow users to see changes in the data in a more intuitive way, making it easier to identify long-term trends and patterns. This is particularly useful for SMEs that want to visualize the impact of their marketing campaigns, customer behavior, or sales evolution over an extended period.

A basic example of an animated chart in Plotly would be representing how a company's sales change in different regions over time.

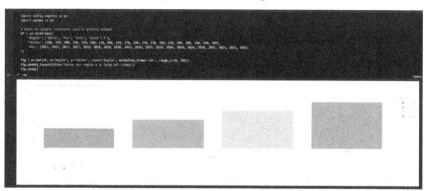

This animated bar chart shows how sales in different regions change over the years. As the animation progresses, users can see the fluctuations and trends in each region, allowing them to identify important patterns, such as sustained growth in one region or a decline in another. For SMEs, this type of animated visualization is extremely useful when illustrating how their market strategies or specific campaigns have affected sales in different geographic areas or how their business has evolved over time.

In summary, Plotly's ability to create interactive graphs, dynamic dashboards, 3D charts, and animations makes it an indispensable tool for SMEs that need to explore and visualize their data effectively. With these features, companies can provide their teams, managers, and clients with a clear and dynamic way to interact with data, improve decision-making, and ultimately optimize their business strategies.

- ## Tools like Tkinter, Streamlit, or Flask for visualizations

In addition to classic visualization tools like Matplotlib, Seaborn, or Plotly, there are options that take visualizations a step further by integrating them into interactive interfaces or more complete applications. These options not only improve the way data is displayed but also allow users to interact directly with it, something especially useful for SMEs looking to customize the data analysis experience according to their specific needs.

In this sense, tools like Tkinter, Streamlit, and Flask offer new possibilities. Each of them provides different approaches to building applications that not only visualize data but also create environments where users can explore that data in greater depth. Unlike static or even interactive charts generated in a console, these platforms allow for presenting visualizations in user-friendly interfaces, whether in a local environment or through web applications.

Throughout the next pages, we will delve into how these tools can be used to integrate visualizations into dashboards, interactive applications, or even more comprehensive web solutions. We will see how each one offers unique features that can be tailored to different types of projects and business needs, allowing SMEs to improve how they manage and present their data efficiently.

- ### Tkinter for local visualizations

Tkinter is Python's standard library for creating graphical user interfaces (GUIs), a robust and straightforward option for those looking to develop local desktop applications without relying on web platforms or external servers. Although it is not as modern or packed with advanced features as other frameworks like Streamlit or Flask, Tkinter remains a highly functional tool for building applications that allow data visualization, generating charts, and managing information directly on the local system. This is especially useful for SMEs or freelancers who need quick and effective solutions without the complexity of setting up network infrastructures or being dependent on a constant Internet connection.

One of the main attractions of Tkinter is its ease of use. Being part of the standard Python installation, there's no need to install anything extra, making it an immediately accessible solution. Additionally, its ability to generate windows, buttons, entry fields, menus, and other basic graphical tools makes it ideal for those looking to create simple yet functional interfaces that allow direct interaction with the user. For SMEs or freelancers who don't have a large technical team or don't need the complexity of a full web application, Tkinter offers a practical and accessible way to build applications that enable data visualization and analysis directly on a local machine.

One area where Tkinter can be especially useful is in creating data visualization applications. Although it doesn't have the advanced graphical capabilities of Plotly or Seaborn, Tkinter can be seamlessly integrated with other Python visualization libraries like Matplotlib. This allows users to create desktop applications that generate and display charts without relying on web browsers or servers. The integration of Matplotlib with Tkinter enables users to generate bar charts, line charts, scatter plots, or even histograms directly in an application window, making data analysis quick and accessible.

For example, a small business managing sales data could develop a simple desktop application in Tkinter that allows the user to load a CSV file with sales data, perform a series of calculations, and generate interactive charts based on that data. This would enable them to analyze sales trends, identify demand peaks, or visualize sales evolution over time, all from a local application that doesn't rely on an internet connection or server infrastructure. This type of application is not only useful for small businesses but also for freelancers who manage their own data and want access to tools that allow them to visualize information without the need for more complex or expensive tools.

To create a basic application that allows for local graph visualization using Tkinter and Matplotlib, you can follow a relatively simple workflow. First, you create a window in Tkinter with the necessary elements for the user to load or input data. Then, Matplotlib is used to generate the graph and display it within the same window. The following example shows a basic code that illustrates how to create such an application:

```
import tkinter as tk
from tkinter import filedialog
import matplotlib.pyplot as plt
from matplotlib.backends.backend_tkagg import FigureCanvasTkAgg
import pandas as pd

# Crear la ventana principal de la aplicación
root = tk.Tk()
root.title("Visualización de datos con Tkinter y Matplotlib")

# Función para cargar el archivo CSV
def cargar_datos():
    file_path = filedialog.askopenfilename()
    if file_path:
        data = pd.read_csv(file_path)
        generar_grafico(data)

# Función para generar el gráfico
def generar_grafico(data):
    fig, ax = plt.subplots(figsize=(6,4))
    ax.plot(data['Fecha'], data['Ventas'], marker='o')
    ax.set_title("Ventas a lo largo del tiempo")
    ax.set_xlabel("Fecha")
    ax.set_ylabel("Ventas")

    # Mostrar el gráfico en la ventana de Tkinter
    canvas = FigureCanvasTkAgg(fig, master=root)
    canvas.draw()
    canvas.get_tk_widget().pack()

# Botón para cargar datos
btn_cargar = tk.Button(root, text="Cargar datos", command=cargar_datos)
btn_cargar.pack()

# Iniciar la aplicación
root.mainloop()
```

This simple example creates a Tkinter window with a button that allows the user to load a CSV file with sales data. Once the data is loaded, a line chart is generated with Matplotlib that shows the sales evolution over time. The interaction is straightforward, and the chart is displayed within the same application window, making it easy for the user to view without having to leave the application or interact with a web browser. This approach is ideal for small businesses that want quick access to their data and visualize it without needing to use external services.

Tkinter also offers the ability to customize the user interface through elements like dropdown menus, radio buttons, and input boxes. This allows companies to develop more sophisticated applications that not only visualize data but also provide additional controls for users to adjust the parameters of the charts or the data to be analyzed. For example, dropdown menus could be added to allow users to select which type of chart they want to see (bar, line, scatter, etc.), or even input boxes that let them filter data by date range or product categories.

Let's suppose a SME wants to create an internal tool to analyze sales by product categories and filter the data by different time periods. With Tkinter, it's possible to add interactive elements that allow selecting the product category and date range to analyze, so the generated chart shows only the relevant information for those selections. Below is an example of how this functionality could be implemented:

```python
import tkinter as tk
from tkinter import ttk
from tkinter import filedialog
import matplotlib.pyplot as plt
from matplotlib.backends.backend_tkagg import FigureCanvasTkAgg
import pandas as pd

# Crear la ventana principal
root = tk.Tk()
root.title("Análisis de ventas por categoría")

# Variables para los filtros
categoria_seleccionada = tk.StringVar()
rango_fechas = tk.StringVar()

# Función para cargar el archivo CSV
def cargar_datos():
    file_path = filedialog.askopenfilename()
    if file_path:
        data = pd.read_csv(file_path)
        generar_grafico(data)

# Función para generar el gráfico
def generar_grafico(data):
    # Filtrar los datos por categoría seleccionada
    categoria = categoria_seleccionada.get()
    data_filtrada = data[data['Categoría'] == categoria]

    # Generar el gráfico
    fig, ax = plt.subplots(figsize=(6, 4))
    ax.plot(data_filtrada['Fecha'], data_filtrada['Ventas'], marker='o')
    ax.set_title(f"Ventas para {categoria}")
    ax.set_xlabel("Fecha")
    ax.set_ylabel("Ventas")

    # Mostrar el gráfico en la ventana de Tkinter
    canvas = FigureCanvasTkAgg(fig, master=root)
    canvas.draw()
    canvas.get_tk_widget().pack()

# Menú desplegable para seleccionar la categoría
label_categoria = ttk.Label(root, text="Seleccionar Categoría:")
label_categoria.pack()
menu_categoria = ttk.Combobox(root, textvariable=categoria_seleccionada)
menu_categoria['values'] = ("Electrónica", "Ropa", "Juguetes", "Hogar")
menu_categoria.pack()

# Botón para cargar datos
btn_cargar = tk.Button(root, text="Cargar Datos", command=cargar_datos)
btn_cargar.pack()

# Iniciar la aplicación
root.mainloop()
```

In this case, the dropdown menu allows the user to select the product category they want to analyze, and the generated chart shows only the data related to that category. This type of functionality is ideal for SMEs that manage multiple product lines and need to analyze their performance in a segmented way. Additionally, being a local application, Tkinter offers the advantage that data visualization and processing are done directly on the user's computer, without the need to send data to a remote server or be connected to the Internet.

Another important aspect of Tkinter is its ability to handle local storage and file manipulation, allowing SMEs to create tools that not only visualize charts but also offer additional functionalities such as loading and saving data, exporting charts in image formats (PNG, JPG), or even generating automatic reports in PDF format. These features make Tkinter a versatile option for companies looking for a complete local data analysis solution.

In addition, Tkinter is fully compatible with other Python libraries, allowing it to be integrated with additional functionalities such as local databases (SQLite), file manipulation tools (os, shutil), and advanced data analysis libraries like NumPy or Pandas. This integration gives Tkinter considerable flexibility for developing applications that cover a wide range of data visualization and analysis needs without the complexity of web-based applications.

In summary, Tkinter is a powerful and accessible tool for SMEs looking for quick and effective solutions for local data visualization without relying on online infrastructures or complex setups. Although it may not be as modern as other options, its ease of use and ability to integrate with libraries like Matplotlib make it a solid choice for those who need to generate charts and analysis applications in a local, controlled environment.

• Streamlit and Flask for web visualization applications

When we talk about real-time data visualization, especially in the context of SMEs, the ability to create interactive web applications that allow not only viewing data but also interacting with it becomes a valuable tool for optimizing decision-making. Unlike local applications, web applications allow information to be shared across the organization, providing access to different teams, such as sales or marketing, regardless of their location. Tools like Streamlit and Flask play a crucial role in this area, as they allow the creation of interactive dashboards and customized internal solutions that display real-time visualizations, facilitating collaboration and shared data analysis.

Streamlit and Flask are two different approaches to developing web visualization applications, each with its strengths. Streamlit is quicker to implement and specifically designed for data applications, with a minimal learning curve and fast integration with popular libraries like Pandas,

Matplotlib, and Plotly. This makes it ideal for SMEs looking for an agile solution without requiring extensive technical knowledge or complex setups. On the other hand, Flask is a more robust web microframework that provides greater flexibility and customization, allowing the creation of web applications that are more tailored to the specific needs of the business. Flask is ideal when the SME has a technical team that can manage the web server infrastructure and needs more control over the application's structure and functionalities.

Next, we will explore each of these options in more detail.

- **Streamlit: simplicity and speed for web visualization applications**

Streamlit has quickly gained popularity in the data science world for its ability to create interactive web applications quickly and easily, without the need for web development experience. Unlike other frameworks, Streamlit focuses on simplifying the process of creating interactive applications, especially for data visualization and real-time analysis. This makes it a perfect tool for SMEs looking to develop interactive dashboards for their internal teams without having to manage web servers or implement complex backend structures.

What sets Streamlit apart from other tools is its minimalist approach. Developers can write code in Python using libraries like Pandas, Matplotlib, or Plotly to generate charts, tables, and other visual elements, and Streamlit automatically turns that code into an interactive web application. This means that an SME already familiar with Python and data analysis libraries can quickly transform their scripts into a web app without needing additional knowledge in HTML, CSS, or JavaScript.

One of Streamlit's strengths is its ability to easily integrate with libraries like Pandas. For example, a sales SME could have a Python script that analyzes sales data stored in CSV files or a database. With Streamlit, it's possible to transform that analysis into an interactive application where sales team members can upload new data files, view real-time sales charts, or apply filters to analyze specific market segments. A typical dashboard in Streamlit could include bar charts to visualize sales by product category, line charts to analyze trends over time, and dynamic tables that allow users to dive into the data with just a few clicks.

Here is a basic example of how Streamlit allows you to create an interactive data visualization app using Pandas and Matplotlib:

```
import streamlit as st
import pandas as pd
import matplotlib.pyplot as plt

# Título de la aplicación
st.title("Dashboard de Ventas Interactivo")

# Subir archivo CSV
uploaded_file = st.file_uploader("Cargar archivo CSV con datos de ventas", type="csv")

if uploaded_file is not None:
    # Leer el archivo CSV
    df = pd.read_csv(uploaded_file)

    # Mostrar tabla de datos
    st.write("Datos cargados:")
    st.write(df)

    # Crear gráfico de ventas
    st.write("Gráfico de ventas por producto")
    fig, ax = plt.subplots()
    ax.bar(df['Producto'], df['Ventas'])
    st.pyplot(fig)

    # Filtrar por producto
    producto = st.selectbox("Seleccionar producto", df['Producto'].unique())
    datos_filtrados = df[df['Producto'] == producto]

    # Mostrar gráfico de ventas filtrado
    st.write(f"Ventas para el producto {producto}")
    fig2, ax2 = plt.subplots()
    ax2.plot(datos_filtrados['Fecha'], datos_filtrados['Ventas'], marker='o')
    st.pyplot(fig2)
```

This example creates an interactive dashboard where users can upload a CSV file with sales data and generate real-time charts. Additionally, Streamlit allows users to filter the data and visualize the filtered results without needing to reload the page or deal with complicated backend configurations. This approach greatly simplifies the development of dashboards in SMEs, enabling teams to make quick decisions based on up-to-date data.

Another great advantage of Streamlit is that it provides native interactivity. Users can interact with the charts and adjust analysis parameters directly from the browser, all in real time. This is ideal for SMEs that need to perform exploratory analysis on their data or present interactive results to other departments without having to reprogram or regenerate the charts manually each time. Marketing teams, for example, can change the filters on a campaign and instantly see the impact on sales.

Streamlit also allows the use of advanced graphics with Plotly, one of the most powerful libraries for creating interactive visualizations. The charts generated with Plotly enable users to zoom in, scroll through the data, and even see specific details at each point of the chart with just a click. This combination of Streamlit and Plotly is extremely useful for SMEs that need a rich and dynamic data visualization, which can also be easily shared with other team members or even with clients.

In summary, Streamlit is a perfect solution for SMEs that need to create interactive web applications for data visualization without complications. Its integration with Pandas, Matplotlib, and Plotly makes it a versatile tool that allows the creation of internal dashboards that facilitate real-time data-driven decision-making, with quick implementation and minimal programming effort.

- **Flask: flexibility and customization for web visualization applications**

Flask, on the other hand, is a more robust and flexible option when it comes to developing more complex and customized web applications. Unlike Streamlit, which is specifically designed for the quick creation of data-centric applications, Flask is a web microframework that allows you to build complete web applications from scratch, meaning SMEs have greater control over every aspect of the application, from business logic to data presentation.

Flask is an ideal tool when the company has more advanced needs or requires complete customization of its application. For example, an SME with a technical team managing large volumes of data or with specific security or user authentication requirements can opt for Flask to build a custom web application that not only visualizes data but also integrates multiple additional functionalities, such as access to databases, authentication systems, report generation, and more.

Flask's main advantage lies in its flexibility. While Streamlit is excellent for quickly creating applications with a simple interface, Flask allows for the development of much more complex applications that can include different web routes, integration with relational and non-relational databases, REST APIs, and custom modules to handle various types of data. This makes it an ideal option for SMEs that need a robust solution that can grow with their business, providing a solid web infrastructure to handle not only data visualization but also advanced information processing and management.

An example of how Flask can be used to create a custom data visualization application is developing an internal dashboard for a sales team that shows daily sales, product performance, and sales forecasts based on historical data in real time. This dashboard should not only display charts but also allow users to filter data, generate reports, and access different sections of the application based on their roles and permissions.

Below is a basic example of how Flask can be integrated with Matplotlib to generate dynamic charts in a web application.

```python
from flask import Flask, render_template, request
import matplotlib.pyplot as plt
import pandas as pd
import io
import base64

app = Flask(__name__)

# Ruta principal
@app.route('/')
def index():
    return render_template('index.html')

# Ruta para generar el gráfico
@app.route('/grafico')
def grafico():
    # Generar datos de ejemplo
    data = {'Producto': ['A', 'B', 'C'], 'Ventas': [100, 150, 200]}
    df = pd.DataFrame(data)

    # Crear gráfico de barras
    fig, ax = plt.subplots()
    ax.bar(df['Producto'], df['Ventas'])
    ax.set_title('Ventas por Producto')

    # Convertir el gráfico a imagen para mostrar en HTML
    img = io.BytesIO()
    fig.savefig(img, format='png')
    img.seek(0)
    plot_url = base64.b64encode(img.getvalue()).decode()

    return render_template('grafico.html', plot_url=plot_url)

if __name__ == '__main__':
    app.run(debug=True)
```

In this example, Flask generates a bar chart based on sample data and displays it on a web page. This application is fully customizable, allowing you to add additional features like data upload, the creation of different charts, or interaction with databases to fetch and visualize data in real-time. Moreover, Flask allows for the integration of security, user systems, and roles, which is ideal for business applications where different users need access to various functionalities according to their permissions.

One of the greatest advantages of Flask is its ability to integrate with other services and systems, allowing you to build complex web applications that interact with various data sources. For example, an SME managing multiple sales and marketing systems could use Flask to develop a centralized application that gathers data from different APIs, databases, and external files, and then presents that data in an interactive dashboard that includes charts, tables, and predictive analysis.

Scalability is another aspect where Flask excels. As a company grows, Flask can grow with it, allowing you to add new features or handle a larger user and data load without needing to switch to a new platform. This makes it an ideal choice for SMEs that anticipate future growth and need a solid infrastructure that can adapt to their changing needs.

In conclusion, both Streamlit and Flask offer powerful solutions for SMEs looking to develop web visualization applications. While Streamlit is perfect for companies seeking a quick and easy-to-implement solution, Flask provides the flexibility and robustness needed to develop customized and scalable applications that meet more advanced business needs.

3.5. Geospatial analysis in Python practical applications for SMEs

Geospatial analysis is a powerful tool for SMEs that rely on the geographic location of their customers, resources, or branches to make strategic decisions. Whether a company seeks to optimize delivery routes, identify new market areas, or simply analyze the geographic distribution of its sales, using tools for geospatial analysis in Python provides a significant competitive advantage. Libraries like Folium and Geopandas allow companies to analyze and visualize spatial data effectively, opening new possibilities for interpreting information and making location-based decisions.

The use of geospatial data has expanded rapidly in recent years, and for SMEs operating in sectors like logistics, retail, or real estate, the ability to visualize data in a geographic context is crucial. For example, a company with multiple physical stores might want to understand where their customers are coming from, which areas have a higher concentration of sales, or where there are opportunities to open new stores. Geospatial analysis can also be essential for optimizing delivery routes, reducing operational costs, or even improving the customer experience, all based on a detailed understanding of how data is distributed in space.

- Geospatial analysis libraries in Python

Within the Python ecosystem, there are several libraries designed to work with geospatial data. Geopandas and Folium are two of the most popular and powerful. Geopandas is an extension of Pandas that allows you to work with spatial data, making it easy to read, manipulate, and visualize geographic data. On the other hand, Folium is specifically designed for creating interactive maps, based on the Leaflet.js library, which allows Python developers to generate dynamic maps that users can explore interactively. Both libraries offer a different but complementary approach to spatial data analysis, with Geopandas being excellent for data processing and analysis, while Folium excels in creating interactive visualizations.

Geopandas is especially useful when working with geographic data in shapefile format or when spatial calculations are needed, such as polygon intersections, spatial joins of datasets, or geographic coordinate projections. Companies that work with spatial data, like customer maps or delivery regions, can benefit from using Geopandas to perform complex geographic operations and gain valuable insights. For example, a company that wants to understand how its sales are distributed by postal code can use Geopandas to load a shapefile of postal codes and overlay its sales data to identify the best-performing areas.

On the other hand, Folium is an excellent choice when the goal is to create interactive maps that allow users to explore data in a visual environment. For example, an SME managing a delivery service can create an interactive map showing delivery areas, highlighting high-demand zones or identifying areas where deliveries are slower. With Folium, it's possible to integrate multiple layers into a single map, allowing the combination of different types of data (such as points of interest, routes, or service area polygons) to provide a rich and detailed visualization.

- Using Geopandas for Geospatial Data Analysis

Geopandas extends the functionality of Pandas to work with geospatial data, allowing you to easily manage objects like points, lines, and polygons. Just like with Pandas, the data is stored in a GeoDataFrame, which can contain a geometry column where the spatial features of the objects are stored, such as the coordinates of points or the shapes of geographical areas. This enables a range of geospatial operations, from reading and manipulating data to executing complex spatial calculations.

A classic example of using Geopandas in an SME could be the analysis of customer locations. Suppose a company has a list of customer addresses and wants to analyze the geographic distribution to identify patterns or areas of concentration. First, this list of addresses can be converted into geographic coordinates using a geocoding service, and then Geopandas can be used to load those coordinates into a GeoDataFrame. Once the data is in geospatial format, it's possible to perform calculations such as finding areas with the highest customer density or identifying the most profitable delivery zones.

The following example shows how to load a shapefile with postal code data and then overlay points representing customer locations to perform a density analysis:

```python
import geopandas as gpd
import matplotlib.pyplot as plt

# Cargar un shapefile de códigos postales
shapefile = 'path_to_shapefile/codigos_postales.shp'
gdf_codigos_postales = gpd.read_file(shapefile)

# Cargar un conjunto de datos de clientes (GeoDataFrame)
gdf_clientes = gpd.GeoDataFrame({
    'Nombre': ['Cliente 1', 'Cliente 2', 'Cliente 3'],
    'geometry': gpd.points_from_xy([10.5, 10.7, 11.2], [55.3, 55.4, 55.1])
})

# Mostrar el mapa con los códigos postales y los clientes superpuestos
fig, ax = plt.subplots(figsize=(10, 10))
gdf_codigos_postales.plot(ax=ax, color='lightblue', edgecolor='black')
gdf_clientes.plot(ax=ax, color='red', marker='o', markersize=50)
plt.title('Distribución geográfica de clientes')
plt.show()
```

In this example, a shapefile containing the boundaries of postal codes for a specific region is first loaded, then points representing customer locations are overlaid. This type of analysis allows you to quickly identify where customers are most concentrated, which can be useful for optimizing marketing campaigns or improving the distribution of sales resources. It's also possible to conduct more advanced analyses, such as calculating the distances between customers and the nearest physical stores or determining the best location to open a new branch based on the current geographic distribution of customers.

Geopandas also allows for complex spatial operations, such as spatial joins between different geographic datasets. For example, a company with sales data by region can join that data with a shapefile containing administrative region boundaries, so each region has a value associated with sales. This is especially useful for visualizing regional differences in sales performance or identifying areas of opportunity.

Another practical use case for Geopandas is calculating buffers or areas of influence. For example, a SME that wants to analyze the coverage of its home delivery service can use Geopandas to create a buffer around its store locations and see if any areas fall outside the delivery coverage. This can be done with a single line of code:

```
# Crear un buffer de 10 km alrededor de las ubicaciones de las tiendas
gdf_tiendas['buffer'] = gdf_tiendas.buffer(10000)

# Mostrar el mapa con las áreas de cobertura de las tiendas
gdf_tiendas.plot()
plt.show()
```

By applying this type of analysis, SMEs can optimize their operations, whether by expanding delivery zones or adjusting marketing strategies to target areas outside the current coverage. Geopandas' flexibility to work with spatial data allows businesses to explore a wide range of solutions that can improve efficiency and profitability.

- **Folium for interactive geospatial visualizations**

Folium is a Python library designed to create interactive maps using Leaflet.js, an open-source JavaScript library for map creation. With Folium, SMEs can generate maps that not only display the location of points or areas but also allow users to interact with the map, zoom into specific areas, add markers, or even overlay additional data layers. This makes Folium a perfect tool for visualizing geospatial data in a more dynamic and accessible context.

While Geopandas is excellent for processing geospatial data and creating static maps, Folium allows you to add interactivity to those maps, which is ideal when you want to present the results to a team or clients who need to explore the data visually. For example, a logistics SME could use Folium to create an interactive map showing delivery routes, allowing users to zoom in on different routes, select specific delivery points, and view additional information about each point, such as the estimated time of arrival or the number of packages delivered.

The following code shows how to create a basic interactive map with Folium, marking the locations of several stores in a geographic area:

```
import folium

# Crear un mapa centrado en una ubicación específica
mapa = folium.Map(location=[40.416775, -3.703790], zoom_start=12)

# Agregar marcadores para diferentes tiendas
folium.Marker([40.416775, -3.703790], popup='Tienda 1').add_to(mapa)
folium.Marker([40.428715, -3.706935], popup='Tienda 2').add_to(mapa)
folium.Marker([40.408825, -3.707520], popup='Tienda 3').add_to(mapa)

# Mostrar el mapa interactivo
mapa.save("mapa_tiendas.html")
```

This example generates an interactive map centered on Madrid, with three markers representing the locations of different stores. Users can click on each marker to see additional information, such as the store's name or any other relevant details. The ability to add multiple layers and customize the markers makes Folium a very versatile tool for geospatial visualization.

Another interesting feature of Folium is the ability to integrate heatmaps. This type of visualization is especially useful for SMEs that want to analyze the density of their customers or sales in different geographic areas. For example, a company that wants to see where most of its customers are concentrated can use a heatmap to highlight high-density areas, making it easier to identify key areas for marketing campaigns or expansion.

The following example shows how to create a heatmap with Folium to visualize the density of customers in different locations.

```
from folium.plugins import HeatMap

# Datos de clientes (latitud y longitud)
clientes = [
    [40.416775, -3.703790],
    [40.428715, -3.706935],
    [40.408825, -3.707520],
    [40.417875, -3.709780]
]

# Crear un mapa centrado en una ubicación específica
mapa_heatmap = folium.Map(location=[40.416775, -3.703790], zoom_start=12)

# Agregar el heatmap al mapa
HeatMap(clientes).add_to(mapa_heatmap)

# Mostrar el mapa interactivo
mapa_heatmap.save("heatmap_clientes.html")
```

This code creates a heat map showing the concentration of customers in a city. Areas with more customers are highlighted with more intense colors, allowing you to quickly see zones with higher activity or customer presence. This type of visualization is extremely useful for SMEs looking to optimize their business strategies based on the geographic density of their customer base.

In summary, both Geopandas and Folium offer powerful tools for geospatial data analysis and visualization. Geopandas allows for complex spatial calculations and working with structured geographic data, while Folium makes it easy to create interactive maps that enhance visual presentation and allow users to explore the data dynamically. Together, these tools provide SMEs with an effective way to leverage the power of geospatial analysis, optimizing their operations and improving location-based decision-making.

3.6. Transform your data into decisions with effective storytelling

Data storytelling has emerged as one of the most valuable skills in the modern business world. It's not just about showing well-crafted charts and tables, but about creating a coherent and engaging narrative that allows the audience to understand the deeper meaning behind the numbers. Telling a story with data means structuring the information in a way that flows logically, enabling observers not only to receive the data but also to interpret its significance and make informed decisions based on it. For SMEs, where resources and time are limited, effective use of data storytelling can make a difference in how results are presented and what actions are taken.

The key to any successful story is structure. In storytelling with data, structure is also crucial. Data is not self-explanatory; it needs to be contextualized, and that is the foundation of the narrative. Without a clear narrative, data visualizations can become confusing or irrelevant, and it's easy for the audience to lose focus on what really matters. To properly structure a narrative with data, you first need to identify the central message. This message is what the data should support, guiding the observer's interpretation. It can be a trend, a significant change, a recurring pattern, or even an anomaly that needs to be highlighted.

Once the central message has been identified, the story must be developed through a narrative flow that guides the audience from the background to practical conclusions. To achieve this, it's essential to choose the right visualizations, avoiding the temptation to overload the story with too many charts or irrelevant information. The goal of data storytelling is to simplify the complex, highlighting the most important information in a visually appealing and clear way. Each chart or visualization should serve a specific purpose within the narrative.

The narrative flow in storytelling with data follows a scheme that, although flexible, is usually structured in the following way. First, it's important to establish the context or starting point. This is where the background of the data is presented, allowing the audience to understand the setting they are in. For example, in a sales analysis for an SME, the context might be the sales behavior over the past year, highlighting seasonal fluctuations or the effects of previous promotions. This first stage of the narrative answers the questions "Where are we now?" and "What has happened so far?

Next, it's crucial to identify a key point or change in the data. This is the moment when the narrative takes a turn and highlights something that has changed, a pattern that has emerged, or an opportunity that has arisen. This key point should be supported visually, preferably with simple charts that allow the audience to easily identify the change or trend. For instance, if sales increased significantly after the implementation of a new marketing strategy, it's important to show this change in a line chart that highlights the before and after of the implementation. This moment in the narrative answers the question, "What has changed?" or "What is the most important thing that has happened?

The next step in the narrative flow is to explain the possible reasons behind the data. This is where analysis and interpretation come in. At this point, you should offer an explanation of why the change has occurred or why the data shows a certain pattern. For SMEs, this is a key moment to extract lessons that can inform future decisions. It's useful to use comparative graphs or visualizations showing different factors influencing the outcome. For example, in a sales analysis, a bar chart comparing sales across different distribution channels can be helpful to understand why one has outperformed the others.

A common mistake in data storytelling is assuming that the data speaks for itself. In reality, data only comes to life when contextualized within a narrative that allows the audience to understand not just the 'what' but also the 'why'. Companies must avoid the trap of using data visualizations simply because they are attractive or sophisticated. Visualizations should be directly related to the narrative, guiding the audience through the key points and simplifying the inherent complexity of the data.

A very useful technique for structuring your narrative is the zoom technique, which allows you to start with an overview and then zoom in on the most relevant details. For example, in an analysis of overall sales throughout the year, you can start by showing a line graph of monthly sales. This gives the audience a clear idea of the general trends. Then, to add value to the analysis, you can zoom in on the months with significant variation and provide more details on those periods, using more specific charts like stacked bar charts to show sales by product during those key months. This technique keeps the focus on what's important, avoiding overwhelming the audience with unnecessary details from the start.

Another key aspect of storytelling with data is the sequence of revelation. You shouldn't show all the information at once, as this can be overwhelming. Instead, it's better to guide the audience through a series of visualizations that gradually build the story. Each visualization should add an additional layer of understanding to the narrative, allowing the audience to discover key information gradually. For example, when analyzing the behavior of an SME's customers at different stages of the sales funnel, you can start by showing a visualization that summarizes how many customers are at each stage of the funnel. Then, you can break down the visualization to show which factors are influencing customer progression, gradually revealing how marketing actions have impacted customer conversion at each stage.

Simplicity is another essential principle in data storytelling. Too often, data is presented in an overly complex manner, with overloaded charts that confuse rather than clarify. It's important to choose the right type of chart and use colors and labels that guide the viewer to the right conclusions. A line chart is ideal for showing trends over time, while a bar chart might be more appropriate for comparing different categories. SMEs should look for visualizations that simplify information without losing depth, making data accessible to the entire team, regardless of their technical level.

The use of annotations within visualizations is also an effective technique to highlight key points and avoid misunderstandings. A chart can clearly show a trend, but without an annotation explaining the context or relevance of that trend, the audience might not interpret the information correctly. For example, in a chart showing an increase in sales during a particular month, an annotation explaining that the increase was the result of a specific marketing campaign can help contextualize the information and guide the audience toward the correct interpretation of the chart.

In the case of SMEs, data storytelling must also be aligned with the company's strategic objectives. Each visualization should be designed to answer a question or solve a specific problem. Stories told with data shouldn't be neutral; they must be intentional and directed towards a clear conclusion that drives action. If a company is looking to improve its operational efficiency, the story it tells with its data should focus on identifying areas for improvement, comparing current performance with previous benchmarks, and highlighting the most important opportunities for change. The narrative should be clear and actionable, providing the audience with a logical path towards implementing the necessary improvements.

A typical example in an SME could be evaluating the performance of digital marketing campaigns. Instead of simply showing graphs that illustrate advertising spend or the number of clicks received, storytelling with data involves guiding the audience through the campaign results and their implications for future marketing strategy. The narrative could start with a line chart showing the evolution of advertising impressions over time, followed by a bar chart comparing the performance of different advertising channels (e.g., Google Ads versus social media). Finally, the narrative would conclude with an ROI (return on investment) analysis, using a scatter plot to show the relationship between spend and conversions for each channel. This type of narrative allows marketing managers not only to see the results but also to understand which channels are providing the highest return and how they can adjust their strategy for future campaigns.

Additionally, the use of colors and typography in visualizations plays an essential role in data storytelling. Colors should be chosen carefully to guide the audience towards the most important elements of the visualization. Stronger and more striking colors should be used to highlight key areas, while softer or neutral colors should be used for secondary information. Typography should be clear and readable, and labels and titles should be precise and concise, providing the audience with the necessary information without unnecessary distractions.

Data storytelling is a powerful tool for transforming seemingly disorganized datasets into useful information that can guide decision-making in SMEs. By structuring data into a clear and coherent narrative, businesses can not only visualize their results but also interpret their meaning, identify areas of opportunity, and improve their operations through more informed and strategic decisions.

Chapter 4 – Boost Your Business with Automation

4.1. How can automation improve your business?

Automation has become a key element for the competitiveness of SMEs in today's business environment. As companies seek to improve their operational efficiency and optimize the use of their resources, automation offers a unique opportunity to simplify processes, reduce costs, and, above all, free up time and energy so that employees can focus on more strategic and high-value tasks. In this chapter, we will explore in depth how automation can significantly improve various aspects of a business, allowing SMEs to adapt and thrive in an increasingly dynamic and demanding market.

Automation is not just about reducing the workload of repetitive tasks; it also helps minimize errors that can occur in manual processes. From invoice management and data entry to sending follow-up emails, there are numerous administrative tasks that, if automated, allow employees to spend more time on activities that require creativity, analysis, and decision-making. This freeing up of human resources not only optimizes team performance but also enhances the quality of the work produced.

Another crucial aspect we will address in this chapter is the scalability that automation offers. For many SMEs, one of the biggest challenges is growing without being overwhelmed by the need to increase staff or operational resources. An automated process can handle thousands of records or transactions with the same efficiency as it manages dozens, providing exponential growth capacity without a proportional investment in labor.

Finally, we cannot underestimate the impact of automation on the customer experience. Tools like chatbots or automated response systems allow companies to provide 24/7 customer service, improve response times, and personalize interactions with users. This not only enhances customer satisfaction but also strengthens loyalty and commitment to the company. In this chapter, we will examine how these benefits can be practically implemented in SMEs, maximizing the value they can deliver to their customers and internal operations.

- ## Automation to Boost Talent and Efficiency in Human Resources

The optimization of human resources is one of the most transformative aspects of automation within a company, especially for SMEs, where resources are often limited and operational efficiency plays a crucial role in competitiveness. Automation allows employees to free up their time and effort from the most repetitive and tedious tasks, giving them the opportunity to focus on higher-value activities, such as strategy and creativity, which directly drive business growth and differentiation. In this context, automation should not be seen as a replacement for employees but as a tool that optimizes the use of their talent and skills, thus improving both productivity and the quality of work.

One of the most obvious fields where automation has a significant impact is in administrative tasks, which are often repetitive processes prone to errors when done manually. A clear example of this is invoice management, where automation can simplify the entire lifecycle of an invoice, from creation and sending to payment tracking. Traditionally, this process can consume a considerable amount of time, as it involves gathering information, generating documents, and managing collections. However, by automating these tasks, companies can send invoices automatically once a sale is completed, track payment status, and schedule automatic reminders in case of delays. This not only saves employees time but also reduces the likelihood of errors, such as missing a payment or sending incorrect invoices. Moreover, it allows financial managers to focus on higher-value tasks, such as strategic planning or cash flow optimization, rather than being constantly bogged down in manual invoice management.

Another practical example is sending follow-up emails, a task that often falls into the repetitive category but is essential for maintaining good customer relationships. Instead of employees spending time manually sending emails after a customer interaction (such as a purchase or a request for information), automation allows these emails to be scheduled to send automatically at key moments. For example, a thank-you email after a purchase, a reminder before a service renewal, or even a follow-up message to survey customer satisfaction. This email automation capability not only improves operational efficiency but also ensures that customers receive consistent communications at the right time, which can significantly enhance the customer experience and foster loyalty. Meanwhile, employees can focus on more important tasks, such as developing new loyalty strategies or improving the product offering.

Human resources management also benefits greatly from automation. An area that used to involve a significant administrative burden is the recruitment process, which includes posting job offers, reviewing resumes, scheduling interviews, and communicating with candidates. By automating parts of this process, companies can reduce the time spent on these tasks without compromising the quality of the selection process. For example, initial resume screening can be automated using software that identifies key skills and relevant experiences in candidates, allowing recruiters to focus on interviewing those who truly meet the job requirements. Additionally, recruitment management platforms enable the automation of interview scheduling, sending emails to candidates, and tracking the stages of the process, which lightens the administrative load on HR departments and allows them to focus on talent retention or developing training plans.

Automation can also have a significant impact on employee performance management. Many SMEs face the challenge of conducting regular performance evaluations and continuously tracking employee performance, which can be a manually intensive task if done traditionally. By automating part of the process, companies can collect real-time data on employee activities and performance through tools that monitor key performance indicators (KPIs) and generate automatic reports. These reports allow managers to have a clear and objective view of employees' progress without having to spend excessive time manually reviewing data. In addition, automating performance tracking can help quickly identify areas for improvement, enabling employees and managers to take corrective action before issues become more significant.

In the field of marketing, automation plays a key role in optimizing human resources, especially when it comes to digital marketing campaigns. Instead of employees spending hours manually creating, scheduling, and sending promotional emails, marketing automation tools allow for the setup of workflows that manage each phase of the campaign automatically. For example, in an email marketing strategy, an SME can automate the sending of a sequence of emails to a segmented group of potential customers based on their behavior, such as visiting the website or making a purchase. This not only ensures that the message reaches the right customer at the right time, but also allows marketing teams to focus on strategy and content creation rather than the technical execution of the campaign. Additionally, with automated analysis of campaign results, marketing managers can gain valuable insights into the performance of their marketing efforts and adjust their strategies in real-time, significantly improving the effectiveness of campaigns without a manual workload overload.

Another sector where automation has proven valuable is customer service, a critical area for SMEs looking to improve customer satisfaction and retention. The implementation of chatbots and automated response systems allows companies to manage customer inquiries much more efficiently. Chatbots can automatically answer frequently asked questions, process simple requests, and even guide users through basic technical support processes, all without direct human intervention. This reduces the burden on customer service teams, allowing employees to focus on solving more complex issues that truly require human intervention. Additionally, by automating initial responses, companies can offer faster and more efficient service to their customers, resulting in a better customer experience and greater satisfaction. Meanwhile, customer service agents can concentrate on improving processes, designing better solutions, and maintaining closer relationships with high-value customers.

In the area of operations, automation can also play a crucial role in optimizing time and resources. For example, in the logistics sector, automating inventory management can help SMEs maintain precise control of their stock without the need for employees dedicated exclusively to manual product oversight. Automated systems can track available stock in real time, alerting managers when it's necessary to restock a product or manage a purchase order. This significantly reduces the possibility of human error and prevents situations of overstocking or product shortages, which in turn improves operational efficiency. Additionally, by freeing employees from constant inventory supervision, they can focus on more strategic tasks, such as improving supplier relationships or identifying growth opportunities in the market.

Another interesting case of optimization through automation is production planning in manufacturing SMEs. Traditionally, production planning involves manually tracking work orders, controlling machines, and allocating resources. However, by using automated Enterprise Resource Planning (ERP) systems, companies can manage the entire production process much more efficiently. These systems not only automate the planning of production orders based on demand but also facilitate the optimal allocation of resources, such as machines and labor, ensuring that products are manufactured on time and without interruptions. Instead of having to manually plan every aspect of production, employees can focus on improving product quality, innovating processes, or working on new product development.

Automation also has a positive impact on project management, a key area for many SMEs that handle multiple initiatives and need to control time and resources effectively. Tools like automated project management systems allow companies to establish workflows that ensure each task is completed on time and by the right person. Automated tracking systems can generate reminders, automatically update task statuses, and send progress reports, reducing the need for managers to constantly supervise every detail. This way, project managers can focus on strategic tasks like long-term planning or solving critical problems, rather than being bogged down by day-to-day micromanagement.

Automation not only helps reduce workload but also improves the quality of the work performed. When employees are freed from tedious tasks, they have more time and energy to focus on activities that truly require their attention, such as solving complex problems, making strategic decisions, or innovating. This not only increases job satisfaction but also has a positive impact on the overall business results. Companies that automate repetitive and administrative tasks often experience a significant improvement in efficiency, a reduction in operating costs, and a greater capacity to adapt to market changes, which is crucial for survival and growth in today's environment.

In summary, automation is a powerful tool for SMEs looking to optimize the use of their human resources. By allowing employees to focus on more strategic and creative tasks, and freeing up time from repetitive tasks, automation not only improves operational efficiency but also enhances the quality of work and the company's ability to grow sustainably.

- **How Automation Minimizes Errors and Optimizes Resources in SMEs**

Error reduction is one of the most clear and immediate benefits that automation brings to any business, especially SMEs. Repetitive and manual tasks are inherently prone to human error. These errors may seem minor in some cases, but when they accumulate or go unnoticed, they can have significant consequences for a company's operations and financial performance. From incorrect data entry to errors in generating financial reports, every operational failure can translate into a loss of time, resources, and ultimately, money. Automation not only saves time by performing these tasks more quickly but also ensures a much higher level of accuracy than what can be achieved manually.

One of the most common examples where automation helps reduce errors is in accounting data entry. In a company, accounting is a critical function that requires absolute precision, as an error in the data can have a significant impact on financial results, budget planning, and even compliance with tax regulations. When this process is done manually, errors are inevitable. From incorrect transcription of numbers to the introduction of duplicate data, each mistake can create discrepancies that are difficult to trace and correct. This is where automation comes into play. Accounting automation tools can handle large volumes of data with accuracy and speed, eliminating the need for manual intervention in tasks such as invoice entry, bank reconciliation, or expense allocation. These tools not only ensure that data is entered correctly, but they can also identify and correct inconsistencies automatically, reducing the likelihood of errors in a process that would otherwise be prone to mistakes.

A practical case would be that of an SME using automated accounting software to manage its billing flow. Instead of an employee manually entering each invoice into the system, the software can automatically capture the information from electronic invoices and record it in the corresponding accounting system. This not only ensures that the information is recorded accurately but also allows invoices to be processed faster and more efficiently. Additionally, the software can automatically verify that the invoices match purchase orders and delivery notes, detecting any discrepancies that may arise, such as an incorrect price or a mismatched quantity. This way, the process becomes not only more efficient but also much more accurate, significantly reducing the possibility of errors that could affect the company's financial results.

Another area where automation plays a key role in reducing errors is in the generation of financial reports. In many companies, financial reports are generated monthly, quarterly, or annually, and are essential for managers to understand the company's financial status, plan strategies, and make key decisions. However, when these reports are generated manually, errors often occur in the data collection process, financial metric calculations, or even in the interpretation of the results. An error in a financial report can lead to an incorrect assessment of the company's economic health or erroneous decisions regarding investments or expenses. By automating the generation of financial reports, SMEs can ensure that the data used is always correct, calculations are accurate, and reports are generated consistently and without errors. Additionally, automated tools can customize reports according to the company's needs, ensuring that the most relevant metrics are included and that reports are available in real-time, facilitating faster and more data-driven decision-making.

Bank reconciliation is another process that, when done manually, is rife with opportunities for errors. Bank reconciliation involves verifying that a company's records match the movements in its bank account, ensuring that all transactions have been correctly recorded. If this process is done manually, it's easy to overlook small errors, such as a transaction being recorded twice or an incorrect amount being entered in the accounting books. However, when bank reconciliation is automated, the system can automatically compare the company's internal records with bank movements, immediately identifying any discrepancies. This not only saves time but also significantly reduces the chance of errors that could create financial problems for the company, such as losing control over available balances or failing to detect fraudulent transactions.

In the field of inventory management, automation also helps reduce common errors in tracking and controlling stock. Companies that manage their inventory manually are more likely to encounter recording errors, whether it's omission of products, incorrect quantity entries, or failure to update inventory levels in real time. These errors can have a direct impact on operational efficiency, causing stockouts or excess products, which translates into financial losses. With inventory automation, every product movement, whether it's a sale, a return, or a new merchandise entry, is automatically recorded in the system, ensuring that inventory levels always reflect reality. This accuracy is essential for SMEs looking to optimize their resources and avoid unnecessary costs due to inventory management errors.

Another example where automation minimizes errors is in the payroll process. For any company, accurately calculating and processing employee payments is crucial. A payroll error, whether overpaying or underpaying an employee, can create problems both financially and in terms of employee satisfaction. Additionally, errors in tax calculations or social security contributions can have serious legal implications. When the payroll process is done manually, the likelihood of these errors is high, especially if the number of employees is significant. However, by automating this process, SMEs can ensure that payroll calculations are accurate, performed on time, and that all tax and contribution aspects are correctly managed. This not only reduces errors but also improves employee satisfaction, as they receive their payments promptly and without discrepancies.

Data recording and analysis also benefit greatly from automation. In many SMEs, employees have to collect, record, and analyze data manually, which is not only a tedious task but also rife with opportunities for errors. A wrongly entered data point or a poorly applied formula can completely distort the subsequent analysis, potentially leading to incorrect conclusions about the state of a project or the viability of a business strategy. By automating these processes, data is recorded and analyzed automatically, ensuring there are no human errors in transcription or calculation. This is especially important when dealing with large volumes of data or complex analyses, where a small error in the input data can have a domino effect on the entire subsequent analysis.

In the case of personalized reports or automated reports, automation not only ensures that the data presented is accurate, but also allows for the continuous updating of these reports with the most recent information. This is especially useful in companies that need to track certain key metrics on a daily or weekly basis, such as sales, production, or financial performance. Instead of having an employee manually generate these reports every day, automation allows the reports to be updated automatically with the latest data, which not only saves time but also eliminates the possibility of errors in data collection and presentation.

Another important aspect of reducing errors through automation is the automatic verification of processes. In many areas of a business, it is essential to ensure that all processes are completed correctly before moving on to the next stage. For example, in a manufacturing company, errors in production or the supply chain can lead to defective products or delivery delays. By automating the verification of each step in the process, companies can ensure there are no failures that affect product quality or delivery timelines. This not only improves accuracy but also reduces the amount of resources needed for manual supervision of each step in the process.

Finally, an area where automation has proven to be extremely useful in reducing errors is document management. The organization, storage, and retrieval of documents is a task that was traditionally done manually, which increased the risk of losing important documents or not archiving information correctly. By automating the document management process, SMEs can ensure that all documents are properly archived, easily retrievable, and that there are no errors in the tracking or organization of key company documentation. This is especially important when it comes to complying with legal regulations or tax laws, where precision in document management is crucial to avoid penalties or fines.

In summary, automation not only saves time in operational processes but also significantly reduces the number of errors that can occur in repetitive and manual tasks. For SMEs, where resources are limited and errors can have serious consequences, automation offers an effective solution to improve accuracy and efficiency, ensuring that data is processed correctly and that key reports and processes are completed without failures.

- ### Limitless Scalability: Automation for SME Growth

Scalability is a crucial concept in the growth of any business, and for SMEs, the ability to scale without proportionally increasing costs or human resources is one of the biggest challenges and, at the same time, one of the most important goals. Scalability means that a company can expand its operations, handle a larger volume of work, or serve more customers without a significant increase in operating costs or business complexity. This is where automation plays a fundamental role, allowing SMEs to grow efficiently and effectively, without the need to hire more staff or invest in additional infrastructure.

One of the most outstanding aspects of automation is that it allows companies to handle increasing workloads without having to double or triple their workforce. For example, an automated process can manage hundreds or even thousands of records, whether they are clients, transactions, or inventories, quickly and accurately. In a scenario where this process is done manually, the company would be forced to hire more staff as the amount of data to process increases, which not only involves additional costs but also greater complexity in team management. However, with automation, the same processes handled by a small team can easily scale to cover a much larger workload without the need to increase staff.

In this context, automation not only saves time, but also enables more efficient resource management. An automated system can work continuously, processing data, generating reports, or managing transactions 24/7, which would be impossible for a human team. This not only increases the company's operational capacity but also ensures that the same level of service and quality can be maintained, even during periods of rapid growth. Additionally, automated systems are more consistent and less prone to errors than human employees, ensuring that processes remain accurate and efficient regardless of the workload.

A concrete example of scalability through automation can be found in customer management. Imagine a SME using a manual or semi-automatic customer relationship management (CRM) system, where employees are responsible for updating customer profiles, tracking interactions, and scheduling marketing campaigns. As the company grows and its customer base increases, managing these tasks manually becomes increasingly difficult and consumes a considerable amount of time and resources. However, with automation, the CRM can automatically update customer profiles based on their interactions with the company, schedule marketing campaigns based on customer behavior, and generate performance reports without human intervention. In this way, the company can serve thousands of additional customers without the need to hire more staff or increase the workload of current employees.

The same principle can be applied to other areas of the business, such as inventory management or order processing. For an SME handling physical products, inventory automation can make the difference between a smoothly running system and one overwhelmed by growth. Instead of having employees manually track every inventory movement or order processing, an automated system can perform these tasks in real-time, updating inventory levels every time a sale is made or a new product is received. This allows the company to handle a much larger sales volume without increasing the number of staff responsible for inventory management. Additionally, automation in this context reduces the risk of errors, such as overstocking or stockouts, which in turn improves customer satisfaction and optimizes operational costs.

Another key aspect of scalability through automation is the ability to process large volumes of data quickly and accurately. In a growing company, the amount of data generated can increase exponentially, from sales and customer data to financial and performance reports. Handling this data manually would be practically impossible without a considerable investment in additional human resources. However, with automated data analysis processes, the company can manage this growing volume without any problem. For example, an automated system can analyze sales data in real-time to identify customer behavior patterns, predict future demand, and suggest marketing or sales strategies based on objective data. This allows the company to scale its analysis capacity without needing to hire more staff, while improving decision-making based on up-to-date and accurate information.

In the realm of finance and accounting, automation also offers great potential for scalability. As a company grows, managing its finances manually becomes increasingly complicated and time-consuming. From data entry to financial report generation, and even bank reconciliation, each of these processes can be automated so that the company can handle a growing volume of transactions and financial data without increasing its accounting team. An automated system can automatically record each transaction, generate real-time reports, and reconcile bank accounts quickly and accurately. This not only reduces the workload of employees but also allows the company to maintain stricter and more precise financial control, even as it grows.

Another example of scalability is found in customer service operations. Companies that provide services to a large number of customers face the challenge of maintaining service quality as demand increases. This is especially difficult if employees have to handle each inquiry or request manually. However, with the automation of customer service through chatbots or automated response systems, companies can manage a much higher volume of interactions without the need to increase their staff. Chatbots can automatically respond to the most common customer questions, direct them to the right solutions, or even escalate more complex inquiries to a human agent when necessary. This allows the customer service team to focus on the more complicated issues that truly need human intervention, while simpler queries are resolved automatically and in real time.

One area that can also benefit greatly from automation in terms of scalability is digital marketing. Marketing campaigns, especially on digital platforms, require constant monitoring, adjustments based on results, and the creation of relevant content for different audiences. If done manually, this can be extremely labor-intensive, especially as the company grows and its campaigns become more complex. However, with marketing automation, SMEs can scale their campaigns without increasing their marketing team. For example, automated marketing tools can manage content distribution across different channels, personalize messages based on customer behaviors and preferences, and analyze campaign performance in real-time, all without human intervention. This allows the company to reach a much larger audience and manage more complex campaigns without needing to hire more staff or spend extra hours on manual oversight.

Email automation is another aspect that allows SMEs to scale their reach without increasing resources. Instead of employees having to create and send emails to each client manually, email automation tools enable businesses to schedule emails based on specific customer actions, such as making a purchase or abandoning a shopping cart. This not only improves the effectiveness of email marketing campaigns but also ensures that customers receive the right message at the right time, all without the need for human intervention. The company can therefore manage large-scale email campaigns and extend its reach without having to increase the size of its team.

In the field of production or manufacturing, scalability through automation is also essential for SMEs looking to increase their production capacity without significantly increasing their operating costs. Automated production planning systems can efficiently manage work order scheduling, resource allocation, and production line oversight, ensuring that the company can increase its production volume without hiring more staff. Additionally, automating machinery monitoring and quality control allows for real-time problem identification and correction, ensuring the company can maintain product quality even as production scales up. This not only reduces the need for manual oversight but also improves efficiency, allowing the company to increase its production capacity without dealing with the operational challenges that usually accompany growth.

An important aspect of scalability is that it allows companies to quickly adapt to changes in demand. If an SME experiences rapid growth, automation allows it to adjust to this increase in demand without having to go through a lengthy process of hiring and training new employees. For example, if an online store experiences a sudden increase in order volume, an automated order management system can handle this surge seamlessly, ensuring that all orders are processed and shipped on time. The same

applies to service companies, where an increase in the number of clients can be managed by automating appointment scheduling, request tracking, or billing, allowing the company to maintain high-quality service without being overwhelmed by the additional workload.

In summary, automation allows SMEs to scale their operations efficiently, handling an increasing workload without the need to proportionally increase their workforce. This not only reduces operating costs but also enables companies to grow sustainably, maintaining service quality and process accuracy. From customer management and marketing to production and finance, automation provides a scalable solution that allows SMEs to adapt to growth without compromising their efficiency or operational capacity.

- **Improving the customer experience through automation**

Automation has radically transformed the customer experience, offering companies the ability to provide faster responses, more efficient services, and continuous attention that doesn't depend on traditional working hours. For SMEs, which often have limited resources and a small staff, automation has become an essential tool for improving the quality of customer service without significantly increasing costs or labor. One of the most noticeable aspects of this impact is the ability to offer 24/7 service, ensuring that customers can get assistance at any time, regardless of staff availability. In addition, automation allows for the personalization of customer interactions, which significantly improves customer satisfaction and strengthens the relationship between the company and its user base.

One of the most important advances in this area is the use of automated response bots. These bots, programmed to handle frequently asked questions and basic inquiries, allow companies to serve customers immediately and in real time. Often, customers need quick answers to common questions like opening hours, order status, or return policies. However, if the customer has to wait several hours or even days for a response, their experience can deteriorate significantly. With automated bots, customers can get immediate answers to these types of inquiries without the intervention of a human agent, reducing frustration and improving their perception of the company. By freeing employees from these repetitive tasks, staff can focus on more complex issues or improving other aspects of the service.

Chatbots are another clear example of how automation can improve the customer experience. A chatbot can be integrated into a company's website or app to provide real-time assistance. If a customer has a question about a product, the chatbot can respond immediately by providing detailed information about the item, showing recommendations for related products, or even guiding the customer through the purchase process. This not only speeds up the buying process but also improves customer satisfaction by offering a personalized and proactive level of support. Additionally, chatbots can handle multiple conversations simultaneously, meaning they can assist hundreds of customers at the same time without compromising service quality.

Another key advantage of automation in customer service is the ability to personalize interactions. Today, customers expect companies to offer personalized experiences based on their preferences and behaviors. Automation allows companies to collect and analyze data on their customers, making it easier to create detailed profiles that include information about their interests, past purchases, and online behavior. With this data, SMEs can automate the sending of personalized emails, offer product recommendations based on the customer's previous purchases, or even adjust promotional messages to be more relevant to each individual customer. This not only improves the customer experience but also increases the likelihood of a purchase, as the customer feels attended to and understood in a more personal way.

A clear example of automated personalization is sending follow-up emails after a purchase. Instead of employees manually sending these emails, the automated system can schedule personalized messages thanking the customer for their purchase, providing additional information about the product, or suggesting complementary products. Moreover, these emails can include discount coupons or personalized promotions based on the customer's purchase history, which not only enhances the post-sale experience but also encourages customer loyalty and promotes future purchases.

Another important aspect of automation in customer service is the ability to offer continuous service. In an SME, where human resources may be limited and customer service teams are usually only available during working hours, providing 24/7 service without automation would be practically impossible. However, with automated tools, companies can ensure that their customers receive assistance at any time of the day, regardless of the hour or location. This type of continuous service is especially important in sectors like e-commerce, where customers make purchases or inquiries outside of regular office hours. With automation, an online store can ensure that customers receive immediate responses about the status of their orders, get technical support, or even manage returns, all without the need for a human agent to be present.

In addition to providing continuous service, automation can also improve the speed and accuracy of the responses customers receive. In many companies, the simplest or most frequent inquiries can be quickly resolved through pre-programmed responses. This means that customers don't have to wait for an employee to read and respond to their query; instead, the system provides an instant reply based on a database of predefined answers. For example, if a customer asks about delivery times or accepted payment methods, the system can immediately respond with the correct information. This not only enhances the customer experience by reducing wait times but also ensures that responses are accurate and consistent in every interaction.

The automation of customer service also allows companies to identify and resolve issues proactively. With the use of machine learning algorithms and artificial intelligence, companies can anticipate common problems that customers might face and offer solutions before the customer even asks for help. For example, if a customer is browsing a company's website and has difficulty completing a purchase, the automated system can detect this behavior and offer real-time assistance, either through a chatbot or with a pop-up notification providing clear instructions. This type of proactive assistance significantly improves the customer experience by preventing frustration and ensuring that customers can complete their transactions without interruptions.

In the case of more complex problems that cannot be solved by an automated bot, the automation of customer service also facilitates the scalability of requests to a human agent. Instead of customers having to navigate a complicated menu system or wait for an employee to be available to answer their query, automated systems can direct the more complex requests to human agents quickly and efficiently. This ensures that customers receive the appropriate attention without unnecessary delays and that employees can focus on solving the most critical issues instead of spending time on basic or repetitive queries.

In addition to improving efficiency and speed of responses, automation also allows companies to collect and analyze data from customer interactions. Every time a customer interacts with a bot or automated system, valuable data is generated that can be used to improve future service. This data can reveal customer behavior patterns, identify recurring issues, or highlight areas where the company could improve its processes. By using these metrics, SMEs can adjust their customer service strategies to make them more effective, ensuring that customers receive high-quality service in every interaction.

Another interesting application of automation in customer experience is the use of virtual assistants that not only provide information but also guide customers through complex processes. For example, a company offering financial services can implement a virtual assistant that helps customers complete online forms, perform financial calculations, or generate personalized reports. Instead of the customer having to search for information on their own or call a customer service representative, the virtual assistant can guide them step by step through the process, ensuring everything is completed correctly and efficiently. This guided interaction capability greatly improves customer satisfaction, as it allows them to solve problems or complete tasks quickly and without hassle.

A less visible but equally important impact of automation in customer service is the improvement in time management for both customers and employees. For customers, the ability to solve problems on their own through automated tools means they don't have to wait for an employee to be available to assist them, saving time and reducing frustration. For employees, automation frees up valuable time that they can dedicate to more strategic tasks or to solving complex problems that truly require human intervention. In this way, automation not only improves the customer experience but also optimizes the use of human resources within the company.

Finally, another crucial aspect of automation in customer experience is its ability to increase customer trust and loyalty. By offering fast, efficient, and personalized service, companies can build stronger relationships with their customers, increasing the likelihood that they will return in the future. Customers value speed and accuracy in service, and when a company can consistently provide both, they develop greater trust in the brand.

Additionally, the ability to personalize interactions and offer continuous service improves the company's perception and reinforces long-term customer loyalty.

In summary, automation has transformed the way SMEs can manage and improve the customer experience. From implementing chatbots and automated response bots to the ability to offer continuous service and personalized interactions, automation allows businesses to enhance service quality, reduce wait times, and increase customer satisfaction without significantly increasing human resources. Additionally, the ability to collect valuable data on customer interactions enables companies to continuously adjust and improve their customer service approach, ensuring they can provide high-quality service that meets the changing needs and expectations of their users.

4.2. Introduction to RPA (Robotic Process Automation) for SMEs

Robotic Process Automation (RPA) has revolutionized the way businesses manage repetitive and manual tasks, allowing them to optimize time and resources. While large corporations have been using advanced automation technologies to improve operational efficiency for years, more and more SMEs are discovering that they too can benefit from these solutions. Although RPA has traditionally been associated with expensive systems and complex implementations, there are actually accessible and low-cost tools that can be easily implemented, even by small businesses, without the need for large investments in software or infrastructure.

In this section, we will explore how SMEs can effectively implement RPA, leveraging available tools to automate everyday processes and free their employees from repetitive tasks that consume time and energy. The goal is to allow teams to focus on more strategic tasks, while manual and routine actions, such as data entry or sending emails, are handled automatically. Through Robotic Process Automation, small businesses can increase productivity, reduce human error, and significantly improve operational efficiency.

One of the main attractions of RPA for SMEs is its accessibility. Unlike large corporations that can afford custom and expensive automation solutions, SMEs can take advantage of open and free tools like Selenium, PyAutoGUI, and Robot Framework, all compatible with Python. These tools allow companies to automate basic processes without needing to modify their internal systems, which is a crucial advantage for those using platforms like CRM or ERP that cannot be altered. The ability to simulate human interaction with desktop or web applications is a distinctive feature of RPA, setting it apart from traditional script or API-based automation.

Throughout this section, we will also look at practical cases that illustrate how SMEs can apply RPA effectively. From automating billing, where systems can generate and send invoices automatically, to creating weekly reports, the impact of RPA on productivity improvement is undeniable. More and more companies are discovering that implementing automation solutions not only saves time but also reduces human errors and facilitates the scalability of operational processes. RPA is not only an accessible tool, but it also offers a quick return on investment, making it an ideal solution for small businesses looking to improve efficiency and reduce costs.

- **What is RPA and how can it be applied in an SME?**

Robotic Process Automation (RPA) is a technology that allows companies to automate repetitive and routine tasks using robots or scripts that mimic human actions in computer systems. RPA has revolutionized the way organizations optimize their processes, enabling companies to manage administrative tasks, collect data, process transactions, and generate reports quickly and without human intervention. This type of automation is especially relevant for SMEs, as it helps improve efficiency and reduce costs without requiring a significant investment in technological infrastructure. For small and medium-sized enterprises, RPA is a tool that allows them to maximize existing resources, eliminate bottlenecks in operational processes, and let employees focus on higher-value strategic tasks.

Unlike large corporations that can afford custom and highly expensive automation solutions, SMEs need more accessible and flexible alternatives. That's why the use of Python-based RPA tools has become so popular in this sector. Python, a widely-used open-source programming language, offers a wide variety of libraries and frameworks that make it easy to create process automations. With libraries like Selenium, PyAutoGUI, and Robot Framework, SMEs can implement RPA processes at low cost and with minimal investment in technical resources. These tools allow small businesses to start automating processes quickly, scalably, and effectively.

To understand the importance of RPA in the context of an SME, it is essential to consider the type of tasks that can be automated and the specific benefits this can bring to small and medium-sized enterprises. In an SME, staff often have to perform multiple functions due to limited resources. For example, the same employee may be in charge of billing, customer service, and report generation. This implies a workload overload and a high risk of human error due to the number of tasks that must be performed in parallel. With the implementation of RPA, companies can delegate many of these repetitive and administrative tasks to software robots, freeing employees from manual tasks and allowing them to focus on more strategic activities, such as data analysis or personalized customer service. Robotic automation allows for a smoother workflow, processes to be carried out with greater precision, and human resources to be used more efficiently.

One of the most common applications of RPA in an SME is data entry into business systems. Data entry is an essential task, but it is also repetitive and prone to errors when done manually. Companies often need to input data into management systems, supplier portals, or e-commerce platforms on a constant basis, which can be time-consuming. With RPA, companies can program bots to perform this data entry automatically, significantly reducing the margin of error and ensuring that information is recorded quickly and accurately. For example, by using Selenium, a Python library designed to interact with web browsers, a company can automate filling out online forms or querying data on different web portals. This not only saves time but also ensures that data is entered correctly, avoiding errors that could lead to operational issues or loss of important information.

Another relevant aspect of RPA in the context of SMEs is the automation of administrative management tasks, such as generating and sending invoices, issuing repetitive emails, or processing customer requests. These activities often take up a significant portion of the administrative staff's time, which could be devoted to more strategic tasks. With tools like PyAutoGUI, a Python library that allows you to control the computer's graphical interface, a company can program automations to perform actions like opening applications, moving files, copying and pasting information, or sending follow-up emails. This streamlines administrative tasks and ensures that processes are completed efficiently and error-free, improving the company's overall productivity.

For an SME, the accessibility of these Python-based RPA tools represents a significant advantage. Unlike traditional automation solutions, which may require access to system APIs or direct modifications to the software, RPA allows you to automate processes without needing backend access to applications. This is particularly useful for companies using third-party software, such as customer relationship management (CRM) systems or enterprise resource planning (ERP) systems, as they don't always have the ability to modify or customize these systems. With RPA, robots can simulate human interaction directly on the user interface, enabling SMEs to integrate automation into their processes without making changes to their internal systems. In this way, RPA becomes a flexible and adaptable tool that can be implemented on any type of system or platform.

One of the most notable benefits of RPA in the context of SMEs is the reduction of errors. When employees have to perform repetitive tasks, such as copying and pasting information from one system to another or doing manual calculations, the risk of making mistakes increases significantly. These errors can have a negative impact on the company's operations, especially if they occur in critical tasks, such as billing or inventory management. With RPA, companies can ensure that these tasks are performed accurately and error-free, improving service quality and reducing the cost associated with fixing mistakes. For example, in the case of billing, an RPA robot can automatically generate and send invoices based on received orders, ensuring that each invoice is issued correctly and without delays. This not only saves time but also avoids billing issues that could affect customer relationships.

In addition to reducing errors, robotic process automation also allows SMEs to increase operational efficiency. With RPA, processes are completed quickly and without interruptions, meaning tasks that used to take hours can now be completed in minutes. This is especially useful for companies that handle large volumes of data or need to process information constantly. For example, a company that receives hundreds of customer requests through its website can use RPA to automatically process these requests, classify the information, and update the database without human intervention. This not only saves time but also allows the company to respond to its customers more quickly and efficiently.

Scalability is another key aspect of RPA in SMEs. As a company grows and its workload increases, implementing RPA allows it to handle the additional load without hiring more staff. RPA bots can be managed in a scalable way, meaning they can run multiple processes simultaneously, handling an increasing number of transactions without the company incurring additional costs. This is particularly beneficial for SMEs looking to grow and expand without losing operational efficiency. Automating critical processes allows companies to maintain a high level of productivity and quality as their operations increase, which is essential to compete in an ever-changing market.

To implement RPA in an SME, it's important to identify the areas where automation will have the greatest impact. Generally, the most suitable tasks for RPA are those that are highly repetitive, rule-based, and have a clear structure. In a small business, these tasks can include data entry, report generation, inventory management, order tracking, account reconciliation, and sending emails. Once these tasks are identified, the company can develop RPA scripts using accessible tools like the aforementioned Selenium, PyAutoGUI, and Robot Framework, which offer a simple and cost-effective way to start automating processes without the need for large investments in technology.

One of the great advantages of RPA for SMEs is its flexibility and ease of implementation. With basic training in Python and knowledge of the available tools, companies can start implementing RPA in their internal processes in no time. Moreover, since many Python-based RPA tools are open-source, companies can adapt and customize them to their specific needs, allowing for an automation solution that perfectly fits their workflows. This means that SMEs can access the same advanced automation technology as large corporations, but in an affordable way and on a scale appropriate for their operations.

In short, Robotic Process Automation (RPA) is a powerful tool that allows SMEs to optimize their processes, reduce errors, improve efficiency, and scale their operations sustainably. Through the use of accessible Python-based tools, small businesses can implement RPA solutions without the need for large investments, allowing them to compete on equal footing with larger companies. RPA thus becomes a strategic tool for SMEs, enabling them to do more with less and focus on what really matters: growth and continuous improvement.

- ## Accessible tools for RPA with Python

RPA (Robotic Process Automation) tools based on Python have opened a new path for SMEs to optimize their operations without the need to invest in costly and complex solutions. The popularity of Python and its ecosystem of automation libraries allows even small businesses to implement RPA in their daily workflows, simplifying and speeding up repetitive tasks. Tools like Selenium, PyAutoGUI, and Robot Framework are excellent options for automating processes without a large investment in advanced technology. These libraries are not only affordable but also offer great flexibility and scalability, making them ideal solutions for the specific needs of small and medium-sized businesses. Next, we will explore in depth how these tools can be used to optimize essential tasks in an SME, from automating web interactions to automating graphical interfaces and administrative processes.

Selenium is one of the most recognized tools for web browser automation and is particularly useful for SMEs that need to interact with web-based systems, such as supplier platforms, customer relationship management (CRM) systems, and other SaaS applications. Instead of having an employee spend time manually entering data into different web systems, Selenium allows these processes to be carried out automatically and without human intervention. This not only saves time but also minimizes the risk of errors that can occur when manually entering large volumes of data. By programming a Selenium bot, an SME can establish automated workflows that input, extract, and manage data on any web platform, whether it's to update order statuses, manage inventories, or retrieve supplier information.

A clear example of how Selenium can assist with data entry in web systems is a company that needs to make recurring orders for materials through a supplier's portal. Normally, this would require an employee to manually enter the quantity of products, check prices, and complete the purchase process. However, with Selenium, a bot can be programmed to perform all these tasks automatically, logging into the system, filling in the necessary fields, and confirming the order without human intervention. Selenium can also be programmed to perform periodic checks, automating the querying of prices, product availability, or shipping status on supplier portals, providing continuously updated information without the need for constant supervision.

In addition to entering data, Selenium can be a valuable tool for automating tests on websites or web applications that an SME might be developing or using. For businesses with internal web platforms or those relying on e-commerce systems, Selenium allows for automated interaction with these platforms, ensuring that functionalities and forms work correctly. By performing automated tests, SMEs can ensure their systems are functioning as they should, detecting potential errors or failures without the need for exhaustive manual testing. This capability is particularly valuable when implementing website updates or making changes to the platform, as Selenium allows for repeated testing quickly and efficiently.

Another powerful tool for process automation in Python is PyAutoGUI, designed for automating graphical interfaces. Unlike Selenium, which focuses on web browser automation, PyAutoGUI allows businesses to interact with desktop applications, simulating mouse clicks, keyboard inputs, and other actions a user would perform manually on their computer. This tool is especially useful for SMEs that rely on multiple desktop applications and need to integrate information between them without human intervention. For example, in the case of a company that uses an inventory management system in a desktop application, PyAutoGUI allows automating the process of entering and updating data in the system, without the need for an employee to manually perform each step.

A common use of PyAutoGUI in an SME could be automating administrative tasks that require interacting with multiple desktop applications. For example, if a company needs to move files between folders frequently, rename documents, or send daily emails, PyAutoGUI can be programmed to perform all these tasks automatically. PyAutoGUI allows you to schedule scripts that perform repetitive actions such as opening and closing applications, clicking on specific buttons, copying and pasting information between different programs, and executing key sequences that a user would normally enter manually. This not only speeds up the workflow but also reduces the likelihood of human errors when performing these tasks.

In the case of email management, a daily activity in many businesses, PyAutoGUI can be integrated with desktop email applications to send messages automatically, whether it's sending regular updates to clients or notifying employees about the status of a project. This type of automation is particularly useful for SMEs that need to send emails constantly, such as payment reminders, order confirmations, or follow-up reports. Instead of having an employee spend time manually sending each email, PyAutoGUI can handle the entire process, ensuring that messages are sent on time without the need for human intervention. This frees up staff to focus on more strategic tasks while automation takes care of basic and repetitive communications.

Another key tool in the arsenal of Python-based RPA is Robot Framework, an open-source automation framework that provides an organized structure for implementing RPA processes efficiently. Unlike Selenium or PyAutoGUI, which are libraries focused on specific tasks, Robot Framework is a broader and more versatile framework that allows for the creation of more complex and structured automation flows. It's an ideal option for SMEs that want to manage multiple automation processes in a centralized way, as it allows for the coordination of different tasks and the monitoring of multiple robots' execution in the same environment.

Robot Framework uses a markup language similar to software testing, which allows use cases to be defined simply and clearly. This means that even employees without advanced programming knowledge can design automated workflows and understand the robots' code. Companies can use Robot Framework to orchestrate complete processes such as report generation, database updates, information extraction from external systems, and sending notifications. Additionally, Robot Framework is compatible with Selenium and other libraries, which allows integration of web, desktop, and other types of automation tasks into a single workflow.

One application of Robot Framework in an SME could be automating the billing process. Instead of having an employee manually generate invoices from received orders, Robot Framework allows you to design a workflow that automatically collects order information, generates a PDF invoice, attaches it to an email, and sends it to the client. This process is carried out quickly and accurately, ensuring that each client receives their invoice on time and without errors. Robot Framework also allows this sequence to be scheduled to run at specific times, ensuring that invoices are sent at regular intervals, regardless of the order volume. This way, the company saves time, reduces errors, and maintains a consistent level of service.

In addition to its utility for generating invoices, Robot Framework is also excellent for automating reports, another repetitive and essential task for many SMEs. For example, a company may need to generate weekly sales or inventory reports for its managers or employees. With Robot Framework, you can design a workflow that collects the necessary information from internal systems, organizes it into a report, and automatically sends it to the appropriate recipients. This eliminates the need for employees to spend time manually generating reports, allowing information to reach managers on time and with consistent accuracy. Robot Framework ensures that the process of collecting and sending reports is error-free and regular, making decision-making in the company easier.

One of the great advantages of these RPA tools in Python is their accessibility for businesses of all sizes. Unlike commercial RPA solutions, which can be expensive and require specialized technical staff, tools like Selenium, PyAutoGUI, and Robot Framework can be learned and managed by employees with basic Python programming knowledge. This allows SMEs to implement RPA in their internal operations without the need to hire additional staff or make a large investment in software. Moreover, the Python community is extensive and offers a wealth of resources, tutorials, and forums where employees can learn and resolve doubts, making these tools especially valuable for companies looking to optimize productivity without incurring high costs.

The automation of administrative processes through these tools also has a direct impact on cost reduction. By eliminating the need to perform repetitive tasks manually, companies can reduce employee workload, which in turn decreases the time and resources devoted to these tasks. This allows employees to focus on activities that truly add value, such as customer service, business strategy development, or innovation. Automation also reduces errors associated with manual tasks, resulting in greater accuracy in records and reports, avoiding operational issues and improving the overall efficiency of the company.

In conclusion, the RPA tools available in Python, such as Selenium, PyAutoGUI, and Robot Framework, provide SMEs with an efficient and affordable way to automate their internal processes. From web task automation to interacting with desktop graphical interfaces and creating structured RPA flows, these tools allow businesses to manage their operations more efficiently and accurately. The ease of implementation and flexibility of these tools make RPA a realistic and viable option for any SME looking to improve productivity, reduce costs, and optimize resources without resorting to expensive solutions. As more small businesses adopt RPA, these tools are becoming an essential competitive advantage to improve operational efficiency in an increasingly digital and demanding business environment.

- ## RPA vs. Traditional Automation

Robotic Process Automation (RPA) and traditional automation represent two distinct approaches to optimizing and streamlining processes in businesses, although they share common goals. Both allow for reducing the burden of repetitive tasks, increasing efficiency, and minimizing human errors, but they achieve this in different ways and with unique functionalities. Traditional automation is mainly based on creating scripts and using APIs to automate processes in systems with direct access, such as databases and servers. In contrast, RPA goes further by allowing companies to simulate human interactions with desktop or web applications without needing direct access to the underlying layers of the systems. This ability to emulate human actions on user interfaces enables SMEs to leverage automation on platforms they cannot or do not wish to modify directly, such as CRM, ERP systems, and other third-party applications.

One of the key differences between traditional automation and RPA lies in how they interact with systems. Traditional automation generally relies on scripts written in languages like Python, Java, or JavaScript to execute commands on systems with direct access. Scripts are designed to automate specific tasks, such as performing calculations, moving files, or updating data in a database. These scripts usually require the user to have access to the system's code or APIs, allowing direct software modification to integrate automation into the workflow.

However, this approach has limitations when dealing with systems to which the user does not have full access or where direct code modification is complex or costly. In these cases, small businesses using third-party solutions like web-based CRM or ERP encounter barriers when trying to implement traditional automation. Instead, RPA allows these businesses to automate tasks in external systems, interacting directly with the user interface in a manner similar to a human. Through specialized software, RPA robots can simulate mouse clicks, keyboard inputs, navigation, and other actions, enabling automation without modifying the underlying code. This is a key advantage for SMEs, as it allows them to use advanced automation tools without having to invest in customization or access permissions to the system's backend.

Another significant difference between traditional automation and RPA is the level of flexibility each offers in terms of interaction with multiple systems and applications. Traditional automation relies heavily on the availability of APIs or direct access to databases and internal system functions. For example, if a company wants to automate the flow of data between its sales system and its billing system, it needs to have access to the APIs of both systems and write scripts that connect these two platforms. While this approach is effective when access is available, it presents challenges if one of the systems does not allow modifications or lacks an API.

RPA solves this limitation by allowing robots to work directly on the graphical interface of each system, which means they can operate independently of the availability of APIs or direct backend access. This is especially beneficial for SMEs that use a combination of custom software and third-party applications, as RPA robots can integrate these systems without code intervention. Additionally, robots can exchange data between systems without needing to create connection bridges between them, simplifying the automation process and reducing the need for advanced technical knowledge.

The implementation and maintenance of each type of automation also differs significantly. In traditional automation, scripts are usually designed to fulfill specific functions within a system and, although effective, may require frequent updates when the system undergoes changes in its structure or when new functions are added. This means developers are needed to maintain and adjust the scripts as the system evolves, which can be costly and time-consuming. For example, if an SME uses an automation script to move data between its sales database and its inventory system, any change in the data format or system architecture could require adjustments to the script code to keep it functioning correctly.

RPA, on the other hand, relies on robots configured to mimic human actions, making it more resilient to certain changes. While a change in the interface might require adjustments in the robot's paths or commands, RPA is not affected by modifications in the system's internal structure. This means that, in general, RPA-based automation can be maintained and adapted less frequently than traditional scripts, reducing maintenance costs and allowing companies to be more agile in their implementation. In the context of an SME, this is crucial, as it reduces the reliance on specialized programmers and allows staff without advanced knowledge to adjust the robots according to business needs.

Scalability is another differentiating factor between traditional automation and RPA. In traditional automation, scaling the process generally requires duplicating infrastructure or adding more servers or processing capacity to handle the increased workload. Additionally, expanding scripts can become complex if you try to integrate them into multiple systems simultaneously. With RPA, scalability is easier, as robots can be replicated and run in different environments without needing to change existing systems. RPA robots can be programmed to execute multiple tasks at once, allowing the process to scale more smoothly and with fewer infrastructure constraints. For SMEs that need to manage a growing volume of transactions, sales, or customer inquiries, the scalability of RPA allows them to automate these tasks without having to redesign their internal systems.

Another key difference lies in the ease of implementation and usability for non-technical users. Traditional automation, which relies on scripts and APIs, often requires advanced programming knowledge, leading to a steeper learning curve. This can be an obstacle for SMEs, which often lack specialized development and programming staff. RPA, on the other hand, is designed so that even those with limited technical knowledge can configure and manage robots. Many RPA platforms offer drag-and-drop interfaces, allowing users to build visual workflows for robots without writing code. This democratizes the use of automation, enabling anyone in the company to set up basic robots, making implementation easier and reducing the reliance on technical staff.

A fundamental aspect that differentiates RPA from traditional automation is its ability to simulate human interaction with desktop or web applications. Instead of executing direct commands in the backend, RPA operates visually, using the user interface to perform tasks like opening applications, clicking buttons, entering data into forms, and navigating web pages. This allows robots to work in systems where there is no API or where changes to the source code are not desired. For an SME using a third-party application in their daily management, like a CRM or an accounting system, the ability to automate tasks in the user interface is extremely useful. RPA robots can open the application, search for the necessary data, enter information, and generate reports without modifying the software.

In this sense, RPA is especially useful in the context of system integration. Many SMEs use multiple systems for their operations, and these systems are not always interconnected. Traditional automation would require creating a communication bridge between these systems, which can be costly and complex. However, RPA allows a robot to work on the interface of each system, transferring data from one to another without needing backend integrations. For example, an RPA robot could extract data from a sales system, transfer it to the billing system, and update the status in the inventory system, all through the graphical interface of each application. This allows SMEs to keep their systems separate while leveraging automation to facilitate workflow between them.

Finally, the resilience of RPA in the face of system changes is also a key advantage. Unlike automation scripts, which can fail if the system's structure or parameters change, RPA robots are less sensitive to backend modifications and can adjust to continue functioning in a changing environment. This allows SMEs to implement automation without worrying about the costs and time required to keep scripts updated. When an application's interface changes, RPA robots can be adjusted simply by redirecting routes and commands without having to rewrite complex code. In summary, RPA's resilience allows automation to remain useful and operational in constantly evolving environments, which is essential for small businesses seeking flexibility and adaptability in their processes.

In conclusion, RPA offers SMEs a powerful and accessible alternative to traditional automation based on scripting and APIs. RPA's ability to operate in systems without backend access, its ease of implementation and maintenance, scalability, and flexibility make it an ideal tool for optimizing processes and improving operational efficiency. For small and medium-sized businesses that want to benefit from automation without relying on costly or complex modifications to their systems, RPA represents an effective solution that allows them to compete on equal footing with larger companies and more complex technological infrastructures.

- ## Practical examples of RPA in SMEs

Implementing Robotic Process Automation (RPA) has proven to be a powerful and accessible tool for optimizing workflow in companies across different sectors, and this is especially true for SMEs. Small and medium-sized enterprises can leverage RPA to automate repetitive, high-volume tasks, reducing errors, saving time, and allowing staff to focus on more strategic, high-value activities. The practical applications of RPA in SMEs are broad and varied, from generating invoices and automating reports to managing inventories and entering data into management systems. Below, we'll explore some specific cases of how different types of companies have implemented RPA in their operations to improve the efficiency and accuracy of their processes.

One of the most common and effective uses of RPA in SMEs is automating the billing process. For companies that receive purchase orders regularly, generating and sending invoices can take significant time and be prone to errors if done manually. A specific example of how RPA can optimize the billing process can be found in a storage and wholesale office supplies company. This company receives numerous daily orders from different clients, each with specific requirements regarding quantities, prices, and delivery times. Traditionally, the administrative team would have to manually generate invoices for each purchase order, verify product data, apply the necessary discounts, and send the invoices to the client.

With RPA, the company has been able to automate the entire billing process. Upon receiving a purchase order, the RPA system accesses the product database and checks inventory availability. Once stock is confirmed, the robot takes the order details, calculates the total with applicable discounts, and automatically generates the invoice in PDF format. Finally, the system sends the invoice to the client via email without the need for human intervention. This automation not only reduces the time the administration team spends on billing but also eliminates calculation errors and ensures that each customer receives their invoice quickly and accurately. Additionally, the system can be programmed to send automatic reminders for pending payments, improving cash flow and allowing the company to maintain more effective control of its accounts receivable.

A similar case can be observed in the car dealership sector, where the billing process is essential and often involves a series of specific details. A car dealership, for example, receives multiple orders from customers interested in different vehicle models, with additional customization options and financing plans. Instead of the administrative team having to generate an individual invoice for each customer, the dealership can implement RPA so that the system automates invoice generation based on order data. The RPA bot accesses customer and vehicle information, calculates the total cost including taxes and financing fees, and sends the invoice to the customer. Additionally, the system can integrate with the dealership's CRM to update the status of each order and send automatic notifications to the customer at every stage of the process. This not only improves the accuracy of invoices and speeds up the purchasing process, but also optimizes the customer experience, as they receive constant updates and quick, efficient service.

Automating reports is another RPA application that has proven very useful for SMEs. In companies that require frequent reports for decision-making, RPA allows for the automation of data collection and report generation, saving time and ensuring that data is always up-to-date and available. A specific example of how RPA can be applied in report automation is in a plastic product factory, such as toys or kitchen items. In this factory, the production and sales teams need weekly reports that reflect stock levels, recent sales, and products in the manufacturing process. Generating these reports manually can be a tedious and error-prone task, as it involves gathering data from different systems and compiling the information into a suitable format.

With RPA, the factory has automated the generation of these weekly reports. The RPA system connects to the inventory and sales databases and extracts the necessary data, such as the quantities of products in stock, the number of units sold in the last week, and the status of ongoing manufacturing orders. The RPA bot then organizes this information into a report and automatically sends it to the managers of each department. This automation ensures that the reports are always available on time, allows managers to make informed decisions, and removes the workload from employees, who can focus on supervision and production optimization tasks. By eliminating manual errors in data collection, the company also improves the accuracy of its decisions, which positively impacts its performance and efficiency.

In the case of an accounting and financial advisory firm, RPA has also become an indispensable tool for generating automatic reports. Advisory firms typically handle large volumes of data from different clients, and generating accurate and personalized financial reports for each of them can be a laborious task. In this context, automation allows the system to generate and send financial reports automatically based on each client's data. An RPA bot accesses each client's accounting databases, collects financial transactions, calculates income and expenses, and generates a monthly financial report. This report is automatically sent to the client, who receives a detailed document about their financial situation without the advisory firm having to spend additional time on manual report generation. This not only improves the efficiency of the advisory firm but also allows them to offer a fast, high-quality service that enhances client satisfaction.

Inventory management is another area where RPA can bring significant value to SMEs, particularly in wholesale and retail warehouses. Managing inventory can be a complex task, especially if the inventory is large and products have a high turnover rate. An automotive supply warehouse, for example, may have thousands of parts and components in its inventory that require constant tracking to avoid both overstocking and stockouts. With RPA, the warehouse can automate real-time inventory tracking, allowing the system to automatically update stock levels each time a new order is received or a sale is made. The RPA bot connects to the inventory system, checks the available quantities, and sends automatic alerts when a product's stock level falls below a set threshold. This allows the warehouse to anticipate demand and place restocking orders in a timely manner, preventing stockouts and ensuring that products are always available for customers.

A law firm can also benefit from process automation through RPA, especially in document management and information gathering. Firms often handle a large volume of legal documents, such as contracts, files, and client correspondence. Automation allows the system to manage these documents in an organized manner, ensuring that each file is complete and that automatic notifications are sent to lawyers when specific actions are required in a case. For example, an RPA bot can be programmed to extract data from contracts, check deadlines for important documents, and send automatic reminders to the lawyers in charge. This allows the team to focus on legal strategy and client service, while automation takes care of the administrative details that, although important, consume time and effort. Improving the accuracy and efficiency of administrative processes enables the firm to provide higher quality service, which in turn enhances client satisfaction.

In the realm of production, such as in a factory producing plastic kitchenware, RPA can also help improve operational efficiency and reduce errors in manufacturing and quality control processes. This factory, which produces kitchen utensils like storage containers, plastic cutlery, and cutting boards, needs to maintain precise oversight of its production and quality processes to comply with food safety standards. With RPA, the factory can automate the collection of production data and quality control at each stage of the process. The RPA robot collects data from production equipment, such as the number of products manufactured, cycle time, and quality specifications. This data is automatically logged into the management system, allowing supervisors to monitor the process in real time and make adjustments as needed. Automation reduces the workload in quality control, ensuring that each product meets the required standards and minimizing errors that could result in defective products.

A final practical example of how SMEs can benefit from RPA is in order and logistics management. A distribution warehouse for construction tools and machinery receives orders from clients of different sizes and geographic locations. Managing these orders manually means staff have to review each request, check product availability, generate shipping documentation, and coordinate logistics. With RPA, the system can automate the entire order management process. The RPA bot reviews each order, checks inventory, generates the invoice, and prepares the shipping documentation. Additionally, the system can integrate with the courier company's platform to schedule the pickup and update the shipping status. This allows the warehouse to handle a higher volume of orders without increasing the workload of its staff, ensuring fast and accurate delivery to each client.

In each of these cases, the value that RPA brings to SMEs is significant. Automating processes, from invoicing to report generation and inventory management, allows small and medium-sized enterprises to optimize their operations, improve task accuracy, and free up time for employees to focus on more strategic and impactful activities. Moreover, by reducing the margin of error in repetitive tasks, RPA contributes to improved customer satisfaction by providing faster, more accurate, and efficient service. Each of these examples illustrates how RPA has become a key tool for SMEs in different sectors, enabling them to compete in the market more effectively and sustainably.

4.3. Automating repetitive tasks with Python and APIs

In today's context, where technology plays a central role in business efficiency and growth, automating repetitive tasks with Python and APIs has become a key strategy for SMEs. Automation allows companies to optimize tasks that are usually repetitive and time-consuming, freeing employees from manual burdens and enabling the team to focus on more strategic and creative activities. Python, with its ease of use and wide range of libraries, offers an accessible and versatile solution for even small and medium-sized businesses to automate everyday processes, from sending emails to managing files and downloading data. Through customized scripts, Python makes it easy to program tasks tailored to each company's specific needs.

Beyond RPA-based automation, Python and the use of APIs allow SMEs to take this strategy a step further, integrating their internal systems with external platforms and services. APIs enable different applications to communicate with each other in an automated way, opening up a world of possibilities for managing and exchanging information in real-time. For example, using APIs, an SME can connect directly to services like Google Sheets, Trello, or Slack to automatically update spreadsheets, manage tasks, or receive instant notifications, thus streamlining collaboration and improving data accuracy. The integration of APIs from e-commerce platforms or payment gateways also allows for the automation of inventory management, order processing, and payment tracking, tasks that in many companies are still done manually.

In this chapter, we will explore practical and specific examples of how SMEs can implement Python and APIs to transform their daily processes. Through use cases applicable to any sector, we will see how these tools can automate everything from personalized email delivery and file management to data analysis and the execution of digital marketing campaigns. The ability to automate tasks through Python and APIs offers companies a significant competitive advantage, increasing efficiency and allowing human resources to focus on developing new business strategies and continuous improvement.

- **Automation of daily tasks with Python**

Automating everyday tasks with Python represents an invaluable opportunity for SMEs looking to optimize their workflow and reduce time spent on repetitive tasks. Python, thanks to its simplicity and flexibility, allows businesses to develop custom scripts that automate manual processes, improving efficiency and accuracy in executing daily tasks. Instead of relying exclusively on third-party software tools or performing tedious tasks manually, SMEs can program their own Python scripts to manage email sending, organize and handle files, or perform real-time data analysis.

With Python, it's possible to implement accessible solutions to perform essential business functions, from programming automatic reminders and organizing accounting documents, to collecting web data for market analysis. Through this automation, companies can free up human resources, minimize errors, and ensure that administrative tasks are executed consistently. Additionally, Python's ability to integrate with other systems and databases makes it an ideal tool for SMEs in any sector looking for a simple and effective way to transform their daily operations. Let's look at some examples.

- **Email delivery automation**

Sending emails is one of the most common tasks in the business world, and for many SMEs, managing communications with clients, suppliers, and collaborators can consume a significant amount of time and resources. Automating this task with Python allows companies to send messages more quickly, efficiently, and accurately. With the smtplib library, Python provides a simple and effective way to send automated emails, facilitating both mass mailings and personalized messages, tailored to the needs of each client or contact.

One of the most effective uses of smtplib is the automation of promotional campaigns. Instead of relying on external marketing platforms, SMEs can schedule their own email campaigns to promote their products or services to a customer list. For example, a small online store that wants to send special offers to loyal customers can use Python to schedule periodic mailings. By using scripts, the company can access a customer database, select the right recipients, and send emails with promotional content. Each message can include specific details for each customer, such as their name, recommended products, or personalized discounts, improving the user experience and increasing the likelihood of conversion.

Another application of smtplib in automation is sending appointment reminders or payment due notices. For SMEs that rely on a constant flow of appointments or client interactions, like consultancies or health centers, scheduling automatic reminders ensures that clients remember their appointments or payment commitments, reducing the risk of cancellations or payment delays. A Python script using smtplib can be programmed to send appointment reminders to clients one or two days before the event, ensuring the client is informed and doesn't forget the date. In the case of payment reminders, businesses can schedule notifications to be automatically sent each month to clients with outstanding payments, customizing each message with the amount due and the due date.

The configuration of smtplib is quite simple. Once the authentication details are set on the email server (SMTP), such as the username and password, you can create an automated message using Python's email module, which allows you to structure the email, define the recipient and sender, and customize the content in HTML or text format. This gives SMEs full control over the design of their emails and ensures that each message aligns with the company's image and tone. Additionally, the library is compatible with many email servers, providing flexibility when integrating with each company's messaging system.

- **Data download and analysis automation**

The ability to obtain up-to-date and relevant data in real-time is essential for decision-making in any business, but collecting this information manually can be a tedious and ineffective process. With Python, SMEs can automate data extraction from websites and other online resources using the requests and BeautifulSoup libraries, enabling web scraping tasks to be performed quickly without human intervention. Requests facilitates connecting to and downloading web pages, while BeautifulSoup allows the extraction of specific information that the business needs in a structured and organized way.

A practical application of requests and BeautifulSoup is obtaining price lists from suppliers. For companies that rely on multiple suppliers, it is crucial to have up-to-date information on prices and product availability. Instead of manually visiting each supplier's website to gather this information, a Python script can be programmed to automatically access each supplier's pages, download the information, and extract the prices of relevant products. This way, the purchasing or logistics team can have an up-to-date price list in real-time, which makes it easier to compare different suppliers and allows for more informed and cost-effective purchasing decisions.

Trend analysis on social media is another example where requests and BeautifulSoup are useful. SMEs that want to stay updated with sector trends or seek market opportunities can use these scripts to monitor keywords and hashtags on news sites, blogs, and social media. A Python script can be programmed to search for brand mentions, products, or related topics, extracting key data and storing it in a database or local file. This data can then be analyzed to identify patterns, such as the frequency of mentions or the context in which certain terms are used. This type of analysis allows the company to identify areas of interest and potential growth opportunities in real time.

Requests and BeautifulSoup can also be applied in monitoring the competition. Companies can program scripts to extract information from competitors' websites, such as new products, prices, or marketing strategies. By doing this, SMEs can stay updated on the actions of their competitors and adjust their own strategies based on the information obtained. For example, a cleaning products company can use Python to gather information about new products launched by competitors, their sales prices, and promotions, in order to adjust its own offering in real time and improve its competitiveness in the market.

- **Managing Files with Python**

For many SMEs, managing large volumes of files is a daily task that consumes time and effort. Whether it's invoices, client documents, or inventory files, organizing these documents can become complex as the volume of data increases. Python offers a practical solution through the os and shutil libraries, which allow you to automate file management tasks such as moving, renaming, and compressing documents quickly and effectively. Automating these tasks not only saves time but also ensures that files are organized and easily accessible when needed.

An example of using os and shutil is organizing invoices and accounting documents. An SME that generates invoices constantly can program a Python script to automatically move each new invoice to a specific folder based on the client or document type. For instance, the script can check the file name, identify the client number or issue date, and then move the file to the corresponding folder. This makes it easier for the accounting team to quickly and neatly access the necessary documents without wasting time searching for each file manually. Additionally, the script can be programmed to rename each file following a standard format, ensuring that all documents have a uniform and consistent naming, further facilitating information management.

Another practical application is file compression and data backup. In many companies, the amount of data generated can consume a large amount of storage space, so automatically compressing old files or backing up critical data is a necessity. A Python script can be programmed to identify files older than a certain age and compress them into ZIP files or move them to a backup folder, thus freeing up system space. This is especially useful for companies that handle large volumes of digital documents, such as architectural firms or engineering companies, where blueprints, designs, and technical documents take up a lot of storage space. Automating backup and compression ensures that data is secure and accessible at all times, without the need to perform these procedures manually.

In addition, automating file organization allows companies to optimize workflow, reducing the time employees spend on filing tasks and enabling the team to focus on higher-value activities. For example, in a financial services company that generates multiple documents for each client, a Python script can automatically sort each file into a specific folder for each client, organizing the documentation according to the transactions or projects carried out. This not only saves time but also improves accuracy and minimizes the risk of errors, as the documents will always be in the right place.

Automating file management also allows SMEs to improve the security of their data. With Python, scripts can be programmed to move sensitive files to protected folders or perform automatic backups to a secure server. For example, a medical clinic handling patient data can use Python to automatically move medical records to a secure folder after each consultation, ensuring that the information is protected and complies with privacy regulations. This type of automation ensures that the company meets security and privacy regulations, reducing the risk of loss or exposure of sensitive data.

In summary, using Python to automate file management allows SMEs to organize and protect their data efficiently and effectively. As businesses generate more digital documents, the ability to automatically sort, move, and back up files becomes essential to maintain an agile and optimized workflow. Thanks to libraries like os and shutil, companies can implement customized automation solutions tailored to their specific needs, improving productivity and ensuring the integrity of their information.

- **Automation with APIs**

Automation with APIs allows SMEs to integrate their internal systems with a variety of external services and platforms, optimizing their workflows and eliminating the need for repetitive manual tasks. By connecting to APIs, businesses can share data, trigger notifications, and synchronize updates in real-time, enabling processes to occur automatically and accurately. This results in greater efficiency, better organization, and the ability to focus human resources on strategic, value-added activities.

For SMEs, the use of APIs offers numerous opportunities, from integrating with external services like Google Sheets or Slack to manage and analyze data, to connecting with ecommerce platforms like Shopify or WooCommerce to automate tasks related to sales and inventory. By understanding how APIs work and how to apply them to their daily operations, small and medium-sized businesses can achieve a transformation in the way they manage their data and improve their communication and response processes. Python facilitates this integration with APIs through the use of libraries and modules that simplify the sending and receiving of data between services, making API automation accessible to any SME looking to adapt to the current digital environment.

- **Integration with external services**

The integration with external services through APIs allows SMEs to automate tasks and maintain continuous synchronization between different applications. Popular tools like Google Sheets, Trello, or Slack are commonly used in many businesses, and the ability to connect them with an SME's internal systems via their APIs offers great value. Python, with its ability to make HTTP requests and handle JSON, enables companies to easily set up scripts that connect these applications, automating processes and improving communication between teams.

A practical example of this integration is the automatic updating of spreadsheets in Google Sheets. In companies where daily sales or inventories require constant monitoring, keeping these sheets updated can consume a lot of time. With the Google Sheets API and Python, it's possible to program a script that takes sales data from the point of sale system or ERP and automatically sends it to a spreadsheet in Google Sheets. Every time a sale is made, the system can update in real time the product stock, total sales, or billing data. This allows managers and accounting teams to access accurate and updated information without relying on manual data entry, improving accuracy and reducing the risk of errors.

Another useful integration is the connection with Trello, a project management tool widely used in SMEs. With the Trello API and a Python script, companies can automate the creation of tasks and update cards on their boards automatically. For example, a company managing customer orders can use a script that connects their order system with Trello so that each new order automatically creates a card on an order tracking board. The card can include relevant information, such as the customer's name, the product purchased, the delivery date, and the order status. This not only organizes the workflow but also allows the sales or operations team to visualize and manage orders centrally, with automatic updates reflecting the progress of each order.

The Slack API is another powerful tool for improving communication in a company through automation. With a Python script, you can send automatic notifications to a Slack channel when an important event occurs in the company, such as a big sale, a new client, or the receipt of an order. For example, in an SME dedicated to wholesale office supplies, a script can monitor the sales system and, whenever an order exceeds a certain amount, automatically send an alert to the sales team's Slack channel. This notification keeps the entire team informed in real-time about important events, facilitating coordination and quick decision-making. Additionally, Slack allows employees to respond and comment on the notification, enhancing collaboration around these events and ensuring better order management and customer relations.

- ▪ **Automation on ecommerce platforms**

For SMEs operating in e-commerce, APIs from platforms like Shopify or WooCommerce offer great automation opportunities that simplify inventory management, order processing, and real-time data updates. In the case of Shopify, one of the most popular e-commerce platforms, its API allows merchants to connect their online store with other internal systems, avoiding the need to perform repetitive tasks that consume time and resources. With Python, SMEs can leverage these APIs to synchronize their inventory, update product data, and automatically manage orders.

A concrete example of automation with the Shopify API is the automatic management of inventory. For companies that sell products both online and in physical stores, keeping inventory synchronized is crucial to avoid errors and ensure that stock is always available for customers. Through a Python script, the company can schedule automatic inventory updates every time a sale is made, whether online or in the physical store. Each time a product is sold, the script communicates with the Shopify API to reduce the quantity of that product in the inventory, ensuring that customers always see the correct product availability on the website. This automation allows the company to manage its inventory accurately and in real-time, avoiding stockouts and improving the customer shopping experience.

Automation of order processing is another practical application in ecommerce platforms. With the Shopify API, SMEs can set up a script that takes each new order placed in the store and processes it automatically. This includes everything from payment verification to generating the shipping label and updating the order status in the company's system. For a company with personalized products, for example, a Python script can be programmed to automatically check if payment has been received and, if so, send the order information to the production team. Additionally, the system can generate a shipping label with the customer's details and send it to the logistics department for processing, thus speeding up order fulfillment without human intervention. This automation allows the company to process orders faster, reduce wait times, and improve customer satisfaction.

In the case of WooCommerce, another popular ecommerce platform for small businesses, the API allows you to manage not only inventories and orders but also integrate sales data with other tools. For example, a company using WooCommerce and Google Analytics can integrate both platforms to better analyze customer behavior on their website. By using a Python script, the company can extract data from WooCommerce, such as the best-selling product categories, purchase times, and customer demographics, and send it to Google Analytics for detailed reports. This analysis allows the company to adjust its marketing strategies, optimize prices, and improve the layout of its online store based on customer behavior.

The WooCommerce API also allows data to be sent to other management tools, such as ERP systems, making financial and accounting management easier. A Python script can be set up so that every time a sale is made in WooCommerce, the system automatically sends order data and billing details to the company's ERP, updating the accounting system in real-time. This ensures that sales data is always up-to-date in the financial system, making it easier to close balance sheets, analyze revenue, and comply with the company's tax obligations.

The integration of ecommerce platforms with other tools through APIs allows SMEs to automate multiple processes, improving efficiency and reducing management times at every step of the workflow. Whether on Shopify, WooCommerce, or any other ecommerce platform, automation through APIs enables small and medium-sized businesses to manage their operations in a professional and scalable way, without relying on repetitive manual tasks. This automation capability not only optimizes the daily operations of businesses but also allows them to focus on providing better customer service, developing growth strategies, and expanding sales more quickly and effectively.

- ## Practical automation: API integration to optimize payments and marketing

Automation through APIs offers SMEs the opportunity to quickly implement processes that improve efficiency in critical areas like payment management and marketing. By integrating external services, businesses can reduce the time and effort required for repetitive tasks and enhance accuracy at every stage of their operations. Using payment APIs like PayPal or Stripe, companies can automate payment processing and transaction tracking, optimizing the customer experience and minimizing errors in financial management. Similarly, APIs from Mailchimp or SendGrid allow for the automation of digital marketing campaigns, facilitating the sending of personalized and segmented emails based on customer behavior. These practical examples of automation are applicable to any SME looking to improve operational efficiency and connect their internal systems with essential external services.

Automation of payments and tracking

The payment process is a fundamental part of any SME, especially in companies offering digital services, subscriptions, or e-commerce. PayPal and Stripe APIs allow businesses to automate the entire payment flow, from payment confirmation to sending notifications and recording transactions in real-time. These integrations ensure that the payment process is fast, secure, and error-free, which is essential for improving the customer experience and ensuring a steady cash flow.

With the PayPal API, a company can automate both individual and recurring payments, making it easier to manage subscriptions or installment payment services. Using a Python script, the system can automatically check if the customer has made the payment, confirm the transaction, and update the status in the company's system. For example, in an online consulting company, once the client makes a payment via PayPal, the system can record the transaction and automatically enable the client's access to the service platform. This eliminates the need to manually verify each payment, reducing management time and ensuring faster service for customers.

PayPal's API also allows for the automation of transaction tracking and payment notifications. In a company that makes sales to international customers, it's important to maintain detailed control of transactions and ensure that each payment meets the specific requirements of each country. Through the API, the system can be programmed to track each transaction, record the details, and send automatic alerts to the finance team when unusual transactions are detected. This not only speeds up payment management but also improves security and reduces the risk of errors or fraud.

Stripe, for its part, offers a versatile and comprehensive solution for automating payments in online stores. A company using Stripe to process payments can automate the confirmation and tracking flow of each transaction through a Python script, which is automatically triggered every time a payment is made in the store. Stripe allows automating payments with credit cards, bank transfers, and other methods, making it easier to manage revenue for businesses with both national and international operations. In the case of a subscription store, for example, a customer can sign up, and the system programmed with the Stripe API takes care of activating the subscription and generating periodic charges based on the selected plan, eliminating the need to process each payment manually.

Another interesting feature of Stripe is the ability to perform automatic refunds. In many sectors, such as e-commerce, it's common for customers to request returns. With the Stripe API, a script can be set up so that when a refund request is received in the customer service system, it is automatically authorized and processed. This not only improves the customer experience by providing a quick solution but also reduces the workload of the customer service team and prevents errors in refund processing.

In addition to payment processing, integrating transaction tracking is another advantage of automation with payment APIs. Both PayPal and Stripe allow you to extract transaction data, including time, amount, and payment method, and automatically record it in an internal database or system. This tracking facilitates sales analysis, revenue control, and the identification of payment patterns that can be useful for financial planning. With this information, an SME can analyze its revenue streams and make informed decisions to optimize its business model and improve customer satisfaction.

- ■ Marketing automation

Marketing automation is another area where SMEs can benefit significantly by using APIs like those from Mailchimp and SendGrid. These platforms allow for automated and personalized email marketing campaigns, making it easier to send emails based on customer behavior, preferences, and interaction history with the company. By implementing this automation, SMEs can save time on planning and executing campaigns, and improve the effectiveness of their messages by reaching the right audience at the right moment.

Mailchimp is one of the most popular marketing tools, and its API allows businesses to integrate their CRM systems and customer databases to automate the sending of segmented emails. With Mailchimp and a Python script, a company can schedule a series of emails that are automatically sent based on customer actions. For example, in a handcrafted products store, when a customer makes a purchase, the system can automatically send a thank-you email. Later, a follow-up message can be scheduled to be sent two weeks later, requesting a review or presenting related products. This customization of content and timing increases the chances of the customer engaging with the messages and becoming a repeat customer.

The Mailchimp API also makes it easy to send personalized emails based on user behavior on the website. For example, if a customer adds products to their cart but doesn't complete the purchase, the system can schedule a reminder email to be sent to the customer automatically. These types of 'abandoned cart' messages are very effective in recovering sales that would otherwise be lost, allowing SMEs to improve their conversion rates without investing time in manual follow-up. Additionally, Mailchimp offers the option to segment emails based on customer demographics, interests, and location, which makes it easier to personalize campaigns and increase their effectiveness.

SendGrid is another widely used platform for bulk email sending, and its API is particularly useful for businesses that need to handle a large volume of messages, such as newsletters, product updates, or event notifications. With the SendGrid API, an SME can schedule and send bulk emails in a matter of minutes. For example, a language school that organizes online classes can automate the sending of reminders and access links to students each week, personalizing each message with the recipient's name and class schedule. This integration ensures that all students receive their notifications on time, improving organization and avoiding cancellations or confusion.

SendGrid also allows businesses to conduct A/B testing on their email campaigns, making it easy to analyze the performance of different message versions and optimize marketing strategies based on the results. With the help of a Python script and the SendGrid API, a company can schedule alternating sends of messages with different subjects or content, and then analyze open rates, clicks, and conversions. This provides valuable insights into which messages are most effective, allowing SMEs to adjust their campaigns to maximize the impact and effectiveness of their communication with customers.

Both APIs, Mailchimp and SendGrid, offer the advantage of accessing real-time metrics that make it easier to track and analyze each campaign. These metrics include open rates, clicks, conversions, and unsubscribe rates, allowing the company to measure the impact of its emails and continuously adjust its strategies. Automating these reports lets marketing managers focus on content creation and strategy, while Python scripts and APIs handle the sending and data collection.

4.4. Real-time monitoring and automated alerts: Improving decision-making

Real-time monitoring and automatic alerts are essential tools that enable SMEs to improve their responsiveness to significant changes in their operating environment. By receiving real-time alerts based on key data, businesses can make informed decisions quickly, optimizing both internal efficiency and customer experience. In competitive sectors, where reaction times are crucial, having automated alert systems helps SMEs stay ahead of potential problems and seize opportunities immediately. These alerts can range from low inventory or sales spikes notifications to critical performance alerts on digital platforms and servers, all of which allow teams to stay informed and act in real time.

One of the most practical benefits of implementing an alert system is the ability to monitor key files and folders in the company using tools like Python's watchdog library. For example, a company that works with large volumes of data and constant updates can benefit from receiving an automatic notification every time a change is made to an important file folder. This facilitates the automatic creation of backups or reports and ensures that the data is always up to date. Real-time monitoring is also valuable in operational areas such as inventory management. By using data analysis tools like Pandas along with smtplib to send emails, an SME can set up alerts to notify them when a product's inventory falls to critical levels, allowing them to make restocking decisions immediately and avoiding sales losses due to stockouts.

For companies managing e-commerce or web platforms, monitoring system performance is essential to ensure stable operation and a satisfactory customer experience. Using monitoring APIs like New Relic or Pingdom, a company can track the performance of its servers and applications, receiving automatic alerts if load speed or availability drops below optimal levels. This capability allows SMEs to take immediate action and resolve technical issues before they impact the user experience or the company's reputation.

In addition to internal systems, integrating third-party tools like Twilio or Slack facilitates the implementation of customized alert systems that notify employees or managers when an important event occurs. Whether it's an SMS notifying about a failed transaction or a Slack message informing about a new important client, these notification systems strengthen internal communication and speed up the response to critical situations. Finally, in the financial area, automatic alerts based on financial data help SMEs maintain constant control over their income and expenses, notifying the management team of sales drops or unexpected increases in spending.

- **Real-time alerts for decision-making**

Real-time alerts based on automated data are an essential tool for any SME to maintain active and effective control over its operations and decisions. Quick and well-founded decisions are the foundation for staying competitive in a constantly moving market. Imagine receiving an instant alert the moment a product is about to run out or when your server performance drops. This kind of information allows you to act at the right moment, preventing issues that could directly impact customer satisfaction, sales, and final results.

The impact of these alerts on the daily operations of an SME is clear: they reduce the margin for error and reaction time to any changes. With them, the management team no longer has to manually oversee every aspect of the business. Instead, they receive real-time notifications when something critical occurs, allowing them to focus on other areas of the company with the peace of mind that an automated system is keeping track of operational details. Moreover, this type of automation improves performance, as it frees employees from repetitive monitoring tasks, enabling them to dedicate their time to more strategic and value-added activities.

Implementing real-time alerts also helps to anticipate problems. For a retail store, a low inventory notification ensures restocking happens before products run out. In an online store, detecting a drop in loading speed in time can lead to corrective actions before customers are affected. These cases show how alerts not only improve operational efficiency but can also be a key factor in customer satisfaction. Being able to react to demand fluctuations, changes in customer habits, or technical issues in real-time allows SMEs to maintain a competitive edge despite their limited resources.

The watchdog library in Python is an ideal tool for monitoring changes in files and folders within a company's work environment. Its implementation allows the system to notify in real time when an update occurs in a relevant file or folder. This is especially useful for automating backup tasks and ensuring that key data is always available and secure. Imagine a situation where a store's inventory file is updated every week. By configuring watchdog, each time the inventory file is updated, the library can execute a series of commands that generate a report and save it in a secure location in the cloud, or even automatically send it to the inventory manager via email.

In addition to file monitoring, watchdog is useful for analysis and reporting processes. Suppose a restaurant uses a spreadsheet system to record the daily consumption of ingredients. If watchdog detects a change in this file, it can generate a daily report that is sent to the purchasing team, allowing the restaurant to place replenishment orders before the most demanded ingredients run out. This way, the risk of operational failures is reduced, and the kitchen team always has the necessary ingredients to meet demand.

For inventory management and sales alerts, we can use a combination of Pandas and smtplib. With Pandas, you can program a script that regularly checks the inventory database. This script can compare the available quantities of each product with the minimum thresholds set for each one. If the inventory of a product falls below the pre-established threshold, the script will generate an alert that will be automatically sent via email or text message using the smtplib library. This approach allows the SME to always be aware of their inventory status without the need for constant manual supervision.

A practical example of this implementation could be in a fashion store that wants to avoid running out of stock of its best-selling products. In this case, the team sets a minimum inventory threshold for each garment, so when the levels of a specific product fall below that limit, the system automatically sends a notification to the purchasing manager. This message could include a direct link to place the restocking order, speeding up the decision-making process and ensuring that high-turnover products are always available for customers.

Implementing automated performance alerts is also crucial for companies managing e-commerce or any digital platform. APIs like New Relic or Pingdom offer continuous monitoring of servers and applications, allowing you to detect issues such as increased response times or website downtime. These APIs not only send real-time alerts but also provide analysis tools to identify patterns and anticipate potential failures before they occur. For example, an e-commerce site noticing a drop in performance over the weekends can investigate the causes and adjust its servers or network to better handle traffic during those periods.

Server monitoring not only improves user experience by ensuring fast load times and stable access, but it also prevents sales losses and damage to the company's reputation. In a context where users expect immediate responses and seamless experiences, a website that operates without interruptions can make the difference between a sale and a dissatisfied customer. Performance alerts are, in this sense, essential for maintaining customer trust in the platform and ensuring a high-quality user experience.

Third-party tools like Twilio or Slack offer very useful options for implementing notification systems that improve internal communication and rapid response to incidents. With Twilio, you can set up the system to send automatic text messages to employees' phones when a relevant event occurs, such as the onboarding of a new important client or the detection of a failed transaction. Slack, on the other hand, allows real-time notifications to be integrated into the company's internal communication channels, ensuring the entire team is informed of critical situations as they happen.

For example, a store that offers exclusive products might want to notify its sales team whenever a VIP customer makes a significant purchase or when a highly sought-after product is about to run out. This immediate notification allows the team to make informed decisions and prioritize certain customers or products as needed, thereby optimizing sales and the customer experience.

In the financial field, automated alerts are powerful tools for monitoring and controlling expenses and income. An SME that sets weekly or monthly sales targets can use scripts to compare current figures with the targets. If sales drop by 10% compared to the previous week, the system can send an alert to management to review possible causes and adjust the sales strategy accordingly. This type of alert is also useful to avoid unexpected expenses. Suppose a service company sets a monthly spending limit for external suppliers. Through an automated system, notifications can be sent when spending reaches 90% of the budget, allowing management to review and adjust expenses before exceeding the limit.

Implementing automatic alerts in the financial sector not only helps prevent budgetary issues but also fosters a culture of control and efficiency within the company. The management and accounting teams can focus on analysis and planning tasks without the need to continuously monitor the figures. By having an alert system that informs them of potential deviations, they can dedicate their efforts to finding solutions and improving the financial efficiency of the company.

Automating these alert systems doesn't require a complex technological infrastructure. With Python and its various libraries, any SME can set up a notification system that sends alerts through the preferred communication channels. The ability to integrate these alerts into messaging platforms like WhatsApp or Telegram further expands communication options, allowing alerts to reach the responsible parties' mobile devices, regardless of their location. This mobility is especially important for small business owners or teams who cannot be physically present at all times.

One interesting aspect of automated alerts is that they also help improve interdepartmental coordination within the company. When all departments are notified of a relevant event, such as a drop in inventory or a decline in sales, teams can collaborate proactively to solve the issue. The sales, inventory, and marketing teams can work together to ensure inventory is available, promote the necessary products, and plan strategies to reactivate sales if needed. This type of collaboration is possible when the entire organization is informed of changes in real time, and it becomes a strategic advantage that strengthens the company's cohesion and agility.

In conclusion, real-time monitoring and automated alerts are crucial tools for SMEs to optimize their decision-making. Thanks to their adaptability, these solutions allow companies in various sectors, from retail to services and technology, to improve operational efficiency and respond quickly to changes in the environment.

- **Monitoring of systems and performance**

Monitoring systems and performance is essential for any company that operates in ecommerce or relies on web platforms to offer its services. In the context of SMEs, having a real-time monitoring infrastructure for server and application performance can make a crucial difference in the quality of service they provide, and ultimately, in the customer experience. For an ecommerce business, every second counts, and a reduction in loading speed or a service interruption can lead to significant revenue losses and decreased customer satisfaction. The ability to detect and resolve performance issues at the exact moment they occur is key to preventing site abandonment and ensuring that customers have a smooth and uninterrupted experience.

Monitoring APIs, such as New Relic or Pingdom, are valuable tools for overseeing the performance of servers and applications in real time. These APIs allow SMEs to have a detailed and continuous view of critical aspects, such as server response time, page load, resource consumption, downtime, and other factors that can directly impact service quality. With these tools in place, the company's technical team receives automatic alerts whenever any metric falls below a previously set threshold, like a significant reduction in load speed or an unexpected increase in server errors. This way, they can quickly intervene to resolve the issue before users experience difficulties.

One of the most notable aspects of APIs like New Relic is their ability to provide detailed and segmented metrics in real time. These tools not only show general data about system performance, but also allow you to break down the information and analyze the behavior of each component of the platform. For example, a SME managing an ecommerce site can configure New Relic to receive specific reports on each page of their site, identifying which ones are causing the most loading issues or at what specific time of day traffic increases, impacting server performance. With this information, the company can make precise adjustments, optimizing the system to improve performance during high demand periods and minimizing access or loading issues.

Real-time monitoring is also an advantage for web platforms that rely on multiple interconnected services and applications. For an ecommerce company, not only is the web server important, but also other elements like the database server, payment system integrations, supplier APIs, and content customization modules. Each of these components can become a point of failure if not properly monitored, and a tool like New Relic allows you to track each one, providing specific alerts if a module becomes slow or unresponsive.

On the other hand, Pingdom offers features that allow businesses to perform performance tests from different geographic locations, which is particularly useful for ecommerce sites with customers in various parts of the world. Load times can vary significantly depending on the user's location, and by using Pingdom to conduct load tests from different points, a company can identify performance patterns affecting certain segments of their audience and optimize resources to improve load speeds where they are needed most. Additionally, Pingdom provides detailed reports that can break down each component of the webpage, from images to scripts and CSS styles, allowing the company's technical team to adjust each element to ensure a fast and efficient experience in all locations.

Automated alerts from Pingdom and New Relic are essential for businesses to anticipate problems. Imagine an online store experiencing a sudden increase in traffic during a special sales event like Black Friday. Without proper monitoring, the server could quickly become overloaded, leading to decreased performance, longer load times, or even a complete website crash. By receiving real-time alerts when the system starts experiencing increased load, the SME team can respond immediately, scaling resources if necessary or adjusting traffic to maintain site stability. This quick reaction capability is particularly valuable during high-impact campaigns, where every second of downtime can mean lost sales and damage to the company's reputation with customers.

New Relic and Pingdom also offer diagnostic and analysis tools that help identify the root cause of problems. Once an alert is received, the team can access a complete set of data that shows not only the symptom of the problem, such as increased response times, but also its likely cause, whether it's a traffic spike, a third-party service failure, or database saturation. With this information, the team can make informed decisions and execute specific solutions instead of making general adjustments that might not solve the underlying issue. These tools also allow for the creation of an incident history that can be consulted to detect performance patterns and anticipate potential future failures.

A crucial aspect of real-time monitoring is the visibility it provides to both development and operations teams simultaneously. By receiving the same metrics and alerts, different departments within an SME can work together in a coordinated way to resolve performance issues quickly and accurately. Monitoring tools allow the creation of custom dashboards displaying the most relevant metrics for each area of the company, so each team can focus on the elements that most affect their responsibilities. This collaborative approach is essential to ensure problems are resolved comprehensively and do not recur in the future.

In addition to detecting and solving problems as they occur, monitoring APIs like New Relic and Pingdom allow for scheduled performance tests to identify potential bottlenecks before they affect users. Through these tests, an SME can identify and resolve scalability issues in its system, ensuring optimal performance even during peak demand times. Regular load testing is also useful for assessing the impact of system updates, such as adding new features or migrating to a more complex infrastructure. By checking how systems respond to changes, the company can implement updates safely, knowing they won't negatively impact the user experience.

The ability to configure custom thresholds is another significant advantage of these tools. Each SME can tailor their alerts to the specific needs of their platform, setting optimal performance levels for each system component. For example, an online store can define that the server response time must always be below two seconds, and any increase above this limit should generate an immediate alert. This way, the team can maintain the service quality that their customers expect and ensure that any performance degradation is detected and resolved immediately.

Automating alerts through these tools also allows SMEs to optimize the time and resources of their technical team. Instead of dedicating time to constant system monitoring, the team can focus on other development tasks or platform optimization, knowing they will receive automatic notifications if any issues arise. This automation is particularly valuable for companies that do not have large tech teams and rely on their resources to manage multiple responsibilities. By having a system that handles monitoring, the company can ensure a stable and high-quality service without overburdening the team with additional monitoring tasks.

Performance alerts can also be integrated with other incident management and communication tools like Slack or Microsoft Teams, so messages reach the channels where support and operations teams are active. This way, any issues detected in the system reach the responsible parties instantly, and they can quickly coordinate to take action. This integration with communication tools is especially useful for distributed teams or companies operating across extended hours, as it ensures alerts reach the appropriate personnel at all times.

An additional benefit of real-time monitoring is its ability to provide valuable information for long-term analysis. By continuously observing performance metrics, a company can identify trends in platform behavior, such as seasonal variations in traffic or recurring resource consumption patterns during certain times of the year. This type of information is useful for planning infrastructure growth and anticipating demand spikes that may require additional server scalability. With this data in hand, SMEs can make strategic decisions about resource investment and optimize their platform's capacity to adapt to demand without affecting the user experience.

Monitoring tools also offer advanced customization options for performance reports, allowing companies to generate detailed reports tailored to their specific needs. These reports can include analysis of page load times, resource consumption per module, and overall server performance. With this information, the tech and management teams can analyze the platform's efficiency and make informed decisions about possible improvements. Additionally, with a well-documented performance history, the company can assess the impact of system updates and optimize its development processes based on the results obtained.

The ability to anticipate problems and act quickly on any issue is essential for SMEs that rely on their digital platforms to generate revenue and maintain customer satisfaction. With tools like New Relic and Pingdom, these companies have a powerful resource at their disposal to keep a stable service, improve the customer experience, and ensure their competitiveness in an increasingly demanding environment. In a market where every second counts, real-time system and performance monitoring is not just a desirable option, but a strategic necessity for any SME that aims to stand out and offer uninterrupted quality service.

- **Implementation of an alert system using third-party services**

The implementation of an alert system with third-party services is a key strategy to improve internal communication and response capacity in an SME, especially in situations where a quick reaction to critical events is required. In a digital environment, the ability to receive automatic notifications through messaging platforms like Slack or via SMS using tools like Twilio allows teams to be informed in real-time of any significant changes in the system. This type of alert is invaluable for decision-making, as it ensures that team members, regardless of their location or availability at the time, can receive important notices and act immediately.

The Twilio messaging service is widely used for its ability to send SMS and automatic notifications through the global telephony infrastructure. This makes it an especially effective option for critical alerts, as SMS is a direct communication channel that reaches the recipient almost immediately. For an SME, implementing an SMS-based alert system can make a big difference in its ability to respond to high-impact events, such as an ecommerce system crash, the rejection of an important transaction, or the acquisition of a new high-value client. With Twilio, it's possible to set up rules that automatically trigger message sending when these events occur, and these messages can be customized to include key information that helps the team quickly understand the nature of the problem or the action that needs to be taken.

On the other hand, Slack has become an essential communication tool for many businesses thanks to its organized channel structure, which facilitates team collaboration. Its integration with monitoring tools allows alerts to reach the specific channel where the responsible team members are active, making it easier to respond quickly and in a coordinated manner. Through Slack, an SME can receive automatic notifications every time a significant change occurs in the system, such as a failed transaction, an inventory file update, or the addition of an important customer to the database. This centralized alert approach ensures that all team members receive the same information at the right time and, in many cases, allows problems to be resolved collaboratively in real-time.

Implementing a notification system with third-party services offers clear advantages in terms of communication efficiency and effectiveness. The ability to configure automated alerts in Slack allows notifications to be directed to specific channels, so each team receives the alerts relevant to them, avoiding information overload and enabling teams to focus on events that directly impact their responsibilities. For example, in an ecommerce company, the sales team can receive Slack notifications for each new major customer purchase, while the technical support team gets automatic alerts in case of server issues or system outages. By directing each notification to the relevant departments, response capacity is optimized, and errors from miscommunication are reduced.

One of Twilio's main advantages is its ability to customize and segment alerts, allowing an SME to adjust the notification system to its specific needs. While automated SMS alerts are associated with critical events, it's possible to set up different rules that trigger these messages based on the urgency of each case. For example, if a company detects that an important transaction has failed, Twilio can send a text message to the finance manager and simultaneously notify the technical support team to review the payment system and determine if there's a platform error. This approach ensures that alerts reach the right people immediately, maximizing the chances of resolving the issue before it affects other clients or the system's functionality.

Another relevant feature of Twilio is its ability to integrate alerts with CRM systems or customer management tools, facilitating personalized attention and improving the customer experience. Imagine a situation where a new high-value customer makes their first transaction on the company's online store. By setting up an automatic alert with Twilio, the sales team or customer service manager can receive an SMS notifying them of this new addition, allowing them to give the customer a personalized welcome or make a special offer. This type of action, driven by automatic alerts, helps create a closer relationship with the customer from the very first moment, which is essential for improving their loyalty to the brand and encouraging future purchases.

Moreover, Slack offers advanced integration options with monitoring and analytics systems. Many companies choose to connect their alert systems with data analysis tools like Google Analytics or performance monitoring services like New Relic to receive automatic alerts directly in Slack. This integration allows marketing and sales teams to stay on top of their campaign performance and web traffic in real-time. For example, if an unusual increase in traffic to a product page is detected, the marketing team can receive an alert in Slack to investigate the source of that traffic, evaluating whether it's due to an ongoing campaign or a viral piece of content. In this way, alerts provide greater visibility into user behavior and offer an immediate opportunity for action that might otherwise go unnoticed.

Implementing an automated alert system also improves the resolution of technical issues by enabling early error detection. In an ecommerce setting, for example, the support team can receive an alert in Slack whenever the system detects a payment failure or an error in the checkout process. This allows technicians to immediately access the area where the error occurred, preventing other customers from experiencing similar issues and ensuring that sales are not affected. Moreover, Slack allows integration with bots and third-party applications that can provide a detailed description of the problem or even suggest solutions based on past errors. This immediate response capability is essential for reducing downtime and improving customer satisfaction by ensuring a seamless shopping experience.

A notification system implemented with Twilio and Slack also facilitates incident management by automatically generating reports and logs. Every time a relevant event occurs, the automatic alerts can record the time, type of event, and the responsible party who responded, creating a history that can be consulted later to identify patterns or areas for improvement. For example, if it is observed that payment system failures are more frequent on certain days or times, the company can investigate the causes and take measures to prevent future disruptions. This type of incident analysis allows the company to improve its infrastructure and reduce the impact of recurring problems on the customer experience.

The use of Twilio and Slack for automated notifications also brings benefits in terms of operational efficiency and time savings. By centralizing alerts in an automated system, work teams no longer have to constantly monitor the platform's status or perform manual checks. Instead, they receive timely notifications when an event requires their attention, allowing them to focus on strategic and value-added tasks without worrying about potential system issues. This proactive approach, based on automated alerts, contributes to improved productivity and more efficient use of resources.

Personalization of alerts in Slack is also a fundamental aspect for an SME, as it allows setting specific notifications for each area of the business. This means that teams can adjust alert thresholds so that only truly critical events are notified, avoiding information overload and ensuring that each alert is relevant to the team that receives it. For example, the finance team can set alerts to notify only high-value failed transactions, while the support team can receive alerts about payment system issues, and the sales team can be aware of each new high-value customer. This customization capability allows for attention to be optimized for each event according to its level of importance.

In addition, with Twilio and Slack, you can create tiered alert sequences that act according to the severity of the event. In the case of a system failure, the first level of alert can be sent to the technical support team, who are responsible for checking and solving the problem. If no confirmation of resolution is received within a certain timeframe, the system can escalate the alert to operations managers or company executives, ensuring the issue is resolved as quickly as possible. This scalability in alerts ensures that no critical problem goes unnoticed and that there is always an additional level of oversight in case of emergencies.

Another significant advantage is the remote access capability offered by both Twilio and Slack. Thanks to Twilio's infrastructure, SMS messages can be received on any mobile device, which is particularly useful for SMEs whose teams work remotely or in different time zones. Slack, on the other hand, allows access to communication channels from mobile devices, tablets, or computers, facilitating collaboration among team members and ensuring that alerts are received regardless of the recipient's location. This connectivity is essential to ensure that the company can respond quickly and effectively to any critical situation, no matter where its employees are at that moment.

The integration options between Twilio, Slack, and other technological platforms also allow for automated and comprehensive incident management. For example, if a server goes down, the monitoring system can trigger an automatic alert that is sent to Slack, where a bot is activated to gather information about the incident. The bot can perform a series of preliminary diagnostics and send the results to the technical support team, providing detailed context about the problem before the technicians step in.

This automated process allows the company to save time in problem resolution and minimize the impact on the customer experience.

Implementing an alert system with Twilio and Slack also offers advantages in long-term decision-making. By maintaining a complete record of all generated alerts and corresponding responses, the company can analyze the incident history to identify patterns or recurring issues. This information is useful for evaluating system performance and planning improvements in the technological infrastructure, anticipating potential failures and strengthening vulnerable areas. Additionally, incident analysis allows the company to optimize its customer service processes and improve its response capacity, which is essential for maintaining high service quality.

The implementation of Twilio and Slack in the alert system also reinforces the culture of responsibility and collaboration within the company. By receiving notifications automatically and in real time, each team member can proactively contribute to problem-solving and continuous system improvement. This open and accessible communication structure promotes greater cohesion between departments, as everyone has the opportunity to stay informed and collaborate to solve problems in a coordinated manner.

Thanks to the advanced features of Twilio and Slack, an SME can tailor its notification system to its specific needs, setting up different types of alerts based on the urgency or importance of the event. This approach allows the company to maintain effective control over its operations, ensuring that each team member receives the information they need at the right time, maximizing responsiveness to any critical situation.

- **Automation of financial alerts**

The automation of financial alerts is a crucial tool for an SME to maintain thorough and real-time control over its economic situation. Implementing this type of notifications allows the company's managers to react quickly to changes in their financial figures and make informed decisions without delays. For an SME, resources are limited, and any imbalance in income or expenses can have a significant impact on its viability. Therefore, having a system that sends automatic alerts when important financial variations occur allows teams to respond efficiently, minimizing losses and maximizing savings opportunities.

Implementing a financial alert system requires integrating data analysis tools and messaging platforms that allow financial managers to receive real-time notifications. One of the most common scenarios for an SME is to set up an automatic alert if sales drop by a specific percentage over a certain period, such as 10% in a week. This notification allows the company to immediately detect any significant decline in revenue and take corrective actions, such as launching promotional campaigns to boost sales, adjusting pricing strategies, or analyzing the causes of the drop to prevent it from happening again.

The process of setting up this type of alert begins with gathering up-to-date financial data, which can be done using dynamic spreadsheets or advanced financial analysis tools. These tools allow you to automate data updates so that the system always has the most recent information. Once the data is organized and centralized, you can define the rules that will trigger the alerts. For example, if the company uses a spreadsheet to record daily sales, a formula can be programmed to calculate the percentage change in sales week over week. If this change reaches a critical threshold, such as a 10% drop, the formula will trigger a macro or script to send an alert via email or text message to the financial manager.

There are various platforms that allow you to automate this process without advanced programming knowledge. Tools like Google Sheets or Excel Online can be configured to send automatic emails when certain data conditions are met, using integration applications like Zapier or IFTTT to connect spreadsheet results with notification platforms. For example, if a clothing store's sales show a declining trend during the first week of a season, the system can send an automatic notification to the marketing team to analyze the situation and consider adjusting promotions or modifying the advertising campaign.

Regarding expense control, implementing automated alerts is equally important to ensure that the SME does not exceed its established budget limits. Setting up an alert that notifies when a certain spending threshold is surpassed allows the company to act responsibly and avoid the risk of unnecessary or excessive expenses. To establish this alert, the finance team can use a shared spreadsheet to record expenses in real time. Through cumulative sum formulas, it's possible to monitor how much the company has spent in a given period, and if this total reaches 90% or 100% of the set budget, the system can generate an alert informing management of the need to review and optimize the remaining expenses for the period.

For SMEs that work with accounting and financial management software, many of these tools already offer the functionality of automatic alerts. Programs like QuickBooks, Zoho Books, or Xero allow users to set up notifications when financial figures reach certain values. In these cases, the system sends an automatic message to the responsible parties when it detects that a spending threshold has been exceeded or when there is a significant change in sales. This integration of alerts into accounting software allows financial and administrative teams to stay informed of the situation without having to manually check the figures every day, which saves time and facilitates decision-making based on reliable and up-to-date data.

Another advantage of automatic financial alerts is that they promote transparency and communication within the company. By receiving constant notifications about changes in income and expenses, both the finance team and management can coordinate their efforts to address any issues before they turn into a crisis. If the alert indicates a drop in sales, the marketing team can review and adjust their strategy, while the sales team can focus on incentivizing customers or reaching out to potential leads to boost numbers again. This constant flow of information allows for more effective collaboration between different departments, ensuring that everyone works towards the same goal of maintaining a stable and sustainable financial situation.

Automating cash flow alerts is another fundamental aspect that allows SMEs to manage their finances with greater precision. Cash flow is one of the most important indicators of a company's financial health, and any imbalance between income and expenses can jeopardize operations. Setting up automatic alerts to receive notifications when cash flow reaches critical levels helps the company make quick decisions to improve liquidity, such as adjusting payment terms with suppliers or speeding up the collection of outstanding accounts. Using a spreadsheet or accounting software, the company can program a system to evaluate cash flow daily or weekly and generate an alert if the balance is insufficient to cover projected operating expenses.

Alerts about profit margins are also very useful for SMEs looking to optimize their profitability. By setting up a notification to inform if the profit margin falls below a critical level, the company can immediately identify which products or services are less profitable and adjust its pricing strategy or reduce associated costs. To implement this alert, a combination of spreadsheets and analysis scripts can be used to calculate the profit margin of each product or service based on production costs and revenue. When one of these margins reaches a low threshold, the system can generate an alert that sends the information to the financial team and management, allowing them to review the production process, analyze the competition, and adjust prices or costs as needed.

Managing alerts for accounts receivable and payable is equally crucial for maintaining a solid financial structure. Setting up alerts to notify when an account receivable is nearing its due date or when an important payment needs to be made helps the SME manage its finances more orderly, avoiding payment delays and maintaining a good relationship with suppliers and customers. This type of notification can be implemented in any accounting system or even in spreadsheets by setting up scheduled reminders. In the case of accounts payable, the alerts allow the company to anticipate important payments and adjust its budget to avoid liquidity issues.

Automated sales trend analysis alerts are also very useful for SMEs looking to anticipate demand fluctuations and adjust their sales strategy according to market behavior. With a system that analyzes sales data in real-time, the company can receive notifications when it detects a downward trend or an unexpected increase in sales of a specific product. This type of alert allows the company to adjust its inventory, plan promotional campaigns, or consider expanding its offerings based on projected demand. For example, if a tech store receives an alert that sales of a smartphone model are rapidly declining, it can assess whether the drop is due to a change in customer preferences or the arrival of new models on the market, and take action to adjust its stock and reduce the risk of losses.

The automation of alerts for tracking financial goals is also an effective strategy for SMEs that set growth targets. By setting up notifications that are automatically sent when a certain percentage of quarterly or annual goals is reached, the company can assess its progress and adjust its sales or spending strategy as needed to meet the established targets. This type of alert is especially useful for companies that want to monitor their growth in real time and seek to dynamically adjust their operations to maximize performance.

Another type of alert that can be successfully implemented in an SME is the notification of compliance with marketing and advertising budgets. Often, companies allocate a significant portion of their budget to promotional activities, and controlling these expenses is essential to ensure a positive return on investment. Setting up alerts that notify the team when advertising expenses reach 80% or 90% of the budget allows the company to review and optimize ongoing campaigns to ensure they are used efficiently and prioritize actions with the greatest impact on sales.

The automation of financial alerts based on key performance indicators (KPIs) is also essential for the financial control of the company. Defining KPIs such as revenue growth, sales conversion rate, or expense-to-income ratio, and setting up automatic alerts that notify when one of these indicators falls short of projected levels, allows the company to reevaluate its strategy and take corrective action immediately. These alerts provide a real-time view of financial performance, helping the SME maintain constant control over results and make decisions based on objective data.

For SMEs operating in highly volatile sectors or markets where input and raw material prices fluctuate constantly, implementing automatic production cost alerts is a valuable practice. By receiving notifications whenever the cost of a key material or component exceeds a certain threshold, the company can evaluate supplier alternatives, adjust its price margins, or consider material substitution. This type of alert allows the SME to remain competitive and protect its profit margins in contexts where input prices can change drastically in short periods of time.

Finally, automating revenue variability alerts is especially useful for SMEs that experience significant sales fluctuations due to seasonal or market factors. Setting up automatic notifications that inform the financial team when revenue exceeds or falls below a certain percentage compared to the previous period allows the company to analyze the reasons behind these variations and adjust its strategy. This type of alert is particularly valuable for companies in the retail or tourism sectors, where sales can be affected by seasonality, enabling constant adaptation to changing market conditions.

In summary, automating financial alerts is a strategic resource for SMEs, helping to optimize the control of income and expenses, strengthen data-driven decision-making, and promote a culture of financial responsibility within the organization.

4.5. Implementation of automated workflows

The implementation of automated workflows is a fundamental strategy for SMEs looking to optimise their operations and improve efficiency without significantly increasing costs. Nowadays, tools like Zapier or Integromat have made it easier for businesses of all sizes to integrate different platforms and systems through APIs, allowing for the automation of complex processes without the need for extensive code development. These tools are particularly useful for SMEs as they simplify repetitive tasks and ensure that teams can focus on strategic activities that add more value to the business.

Zapier is one of the most popular automation platforms and offers an intuitive interface that allows users to create 'Zaps,' which are workflows made up of a series of automated steps triggered by a specific initial condition. For example, if an SME wants to automate customer data entry, they can create a Zap that, upon receiving a contact form through their website, automatically extracts the information provided by the customer and enters it into their CRM system, such as Salesforce or HubSpot, or into a Google Sheets spreadsheet. This integration allows the sales team to save time and ensures that customer information is always up to date without the need for manual entries.

Integromat, on the other hand, offers a drag-and-drop interface that allows you to set up complex workflows known as 'Scenarios'. These scenarios work similarly to Zaps in Zapier but offer a higher level of customization, enabling businesses to handle more advanced integrations. Integromat stands out for its processing capabilities, allowing SMEs to manage large volumes of data from multiple platforms simultaneously and perform complex transformations at each stage of the workflow. An SME that wants to automate its order tracking system, for example, can use Integromat to integrate its ecommerce platform with its inventory management software and a messaging platform like Slack, so that every time a sale is made, the inventory is updated, and the logistics team receives an automatic notification with the order details.

One of the most important aspects of these automation tools is their ability to connect multiple platforms using APIs. APIs, or application programming interfaces, allow different applications to exchange information with each other automatically and without manual intervention.

Both Zapier and Integromat enable SMEs to create workflows that integrate common applications such as email, CRM, accounting software, communication tools, and ecommerce platforms, making it easy for data to flow seamlessly across the various systems that make up the company's digital infrastructure.

One example of using automated workflows is real-time lead management. Imagine a SME receives leads through forms on its website, LinkedIn profile, and email marketing campaigns. Using Zapier, the company can set up a workflow that automatically detects each new lead on any of these platforms and imports it into its CRM system. The workflow could then tag the lead according to its source, assign it to a sales representative, and send a personalized welcome message to the client. With this automated process, the sales team not only saves time but also ensures that each lead receives timely and personalized attention, increasing the likelihood of conversion and improving the customer experience.

Regarding Integromat, its ability to handle more complex processes makes it an ideal choice for SMEs looking to optimize their supply chain. For example, an ecommerce business selling products nationwide can use Integromat to connect its sales platform with its inventory software and shipping system. Every time a sale is made, Integromat automatically updates the inventory, assigns the order to the corresponding supplier, and notifies the logistics team to prepare the shipment. Additionally, the customer receives an order confirmation email with the tracking number, providing a seamless and frictionless experience. This automation minimizes the risk of human error, prevents stockouts, and ensures the purchasing and delivery process is fast and efficient.

For SMEs operating with multiple sales channels, integrating these automated workflows is particularly useful. Imagine a fashion store that sells both in its physical store and on an ecommerce platform, as well as on social media like Instagram. With Zapier, the company can set up a workflow that centralizes all sales data in a single inventory system and synchronizes stock information in real time across all channels. This way, every time an item is sold on any platform, the inventory is automatically updated, reducing the risk of selling out-of-stock products and improving inventory control accuracy. This allows the company to respond quickly to demand and enhance the customer experience by ensuring that the products they see online are available.

Tools like Zapier and Integromat are also essential for automating marketing processes in SMEs. A company running email marketing campaigns can use Zapier to automate the registration and segmentation of contacts. For example, every time a customer subscribes to the company's mailing list, the system can automatically add the customer's information to an email marketing platform like Mailchimp, segment them based on their preferences, and send a personalized welcome message. This automation not only simplifies the registration process but also improves campaign personalization and ensures that each customer receives relevant content, which can increase open and conversion rates.

Another relevant application of automated workflows is the management of billing and payments. Many SMEs face the challenge of manually coordinating income and expense records, which can be error-prone and time-consuming. With Integromat, the company can set up a workflow that connects its sales platform with its accounting system, so that every time a sale or order is made, the system automatically creates an invoice, logs it into the accounting software, and sends a confirmation email to the customer with the payment information. This way, the administrative team can focus on financial analysis and strategic decision-making instead of spending time on repetitive tasks.

Human resources management is another area where SMEs can benefit from automated workflows. Imagine a company using a recruitment platform and wanting to streamline the onboarding process for new employees. With Zapier, the company can set up a workflow that, upon receiving a hiring confirmation from the recruitment platform, automatically adds the new employee's information to the HR database, creates an email account for the employee, sends a welcome message, and provides access to the necessary documents for onboarding. This automation simplifies the onboarding process and ensures that the new employee has everything they need from day one, contributing to a smooth and positive integration experience.

Automatic alerts and incident management can also benefit greatly from automation. An SME that wants to maintain strict control over its ecommerce performance can use Integromat to connect its website with a monitoring platform like Pingdom or Google Analytics, and set up a workflow that sends automatic alerts to the support team whenever a performance issue is detected, such as an increase in load time or a server crash. This workflow can also send a notification to the affected customer, informing them that the technical team is working to resolve the issue. This automation allows the company to react immediately to incidents, ensuring the customer experience is not affected and minimizing downtime.

Cash flow automation is another important application that benefits SMEs. By using Zapier, the company can connect its sales system with its accounting software, so that every time a sale is made or an expense is incurred, the system automatically records the transaction in the cash flow. Additionally, automatic alerts can be set up to notify management when the cash flow falls below a critical level, allowing the company to make quick decisions to adjust expenses or increase revenue. This integration not only improves the accuracy of financial records but also ensures that the management team is aware of the financial situation in real time.

Automated workflows are also useful for managing customer relationships. With Integromat, an SME offering personalized services can create a workflow that, upon receiving a new order or information request, automatically gathers relevant customer information and records it in the company's CRM. Furthermore, the system can send a thank you or welcome message and assign the customer to a sales or customer service representative for follow-up. This type of automation ensures that each customer receives personalized and timely attention, which is essential for building a long-term relationship and improving loyalty.

For SMEs managing inventories, automating stock control is essential to ensure product availability and avoid the risk of stockouts. With Zapier, the company can integrate its sales platform with its inventory system so that each time a sale is made, the system automatically updates the available stock and sends an alert when the inventory of a specific product falls below a certain threshold. This allows the purchasing team to efficiently manage restocking and ensures that products are always available for customers, reducing the risk of losing sales due to lack of inventory.

Finally, automating performance reports is an application that helps SMEs make strategic, data-driven decisions. With Integromat, the company can set up a workflow that collects data from multiple platforms, such as Google Analytics, the CRM, and the sales system, and consolidates it into a monthly or weekly report. This report can be automatically sent to the management team, providing a clear view of key metrics and allowing the company to identify trends, analyze performance, and adjust its strategy based on the results obtained.

The automation of workflows with tools like Zapier and Integromat gives SMEs a significant competitive advantage by optimizing efficiency, reducing human errors, and improving the customer experience.

Chapter 5 - Introduction to Artificial Intelligence

5.1. What is artificial intelligence?

Artificial intelligence (AI) has become a fundamental pillar of technological innovation, transforming industries and processes in ways that once seemed unattainable. In general terms, AI is a branch of computer science that seeks to equip machines with the ability to perform tasks that require human intelligence, such as recognizing patterns, learning, making decisions, and solving problems. It is a technology designed so that systems can perceive, reason, act, and learn in complex and changing environments, opening up new opportunities for businesses of all sizes, including small and medium-sized enterprises (SMEs).

AI is not just about replicating human intelligence; it also allows for processing large volumes of data quickly and accurately, extracting insights, and automating decisions that previously required human intervention. In SMEs, this translates into the ability to perform tasks like customer segmentation, sales data analysis, experience personalization, and process automation more quickly and effectively. It's crucial for small businesses to understand that AI is not an unattainable technology and that today there are accessible tools that allow them to leverage its capabilities with a limited budget.

There are several types of AI that can be classified based on their complexity and autonomy. Weak or narrow AI is designed to perform specific tasks, such as natural language processing, virtual assistants, or chatbots that many companies use in their customer service. This type of AI can perform its function efficiently in a specific environment but lacks understanding or awareness beyond that task. Weak AI is currently predominant in commercial applications as it allows for process automation and efficiency improvement in key areas without needing complex systems.

On the other hand, strong AI aims to imitate human intelligence more comprehensively, with capabilities like autonomous reasoning and problem-solving in varied contexts. Despite its appeal, strong AI is still in the research and development phase, and its practical applications are very limited in the commercial sphere. Strong AI seeks to create systems that can adapt to new environments and situations without relying on human intervention, a long-term goal that poses both technological and ethical challenges.

The applications of AI in the business sector cover multiple key areas. Among them, machine learning is an essential subfield, as it allows machines to learn from data without being explicitly programmed. With machine learning, systems can analyze historical data, identify patterns, and make predictions, optimizing decisions in areas such as sales, marketing, and customer service. Another relevant area is natural language processing (NLP), which enables machines to interpret and generate text, facilitating applications like chatbots and sentiment and emotion analysis systems on social media. Computer vision is also one of the growing areas of AI, helping to interpret images and videos for applications in sectors like manufacturing, ecommerce, or medicine. Lastly, robotics uses AI to give machines autonomy in performing repetitive or dangerous physical tasks, an area particularly relevant for industries that rely on automation to optimize processes and reduce workplace risks.

This chapter will delve into the essential concepts of artificial intelligence, its applications, types, and the importance of each of its key areas, allowing readers to gain a comprehensive and applied view of AI in a business context accessible to SMEs and freelancers.

• Definition of artificial intelligence

Artificial intelligence (AI) represents one of the most impactful revolutions in modern technology. Its main goal is to develop systems and algorithms capable of performing tasks that normally require human intelligence, a process that ranges from recognizing complex patterns and learning from experiences to autonomous decision-making and solving complex problems. Unlike traditional tools and technologies that operate by following specific instructions, AI allows machines to act and learn autonomously, opening up a range of possibilities that transcend multiple sectors and applications.

To accurately understand what artificial intelligence means, it's crucial to grasp its focus and scope in the field of computing. In basic terms, AI aims to equip machines with cognitive abilities that, until now, only humans have been capable of performing. This includes processing information in an intelligent and adaptive way; that is, not just receiving and processing data but also analyzing it and responding based on previous patterns or rules derived from experience. AI encompasses complex techniques and models designed so that systems are not limited to merely executing instructions but can improve and evolve their performance over time through data analysis.

One of the fundamental aspects that defines AI is its ability to perform pattern recognition. This capability allows machines to identify regularities in large datasets, enabling them to classify and predict future behaviors or events. In practice, this process allows, for example, recognizing faces in photographs, classifying emails as spam, or identifying fraud patterns in financial transactions. To achieve this level of recognition, AI systems use advanced algorithms that are trained with a large number of examples (data) from which they learn to identify the key features that define each specific pattern.

Another distinctive feature of AI is its ability to learn. This property, known as machine learning, allows systems to improve their performance without direct intervention from a programmer. Instead of receiving explicit instructions for each situation, AI systems can process large volumes of data and learn from them, adjusting their responses and decisions based on past experiences. In a commercial environment, for example, an AI applied to marketing can analyze data from past customer interactions and adapt its recommendations according to purchasing preferences. This type of learning is what makes AI useful in complex and variable contexts, as it adapts and evolves over time, making its predictions increasingly accurate.

Decision-making is another crucial aspect of artificial intelligence, as it allows AI to act autonomously in situations where human intervention would previously have been necessary. For a machine to make decisions independently, mathematical and statistical models are used to select the most optimal option based on a series of criteria and constraints. In this process, AI considers complex variables that can influence the outcome of a decision and can adjust its choice based on the probability of success, cost, and efficiency. A clear example of this is the use of AI in inventory management or logistics route planning, where decisions adapt in real-time to changes in demand, prices, or traffic.

Artificial intelligence is also defined by its ability to solve complex problems. In many cases, this involves using specialized algorithms capable of exploring multiple alternatives and choosing the best solution for a given situation. AI systems can tackle problems that require calculations and decisions in dynamic environments with high uncertainty, something that would be extremely laborious and costly for a person. Through techniques like predictive analysis, AI can anticipate future scenarios, allowing businesses to plan ahead and make informed decisions. For example, in e-commerce, AI can predict product demand for the coming months, helping to avoid overstock or inventory shortages.

From a structural standpoint, AI is based on algorithms and mathematical models that allow it to process information and generate useful results from large amounts of data. Unlike conventional programs, where each step is specified, AI algorithms are designed to learn iteratively, continuously improving as they are exposed to new data. This iterative process is what makes AI particularly effective in tasks involving variability and complexity, such as financial data analysis or medical diagnosis. AI can integrate real-time data and adjust its models according to changes in the environment, making it a powerful and flexible tool for multiple applications.

Over the past few years, artificial intelligence has advanced thanks to the combination of three main factors: increased computing power, availability of large volumes of data, and the development of increasingly sophisticated algorithms. Computing power has enabled the processing of millions of data points in a matter of seconds, while the availability of data has given algorithms the ability to train in broader and more diverse contexts. At the same time, advancements in algorithms, such as deep neural networks and optimization methods, have allowed AI to achieve results that were previously unattainable, such as natural language interpretation or image recognition.

When considering AI as a tool in the business world, especially for SMEs, it's important to understand that this technology has transformed the way companies approach their operations and strategies. AI not only allows for greater automation of repetitive tasks, but it also offers SMEs the possibility to optimize their resources, improve efficiency in their operations, and make more accurate decisions. AI, for example, can identify which products have the highest demand during certain periods, optimizing purchasing and storage processes, or it can detect abandonment patterns in customers who don't complete online purchases, allowing companies to adopt data-driven customer recovery strategies.

Furthermore, AI has facilitated the development of solutions that personalize the customer experience, which is crucial to staying competitive in markets where consumer expectations are constantly changing. AI systems can analyze each user's data individually, offering recommendations or suggestions that align with their preferences and past behaviors. In an online store, for example, AI can analyze purchase history, browsing behavior, and viewed products to offer relevant product recommendations. This personalization not only improves customer satisfaction but also increases the likelihood of additional purchases.

Artificial intelligence, by redefining how data is processed and decisions are made, also drives the development of data-driven business strategies. Through advanced analysis, AI enables companies to identify new business opportunities and market trends that might otherwise go unnoticed. AI can process large volumes of information from various sources (such as social media, sales records, and consumption patterns) and extract insights that form the basis for strategic decisions. In a competitive environment, where speed of reaction and adaptability are crucial, this technology gives companies a significant advantage by allowing them to quickly respond to changes in consumer preferences or competitor behavior.

In summary, artificial intelligence is a field that combines the power of data, algorithms, and computing to create systems capable of performing tasks that were previously only possible for humans. AI can interpret complex patterns, learn from past experiences, make autonomous decisions, and solve problems, which opens up immense possibilities in different sectors and business areas. Although in its early stages, AI was a technology reserved for companies with large resources and technical capabilities, recent advances have made it possible for small and medium-sized enterprises to implement it. Today, AI is an accessible and transformative tool that is revolutionizing the way companies operate, optimize their processes, make decisions, and interact with their customers.

- **Types of AI**

Artificial intelligence (AI) has become a transformative tool for many sectors, driving innovations and improving efficiency in business processes, from multinationals to small and medium-sized enterprises (SMEs). However, it's important to understand that AI is not a homogeneous concept; within it, there are different types with varying characteristics and levels of complexity that determine their application in different contexts. Primarily, AI is classified into weak AI and strong AI, two categories that differ in their objectives and capabilities.

Weak AI, also known as narrow AI, is designed to perform specific tasks and represents the most common type of AI in use today, especially in SMEs. This type of AI is limited to carrying out concrete functions such as answering questions, performing calculations, or managing customer service flows through chatbots. On the other hand, strong AI is a theoretical vision aimed at creating systems with general intelligence similar to that of humans, capable of learning and adapting to a wide range of situations without predefined restrictions. Although it does not yet exist fully, it represents a research horizon with fascinating possibilities. For the current environment, it is weak AI that makes a difference in the daily operations of businesses, providing them with accessible tools to improve customer experience and optimize their internal processes.

- **Weak or narrow AI**

Weak or narrow AI is a type of artificial intelligence specialized in performing specific tasks, and by design, it is confined to certain application domains. In other words, this AI does not have a general understanding of the world like a human would; it is developed to execute specific functions effectively. Therefore, it is a specialized intelligence that cannot reason beyond its area of application, although it can achieve very high performance within those limits.

In the realm of SMEs, weak AI is the most accessible and useful due to its low cost and the wide range of tools available that don't require a complex technological infrastructure or advanced technical knowledge. Virtual assistants and chatbots are common examples of weak AI, and their application in businesses has revolutionized how they interact with customers and manage user support. A virtual assistant can resolve basic queries, redirect users to the correct sections of the website, or even process basic transactions without human intervention. This type of application allows SMEs to offer 24/7 customer service, something that was previously out of reach for many due to the high costs associated with traditional support services.

Weak AI systems work through specific algorithms and supervised learning, where the machine is trained with labeled data to learn to identify patterns and make decisions based on those patterns. An example is a chatbot programmed to recognize frequently asked questions about a product and automatically respond with relevant information. This weak AI can process natural language to identify the customer's intent and respond according to a set of predefined answers, improving the accuracy of its responses over time. Although these chatbots don't 'understand' language like a human would, they can analyze phrases and keywords to provide useful and practical responses, offering a personalized experience to the customer.

The use of weak AI also extends to data analysis and trend prediction, areas where SMEs can gain significant benefits. For example, using machine learning algorithms, an AI can analyze customer purchasing behavior and predict which products will be in high demand next month. This way, a small e-commerce store can optimize its inventory and prepare for high-demand events, such as sales seasons or special offer days. Similarly, this type of AI also allows for personalized offers and content for each customer, improving satisfaction and increasing the likelihood of sales.

Weak AI is also crucial in digital marketing. Advertising platforms like Google Ads and Facebook Ads use weak AI algorithms to analyze user behavior and display targeted ads to specific audiences, based on behavioral data and preferences. For SMEs, this advanced segmentation capability results in a competitive advantage that allows them to maximize the return on investment in advertising without resorting to massive marketing strategies. In this way, weak AI offers businesses practical tools that can be integrated without large investments, enabling them to compete in an increasingly competitive and digitalized market.

In summary, weak AI is an accessible and valuable tool for SMEs, as it allows them to optimize specific processes and improve customer experience without the need for costly infrastructure or advanced technical knowledge. Although its capabilities are limited to specific tasks, the effectiveness of weak AI in fulfilling those tasks represents a considerable advantage for businesses, providing the possibility to automate repetitive tasks, analyze data in real time, and make informed decisions based on the analysis of large amounts of information.

- **Strong AI**

Strong AI, also known as General AI or AGI (Artificial General Intelligence), is a concept that represents one of the most ambitious goals in the field of artificial intelligence. Unlike weak AI, which is designed to perform specific and limited tasks, strong AI aims to develop systems with a cognitive capacity similar to that of humans. This means that strong AI would be able to perform a wide range of tasks, from solving complex problems to learning and adapting autonomously to new contexts, in a way similar to how a person would. In other words, strong AI would have a general intelligence capable of tackling multiple domains and understanding the world in a comprehensive manner.

Currently, strong AI is in the research and development phases, and scientists have not yet managed to create a system that fully meets the characteristics of general intelligence. However, strong AI is a topic of great interest and discussion in the scientific community, as it poses not only technical challenges but also ethical and social ones. Developing an AI capable of understanding and reasoning like a human being involves significant advances in areas such as natural language processing, visual perception, and autonomous decision-making. This type of intelligence would need to learn in an unsupervised manner, meaning it wouldn't require detailed instructions for each task, and adapt to new situations with ease.

In theory, strong AI would be capable of reasoning, planning, learning, and acting autonomously across a wide range of environments. This means that instead of being limited to a specific function, like sorting emails or analyzing customer data, strong AI could interpret and respond to multiple contexts without predefined restrictions. For example, in a business environment, a strong AI could simultaneously analyze financial data, market trends, and consumer behavior to generate innovative business strategies and make decisions autonomously, all without human intervention.

The development of strong AI presents various technical challenges. One of the biggest hurdles is the need to equip systems with a level of understanding of the world that goes beyond patterns or correlations, encompassing deeper contextual and semantic aspects. This would require creating algorithms that not only interpret data but also understand the context and intention behind each situation. Additionally, there are processing and storage limitations, as an AI with these capabilities would demand enormous amounts of data and an unprecedented computational infrastructure.

From an ethical standpoint, the development of strong AI also raises complex questions, such as the possibility that these systems could acquire a level of autonomy that might be difficult to control or regulate. Strong AI carries the risk that, if not developed and supervised properly, it could make decisions beyond human control, with potentially unpredictable consequences. For this reason, many experts believe that the development of strong AI should be approached with caution and strict ethical regulation, ensuring that systems are responsible and aligned with society's values and goals.

It is important to clarify that, although strong AI has been widely explored in literature and the media, there is still no fully operational system that can be considered as such. Most current systems, even the most advanced ones, are still examples of weak AI, as they are designed to perform specific and limited tasks within certain parameters. However, interest in strong AI continues to grow, and it is expected that in the future, advances in quantum computing, deep learning algorithms, and neural networks will contribute to the development of increasingly advanced systems capable of performing tasks that were once considered impossible for a machine.

For SMEs and businesses in general, strong AI is not yet a technology applicable in the short term, but its development presents interesting possibilities on the horizon. As research in strong AI progresses, businesses could benefit from more autonomous and intelligent applications that go beyond the automation of specific, limited tasks. However, in the current context, weak AI remains the most viable and accessible option, and it offers practical and affordable solutions to improve efficiency and customer experience in businesses of all sizes.

In summary, while weak AI represents the current reality of artificial intelligence in business applications, strong AI is a long-term vision with the potential to radically change our relationship with technology and redefine the capabilities of intelligent systems.

- **Key areas of artificial intelligence**

Artificial intelligence (AI) encompasses various specialized areas that together form an ecosystem of capabilities and technological applications designed to replicate or imitate aspects of human intelligence in computational systems. These key areas of AI not only drive the development of innovative technologies but also allow businesses, from large corporations to small and medium-sized enterprises (SMEs), to access advanced tools that optimize processes, improve customer experience, and enhance their competitiveness in an increasingly digitalized market. By exploring the main areas of AI, a range of possibilities opens up for understanding how and in what aspects AI can transform the business world.

Within the fundamental areas of AI are machine learning, natural language processing (NLP), computer vision, and robotics, each with its own specific goals and applications. Machine learning, for example, is one of the most prominent subfields of AI, where machines acquire the ability to learn from data and make predictions or decisions without explicit programming. This feature is crucial in applications such as predicting consumer trends, detecting fraud, and optimizing inventory.

Natural Language Processing (NLP) allows machines to understand and generate human language, a fundamental capability in creating chatbots and virtual assistants that can significantly improve customer service. Computer vision, another relevant area, focuses on the analysis of images and videos, enabling machines to identify and categorize objects in images, which is essential in sectors like manufacturing, where it can be used for real-time product inspection. Finally, robotics combines AI principles with hardware, allowing the automation of repetitive or dangerous physical tasks, and finds applications especially in the manufacturing and logistics industries.

These areas not only stand out for their applicability in specific sectors but also for their potential for integration to solve complex and multifaceted problems. Thus, by understanding the key areas of artificial intelligence, SMEs can identify which of them can add the most value to their operations and customers, helping them transform their processes and strategies through advanced technology.

- Machine Learning

Machine learning is one of the most popular and effective subfields of artificial intelligence in terms of applicability for businesses of all sizes. Through machine learning, machines can learn patterns and relationships in large volumes of data to make predictions and decisions without the need for a human to explicitly program them for each case. This process allows machines to 'learn' from previous examples, improving their performance as more information is provided.

The concept of machine learning revolves around the principle that machines can develop 'intelligence' based on data, allowing them to recognize patterns and trends that may be invisible to the human eye. In the context of SMEs, machine learning has democratized access to predictive tools that were unthinkable just a few years ago, giving these companies the ability to anticipate changes in customer behavior, adjust their inventories, or personalize their product offerings in an advanced and precise way.

There are various approaches and algorithms in machine learning, each designed for specific tasks and objectives. One of the most well-known and widely used types of algorithms is supervised learning, where the model is trained with data that includes both inputs and expected outputs, allowing the machine to "learn" the relationship between them. This technique is particularly useful in classification tasks, such as customer segmentation, where the goal is to group customers into categories based on relevant characteristics. For example, a clothing store can use a supervised learning algorithm to classify its customers according to their shopping preferences and offer them personalized promotions.

Another approach in machine learning is unsupervised learning, where the model analyzes data without labels or prior information about categories. This approach is useful in tasks like detecting unknown patterns, where the model identifies similarities in the data without specific instructions. For an SME, this technique can be useful for discovering behavioral patterns in their customers, allowing them to adjust their marketing or product development strategies based on these patterns. Clustering algorithms, such as k-means, are common in unsupervised learning and are used to group similar items, like identifying products that are often bought together.

Within supervised models, some of the most common algorithms include linear regression and logistic regression, widely used in sales predictions and trend analysis. Linear regression is used when the goal is to predict a numerical value, such as the monthly sales of a product, based on variables like price, season, or marketing investment. On the other hand, logistic regression is useful in binary classification problems, such as predicting whether a customer will make a purchase based on their browsing history on a website.

Another type of supervised machine learning model is the decision tree, which is used to create a rule-based decision model. This approach is useful for segmenting customers or making decisions in business processes that depend on multiple variables. In the context of an SME, a decision tree can help predict which type of customer is more likely to respond to a marketing campaign, based on variables such as age, purchase history, and frequency of website visits.

Machine learning also includes advanced techniques like deep learning, which involves artificial neural networks with multiple layers that can identify complex patterns in massive datasets. Deep learning has revolutionized fields like image recognition and computer vision, and although these models require more computational resources, they have become accessible through cloud platforms that allow SMEs to leverage their power without needing to invest in specialized hardware.

One of the great advantages of machine learning is its practical applicability in optimizing business operations. In SMEs, machine learning can be used for tasks such as demand forecasting, customer segmentation, and product recommendation personalization. A clear example of its application is using machine learning to analyze past sales data and predict which products will be in high demand in the coming months, allowing the company to adjust its inventory and place orders with suppliers in advance to avoid stockouts.

Machine learning techniques also allow for improved operational efficiency in areas such as logistics and inventory management. A machine learning algorithm can analyze sales patterns and recommend optimal inventory levels, minimizing storage costs and avoiding both shortages and overstocking. Additionally, in the realm of digital marketing, machine learning can analyze customer interactions with a company's website to determine which products are most appealing and how to target advertising campaigns more effectively.

Machine learning is not just limited to sales prediction or inventory optimization; it is also a key tool in personalizing the customer experience. Thanks to its ability to analyze large volumes of data, a machine learning system can identify patterns in customer behavior, such as the product categories they are usually interested in, the times of day they make purchases, or the promotions that are most effective. This information allows SMEs to personalize recommendations and offers, creating a more relevant and engaging experience for each customer and increasing the chances of conversion.

Finally, it is important to highlight that machine learning is a constantly evolving technology, with an increasing availability of tools and platforms that make its implementation easier. Nowadays, SMEs can access cloud-based machine learning platforms that offer scalable infrastructure and pre-trained models, significantly reducing entry costs. Services like Amazon SageMaker, Google Cloud AI, and Microsoft Azure AI allow companies to train custom models without advanced technical knowledge, democratizing access to machine learning and expanding innovation possibilities for businesses of all sizes.

In conclusion, machine learning represents a powerful and versatile tool that is transforming the way businesses operate and make decisions. Its ability to deeply analyze data and extract actionable insights makes it an indispensable resource for SMEs that want to optimize their processes, improve customer experience, and compete in an increasingly data-driven market. By applying machine learning algorithms, these companies can make more informed decisions, anticipate market needs, and quickly adapt to changes in consumer behavior, thus maximizing their efficiency and profitability.

- **Natural Language Processing (NLP)**

Natural Language Processing (NLP) focuses on the ability of machines to understand and generate human language in a coherent and relevant way. It is one of the most visible AI applications in daily life, as it is present in many tools and services we use every day. NLP allows machines to "read" or "listen" to human language, interpret it, and respond based on what they have learned, enabling smooth communication between people and computer systems. This ability to understand and generate text or voice is essential in applications such as virtual assistants, chatbots, and sentiment analysis systems, which are particularly useful for improving customer experience and optimizing data management in SMEs.

One of the main focuses in natural language processing is sentiment analysis, which allows companies to understand customer emotions and opinions in real time. For example, by analyzing comments on social media, emails, or satisfaction surveys, an SME can identify whether the customer's perception is positive, negative, or neutral and act accordingly. This approach can be applied in customer service, where the machine evaluates if the tone of the message is satisfactory or if there is an implicit complaint, generating automatic alerts for the support team to take specific actions. Sentiment analysis is a tool that enables real-time decision-making, improves customer satisfaction, and adjusts business strategies.

Another fundamental aspect of NLP is the ability to process large volumes of unstructured data in the form of text, such as emails, product reviews, or social media interactions. Through NLP algorithms, SMEs can extract patterns and trends in customer comments, identify keywords indicating frequent issues, or analyze the most popular topics. This functionality allows companies to make adjustments to their products, campaigns, or services according to customer needs, optimizing their offerings and improving the overall user experience.

NLP also enables the creation and deployment of intelligent chatbots that automate customer service, answering frequently asked questions and resolving basic issues immediately. These chatbots are especially useful for SMEs that want to offer 24/7 customer service without hiring additional staff. With NLP, chatbots can maintain a coherent conversation with users, respond to simple questions, and even transfer the conversation to a human agent if the query is complex. This automation helps improve operational efficiency, reduce wait times, and provide a consistent and satisfying customer experience.

In addition, NLP can also be integrated into automatic translation and voice-to-text transcription tools, which expands communication possibilities and facilitates access to information in different languages or formats. For example, an ecommerce business can use NLP to translate product descriptions into multiple languages, expanding its international reach and improving the accessibility of its services. Similarly, voice recognition can be used in customer service systems that allow users to interact through voice commands, improving accessibility and process efficiency.

NLP has advanced considerably thanks to state-of-the-art language models like GPT-3 or BERT, developed by leading technology companies. These models enable machines to understand and generate language more accurately and coherently, offering a more natural and humanized experience in interactions. For SMEs, these advances mean the possibility of accessing chatbots and language data analysis systems with advanced precision, improving the analysis and response to customer interactions.

- **Computer Vision**

Computer vision is another key area of artificial intelligence that enables machines to 'see' and 'understand' the world through images and videos. Through computer vision, machines can analyze and recognize patterns in visual data, which is especially useful in sectors like manufacturing, ecommerce, security, and healthcare. Advances in computer vision allow SMEs to perform tasks that previously required human intervention, such as quality inspection, product tracking, or object identification, in a fast, accurate, and cost-effective manner.

In manufacturing, for example, computer vision is used to inspect products on the production line and automatically detect quality defects. Computer vision systems can analyze each piece or product in real time, identifying variations or faults based on previously established parameters. This helps reduce production costs associated with defective products and improves the final product quality. In an SME that produces food or consumer goods, computer vision can be an invaluable tool for maintaining quality standards without the need for additional staff to supervise the production process.

In ecommerce and retail, computer vision enables advanced features like visual product recommendations or image-based search. By analyzing a product image, an online store can suggest similar or complementary products, enhancing the user experience and increasing conversion rates. Additionally, customers can search for products by taking a photo with their mobile device, which simplifies the buying process and improves the overall user experience.

Security is another area where computer vision has practical applications. Smart camera systems, using computer vision algorithms, can analyze in real time what is happening in a specific area and detect suspicious behavior, automatically alerting security personnel. These systems are particularly useful in stores or warehouses, where they can help prevent theft or control unauthorized access. For SMEs, this means a reduction in surveillance costs and an overall improvement in the security of the facilities.

Another key application of computer vision is found in advertising and marketing, where it is used to analyze consumers' facial expressions and emotions while interacting with ads or products at the point of sale. This type of analysis can help companies understand how customers react to a specific campaign and adjust their marketing strategy based on this data. In addition, computer vision is also used in market research, analyzing the flow of people in a physical store to determine which areas are of greatest interest and optimize product placement.

Vision techniques are based on Convolutional Neural Networks (CNNs), which are specifically designed to process visual data. CNNs allow vision systems to detect and classify objects with high accuracy, regardless of their size, shape, or position in the image. These neural networks are the foundation of many recent advances in image recognition and are crucial for applications like object detection, image segmentation, and facial recognition. Thanks to these advances, SMEs can access affordable vision tools that enable them to automate complex processes and improve operational efficiency.

- **Robotics**

Robotics is the area of artificial intelligence responsible for designing, building, and programming robots to perform physical tasks in the real world. Unlike AI applications that operate solely in the digital realm, robotics combines software and hardware to create machines capable of interacting with their physical environment autonomously or semi-autonomously. Robotics has applications in numerous sectors, especially those that require repetitive, dangerous, or highly precise tasks, such as manufacturing, logistics, and construction.

In manufacturing, robots have revolutionized production lines by performing tasks such as assembly, painting, packaging, and handling heavy materials. Industrial robots can work continuously without needing breaks, which increases productivity and reduces production costs. These robots are programmed to execute precise and repetitive movements, ensuring a level of accuracy and consistency that is difficult to achieve with human labor. Additionally, in industries like automotive, robotics allows for assembly tasks that require complex welding and adjustments with millimetric precision.

Logistics is another sector where robotics is having a significant impact. In warehouses, autonomous transport robots can move products from one place to another efficiently, optimizing the flow of goods and reducing order preparation time. These robots can navigate autonomously through the warehouse, avoiding obstacles and adapting to changes in the environment. In an SME focused on e-commerce, logistics robots can significantly speed up inventory management and order preparation, allowing for greater efficiency and faster deliveries.

Robotics is also crucial in construction, where it is used to perform tasks that involve a high level of risk for workers. Robots can handle jobs such as demolition, material cutting, or drilling in hazardous environments, reducing the risk of workplace accidents. In some advanced applications, robots can work in conjunction with drones, inspecting structures and assessing the safety of construction sites. This allows construction companies to better manage their projects and reduce associated times and costs.

In the SME sector, robotics also offers opportunities for automation in areas like packaging and material handling, allowing companies to reduce employee workloads and assign them to higher-value tasks. For example, a collaborative robot or 'cobot' can work alongside employees on assembly or packaging tasks, making the job easier and increasing the overall efficiency of the company. These collaborative robots are designed to interact safely with humans and are a viable solution for small and medium-sized businesses looking to automate certain tasks without replacing their staff.

Moreover, robotics has important applications in customer service and hospitality. Robots can handle visitor reception, product transportation in hotels, or assistance at points of sale. This type of robot improves the customer experience, reduces wait times, and allows employees to focus on more personalized service tasks. In an SME, service robots can be a valuable resource for enhancing the customer experience and optimizing operations in sectors like hospitality or retail.

Thanks to advances in artificial intelligence, robots are increasingly capable of adapting and learning from their environment, allowing them to perform complex and unstructured tasks. With the integration of sensors and computer vision technologies, robots can perceive their surroundings, identify objects, and adapt to unexpected situations. For example, in a warehouse, a robot with computer vision can identify specific products, adjust its path based on obstacles, and efficiently organize items on shelves.

In conclusion, natural language processing, computer vision, and robotics represent fundamental areas of artificial intelligence with practical applications in industry. These technologies enable SMEs to improve efficiency, reduce costs, and offer personalized experiences to their customers. With the continuous development of these areas, AI will continue to provide opportunities to automate complex tasks and enhance the competitiveness of businesses in an ever-changing market.

5.2. Why is artificial intelligence important today?

Artificial intelligence (AI) has become one of the most disruptive and innovative technologies of the past decade, impacting virtually every aspect of our personal and professional lives. In the current context, its importance lies in its ability to transform processes, optimize operations, and facilitate data-driven decision-making across multiple sectors. From healthcare and education to logistics and marketing, artificial intelligence offers solutions that allow companies not only to be more efficient but also to develop new business models and improve the customer experience.

- **Global impact of AI**

The global impact of artificial intelligence is vast and increasingly visible across different industries. This change is no longer a projection into the future but a tangible reality that influences the strategies and decisions of companies of all sizes, from large corporations to small and medium-sized enterprises (SMEs). Advances in AI algorithms, greater data availability, and processing power have made artificial intelligence more accessible and affordable than ever. Its impact ranges from automating routine tasks to creating new products and services, and it's transforming the global economy in multiple dimensions.

In the healthcare sector, AI has enabled advances in disease diagnosis and the creation of personalized treatments. Machine learning applications in medical image analysis, for example, allow for the detection of diseases like cancer in their early stages, significantly improving patient prognosis. Additionally, processing large amounts of clinical data allows researchers to identify patterns and trends in disease spread, facilitating better prevention and response to epidemics. This shows that AI not only optimizes medical care but can also save lives.

Logistics and transportation is another sector that has experienced a significant change due to AI. Logistics companies use route optimization algorithms to reduce costs and improve delivery times, resulting in greater customer satisfaction. Computer vision also plays an important role, especially in inventory management, where automated systems can monitor stock in real time and prevent shortages or overstocking. These improvements in the supply chain allow for greater efficiency in resource management, which is essential for any company that wants to remain competitive in a global market.

In the field of education, artificial intelligence has facilitated the development of personalized learning platforms that adapt to each student's pace and learning style. AI tools allow for the assessment of students' progress and recommend additional content based on their needs, thus improving the quality of learning. These solutions are especially valuable in remote education environments, where interaction between teachers and students is limited, and AI can provide additional support to optimize results.

Trade and marketing have also greatly benefited from advances in artificial intelligence. AI algorithms allow the analysis of large volumes of customer data in real-time, which facilitates the personalization of marketing campaigns and improves the customer experience. AI enables companies to anticipate their customers' needs, offer recommended products, and customize interactions, resulting in greater loyalty and higher conversion rates. In a world where competition is fierce and customer retention is essential, AI has become a key tool for success in digital marketing.

In addition to its impact on specific sectors, AI is changing the work environment and the global economy. The automation of routine tasks allows employees to focus on higher-value activities, which not only increases efficiency but also enhances job satisfaction and well-being. Although the impact of AI on employment has raised concerns, especially in repetitive and low-skilled jobs, the technology also creates new job opportunities in areas like AI development, data management, and cybersecurity. The key to making the most of this positive impact lies in the continuous training and updating of professionals, who must acquire the skills needed to work in an increasingly digital and automated environment.

- **Automation and efficiency**

One of the main benefits of artificial intelligence is its ability to automate repetitive tasks and improve efficiency in a company's operations. Automation through AI has become an essential component for businesses that want to reduce costs and optimize their use of resources, especially in an environment where digitalization is increasingly necessary for competitiveness.

In many cases, AI can perform tasks that previously required human intervention, more quickly and accurately. This is particularly useful in manufacturing and production sectors, where AI can handle tasks like assembly, quality inspection, and predictive maintenance. For example, computer vision systems can automatically identify defects in products, allowing quality issues to be corrected in real time and reducing waste. Automating these tasks not only improves production efficiency but also ensures that products meet quality standards, reducing the need for costly control processes.

In the field of human resources management, AI also has a significant impact. AI systems allow for the automation of administrative tasks such as staff selection, resume analysis, and payroll management. AI algorithms can analyze large volumes of candidate data to identify those who best fit the job requirements, reducing the time and costs associated with the hiring process. Additionally, AI can facilitate employee retention by analyzing job satisfaction data and identifying potential problems before they become crises, which contributes to greater efficiency in talent management.

Another clear example of automation in the financial sector is the use of AI algorithms in fraud detection. AI systems can analyze large volumes of transactions in real time to identify unusual or suspicious patterns, allowing financial institutions to prevent fraud more effectively. Additionally, AI enables banks and financial entities to offer personalized services and improve customer experience through the automation of services like account management and customer support. These advances are essential in a sector where security and efficiency are priorities.

In SMEs, automation through AI also has practical applications. Small and medium-sized enterprises can use AI tools to automate tasks like order processing, inventory management, and customer service. Chatbots, for example, can respond to frequently asked customer questions immediately, which improves the user experience and allows company staff to focus on more complex tasks. Automating these processes not only reduces operating costs but also enables SMEs to compete with larger companies by offering fast and efficient service.

Moreover, AI can improve marketing efficiency by enabling personalized advertising campaigns and audience segmentation. AI algorithms can analyze user behavior in real-time and adjust ads based on their interests and preferences. This allows companies to maximize their return on investment in advertising and increase conversion rates. In an environment where the marketing budget may be limited, automation and efficiency in digital marketing are key for SMEs to achieve better results with fewer resources.

In summary, AI's ability to automate repetitive tasks and improve operational efficiency allows companies to reduce costs, optimize resource use, and enhance overall productivity. This is especially important in a context where the demand for high-quality products and services is constantly increasing and competition is fierce. Automation through AI is a crucial competitive advantage that enables companies to respond quickly and efficiently to market changes, meet customer expectations, and adapt to new trends in business digitalization.

- **Data-driven decision making**

Another important advantage of artificial intelligence is its ability to facilitate data-driven decision-making. In an environment where data is increasingly abundant, AI allows companies to analyze large volumes of information in real time, enabling them to make faster, more accurate, and well-founded decisions. For SMEs and freelancers, data-driven decision-making is an invaluable tool that allows them to identify opportunities, reduce risks, and improve the efficiency of their operations.

AI facilitates real-time decision-making by analyzing data from multiple sources, such as social media, customer transactions, market data, and performance statistics. This allows companies to gain a comprehensive and up-to-date view of their situation, which is essential for strategic planning and quick market response. For example, a retail company can analyze real-time customer behavior on its online store and adjust its sales strategy based on the most demanded products or the promotions generating the most interest.

In the realm of SMEs, AI also enables the personalization of offers based on customer data. By analyzing historical and real-time data, businesses can identify customer preferences and tailor their product or service offerings accordingly. This is particularly useful in the e-commerce sector, where personalizing the customer experience is key to increasing satisfaction and loyalty. Additionally, data-driven decision-making allows companies to forecast product demand, which is crucial for inventory management and order planning.

Data-driven decision-making also has practical applications in risk management. AI algorithms can analyze historical data and detect patterns that indicate an increased risk of certain events, such as customer loss or a drop in sales of a specific product. This allows companies to anticipate problems and take preventive measures to mitigate the impact of these risks. For example, a predictive AI model can identify customers at risk of leaving the brand and recommend personalized retention strategies, such as offering discounts or special incentives.

Moreover, AI allows for simulations and predictive analysis that facilitate long-term planning. AI models can predict the impact of different decisions and scenarios on the company's performance, enabling managers to assess potential outcomes before making changes. This is especially useful in financial management, where AI allows for the analysis of the impact of decisions such as investing in new products, expanding into new markets, or adopting new technologies.

In conclusion, artificial intelligence has proven to be a transformative technology that is changing all industries globally. Its impact extends from task automation to data-driven decision-making, and its adoption is constantly growing in companies of all sizes. For SMEs and freelancers, AI offers a key competitive advantage that allows them to optimize operations, reduce costs, improve customer experience, and make more informed and less risky decisions. The importance of AI in today's business environment lies in its ability to turn data into value and facilitate an agile and efficient response to market changes and customer needs.

5.3. Why is artificial intelligence important for SMEs and freelancers?

Artificial Intelligence (AI) is no longer an exclusive technology for large corporations and has become a fundamental tool for small and medium-sized enterprises (SMEs) and freelancers. Today, AI solutions have been democratized, offering businesses of any size the opportunity to improve their operations, optimize resources, and provide a better customer experience. This democratization means that advanced tools for data analysis, natural language processing, and task automation are now within reach of companies that previously couldn't afford or implement such technologies.

Democratization of technology

One of the most significant advances in the field of artificial intelligence is its democratization. Until recently, AI was perceived as an expensive and complicated technology, restricted to companies with large budgets and technical resources. However, changes in software development, data accessibility, and computing power have made it possible for AI to be used today by companies of all sizes. Platforms like Google Cloud AI, Amazon Web Services (AWS), and Microsoft Azure AI have pioneered the offering of scalable AI services, meaning any company can access these services without the need for costly infrastructure or a specialized technical team.

The democratization of AI allows SMEs to access tools that were previously only available to large corporations. For example, cloud-based machine learning models offer companies the ability to implement prediction models, natural language processing, and advanced data analysis with a relatively low investment. These services are designed to be flexible and scalable, allowing companies to pay only for what they use. This way, SMEs can start with pilot AI projects and, if they prove successful, expand their use progressively.

The accessibility of these cloud platforms means that companies can perform advanced tasks, such as predictive analytics, without having a technical team or data scientists on staff. For example, Google Cloud AI offers AutoML, a tool that allows companies to train custom machine learning models without writing code. These platforms often include intuitive graphical interfaces and pre-trained libraries, making it easier to set up and use AI models. This is crucial for SMEs, as it allows them to experiment with the technology and adapt their processes affordably and flexibly.

In addition to cloud platforms, specialized AI tools have emerged, designed specifically for the SME market. Tools like OpenAI's ChatGPT, Microsoft's Lobe, or Google Analytics itself offer affordable and accessible solutions that don't require advanced knowledge to implement. These tools allow SMEs to analyze large volumes of data, better understand their customers, and respond to their needs more quickly and efficiently.

This democratization of AI is changing the landscape for SMEs, allowing them to innovate, reduce costs, and improve competitiveness. The accessibility of AI technology represents a significant advantage for SMEs, enabling them to compete on equal footing with larger companies, achieving significant improvements in their operations and customer relations.

- ## Improvement in customer experience

Artificial intelligence also plays a crucial role in improving the customer experience, a key aspect for loyalty and growth in any business. For SMEs and freelancers, AI allows for the implementation of personalized customer service and sales strategies that were previously only available to large corporations. This is especially useful in a market where the customer experience is one of the most important differentiators. Thanks to AI tools like chatbots, recommendation systems, and marketing personalization techniques, companies can offer a much more agile, effective, and personalized customer service.

One of the most common uses of AI to improve customer experience is through chatbots and virtual assistants. These tools allow companies to provide immediate and constant customer support, resolving queries or processing requests without the need for human intervention. For example, an online store can implement a chatbot that guides users through the purchase process, answering questions about product availability, shipping options, and payment methods. This type of technology can also be customized to respond to frequently asked questions, streamlining service and enhancing customer satisfaction. By reducing the need for traditional customer service, SMEs can also cut costs and optimize the use of their human resources.

Moreover, AI facilitates the personalization of customer interactions, allowing each user to receive a unique experience. Product recommendation systems, for example, use machine learning algorithms to analyze each customer's interests and purchasing behavior and, based on this information, suggest specific products or services. This increases the likelihood of purchase while making the customer feel valued, as they perceive that the recommendations align with their preferences. For an SME, personalization is an effective strategy to increase customer loyalty and generate greater satisfaction.

When it comes to personalizing marketing campaigns, AI allows SMEs to develop messages and promotions tailored to each segment of their audience. This is possible thanks to the analysis of large volumes of data, which allows for the identification of patterns in customer behavior. For example, a fashion company can use AI to identify which products are most popular among its customers and, based on this information, design specific promotional campaigns. Likewise, AI can analyze user behavior on the company's website, personalizing offers and messages in real-time according to the visitor's profile. The personalization of campaigns increases marketing effectiveness and improves return on investment, which is especially important for SMEs with limited budgets.

Moreover, AI allows SMEs to improve customer experience through feedback analysis. Natural Language Processing (NLP) algorithms can analyze customer comments on social media, satisfaction surveys, and online reviews. This provides a more comprehensive view of customer perceptions and allows for real-time identification of areas for improvement. Ultimately, the enhancement of customer experience driven by AI contributes to greater engagement and loyalty, which is vital for the growth and sustainability of SMEs in a competitive market.

- **Resource optimization**

Another significant advantage of artificial intelligence for SMEs is its ability to optimize a company's internal resources. This includes both inventory optimization and automated operations management, which are essential for improving efficiency and reducing costs in a business. For SMEs, which often operate with limited resources, optimization through AI can make a big difference in their competitiveness and profitability.

Inventory management is one of the areas where AI can add considerable value. Through machine learning algorithms, SMEs can analyze historical sales patterns, identify trends, and forecast future product demand. This allows them to adjust their inventory levels to avoid both overstock and stockouts, reducing storage costs and improving product availability. For example, a retail store can use AI to predict increased demand for certain products during holiday seasons, allowing them to place orders in advance and optimize storage space. AI also enables automated reordering of inventory when levels are low, reducing the risk of stockouts.

In addition to inventory management, AI facilitates the automation of operations in multiple areas of the business. Automation reduces the time needed for administrative tasks like invoice processing, order management, and accounting. AI tools can process large volumes of data quickly and accurately, reducing the time and effort required for repetitive tasks and minimizing the risk of errors. In this sense, AI allows SMEs to focus their human resources on higher value-added activities such as customer service, innovation, and the development of new products.

AI also enables the optimization of financial resources through the automation of cash flow management and expense forecasting. SMEs can use AI to analyze their historical income and expenses, identifying patterns and potential liquidity issues before they become a problem. This allows them to make informed decisions about when to invest, when to save, and how to manage their financial resources more effectively. This ability to anticipate financial needs allows SMEs to reduce risk and improve their long-term sustainability.

In conclusion, resource optimization through artificial intelligence is a key factor that allows SMEs to manage their operations more efficiently and profitably. AI's ability to automate tasks, forecast demand, and optimize inventory and financial management represents an important competitive advantage that enables SMEs to improve profitability and adapt quickly to market demands.

- Scalability

Artificial intelligence allows SMEs and freelancers to scale their operations without significantly increasing operating costs or hiring more staff. This is especially relevant in a context where many SMEs want to expand their market or handle a larger volume of clients without losing efficiency or quality in their service. With the help of AI, SMEs can increase their service and production capacity in proportion to their growth.

One of the main advantages of AI in terms of scalability is its ability to automate processes, allowing SMEs to handle a larger volume of operations without increasing their staff. For example, a company using chatbots for customer service can attend to a large number of clients simultaneously, something that would be impossible to achieve with human staff without incurring high labor costs. Additionally, chatbots allow companies to offer 24/7 customer service, which improves customer satisfaction and helps increase sales without the need to proportionally raise costs.

Moreover, AI allows SMEs to handle large volumes of data more efficiently. For many companies, growth involves a larger amount of data that needs to be processed and analyzed, whether for inventory management, customer analysis, or resource planning. Machine learning algorithms can handle large data volumes and perform advanced real-time analysis, enabling SMEs to make informed decisions quickly and efficiently. For example, an online store experiencing a sales increase can use AI to analyze customer behavior, identify buying patterns, and adjust its marketing campaigns in real-time to maximize revenue.

Another advantage of AI in terms of scalability is its ability to adapt to new demands and challenges quickly and effectively. The flexibility of AI algorithms allows SMEs to adjust to changes in the market and customer preferences without needing significant modifications to their infrastructure. This is especially useful in sectors where trends and customer demands change frequently, such as e-commerce, fashion, and tourism. For example, a company using AI for inventory management can automatically adjust its stock levels based on demand, allowing it to respond quickly to an unexpected increase in sales or a decrease in demand for certain products.

Finally, the scalability offered by AI also allows SMEs to expand their market and reach new customers without the need to invest in physical infrastructure. AI tools enable companies to offer their products and services globally, which is especially useful for businesses looking to expand their operations internationally. AI's ability to handle large volumes of data and perform real-time analysis allows companies to efficiently adapt their strategies and provide high-quality service to their customers worldwide.

5.4. Artificial intelligence is not just for big companies

Artificial intelligence is by no means a technology exclusive to large companies. Although in its early days AI was limited to organizations with large research teams and high budgets, today the landscape has changed radically. The democratization of AI has allowed advanced tools and platforms to adapt to the needs of small and medium-sized enterprises (SMEs) as well. This change means that artificial intelligence is no longer a luxury or a tool reserved for a specific sector of the market. It is now an essential technology available to companies with tight budgets and small teams, allowing them to automate processes, improve efficiency, and offer a more personalized customer experience.

- ### Accessibility of AI tools for SMEs

AI tools have become accessible and scalable solutions that can be leveraged by companies of all sizes. Today, there are multiple platforms specifically designed to allow SMEs to develop and implement machine learning models without the need for large development teams or advanced AI knowledge. These platforms offer intuitive interfaces and pay-as-you-go options, eliminating the barrier of initial costs and providing flexibility for companies based on their growth and needs.

Among these platforms, AutoML and Lobe stand out, allowing users to create and train machine learning models without advanced technical knowledge. AutoML, from Google, offers an automated solution for creating predictive, classification, and regression models, and its interface guides the user through each stage of the process. This makes it easier for teams in SMEs to work directly on AI model development without needing programming or advanced statistics experience. Additionally, platforms like Amazon Web Services (AWS) and Microsoft Azure have also launched similar services designed to be intuitive and scalable.

Lobe, a Microsoft tool, allows any user to train AI models in just a few steps, focusing on areas like image recognition and data classification. Lobe's simplified interface lets users drag and drop data to train a model without writing any code, making artificial intelligence accessible to marketing, sales, and other departments within a company. Additionally, these models can be exported to mobile applications or other environments, allowing easy integration into the company's daily operations.

Just like AutoML and Lobe, TensorFlow Lite and Google Colab offer solutions tailored for small businesses and individual developers. Google Colab allows you to train machine learning models in the cloud for free, eliminating the need for specialized hardware. TensorFlow Lite, on the other hand, is a tool designed for mobile devices and IoT applications, which is ideal for companies wanting to implement AI in low-energy environments or devices with limited resources. This is particularly useful for SMEs in sectors like retail, logistics, and manufacturing, which can benefit from artificial intelligence without having to invest in expensive computing equipment.

The accessibility of these tools represents an opportunity for SMEs to compete on equal terms with larger companies. The flexibility of cloud platforms allows businesses to adjust their use of AI according to their needs, paying only for the resources they use. Moreover, many of these tools come with pre-trained libraries and models that enable complex tasks, such as natural language processing or image classification, without the need to set up an AI environment from scratch. This democratization of AI gives SMEs the power to transform their data into valuable insights and allows them to make informed decisions, optimize processes, and improve their customers' experience in a cost-effective and accessible way.

- **Examples of AI in SMEs**

SMEs are discovering innovative ways to apply artificial intelligence in different areas of their business, from marketing and customer service to logistics and inventory management. The versatility of AI allows these companies to automate processes, personalize their interactions, and optimize their operations in a way that, until a few years ago, was only accessible to large corporations. Two key areas where AI is having a significant impact on SMEs are marketing automation and customer service.

- **Marketing automation**

The automation of marketing is one of the most popular AI applications among SMEs, as it allows maximizing the impact of marketing campaigns with limited resources. AI tools enable audience segmentation, user behavior analysis, and personalized marketing content based on each customer's preferences. This personalization improves the effectiveness of campaigns and increases the likelihood of conversion. Tools like Mailchimp and HubSpot have integrated artificial intelligence to optimize the creation, distribution, and analysis of marketing campaigns.

Mailchimp, for example, uses AI to recommend the best times to send emails based on subscriber opening patterns and behavior. This functionality ensures that messages reach recipients at the optimal time, increasing the likelihood that the message will be read and converted into a sale. Mailchimp's AI also allows for personalizing email content based on each segment's interests, which improves the relevance of the message and, therefore, the conversion rate.

HubSpot, on the other hand, uses artificial intelligence to help companies manage their contacts and leads more efficiently. HubSpot's AI automatically classifies leads based on their conversion potential and prioritizes those with a higher likelihood of becoming customers. This allows sales teams to focus on the most promising leads, optimizing the time and resources invested in the sales process. Additionally, HubSpot uses AI to suggest topics and keywords for marketing content, making it easier to create relevant and engaging content for the audience.

In addition to Mailchimp and HubSpot, there are other tools that use AI to automate content marketing, social media advertising campaigns, and customer data analysis. These tools allow SMEs to optimize their marketing efforts and achieve better results without the need for a large team or a high budget. AI also enables companies to analyze the performance of their campaigns in real time, allowing them to make quick adjustments and improve the effectiveness of their marketing actions.

- **Customer support**

Customer service is another area where artificial intelligence is having a major impact on SMEs. Intelligent chatbots and virtual assistants enable companies to offer fast, efficient, and 24/7 customer service. This is especially useful for SMEs, which often lack the resources to maintain a dedicated support team. Chatbots and virtual assistants can answer frequently asked questions, process simple requests, and guide customers through the purchase process, improving the customer experience and freeing up time for the human team to focus on more complex tasks.

Customer service chatbots use natural language processing (NLP) techniques to understand user questions and provide relevant answers in real time. These tools can resolve most customer inquiries without human intervention, reducing wait times and improving customer satisfaction. For example, an online store can implement a chatbot that answers questions about product availability, payment methods, and delivery times. If the chatbot cannot resolve a specific query, it can redirect the customer to a human representative, ensuring that each customer receives the appropriate attention.

In addition to chatbots, virtual assistants are also being adopted by SMEs to improve customer service. These assistants can perform more complex tasks, such as scheduling appointments, processing payments, and tracking orders. Virtual assistants can also integrate with other platforms, like email and social media, allowing businesses to offer an omnichannel customer service experience. This improves the consistency and efficiency of customer service, as users can receive support on their preferred platform and whenever they need it.

AI in customer service not only improves the user experience but also provides valuable insights for businesses. Chatbots and virtual assistants can collect data on the most common questions and issues from customers, allowing companies to identify areas for improvement in their products or services. This information can be used to optimize internal processes, develop proactive solutions, and personalize future interactions with customers, further enhancing the customer relationship and fostering loyalty.

- **Costs vs. benefits**

Although the implementation of artificial intelligence may require an initial investment, the long-term benefits far outweigh the cost. Many AI solutions offer a pay-as-you-go model, allowing SMEs to control their expenses based on their activity level and avoid high costs of licenses and annual subscriptions. This flexible approach allows companies to adjust their AI investments according to their growth and the results they are achieving.

The adoption of AI under a pay-per-use model allows SMEs to test and experiment with different applications without committing large budgets. This reduces the risk associated with implementing new technologies and allows companies to optimize their spending based on the return on investment generated by AI solutions. For example, a company can start using AI to improve customer service and, depending on the results, scale its investment to other areas such as marketing automation or inventory management.

The benefits of AI for SMEs go beyond simple cost reduction. By implementing AI, SMEs achieve significant improvements in operational efficiency, which translates into greater productivity and more efficient use of resources. AI allows for the automation of repetitive tasks that would otherwise consume a lot of time and human effort. For example, an e-commerce company can automate sales data analysis to identify popular products and adjust inventory strategies based on projected demand. This automation allows employees to focus on higher value-added activities, such as product development, sales strategy, or improving the customer experience.

Beyond cost reduction, implementing AI also helps improve customer satisfaction. AI enables personalized and fast customer service, which translates into a better user experience. AI can predict customer needs based on past behavior, allowing for tailored recommendations and improving customer relationships. This is especially valuable in today's digital environment, where customers expect quick and personalized interactions with brands. The ability of AI to process large volumes of data and generate real-time insights allows SMEs to respond quickly and proactively to customer needs, resulting in greater loyalty and increased sales.

On the other hand, AI allows SMEs to gain a competitive advantage in their sector. By automating processes and improving operational efficiency, companies can offer more competitive prices and reduce response times, increasing their ability to attract and retain customers. Additionally, AI enables SMEs to identify market trends and opportunities, making it easier to create innovative products and services that meet changing consumer needs. For example, a company can use AI to analyze customer preferences and launch personalized products that align with those preferences. This ability to adapt and personalize helps SMEs differentiate themselves from competitors and strengthen their market position.

For many SMEs, the return on investment in AI is visible in a relatively short period. Automating processes and optimizing resources lead to significant savings in operational costs, while improving the customer experience translates into increased sales and greater customer loyalty. AI also allows SMEs to anticipate problems and opportunities, facilitating strategic decision-making and reducing risk in business management. This positive impact on operational and financial results makes AI implementation an attractive and profitable investment for SMEs, even for those with limited budgets.

In conclusion, AI is no longer a technology exclusive to large corporations; it has become an accessible and affordable tool for SMEs. The democratization of AI and the availability of tools and platforms tailored to the needs of small businesses allow them to leverage the potential of artificial intelligence to improve operational efficiency, personalize the customer experience, and compete on equal footing with larger companies.

With the right approach, AI can become a driver of growth and differentiation for SMEs, enabling them to achieve their business objectives and enhance their competitiveness in today's market.

5.5. Mathematics in Artificial Intelligence

Mathematics plays a fundamental role in artificial intelligence, forming the foundation upon which algorithms and models are developed, allowing AI systems to learn, interpret, and make decisions. Although modern interfaces and platforms have made AI implementation more accessible, removing the need for deep mathematical knowledge, understanding certain basic mathematical concepts is still valuable, even for those without a specialized technical background. This knowledge helps entrepreneurs and decision-makers better understand how AI works and evaluate its performance in an informed manner, which is especially relevant for SMEs looking to apply AI effectively in their operations.

- **Mathematical Foundations of AI**

AI, at its core, is based on algorithms that use mathematical techniques to identify patterns, process large volumes of data, and make predictions. These algorithms require a series of calculations that allow models to be adjusted and their performance optimized so they can learn from the data. The three main mathematical pillars that support AI are linear algebra, differential calculus, and optimization, each of which uniquely contributes to the development and precision of AI models.

In practice, AI algorithms must be able to handle complex data and make decisions based on that data. This is where linear algebra allows algorithms to work with large sets of structured data, and differential calculus helps find optimal solutions by adjusting models. In turn, optimization enables continuous improvement of model performance by minimizing errors in predictions and improving response accuracy. For SMEs, this mathematical structure may not be directly visible in the AI platforms they use, but understanding these concepts helps gain a better insight into how models are trained and applied, and why a model's performance can vary depending on the data and parameters used.

- **Linear Algebra**

Linear algebra is one of the key mathematical areas in artificial intelligence and machine learning. This field focuses on the study of vectors, matrices, and the operations between them, providing the necessary tools to represent and manipulate data efficiently. In the context of AI, linear algebra is essential for representing data in a structured format that can be processed and analyzed by machine learning algorithms.

For neural networks, one of the most common models in AI, linear algebra is essential. Neural networks are composed of layers of interconnected 'neurons,' and each connection between neurons can be represented by a series of matrix multiplication operations. These operations allow data to flow through the network, activating different neurons and enabling the model to learn patterns in the data. Matrix multiplication allows neural networks to combine data and extract complex information from it, transforming input data into predictions.

Another key application of linear algebra in AI is the processing of large volumes of data. Data is commonly represented in matrices, where each row can represent an observation (for example, a customer transaction) and each column can represent a feature (such as price, quantity, or product type). This structure facilitates parallel processing, where algorithms can handle thousands or millions of observations efficiently and quickly, which is essential for machine learning in large-scale commercial applications.

Furthermore, linear algebra allows for data transformations such as dimensionality reduction using techniques like Principal Component Analysis (PCA). Dimensionality reduction is a process that simplifies data while retaining as much relevant information as possible, which is especially useful for improving the speed and efficiency of AI models. For SMEs, dimensionality reduction can make it easier to analyze large volumes of data without the need for advanced computational infrastructure.

- **Calculation**

Differential calculus is another fundamental mathematical pillar in AI, as it is used to optimize machine learning models and improve their accuracy. In particular, differential calculus allows learning algorithms to adjust their predictions and find patterns in the data through an iterative process of error minimization.

In machine learning, models often work with objective functions or cost functions, which measure the difference between the model's predictions and the actual observed values. These cost functions are minimized to improve the model's accuracy and reduce the margin of error in predictions. Differential calculus allows for the calculation of the gradient of the cost function, which is the rate of change of the function with respect to the model's parameters. By adjusting the parameters in the direction of the gradient, machine learning algorithms can 'learn' from the data, minimizing errors and optimizing their predictions.

In neural networks, this process is carried out using an algorithm called backpropagation, which uses differential calculus to adjust the weights of each connection in the network. Backpropagation allows the network to "learn" from errors, making adjustments based on the difference between predictions and actual results. This process is essential for improving the accuracy and performance of the model as it is trained with more data.

For SMEs, understanding the role of calculus in AI can help make informed decisions about the type of model that best suits their needs and the adjustments needed to improve model performance based on the available data. For example, in sales forecasting applications, a model optimized using differential calculus can more accurately predict product demand, making it easier to plan inventory and manage resources.

- **Optimization**

Optimization is a crucial mathematical process for artificial intelligence, as it allows for continuous improvement of model performance and maximizes prediction accuracy. Optimization is used in all aspects of AI, from training machine learning models to hyperparameter tuning, enabling algorithms to learn from data and improve over time.

Optimization in AI involves finding the optimal value of the model parameters that minimize the cost function. This process is carried out using optimization algorithms, such as gradient descent, which iteratively adjust the model parameters until a minimum value of the cost function is reached. Gradient descent is particularly useful in machine learning models, as it allows algorithms to learn from large volumes of data and improve their accuracy without human intervention.

In commercial applications, optimization allows AI models to adapt to changes in the environment and data. For example, an AI model used for demand forecasting can be adjusted to improve its accuracy as consumer behavior changes. Optimization also allows models to be adjusted based on data variability, such as seasonal fluctuations or economic changes, enabling SMEs to adapt quickly to market conditions.

Moreover, optimization is fundamental for hyperparameter tuning, which involves the parameters that control the performance and configuration of the model. Hyperparameters determine aspects like model complexity, learning rate, and the number of training iterations, and they can significantly affect the model's accuracy and speed. For SMEs, hyperparameter tuning is a valuable tool that allows them to tailor AI models to their specific needs, maximizing the return on investment in AI technology.

- **Why is it relevant for SMEs?**

While SMEs don't need mathematicians on their team, it is beneficial for them to understand the basic concepts of mathematics in artificial intelligence, as these foundations allow AI models to be accurate, efficient, and scalable. Understanding the mathematical concepts behind AI enables decision-makers to assess model performance and make informed adjustments to improve the accuracy and relevance of predictions.

By understanding the role of linear algebra in data representation, SMEs can optimize their data before inputting it into an AI model, improving efficiency and reducing processing time. Additionally, an understanding of differential calculus and optimization allows SMEs to adjust their models based on changes in data and the business environment, enhancing the adaptability and responsiveness of AI models to new opportunities and challenges.

AI offers SMEs a competitive advantage in an increasingly digitized and globalized market, and understanding the mathematical fundamentals of AI allows them to maximize that advantage. Well-tuned AI models enable SMEs to accurately forecast demand, efficiently manage resources, and improve the customer experience, resulting in sustainable growth and higher long-term profitability. Additionally, understanding the mathematical fundamentals allows SMEs to better evaluate AI solutions offered by third parties and make informed decisions about which tools and technologies are best suited for their business.

With a basic understanding of the mathematical concepts in AI, SMEs can fully leverage the opportunities offered by artificial intelligence to optimize their operations, improve customer experience, and stay competitive in a rapidly evolving environment.

5.6. Statistics in Artificial Intelligence

Statistics play a central role in artificial intelligence, being one of the fundamental bases of many of its applications, especially in the field of machine learning. In essence, AI relies on the ability of algorithms to analyze and learn from large volumes of data, and this is precisely where statistics provide their techniques and approaches to transform data into valuable insights. Statistics provide the framework for identifying patterns, making inferences, and creating predictive models that help AI systems make informed decisions.

In the context of machine learning, statistics allow algorithms to analyze structured and unstructured data effectively, interpreting patterns in a way that would be impossible for traditional methods. Through the use of statistical techniques, AI models can be adjusted to handle uncertainties, improve their accuracy, and make predictions in situations where data may be incomplete or noisy. For SMEs, the application of statistics-based AI is an opportunity to make informed, data-driven business decisions, covering everything from sales forecasting to inventory optimization and the personalization of marketing campaigns.

- **Applied Statistics in AI**

Statistics in AI not only allow algorithms to analyze data, but also provide a methodological foundation for evaluating the performance and accuracy of models. In machine learning, statistics are applied through various techniques that help algorithms identify meaningful relationships in the data and make predictions based on those relationships. Statistical techniques are especially useful for working with complex, high-dimensional data, where simplifying and selecting relevant variables is essential.

One of the most important applications of statistics in AI is uncertainty modeling. In situations where data is incomplete or noisy, AI models can use probabilities to quantify uncertainty and adjust their predictions accordingly. This allows AI algorithms to be more robust and adaptable to different types of data and environments. Statistical techniques also enable rigorous testing and evaluation of AI models, ensuring that predictions are accurate and reliable before implementation in the business environment.

In supervised machine learning, for example, statistics are used to train algorithms to recognize patterns in labeled data and then apply that knowledge to make predictions on new data. In unsupervised machine learning, statistical techniques help uncover hidden relationships in unlabeled data, which is key for tasks like customer segmentation and consumption pattern detection. These techniques, ranging from regression and probability to statistical inference, help SMEs gain a deeper understanding of their data and leverage business opportunities based on it.

- Probability

Probability is one of the key foundations in AI, especially when it comes to modeling uncertainty and making predictions. In the context of artificial intelligence, probability allows algorithms to handle scenarios where there is no absolute certainty about the outcomes, only possibilities and trends. Probability provides a framework for quantifying uncertainty in data and for assessing the confidence in the model's predictions.

Probability theory is used in AI to calculate the likelihood of certain events occurring based on historical data. For example, in a predictive marketing application, an AI model could calculate the probability of a customer making a purchase based on their previous behaviors and the buying patterns of similar customers. This allows companies to anticipate customer behavior and tailor their strategies according to the conversion probabilities.

A practical example of applying probability in AI is the use of Bayesian networks, which are probabilistic graphical models that represent the relationship between a set of random variables. Bayesian networks use probability to make inferences about uncertain or incomplete data and are especially useful in scenarios where it's necessary to combine different sources of information to make informed decisions. This approach allows AI models to adapt to changes in data and work under conditions of uncertainty, which is especially valuable for SMEs operating in variable and constantly changing markets.

Another key probabilistic approach in AI is the use of probability distributions to model data. Distributions allow us to describe variability in data and assign probabilities to different possible outcomes. Probability distributions, such as the normal distribution or the binomial distribution, are fundamental for understanding how data is distributed and for making inferences about it. In the context of SMEs, probability distributions can be used to forecast product demand, assess risk in investment decisions, and anticipate customer responses to different marketing strategies.

- **Regression**

Regression is an essential statistical technique in machine learning that allows models to identify relationships between variables and make predictions based on those relationships. In simple terms, regression helps predict a continuous value based on one or more input variables. There are several types of regression, such as linear regression, polynomial regression, and logistic regression, each applied depending on the nature of the data and the prediction objective.

Linear regression is one of the most common methods in AI and is especially useful when you want to predict a continuous variable based on one or more predictor variables. In the context of SMEs, linear regression can be used to forecast product sales based on factors such as price, advertising, and the time of year. This model aims to fit a line that minimizes the distance between the observed data points and the predicted values, allowing for accurate predictions based on the linear relationship between variables.

Polynomial regression is an extension of linear regression that allows for modeling non-linear relationships between variables. In situations where the relationship between variables is not linear, polynomial regression allows for fitting curves instead of straight lines, providing better accuracy in predictions. In business applications, polynomial regression can be useful for predicting complex phenomena that follow non-linear patterns, such as seasonal fluctuations in product demand.

Logistic regression, although technically not a regression model in the strictest sense, is another important AI technique used to predict binary or categorical outcomes. Unlike linear regression, which predicts a continuous value, logistic regression predicts the probability that an event will occur or not. For example, a company can use logistic regression to predict whether a customer will make a purchase or leave the website without completing the transaction. Logistic regression allows data to be classified into categories and is particularly useful in marketing applications and customer segmentation.

- Statistical inference

Statistical inference is the process of making generalizations about a population based on a data sample. In AI, statistical inference is crucial for analyzing data from a representative sample and drawing conclusions that can be applied to a broader dataset. Inference allows AI algorithms to make predictions and informed decisions based on the observed data, even when all possible data is not available.

One of the most common inference techniques in AI is the analysis of confidence intervals. Confidence intervals allow AI models to estimate the range within which the true values of the data are expected to fall with a certain level of confidence. This is useful for assessing the accuracy of predictions and understanding the uncertainty in the results. In business applications, confidence intervals enable SMEs to evaluate the level of confidence in sales forecasts or the effectiveness of a marketing campaign, helping to make decisions with a lower level of risk.

Another important statistical inference technique in AI is hypothesis testing, which is used to determine if there is a significant relationship between variables or if an observed difference in the data is statistically significant. Hypothesis tests allow AI models to evaluate the effectiveness of different strategies and make informed decisions based on the data results. In the context of SMEs, hypothesis testing can be used to assess the effectiveness of a new marketing strategy or to determine if a price change for a product has had a significant impact on sales.

- Importance for SMEs

Basic statistical knowledge is a powerful tool for entrepreneurs and SME managers, as it allows them to better understand the reports and results from AI models and make informed, data-driven decisions. Statistical techniques not only help interpret the results of AI models but also enable the evaluation of the accuracy and validity of predictions, which is essential to ensure that business strategies are well-founded.

For SMEs, applied statistics in AI allows them to optimize operations and improve competitiveness in a dynamic market. For example, by using regression models, SMEs can forecast sales trends and adjust inventory based on expected demand. Probability allows them to anticipate customer behavior and personalize marketing strategies based on conversion probabilities. Statistical inference enables them to evaluate the effectiveness of business strategies and adjust decisions based on the results obtained.

5.7. History and evolution of AI

The history of artificial intelligence is a fascinating journey spanning more than half a century, from its beginnings in theory and experimentation to its widespread adoption in everyday life and business. AI, both as a concept and a field of study, began with the ambition of emulating human intelligence and endowing machines with the ability to think and learn. Today, AI is present in virtually all sectors, and its advancements have been driven by significant improvements in computing power, the availability of massive data, and developments in learning algorithms. This journey has been marked by key milestones and a technological and theoretical evolution that has redefined what can be achieved with AI.

- **The first steps: Theoretical foundations and the beginnings of AI (1950s)**

The origin of modern AI can be traced back to the 1950s when scientists began exploring whether machines could emulate human cognitive functions such as reasoning and learning. One of the pioneers of this idea was Alan Turing, a British mathematician who in 1950 published an influential paper titled Computing Machinery and Intelligence. In this document, Turing posed one of the most fundamental questions: "Can machines think?" In the paper, Turing proposed the famous Turing Test, a test designed to determine whether a machine can exhibit intelligent behavior indistinguishable from that of a human. This idea laid the groundwork for future research and debates about machines' ability to think and learn.

In 1956, the term "artificial intelligence" was officially used for the first time at the Dartmouth Conference, a key event that brought together prominent scientists interested in developing intelligent machines. This event is considered the formal beginning of AI as a field of study. Several objectives were outlined, such as the development of algorithms capable of solving complex problems. During this period, progress was made in areas like problem-solving and symbol processing, which are essential in programming intelligent systems.

- ## The rise and expectations: 1960s to 1970s

In the 1960s and 70s, AI experienced a surge of interest and funding. Researchers were excited about the possibility of creating intelligent machines, and significant advances were made in areas such as natural language processing, computer vision, and expert systems. During these years, the first AI programs were developed that could play strategy games, like chess, and solve basic mathematical problems. One of the most well-known systems from this era was ELIZA, a natural language processing program designed by Joseph Weizenbaum that simulated a human conversation. Although rudimentary, ELIZA was one of the first systems to interact with users in a way that mimicked intelligence.

During this period, however, the limitations of AI technology at the time also began to show. The first AI systems, which were based on predefined rules rather than learning, required enormous amounts of time and computing power. Additionally, these systems struggled to solve complex real-world problems, causing the expectations of previous years to deflate. By the late 1970s, enthusiasm for AI waned due to these issues and the high cost of research projects, leading to what is known as the first 'AI winter.

- ## Advances in algorithms and the revival of AI: 1980 to 1990

In the 80s, AI experienced a renaissance driven in part by the development of expert systems, programs designed to simulate the decision-making of a human expert in a specific domain, such as medical diagnosis. Expert systems were successfully used in various industries, from medicine to finance, demonstrating that AI could be applied to solve specific problems effectively. During this period, more advanced machine learning algorithms were also created, such as artificial neural networks, which sought to mimic the functioning of the human brain. Although these models were still rudimentary compared to today's neural networks, their development marked an important milestone in AI.

However, the neural networks of that time also faced limitations, mainly in terms of computational power and processing capacity to handle large volumes of data. Without sufficient power to train deep and complex networks, these algorithms did not reach their full potential. Despite these challenges, interest in AI and machine learning continued to grow, and the theoretical foundations established during this period laid the groundwork for future advances.

- **The revolution of deep learning and Big Data: From 2000 to the present**

With the arrival of the Internet era and the explosion of digital data, the possibilities of AI expanded enormously. In the early 2000s, new technologies allowed AI to enter a phase of accelerated evolution. Two key factors contributed to the AI renaissance during this period: the increase in processing power thanks to graphics processing units (GPUs) and the availability of Big Data, which provided researchers with an unprecedented volume of information to train their algorithms.

One of the most important advances during this period was the development of deep learning, a subfield of machine learning that uses deep neural networks to analyze data more precisely and complexly than ever before. Unlike traditional neural networks, deep networks have multiple layers that allow them to learn complex data features without human intervention. In 2012, a notable breakthrough in deep learning was the AlexNet model, which significantly outperformed other models in an image recognition competition. This achievement spurred a new boom in AI, as it demonstrated that deep learning algorithms could outperform traditional methods in complex tasks.

Since then, deep learning has been applied to a wide range of areas, including natural language processing (NLP), computer vision, and autonomous decision-making. The commercial applications of AI also began to expand rapidly, with companies implementing AI in marketing, customer service, and operations management. AI became accessible not only to large companies but also to small and medium-sized enterprises thanks to cloud platforms and open-source libraries, which democratized access to this technology.

• AI Today: Mass Adoption and the Near Future

Today, AI is present in practically every sector of the economy, from healthcare and finance to logistics and retail. The applications of AI have grown enormously, and its adoption has accelerated with the development of accessible technologies and low-cost platforms that allow any company, regardless of size, to implement AI in their operations. In the healthcare sector, for example, AI is used to diagnose diseases, analyze medical images, and personalize treatments. In e-commerce, it is employed for personalized recommendations and chatbots that enhance the customer experience.

In addition to its adoption in the business world, AI has also started to play an important role in the daily lives of users. From virtual assistants like Siri and Alexa to navigation and real-time translation apps, AI is becoming increasingly common in people's lives. As AI continues to evolve, its role in society and business is expected to grow, especially in areas like robotics, autonomous driving, and the automation of administrative tasks.

In the near future, AI will continue to benefit from advances in processing capacity and learning models, such as generative models and general AI systems that have the potential to further improve the accuracy and versatility of intelligent systems. Researchers are also exploring methods to make AI models more explainable and transparent, which is crucial for increasing trust in these systems and for their adoption in sensitive sectors like finance and law.

The history of AI is, ultimately, a testament to the progress of technology and how the pioneering ideas of visionary scientists have led to systems that now impact every aspect of our lives. As technology continues to evolve, AI will continue to play a crucial role in the digital transformation of businesses, providing them with powerful tools to adapt and thrive in an increasingly data-driven world.

Chapter 6 - Machine Learning in SMEs

6.1. Introduction to predictive models: Practical applications in SMEs

Predictive models are powerful tools that allow businesses to anticipate future events based on historical data and behavioral patterns. For an SME, this forecasting ability can transform how decisions are made in critical areas like sales, marketing, inventory management, and customer loyalty. While it may seem like a technical concept reserved for large companies, the reality is that predictive models are accessible and applicable to businesses of any size. Using structured data and statistical algorithms, predictive models help answer fundamental questions about the future, from what the demand for a product will be next month to which customers are most likely to make a repeat purchase.

Unlike other methods that only describe or analyze the past, predictive models focus on forecasting future behaviors and outcomes based on observed trends. These models are not magic; they are statistical and mathematical tools that 'learn' patterns by analyzing large amounts of historical data. In its simplest form, a predictive model identifies the relationships between different variables and projects those patterns into the future, providing key insights for strategic decisions. For example, by analyzing past sales data, a predictive model can identify that certain products tend to have high demand during specific seasons and adjust stock projections accordingly.

For SMEs, predictive models offer a great opportunity for optimization in multiple areas. With sales forecasting models, for example, a small business can anticipate peak periods and prepare with the right resources, improving planning and reducing costs. In marketing and customer behavior, predictive models can help identify which customers are at risk of leaving, allowing the company to anticipate with personalized retention campaigns. Additionally, with inventory optimization based on predictions, an SME can avoid overstock or stockout issues by adjusting decisions to forecasted demand.

The accessibility of machine learning technologies and software tools like Python and libraries such as Scikit-Learn makes it easier for SMEs to implement these models in a practical way. These models offer the possibility to integrate predictive analysis into daily processes, resulting in continuous improvement in decision-making and business competitiveness.

- ## What is a predictive model?

A predictive model is a mathematical and statistical tool that allows companies to anticipate future events based on patterns observed in historical data. For an SME, this forecasting ability can be crucial in making strategic decisions, as it facilitates planning and allows them to react to possible scenarios with the necessary foresight to reduce risks or seize opportunities. In essence, predictive models don't predict the future in the sense of fortune-telling, but through rigorous data analysis, they identify recurring patterns and project those patterns into the future. This results in informed predictions based on previous trends that can be observed in the available data.

To understand how these models work, it's important to consider that they are based on the premise that certain behaviors tend to repeat over time, and by analyzing large amounts of past data, it's possible to discover relationships and patterns that can be used for making predictions. Predictive models use algorithms that process these data intensively, looking to identify relationships between different variables and using those relationships to make forecasts. For example, a sales predictive model can analyze how a company's sales have evolved over the past five years, taking into account factors such as marketing campaigns, seasonal changes, and economic conditions, and use that information to estimate sales behavior in the next quarter.

The historical database is essential for the model to learn. By being fed with previous data, the model detects patterns and trends, building a mathematical representation of the relationship between different variables. This learning process is known as model training, as the model 'learns' from the input data to make estimates about future data. It's important to highlight that, although these models can be very accurate in their predictions, they are not perfect or infallible. Their accuracy depends on several factors, such as the quality of the historical data, the choice of the right algorithm, and the amount of data available for training. The more data and better quality the model has, the greater its ability to capture underlying trends and make accurate predictions.

When explaining what a predictive model is, it's important to emphasize that these models are far from being a form of 'magic.' It's not a mystical or supernatural process; on the contrary, it is a strictly technical and mathematical process, applying statistical and probabilistic principles to detect patterns. A predictive model cannot anticipate events that don't have a basis in historical data; that is, it can only predict what shows some form of recurrence or regularity. If faced with a radical change that has no precedent in the data, the model won't be able to forecast it accurately. This limitation is inherent to all predictive models, so it's crucial to have realistic expectations about their capabilities and understand that their predictions are always subject to a margin of error.

There are different types of predictive models that adapt to various goals and types of data. Regression models are particularly useful when you want to predict a continuous numerical value, such as future sales of a product or the price of an asset in the market. On the other hand, classification models are more suitable for situations where you want to predict a category or label, such as whether a customer will leave a service or if a transaction is potentially fraudulent. Both types of models are applicable to specific situations and allow businesses to tailor their use according to their needs.

A clear example of the application of a predictive model is in forecasting a company's sales. Let's say an SME has sales data from the last five years and wants to predict demand for the next quarter. By feeding this data into a linear regression model, the model will identify relevant factors such as seasonal trends, sales spikes during specific marketing campaigns, or the effects of economic changes. Based on these factors, the model projects an estimate of future sales. This allows the company to plan its production and adjust its resources to efficiently meet the expected demand. Additionally, this type of model can be tuned and improved over time, as the system can be continuously updated with new data and recalibrated to better reflect the latest trends.

Another common use of predictive models is in customer segmentation and behavior prediction. A company using a classification model can segment its customers based on their purchasing behavior and predict, for example, which customers are most likely to make a repeat purchase or, conversely, those who might leave the brand. This prediction allows the company to carry out personalized retention campaigns, offering special incentives to customers at risk of leaving, or specific promotions to those showing interest in additional products. In this way, the company can maximize loyalty and optimize its marketing resources by focusing on the customers who truly need personalized attention to stay engaged with the brand.

Inventory optimization is another area where predictive models have a significant impact. An SME selling products with fluctuating demand can use a predictive model to anticipate restocking needs and avoid both excess inventory and stockouts. This type of model analyzes sales trends, identifies high-turnover products, and adjusts inventory forecasts based on seasonality and other demand factors. For example, a clothing store can predict which garments will be most in demand during the Christmas season, allowing it to adjust its inventory orders to meet that demand optimally. This type of automation not only saves costs but also improves business efficiency, as the company can avoid losses from excess inventory or missed sales due to stock shortages.

The process of developing a predictive model generally begins with the selection and preparation of data. This is an essential step, as the quality of the data directly affects the accuracy of the predictions. The data must be clean, structured, and representative of the situation you want to predict. For example, if an SME wants to forecast product demand, it will need historical sales data, as well as additional data on external factors that may influence it, such as marketing campaigns, special promotion dates, price variations, or even weather in specific cases. The model will process this data, assessing the importance of each factor in the prediction, and then adjust its parameters to reflect the relationships found in the data.

Once the data is ready, the next step is to select the right algorithm for the type of prediction needed. For numerical predictions, linear regression models, polynomial regression, and neural networks are often very effective. For category predictions, classification models like decision trees, random forests, and logistic regression are popular choices. Choosing the right model is crucial, as each algorithm has strengths and limitations that make it more suitable for certain types of data and specific problems. A classification model, for example, can be very effective in predicting customer churn, while a regression model is ideal for forecasting a product's future sales.

After selecting the algorithm, training the model is the stage where the system learns from historical data to make predictions. This training involves feeding the model a set of labeled data, meaning data where the outcomes are known. The model adjusts its internal parameters until its predictions closely match the actual results. This process can be repeated many times, optimizing the model with each iteration to improve its accuracy and minimize error. Finally, the model is evaluated on a test data set, allowing it to predict on unseen data. This validation step is essential to ensure that the model can generalize its predictions beyond the specific data it was trained on.

It is important to note that predictive models do not always offer 100% accurate predictions. Each prediction is associated with a degree of uncertainty, as the models are based on probabilities and historical trends that may change due to external or unexpected factors. A sales prediction model may estimate that a company will sell 10,000 units of a product next month, but if there is an unexpected change in consumer preferences or a new competitor arises, actual sales may differ significantly from the prediction. Despite this limitation, predictive models remain valuable tools because they provide a solid information base that allows companies to plan more accurately and respond more quickly to changes.

Another advantage of predictive models is their ability to improve over time. As new data is collected, the models can be updated and retrained to reflect the latest trends, continuously improving their accuracy. This process, known as continuous learning, allows models to adapt to changes in the environment and new situations that may arise. In an SME, this continuous learning capability is particularly useful, as it allows the company to respond swiftly to market changes and adjust its predictions according to the current reality.

In summary, a predictive model is a fundamental tool that relies on historical data to make projections about the future. By analyzing patterns and relationships between variables, these models provide businesses with foresight that allows them to make informed decisions and plan strategically. Although predictive models cannot foresee radical and unexpected changes, their ability to detect and project recurring trends makes them a key resource for improving efficiency, reducing risks, and seizing opportunities. For an SME, implementing these models represents an opportunity to compete on equal footing with larger companies, as it enables them to optimize resources and respond precisely to market demands.

- ## Practical application cases in SMEs

Prediction through predictive models represents a highly valuable tool for SMEs, as it allows them to anticipate product demand, better understand customer behavior, and manage inventories more efficiently. In an increasingly competitive market, having the ability to foresee the future based on historical data and known patterns becomes a strategic advantage. Predictive models enable companies not only to save on operational costs but also to improve customer experience, optimize their resources, and increase profitability. Let's explore three key applications for SMEs: sales prediction, customer behavior prediction, and inventory optimization.

- ### Sales Forecasting

For any SME, the ability to forecast future sales is a fundamental aspect of planning and resource allocation. By analyzing historical sales data, past marketing campaigns, and seasonal patterns, predictive models allow you to estimate future product demand, making it easier to prepare suitable strategies during high-demand periods.

- Black Friday and Christmas campaigns: During Black Friday and the Christmas season, sales usually experience significant peaks, and accurate forecasting can be crucial to responding to this demand. For example, an electronics store that has collected sales data over the past three years could analyze how sales varied each Black Friday and use a linear regression model to forecast sales for the next period. This model will consider factors such as the effectiveness of discount campaigns, the most popular products during those dates, and customer responses in previous years. With this prediction, the store can ensure it has the necessary inventory, avoid losses due to stockouts, and capitalize on the moment to the fullest.

- Seasonal promotions: For businesses whose products are sensitive to seasonality, such as clothing stores or garden product retailers, sales forecasting becomes a key tool. Imagine a garden store that sees an increase in demand for plants and accessories during the spring. By analyzing previous sales data, the predictive model can help project how many products will be sold in the upcoming season. This allows for proactive planning, avoiding both product shortages and overstock, optimizing resources, and ensuring a quick response to customer needs at the right time.

- New product launches: SMEs looking to introduce new products to the market can also benefit from predictive models. A practical example is a cosmetics store that, after launching a new product line, can analyse initial sales and customer response during the first few weeks. By feeding this data into a machine learning model, the store can adjust sales projections for the following months, thus managing its inventory and tailoring marketing campaigns according to estimated demand. This approach reduces the risks associated with product launches and allows the company to adjust its strategy based on the real market reaction.

- **Customer Behavior Prediction**

Understanding customer behavior and anticipating their actions is essential to improving relationships, fostering loyalty, and increasing repeat sales. Predicting customer behavior through classification models allows SMEs to identify which customers are more likely to make a repeat purchase or, conversely, to leave the brand. This predictive segmentation is key to designing more personalized and effective retention campaigns.

- Customer segmentation and retention campaigns: Imagine a subscription service SME that wants to prevent customers from leaving the service (a phenomenon known as churn). By analyzing historical behavioral data, such as service usage frequency, customer service interactions, and participation in promotions, a classification model can help identify the factors contributing to churn. This model can predict which customers are at risk of leaving and classify each customer based on their likelihood of churn. The company can then design a personalized retention campaign offering incentives to high-risk customers, thereby improving retention rates and strengthening customer relationships.

- Loyalty campaigns: For SMEs in the retail sector, such as a fashion store, customer loyalty is essential. A predictive model that analyzes purchase behavior and the interaction history of each customer can help segment customers into different categories: frequent buyers, seasonal buyers, new customers, and inactive customers. Based on this segmentation, the store can design specific loyalty campaigns for each group. For example, frequent buyers can be offered exclusive discounts to maintain their loyalty, while inactive customers can be sent a special offer to encourage them to return to the store. This prediction-based approach allows for personalized marketing campaigns and maximizes the effectiveness of promotions.

- Personalized offers and product recommendations: SMEs with a large product catalog can use predictive models to recommend relevant products to each customer based on their past purchases and preferences. For example, an e-commerce site selling tech products could use a supervised learning model to analyze previous purchases and recommend accessories or complementary products. If a customer buys a mobile phone, the system could suggest a protective case or a wireless charger, increasing cross-selling opportunities. This type of prediction not only enhances the customer experience but also increases the average purchase value, optimizing sales opportunities.

  ▪ **Inventory Optimization**

Inventory management is a critical aspect for any SME, as the balance between maintaining enough stock and avoiding excess inventory can directly influence the business's profitability. Predictive models allow you to anticipate which products will have higher demand and when, thus facilitating efficient inventory management and reducing the costs associated with overstock or stock shortages.

- Anticipated restocking: An SME using predictive models for inventory management can anticipate product shortages based on past sales patterns. For example, a grocery store could analyze its sales data to predict the demand for staples like milk, bread, and fresh produce. A predictive model that analyzes daily demand can alert the purchasing team when a product is close to running out, allowing them to place an order in time to avoid shortages and meet demand without interruptions.

- Storage cost reduction: Keeping an excessive inventory involves storage costs that many SMEs cannot afford. For a bookstore, for example, anticipating periods of lower demand can make a big difference in terms of costs. By analyzing sales data from previous years and business seasonality, the bookstore can use a prediction model to adjust its orders and reduce inventory during low-demand periods. This inventory optimization allows for reduced storage costs while maintaining the availability of the most in-demand titles each season.

- Inventory management in ecommerce: SMEs selling products on ecommerce platforms must ensure that their inventory always reflects real availability, avoiding sales of out-of-stock products. A fashion ecommerce, for example, can use a predictive model to manage inventory in real time. By analyzing historical sales and purchasing behavior on the platform, the model can forecast demand for each item and update inventory dynamically. Thus, if a high-demand item starts to run out, the system sends an alert for the purchasing team to restock in a timely manner. This approach not only optimizes inventory but also improves the customer experience by ensuring the availability of popular products.

Each of these examples shows how predictive models can be applied in key areas of a SME's operations, facilitating data-driven decision-making and improving both internal efficiency and customer satisfaction. From sales prediction and customer behavior to inventory optimization, these models help SMEs adapt to market needs, maximize their resources, and build a competitive advantage in their sector. By automating and personalizing their strategies through informed predictions, SMEs can make proactive decisions that lead to sustainable growth and long-term customer relationships.

- ## Difference between classification and regression models

Classification and regression models are two main types of predictive models used in machine learning and data science to make forecasts and solve specific problems based on available data. Both models are based on mathematical and statistical principles that allow for the identification of patterns in historical data and making informed predictions. However, the goals and approaches of these models are different. While regression models focus on predicting continuous numerical values, such as sales volume or product price, classification models aim to assign labels or categories to data, such as determining whether a customer will churn or if a transaction is fraudulent.

▪ Regression Models

A regression model is a type of predictive model used to predict continuous or quantitative values. These values are numerical and can take on a wide range of values within an interval. Regression is based on analyzing the relationship between a dependent variable and one or more independent variables. In this context, the dependent variable is the value you want to predict, while the independent variables are the factors that influence that prediction. Regression models aim to establish a mathematical relationship between these variables, and by doing so, they allow us to estimate the value of the dependent variable based on the values of the independent variables.

For example, if an SME wants to forecast the sales amount of a product for the next quarter, they can use a regression model to analyze historical sales data, considering factors like marketing campaigns, seasonal variations, and past promotions. The model will generate a mathematical function that relates these factors to sales, and using that function, the company can estimate how much it will sell in the future.

There are various types of regression models, and each is suitable for different types of data and problems. Some of the most common regression models include:

- Linear Regression: Linear regression is one of the simplest and most widely used regression models. This model assumes that there is a linear relationship between the dependent variable and the independent variables, meaning that as an independent variable increases or decreases, the dependent variable changes proportionally. Linear regression is useful for situations where the relationship between variables is approximately linear, such as predicting sales based on advertising investment or estimating the price of a product based on its features.

- Polynomial Regression: Unlike linear regression, polynomial regression allows for modeling non-linear relationships between the dependent variable and the independent variables. This model is useful when data shows curved or complex patterns that cannot be captured by a straight line. Polynomial regression is used in cases where data trends are more complex and require a more flexible fit.

- Logarithmic and Exponential Regression: Logarithmic and exponential regression models are applied when the relationship between variables follows a growth or decay curve. These models are useful for analyzing data that grows rapidly at first and then stabilizes over time, or vice versa. In the case of an SME, these models could be useful for predicting the adoption of a new product in the market, where sales might increase rapidly at first and then level off.

- Multiple Regression: Multiple regression is used when there are several independent variables influencing the dependent variable. For example, if an SME wants to predict product sales, it can consider multiple factors such as price, seasonality, and marketing campaigns. Multiple regression analyzes how each of these variables affects the final value and generates a function that relates all the variables to the projected sales.

Regression models are essential in business because they allow you to quantify and forecast specific results. In an SME, this type of model can be used to predict product demand, production costs, or the budget needed for an advertising campaign. The ability to predict continuous values enables companies to plan accurately, optimize resources, and make decisions based on grounded projections.

- **Classification Models**

Unlike regression models, classification models do not focus on predicting a numerical value, but rather on assigning categories or labels to the data. The goal of a classification model is to determine which group or class a data set belongs to. This type of model is particularly useful in situations where decisions need to be made based on specific characteristics and each entry must be classified into a defined category. For example, an SME can use a classification model to predict if a customer will leave the service or if a transaction is potentially fraudulent.

Classification models work by analyzing patterns in the data and, based on these patterns, assign a label to each new piece of data. To train a classification model, a labeled dataset is used where each example is associated with a known category or class. The model learns to recognize the features that define each class and can then use that knowledge to classify new data.

There are different types of classification models, each with specific approaches and algorithms:

- Logistic Regression: Although its name includes the word "regression," logistic regression is actually a classification model. This model is used to predict the probability that an observation belongs to a specific class. Logistic regression is particularly useful for binary classification problems, such as predicting whether a customer will churn or not. This model calculates a probability between 0 and 1 and classifies the observation based on a predetermined threshold.

- Decision Trees: Decision trees are classification models that split data into groups using decision rules in a tree-like structure. At each step of the tree, the model selects the variable that best separates the data based on the target class. This model is easy to interpret and clearly visualizes how decisions are made at each level. It is useful for cases where a clear interpretation of classification rules is needed.

- Random Forests: Random forests are an extension of decision trees and consist of a set of decision trees working together. Each tree makes decisions based on a random sample of the data, and the forest ultimately combines the decisions of all the trees to achieve an accurate classification. Random forests are effective in complex problems and are resistant to overfitting, as they promote a balanced classification based on multiple perspectives.

- Support Vector Machines (SVM): SVMs are classification models that aim to separate data classes using a line or hyperplane that maximizes the distance between groups. This model is suitable for problems where the classes are clearly separable, and its goal is to find the optimal boundary for accurate classification. SVMs are particularly useful in high-dimensional problems.

- Neural Networks: Neural networks are advanced classification models that can learn complex patterns in data through multiple layers of processing. These models are useful in classification problems where there are multiple variables and non-linear patterns that require precise tuning. Neural networks are applied in problems such as predicting the likelihood of customer churn or detecting fraud.

- **Key Differences Between Regression and Classification Models**

The main difference between regression and classification models lies in the type of prediction they make and the results they generate. While regression models focus on estimating continuous numerical values, classification models aim to assign categories or labels to the data. This difference is fundamental as it defines the type of problem each model can solve and the type of data it needs for training.

Regression models are usually more suitable for problems where the goal is to predict a numerical value, such as projected sales or the price of a product. On the other hand, classification models are ideal for problems where decisions need to be made based on categories, such as determining whether a customer will make a purchase or if a credit application is high or low risk.

In terms of interpretation and business use, regression and classification models have distinct applications. Regression models provide a concrete value that can be used in financial analysis and operational planning. For example, an SME using a regression model to forecast future sales of a specific product can make inventory decisions and allocate resources based on the predicted value. On the other hand, classification models generate a category or label that can be used in strategic decision-making. For instance, a service company can use a classification model to identify customers who are most likely to cancel their subscription, thereby designing a personalized retention campaign.

Another significant difference between regression and classification models is the type of evaluation used to measure the model's accuracy. In regression models, metrics such as Mean Squared Error (MSE) and R^2 are used, which measure the distance between predicted and actual values. These metrics allow us to assess how well the model fits the data and whether the predictions are accurate enough. In classification models, evaluation metrics include precision, recall, F1-score, and the confusion matrix, which measure the model's ability to correctly classify data into the corresponding categories. These metrics help evaluate whether the classification model is effective in predicting labels and can correctly identify the relevant classes.

- **Practical Applications in SMEs**

The practical applications of regression and classification models are diverse and offer SMEs the opportunity to optimize their operations and improve their business strategies through informed predictions.

For regression models:

- SMEs can use regression models to forecast future sales based on historical data and plan production and inventory. This allows the company to ensure an adequate supply of products and improve operational efficiency.

- Service companies can use regression models to estimate the budget needed for advertising campaigns based on the relationship between marketing investment and revenue. This approach helps optimize resources and maximize return on investment.

- Regression models can also be used to predict production costs based on raw material prices and other inputs. This allows SMEs to calculate their costs accurately and adjust sales prices according to projections.

For classification models:

- SMEs can use classification models to identify customers at high risk of churn and design personalized retention campaigns. This allows the company to reduce churn rates and increase loyalty.

- Companies managing ecommerce platforms can use classification models to detect fraudulent transactions and avoid financial losses. By analyzing the characteristics of each transaction, the model can identify fraud patterns and alert the security team.

- SMEs that want to segment their customers into different groups based on their behavior can use classification models to identify profitable customers, frequent customers, and inactive customers. This segmentation allows for the design of personalized marketing strategies and promotions for each group, optimizing results.

In conclusion, the choice between regression and classification models depends on the type of problem a SME wants to solve and the specific results it seeks to achieve. While regression models provide quantitative and continuous values, classification models allow data to be labeled and strategic decisions to be made based on categories. Both models offer companies an opportunity to improve their processes and make data-driven decisions, which contributes to sustainable growth and better management of business resources.

6.2. Sales and Customer Behavior Prediction with Scikit-Learn

Sales and customer behavior prediction is a key strategy for SMEs looking to anticipate customer needs, optimize operations, and improve decision-making. These predictions can help companies adjust their inventory, plan more effective marketing campaigns, and personalize their customer retention strategies. Scikit-Learn, one of the most comprehensive and accessible machine learning libraries in Python, is a powerful tool for building predictive models that allow SMEs to leverage the value of their data. Scikit-Learn offers a wide variety of machine learning algorithms for classification, regression, and clustering tasks, making it a versatile option for both novice and advanced users.

One of the biggest advantages of Scikit-Learn is its simplicity and ease of use. The library is designed so that even those without a deep knowledge of machine learning can implement it. Scikit-Learn provides intuitive user interfaces and a modular structure that makes it easy to create, train, and validate models quickly. For advanced users, it offers tools to fine-tune complex models and work with large volumes of data. From basic models like linear regression to advanced algorithms like random forests and support vector machines, Scikit-Learn covers a wide range of needs for companies wanting to leverage predictive analytics.

For an SME, Scikit-Learn allows you to create sales prediction models that help estimate future demand based on historical patterns, such as seasonality, past promotions, and other relevant factors. These models not only allow you to forecast sales but also identify the key factors influencing demand fluctuations. Additionally, Scikit-Learn facilitates customer segmentation through classification models, enabling you to predict customer behavior, such as the likelihood of churn or lead conversion probability. This is crucial for personalizing marketing and retention campaigns and for optimizing resources focused on customers with the highest growth potential.

In this chapter, we will analyze the key steps to build a sales prediction model with Scikit-Learn, from feature selection and data preprocessing to training a regression model. It will also explain how to use classification models to segment customers based on their historical behavior, and explore practical examples such as churn prediction and lead conversion. Finally, it will show how transactional data can be analyzed to identify patterns of repeat purchases, allowing SMEs to customize their marketing strategies and improve the customer experience.

- ## Introduction to Scikit-Learn

Scikit-Learn is one of the most popular and powerful libraries for implementing predictive models in Python, widely used in the fields of data science and machine learning due to its flexibility, accessibility, and ability to solve a variety of complex problems. Developed as an open-source library, Scikit-Learn provides a wide range of machine learning algorithms and tools for data preprocessing, feature selection, model evaluation, and parameter tuning. This combination of features makes it an indispensable tool for both beginners and advanced users looking to implement predictive models efficiently and effectively.

One of the main advantages of Scikit-Learn is that it is designed to be easy to use and accessible for those without a deep understanding of machine learning. The simplicity of its user interface allows beginners to apply complex algorithms without needing extensive training in advanced mathematics or statistics. At the same time, it offers great flexibility and depth, which is useful for advanced users who want to customize their models and make specific adjustments in their analyses. The library follows a clear and consistent structure, where each algorithm and machine learning method is designed to be intuitive and easy to apply. This allows users to quickly become familiar with the functions and adapt them to their needs without the steep learning curve that many other machine learning tools require.

Scikit-Learn is particularly powerful in implementing predictive models, which is key for SMEs and companies looking to apply machine learning in their operations without the need for sophisticated technological resources. This library includes a wide range of regression, classification, clustering, and dimensionality reduction algorithms, making it easy to apply to different types of problems. For example, a company can use linear regression models to forecast future sales based on historical data patterns, or use classification algorithms like random forests or support vector machines to segment customers and analyze their behavior. The versatility of Scikit-Learn allows the same organization to implement models in various areas of their business without needing to switch tools or invest in expensive software.

A fundamental feature of Scikit-Learn is its ability to integrate with other popular Python libraries, such as NumPy, Pandas, and Matplotlib. These integrations allow users to manipulate and visualize data efficiently, which is essential in the preprocessing and analysis stages before building models. NumPy is ideal for handling large volumes of numerical data, while Pandas organizes this data into DataFrame structures, making exploration and analysis easier. On the other hand, Matplotlib creates charts and visualizations that help better understand the data and identify patterns that may be relevant for modeling. This synergy between libraries not only streamlines the workflow for data scientists but also allows users to conduct a complete and detailed analysis at every stage of the project, from initial data exploration to interpreting the results.

Another advantage of Scikit-Learn is its ability to simplify data preprocessing, a crucial stage in building machine learning models. Data in its raw state often contains noise, outliers, or is on different scales, which can affect the model's performance if not corrected. Scikit-Learn provides tools for normalizing, standardizing, and handling missing values, as well as allowing feature selection and dimensionality reduction. These steps are important for optimizing model performance and ensuring that only the most relevant variables are included in the analysis. Normalization and standardization, for example, are techniques that adjust the data scales to have a uniform distribution, improving the performance of algorithms sensitive to the magnitude of variables, such as distance-based models, and enabling the model to function more efficiently and accurately.

Scikit-Learn also stands out for its advanced model validation and evaluation options, which are essential to ensure that predictive models are highly accurate and generalizable to new data. The library offers several cross-validation tools that allow you to evaluate a model's performance on multiple data subsets. Cross-validation is crucial to avoid overfitting, a common problem in machine learning where the model fits too closely to the training data and loses its ability to generalize. Scikit-Learn makes this process easier by offering methods like KFold and StratifiedKFold, which systematically split the data, providing more reliable estimates of the model's ability to make predictions on new data. In addition, evaluation metrics such as mean squared error (MSE) for regression and accuracy or F1-score for classification allow you to measure model performance and compare different algorithms to choose the most suitable one.

For SMEs and other organizations looking to obtain practical and applicable predictions, Scikit-Learn allows automating hyperparameter tuning with the GridSearchCV tool. Hyperparameter tuning is the process of optimizing the model's configurations to maximize its accuracy and performance. This manual tuning is often tedious and time-consuming, but Scikit-Learn simplifies the process by offering a systematic approach to searching for model parameter values to identify the combination that maximizes performance on the dataset. GridSearchCV tests various parameter combinations and selects the best configuration according to the defined evaluation metrics. This functionality not only improves model efficiency but also allows users to make adjustments without the need for complex manual intervention.

In addition to its ability to build and train models, Scikit-Learn facilitates the creation of pipelines, which are automated processing sequences that combine all the necessary steps for building and evaluating a model. Pipelines simplify the workflow by combining preprocessing, feature selection, model tuning, and evaluation into a single process. This approach is particularly useful in machine learning projects that require several steps before reaching the final model. Instead of processing each stage separately, Scikit-Learn pipelines allow all steps to be performed together, minimizing errors and making the model more replicable. For an SME, pipelines can reduce the time and effort required to implement predictive models, optimizing resources and allowing more time to be spent on interpreting and applying the results.

Scikit-Learn offers a wide variety of machine learning algorithms, both supervised and unsupervised, allowing you to adapt the type of model to the data and the needs of the company. In supervised learning, where labeled data is used, the library provides classification algorithms such as logistic regression and random forests, as well as regression models like linear regression and polynomial regression. These algorithms are useful for problems where the desired outcome is known, such as predicting product sales or identifying the type of customer most likely to make a purchase. In unsupervised learning, where there are no labels and the goal is to find patterns within the data, Scikit-Learn offers clustering and dimensionality reduction algorithms, such as the K-means clustering algorithm and principal component analysis (PCA). These models are useful for segmenting customers, identifying behavior patterns, and simplifying data before building a predictive model.

For companies that require segmentation and customer behavior analysis, Scikit-Learn offers classification algorithms that allow them to identify specific groups of customers based on their characteristics and behaviors. Logistic regression, decision trees, and random forests are powerful classification tools that enable the analysis of large volumes of customer data and the accurate assignment of labels. For example, an ecommerce company can use these algorithms to identify customers who are more likely to make repeat purchases or those who have a high probability of churning. This analysis allows the company to design more effective and personalized marketing campaigns, focusing on customer segments with the greatest growth potential or at risk of leaving.

Another notable aspect of Scikit-Learn is its comprehensive documentation and support from an active community. The Scikit-Learn documentation includes practical examples and step-by-step guides for implementing each available model and method, making it easy to learn and apply the library for users of all levels. Additionally, the active community of developers and users who work with Scikit-Learn constantly contributes tutorials, articles, and solutions to common problems, enriching the learning experience and allowing users to quickly resolve doubts. This community has made Scikit-Learn not only a powerful tool but also a continuous learning platform for those who want to expand their knowledge in machine learning.

In terms of implementation in real projects, Scikit-Learn allows users to perform predictive analysis in different areas of business, from marketing to inventory management. Sales prediction models and customer behavior analysis are two common applications where Scikit-Learn demonstrates its versatility and power. These models can be implemented at any stage of the business cycle to improve planning, optimize resources, and maximize growth opportunities. For example, an SME that wants to anticipate product demand during a Black Friday campaign can use Scikit-Learn to build a regression model that estimates future sales based on data from previous campaigns. This allows them to prepare their inventory and adjust their marketing strategy to make the most of the increase in demand.

Scikit-Learn's accessibility and focus on usability have made it possible for artificial intelligence and machine learning to be applicable in businesses of any size, including SMEs that do not have extensive data science teams. Its ease of integration into existing platforms and workflows allows even the smallest organizations to implement machine learning models without incurring high costs. By offering a variety of algorithms and tools for parameter tuning and evaluation, Scikit-Learn democratizes access to predictive analysis, enabling companies to adopt advanced machine learning practices without the need for complex infrastructure or deep technical knowledge.

Scikit-Learn is also designed to facilitate the implementation and scalability of models in production, which means that companies can integrate their predictive models into real-time systems, such as ecommerce platforms, CRMs, and ERPs. Thanks to its compatibility with tools like Flask and Django, Scikit-Learn allows the development of web applications that run predictive models continuously, updating predictions based on new data and enabling companies to make real-time decisions. This scalability is crucial for SMEs that want to incorporate machine learning into their business processes in an agile way, optimizing both operational and strategic decision-making.

In summary, Scikit-Learn is a machine learning library in Python that combines accessibility, power, and flexibility, making it an ideal choice for implementing predictive models in SMEs. Its ability to integrate with other Python tools, its variety of algorithms, and its focus on simplicity allow companies to build effective predictive models without requiring deep technical training. Additionally, its extensive documentation and support from an active community make it an accessible and useful tool for any user wishing to apply machine learning in their organization. Scikit-Learn offers a full range of advanced solutions that allow for everything from creating basic models to implementing automated and scalable workflows, providing companies with the ability to predict, optimize, and improve their processes using real-time data.

- **Building a Simple Sales Prediction Model**

Building a sales prediction model using Scikit-Learn allows businesses to anticipate product demand, better manage resources, and optimize decision-making in their daily operations. This section will guide the reader through the steps required to develop a sales prediction model in Python with Scikit-Learn, covering feature selection, data preprocessing, and training a linear regression model. This approach provides a solid foundation that any company, regardless of size, can adapt to improve the accuracy of their predictions and ensure optimal inventory and production management.

- **Feature selection**

Feature selection is one of the first steps in building any predictive model. In the context of a sales prediction model, features are the data containing relevant information to forecast future sales. The choice of these features can significantly influence the model's accuracy, as they determine the factors the model will use to learn patterns and make predictions.

For an effective sales prediction, it's crucial to identify the most relevant features. These can include a variety of data, such as:

- Historical sales: This data is essential, as it allows the model to learn patterns over time. The time series of past sales can reflect both general trends and specific fluctuations, providing the model with a solid foundation to estimate future sales. You can include daily, weekly, or monthly sales, depending on the granularity of the analysis.

- Public holidays and special events: Sales are often influenced by seasonal factors and special events, such as Christmas holidays, Black Friday, and other festivities. Including these dates as features in the model allows it to adjust predictions based on seasonality, which is especially useful for businesses that experience sales peaks at certain times of the year.

- Marketing campaigns: Marketing and promotional activities also have a direct impact on sales. By including features that represent marketing campaigns (e.g., a binary variable indicating whether there was a campaign during a specific week), the model can capture the effect of these campaigns on sales.

- Seasonality: In addition to holidays, some products or services exhibit broader seasonal patterns. For example, a clothing store may see sales peaks in summer and winter. By including a feature that reflects the season or month, the model can adjust predictions to account for these seasonal demand patterns.

- Economic variables: External data, such as consumer confidence index, unemployment rate, or interest rate, can indirectly affect a company's sales. Although not always necessary, these features can add value, especially in long-term forecasting models.

To select the right features, you can perform a preliminary correlation analysis to identify which ones are most related to sales. Tools like Pandas and Matplotlib are useful for this analysis, as they allow you to visualize the relationship between variables and better understand how each feature might influence the model.

Data preprocessing

Data preprocessing is a crucial stage in building any machine learning model, as raw data often contains noise, outliers, or is on different scales. The goal of preprocessing is to prepare the data so the model can interpret it effectively, which often results in improved performance and accuracy. In this case, preprocessing will include cleaning, normalizing, and standardizing the data, as well as creating time variables.

Data cleaning

Before starting to train the model, it is important to ensure that the data is complete and does not contain missing or duplicate values. In Python, the Pandas library provides tools to identify and manage null values. In the case of missing values, you can apply imputation techniques (for example, replacing missing values with the mean or median of the series) or remove incomplete rows, depending on the context and the amount of data available. The goal is to ensure that the dataset is complete and representative of the company's reality.

Creating time variables

To capture seasonality and other time patterns, it's useful to transform the date into additional features that can help the model identify temporal patterns. For example, you can break down the date into month, week of the year, or day of the week to reflect how sales vary in different time periods. Additionally, you can create binary variables indicating whether the date corresponds to a holiday or a special campaign, allowing the model to adjust its predictions based on these events.

- **Normalization and standardization**

Normalization and standardization are techniques used to adjust the scale of data, especially when features have different units or value ranges. Normalization scales values to a specific range (usually between 0 and 1), while standardization adjusts data to have a mean of 0 and a standard deviation of 1. Scikit-Learn provides simple functions to apply these transformations using the MinMaxScaler and StandardScaler methods. The choice between normalization and standardization will depend on the algorithm being used; in the case of linear regression, standardization is generally a good option as it helps the model converge more quickly during training.

- **Encoding categorical variables**

In some cases, the features may include categorical variables, such as types of marketing campaigns or seasons. Since most machine learning algorithms require numerical data, it's necessary to convert these categories into numerical values through a process known as encoding. Scikit-Learn offers the OneHotEncoder method to perform this encoding, which transforms each category into a separate binary column. This allows the model to use the categories as features without introducing biases or incorrect interpretations.

- **Training a linear regression model**

Once the features have been selected and preprocessed, the next step is to train a linear regression model using Scikit-Learn. Linear regression is a simple yet effective statistical method for predicting continuous values, and in this case, it is ideal for forecasting sales. Linear regression assumes a linear relationship between the features and the target variable (in this case, sales), allowing the model to fit a straight line that minimizes the error between predictions and actual values.

- **Import and split the data**

To train the model, it's important to split the dataset into two parts: a training set and a test set. This division allows the model to learn from one part of the data and be evaluated on performance with data it hasn't seen during training. Scikit-Learn makes this division easy with the train_test_split method, allowing you to specify the proportion of data allocated to each set (for example, 80% for training and 20% for testing).

```
# X: Características
X = [
    [300, 2, 5, 200, 1], # Día con 300 clientes, 2 promociones, 5 productos nuevos, 200 visitas web, y 1 evento especial
    [250, 1, 3, 180, 0],
    [280, 3, 6, 210, 1],
    [220, 1, 2, 160, 0],
    [310, 4, 7, 230, 1],
    [260, 2, 4, 190, 0],
    [290, 3, 5, 200, 1],
    [240, 1, 3, 170, 0],
    [320, 4, 6, 220, 1],
    [270, 2, 4, 180, 0]
]

# y: Variable de destino (ventas en euros)
y = [5000, 4000, 5200, 3900, 5600, 4500, 5300, 4100, 5800, 4700]
```
```
from sklearn.model_selection import train_test_split

# Supongamos que X son las características y y es la variable de destino (ventas)
X_train, X_test, y_train, y_test = train_test_split(X, y, test_size=0.2, random_state=42)
```

- Training the linear regression model

With the training set ready, it's possible to train the linear regression model. Scikit-Learn provides a linear regression implementation through the LinearRegression method, which fits a straight line to the training data by minimizing the sum of squared errors. Once trained, the model can make predictions based on the input features.

```
from sklearn.linear_model import LinearRegression

# Crear el modelo de regresión lineal
modelo = LinearRegression()

# Entrenar el modelo con los datos de entrenamiento
modelo.fit(X_train, y_train)
```

- Model Evaluation

Once the model is trained, it is important to evaluate its accuracy using the test set. The evaluation allows us to measure how well the model has learned and whether its predictions are accurate. In the case of linear regression, a commonly used metric is the Mean Squared Error (MSE), which measures the average of the squared errors between predictions and actual values. Scikit-Learn offers the mean_squared_error method to calculate the MSE easily.

287

```
from sklearn.metrics import mean_squared_error

# Realizar predicciones con el conjunto de prueba
predicciones = modelo.predict(X_test)

# Calcular el error cuadrático medio
mse = mean_squared_error(y_test, predicciones)
print(f"Error cuadrático medio: {mse}")
```

`[11]` ✓ 0.0s

··· Error cuadrático medio: 3182.3216137248887

- **Interpretation of results and adjustments**

The MSE provides an indication of the model's accuracy, and a low MSE value indicates that the predictions are close to the actual values. However, the interpretation of this value also depends on the magnitude of the data and the expected level of precision. If the error is too high, it is possible to adjust the model by trying different features, preprocessing techniques, or even using more advanced models, such as polynomial regression or decision trees.

- **Future predictions with the model**

Once the model is evaluated, it can be used to make predictions with future data. This is especially useful for forecasting sales in specific periods and for making more informed business planning. To make predictions with future data, it's necessary to create a set of features that represent the conditions of the future period, such as the date, special events, and any other relevant factors.

```
# Crear un nuevo conjunto de datos para predicciones futuras
X_nuevo = [
    [310, 3, 5, 210, 1],  # Día futuro con 310 clientes, 3 promociones, 5 productos nuevos, 210 visitas, y 1 evento especial.
    [280, 2, 4, 190, 0],  # Día futuro con 280 clientes, 2 promociones, 4 productos nuevos, 190 visitas, sin evento especial.
    [330, 4, 6, 220, 1],  # Día futuro con 330 clientes, 4 promociones, 6 productos nuevos, 220 visitas, y 1 evento especial.
    [260, 1, 3, 180, 0],  # Día futuro con 260 clientes, 1 promoción, 3 productos nuevos, 180 visitas, sin evento especial.
    [300, 3, 5, 200, 1]   # Día futuro con 300 clientes, 3 promociones, 5 productos nuevos, 200 visitas, y 1 evento especial.
]

# Supongamos que X_nuevo contiene las características futuras
predicciones_futuras = modelo.predict(X_nuevo)
```

`[17]` ✓ 0.0s

With the future predictions generated, the company can make informed decisions in areas such as inventory, production, and marketing campaigns, ensuring it is prepared to respond to expected demand.

To do this, we can visualize it as follows to make those decisions:

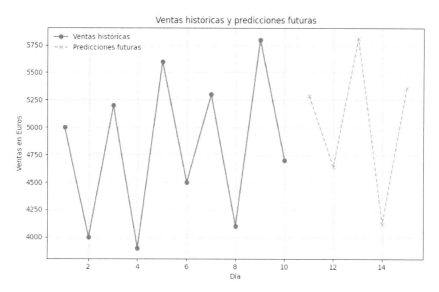

We have generated a combined visualization of historical sales and future predictions, which allows for a clear comparison between actual data and the model's projections. The blue line represents historical sales, showing past sales behavior, while the red, dashed line shows the predictions for future days. This visualization helps to interpret more tangibly how the model anticipates sales trends, whether indicating possible increases, decreases, or stabilization of demand during the analyzed period. The markers on each point also allow for precise evaluation of daily sales and comparison of the predictions against historical data.

By looking at the resulting graph, the company can understand how its prediction model fits reality and how it anticipates future demand. This comparison between past data and projections provides the team with an informed perspective on sales trends, which is crucial for optimizing decisions in key areas such as inventory adjustment, production planning, or designing marketing campaigns for strategic dates.

In summary, developing a sales prediction model with Scikit-Learn allows companies to accurately and efficiently anticipate demand. By selecting relevant features, proper preprocessing, and training a linear regression model, SMEs can optimize their operations and improve their ability to make data-driven strategic decisions.

• Customer segmentation with classification models

Customer segmentation using classification models is a key tool that enables SMEs to better understand their customers' behavior and make informed decisions to improve loyalty and optimize marketing campaigns. These classification models allow the analysis of historical behavior patterns and classify customers based on their likelihood of taking specific actions, such as churning or becoming customers after showing interest. The ability to anticipate these behaviors is invaluable, as it allows companies to tailor their retention and conversion strategies, improving the effectiveness of their efforts and maximizing available resources.

Here are two of the most common applications of classification models in customer segmentation for SMEs: churn prediction and lead conversion prediction. These applications offer great potential to increase profitability and efficiency in marketing and sales operations, allowing companies to focus on customers who need specific attention or have a high potential to become active clients.

▪ Churn Prediction

Customer churn prediction refers to identifying customers who are likely to stop using a product or service. For many SMEs, customer churn is a problem that directly impacts profitability, as acquiring new customers is often more expensive than retaining existing ones. Implementing a classification model to predict which customers are most likely to leave allows the company to act in time, launching personalized retention campaigns and offering specific incentives to reduce the churn rate.

▪ Selection of relevant features for churn prediction

To build an effective churn prediction model, it's essential to identify the features that best reflect customer behavior and engagement with the company. Among the most common and relevant features for this type of model are:

- Service usage frequency: A customer who has significantly reduced their service usage in recent months may be considering leaving. Usage frequency helps assess the level of interest and commitment the customer has with the product.

- Interaction with customer service: The number of interactions with support and the nature of the queries can reflect the level of customer satisfaction. Frequent complaints or unresolved queries are often indicators of an unsatisfied customer.

- Time since last purchase or visit: A customer who hasn't made a purchase or visited the website for an extended period may be at risk of churn. This variable helps identify less engaged customers.

- Customer tenure: The length of the relationship with the customer can also be an important factor. In many cases, recent customers tend to be less loyal than those who have been using the service for a longer period.

- Responses to previous retention campaigns: If the customer has responded negatively to retention campaigns in the past, there may be a higher likelihood that they are considering leaving. Therefore, this information can be useful for predicting churn.

  - Implementing the churn prediction model with Random Forest

A very effective algorithm for churn prediction is the random forest, which consists of a series of decision trees working together to classify customers based on their likelihood of leaving. This method is robust and tends to deliver good results in classification problems, as it uses multiple trees to reduce error and improve accuracy.

Implementing the random forest model in Scikit-Learn is straightforward and allows for hyperparameter tuning to optimize accuracy. Below is the basic process to train a churn prediction model:

1. Data preparation: First, the dataset must be organized, ensuring that the features (e.g., frequency of use, tenure, and last purchase) and the target variable (churn or no churn) are properly structured.

2. Data splitting: Then, the dataset is divided into a training set and a test set. This allows training the model with part of the data and evaluating its performance on new data, ensuring it is not overfitting.

3. Training the model: With the data prepared, the model is trained using the random forest algorithm. Scikit-Learn offers an efficient implementation of this algorithm through the RandomForestClassifier method.

4. Model evaluation: Once trained, the model is evaluated using metrics such as precision, recall, and F1-score, which indicate its ability to correctly predict customers at risk of churn.

5. Interpretation of results and model adjustment: Finally, the results are interpreted and, if necessary, the model's hyperparameters are adjusted to improve performance.

This predictive approach allows the company to identify customers at risk of leaving and direct specific efforts towards them. For example, it can offer discounts or service improvements, designing personalized retention strategies that help reduce the churn rate and improve customer loyalty.

- ### Alternative implementation: Logistic Regression

Another option for churn prediction is the use of logistic regression, a classification algorithm that is particularly suited for binary classification problems (such as yes or no). Logistic regression calculates the probability of a customer leaving the service based on their characteristics and allows you to identify the factors that contribute most to the risk of churn.

Implementing logistic regression in Scikit-Learn is straightforward and allows for quick model fitting. Unlike random forests, logistic regression offers interpretability, as its coefficients indicate the influence of each feature on the likelihood of churn. This interpretability enables the company to better understand which factors are driving churn and adjust their strategies accordingly.

- ### Lead Conversion Prediction

Lead conversion prediction is another valuable use of classification models for SMEs, allowing them to identify which prospects or leads have the highest likelihood of becoming active customers. By anticipating the conversion probability of each lead, the company can focus its sales and marketing efforts on those with the most potential, thus improving the conversion rate and optimizing resource use.

- ### Selecting relevant features for conversion prediction

To build a conversion prediction model, it's essential to select features that reflect the behavior of leads and their level of interest in the product or service. The most common features for conversion prediction include:

- Frequency of website visits: A lead who frequently visits the website shows a higher interest in the products or services offered, which may indicate a greater likelihood of conversion.

- Interaction with marketing campaigns: Responses to promotional emails, ads, and other marketing content are an indicator of the lead's level of engagement. The more positive interactions a lead has with campaigns, the higher their likelihood of converting into a customer.

- History of purchases or previous inquiries: Leads who have made specific inquiries or shown interest in certain products tend to be closer to making a purchase, making this feature relevant for the model.

- Duration of the relationship with the lead: The time that has passed since the first contact with the lead can also influence the likelihood of conversion, as leads that have been in contact for longer periods are usually more likely to convert.

  - **Implementation of the lead conversion model with Random Forest**

Random forest is also an excellent option for lead conversion prediction, as it allows you to classify leads based on their likelihood of becoming customers. The implementation process is similar to churn prediction, although in this case, the target variable will be lead conversion (yes or no) instead of customer retention.

1. Data preparation: First, the dataset of leads is structured with the relevant features and the target variable, which indicates whether the lead has converted into a customer or not.

2. Data splitting: The dataset is divided into a training set and a test set.

3. Training the model: The model is trained using RandomForestClassifier in Scikit-Learn.

4. Model evaluation: Accuracy, recall, and F1-score are used to assess how well the model predicts the probability of conversion.

5. Interpretation of results: Finally, the results are interpreted and the hyperparameters are adjusted to optimize the model's accuracy.

- **Alternative implementation: Logistic Regression**

Logistic regression can also be used to predict lead conversion. Since this model is interpretable, it allows understanding the weight of each feature in the probability of conversion, helping the company identify the key factors that drive leads to become customers. For example, the company might discover that interactions with specific campaigns have a greater influence on conversion, which could guide marketing efforts towards content strategies or promotions that generate higher engagement.

- **Practical application of segmentation models in SMEs**

Once the churn prediction and lead conversion prediction models are trained, SMEs can apply them in their daily operations to optimize marketing efforts, reduce customer acquisition costs, and improve retention. Implementing these models allows the company to anticipate the needs and behavior of its customers, which in turn strengthens the relationship with them and increases their loyalty to the brand.

By predicting customer churn, the company can identify and address those at risk before they decide to leave the service, which not only reduces the churn rate but also saves on acquisition costs. In the case of leads, the model allows identifying prospects with the highest conversion potential, helping the company focus its resources on the leads with the greatest potential. With strategies based on these classification models, SMEs can maximize their resources and ensure a better experience for both current and future customers.

The combination of classification algorithms with data analysis and machine learning allows SMEs to transform data into a strategic tool for accurately segmenting customers, anticipating their needs, and creating highly effective retention and conversion campaigns.

- **Transactional data analysis for personalized predictions**

The analysis of transactional data is a fundamental practice for SMEs looking to maximize the value of each customer and improve their marketing effectiveness. By leveraging the data generated in each transaction, a company can identify purchasing patterns and anticipate future customer needs, allowing for the development of personalized campaigns and optimized inventory management. Transactions reflect the actual behavior of the customer and, unlike other more general data, provide precise information about when a customer makes a purchase, what products they buy, and how often. This information is valuable because it allows for highly accurate predictions of when a customer is likely to make their next purchase, which in turn facilitates the design of data-driven marketing and retention strategies.

Transactional analysis not only improves the understanding of customer behavior but also helps segment the database into groups of customers with similar purchasing patterns. To perform an effective analysis, it's necessary to understand the various metrics and predictive models that can be applied to transactional data, such as recurrence analysis, purchase timing models, and repurchase probability analysis. By identifying these patterns, SMEs can implement automated marketing strategies and design retention campaigns tailored to each type of customer, thereby maximizing the retention rate and the lifetime value of each customer.

- **Collection and preparation of transactional data**

The first step in leveraging transactional data is collecting and organizing the data generated from each sale. Transactional data contains key information such as the date and time of the transaction, the total purchase value, the specific products purchased, the payment method used, and the purchase channel (whether it's a physical store, a website, or an app). This data allows you to build a detailed timeline of the customer's buying behavior, accurately identifying their preferences and consumption patterns.

Once collected, the data must be structured and processed properly. Organizing this data into a coherent structure facilitates analysis and allows the predictive model to work efficiently. For most transactional analyses, it's useful to create a database where each row represents a unique transaction, including customer data and specific purchase details. The data should be clean, meaning free of errors or duplicates, and organized in a way that allows easy grouping by customer to analyze the frequency and value of purchases.

Moreover, it's important to note that some customers may have more erratic or less consistent purchasing patterns, while others may follow very regular patterns. The ability to identify both types of behavior allows the company to adapt its strategy more accurately. For example, customers who purchase regularly at specific intervals, such as monthly or quarterly, are ideal candidates for personalized retention campaigns that activate just before their next estimated purchase. Customers with less consistent patterns can be segmented to receive reactivation campaigns or incentives to encourage them to return.

- ▪ **Recurring purchase pattern identification**

Identifying patterns of repeat purchases is essential for understanding customer buying cycles and anticipating their future needs. There are several metrics and methods that allow for the evaluation of recurrence in transactional data. Among them are purchase frequency analysis, recency, and the monetary value of transactions. These metrics form the basis of the RFM (Recency, Frequency, Monetary) model, which classifies customers based on three main aspects.

- Recency (R): The amount of time since the customer's last purchase. Customers who have made recent purchases are usually more engaged and have a higher likelihood of making another purchase in the near future.

- Frequency (F): The number of times a customer has made purchases in a given period. Customers who buy frequently tend to be more loyal and generate more value over time.

- Monetary Value (M): The total amount the customer has spent on their purchases. This metric helps identify the most valuable customers, those who not only buy frequently but also make higher-value transactions.

RFM analysis allows you to segment customers into different categories and accurately predict who is most likely to make a purchase in the future. This analysis is also useful for designing personalized marketing campaigns and adjusting retention strategies. For example, customers with high frequency and recency can receive loyalty incentives, while those with high recency but low frequency could benefit from reactivation campaigns to motivate them to increase their purchase frequency.

- ▪ **Prediction of the time of the next purchase**

One of the key objectives in transactional data analysis is predicting the time of the next purchase. By understanding the intervals between a customer's purchases, it is possible to estimate when they are likely to make their next transaction. There are several statistical and machine learning methods that can be used to predict the time of the next purchase based on each customer's historical data.

The time-to-purchase model, or survival model, is a technique that calculates the probability of a purchase occurring within a specific time interval. To implement this model, the purchase history of each customer is analyzed, evaluating the time between one purchase and the next. This technique is based on statistical survival analysis methods that estimate the 'lifetime' of an activity, in this case, purchase recurrence. This type of model is well-suited to customers with consistent purchasing patterns, as it allows you to anticipate the likelihood of them making a purchase in the near future.

Another popular method is the use of time series models to project purchasing behavior over time. Time series models, such as ARIMA (AutoRegressive Integrated Moving Average) and exponential smoothing models, are techniques that allow for the analysis of patterns over time and the prediction of future values based on these patterns. Time series models are useful for analyzing recurrent purchasing behaviors in high-turnover products, such as daily or weekly consumer goods.

Predicting the next purchase allows the company to plan its marketing campaigns more precisely. For example, if a purchase timing model predicts that a customer will make a purchase in the next 15 days, the company can send a reminder or special promotion a week before to encourage the purchase. This not only increases the likelihood of the customer returning, but also helps strengthen their loyalty to the brand.

- ▪ **Implementation of Machine Learning Models for Personalized Prediction**

The use of machine learning models for personalized prediction offers a significant advantage by combining transactional data analysis with advanced algorithms that can identify complex patterns in customer behavior. Some of the most common and effective algorithms for this type of analysis include decision trees, random forests, and neural networks.

A popular approach is implementing classification models that identify customers with a high likelihood of making a purchase in the short term. These models can be trained with relevant features, such as time since last purchase, number of purchases in the last quarter, and interaction with recent marketing campaigns. Based on this information, the model can classify customers according to their likelihood of repurchasing, allowing the company to design personalized strategies for each group.

Another option is to use regression models to predict the exact time of the next purchase based on customer characteristics. These models allow for a more precise estimation of the purchase period, which is useful for products with regular or seasonal buying patterns. For example, a clothing store can use a regression model to predict when a customer is likely to return for the next season, and adjust their marketing campaigns accordingly.

- **Personalization of marketing strategies**

The ability to predict customer buying behavior allows SMEs to tailor their marketing strategies based on each client's individual needs. With the information obtained from transactional analysis and purchase predictions, the company can design campaigns that fit each client's lifecycle, ensuring greater effectiveness and a more personalized experience.

For example, for customers with a high probability of making a purchase in the short term, the company can send personalized reminders or discount coupons to incentivize the purchase. Less active customers can receive reactivation campaigns, such as special offers or loyalty programs, designed to regain their interest. This approach allows maximizing the return on marketing investment, as each campaign is directed at the most relevant customers at the most appropriate time.

In addition to marketing campaigns, predicting buying patterns also allows for optimized inventory management. If a company can anticipate which products will be in demand during a specific period, it can adjust its inventory accordingly and avoid both stockouts and overstock. This not only improves operational efficiency but also enables the company to better meet customer needs, ensuring that desired products are always available.

- **Transactional data analysis and customer loyalty**

The information obtained from transactional data analysis allows companies to strengthen their loyalty strategy by improving the customer experience and increasing their loyalty to the brand. By understanding each customer's buying patterns, the company can design more effective loyalty programs tailored to each customer's individual habits and preferences.

An example of this is the design of personalized reward programs that reward customers for their loyalty and purchase frequency. By using transactional data to identify the most active and loyal customers, the company can offer specific incentives, such as exclusive discounts or early access to products, which reinforce their commitment and increase their satisfaction.

Moreover, the analysis of transactional data allows us to detect changes in customer behavior that might indicate a decrease in their interest or engagement with the brand. These changes, such as a reduction in purchase frequency or a decrease in the average transaction value, are signs that the customer might be at risk of leaving. By identifying these patterns in time, the company can implement retention strategies and reactivation campaigns that reduce the risk of churn and strengthen the customer relationship.

- **Integration of predictive models into the sales system**

For transactional data analysis to be truly effective, it's essential that predictive models are integrated into the company's sales and CRM systems. This integration allows the sales and marketing team to access real-time information about customer behavior, making it easier to personalize interactions and improve decision-making.

For example, by integrating a next purchase prediction model into the CRM, the sales team can receive automatic alerts when a customer is about to make a purchase, allowing them to send a personalized offer or reminder at the right time. Additionally, this integration facilitates the automation of marketing campaigns, as it allows emails and promotions to be scheduled based on the forecasts generated by the model, optimizing resource management and improving the effectiveness of the campaigns.

Ultimately, the analysis of transactional data and the use of predictive models provide SMEs with a powerful tool to understand customer behavior and anticipate their needs. This predictive ability allows the company to design personalized marketing strategies, optimize inventory management, and improve loyalty, which helps build stronger relationships with customers and maximize the value of each transaction.

6.3. Implementation of classification and regression models in daily operations

The implementation of classification and regression models in the daily operations of an SME is a fundamental strategy to maximize the value of data and improve operational efficiency. Although training predictive models is a crucial step, their true power unfolds when integrated into daily business processes, allowing for informed and agile decisions in key areas such as sales, marketing, and pricing management. In this sense, predictive models go beyond being mere analytical tools to become strategic assets that drive the company's ability to anticipate market demands and quickly adapt to trends.

One of the advantages of predictive models in the SME environment is that they can automate the generation of periodic predictions. With Python, you can set up automated scripts that update the data daily or weekly, run the model, and generate predictions for the next period. This approach saves time and allows the team to have updated projections without manual effort, whether to forecast weekly sales or adjust inventory. Automation turns models into efficient and scalable business processes, ready to adapt to the pace of the company.

Additionally, SMEs can benefit from interactive and simple dashboards to visualize predictions clearly and accessibly for the team. Tools like Jupyter Notebooks, Streamlit, or Plotly's Dash facilitate the creation of customized dashboards where company managers can access predictions and view trends at a glance. These dashboards simplify decision-making, allowing managers to visualize how sales, customer behavior patterns, or marketing campaign performance are expected to evolve.

In this chapter, practical implementation examples are explored, such as using classification models for quick decisions in personalized promotions, regression models to optimize prices based on projected demand, and predictive analysis to improve marketing campaigns. The integration of these models allows SMEs to use data to make more precise decisions, personalize their offers, and optimize performance across all business areas. Thus, predictive analysis becomes a tool that boosts the company's competitiveness and enables them to make the most of the knowledge generated from their own data.

- ## How to integrate predictive models into business processes

The integration of predictive models into business processes allows SMEs to incorporate informed, real-time predictions into their daily decision-making, benefiting from the practical value offered by data and advanced analytics. This implementation transforms machine learning models from simple analysis tools into active business elements that drive strategy in areas such as sales, marketing, production, and customer service. By automating prediction generation and visualizing the results in an accessible way, companies can quickly react to changes in customer behavior, optimize inventory management, and adjust their strategies to maximize performance.

Once the model has been trained and validated, the opportunity arises to integrate it into the daily workflow. This integration process includes two main aspects: automating periodic predictions and using interactive dashboards to visualize predictions, which simplify the interpretation of results and their application in decision-making. Each of these steps provides specific benefits for SMEs, allowing for efficient use of models and improved accessibility for the entire team.

- ### Automation of predictions: Scripts for periodic forecasts

Automating periodic predictions is essential for a company to have up-to-date forecasts without constant manual intervention. This automation allows the predictive model to run at specific intervals, whether daily, weekly, or monthly, generating accurate predictions for the next period. Python, with its versatility and extensive library of tools, provides an ideal environment for setting up scripts that perform this task automatically. Automation saves time, reduces the margin for error, and ensures that the company is always informed about the key forecasts for its operations.

A practical example would be predicting daily or weekly sales. If an SME has trained a regression model to forecast sales, automating the predictions allows the model to run every day or every week, so the team can anticipate changes in demand and adjust inventory or marketing campaigns based on the forecasts. Below, we'll show how to set up this automation in Python, highlighting the most effective libraries and methods to achieve this.

- ▪ **Setting up an automation script in Python**

The schedule library is an effective option for configuring the execution frequency of a script in Python. This package allows you to schedule specific tasks at defined intervals, such as running daily or weekly predictions. Once the script is set up, schedule will automatically execute the prediction process, updating the data and generating results for the next period without manual intervention.

To illustrate how an automation script could be set up, let's consider the example of a company that wants to run its sales prediction model every day at the end of the day, updating the data with that day's sales and generating a forecast for the next day. The script will include the process of loading and preprocessing the data, running the predictive model, and saving the results.

Here is an example of code to set up an automation script using schedule:

```python
import schedule
import time
import pandas as pd
from sklearn.externals import joblib

# Función para cargar y preprocesar los datos
def cargar_datos():
    # Cargar los datos actualizados
    datos = pd.read_csv("ventas_diarias.csv")
    # Realizar preprocesamiento si es necesario
    return datos

# Función para hacer la predicción
def hacer_prediccion():
    # Cargar el modelo previamente entrenado
    modelo = joblib.load("modelo_prediccion_ventas.pkl")

    # Cargar y preprocesar los datos
    datos = cargar_datos()

    # Hacer predicción con los datos más recientes
    prediccion = modelo.predict(datos)

    # Guardar las predicciones
    predicciones_df = pd.DataFrame(prediccion, columns=['Prediccion'])
    predicciones_df.to_csv("predicciones_futuras.csv", index=False)
    print("Predicción generada y guardada.")

# Programar la tarea para que se ejecute diariamente
schedule.every().day.at("20:00").do(hacer_prediccion)

# Loop para mantener el script en ejecución y revisar la programación
while True:
    schedule.run_pending()
    time.sleep(60)  # Esperar 60 segundos entre cada ejecución
```

In this script, the function hacer_prediccion loads a previously trained prediction model, extracts the most recent data, and calculates the sales forecast for the next period. The script also saves the predictions in a CSV file so they're available for the team. At the end of the script, the method schedule.every().day.at("20:00") ensures that the function runs every day at 8:00 p.m. and automatically makes the predictions.

- **Maintenance and updating of the automated model**

Over time, company data evolves and customer behavior patterns can change, so it's important to keep the predictive model up to date. Automation also allows for setting up a model retraining process at specific intervals, so the model adjusts to new data and maintains its accuracy. This retraining can be scheduled using logic similar to the prediction script.

Python, along with tools like Scikit-Learn and joblib, makes it easy to implement updatable models and allows them to adjust to current data without needing to retrain from scratch. This reduces workload and ensures that the model remains relevant and accurate for future predictions.

- **Visualizing Predictions with Simple Dashboards**

The visualization of predictions through interactive dashboards is a fundamental tool for translating the results of predictive models into visual and accessible information for the entire team. Dashboards become a platform where business leaders can explore, understand, and make data-driven decisions without needing deep technical knowledge. Visual clarity helps users immediately see the behavior of projected trends and respond quickly to changes in market conditions.

There are several tools in the Python ecosystem that make it easy to create custom dashboards, each with specific features that cater to different levels of complexity and business needs. Among the most popular options are Jupyter Notebooks, Streamlit, and Dash by Plotly. The choice between these tools will depend on the specific functionalities the company requires, the nature of the analysis, and the level of customization needed for data visualization.

- **Jupyter Notebooks: Flexibility and Accessibility in Interactive Documents**

Jupyter Notebooks is a widely used platform in data science that allows you to create interactive documents combining text, visualizations, and code in a single environment. This tool is ideal for companies looking for accessible and flexible visualization, especially if users need to make manual adjustments to model parameters or perform additional real-time analysis. Jupyter Notebooks offers a modular structure where each code cell can be executed independently, allowing for progressive data exploration tailored to the needs of each analysis.

Notebooks allow for immediate visualization of the model's predictions. A company can use line or bar charts to compare historical sales with future projections in an interactive environment. This type of visualization enables the team to interpret the continuity of sales data and clearly see the projected fluctuations. Additionally, interactive cells allow for real-time adjustment of the model's parameters and show how these adjustments impact predictions, which is especially useful for exploring hypothetical scenarios in sales or inventory and conducting sensitivity analysis.

Another advantage of Jupyter Notebooks is their flexibility to integrate other Python libraries, such as Matplotlib or Seaborn, to create advanced charts that complement the analysis. While this tool may not be as accessible for users unfamiliar with programming, its flexibility makes it an ideal choice for those with basic Python knowledge who want to create custom visualizations without relying on external platforms.

- **Streamlit: Creating Interactive Dashboards in Real Time**

Streamlit is a library designed to simplify the development of interactive dashboards and web applications in Python. This tool is especially useful for SMEs that want to share predictive model results with non-technical users in an accessible environment without requiring programming knowledge. Unlike Jupyter Notebooks, Streamlit offers a more user-friendly interface, as it allows visualizations and controls to be deployed directly in the web browser, making it easy for all team members to access from any location.

The implementation of a dashboard in Streamlit allows the inclusion of sliders, buttons, and selectors that users can manipulate to adjust the model's variables, making it ideal for exploring real-time scenarios. For example, a company analyzing sales projections for the coming weeks could develop a Streamlit dashboard with controls to adjust parameters such as marketing budget, seasonality, or promotions. As the user modifies these values, the model recalculates the predictions and updates the graphs, providing an immediate visualization of how these variables influence sales projections. This type of interactivity allows company executives to evaluate the impact of strategic decisions without needing to reprogram the model or wait for a new execution.

Streamlit also allows the integration of advanced graphics and visualizations generated with Plotly and Matplotlib, which enhances data presentation and enables combining different types of charts in the same dashboard. Streamlit's ability to render graphics and respond in real-time to user adjustments makes it ideal for collaborative analysis in sales and marketing, where agility in decision-making is crucial.

- Plotly Dash: Advanced Visualization and Full Interactivity

Dash from Plotly is a Python library that allows the creation of interactive web applications and advanced dashboards. By combining the graph functionality of Plotly with the web environment of Dash, this tool offers a high degree of customization and visual power for SMEs that need a more sophisticated level of data analysis and presentation. Dash is particularly useful for high-complexity visualizations, such as sales time series, seasonality analysis, or advanced customer segmentation, and is ideal for companies looking to integrate interactive dashboards into their information systems.

Dash allows you to create complete dashboards with a wide range of complex charts, such as scatter plots, heat maps, and 3D visualizations, which is essential for companies that need to perform in-depth analysis and present data from multiple angles. For example, a company evaluating the impact of a marketing campaign on different customer segments can use a Dash dashboard to compare the response rate of each segment, visualize conversion based on different variables, and analyze revenue projections for each segment.

Dash's interactivity allows users to explore predictions in depth, adjusting variables in real-time and visualizing their impact on the graph. This facilitates scenario analysis and decision-making based on precise data. Additionally, Dash allows you to integrate multiple pages or sections into a single dashboard, so you can organize visualizations into tabs, enabling users to navigate between sales forecasts, inventory analysis, and customer segmentation without switching applications. Dash also supports the implementation of real-time machine learning models, allowing trained models to be loaded directly into the dashboard and data to be automatically updated according to new sales or customer behavior records.

- **Example of application: Dashboard for sales predictions in Dash**

To illustrate how Dash can be integrated into a business environment, let's consider the case of a company that wants to monitor sales forecasts and evaluate the performance of its campaigns in real-time. Using Dash, you could create a dashboard that shows historical sales data along with projections for the next month, allowing the team to compare current results with projected targets.

1. Visualization of Historical Sales and Future Predictions: The dashboard would include a line chart showing actual sales to date, with a different colored line for predictions. This allows the team to visualize sales performance and see if the projected trend is being maintained.

2. Scenario Analysis: With sliders and dropdown selectors, users can adjust variables such as marketing investment, product pricing, or seasonality, and see how these adjustments impact sales forecasts. This ability to explore scenarios allows sales managers to assess the impact of potential strategies before implementing them.

3. Customer Segmentation Visualization: A heat map could show the conversion rate by customer segments in different regions or product categories, making it easier to identify areas of opportunity and adjust the marketing strategy to optimize segmentation.

4. Alerts and Notifications: Dash allows you to schedule alerts on the dashboard, which can be triggered when the sales forecast deviates significantly from expectations. This enables a quick reaction and adjustment of strategy if the company observes that sales are below expectations.

5. Key Metrics Panel: A side panel would display key metrics such as the model's mean squared error (MSE), average conversion rate, and real-time sales growth, providing an accessible summary for executives.

The dashboard in Dash makes it easy for the company to analyze its projections and performance in depth, allowing them to make informed decisions based on visual and real-time data.

▪ Integration and access to Dashboards

Once the dashboard is created, SMEs can deploy it in their work environment and share it with the team via a web server or an internal network. Dash and Streamlit make it easy to deploy dashboards on a server, allowing users to access them from any device with an internet connection. This is especially useful in collaborative environments where multiple departments need to consult the same data.

In conclusion, interactive dashboards are a key tool for the visualization and analysis of predictions generated by machine learning models, providing SMEs with easy and understandable access to complex data that would otherwise be difficult to interpret and use in daily business decision-making.

● **Classification model for quick decision-making**

Classification models have become an invaluable tool for SMEs looking to make quick, data-driven decisions, especially when it comes to direct marketing strategies and promotional personalization. The ability of these models to analyze and categorize large volumes of information in real time offers companies the opportunity to act with precision, thus optimizing their resources and maximizing the impact of their marketing actions. In the daily context of an SME, a classification model can answer a key, recurring question: should we offer a promotion to this particular customer? Based on historical customer behavior data, such as purchase frequency and response to previous offers, the classification model allows for more certainty in deciding if the customer is a suitable candidate for a personalized offer, ensuring that each marketing action aligns with the specific profile of each consumer.

To understand how this strategy works, it's important to first analyze the characteristics of the data that the classification model uses as input. In most cases, the historical information about the customer includes variables such as purchase frequency (how regularly the customer has made purchases in the past), recency of the last purchase (how much time has passed since the last transaction), and their response history to previous offers (whether they have shown interest or ignored similar marketing campaigns in the past). Additionally, extra variables like preferred product or service type, average purchase ticket, and interactions on specific channels such as promotional emails, social media, or website visits are integrated to improve the model's accuracy. This type of data not only reflects the customer's behavior patterns but also their level of engagement with the brand and their willingness to participate in loyalty and repurchase campaigns.

Once the relevant features have been selected and structured, a classification model is trained to analyze this historical behavior and predict the likelihood of a customer responding positively to a new offer. Some of the most common algorithms for these classification models include random forest and logistic regression, which are known for their accuracy in binary classification, that is, deciding between two categories like 'yes' or 'no.' A random forest model works by creating a series of decision trees, each evaluating different combinations of variables to determine if a customer should receive a promotion. The votes from all the trees are aggregated to give a final prediction, which allows for consistent results and reduces the margin of error. In contrast, logistic regression estimates the probability of response to the promotion based on each variable, allowing for coefficient adjustments to maximize model accuracy. Both approaches offer practical and effective solutions for making quick decisions, and the choice between them will depend on the nature of the data and the specific objectives of the campaign.

As a classification model is implemented in an SME's environment, integration into the company's operational and marketing systems allows for automated decision-making regarding the allocation of promotions. For example, the model can be set up so that, upon receiving updated data from a recent transaction, it determines whether the customer qualifies for a special offer based on their profile and previous behavior. This automation allows the marketing team to focus on developing higher-impact strategies while the system executes decisions quickly and accurately. In an automated marketing environment, the model's results are applied directly to email marketing or SMS campaigns that reach the customer at the right time with a specific offer tailored to their needs and preferences. This personalization ensures a positive customer experience and increases the likelihood of conversion, avoiding indiscriminate promotions that could result in wasted resources and a reduction in the customer's perceived value of the brand.

One of the key advantages of using a classification model in promotions is that it allows you to maximize the relevance of each offer for the customer. This is achieved by analyzing patterns that identify whether a customer is more likely to respond to a promotion based on their past behavior. For example, if a customer has shown interest in specific product discounts or seasonal promotions, the model can identify them as a good candidate for a related offer, while a customer who has ignored similar campaigns in the past might be excluded from receiving the promotion, thus avoiding an ineffective marketing effort. This approach not only optimizes resource allocation but also improves the customer's perception of the company, as they receive offers that are relevant and personalized, increasing their satisfaction and loyalty to the brand.

The value of this classification model for an SME goes beyond making real-time decisions. The data generated by the model and the results of each campaign allow for continuous learning, where the model is adjusted and improved with each iteration. This process is known as feedback, and it's essential for the model to evolve and adapt to changes in customer behavior. For example, a customer who initially responded to basic product promotions might, over time, start showing interest in higher-value product categories. The model's ability to adjust its predictions based on these changes allows the SME to optimize its strategies and ensure that offers remain relevant over time.

For optimal integration, it is recommended that the classification model be implemented in a customer relationship management (CRM) system or a marketing platform that coordinates the model's results with campaign execution. In a CRM, the information generated by the model can be directly linked to each customer profile, providing the sales or marketing team with instant access to each customer's likelihood of responding to a promotion. Furthermore, when combined with an automated marketing system, the CRM can activate campaigns automatically, sending offers to customers with high conversion probabilities and adjusting the strategy for those with lower predispositions, achieving a much more effective and precise campaign execution. Using marketing platforms that directly integrate the classification model ensures that decisions are consistent and fast, which is especially important in time-limited campaigns, such as seasonal promotions, weekend discounts, or flash sales.

Using a classification model to decide on the allocation of promotions also allows experimenting with different marketing strategies and measuring the impact of each one. By dividing customers into control and treatment groups, the SME can evaluate how customers respond to different campaigns and adjust the model's variables based on these results. For example, they could experiment by offering a promotion to customers with a high conversion probability score and measure whether the outcome is greater than with customers with a medium score. This methodology allows adjusting marketing strategies based on concrete data, improving the effectiveness of campaigns and maximizing return on investment.

Moreover, a well-implemented classification model contributes to enhancing the overall customer experience by offering a more personalized service. Instead of receiving general campaigns, the customer feels that the company understands them and offers products and services that truly interest them. This approach not only improves response rates but also strengthens the relationship between the brand and the customer, increasing the likelihood of repeat purchases and fostering long-term loyalty. A customer who feels the company understands their needs is more likely to recommend the brand to others, naturally and organically expanding the customer base.

From a strategic perspective, implementing a classification model for promotions allows the company to align its marketing efforts with its overall business objectives. For example, an SME looking to increase sales of a specific product can adjust the model to identify customers who have shown interest in related categories, targeting campaigns towards them. Similarly, a company trying to increase purchase frequency among sporadic customers can adapt the model to classify these customers into a segment that receives more frequent promotions, encouraging them to make purchases more regularly.

The ability to make quick, data-driven decisions is particularly useful in highly competitive markets, where agility is key to staying relevant. A classification model allows for a swift response to changes in customer behavior, adapting campaigns based on real-time results and proactively adjusting the strategy. This is especially relevant during high-demand periods like holidays, sales seasons, and special events, where the model can be recalibrated to maximize the impact of each campaign and ensure the company makes the most of every sales opportunity.

Finally, using a classification model for promotion assignment provides valuable insights into the factors driving customer response, allowing the company to better understand what motivates each customer to respond positively to an offer. This analysis enables continuous adjustment and refinement of the model's variables, making the promotional strategy increasingly precise and effective. Additionally, the company can identify specific patterns within its customer base that would not be visible without the model, allowing it to identify customer segments with similar characteristics that could benefit from personalized marketing strategies.

In summary, a classification model is an essential tool for SMEs looking for a competitive edge in personalizing promotions and optimizing their marketing campaigns. By providing a clear view of each customer's likelihood of response, the model allows you to maximize the impact of each promotion, reduce resource waste, and build long-term relationships with customers, thereby increasing the total value of each customer for the company.

- ## Regression models for price optimization

Regression models are essential tools for SMEs looking to optimise their pricing strategies, as they allow businesses to analyse and predict how changes in product prices directly affect sales and revenue. Pricing is a key aspect of commercial strategy and can significantly impact a company's profitability and competitiveness in the market. Through regression models, an SME can adjust its prices in an informed manner, using historical data to estimate the impact that various pricing policies might have on the demand for its products or services. By conducting predictive analysis based on historical data, the company gains an objective and solid foundation for its pricing decisions, rather than relying on assumptions or generalized strategies.

A regression model, essentially, analyzes the relationship between dependent and independent variables to predict the behavior of one variable based on changes in another. In the case of price optimization, the dependent variable could be sales volume, while the independent variable would be the product price. Through a simple linear regression model, it's possible to observe the relationship between both variables, allowing the company to identify demand elasticity, that is, the sensitivity of customers to price changes. This demand elasticity is a key concept in economics and marketing, as it helps predict whether a price increase will lead to a significant drop in sales, or if, on the contrary, consumers would be willing to pay more without a substantial impact on the quantity sold.

A linear regression model is a suitable starting point for companies exploring how to establish a data-driven pricing strategy, as it offers a simple approach to analyze the correlation between prices and sales. This model assumes a linear relationship between price and demand. In this context, an SME could train a linear regression model using historical sales and pricing data, introducing additional variables such as time of year, seasonality, or promotions, which often influence consumer behavior. For example, in certain sectors, like consumer goods, demand may be more elastic during periods like Black Friday, where consumers look for discounts and promotions, while in other sectors, prices may remain constant throughout the year.

Collecting and preparing historical data is essential for training an effective regression model. To build a robust model, the company must have detailed information on sales and prices for each product over a long period, which allows for capturing demand variations and analyzing how customers have responded to different price levels. If the data includes other factors such as promotions, seasonal discounts, or changes in product quality, the model can be adjusted to account for these variables and provide more accurate predictions. Additionally, it's important to consider the possible presence of external factors, such as the economic situation or market competition, which can also influence demand and should be incorporated into the model if sufficient data is available.

Once the necessary data has been collected, the company can use Python and the Scikit-Learn library to train a regression model that fits the relationship between price and sales volume. The first step in implementing the model is to split the dataset into two subsets: one to train the model and another to validate it, which allows for evaluating the model's accuracy on unseen data. This ensures that the model can generalize the results and make accurate predictions in the future. The linear regression technique estimates the coefficients of the linear function that best explains the relationship between price and sales, enabling the company to forecast the impact of different price levels on demand and optimize the pricing strategy to maximize revenue.

To illustrate how a regression model can optimize pricing, let's consider the example of an SME that sells a specific product and wants to know the optimal price to maximize revenue. The company has collected sales and pricing data over the past few years and has observed that sales tend to decrease as the price increases, indicating that the product has elastic demand. By training a regression model with this data, the company can calculate the equilibrium price, that is, the price at which revenue would be maximized without losing a significant number of sales. The model can also identify the inflection point where a price increase would start to reduce sales more sharply, allowing the company to avoid price levels that could be detrimental.

For this SME, the regression model not only provides a prediction of sales volume based on different prices, but also allows for experimentation with hypothetical scenarios, analyzing how different pricing strategies might affect revenue. For example, the model can predict whether a 5% price reduction would lead to an increase in demand sufficient to offset the decrease in unit revenue. This simulation capability gives the company a detailed view of the financial impact of each strategy and allows them to choose the one that maximizes revenue or profitability.

In addition to the linear regression model, SMEs can use more advanced regression approaches to capture non-linear relationships or complex effects in demand. In some cases, the relationship between price and sales may not be strictly linear, especially if there are customer segments that respond differently to price changes. In these situations, a polynomial regression model can be useful, as it allows for capturing second or third-degree effects in the relationship between price and demand, better fitting complex demand curves. Polynomial regression adds additional terms to the model, such as the square or cube of the price, which allows for reflecting demand sensitivity at different price ranges and optimizing the price to maximize sales in each customer segment.

In a highly competitive market environment, where the company must adjust prices based on the dynamics of supply and demand, regression models offer a significant competitive advantage as they allow the business to anticipate consumer reactions and adjust pricing strategy in real time. For example, if a company knows that a competitor has reduced the price of a similar product, it can use its regression model to predict how this change will affect the demand for its own product and adjust its price to maintain market share. This proactive approach enables the SME to act quickly and minimize the impact of competitors' actions on its revenue and customer loyalty.

Multiple regression is another method that can be very useful for price optimization, as it allows for the inclusion of several independent variables in the model, in addition to price. This means that, besides analyzing how price affects sales volume, the company can consider additional factors such as sales channel, product features, or parallel promotions. Multiple regression is especially useful in markets where consumer behavior depends on a combination of factors, and not just price. By analyzing the effects of each variable together, the multiple regression model provides a more detailed view of how price interacts with other elements of the commercial strategy, which is crucial for designing more effective pricing campaigns.

At the implementation level, a regression model for price optimization can be directly integrated into the company's analysis and planning systems, making real-time decision-making easier. SMEs can use data visualization tools, like dashboards, to monitor sales performance based on current prices and the projections generated by the model. A dashboard can show how sales will change if prices are adjusted by a certain percentage, allowing the company to immediately see the impact of these adjustments on projected revenues. This type of visualization makes it easier to interpret the results and allows company decision-makers to experiment with different price levels to find the ideal balance.

Another advantage of regression models in price optimization is the ability to perform analysis at the customer segmentation level. Models can be tailored to analyze price sensitivity in different customer segments, allowing for price strategies specific to each segment. For example, if the model reveals that younger customers are more price-sensitive than older customers, the company could implement discounts exclusively targeted at the young, thus optimizing prices for each group and maximizing the value received from each segment. This segmented pricing approach allows capturing a larger market share without sacrificing profitability in less price-sensitive segments.

Furthermore, regression models allow businesses to swiftly adapt to market changes by adjusting prices based on economic conditions or seasonal demand. In sectors where prices fluctuate seasonally, such as fashion or tourism, regression models can help anticipate the impact of these changes and adjust prices at the right moment. This adaptability is crucial for SMEs that want to maximize revenue during peak demand or minimize losses during low activity periods. The regression model provides an objective guide to adjusting prices without losing competitiveness and allows businesses to maximize revenue according to market conditions.

Finally, regression models can be used to track the results obtained with each pricing strategy. By comparing the model's predictions with actual results, the company can assess the effectiveness of its price adjustments and improve its future projections. This feedback process allows the model to be adjusted with updated data and the pricing strategy to be refined with each sales cycle, achieving continuous optimization based on market changes and consumer behavior. The model's learning capability becomes a competitive advantage that allows the SME to respond quickly to new trends and market demands, adjusting prices to maintain profitability and customer satisfaction.

In short, regression models provide SMEs with a valuable tool to strategically optimize their pricing, aligning their revenue goals with the real market demand. By analyzing how price changes affect sales, these models allow the company to set prices that maximize revenue, maintain competitiveness, and adapt to customer needs.

- **Marketing optimization**

Marketing optimization using classification models is an effective strategy for SMEs to maximize the efficiency of their marketing campaigns, increase their return on investment, and reduce unnecessary costs. Classification models allow the analysis of large volumes of customer behavior data and predict, with high precision, which profiles are most likely to respond positively to a specific offer or campaign. This data-driven approach improves the personalization of marketing strategies and facilitates the segmentation of customers into groups with different levels of conversion potential, ensuring that the company focuses its efforts only on those customers with the highest likelihood of responding favorably.

Optimizing marketing through classification models allows SMEs to adapt to the current context, where consumers are increasingly demanding and selective with the advertising they receive. The traditional mass marketing approach is ineffective in meeting the expectations of modern customers, who seek relevant and personalized messages. Classification models provide a practical solution to this challenge, as they enable companies to identify patterns in customer behavior and define which types of campaigns are most likely to succeed in each customer segment. By classifying customers based on their characteristics and behaviors, SMEs can optimize their marketing efforts, ensuring that each campaign is targeted at the right audience and avoiding wasting resources on generic or ineffective campaigns.

A typical classification model in the context of marketing uses historical customer data, such as purchase history, brand interaction frequency, and response to previous campaigns, to predict the likelihood of conversion or response to a specific offer. To train this type of model, the company needs a dataset with enough descriptive customer features to reflect consistent behavior patterns. The most common variables in these models include purchase frequency, average transaction value, preferred communication channel, and the types of promotions that have been most effective in the past. Additionally, contextual variables such as product type or season can be included, allowing campaigns to be tailored to specific times of the year when certain customers tend to be more active or receptive to promotional offers.

Once the data is structured, the next step is to train the classification model using machine learning algorithms such as random forest, logistic regression, or decision tree models. Each of these algorithms offers specific advantages depending on the complexity of the dataset and the required accuracy. Random forest, for example, is particularly useful for complex classifications, as it generates multiple decision trees that capture different aspects of customer behavior and reduce the margin of error in the classification. Logistic regression, on the other hand, is an ideal option when a simple binary classification is desired, such as classifying customers into two categories like 'potential' or 'not potential'. The choice of algorithm will depend on the specific objective of the marketing campaign and the type of data available.

Once the model is trained, SMEs can use it to classify their customers based on their likelihood of responding to an offer. This classification process helps identify customer groups that are more likely to respond positively to the campaign, making it easier to personalize offers and design marketing strategies tailored to each segment. For example, a classification model might reveal that a specific group of customers responds better to discount campaigns on high-value products, while another group is more sensitive to promotions on new or exclusive products. By tailoring campaigns to each segment's preferences, the company can maximize the effectiveness of its marketing efforts and improve customer satisfaction, as each customer receives offers that align with their specific interests and needs.

The ability to predict customer responses also allows SMEs to design more financially efficient marketing campaigns. Traditionally, a company launching a marketing campaign incurs significant costs to reach its entire customer base without knowing for sure if everyone will respond positively. However, by using classification models to identify the customers most likely to respond, the company can significantly reduce marketing expenses by focusing only on the segments with the highest probability of conversion. This not only reduces the total campaign cost but also improves the return on investment, as every euro invested in marketing has a greater impact and directly contributes to conversion.

In addition to directing campaigns to the right customers, classification models allow businesses to measure the real impact of marketing strategies. By classifying customers before launching a campaign, the company can divide its database into treatment and control groups. The treatment group receives the campaign, while the control group remains unexposed to the offer. This methodology allows for an objective evaluation of the campaign's impact and helps determine if the model's predictions were accurate, providing constant feedback to adjust and improve the model for future campaigns. Analyzing the results of each campaign also helps identify which customer factors or characteristics were most relevant for conversion, enabling the company to adjust its segmentation strategies and campaign design to maximize effectiveness.

Another advantage of classification models is that they allow businesses to analyze customer behavior across different communication channels and adapt campaigns based on the results from each channel. For example, a company using both email marketing and social media advertising can analyze how each customer group responds in these channels and adjust its communication strategies accordingly. If the classification model reveals that one customer segment responds better to social media campaigns while another segment is more receptive to emails, the company can tailor its strategy to allocate resources more efficiently and achieve the best results in each channel.

The implementation of these models also allows SMEs to engage in proactive marketing, anticipating customer needs and reaching out at the right time. By analyzing behavioral patterns and temporal variables, classification models can predict when a customer is most likely to make a purchase or be receptive to a promotion, enabling the company to schedule campaigns at the time they are most likely to succeed. This proactive approach to marketing not only improves response rates but also helps strengthen the relationship between the company and the customer, as the brand demonstrates a deep understanding of their preferences and presents itself as a timely solution to their needs.

Classification models for marketing optimization also allow companies to develop more effective customer loyalty strategies. By classifying customers based on their likelihood to churn or repurchase, the company can identify those at risk of leaving the brand and design specific campaigns to retain them. For example, a classification model can identify customers who have reduced their purchase frequency in recent months, indicating a possible risk of churn. In response, the company can implement a retention campaign with specific incentives for these customers, such as exclusive discounts or additional benefits, to motivate them to continue buying. This loyalty strategy not only reduces the churn rate but also maximizes the value of each customer over time.

The personalization of marketing campaigns is another major benefit of classification models, as it allows each campaign to be tailored to the individual characteristics and preferences of customers. A well-trained classification model can segment customers based on factors such as age, gender, geographic location, and purchase history, making it easier to create personalized offers that meet the specific needs of each group. This personalization significantly improves the effectiveness of campaigns, as customers are more likely to respond to offers they find relevant and aligned with their interests. Additionally, personalization helps improve the brand image, as customers perceive that the company understands their needs and strives to offer products and services that truly interest them.

From a strategic perspective, classification models also offer SMEs the possibility of conducting predictive marketing, anticipating customer behavior trends and designing campaigns based on future projections. Instead of relying solely on historical data, predictive marketing uses the classification model to forecast how customer needs and preferences will change in the future, allowing the company to plan its campaigns in advance and quickly adapt to market changes. This ability to adapt is especially valuable in dynamic and competitive market environments, where speed in decision-making can make the difference between the success and failure of a campaign.

Finally, classification models allow SMEs to maximize the value of each customer by identifying those with the greatest profit potential and focusing their efforts on them. In many companies, a small portion of the customers generates a large part of the revenue, and classification models help identify these high-value customers and design retention and repurchase strategies specifically for them. This segmented approach optimizes marketing resources and increases return on investment, as each campaign targets the customers who bring the most value to the company.

In conclusion, classification models are an essential tool for marketing optimization in SMEs, as they allow for precise and efficient segmentation and targeting of campaigns. By identifying the customers most likely to respond positively to an offer, the company can reduce costs, maximize the impact of its campaigns, and improve customer satisfaction. Implementing these models not only helps improve the profitability of marketing campaigns but also allows for building stronger and longer-lasting relationships with customers, thus achieving a sustainable competitive advantage in the market.

6.4. Techniques for model evaluation and validation to ensure accuracy

The evaluation and validation of models are crucial steps in the machine learning process, as they ensure that the predictions generated by the model are accurate and consistent. For SMEs to make the most of predictive models in their business decisions, it is essential to understand how to measure the model's performance and adjust its settings to optimize accuracy. The accuracy of a model is the measure of how well it can generalize to new data, and a solid evaluation allows for identifying potential failures, adjusting predictions, and ensuring that the model maintains stable performance as it encounters new data.

One of the first techniques in model evaluation is to split the data into training and test sets. This step allows the model to learn with a subset of the data (training) and have its performance evaluated on another subset (test) it hasn't seen before, thus measuring its ability to generalize. Additionally, using techniques like cross-validation allows for a more robust evaluation of the model, as multiple partitions of the data are made to ensure the results do not depend on a single training or test set. This is key to avoiding issues like overfitting, where the model becomes too tailored to the training data and loses accuracy on new data.

To assess the accuracy of models in specific tasks, there are performance metrics that help interpret the results in detail. In regression models, which aim to predict continuous values, metrics such as mean squared error (MSE) and the coefficient of determination (R^2) are key indicators of how close the predictions are to the actual values and what percentage of the data variability is explained by the model. In classification models, used to categorize data, metrics such as precision, recall, and the F1-score are used to analyze the percentage of hits in different classes and understand if the model correctly detects each category.

Finally, adjusting the model's hyperparameters allows for performance optimization. With tools like GridSearchCV in Scikit-Learn, you can find parameter combinations that maximize model accuracy, achieving a balance between model simplicity and predictive capability. These tuning and validation techniques are essential for SMEs to have reliable and optimized models, ensuring that their decisions are based on solid and accurate predictions.

- **Data splitting into training and test set**

Splitting the data into a training set and a test set is a fundamental machine learning technique that allows us to evaluate a model's ability to generalize its predictions to new data, meaning situations and records it hasn't seen before. This technique is essential for the model to not only learn patterns in historical data but also to apply them effectively in new scenarios, thereby improving its accuracy and usefulness in business environments. In the context of an SME, a model's ability to generalize is crucial, as past data is rarely identical to future data; there are always small variations and external factors that can influence the results.

The training set is used to teach the model patterns and relationships in historical data. This set, usually comprising between 70% and 80% of the available data, contains most of the records and allows the model to identify connections between variables. In this learning process, the model adjusts its internal parameters to minimize prediction errors, aiming for a proper fit to the data structure. However, training the model solely with this set is not enough to ensure its accuracy on new data. Therefore, the test set plays a key role: it is the subset of data the model hasn't seen during training and is used exclusively to evaluate its performance once trained. By applying the model to this data set, the company can obtain a measure of how well the model will perform in practice.

The proportion in which data is divided between the training and test sets can vary depending on the size and nature of the dataset. In large datasets, an 80/20 split (i.e., 80% of the data for training and 20% for testing) is usually adequate, as it provides enough data for training without sacrificing the accuracy of the evaluation. In smaller datasets, however, a 70/30 split may be more useful to ensure a robust evaluation, although it also limits the amount of data available for learning. As the model is trained with the training set, parameter tuning techniques are used to reduce prediction error, making the model as close as possible to the real values. However, if the model fits the training data too closely, it can lose the ability to generalize, resulting in what is known as overfitting.

Overfitting is one of the most common problems in machine learning, and it occurs when the model becomes too tailored to the details and peculiarities of the training set, losing accuracy on new data. In an overfitted model, predictions tend to be accurate on the training set, but accuracy drops significantly when applied to the test set. This problem is particularly concerning for SMEs, which need reliable predictions in everyday situations. To mitigate overfitting, cross-validation is essential, as it allows for a more thorough evaluation of the model and ensures it doesn't rely too heavily on a single dataset.

Cross-validation is a process that involves dividing the data into multiple subsets or "folds," so that the model can be trained and evaluated several times on different data combinations. The most common version of cross-validation is k-fold cross-validation, where the data is divided into k subsets or folds. For example, if a value of k=5 is chosen, the data will be divided into five subsets, and the model will be trained five times, using four folds for training and one for evaluation in each iteration. This process allows each observation in the data to be used for both training and evaluation, providing a more robust measure of the model's accuracy. K-fold cross-validation offers several advantages over a simple train-test split, as it reduces variability in the results and allows for more effective detection of potential overfitting issues.

The implementation of cross-validation in Python is facilitated by libraries like Scikit-Learn, which include functions to perform cross-validation automatically. By using Scikit-Learn, the user only needs to define the desired number of folds, and the cross_val_score function will execute the cross-validation process, returning an accuracy measure for each fold. This approach allows companies to quickly and effectively assess model performance without manually splitting the data in each iteration. Cross-validation is also useful for tuning model hyperparameters, as it provides an accurate evaluation of how these adjustments affect the model's accuracy and generalization ability.

A practical example of cross-validation could be a small business that wants to predict product demand based on variables such as price, seasonality, and sales channel. In this case, the model could be trained using a k-fold cross-validation with k=10, providing 10 evaluations of the model's accuracy on different data subsets. By observing the results, the company could identify whether the model maintains stable accuracy across all folds or if some folds show significantly lower accuracy, indicating potential overfitting issues.

Cross-validation is especially valuable when you have limited datasets, as it maximizes the use of data by allowing each observation to be used for both training and evaluation. This is important in the context of an SME, where data is often more scarce compared to larger companies. However, cross-validation also has limitations; one of the main drawbacks is processing time, as the model must be trained and evaluated multiple times, which can be costly in terms of time and computational resources. In these cases, you can opt for cross-validation with a lower k value or use more advanced cross-validation techniques, such as stratified cross-validation, which ensures that each fold contains a balanced representation of the different classes in the dataset.

Another important technique used in combination with data splitting and cross-validation is hyperparameter tuning. Hyperparameters are model-specific parameters that are not learned directly from the data but must be predefined by the user, and they can have a significant impact on the model's performance. Examples of hyperparameters include the number of trees in a random forest model, the learning rate in a logistic regression model, or the maximum depth of the trees in a decision model. Choosing the optimal values for these hyperparameters can improve the model's accuracy and stability, reducing the risk of overfitting and maximizing its generalization capacity.

Hyperparameter tuning is often done through a process called Grid Search, which evaluates different combinations of hyperparameters and selects the combination that maximizes the model's accuracy. By combining Grid Search with cross-validation, SMEs can ensure that the model is optimized and capable of delivering accurate predictions on new data. The GridSearchCV tool from Scikit-Learn makes this process easier by automatically testing multiple hyperparameter combinations and evaluating each one using cross-validation.

Cross-validation and hyperparameter tuning are tools that, when combined, significantly improve model performance and generalization capabilities. For SMEs looking to optimize their operations and minimize errors in business decisions, these processes provide a rigorous approach to model evaluation and tuning, ensuring that predictions are as accurate and reliable as possible. The combination of training and test set division, cross-validation, and hyperparameter tuning allows companies to implement machine learning models that not only offer short-term accuracy but also maintain robust performance as they encounter new data and scenarios. This strategy ensures that models can adapt to changes in data and that decisions based on them are always supported by reliable and well-founded predictions.

The division of data into training and test, complemented by cross-validation techniques and hyperparameter tuning, establishes a solid foundation for SMEs to trust the performance of their machine learning models.

- **Evaluation metrics for regression models**

Evaluation metrics in regression models are essential for determining the accuracy and reliability of predictions that a model can offer in a practical context. Regression, being a predictive technique focused on forecasting continuous values, is widely used in SMEs for tasks such as estimating future sales, inventory forecasting, or revenue prediction. When evaluating a regression model's performance, it's crucial to use metrics that provide a clear interpretation of how close the predictions are to the actual values. Two of the most common and effective metrics for this purpose are the mean squared error (MSE) and the coefficient of determination (R^2). These metrics not only allow for comparing different regression models but also offer a detailed understanding of a model's behavior in terms of accuracy and explanatory capacity.

Mean Squared Error (MSE) is an evaluation metric that measures the average of the squared errors between the model's predictions and the actual values. MSE is calculated by squaring the difference between the predicted and actual values and then averaging these values. This results in a positive number, where lower values indicate a better fit of the model to the data. MSE is a metric that penalizes large errors more than small ones, due to the quadratic nature of the formula, meaning that if the model has significant errors in some predictions, the MSE will increase considerably. This is useful in many business scenarios as it allows for the detection of models that, while they might offer good predictions overall, struggle with extreme cases. This is especially relevant in sales or revenue forecasting, where errors in high or low predictions can significantly impact decision-making.

To calculate the MSE in Python with Scikit-Learn, you need the model's prediction set and the actual values of the data being evaluated. Scikit-Learn provides the mean_squared_error function, which allows you to calculate the MSE directly. In a practical implementation, after splitting the data into a training set and a test set, the model is trained on the training data and then used to make predictions on the test set. From the generated predictions, mean_squared_error is applied to obtain the MSE, which indicates how well the model predicts the test data. In the context of sales forecasting, a low MSE means that the sales projections are close to the actual values, making the model accurate and reliable.

Interpreting the MSE is essential for evaluating the practical usefulness of the model. Since the MSE is measured in the same units as the target variable squared, it's important to contextualize its value. For example, if an SME uses a model to forecast sales and obtains an MSE of 10,000, this suggests that the mean squared error of the predictions is 100 sales units (by taking the square root of 10,000), which allows the company to judge whether this margin of error is acceptable or if the model needs adjustment. A good practice for interpreting the MSE is to compare it with the average sales: if the MSE represents a small percentage of total average sales, the model can be considered sufficiently accurate; however, if the MSE is high in relation to the average sales, the model may need improvements in its features or tuning.

The coefficient of determination (R^2), on the other hand, is another fundamental metric for evaluating the performance of regression models. Unlike the MSE, R^2 does not measure errors in the units of the dependent variable but indicates the proportion of variance in the data explained by the model. R^2 is interpreted on a scale from 0 to 1, where values close to 1 suggest that the model explains a large part of the variability in the data, while values close to 0 indicate that the model cannot capture significant patterns in the data and that the predictions are no better than a simple mean. A high R^2 is desirable because it indicates that the model correctly captures variations in the data and can make predictions based on these trends.

In mathematical terms, R^2 compares the sum of the squared errors of the model with the total variance in the data and calculates what fraction of that variance is captured by the model. If the model fits the data perfectly, the R^2 will be equal to 1, as there will be no difference between the actual values and the predictions. However, if the model has limited explanatory power and does not capture the patterns in the data, the R^2 will be low, suggesting that the model may require additional adjustments or may not be suitable for the data in question. When evaluating R^2 in a sales prediction model, a value of 0.8, for example, would indicate that 80% of the variation in sales can be explained by the model, which is generally a good result in terms of accuracy.

To calculate R^2 in Python, Scikit-Learn offers the r2_score function, which evaluates the model's accuracy based on the predicted and actual values. Calculating R^2 is useful not only for interpreting a specific model but also for comparing the performance of different models and selecting the one that offers the best fit. In the context of an SME looking to optimize its sales predictions, R^2 can serve as an objective indicator of which model offers greater explanatory power and, therefore, more value in terms of prediction and decision-making.

The combined use of MSE and R^2 allows for a comprehensive evaluation of the regression model. While MSE provides a direct measure of errors in predictions, R^2 helps understand the model's ability to capture patterns and variations in the data. In scenarios where precision in terms of absolute error is critical, such as revenue forecasting, MSE can be a priority metric. On the other hand, in situations where a model with high explanatory power is desired, R^2 is more relevant as it shows how well the model describes the relationship between variables. These two approaches are not mutually exclusive but complementary, allowing SMEs to assess both the accuracy and robustness of their regression models.

Interpreting R^2 also has its nuances, as a value close to 1 doesn't always mean the model is suitable. In some cases, a high R^2 might indicate overfitting, especially if the model has captured noise or specific details from the training set that aren't representative of the data overall. It's important to remember that R^2 measures explanatory power on the dataset where it was calculated, and if the model is overfitted, its generalization ability may be compromised. To avoid this issue, it's essential to evaluate both MSE and R^2 on an independent test set, ensuring that predictions maintain their accuracy and explanatory power on new data.

In addition to MSE and R^2, there are variants of these metrics that can provide additional insights into the model's performance. For example, the mean absolute error (MAE) is another error metric that measures the average of the absolute errors without squaring them, offering a more direct measure of errors without disproportionately penalizing large errors. MAE is useful in cases where a more intuitive interpretation of errors in terms of the dependent variable's units is desired, although it does not provide the same sensitivity to extreme errors as MSE. SMEs can choose to use MAE in combination with MSE and R^2 to obtain a more complete view of the model's performance in terms of accuracy and variability.

Another complementary metric is the relative root mean squared error (RMSE), which is calculated by taking the square root of the MSE, thus providing an error measure in the same units as the dependent variable. This metric is useful when you want to interpret errors in the same units as sales, revenue, or any other continuous variable being predicted. In an SME looking to forecast sales, the RMSE provides an intuitive measure of how far, on average, the predictions are from the actual values, allowing for a more accurate assessment of the magnitude of the errors.

The combination of these metrics allows SMEs to perform a detailed analysis of the model's performance and make informed decisions about its applicability. While MSE and RMSE provide a measure of the average error in predictions, R^2 offers insight into the model's ability to explain variations in the data. Together, these metrics help identify strengths and weaknesses in the regression model, providing a balanced assessment of both its accuracy and explanatory power. For a company that relies on accurate forecasts, such as an SME that adjusts its inventory or pricing strategies based on projected demand, these metrics are essential to ensure the model is reliable and well-suited to its business objectives.

Evaluating a regression model involves much more than looking at a specific metric. It requires a comprehensive analysis that combines several metrics to ensure the model is suitable in terms of both error and explanatory power. A low MSE and a high R^2 are generally indicative of a robust model, but it's important to remember that these results must be interpreted in the specific context of the data and the company's objectives.

By deeply understanding how to calculate and interpret these metrics, SMEs can implement regression models more effectively and obtain accurate predictions that facilitate informed strategic decision-making aligned with their business goals.

- ## Evaluation metrics for classification models

In the evaluation of classification models, metrics are essential to understand the effectiveness and accuracy with which the model can make predictions. These models, which are fundamental in business applications such as predicting customer churn, lead conversion, and fraud detection, categorize observations into different classes, such as "yes" or "no," "repeat customer" or "new customer." To determine if the model correctly classifies these categories, metrics such as accuracy, recall, and F1-score are used, providing a detailed measure of performance. Additionally, tools like confusion matrix and ROC and AUC curves allow for visualizing and understanding the model's performance at a deeper level.

Precision is a basic metric in classification models that represents the percentage of correct predictions made by the model out of the total observations. It is calculated as the number of correct predictions divided by the total predictions. In practical applications, such as predicting customer churn, precision allows us to see how well the model correctly classifies customers who will leave or stay, compared to the actual data. However, precision has an important limitation: it does not distinguish between the types of errors the model can make. If the data is imbalanced, as often happens in problems where the positive class (customer churn) is less frequent than the negative class (loyal customers), precision could appear high simply because the model mostly predicts the more common class. For this reason, in imbalanced classification problems, additional metrics like recall and F1-score are essential.

Recall, also known as sensitivity or true positive rate, is another important evaluation metric that measures the model's ability to correctly identify positive cases, meaning those that truly belong to the class being detected. In the context of predicting customer churn, recall indicates what percentage of customers who will actually leave have been correctly identified by the model. A high recall means the model is effective at detecting positive cases, although it may have some false positives. This metric is particularly relevant in situations where false negatives have a high cost. For example, in detecting customers who will churn, a false negative (failing to detect that a customer will leave when they actually will) could result in losing a customer, which can have a direct financial impact. On the other hand, a false positive in this context would only mean additional effort in trying to retain a customer who may not leave.

The F1-score is a metric that combines precision and recall into a single harmonic measure, providing a balance between the two. It is especially useful when both precision and recall need to be considered, which is common in imbalanced classification problems. In the context of lead conversion, the F1-score helps assess how well the model correctly identifies leads that will convert into customers without making too many errors. A high F1-score means that the model not only correctly identifies positive cases but also minimizes false positives and false negatives. This metric is particularly useful in marketing campaigns where the goal is to optimize resources, ensuring that efforts are focused on leads with the highest conversion probabilities.

The confusion matrix is another essential tool in evaluating classification models, as it provides a detailed view of the types of errors the model makes. This matrix is a table that organizes the model's predictions into four categories: true positives (TP), true negatives (TN), false positives (FP), and false negatives (FN). In the context of predicting customer churn, the confusion matrix allows you to see how many customers were correctly classified as churners or loyal, as well as the cases where the model made errors. True positives represent customers who will indeed churn and were classified as such, while true negatives are the loyal customers correctly identified. False positives correspond to loyal customers who were mistakenly classified as churners, and false negatives represent customers who will churn but were classified as loyal.

Reading the confusion matrix allows the company to identify patterns in the model's errors and make adjustments to improve its performance. In Python, Scikit-Learn makes it easy to create a confusion matrix using the confusion_matrix function, which can be implemented after training the model and making predictions on a test set. Analyzing this matrix is crucial for a comprehensive evaluation of the model, as it helps understand whether classification errors are higher in false positives or false negatives, allowing for informed decision-making based on this information. For example, in a customer retention campaign, a high number of false negatives would indicate that the model is not adequately capturing customers who will leave, suggesting that the model might need adjustments in its features or parameters to improve recall.

Another advanced metric for evaluating classification models is the ROC curve (Receiver Operating Characteristic), along with the AUC (Area Under the Curve). The ROC curve is a graphical representation that allows you to visualize the model's performance at different classification thresholds. On the y-axis of the ROC curve, you have the true positive rate, while on the x-axis, you have the false positive rate. As you adjust the model's classification threshold, the ROC curve shows how these rates change, allowing you to observe the balance between sensitivity (recall) and specificity. A model with a good ability to distinguish between classes will tend to have a ROC curve that approaches the upper left corner of the graph, where the true positive rate is high and the false positive rate is low.

The AUC, or area under the ROC curve, is a numerical value that summarizes the performance of the ROC curve in a single metric, ranging from 0 to 1. An AUC of 1 indicates a perfect model, while an AUC of 0.5 suggests that the model is no better than random classification. In practice, an AUC close to 1 means that the model has a high capacity to distinguish between classes, and it is particularly useful in problems where the balance between false positives and false negatives is critical. In the context of lead conversion, a high AUC allows the company to be confident that the model can correctly identify leads with a higher probability of conversion, making it easier to optimize the allocation of marketing resources.

The ROC curve and AUC are useful metrics for comparing different models and selecting the one with the best overall performance in terms of sensitivity and specificity. In Python, the roc_curve and auc functions from Scikit-Learn allow you to calculate and plot the ROC curve and AUC quickly and easily. These tools are especially useful in imbalanced classification problems, as they allow you to assess the model's effectiveness in conditions where precision and recall alone are not always sufficient to determine the model's optimal performance.

The combined use of precision, recall, F1-score, confusion matrix, ROC curve, and AUC provides a comprehensive view of a classification model's performance. Precision helps understand the overall proportion of correct predictions, while recall shows the model's ability to correctly identify positive cases. The F1-score balances these metrics, providing a harmonized measure of precision and recall that is useful in imbalanced problems. The confusion matrix allows for the analysis of the model's specific errors and the identification of areas for improvement. Finally, the ROC curve and AUC offer a graphical representation and a global metric that facilitate the comparison of models in terms of their discrimination ability.

In the context of an SME, using these metrics allows for a comprehensive evaluation of the classification model and ensures that the predictions are accurate and useful in practical applications. If a company is launching a campaign to convert leads into customers, precision and recall will measure how well the model identifies the leads most likely to convert. If the model has a high F1-score, the company can be confident that marketing resources are being optimally directed towards the right leads. The confusion matrix allows you to see if there is a high number of false negatives or false positives, which could affect the campaign's effectiveness. The ROC curve and AUC together provide an advanced assessment of the model's ability to distinguish between leads that will convert and those that won't, ensuring that the model offers adequate performance in all situations.

These evaluation metrics allow for informed decision-making and adjusting classification models according to the specific needs of the business. In practice, the results of each metric are used to optimize model parameters, adjust decision thresholds, and improve feature selection. This continuous optimization is essential to maintain the accuracy and relevance of classification models in constantly changing business environments.

- **Cross-validation**

Cross-validation is an evaluation technique in machine learning that provides an accurate and robust estimate of a model's performance, ensuring it can generalize its predictions to new, unseen data. Its main advantage lies in maximizing the use of available data, avoiding overfitting, and providing a more reliable view of the model's accuracy. This is especially important for SMEs, which often have limited datasets and need to evaluate their models effectively, optimizing their ability to predict in various scenarios.

In the traditional approach, the data is divided into two sets: one for training and one for testing. However, this division has some limitations, especially if the data is scarce or if the model struggles to capture complex patterns. In cross-validation, the dataset is divided into multiple subsets or partitions, allowing the model to be trained and tested several times on different data combinations. This results in a more comprehensive and robust evaluation, reducing the risk of the model's performance relying solely on a single data split.

K-fold cross-validation is the most common type of cross-validation, where the dataset is divided into k equal-sized subsets or folds. In each iteration, one of these folds is used as the test set, while the remaining folds are used for training. This process is repeated k times, so that each fold serves as the test set once, and the model is trained on the rest of the folds. At the end of the iterations, an average of the metrics obtained in each test is calculated, providing an overall evaluation of the model. This technique ensures that the model has been thoroughly evaluated on all available data, reducing variance in performance metrics and allowing for a reliable estimate of the model's accuracy.

The choice of the number of folds (k) is a fundamental aspect of cross-validation. In general, a value of k between 5 and 10 is suitable for most problems, providing a good balance between evaluation accuracy and processing time. A lower value, such as k=3, may not be sufficient to ensure a robust evaluation, as some important data might not be used as a test set. On the other hand, a very high value, like k=20 or k=30, increases processing time and can introduce some variability in the results, especially if the data is limited. For an SME handling smaller databases, a value of k=5 or k=10 is recommended, as it allows for a thorough evaluation of the model without compromising the available time and computational resources.

In addition to k-fold, there are other variants of cross-validation that can be useful in specific scenarios. Stratified cross-validation is a technique that ensures each fold contains a balanced representation of classes in the dataset, which is crucial when classes are imbalanced. For example, in problems where a positive class is much less frequent than the negative one (such as predicting customer churn), stratified cross-validation helps ensure both classes are represented in each fold, preventing the model from learning biased patterns. Stratification is particularly valuable in classification, as it helps the model generalize to both classes and ensures its performance is not affected by the lack of representation of any of them.

Another variant is leave-one-out cross-validation (LOOCV), where the number of folds equals the number of observations in the dataset. In each iteration, a single observation is used as the test set, while the rest are used for training. This process is repeated as many times as there are observations in the data, providing a thorough evaluation of the model on each data point. Although LOOCV offers an extremely detailed view of the model's performance, it is a resource-intensive technique and can be impractical for large datasets. However, in small datasets, LOOCV allows for maximizing the use of each observation and obtaining an accurate measure of the model's ability to generalize to new data.

The implementation of cross-validation in Python is straightforward thanks to libraries like Scikit-Learn, which provide built-in functions to perform cross-validation automatically. The cross_val_score function allows you to train and evaluate the model across multiple folds, returning a list of performance metrics that can then be averaged for an overall assessment. This approach simplifies the validation process and allows SMEs to evaluate their models quickly and reliably. Additionally, Scikit-Learn allows you to specify the number of folds and the type of cross-validation you want to perform, offering flexibility to tailor the process to different types of problems and data sizes.

Cross-validation is also a useful tool for model selection and hyperparameter tuning. In many cases, an SME may be evaluating different machine learning algorithms to solve a specific problem, such as sales prediction or customer classification. Cross-validation allows for a fair comparison of different models, as each is evaluated on the same set of folds and under the same conditions. By observing the average metrics of each model, the company can select the one that offers the best overall performance, without relying on a single data split. This approach helps avoid biased decisions and ensures that the selected model is the most suitable for the business's needs.

In hyperparameter tuning, cross-validation is key to optimizing model performance. Hyperparameters are specific model parameters that are not learned directly from the data but must be defined by the user. Examples of hyperparameters include the number of trees in a random forest or the learning rate in a gradient model. Cross-validation allows evaluating the impact of different hyperparameter combinations, identifying those that maximize the model's accuracy and generalization ability. Scikit-Learn's GridSearchCV tool facilitates this process, combining grid search with cross-validation to automatically evaluate each hyperparameter combination across multiple folds. At the end of the process, GridSearchCV selects the optimal hyperparameter configuration, allowing the company to obtain a tuned model ready for deployment.

In the context of an SME, cross-validation not only helps to select and fine-tune models but also allows for the identification of potential issues in the model's performance. If significant variations in metrics are observed across folds during cross-validation, this may indicate that the model is sensitive to changes in the data and could have generalization problems in production. This type of analysis is crucial to avoid overfitting the model to specific features of the training data and to ensure stable performance in different situations. Additionally, by reviewing the metrics in each fold, the company can identify if certain data subsets have particular characteristics that affect the model's performance and consider adjustments to the features or the model itself.

The use of cross-validation is also crucial in continuous model evaluation processes. In many business applications, data changes over time due to seasonality, shifts in consumer behavior, or market fluctuations. Cross-validation allows you to periodically assess the model's performance using new data to ensure it maintains its accuracy and relevance. This continuous assessment is especially important in dynamic environments, where a model's predictions can lose accuracy if not regularly updated. Cross-validation helps identify these issues and allows you to decide whether the model needs retraining or its features adjusted to remain effective.

Ultimately, cross-validation provides a comprehensive and reliable assessment of the model's performance, maximizing data usage and ensuring that decisions based on the model's predictions are as accurate and robust as possible. For SMEs, which often rely on small datasets and limited resources, cross-validation is an invaluable tool that allows for efficient model evaluation and adjustment, optimizing their generalization capacity and providing a solid foundation for data-driven decision-making.

- **Hyperparameter tuning**

Hyperparameter tuning is a crucial stage in the development and optimization of machine learning models, as it allows maximizing the model's performance by adjusting certain parameters that are not learned directly from the data. Hyperparameters are configurations that control the behavior and structure of the model before the training process, significantly influencing the model's accuracy, generalization ability, and efficiency. Unlike parameters, which are internal values of the model automatically adjusted during training, hyperparameters must be defined by the user and adjusted according to the specific problem and available data. The proper choice of hyperparameters can make a significant difference in the model's performance, which is particularly relevant for SMEs looking to achieve optimal results and maximize the value of their data.

The process of hyperparameter tuning allows experimenting with different model configurations and selecting the combination that offers the best performance in terms of accuracy and generalization capability. In classification models like decision trees and random forests, hyperparameters can include the number of trees in the forest, the maximum depth of each tree, and the minimum number of samples required to split a node. Each of these hyperparameters affects the model's behavior in a different way. For example, in a random forest model, increasing the number of trees usually improves accuracy by reducing the risk of overfitting; however, this also increases processing time. Similarly, in logistic regression algorithms, the learning rate is a key hyperparameter that defines the speed at which the model adjusts its internal weights during training. If the learning rate is too high, the model can become unstable and fail to converge, while a rate that is too low can lead to extremely slow training and suboptimal results.

To systematically and efficiently tune hyperparameters, it's common to use techniques like Grid Search and Random Search. Grid Search is an exhaustive method that evaluates all possible combinations of hyperparameters within a defined range, identifying the optimal configuration that maximizes the model's performance. In Grid Search, the user defines a range of values for each hyperparameter, and the algorithm evaluates every possible combination of these values, ultimately selecting the combination that offers the best average performance on a validation set. Although Grid Search ensures a complete exploration of the hyperparameter space, it can be costly in terms of time and resources, especially for complex models or large datasets. However, for simpler models or when working with a limited set of hyperparameters, Grid Search is an effective option to obtain an optimized and robust model.

In Python, the Scikit-Learn library makes hyperparameter tuning easy with the GridSearchCV function, which combines grid search with cross-validation. GridSearchCV allows each hyperparameter combination to be evaluated across multiple cross-validation folds, improving the reliability of the results and reducing the risk of selecting configurations that only work on a specific data partition. The user defines a dictionary of hyperparameters and their possible values, and GridSearchCV evaluates all combinations based on a specified performance metric, such as accuracy, recall, or F1-score. At the end of the process, GridSearchCV returns the model with the best combination of hyperparameters, along with an estimate of its average performance, enabling the company to select the optimal configuration quickly and efficiently.

On the other hand, random search is an alternative to grid search that randomly selects a subset of hyperparameter combinations within the search space. Instead of testing all possible combinations, random search evaluates only a sample of these combinations, which reduces processing time and is especially useful when the hyperparameter space is large or the model is very complex. Random search offers good results in a reduced time, although it does not guarantee a thorough exploration of all possible configurations. In Scikit-Learn, the RandomizedSearchCV function allows you to implement this technique easily, providing a quick evaluation of multiple hyperparameter combinations without the need to test each configuration. Random search is useful in problems where quick optimization is needed or in situations where an initial exploration of the hyperparameter space is desired before performing a more detailed grid search.

To illustrate how hyperparameter tuning works, let's consider a practical example of an SME using a random forest model to predict customer churn probability. In this case, some of the key hyperparameters to adjust include the number of trees in the forest, the maximum depth of each tree, and the minimum number of samples required to split a node. By using GridSearchCV, the company can define a range of values for each of these hyperparameters and conduct an exhaustive search to identify the combination that maximizes accuracy on a validation set. For example, they could set a range of 50 to 200 trees, with maximum depths varying between 5 and 20 levels, and a minimum number of samples to split a node between 2 and 10. Once the search is complete, GridSearchCV will return the optimal configuration and the model trained with these values, ready for production deployment.

Hyperparameter tuning not only improves the accuracy of the model, but also optimizes its ability to generalize and its efficiency in resource usage. Some hyperparameters can enhance performance at the expense of processing time, while others help simplify the model to make it more efficient without losing accuracy. In the case of logistic regression, a key hyperparameter is the regularization parameter, which controls the level of penalty applied to the model's weights to prevent overfitting. Proper regularization prevents the model from fitting too closely to the training data, improving its ability to generalize to new data. In GridSearchCV, the user can define a range of values for the regularization parameter and evaluate its impact on model accuracy through cross-validation, allowing them to select the value that best balances accuracy and robustness.

In addition to grid search and random search, there are more advanced methods for hyperparameter tuning, such as Bayesian optimization and Hyperband, which offer more sophisticated solutions for finding the optimal hyperparameter configuration. Bayesian optimization is an approach that uses a probabilistic model to explore the hyperparameter space, prioritizing combinations that have a higher probability of improving the model's performance. Instead of exhaustively or randomly testing each combination, Bayesian optimization evaluates configurations iteratively, learning from each previous test and adjusting its search strategy. This approach significantly reduces the number of combinations needed to find an optimal solution, and it is useful in complex models where processing time is a critical factor. Although it is not as common in Scikit-Learn, there are additional libraries like Optuna and Hyperopt that allow the implementation of Bayesian optimization in Python, and they can be combined with machine learning models.

Hyperband is another hyperparameter tuning method that uses an adaptive strategy to allocate processing resources to the most promising configurations. Instead of evaluating all combinations equally, Hyperband starts by evaluating a large number of combinations with fewer resources and, in each iteration, discards the less effective configurations. This approach allows resources to be focused on the configurations that show better performance, achieving faster and more efficient optimization in complex problems. Hyperband is especially useful in deep learning models, where hyperparameter tuning can require very long processing times.

Hyperparameter tuning is not only a valuable technique for maximizing model accuracy, but it also allows us to explore configurations that optimize other objectives, such as resource efficiency, generalization capacity, or processing speed. Each machine learning model has its own specific hyperparameters, and their choice depends on the type of data, the problem to be solved, and the company's time and resource constraints. For SMEs, which often have limited resources, it's important to find a suitable balance between accuracy and efficiency, ensuring the model is precise without incurring excessive processing times or complex configurations that are difficult to implement in production.

Ultimately, hyperparameter tuning allows the model to be tailored to the specific needs and characteristics of each application. A model optimized through hyperparameter tuning is not only more accurate but also more robust and capable of delivering reliable predictions across various scenarios. Scikit-Learn's ability to combine grid search and cross-validation techniques in GridSearchCV simplifies this process, providing businesses with an accessible and effective tool to fine-tune their models and get the most out of their data.

6.5. Advanced feature engineering techniques

Advanced feature engineering techniques allow SMEs to maximize the value of their data, significantly improving the performance and accuracy of their machine learning models. Feature engineering is the process of transforming and enriching the original data, creating new features or modifying existing ones to better capture the relationships between variables and enable the model to identify useful patterns for predictions. In the context of an SME, this practice is especially valuable, as their data may often be limited in size or detail. However, through the creative use of available data and the generation of new features, it's possible to overcome these limitations and build robust and effective models.

For SMEs, advanced feature engineering can make a big difference, as it allows them to make the most of their business knowledge and turn raw data into useful, actionable information. An example of this could be an e-commerce company that, by combining the purchase history of its customers with their activity on social media, can create advanced features to predict future purchases. This type of feature could reflect the likelihood of a customer making a purchase based on variables such as the frequency of interaction with the brand on social media or the nature of those interactions, allowing the model to capture more complex behavior patterns. These additional features provide the model with a richer information base and increase its accuracy, as they allow it to consider both historical behavior and recent customer interest.

Among the advanced feature engineering techniques, combining variables is one of the most effective for creating new features that capture complex relationships within the data. By combining two or more variables, it is possible to create derived features that represent specific interactions or patterns in the data. For example, in a retail company, a feature could be created that combines the number of products purchased and the total amount spent into a single 'purchase intensity' indicator to measure customers' spending tendency. This feature allows the model to consider both the frequency and the value of purchases, providing a more accurate reflection of buying behavior. In a business environment where variables like spending and frequency are correlated with customer value, these combinations can significantly improve the model's ability to predict future behavior.

Another advanced technique is the creation of temporal features, which is especially useful for data with a temporal structure, such as daily sales, website visits, or social media interactions. Temporal features include aspects like the day of the week, month, seasonality, and trend, all of which can influence customer behavior patterns. For example, a fashion company might observe that its sales tend to increase on specific days of the month or during certain seasons, like year-end sales. By creating temporal features, the company allows the model to capture these seasonal patterns and improve the accuracy of its predictions. In many cases, adding features like 'day of the month' or 'sales season' can enhance the model's ability to anticipate demand spikes or sales slumps, enabling the company to better plan its inventory and marketing campaigns.

Feature extraction from text is another advanced technique that is gaining importance in the analysis of unstructured data, such as social media comments, customer reviews, and service interactions. Text data contains rich information about customers' opinions and preferences, which can help build more accurate prediction models aligned with customer needs. To extract useful features from this textual data, techniques like word frequency (TF-IDF) can be applied to identify the most relevant words in the data context, or sentiment analysis, which measures the positive or negative tone of the comments. For example, a company managing product reviews could create features that reflect the average sentiment of each customer's reviews, which would help identify those with a higher likelihood of repurchase or churn. Text feature extraction can improve customer segmentation and marketing campaign personalization, as it provides the model with emotional and subjective context that numerical data alone cannot capture.

Another advanced feature engineering strategy is the use of data aggregations, which involve calculating specific statistics on data groups to create new features. In a subscription service company, for example, you could create aggregated features that reflect the average time between renewals or the average duration of subscriptions across different customer segments. These aggregations provide the model with a more detailed view of customer behavior over time, allowing it to capture patterns of recurrence or loyalty. Aggregations can include means, medians, maximums and minimums, frequencies, and rates of change, and they are especially useful in time series problems or situations where data reflects repetitive customer behavior. By including aggregated features, the model gains a more complete context of variations in customer behavior, enabling it to improve accuracy in predicting future patterns.

Normalization and standardization of features is a preprocessing technique that allows machine learning models to better interpret data. Although it's not a feature creation technique per se, its impact on feature engineering is notable, as it improves the quality of features and allows the model to focus on underlying relationships. Normalization transforms data to a standard scale (such as between 0 and 1), while standardization adjusts them to have a mean of zero and a standard deviation of one. These transformations are especially important in algorithms like logistic regression and SVM, which are sensitive to scale differences in variables. For an SME managing variables in different units of measure, normalization and standardization allow the model to capture relationships between variables that might otherwise go unnoticed.

Interactions between variables are another advanced feature engineering technique that allows complex relationships in the data to be captured by creating new features based on the multiplication or combination of two or more variables. In a sales prediction model, for example, it might be useful to create a feature representing the interaction between product price and purchase frequency, as this interaction can reflect customers' price sensitivity. By including these interactions, the model gains a more detailed view of how variables influence each other, allowing it to capture more subtle patterns in the data. Creating interactions is especially valuable in regression and classification models, where relationships between variables can significantly influence the outcome.

The use of embeddings is another advanced feature engineering technique that is particularly useful for working with high-dimensional categorical data, such as customer IDs or product names. Embeddings are reduced-dimensional vector representations that encode categorical information in a continuous structure, capturing relationships and similarities between categories. For an SME managing thousands of different products or customers, embeddings allow the dimensionality of these data to be reduced, avoiding the risk of overfitting and improving model efficiency. In a product recommendation context, for example, embeddings can represent the similarity between products and enable the model to recommend relevant products based on past customer preferences.

The technique of imputing missing values is fundamental in feature engineering, as it allows for effective handling of incomplete data. In many cases, SMEs may face data with null or missing values, which can affect the model's performance if not properly managed. Missing values can be imputed using methods such as mean, median, mode, or predictive models that estimate the missing values based on observed features. This technique is important because it preserves the integrity of the dataset and prevents missing values from introducing biases into the model. By performing imputation, SMEs can ensure that the model is trained on a complete dataset, improving its generalization capability.

The encoding of categorical variables is another advanced technique that transforms categorical variables into a numerical representation that the model can process. Some common encoding techniques include one-hot encoding, which creates a column for each category, and target encoding, which replaces each category with the mean of the target variable in that category. In the case of a company that handles categorical information such as product type or region of origin, encoding allows these variables to be effectively used in the model without introducing collinearity or redundant information. The choice of encoding type depends on the nature of the data and the model to be used, as each technique has its advantages and disadvantages in terms of accuracy and efficiency.

Ultimately, the use of advanced feature engineering techniques allows SMEs to build more accurate and robust models, even when working with limited datasets or unstructured data. These techniques maximize the value of the data, transforming it into relevant features that capture complex patterns and relationships, enabling the model to make more precise predictions.

6.6. Using XGBoost for SMEs

XGBoost (eXtreme Gradient Boosting) is one of the most powerful and versatile machine learning algorithms, especially popular for its superior performance in classification and regression tasks. This algorithm has become an essential tool in business environments and is widely used in machine learning competitions for its ability to produce accurate, high-quality models across a variety of predictive problems. For an SME looking to implement a machine learning strategy with the goal of improving predictions and optimizing processes, XGBoost represents an accessible and powerful option that can solve complex problems effectively.

XGBoost is an algorithm based on boosting, a machine learning technique focused on improving a model's accuracy by combining several low-performing models, known as weak models, into a single strong model. In simple terms, boosting involves training multiple models sequentially, where each model tries to correct the errors of the previous one. In the case of XGBoost, it uses the gradient boosting algorithm, which successively adjusts each model to minimize prediction error through a gradient-based optimization technique. This allows XGBoost to be extremely accurate and efficient at capturing complex patterns in data, often outperforming other machine learning algorithms, such as individual decision trees or linear regressions.

One of the reasons why XGBoost is particularly suitable for SMEs is its ability to handle both classification and regression tasks. This means it can be used for a variety of problems, from predicting future sales and credit risk analysis to customer segmentation and fraud detection. Additionally, XGBoost is highly flexible and allows users to adjust a wide range of hyperparameters that control its behavior, which means the model can be tailored to the specific characteristics of the data to improve performance. This precise control over the model enables SMEs to adjust the algorithm according to their particular needs, optimizing both the accuracy and efficiency of their predictions.

To implement XGBoost in an SME, the first step is to prepare the data, ensuring it is clean, complete, and correctly labeled for the classification or regression task at hand. As with other machine learning models, data quality is crucial for XGBoost's performance. This involves cleaning processes such as imputing missing values, normalizing or standardizing features, and transforming categorical variables into numerical values using techniques like one-hot encoding or target encoding. Proper data preparation ensures that XGBoost can accurately identify patterns in the data and maximize the quality of its predictions.

To train an XGBoost model in Python, you can use the xgboost library, which allows you to implement the model quickly and directly. Once the data is prepared, you create an instance of the XGBClassifier model for classification tasks or XGBRegressor for regression tasks, specifying the necessary basic parameters. The flexibility of XGBoost lies in its ability to define a wide variety of hyperparameters that can be tuned to improve the model's performance, such as tree depth, number of estimators, learning rate, and regularization method. Each of these hyperparameters affects the model's accuracy and generalization ability, allowing it to be finely tuned for specific problems.

One of the main hyperparameters in XGBoost is the number of estimators or trees in the model, which defines how many trees will be used in the boosting process. A higher number of estimators tends to increase the model's accuracy, but it also raises processing time and the risk of overfitting. On the other hand, the maximum depth of the trees controls the level of detail with which the model can capture patterns in the data. Greater depth allows the model to capture more complex relationships, but it can also lead to overfitting if the model becomes too tailored to the training data. For an SME, finding a balance between these hyperparameters is crucial, as the goal is a precise and generalizable model that can be implemented efficiently without consuming excessive resources.

The learning rate is another fundamental hyperparameter in XGBoost, which controls how quickly the model adjusts its internal weights in each iteration. A lower learning rate allows the model to make more precise adjustments and reduces the risk of overfitting, although at the cost of longer training times. Regularization is also an essential aspect of XGBoost, helping to avoid overfitting by penalizing overly complex models. In XGBoost, there are two main regularization parameters: lambda (also called L2) and alpha (or L1). These parameters control the level of penalty applied to the model's coefficients and allow you to adjust its complexity to improve its generalization ability.

In addition to its advanced predictive capabilities, XGBoost includes additional features that make it especially efficient and suitable for use in SMEs. For instance, XGBoost has a parallel processing system that allows multiple trees to be trained simultaneously, which significantly reduces processing time and facilitates model use in resource-constrained environments. It also offers memory optimization through data compression and storage in specialized data structures, enabling SMEs to work with large datasets without the need for advanced hardware resources. This resource optimization capability makes XGBoost an ideal choice for companies looking to maximize model performance without incurring additional infrastructure costs.

XGBoost also adapts well to problems where data may be imbalanced, such as in customer churn prediction, where there are usually fewer churn cases compared to retention. In this context, the model allows you to adjust class weights so that observations of the minority class (churn) receive greater weight during training, balancing the impact of both classes and improving the model's ability to correctly detect minority cases. This feature is especially useful for SMEs in sectors like e-commerce, where customer churn represents a significant risk and early detection of customers likely to leave can facilitate the design of effective retention strategies.

The ability of XGBoost to perform regression tasks makes it a valuable tool for SMEs looking to predict continuous variables, such as sales, revenue, or costs. In a regression task, XGBoost builds decision trees that attempt to minimize error at each iteration through gradient adjustment. This approach allows the model to capture non-linear patterns and complex relationships between the independent variables and the dependent variable, which is particularly useful in businesses where sales and cost data can be affected by multiple factors, such as seasonality, market trends, and changes in consumer demand. By properly tuning the hyperparameters and applying regularization techniques, an SME can build a regression model with XGBoost that provides accurate and high-value predictions for strategic planning and decision-making.

To evaluate the performance of an XGBoost model, specific metrics can be used depending on the task, such as accuracy, recall, or F1-score for classification, and mean squared error (MSE) or the coefficient of determination (R^2) for regression. XGBoost also allows for the generation of a feature importance metric, which shows which variables have the greatest impact on the model's predictions. For an SME, this information is invaluable as it helps identify which factors most influence the likelihood of lead conversion or revenue forecasting, aiding in prioritizing business areas and adjusting marketing, sales, and operations strategies.

Another key advantage of XGBoost is that it can easily integrate with hyperparameter optimization tools like GridSearchCV and RandomizedSearchCV from Scikit-Learn, allowing SMEs to optimize the model quickly and effectively. These tools facilitate the search for hyperparameter combinations that maximize the model's performance, which is crucial in business environments where prediction accuracy can directly translate into financial benefits or resource optimization.

In terms of implementation, deploying an XGBoost model in a production environment is also relatively straightforward. XGBoost allows the model to be exported in formats like PMML or ONNX, which facilitate integration with enterprise systems and real-time data analysis applications. This enables the predictions generated by the model to be used directly in business decision-making, improving the agility and accuracy of the company's responses to market fluctuations and customer needs.

Ultimately, XGBoost offers SMEs a powerful and accessible machine learning tool that optimizes both classification and regression tasks. With its ability to capture complex patterns and its flexibility in hyperparameter tuning, XGBoost makes it easy to create accurate and generalizable models that can be applied to a wide range of business predictive problems.

6.7. Real-time prediction

Real-time prediction represents one of the most advanced and valuable applications of machine learning in the business world, offering SMEs a tool to improve their operations and optimize customer experience. With the integration of real-time predictive models, SMEs can respond immediately to changes in customer behavior, anticipate needs, and quickly adapt to market fluctuations. In sectors such as e-commerce, financial services, logistics, and customer service, this ability to make instant predictions allows for the implementation of personalized solutions, inventory adjustments, and the launch of effective marketing campaigns at the right moment, achieving a direct impact on customer satisfaction and business results.

In the case of an ecommerce site, real-time prediction allows for personalized recommendations based on the customer's current behavior, resulting in a more appealing shopping experience tailored to the user's interests. By analyzing real-time data such as browsing history, recent searches, and viewed products, the system can identify behavioral patterns and suggest relevant products, increasing conversion rates and improving customer satisfaction. This ability to make instant recommendations also enables SMEs to compete more effectively with large ecommerce platforms by offering a level of personalization that was traditionally only available to companies with advanced resources.

For an SME to implement real-time predictions, it is essential to have a technological infrastructure capable of collecting, processing, and predicting data on the spot. One of the most widely used technologies for this purpose is data streaming, which allows for the capture and processing of information in real time, maintaining a constant flow of data without interruptions. Real-time processing tools like Apache Kafka and Apache Flink can manage large volumes of data and prepare them for continuous use by predictive models. These processing platforms are compatible with machine learning models and can be easily integrated into the company's workflow, enabling real-time predictions without the need for pauses to process historical data.

Once the data streaming infrastructure is up and running, it's possible to integrate a machine learning model that processes this data in real time. In the context of an ecommerce site, the predictive model could be a recommendation engine based on a collaborative filtering algorithm, where recommendations are made based on the behavior of other users with similar browsing and purchasing patterns. As the customer interacts with the site, the model analyzes their behavior in real time and adjusts the recommendations to offer products that are more likely to interest them. This type of personalized recommendation not only improves the customer experience but also increases the time spent on the site and the likelihood of making additional purchases.

Another option for making real-time recommendations is the use of deep learning models, which are particularly effective at processing large volumes of data and capturing complex patterns in user behavior. A neural network model, for example, can analyze multiple variables at the same time, such as user characteristics, purchase history, browsing time, and previous interactions, generating recommendations in a matter of milliseconds. Recurrent neural networks (RNN) and convolutional neural networks (CNN) are particularly suitable for this type of prediction, as they are designed to process data sequences and can quickly adapt to changes in customer behavior. SMEs that integrate deep learning models into their ecommerce platform can offer more accurate recommendations and achieve a level of personalization that boosts customer loyalty and increases purchase value.

To facilitate the use of predictive models in real time, some machine learning platforms like TensorFlow Serving and Amazon SageMaker allow for efficient model deployment. TensorFlow Serving, for example, is a library specifically designed to serve machine learning models in production and allows for managing multiple versions of a model simultaneously, which is ideal for continuous updates without interrupting service. Amazon SageMaker, on the other hand, offers a complete machine learning platform that enables training, tuning, and deploying models in real time, optimizing workflow and facilitating integration with other company tools and systems. For an SME looking for quick and accessible implementation, these platforms represent a practical and effective solution that allows for real-time predictions without the need for complex internal infrastructure.

In the case of an SME managing its own website or ecommerce application, integrating real-time predictions can be done through APIs that communicate with the machine learning model. The APIs allow the model to receive current user data (such as site interactions or purchase information) and return a real-time prediction, like a product recommendation or a personalized offer. This approach is particularly useful when the model is hosted in the cloud, as it enables access to machine learning services from providers like Google Cloud, Amazon Web Services, or Microsoft Azure without the need for additional infrastructure. For SMEs, using APIs facilitates scalability and allows real-time predictions to adapt to user volume without compromising system performance.

Real-time prediction can also be applied to inventory management in an SME, especially in sectors where product demand fluctuates constantly, such as retail and fashion. With a real-time predictive model, it's possible to anticipate the demand for specific products and adjust inventory proactively, avoiding both overstocking and stockouts. A real-time inventory prediction system can analyze factors like buying trends, active promotions, and recent sales to estimate future demand in real time, allowing the company to maintain the right inventory and reduce operational costs. In an ecommerce environment, this translates to a smoother shopping experience for the customer, who always finds products available, and resource optimization for the company, which can avoid sales losses due to stock shortages.

In customer service, real-time prediction allows for optimizing response times and improving service quality. By using natural language processing (NLP) models, it's possible to analyze customer interactions with support agents in real time and predict satisfaction levels or the risk of customer churn. A real-time prediction system can alert agents when it detects signs of frustration or dissatisfaction in customer responses, allowing the support team to take proactive measures to resolve the issue. This ability to predict customer satisfaction in real time is especially useful in sectors like financial services and e-commerce, where the customer experience is a key factor for retention and loyalty.

Another relevant application of real-time prediction is fraud detection, especially for SMEs that process online payments or handle financial transactions. Real-time classification models can identify unusual patterns in user behavior, such as high-value purchases in a short period or access attempts from unusual locations, and send immediate alerts to prevent fraudulent activities. Real-time fraud detection reduces the risk of financial losses and protects customer security, thereby enhancing trust in the company's platform. Additionally, the model can be continuously updated with new fraud data, improving its responsiveness and accuracy as it encounters new types of threats.

In the context of logistics and supply chain, real-time forecasting can facilitate route optimization and efficient delivery management. By analyzing traffic, weather, and vehicle availability data, real-time predictive models can suggest optimal routes for drivers and adjust delivery schedules according to current conditions. This allows SMEs managing product deliveries to reduce transportation costs, improve delivery punctuality, and offer a more reliable service to their customers. In an environment where delivery demand can constantly vary, real-time forecasting helps the company maintain precise control over its operations and quickly adapt to changes in demand or distribution network conditions.

Implementing real-time predictions also requires proper management of computing resources, especially when working with complex machine learning models that require intensive data processing. The use of GPUs (Graphics Processing Units) and TPUs (Tensor Processing Units) can significantly speed up the model's response time, allowing it to make instant predictions without compromising system performance. For SMEs that lack these resources, cloud implementation is a viable alternative, as many cloud service providers offer on-demand GPUs and TPUs, enabling companies to deploy their models in a scalable and efficient way.

Ultimately, real-time prediction offers SMEs a significant competitive advantage, as it allows them to anticipate their customers' needs and optimize their operations in a dynamic and ever-changing environment. The ability to make recommendations, manage inventories, improve customer service, detect fraud, and optimize logistics in real-time creates a more agile and proactive business experience that directly responds to the challenges of the modern market.

6.8. Automation of the model lifecycle

The automation of the lifecycle of machine learning models is essential to ensure that a model's predictions and recommendations remain accurate and useful over time. Most machine learning models tend to lose precision and effectiveness over time due to changes in data, user behavior, or environmental conditions. This phenomenon, known as data drift or model drift, poses a significant challenge, especially in dynamic business environments like SMEs. To address this issue and ensure that models remain effective, it's crucial to implement MLOps (Machine Learning Operations) practices that automate key stages of the model lifecycle, from development and monitoring to retraining.

MLOps is an approach that integrates DevOps (development and operations) practices in the context of machine learning, allowing comprehensive management of the building, deployment, monitoring, and maintenance of models in production. Implementing MLOps offers SMEs the ability to automate the operation of their machine learning models, reducing the need for manual intervention and ensuring that models remain up-to-date and aligned with changing business conditions. One of the pillars of MLOps is continuous model performance monitoring, which allows for the detection of any decline in model accuracy and triggers automatic retraining if a significant performance loss is identified. This proactive model maintenance approach is essential to maintaining the accuracy and relevance of predictions over time.

Continuous monitoring of the model is a practice that involves constantly observing and evaluating the model's performance in production, using specific metrics to detect any changes in its behavior. In the case of a sales prediction model, for example, you can monitor metrics such as mean squared error (MSE) and the coefficient of determination (R^2) to check if the model continues to make accurate predictions. If the error starts to increase or the coefficient of determination decreases, these changes may indicate that the model is losing accuracy due to data drift. Continuous monitoring allows you to detect these issues before they negatively impact business decisions, and in many cases, it is possible to set performance thresholds that automatically trigger the retraining process when the metrics reach certain critical values.

To carry out continuous monitoring effectively, it is necessary to implement tools and platforms that facilitate the collection and analysis of real-time metrics. Tools like Prometheus and Grafana allow you to monitor model performance and visualize metrics through interactive dashboards, making it easier to detect model drift patterns. These monitoring tools are especially useful for SMEs, as they allow you to centralize the tracking of all models in a single environment, simplifying the monitoring process and reducing the operational burden on the data team. By having a clear view of real-time metrics, it is possible to identify any anomalous changes in model behavior and act immediately to correct them.

In addition to metric monitoring, the lifecycle of models in MLOps includes the automated management of model retraining. Retraining is the process by which the model is trained again with new or updated data, adjusting its parameters to adapt to changes in the environment or user behavior. Automating retraining allows the model to adjust proactively, without the need for manual intervention each time a loss in accuracy is detected. For an SME, this type of automation is crucial, as it avoids interruptions in the use of models and ensures that predictions remain accurate without resorting to costly manual adjustment processes.

The automatic retraining process can be structured in various ways, depending on the company's specific needs and how often the data is updated. One of the most common approaches is scheduled retraining, where the model is retrained at regular intervals, such as weekly or monthly.

This method ensures that the model continuously adapts to gradual changes in the data without requiring constant monitoring. Another option is event-based retraining, where the model is retrained only when performance metrics reach specific thresholds indicating a loss of accuracy. This approach is particularly useful for SMEs operating in dynamic environments, where sudden changes in data can unpredictably affect model performance. By combining continuous monitoring with event-based retraining, it is possible to keep the model up-to-date and avoid issues of overfitting or loss of accuracy.

The automation of the model lifecycle also involves model version management, which allows storing and controlling different versions of the same model as improvements or retraining are carried out. Version management is an important practice in MLOps because it enables the comparison of different model versions' performance and ensures that any changes or adjustments are evaluated before being implemented in production. If an updated version of the model does not meet the established performance criteria, it is possible to revert to a previous version without disrupting the system's operation. This practice is particularly useful for SMEs that implement models in critical environments where prediction accuracy and stability are essential for daily operations.

When it comes to MLOps tools that allow you to manage the lifecycle of models, there are platforms like MLflow and Kubeflow that facilitate automation and monitoring of models in production. MLflow, for example, is an open-source platform that enables you to manage the complete lifecycle of models, from tracking experiments and version control to deployment in production and monitoring. For SMEs, MLflow represents an accessible option that allows them to implement advanced MLOps practices without the need for complex infrastructure. Kubeflow, on the other hand, is a platform based on Kubernetes that allows for deploying and managing machine learning models in distributed environments, which is especially useful for businesses that need to scale their models according to demand.

The automation of the model lifecycle also requires the implementation of continuous testing and validation processes to evaluate the performance and stability of the models after each retraining. This type of testing ensures that the model is not only accurate but also stable and robust under different operating conditions. In MLOps, continuous validation involves conducting performance tests on the model before its final deployment, comparing its predictions with historical or simulated data. In the context of an SME, continuous validation ensures that any changes or adjustments to the model meet accuracy and quality requirements before being implemented in the production environment, reducing the risk of errors and improving the reliability of the predictive system.

Another key aspect of MLOps is the implementation of automatic alerts, which notify the data or operations team when there's a significant drop in model accuracy or a critical error threshold is exceeded. These automatic alerts are essential for SMEs that want to respond quickly to performance issues in their models, as they allow immediate action to prevent incorrect predictions from affecting decision-making. On platforms like Prometheus and Grafana, you can set up customized alerts that trigger automatically based on model performance metrics, making monitoring easier and improving the team's responsiveness to any eventuality.

Managing security and access in the lifecycle of models is another important aspect of MLOps, as it ensures that only authorized users have access to the models and associated data. In many SMEs, the data used to train and retrain models may contain confidential or sensitive information, such as customer or financial data. For this reason, it is essential to implement security controls and access policies that protect data integrity and ensure compliance with privacy regulations. Permission management in MLOps allows control over who has access to each stage of the model's lifecycle and ensures that any changes to the model are properly recorded and audited.

For an SME, automating the lifecycle of models through MLOps is a valuable investment that optimizes resources and improves the efficiency of the machine learning process. By implementing an MLOps infrastructure, the company can reduce reliance on manual tasks and ensure that its machine learning models remain up-to-date and effective over time. This automation not only improves model accuracy but also facilitates scalability and the deployment of new models based on business needs.

In the context of SMEs, where time and budget resources can be limited, implementing MLOps allows you to maximize the value of machine learning models, ensuring they remain an effective tool for decision-making and process optimization.

Chapter 7 - Clustering and Predictive Analysis Techniques in SMEs

7.1. Customer segmentation using clustering and k-means

Customer segmentation is a key strategy in marketing and data analysis to identify and understand different groups of customers with similar characteristics or behaviors, allowing companies to create personalized marketing campaigns, tailor their services, and optimize resources. Segmentation through clustering, particularly using the k-means algorithm, is one of the most effective and accessible techniques for this type of analysis, as it allows you to divide customers into homogeneous groups based on their purchase data, preferences, and behaviors, among others. For SMEs, this methodology is especially useful as it provides valuable insights without requiring complex resources or advanced infrastructure.

Clustering is an unsupervised machine learning technique that groups data into clusters, meaning that the elements within each group are more similar to each other than to elements in other groups. In the context of customer segmentation, clusters represent groups of customers with similar behavioral profiles, such as frequent customers, high-value buyers, or potential customers at risk of leaving. Through this process, SMEs can identify the patterns that define each segment and direct their marketing and sales efforts more strategically and efficiently. For example, customers grouped in a 'high purchase frequency' cluster can receive loyalty campaigns, while those with occasional buying patterns can be offered specific promotions to incentivize their activity.

The k-means algorithm is one of the most popular and widely used clustering options due to its simplicity, effectiveness, and ease of implementation. The algorithm works by assigning each customer to a cluster based on the distance between the customer data and the centroid (midpoint) of each cluster. As the algorithm iterates, it recalculates the centroids of each group until the customers are optimally assigned to the clusters, meaning the distance within the clusters is minimized and the distance between them is maximized. For an SME, this technique is ideal because k-means is fast, scalable, and provides segmentation results that are interpretable and applicable to marketing campaigns. Additionally, being an unsupervised algorithm, it doesn't require prior labels or predefined examples, making it easy to implement with historical customer data.

Implementing segmentation with k-means in Python using libraries like Scikit-Learn and Pandas allows SMEs to build a robust and visually clear clustering analysis. This enables them to leverage their data and gain actionable insights that increase the effectiveness of their campaigns, improve customer retention, and optimize their business strategies.

- ## Introduction to clustering and k-means

Clustering is a data analysis technique that allows you to group elements, in this case, customers, with similar characteristics into different groups or clusters. In the field of customer segmentation, clustering helps identify patterns in user behavior and classify customers based on these patterns. This technique is especially valuable for personalizing marketing strategies, as it allows you to target campaigns in a much more precise and focused way, significantly impacting their effectiveness. Customers who share characteristics and behaviors can have similar needs and expectations, which makes it easier to design campaigns, products, and services tailored to each specific group.

The k-means algorithm is one of the most popular and widely used clustering methodologies due to its simplicity and effectiveness. Its goal is to divide a dataset into a predetermined number of clusters, grouping the data so that the elements of each cluster are more similar to each other than to elements in other clusters. This clustering process allows underlying patterns in the data to be discovered and helps businesses identify different customer profiles. For an SME, k-means is an extremely useful tool because, in addition to being easy to implement, it allows for a clear interpretation of the results, enabling marketing managers to understand the resulting segments and make informed decisions.

The operation of k-means begins by setting the number of clusters or groups you want to identify in the data, represented by the letter 'k' in the algorithm's name. Once this number is chosen, the algorithm randomly assigns 'centroids' or central points for each of the clusters. The centroids are initial reference points and do not represent specific data, but rather theoretical positions in the data space. From these centroids, the algorithm assigns each customer in the data to the cluster whose centroid is closest in terms of distance. The most commonly used distance metric in k-means is Euclidean distance, which measures the closeness between two points in a multidimensional space. As the algorithm assigns data to clusters, it recalculates the centroids of each, moving them toward the center of the observations in the cluster. This process of assignment and recalculation repeats until the centroids no longer change significantly in position, indicating that an optimal point in the data grouping has been reached.

One of the most important benefits of k-means is its ability to reveal customer segments that might not be obvious at first glance. Customer data is often complex and multidimensional, including various characteristics such as purchase value, purchase frequency, types of products bought, and interaction with the company across different channels. These combined factors can make behavior patterns difficult to identify. However, by applying k-means, you can group customers according to these factors, making it easier to identify specific groups like 'high-value frequent customers', 'occasional customers', or 'premium product customers'. These categories provide SMEs with clear and specific insights that enable a much more personalized marketing strategy.

A typical example of applying k-means in customer segmentation can be seen in an ecommerce company. Suppose this company wants to identify different types of customers based on their purchasing behavior. With k-means, variables such as total purchase value, purchase frequency, and product diversity can be used to create different clusters. After applying the algorithm, the company might find that it has a group of customers who buy frequently and place high-value orders, another group that buys occasionally but spends less, and a third group that mainly purchases low-cost products. This information allows for the design of marketing campaigns focused on each segment. For example, high-frequency, high-value customers could receive exclusive offers to retain their loyalty, while occasional buyers could be offered promotions to encourage them to purchase more frequently.

Another benefit of k-means is its computational efficiency. Since it is a relatively simple algorithm in structure, the clustering process is usually fast even when working with large volumes of data. This makes it a viable option for SMEs that often lack large processing resources and require practical and effective solutions for data analysis. Additionally, k-means allows companies to experiment with different values of k, choosing the optimal number of clusters through a process known as the "elbow method." This method consists of running the algorithm with different values of k and observing how the "sum of squared distances" within clusters changes. By plotting these values, an "elbow" is formed at the point where the gain in cluster compactness starts to diminish. This point marks the ideal number of clusters that offers good segmentation without creating unnecessary or redundant groups.

In addition to being a useful technique for understanding a company's customer base, k-means also facilitates a series of practical applications in SME marketing. For example, once customer clusters are identified, the company can use these segments to personalize email marketing campaigns, offering products and services aligned with the interests and behaviors of each group. If a cluster of customers who usually buy products on promotion is identified, a specific marketing strategy can be designed for them, sending alerts when there are discounts or special promotions. This level of personalization not only improves the effectiveness of campaigns but also increases customer satisfaction, as the company demonstrates a deep understanding of their needs and preferences.

The ease of implementing k-means in programming tools like Python has popularized its use in SMEs. In Python, libraries such as Scikit-Learn and Pandas allow you to implement k-means with just a few lines of code, making the segmentation process accessible even for those without advanced machine learning experience. Scikit-Learn includes a clustering function called KMeans, which lets you define the number of clusters and apply the algorithm directly to the data. Once the clustering process is complete, you can use Python's visualization tools, like Matplotlib and Seaborn, to graphically represent the results and gain a visual interpretation of the customer segments. Visualizing the clusters in scatter plots helps marketing and sales teams better understand the distribution of customers and the characteristics of each group, enabling informed decisions about which marketing strategies to implement.

Clustering can also be combined with other data analysis techniques to achieve a more precise and robust segmentation. For example, the clusters resulting from k-means can be combined with behavioral analysis techniques to better understand the consumption patterns of each segment. If a retail company uses k-means to segment its customers based on purchase frequency and transaction value, it can then analyze the behavior data of each cluster to identify preferences in terms of product categories. By adding this level of detail, the company not only classifies its customers according to their general purchasing behavior but also identifies their favorite products, allowing for a much richer and more detailed segmentation.

Additionally, clustering is an adaptable technique that can be tailored to different needs and types of data. While traditional clustering usually relies on numerical data, such as purchase quantities or visit frequency, it's possible to adapt k-means to work with transformed or standardized data, which enhances its ability to identify relevant patterns in more complex or heterogeneous data. This is particularly useful in sectors like ecommerce, where customer data includes both numerical and categorical variables (such as product type, payment method, or purchase channel). By preprocessing these data and converting them into an appropriate numerical representation, k-means can be effectively applied in a wide range of scenarios.

Finally, segmentation using k-means allows SMEs to adopt a more proactive approach to customer retention and improving the user experience. When a company better understands its customers and their preferences, it can anticipate their needs and adjust its communication, sales, and customer service strategies to meet those needs more precisely. Customer retention is a fundamental goal for most businesses, and clustering helps identify groups that may be at risk of churn. For example, if a cluster of customers is detected with decreased purchase frequency, specific campaigns can be implemented to rekindle their interest in the brand, offering personalized promotions or discounts. This strategy not only increases retention but also improves long-term customer satisfaction and loyalty.

- ## Implementation process with Python

The process of implementing the k-means algorithm in Python is essential for an SME to take advantage of data analysis and segment its customer base effectively. This process allows for the identification of hidden patterns and trends in the data, providing insights that facilitate the personalization of marketing campaigns and improve the customer experience. The implementation of k-means can be divided into several key stages, starting with data preprocessing, which includes cleaning, normalization, and transformation of the necessary variables to ensure the model functions accurately. Next, a practical segmentation example can be built using features such as purchase value, purchase frequency, and the type of products acquired, allowing the company to categorize its customers into different behavioral groups.

Data preprocessing is an essential step in any machine learning project, as data is often not in a format that can be directly used by the algorithm. Without proper preparation, the model is likely to produce inaccurate or difficult-to-interpret results. In the context of clustering, this preprocessing includes several important steps: cleaning, handling null values, normalizing numerical variables, and transforming categorical variables into numerical values. Cleaning ensures that the model works only with relevant and complete data, while normalization and variable transformation improve the algorithm's accuracy and efficiency, ensuring that the different data dimensions are on a comparable scale.

Data cleaning is the first step in preprocessing and usually involves removing or imputing missing values, handling outliers, and transforming data into the correct format. In an SME looking to segment its customers, null values may come from incomplete purchase records, satisfaction surveys, or customer profiles. There are several ways to handle these missing values; one of the most common options is value imputation, where the missing value is replaced with the mean or median of the corresponding column, as long as it makes statistical sense. For example, if a customer's purchase frequency value is missing, it can be imputed with the average purchase frequency of other customers. Alternatively, in cases where the missing data is too extensive or irrelevant, incomplete records can be removed to avoid interfering with the model's accuracy.

Outlier treatment is another crucial aspect of data cleaning. For an SME, outliers may arise from customers with anomalous purchasing behavior, such as those making excessively large or very frequent purchases compared to the average. These values can distort clustering results, so careful analysis is recommended. If the outlier is due to a recording error, it can be removed. If the anomalous behavior is real and represents a unique group of customers, it's better to keep the value and analyze its impact on the model to determine whether a separate cluster should be created for these customers.

Once the data is clean, it's essential to normalize the numerical variables. Normalization is the process of scaling variables so they all have a similar range, which is particularly important in algorithms like k-means that use Euclidean distance to measure similarity between points. In practical terms, if an SME uses variables such as purchase value (in euros) and purchase frequency (in days), the difference in the scales of these variables could cause the model to assign undue importance to one of them. Data normalization, through techniques like standardization (where variables are scaled to have a mean of zero and a standard deviation of one) or normalizing to a specific range of values (such as 0 to 1), ensures that all variables have a balanced influence in forming clusters.

Categorical variables, such as customer type (new or returning), purchase preferences, or region, must be transformed into numerical data before applying clustering, as k-means only works with numerical values. There are several techniques for transforming categorical variables; one of the most common is one-hot encoding, where each category is converted into a binary column (0 or 1). For example, if you have a 'customer type' variable with categories 'new' and 'returning', two columns are created: one for 'new' and another for 'returning'. Each customer receives a value of 1 in the column corresponding to their type and a value of 0 in the other. Another transformation technique is label encoding, where each category is represented by a number. Although it's a simpler technique, it may be less suitable when the categories have no specific order, as the algorithm might interpret the numerical value as hierarchical, giving undue importance to one category over another.

Once the data has been preprocessed and is in the right format, we can proceed to implement k-means in Python to segment the customers of an SME. For this example, we'll consider a small e-commerce company that wants to classify its customers into different behavioral groups based on three variables: purchase value, purchase frequency, and type of products purchased. This segmentation will allow the company to develop personalized marketing campaigns, optimize its sales strategy, and improve customer retention.

The first step in the implementation process is to import the necessary libraries in Python. The essential libraries for working with data and machine learning in this case are Pandas for data manipulation, Scikit-Learn for implementing the k-means algorithm, and Matplotlib or Seaborn for visualizing the results. Here's how to get started:

```
import pandas as pd
from sklearn.cluster import KMeans
from sklearn.preprocessing import StandardScaler
import matplotlib.pyplot as plt
import seaborn as sns
```
✓ 1.4s

Let's assume the company already has a dataset with the mentioned variables, which might have the following structure:

Cliente_ID	Valor_Compra	Frecuencia_Compra	Tipo_Producto
1	200	5	1
2	150	10	0
3	300	3	1
4	250	8	0
5	180	6	1

```
# Por si quieres crearlo en Python
data = {
    'Cliente_ID': [1, 2, 3, 4, 5],
    'Valor_Compra': [200, 150, 300, 250, 180],
    'Frecuencia_Compra': [5, 10, 3, 8, 6],
    'Tipo_Producto': [1, 0, 1, 0, 1]
}
df = pd.DataFrame(data)
```
✓ 0.0s

In this dataset, the column Valor_Compra represents the total amount spent by the customer, Frecuencia_Compra indicates the number of days since the last purchase, and Tipo_Producto is a categorical variable that indicates the type of product preferred by the customer (for example, 1 for high-value products and 0 for everyday use products).

First, data preprocessing is performed, ensuring there are no null values and normalizing numerical variables. Normalization can be done using Scikit-Learn's StandardScaler.

```
# Eliminar valores nulos si los hubiera
df.dropna(inplace=True)

# Seleccionar las columnas numéricas para normalizar
X = df[['Valor_Compra', 'Frecuencia_Compra']]

# Normalizar los datos
scaler = StandardScaler()
X_normalized = scaler.fit_transform(X)
```
[23] ✓ 0.0s

K-means is then applied to segment the customers. Before defining the number of clusters, it is useful to apply the elbow method to determine the optimal value of k, which is the number of groups in which you want to divide the customers. The elbow method evaluates the sum of squared distances within the clusters and helps identify the point where adding more clusters no longer significantly improves data compactness.

```
# Método del codo
sse = []
k_values = range(1, 6)

for k in k_values:
    kmeans = KMeans(n_clusters=k, random_state=42)
    kmeans.fit(X_normalized)
    sse.append(kmeans.inertia_)

# Graficar el método del codo
plt.figure(figsize=(10, 6))
plt.plot(k_values, sse, marker='o')
plt.xlabel('Número de clusters (k)')
plt.ylabel('Suma de distancias al cuadrado (Inercia)')
plt.title('Método del codo')
plt.show()
```
[25] ✓ 0.3s

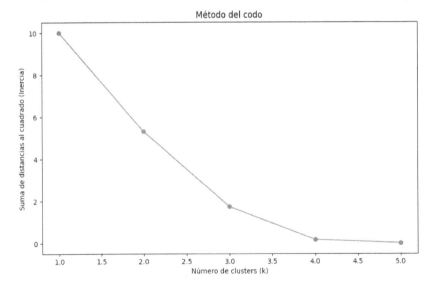

Once the optimal number of clusters has been determined (let's assume it's 3 in this case), k-means is applied with this value:

```
# Aplicar K-means con el número óptimo de clusters
kmeans = KMeans(n_clusters=3, random_state=42)
df['Cluster'] = kmeans.fit_predict(X_normalized)
```

Each customer in the dataset has now been assigned to one of the three clusters, indicating the group they belong to based on their purchasing behavior. To visualize the clusters and better understand the distribution of customers, a scatter plot can be used.

```
# Visualizar los clusters
plt.figure(figsize=(10, 6))
sns.scatterplot(x=X_normalized[:, 0], y=X_normalized[:, 1], hue=df['Cluster'], palette='viridis', s=100)
plt.xlabel('Valor de compra (normalizado)')
plt.ylabel('Frecuencia de compra (normalizado)')
plt.title('Segmentación de clientes con k-means')
plt.show()
```

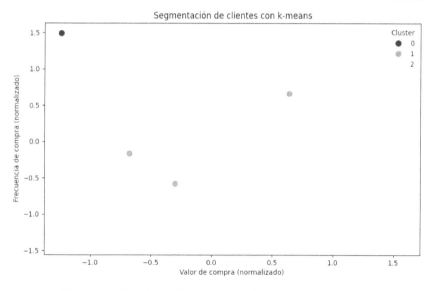

The resulting visualization allows us to observe the groups of customers according to their purchase value and purchase frequency, which makes it easier to identify patterns. For example, cluster 0 might consist of customers with low-value and infrequent purchases, while cluster 1 could represent customers who frequently buy high-value products. This type of segmentation allows the SME to design specific marketing strategies for each group: loyalty campaigns for the frequent customer cluster or discounts for the less frequent group to encourage their purchasing activity.

The described process represents a basic implementation of k-means, but in a production environment, the company can expand the model by incorporating additional variables or adjusting parameters as needed. The advantage of this methodology is its flexibility and the ability to customize it according to the company's specific data and objectives, allowing for advanced segmentation that is useful for strategic decision-making in marketing and sales.

- **Visualization of the clusters**

Customer cluster visualization is a fundamental part of the segmentation process, as it allows for easy interpretation and understanding of the behavior patterns and characteristics of each group. While numerical analysis is essential to ensure the accuracy of clustering, visualization transforms this data into accessible and understandable information for marketing managers and other departments within the company. Visualization tools like Seaborn and Matplotlib are excellent options in Python for visually representing customer clusters, as they offer a variety of charts and customization options that allow you to explore and communicate relationships between data clearly and effectively.

In the context of an SME looking to implement k-means to segment its customer base, the visualization of clusters helps to easily identify different customer profiles based on selected key variables, such as purchase value, purchase frequency, or type of product purchased. A well-designed visualization not only facilitates data interpretation but also allows marketing managers to make informed decisions on how to target each customer group with personalized strategies. The ability to observe these groups in a visual space helps highlight the differences between segments, which is crucial for creating effective and personalized marketing campaigns.

To visualize clusters in Python, you need data in a format that allows you to observe the distribution of points (i.e., the customers) based on the selected variables. In the case of k-means, the clusters are represented in a coordinate space where each customer is a point, and points within the same cluster share similar characteristics. One of the most common charts for visualizing clusters is the scatter plot, which shows the relationship between two variables in a two-dimensional plane. Matplotlib and Seaborn are useful tools for creating scatter plots and for enhancing the presentation and clarity of the data through labels, colors, and point styles that distinguish each cluster.

To begin visualizing clusters, let's assume an e-commerce company has segmented its customers using k-means based on the variables 'purchase value' and 'purchase frequency.' In this case, a scatter plot could be used to represent each customer as a point based on these two variables, assigning a different color to each cluster. The Seaborn library makes this type of visualization easy with the scatterplot function, which allows you to assign the 'Cluster' variable as a color differentiator, thus facilitating visual interpretation of the results. Identifying each cluster by color allows marketing managers to quickly see the customer groups and their behavior.

To follow the explanation, the first thing I propose is to create a DataFrame with random numbers for clients, following the example from the previous section. Here's how you can do it and modify it to your liking:

Once done, we apply k-means with the optimal number of clusters, and we can visualize it with the following code that demonstrates how to create a scatter plot using Seaborn.

```python
import seaborn as sns
import matplotlib.pyplot as plt

# El df es el DataFrame con los datos de clientes y sus clusters
# X_normalized contiene las variables normalizadas para valor de compra y frecuencia de compra
df['Cluster'] = kmeans.labels_

# Visualización de los clusters con Seaborn
plt.figure(figsize=(12, 8))
sns.scatterplot(x=X_normalized[:, 0], y=X_normalized[:, 1], hue=df['Cluster'], palette="viridis", s=100)
plt.xlabel("Valor de Compra (normalizado)")
plt.ylabel("Frecuencia de Compra (normalizado)")
plt.title("Segmentación de Clientes usando k-means")
plt.legend(title="Cluster")
plt.show()
```

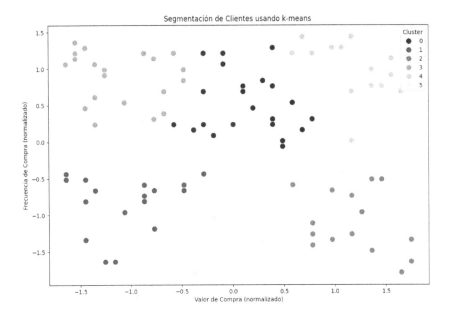

In this visualization, each point represents a customer, and the colors represent the different clusters to which each customer belongs. Using different colors for each cluster allows you to clearly see the separation between groups and the density of customers in different areas of the chart. For example, if cluster 0 represents high-value customers with low purchase frequency, and cluster 1 represents customers with more frequent purchases but lower value, this information becomes evident in the chart.

In addition to the scatter plot, another useful visualization in cluster analysis is the density plot, which helps observe the distribution of a variable's values within each cluster. This type of chart is useful when you want to analyze how certain characteristics are distributed in each customer group. For example, a density plot of 'purchase value' for each cluster can show if there are notable differences in buying patterns between the groups. With Seaborn, you can create a density plot as follows:

```
plt.figure(figsize=(12, 6))
sns.kdeplot(data=df, x="Valor_Compra", hue="Cluster", fill=True, palette="viridis")
plt.title("Distribución del valor de compra por cluster")
plt.xlabel("Valor de compra")
plt.ylabel("Densidad")
plt.show()
```

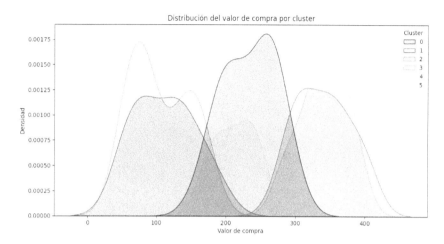

This visualization shows the purchase value density for each cluster, allowing us to see if some clusters tend to have significantly higher or lower purchase values than others. This density analysis is especially useful for understanding the purchasing behavior of each customer segment and designing specific pricing or promotional strategies for each group.

For companies working with multiple dimensions of data, it can be helpful to create 3D plots using Matplotlib, which allows you to represent three variables in the same graph. This three-dimensional visualization is especially useful when clustering has been done based on several variables, and you want to observe how they interact with each other. In Matplotlib, a 3D scatter plot can be created as follows:

```python
from mpl_toolkits.mplot3d import Axes3D

fig = plt.figure(figsize=(10, 8))
ax = fig.add_subplot(111, projection='3d')

# Variables para el gráfico en 3D
x = X_normalized[:, 0]  # Valor de Compra
y = X_normalized[:, 1]  # Frecuencia de Compra
z = df["Tipo_Producto"]  # Variable adicional, por ejemplo tipo de producto

# Crear el gráfico en 3D
ax.scatter(x, y, z, c=df['Cluster'], cmap="viridis", s=50)
ax.set_xlabel("Valor de compra (normalizado)")
ax.set_ylabel("Frecuencia de compra (normalizado)")
ax.set_zlabel("Tipo de producto")
plt.title("Visualización 3D de clusters de clientes")
plt.show()
```

✓ 0.2s

Visualización 3D de clusters de clientes

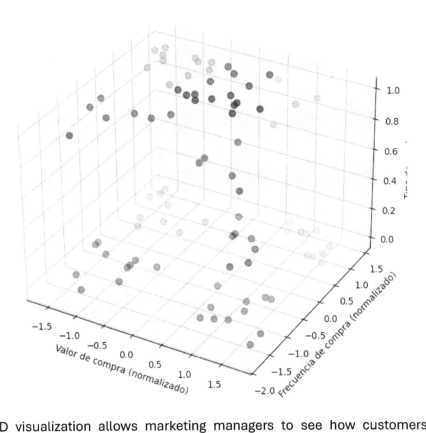

3D visualization allows marketing managers to see how customers behave based on several variables simultaneously, providing additional context in cluster analysis. This representation is particularly valuable when analyzing behavior patterns in a multidimensional environment, allowing for observations that would be difficult to capture in a two-dimensional visualization. For example, in 3D space, you might see a cluster of customers who frequently purchase high-value products, which might not be as evident in a two-dimensional scatter plot.

Another advanced option for representing clusters is the heatmap, which allows you to observe the relationships between different variables and how they are distributed across clusters. In a customer segmentation, a heatmap can show, for example, the relationship between product type and purchase frequency by cluster. In Seaborn, a heatmap can be easily created with the heatmap function:

```
# Crear una tabla cruzada con la frecuencia de compra y tipo de producto para cada cluster
heatmap_data = pd.crosstab(df['Frecuencia_Compra'], df['Cluster'])

# Visualizar el heatmap
plt.figure(figsize=(10, 6))
sns.heatmap(heatmap_data, annot=True, cmap="viridis", fmt="d")
plt.title("Mapa de calor de frecuencia de compra por cluster")
plt.xlabel("Cluster")
plt.ylabel("Frecuencia de compra")
plt.show()
```

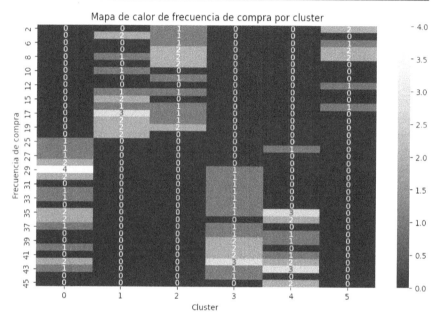

This type of visualization is ideal for identifying correlations or specific trends within each cluster and allows you to see how certain characteristics, like purchase frequency, are distributed across different customer groups. For a company, this information can be key in creating marketing strategies tailored to each customer group, as it helps identify behavior patterns and respond proactively to their needs.

Cluster visualizations not only allow you to observe segmentation in isolation, but they can also be combined into an interactive dashboard that integrates scatter plots, density plots, and heat maps. An interactive dashboard makes it easier to explore the data and allows marketing managers to delve deeper into cluster analysis, observing how customers behave based on different combinations of variables. Creating interactive dashboards with Python can be achieved using libraries like Plotly Dash or

Streamlit, which allow you to integrate multiple charts and create an intuitive interface for real-time data analysis.

Ultimately, the visualization of the clusters not only facilitates the interpretation of the clustering results but also allows marketing, sales, and other departments to make informed decisions based on the visual analysis of the data. The graphical representation of the clusters turns segmentation into an accessible and valuable tool for business strategy, enabling the company to optimize its campaigns and improve the customer experience.

- **Practical Applications in SMEs**

The application of k-means in SMEs is particularly useful for optimizing marketing strategies and customer retention, as it allows you to identify behavior patterns that would otherwise go unnoticed. Thanks to clustering, companies can personalize marketing campaigns and tailor their retention strategies according to customer segments, thus maximizing the effectiveness of their commercial efforts and increasing customer loyalty. By using k-means, an SME can divide its customer base into homogeneous groups, making it easier to target each group specifically aligned with their characteristics and behaviors. These practical applications offer a significant competitive advantage, as they allow companies to leverage customer data to make informed decisions and ultimately optimize their resources.

One of the most direct applications of k-means is the personalization of marketing campaigns, as it allows for segmenting customers based on their purchasing patterns and preferences, making it easier to tailor campaigns to be more relevant for each group. Instead of sending a generic promotion to the entire customer base, a company can identify, for example, customers who purchase frequently and send them exclusive offers or loyalty rewards. On the other hand, customers who buy less frequently can be offered incentives or discounts to motivate them to increase their purchase activity. This personalization not only increases the probability of conversion for each campaign but also improves the customer experience, as they receive content that is relevant and aligned with their interests and behaviors.

To personalize a campaign using k-means, an SME can group customers based on variables such as total purchase value, purchase frequency, and types of products purchased. After applying clustering, the different segments can be represented with distinct characteristics, such as high-value, low-frequency customers or frequent, low-value buyers. This segmentation allows for the design of campaigns that leverage the specific traits of each group. For example, high-value, low-frequency customers can receive notifications about exclusive product launches, while frequent, low-value buyers can be offered loyalty programs to encourage continued purchases. By tailoring campaigns to each group, the company increases the relevance of its communication and reduces the likelihood of customers perceiving promotions as intrusive or unattractive.

Data analysis with k-means also allows companies to identify patterns of seasonal consumption or those related to specific events, which is useful for planning campaigns throughout the year. For example, if a cluster of customers typically buys during sales periods or on specific days like Black Friday, the company can anticipate this and create targeted campaigns for these customers at the right times. This proactive approach not only increases the effectiveness of campaigns but also helps the company optimize inventory and better manage its resources based on the expected demand in each customer segment.

Another important practical application of k-means is segmentation to improve customer retention, a key strategy for reducing customer churn and maximizing loyalty. Cluster analysis allows you to identify groups of customers at risk of leaving, making it easier to develop specific retention strategies for those segments. Customer retention is especially critical for SMEs, as acquiring new customers is usually more expensive than retaining existing ones. Through segmentation, a company can analyze customer behavior patterns and detect warning signs of churn, such as a decrease in purchase frequency or a change in the type of products bought.

To identify groups at risk of churn, an SME can apply k-means using variables such as the time since the last purchase, total purchase value, and purchase frequency. Based on these variables, the algorithm groups customers and allows the observation of specific clusters that show characteristic behaviors of at-risk customers. For example, a cluster with a long interval since the last purchase and low purchase value could represent customers close to leaving the brand. With this information, the company can implement retention strategies that address the needs and expectations of these customers in a specific way.

K-means retention strategies can include personalized incentives, such as limited-time discounts or rewards programs, to motivate at-risk customers to make another purchase. Additionally, the company can use insights from the clusters to tailor its communication and closely monitor these customers. For example, if certain customers reduce their activity after a period of intense shopping, a strategy can be designed that includes reminders or recommendations for similar products to keep the customer interested in the brand.

Customer segmentation using k-means also allows companies to identify opportunities to offer a more personalized and closer service, which is especially important in sectors where the customer relationship directly influences loyalty. If a cluster of customers is characterized by a frequent purchase pattern of high-value products, these customers may respond positively to exclusive treatment or additional benefits. In this case, the company could offer them priority access to product launches or personalized service, which increases the perceived value and the likelihood of retention.

In addition, retention segmentation allows SMEs to establish churn prevention strategies before the customer is at obvious risk of leaving. By identifying early behavior patterns that suggest dissatisfaction or disinterest, the company can implement preventive strategies, such as satisfaction surveys or adjustments in offers. This proactive prevention is especially useful in sectors where competition is high and customers have many options, as it allows for customer loyalty before they are tempted to explore alternatives.

7.2. Segmentation based on behavior and transactional data

Behavioral and transactional data-based segmentation allows SMEs to gain a more detailed and accurate view of their customers, facilitating the creation of personalized campaigns tailored to the specific needs and preferences of each segment. Unlike other segmentation techniques that focus on demographic or geographic characteristics, this strategy focuses on analyzing customer actions and consumption patterns, such as their purchase history, frequency of interaction with the brand, or response to marketing campaigns. This behavior-based segmentation enables companies to make decisions based on concrete data, optimizing resources and maximizing return on investment.

A widely used technique in segmentation based on transactional data is the RFM model (Recency, Frequency, Monetary), which relies on three key variables: the recency of the last purchase, the frequency of purchases, and the total monetary value of each customer's purchases. This model is particularly effective for identifying the most valuable customers and creating retention, reward, or reactivation campaigns for those at risk of leaving. Additionally, the RFM model is easy to implement and requires simple, accessible data for most SMEs, making it a powerful tool to improve customer relationships and increase loyalty.

Segmentation based on online interaction also provides key insights for understanding customer behavior in digital environments. By analyzing data on clicks, visit durations, and conversion rates, companies can better understand their customers' journey and optimize the design of their websites or apps to improve the user experience. Similarly, data from conversion funnels allow businesses to identify the stages of the purchasing process where customers tend to drop off, facilitating the design of specific strategies for each funnel stage and for each segment.

Finally, transactional data provides insights into purchasing patterns and preferences that are essential for creating accurate and useful business segments. Segmentation by type of products purchased or by the customer lifecycle allows SMEs to design campaigns that respond to the specific needs of each group, from new customers to loyal ones, thus optimizing marketing efforts and strengthening the customer relationship. The implementation of this segmentation based on behavior and transactional data drives personalization, increases the relevance of campaigns, and improves long-term retention.

- **Customer Behavior Analysis**

Customer behavior analysis is a key strategy for SMEs as it provides detailed insights into customer preferences, habits, and motivations, enabling precise segmentation aimed at maximizing the effectiveness of marketing campaigns. A deep understanding of customer behavior allows companies to proactively respond to their needs, improving the customer experience and increasing the likelihood of conversion. This analysis is mainly conducted by collecting and studying data from various sources, such as purchase history, website interactions, or responses to previous marketing campaigns. Behavior analysis not only provides a retrospective view but also helps predict future behaviors, which is particularly valuable for designing personalized campaigns that optimize the impact of each marketing effort.

One of the most effective and accessible approaches for SMEs in transactional data analysis is the RFM (Recency, Frequency, Monetary) segmentation model. This technique allows classifying customers based on three simple yet highly relevant variables: the recency of the last purchase (R), the frequency of purchases in a given period (F), and the total monetary value of purchases made by the customer (M). The combination of these variables allows SMEs to group their customers into meaningful and useful segments for strategic decision-making, facilitating the personalization of campaigns and the targeting of resources toward the customers with the greatest potential.

The Recency variable represents the time elapsed since the customer's last purchase. This variable is key because it allows you to identify which customers have interacted recently with the company and which have decreased their purchasing activity. Customers who made a recent purchase are usually more receptive to marketing campaigns, as the brand is fresh in their memory. On the other hand, those customers whose last purchase was made a considerable time ago may be at risk of churn, indicating the need for specific strategies to rekindle their interest. The Recency variable is, therefore, an indicator of the current relationship between the customer and the company, enabling the design of campaigns aimed at fostering loyalty and retention.

The Frequency variable indicates the number of times a customer has made purchases in a specific period. This metric reflects the degree of customer loyalty to the brand and is particularly useful for identifying the most engaged customers. High-frequency customers are those who buy regularly and have a strong relationship with the company, making them the most profitable. Frequency also helps identify customer segments that could benefit from loyalty programs, discounts, or exclusive rewards that further strengthen their commitment to the brand. On the other hand, low-frequency customers represent an opportunity for the company to increase their purchasing activity through incentives or specific campaigns that motivate them to make additional purchases.

The third variable, Monetary (Monetary Value), refers to the total accumulated spending of each customer over a given period. This variable provides a measure of the economic value of each customer and is essential for identifying those who generate the most revenue for the company. Customers with a high monetary value are often more receptive to premium offers, higher-quality product recommendations, and exclusive loyalty programs. On the other hand, low-value customers may respond better to campaigns that offer discounts or promotions on affordable products. The Monetary variable allows the company to segment its customers based on their spending capacity, optimizing marketing campaigns for each group and thus maximizing return on investment.

The implementation of the RFM model is relatively straightforward, as it uses data that most SMEs already collect as part of their daily operations. To calculate and apply the RFM model in Python, you can use the Pandas library, which makes data handling and analysis easier. In this context, the process of implementing the RFM model in Pandas includes several steps: calculating the Recency, Frequency, and Monetary values, classifying customers into different segments, and finally, personalizing campaigns based on the obtained segments.

To implement RFM in Pandas, you first need a dataset that includes customer data such as the unique customer ID, the date of each transaction, and the monetary value of each purchase. Below is a practical example of how to calculate RFM values using Pandas.

First, let's create an example DataFrame:

```
import pandas as pd
import numpy as np
import datetime as dt

num_clients = 100
num_transactions = 500  # Número de transacciones aleatorias

data = {
    'Cliente_ID': np.random.choice(range(1, num_clients + 1), num_transactions),
    'Fecha_Compra': np.random.choice(pd.date_range(start="2023-01-01", end="2024-09-30"), num_transactions),
    'Valor_Compra': np.random.choice(range(50, 401, 10), num_transactions)  # valores entre 50 y 400, múltiplos de 10
}

df = pd.DataFrame(data)
```
`✓ 0.0s`

And now we calculate the RFM values:

```
import pandas as pd
import datetime as dt

# Supongamos que df es el DataFrame con las transacciones de los clientes
# Las columnas incluyen: Cliente_ID, Fecha_Compra, y Valor_Compra

# 1. Definir la fecha de referencia para el cálculo de Recency
fecha_ref = dt.datetime(2024, 10, 1)

# 2. Calcular R, F, y M para cada cliente
# Recency: tiempo desde la última compra
rfm = df.groupby('Cliente_ID').agg({
    'Fecha_Compra': lambda x: (fecha_ref - x.max()).days,
    'Cliente_ID': 'count',
    'Valor_Compra': 'sum'
}).rename(columns={'Fecha_Compra': 'Recency', 'Cliente_ID': 'Frequency', 'Valor_Compra': 'Monetary'})

# 3. Revisar el resultado de los cálculos de RFM
print(rfm.head())
```

```
✓ 0.0s

           Recency  Frequency  Monetary
Cliente_ID
1              177          4       880
2              471          1       290
3              361          2       290
4              160          4      1180
5               57          6      1440
```

This code calculates the values of Recency (days since the last purchase), Frequency (number of purchases), and Monetary (total sum of purchase values) for each customer. Once these values are obtained, customers can be classified into different segments according to their value in each variable. A common strategy is to group the Recency, Frequency, and Monetary values into quartiles or quintiles, so that each customer receives a score from 1 to 4 (or 1 to 5) based on their relative position within each metric. The combination of these scores provides an RFM profile for each customer.

The next phase involves assigning these scores and segmenting the customers:

```
# Asignar puntuaciones de R, F, y M en función de los cuartiles
rfm['R_score'] = pd.qcut(rfm['Recency'], 4, labels=[4, 3, 2, 1])
rfm['F_score'] = pd.qcut(rfm['Frequency'], 4, labels=[1, 2, 3, 4])
rfm['M_score'] = pd.qcut(rfm['Monetary'], 4, labels=[1, 2, 3, 4])

# Combinar las puntuaciones en un único puntaje RFM
rfm['RFM_Score'] = rfm['R_score'].astype(str) + rfm['F_score'].astype(str) + rfm['M_score'].astype(str)

print(rfm.head(10))
```

[42] ✓ 0.0s

...

Cliente_ID	Recency	Frequency	Monetary	R_score	F_score	M_score	RFM_Score
1	177	4	880	2	1	2	212
2	471	1	290	1	1	1	111
3	361	2	290	1	1	1	111
4	160	4	1180	2	1	3	213
5	57	6	1440	3	3	3	333
6	126	8	1410	2	4	3	243
7	105	4	1050	2	1	2	212
8	6	3	890	4	1	2	412
9	34	5	980	4	2	2	422
10	47	4	780	3	1	2	312

At this stage, each customer receives a unique combination of scores in R, F, and M, which are combined into an RFM_Score. This score allows you to group customers based on their purchasing characteristics and determine, for example, which customers are of the highest value (RFM_Score of 444) or which are at risk of churning (RFM_Score of 111). This segmentation facilitates the creation of marketing campaigns tailored to each group. High-value customers, for instance, can receive loyalty programs or exclusive benefits, while customers at risk of churning can receive incentives to reengage with the brand.

RFM segments allow for precise campaign personalization, directing marketing resources towards customers with the highest potential response. High-frequency, high-value customers are ideal candidates for special offers and premium product recommendations, as they can provide the greatest return to the company. Meanwhile, low-frequency, low-value customers can benefit from discount or promotion campaigns designed to increase their purchasing activity and strengthen their relationship with the brand.

The analysis of transactional and behavioral data also allows companies to tailor their retention and loyalty strategies based on RFM segments. Customers with low purchase frequency and high recency may be at risk of leaving the brand, so a reactivation campaign, such as a personalized offer or a purchase reminder, can effectively regain their attention. Similarly, customers with high purchase frequency and medium monetary value can be given incentives to increase their spending with the brand, thus strengthening their loyalty and maximizing their long-term value.

In short, the RFM model is a practical and powerful tool for SMEs as it allows for detailed customer segmentation using simple, easy-to-collect data. This segmentation, based on behavior and transactions, increases the precision and effectiveness of marketing campaigns and helps businesses optimize their resources by focusing efforts on the customer segments most likely to respond and generate value for the business.

- ## Segmentation based on interaction with the website or app

Segmentation based on interaction with the website or app is an essential strategy in today's digital environment to understand and adapt customer experiences based on their online behavior. Unlike traditional segmentation that focuses on demographic characteristics or transactional data, interaction-based segmentation allows SMEs to gain a detailed view of their customers' preferences and habits in the digital realm. By tracking key events and analyzing conversion funnels, companies can better understand how customers interact with their website or app, identify drop-off points, and tailor their marketing and sales strategies based on the specific behavior of each segment.

Tracking events on online platforms is one of the most effective techniques for gathering real-time behavioral data and understanding how customers interact with the website or app. Analytics tools like Google Analytics allow you to track key events such as product clicks, time spent on a page, scrolls, or interactions with specific buttons. This data provides valuable insights into users' areas of interest, their level of engagement, and their journey through the site. For SMEs, implementing tools like Google Analytics is affordable and offers a complete set of metrics that facilitate behavior-based segmentation. Moreover, the data obtained can be processed and transformed into specific features that describe each user's profile and interests, enabling much more precise personalization.

In an online store, for example, you can set up events to track the number of clicks on products from different categories, allowing you to segment customers according to their preferences and direct personalized campaigns to each group. A customer who repeatedly clicks on products from a specific category, such as 'sports' or 'technology,' can be labeled as a 'sports enthusiast' or 'tech-savvy customer,' making it easier to send them promotions or recommendations aligned with their interests. Additionally, tracking the duration of visits offers insights into the level of customer interest, as those who spend more time exploring certain categories or products tend to show a higher purchase intent. In this way, time spent on the website and click analysis become indicators of each user's behavior and profile, enabling segmentation into meaningful groups that help personalize the shopping experience.

To implement event tracking in Google Analytics, you can define custom events tailored to the SME's specific goals. Events are configured so that every relevant interaction on the page is recorded, allowing you to classify user behavior and visualize it in Analytics reports. For example, you can define an event that logs each time a user clicks the 'Add to cart' or 'View product details' button. With this information, businesses can segment users who show a high purchase intent from those who are just browsing without adding products to the cart, allowing for targeted campaigns for each group.

In addition to Google Analytics, SMEs can use their own interaction data by implementing custom analytics systems that collect information directly from their website or app. By integrating tracking scripts into their own platform, companies can define specific metrics and events that better fit their business goals and marketing needs. This approach allows for the customization of the collected data and deeper analysis, identifying patterns that might not be evident in standard analytics tools. Internal data also offers an additional advantage in terms of ownership and privacy, as it remains under the company's control and can be integrated with other CRM systems for more comprehensive segmentation.

Another key aspect of interaction-based segmentation is the analysis of conversion funnels, a tool that allows businesses to identify customer behavior throughout the purchasing process and analyze which stages they tend to abandon. Conversion funnels are visual representations that show the customer's journey from their first contact with the brand to the final conversion (such as a purchase or registration). Each stage of the funnel represents a critical step in the customer's journey, and by analyzing the drop-off rate at each phase, SMEs can accurately identify friction points that prevent customers from moving forward in the purchasing process. This insight is especially valuable for adjusting marketing strategies and creating specific messages or incentives that address customer needs at each stage of the funnel.

Conversion funnel analysis can be done using tools like Google Analytics, which offer customizable funnel features, or by using proprietary analysis systems that track events throughout the buying process. In the case of an online store, the funnel might start on the homepage, move through product views, add to cart, and finally, the payment stage. Each of these stages can have a different abandonment rate, and by segmenting customers based on where they drop off in the funnel, the company can create specific strategies for each group. For example, customers who abandon at the 'add to cart' stage can receive email reminders with incentives or additional product recommendations, while those who drop off at the payment stage might receive a notification addressing common questions or offering additional payment options.

By identifying customer behavior in the funnel, SMEs can also create remarketing strategies specific to each group. Remarketing allows you to target users who have dropped out of the funnel at a particular stage and bring them back to the website through personalized ads on social media, search engines, or email marketing campaigns. Remarketing ads are especially effective for those customers who have shown a high purchase intention, such as those who added products to the cart but did not complete the purchase. In this case, remarketing campaigns can remind the customer of the products left in the cart and offer a special incentive to complete the transaction, thus increasing the likelihood of conversion.

Another advantage of conversion funnel analysis is that it allows companies to optimize the design and user experience on their website or app, improving conversion rates through specific changes in the purchase process. If it's observed that a high percentage of users abandon the funnel at a particular stage, such as product viewing or the payment page, this may indicate navigation issues, slow loading times, or barriers in the payment process. By analyzing these drop-off points and making adjustments to the interface or web design, SMEs can reduce abandonment rates and enhance the overall user experience, encouraging customers to complete the purchase process.

For interaction-based segmentation, behavioral data obtained from event tracking and funnel analysis can be transformed into segmentation features that describe each customer's patterns and engagement. These features allow you to identify customer segments based on their level of interest and purchase intent, making it easier to personalize the browsing experience in real-time. For example, a customer who spends a lot of time exploring a specific product category can receive recommendations for related products or content that highlights the benefits of that category. This type of interaction-based segmentation personalization increases the relevance of communication and the likelihood of conversion, as the customer perceives a higher level of alignment with their interests and needs.

In addition to optimizing marketing campaigns, interaction-based segmentation allows companies to develop more effective loyalty strategies by identifying the engagement patterns of their most loyal customers. Customers who frequently interact with the website or app, visit multiple pages, or explore various categories often have a strong relationship with the brand and, therefore, may respond well to loyalty programs or exclusive rewards. Segmentation allows targeting these customers with appreciation campaigns, early access sales, or special discounts, thereby strengthening their relationship with the brand and increasing their long-term loyalty.

Funnel analysis also helps identify customer segments at risk of churn, especially those who drop out of the purchasing process at critical stages like product selection or the payment phase. These customers can be incentivized through retention campaigns that include reminders, personalized support, or more flexible purchasing conditions. By targeting these at-risk segments, SMEs can reduce the dropout rate and improve retention, maintaining an ongoing relationship with their customers and minimizing revenue losses.

- **Transactional data for segmentation**

The analysis of transactional data is essential for SMEs to segment their customers based on purchase patterns and the lifecycle of the relationship between the customer and the brand. Transactional data offers a detailed and quantifiable view of consumption habits, making it easier to identify specific segments and create marketing strategies targeted at each one. By observing how, when, and what customers spend on, companies can better understand their needs, preferences, and motivations, allowing for a much more personalized and effective marketing approach. Segmentation based on transactional data provides key insights to optimize the customer experience, improve retention, and ultimately increase the value of the relationship with each customer.

Purchase pattern analysis is one of the most common techniques in segmentation based on transactional data, as it allows identifying trends and recurring buying behaviors within the customer base. Purchase patterns reveal customer preferences regarding products, purchase frequency, and spending amounts, which helps group customers into meaningful segments. For example, by analyzing transactions from an online store, an SME can identify customer segments that mainly buy high-value products, daily use products, or promotional items. Each of these segments represents a distinct customer profile, with different motivations and expectations, which makes it easier to create marketing strategies tailored to each group.

To identify purchasing patterns, it's essential to have a data management system that records each transaction, including details such as the type of product purchased, the value of the purchase, the date, and the purchase frequency. With this information, you can analyze the data in aggregate to spot trends and classify customers according to the type of products they buy most frequently. Customers who purchase high-value products, for example, tend to be interested in quality products and often respond well to campaigns that emphasize the benefits and exclusivity of certain items. On the other hand, customers who buy everyday products are usually more motivated by price and promotions, so campaigns targeting this segment can focus on discounts or savings packages.

Identifying buying patterns also allows SMEs to adapt their inventory and sales strategies based on the demand of each segment. By understanding their customers' preferences, companies can anticipate their needs and optimize inventory to ensure that the most in-demand products are always available. This proactive approach not only improves customer satisfaction but also reduces costs associated with stockouts or excess inventory in low-demand products. Additionally, identifying buying patterns allows for the creation of personalized product recommendations, which increases the likelihood of purchase and enhances the customer experience by providing suggestions that align with their preferences.

Another important aspect of analyzing purchase patterns is identifying seasonal peaks or special events that impact customer behavior. In many sectors, customers show specific buying patterns on key dates, such as the January sales, Black Friday, or back-to-school campaigns. By segmenting customers based on their seasonal behavior, SMEs can create campaigns that respond to demand during these periods, maximizing sales and optimizing resources. For example, if a segment of customers tends to make high-value purchases during Black Friday, the company can offer exclusive promotions to this group on that date, encouraging purchases and creating a valuable experience.

In addition to analyzing purchasing patterns, segmentation by customer lifecycle is another effective strategy that allows you to classify customers based on their temporal relationship with the brand. This approach segments customers according to how long they've been interacting with the company and their level of engagement. The main segments in the lifecycle typically include new customers, repeat customers, and loyal customers. This classification allows SMEs to develop specific marketing strategies for each stage of the lifecycle, adjusting communication and incentives according to the customer's level of familiarity and loyalty with the brand.

New customers are those who have made one or a few recent purchases and are in the initial stage of their relationship with the company. This segment is critical, as it represents an opportunity to establish a strong relationship with the customer from the start. The marketing strategy for new customers should focus on offering a positive and attractive experience that encourages the customer to return. Welcome discounts, product samples, or referral programs are examples of strategies that are often effective in capturing the attention of new customers and driving repeat purchases. Additionally, communication with this group should be clear and personalized, providing relevant information about products and services to facilitate their decision-making process.

Repeat customers are those who have made several purchases and show a consistent interest in the company's products or services. This segment represents a developing relationship, where the customer already has a certain level of trust in the brand and is therefore more likely to respond to loyalty campaigns or reward programs. Marketing strategies aimed at repeat customers can include point programs, exclusive offers, or recommendations of complementary products that encourage increased purchases. At this stage, it is essential to maintain continuous and personalized communication, reminding the customer of the benefits of continuing to shop with the brand and motivating their long-term loyalty.

Loyal customers are those who have maintained a long-term relationship with the brand, have made multiple purchases, and usually have a high value for the company. This segment is especially valuable because these customers tend to be the most profitable and often act as brand ambassadors, recommending it to friends and family. Marketing strategies for loyal customers should focus on further strengthening their relationship with the brand by offering them exclusive benefits, early access to new products, or personalized services. Additionally, loyal customers appreciate feeling recognized, so companies can implement loyalty programs that include special rewards, customer anniversary celebrations, or even thank-you campaigns that reinforce their emotional connection with the brand.

Lifecycle segmentation also facilitates the implementation of effective retention strategies, as it allows you to identify segments at risk of leaving the brand and design specific campaigns to motivate them to continue buying. Customers who have decreased their purchase frequency, for example, can receive reactivation campaigns with personalized offers or reminders of the brand's benefits. Additionally, lifecycle segmentation helps manage the customer relationship proactively, anticipating their needs and ensuring that the company provides a consistent and satisfying experience at every stage of the cycle.

To implement segmentation by life cycle and purchasing patterns, SMEs can leverage data analysis tools and CRM systems to collect, store, and analyze customer information continuously. These tools facilitate the classification of customers into specific segments and automate the personalization of marketing campaigns, tailoring messages and offers based on each customer's data. CRM systems also allow for detailed tracking of customer interactions with the brand, which is essential for understanding their behavior over time and optimizing retention and loyalty strategies.

The combination of segmentation by purchase patterns and lifecycle offers an integrated view of the customer, allowing SMEs to develop marketing strategies aimed at maximizing the value of each customer and building long-term relationships. By classifying customers based on their transactions and their relationship with the brand, companies can target each group specifically, maximizing the return on marketing investment and improving the customer experience at every stage of the lifecycle.

7.3. Creating personalized marketing strategies using advanced analytics

The creation of personalized marketing strategies through advanced analytics allows SMEs to achieve a level of precision in their campaigns that significantly improves the effectiveness and relevance of communication with customers. As data becomes more detailed and accessible, advanced analytics offers a unique opportunity to segment customers accurately, identify their interests, and anticipate their needs, thus adapting marketing campaigns to each segment in a specific way and achieving a stronger connection with the target audience. This personalized approach not only increases the likelihood of conversion but also enhances the customer experience and strengthens the brand relationship.

One of the keys to creating personalized strategies is the use of advanced segmentation, which allows businesses to divide customers into detailed groups based on their behavior, preferences, and characteristics. This detailed segmentation makes it easier to design marketing campaigns that are tailored to the specifics of each group, achieving much more relevant and effective communication. For example, a SME that understands the purchase patterns and online interactions of its customers can design multichannel campaigns targeted at each segment, using emails, social media, and SMS to offer content and promotions aligned with each customer's interests. This type of multichannel approach is especially useful in today's marketing environment, where consumers interact with brands across multiple platforms and expect consistent and personalized experiences on each one.

Automation of campaigns is another key pillar in advanced marketing personalization, as it allows for efficient management of sending specific content to each segment without manual intervention. Tools like Mailchimp, ActiveCampaign, or HubSpot, along with the integration of APIs and programming languages like Python, make it easy to automate campaigns based on recent customer behavior. With this technology, an SME can send personalized emails at the right time, such as exclusive offers to customers who have shown particular interest in certain products or targeted discounts to those who haven't purchased recently.

Finally, predictive analysis expands the scope of personalization by forecasting future customer behavior. SMEs can leverage these predictive models to anticipate which customer segments could benefit from a specific promotion or require incentives to increase their loyalty. This proactive approach allows businesses to respond to customer needs before they arise, optimizing campaign results and improving long-term customer relationships. Together, these advanced analytics-based marketing strategies not only maximize marketing efficiency but also position SMEs as brands that are close and responsive to the individual needs of their customers.

- ## Advanced segmentation-based marketing strategies

Advanced marketing analysis allows SMEs to carry out customer segmentation with a level of precision that facilitates the creation of highly personalized strategies for each group, maximizing campaign effectiveness and optimizing resource use. Personalization is a key component in today's marketing, as customers not only expect a relevant experience but also demand interactions tailored to their interests, needs, and behaviors. As SMEs adopt advanced analytical techniques, they gain a detailed view of their customers that allows them to tailor marketing messages, channels, and content according to each segment. This approach ensures that campaigns are not only relevant but also timely and meaningful, creating a stronger connection between the customer and the brand.

Advanced segmentation is a process that goes beyond demographic or geographic segmentation traditionally used in marketing. With advanced analysis, SMEs can group their customers based on behavioral patterns, transactional data, digital interactions, and other factors that provide a deeper understanding of the customer. With such precise segmentation, the company can design personalized messages for each customer group, aligning campaigns with the interests and behaviors of each segment. This level of personalization allows for strategies that not only aim to increase sales but also improve customer satisfaction and build long-term relationships. For example, by identifying customer segments that make recurring purchases or tend to buy high-value products, SMEs can tailor their campaigns to recognize their loyalty and offer them exclusive benefits, thereby increasing the likelihood that they will continue buying from the company.

Among these strategies, personalized multichannel campaigns are one of the most powerful tools, as they allow SMEs to reach their customers at various digital touchpoints, such as email, social media, and WhatsApp messages. This multichannel approach ensures that the message is delivered through the customer's preferred channel, increasing the likelihood of interaction and response. For example, sending personalized emails is an effective way to maintain communication with the most valuable customers, while WhatsApp can be useful for sending reminders or promotions to those who haven't purchased recently. By integrating multiple channels into a unified strategy, SMEs not only increase the visibility of their campaigns but also create a consistent and seamless brand experience, where each channel reinforces the others' message.

Email remains an effective and highly customizable channel, especially when used in combination with advanced segmentation data. For high-value customers or those who make frequent purchases, emails can include exclusive offers, premium product recommendations, or invitations to special events that make them feel appreciated and valued by the brand. To implement these personalized campaigns, SMEs can use marketing automation tools that allow them to segment customers according to their behavior, sending messages to the right segments at the right time with the most relevant content. Automation allows, for example, scheduling thank-you emails for customers who have reached a certain spending level, reinforcing the brand relationship and increasing retention probability.

Social media is another important channel within multichannel campaigns, as it facilitates direct interaction with customers and allows for even more detailed segmentation based on user preferences and behavior. SMEs can leverage platforms like Facebook and Instagram to show personalized ads to different customer segments, based on their previous interactions with the brand. For example, a customer who has visited a specific product page on the website may see an ad on their social media reminding them of that product or showing them related products. Additionally, social media allows for two-way communication with customers, which is ideal for answering their questions, gathering their opinions, and adjusting campaigns based on their feedback. This direct interaction helps improve customer satisfaction and creates a sense of community and connection with the brand.

WhatsApp and other messaging apps also offer a personalized and direct channel for communication with customers. WhatsApp allows you to send instant messages to clients, ensuring quick and personalized communication, which is especially useful for sending reminders or last-minute promotions. For example, a company can send a WhatsApp message to customers who haven't made purchases recently, reminding them of the benefits of the products or inviting them to take advantage of a special promotion. These types of messages can include direct links to the online store, making it easy for the customer to take action immediately. Additionally, WhatsApp allows for less formal and closer communication, which can be effective for certain customer segments that value immediacy and simplicity in communication.

Multichannel personalized campaigns can also integrate real-time behavioral data, adapting messages and offers based on recent customer interactions. For example, a company that detects a customer has abandoned their shopping cart can send an email or WhatsApp message to remind them of their cart, encouraging them to complete the purchase with a special discount. This ability to respond quickly and personally increases the likelihood of conversion and reduces cart abandonment, which is especially valuable in an ecommerce environment where competition is high and customers have multiple options.

Advanced analysis allows SMEs to create personalized multichannel campaigns that not only adapt to each customer's preferences but also respond to their needs and behaviors in real time. As companies collect more detailed data about their customers, they can dynamically adjust their marketing strategies, improving the precision and relevance of each message.

• Automation of personalized campaigns

The automation of personalized campaigns is an advanced marketing strategy that allows SMEs to manage campaigns efficiently and effectively, ensuring that messages reach the right audience at the optimal time. Marketing automation has become a fundamental tool for companies that want to maximize the impact of their campaigns without incurring high personnel costs or managing manual processes. As customer data becomes more accessible and detailed, automation allows companies to segment their customers precisely, personalize the content of their campaigns, and send specific messages that generate a greater response. Tools like Mailchimp, ActiveCampaign, and HubSpot have positioned themselves as accessible and powerful platforms for implementing these strategies in the SME environment, facilitating the creation, management, and optimization of personalized marketing campaigns.

Marketing automation offers a considerable advantage by reducing the operational workload while improving the accuracy and relevance of each message sent. Instead of sending emails or messages en masse, automation allows each customer to receive communications tailored to their specific behavior and interests. This is achieved through the integration of advanced segmentation data, which ensures that each campaign is directed at a clearly defined group of customers. For example, SMEs can create automated welcome campaigns for new customers, send abandoned cart reminders to those who left products in the cart without completing the purchase, or send product recommendations based on each customer's purchase history.

Automation tools like Mailchimp provide an intuitive platform that allows SMEs to segment their customer database and schedule the sending of personalized emails automatically. Mailchimp lets you import segmented customer lists and design automated workflows for each segment. For example, an SME with a high-value customer segment can schedule thank-you emails and offer exclusive discounts to this group. At the same time, they can schedule reactivation emails for customers who haven't purchased in a certain period, incentivizing them with special promotions. Additionally, Mailchimp allows you to track the performance of each campaign, showing metrics like open rate, click-through rate, and conversion, which helps adjust the strategy based on the results obtained.

ActiveCampaign is another automation platform that offers a comprehensive approach to personalized marketing, integrating both email automation and customer relationship management (CRM). ActiveCampaign makes it easy to send personalized emails based on customer behavior, allowing SMEs to set up automated campaigns that respond to specific actions. For example, if a customer visits a product page on the website, ActiveCampaign can automatically send a follow-up email with additional information about the product or similar recommendations. This fast response capability allows businesses to leverage every customer interaction opportunity, optimizing the conversion funnel and improving the user experience.

HubSpot is another popular option in marketing automation, known for its ability to integrate with other platforms and its focus on managing the entire customer lifecycle. HubSpot allows you to create personalized campaigns that not only send automated emails but also integrate with social media and other communication tools. With HubSpot, an SME can design advanced workflows that segment customers based on their web interactions and responses to previous campaigns. For example, if a customer responds to a welcome email, HubSpot can schedule a follow-up email offering an additional discount or a free product sample. This automation ensures that the customer experience is consistent and personalized at every touchpoint with the brand.

The integration of automation with advanced segmentation data is key to maximizing the impact of each campaign. By having data on each customer's behavior and preferences, SMEs can create detailed segments and design specific messages for each group. For example, frequent buyers can receive product recommendations based on their previous purchases, while customers who haven't bought in a certain period can receive reactivation incentives, such as discounts or free shipping. This level of personalization not only increases the likelihood of conversion but also improves the customer's perception of the brand, as they feel the messages are relevant and useful.

Marketing automation is not limited to platforms like Mailchimp, ActiveCampaign, or HubSpot; it can also be complemented with development tools and programming languages like Python. Python offers a wide range of libraries and APIs that allow SMEs to create customized automation solutions tailored to their specific needs. One of the most common applications of Python in the field of marketing automation is integration with email APIs, such as Mailchimp's, to schedule and send automated messages based on customer behavior.

For example, using the Mailchimp API and Python, an SME can automate the sending of welcome emails to new customers who register on their website. The Mailchimp API allows developers to interact with the platform's data and customize the email content based on defined segments. Below is an example of how to use Python and the Mailchimp API to send personalized emails to a specific segment based on their recent behavior.

First, you need to install the Python requests library, which makes it easier to interact with the Mailchimp API.

Next, you need to set up the Python script to make a call to the Mailchimp API. This example shows how to send an email to a group of customers who haven't made purchases in the last three months. To use the Mailchimp API, you need a valid API key, which can be obtained from your Mailchimp account, and the ID of the contact list to which the email will be sent.

```
import requests
import json

# Configuración de la API de Mailchimp
api_key = 'TU_CLAVE_API'
server = 'usX'  # El servidor depende del subdominio de tu cuenta en Mailchimp
list_id = 'TU_LIST_ID'

# Definir la URL de la API y los headers
url = f'https://{server}.api.mailchimp.com/3.0/lists/{list_id}/members'
headers = {
    'Authorization': f'Bearer {api_key}',
    'Content-Type': 'application/json'
}

# Datos del cliente
cliente_email = 'cliente@example.com'
data = {
    "email_address": cliente_email,
    "status": "subscribed",
    "merge_fields": {
        "FNAME": "Nombre",
        "LNAME": "Apellido"
    }
}

# Realizar la solicitud POST para añadir al cliente a la lista y enviar el correo
response = requests.post(url, headers=headers, data=json.dumps(data))

# Verificar la respuesta
if response.status_code == 200:
    print("Correo enviado exitosamente")
else:
    print("Error en el envío del correo:", response.json())
```

This script automates the sending of emails to customers registered on the Mailchimp list, allowing the customization of FNAME and LNAME fields with each customer's first and last name. Additionally, the Mailchimp API allows you to segment the list based on various criteria, such as purchase history, web behavior, and frequency of interaction with the brand. In this way, SMEs can send specific emails to each customer segment without the need for manual intervention, improving the efficiency and effectiveness of campaigns.

In addition to sending emails, Python also allows for the integration of marketing automation with other tools and platforms using APIs, such as the company's CRM, website, and social media. This integration facilitates the real-time collection and analysis of data, which is crucial for adjusting marketing campaigns based on customer behavior. For example, if an SME detects that a customer has abandoned a shopping cart on their website, it can trigger an automated flow that sends a reminder email or a message on social media, encouraging the customer to complete the purchase. This quick response capability increases the likelihood of conversion and improves the customer experience.

The automation of campaigns also allows for continuous A/B testing, evaluating the effectiveness of different content, calls to action, and segmentations. For example, a company can send two different versions of an email to a segment of customers and analyze which version has a higher open or click rate. This information allows for adjusting campaign content based on the results, thus optimizing the effectiveness of each message and ensuring that the communication is as relevant as possible for each customer segment.

- **Predictive Analysis-Based Strategies**

Predictive analytics is a powerful tool for SMEs looking to optimize their marketing and sales strategies by anticipating customer behavior. By using predictive analytics, businesses can leverage historical and current data to identify patterns and trends that allow them to foresee future customer actions. This is especially useful for personalizing campaigns, retaining customers, and increasing profitability, as it enables marketing efforts to be directed towards the right customers at the right time. Instead of relying on assumptions, predictive analytics allows companies to base their decisions on objective data, improving the accuracy of their campaigns and their impact.

For an SME, predictive analysis can involve implementing machine learning algorithms that use transactional, demographic, behavioral, and interaction data to identify patterns that can be extrapolated over time. By applying these models to the customer database, the company can forecast future behavior, such as the likelihood of a customer making a purchase, their buying frequency, or even their propensity to leave the brand. The most common predictive models include classification and regression algorithms, such as decision trees, random forests, logistic regression models, and neural networks, which allow for the analysis of variables and relationships within the data to make precise and useful predictions for strategic decision-making.

One of the most common uses of predictive analytics in marketing is identifying customers who may need a special offer in the future. In this case, the company analyzes purchasing behavior and other data to detect early signs of disengagement or loss of commitment from customers. For example, if a customer who used to buy monthly hasn't made a purchase in two months, the predictive model could identify them as at risk of churn. In response, the company could automate the sending of a personalized promotion or incentive to rekindle the customer's interest in the brand. This type of strategy, known as proactive marketing, allows companies to anticipate customer needs, increasing the likelihood of retention and maintaining a stable, long-lasting relationship.

Another key aspect of using predictive analysis is customer segmentation based on their likelihood of future purchases, which allows marketing resources to be prioritized and campaigns optimized. Predictive segmentation divides customers into different categories according to their propensity to make a purchase or engage with the brand. Customers with a high likelihood of purchase are considered 'priority customers' and receive campaigns aimed at maximizing their purchase frequency, while customers with a low likelihood of purchase can receive additional incentives to motivate them to make a purchase or increase their level of engagement. By focusing on each group according to their conversion potential, the company optimizes its marketing spend and improves the profitability of each campaign.

Predictive analysis also allows for personalized recommendations for each customer, a process known as recommendation systems. These recommendations are based on behavioral data and past purchases, enabling the company to suggest specific products that might interest each customer according to their preferences and buying patterns. This recommendation approach not only increases the likelihood of cross-selling or upselling but also enhances the customer experience by providing relevant content tailored to their tastes. For example, if a customer has purchased pet products in the past, the recommendation system could suggest related food or toys. This type of personalization increases customer satisfaction and loyalty to the brand.

Churn prediction is another critical use of predictive analytics in SME marketing. The churn prediction model identifies customers who are likely to leave the brand in the near future. This is essential in industries where customer retention is crucial for maintaining a steady revenue flow and reducing the costs of acquiring new customers. By identifying these customers in advance, the company can implement specific strategies to retain them, such as personalized discounts, proactive customer service, or loyalty incentives. These retention strategies allow the company to maintain a positive relationship with the customer and avoid the loss of revenue associated with churn.

In addition to retaining customers, predictive analysis can optimize a company's pricing strategies. Predictive analysis models can anticipate how different customer segments will respond to price variations and promotions, allowing SMEs to adjust prices to maximize revenue without affecting the brand's perceived value. For example, if the analysis indicates that a specific segment is less price-sensitive, the company can launch a campaign for premium products or additional services at higher prices, increasing profitability in that segment. At the same time, it can identify more price-sensitive customers and offer them personalized discounts that increase their interest and purchase frequency.

In practical implementation, predictive analysis is integrated with marketing automation tools, allowing the company to automatically send personalized campaigns based on the predictive model's results. For example, a company using a predictive model to identify customers most likely to respond to a seasonal product campaign can schedule automated emails or targeted ads to these customers at a specific time, maximizing the campaign's effectiveness. Marketing tools like Mailchimp, ActiveCampaign, or HubSpot can be integrated with these predictive models to manage the delivery of personalized content, ensuring the message reaches the right customer at the right time.

A practical example of how an SME can use predictive analytics is by using Python and the Scikit-Learn library, a common tool for building machine learning models. Suppose an online store wants to predict which customers are likely to make a purchase during an end-of-season promotion. By using a classification model, such as a random forest, the company can analyze historical data to identify patterns in the behavior of customers who bought during past promotions. The data used in the model can include purchase frequency, average spending, last purchase date, and types of products bought. From this data, the model predicts the likelihood of a customer participating in the next promotion. This prediction allows the company to focus its marketing campaigns and optimize the advertising budget by targeting customers with the highest conversion potential.

Predictive analysis also allows SMEs to anticipate demand peaks and adjust their inventory and logistics accordingly. For example, by analyzing data from previous seasons and external factors like marketing campaigns or holidays, the company can forecast when there will be an increase in demand for certain products. This facilitates inventory planning and supply chain management, reducing the risk of stockouts or excess inventory. In this way, the company not only improves its operational efficiency but also better meets customer expectations, ensuring that products are available when they need them.

Another practical application of predictive analysis in marketing is the optimization of the advertising budget by identifying the most effective marketing channels for each customer segment. Through data analysis, SMEs can predict how different customer groups respond to ads on social media, emails, or paid search campaigns. This allows the company to allocate the advertising budget more precisely, maximizing the return on investment in each channel. For example, if the predictive model indicates that a group of customers responds better to ads on Instagram than on Facebook, the company can shift resources towards Instagram to optimize results.

The application of predictive analytics in marketing also facilitates real-time content personalization on the company's website. Predictive models can analyze interactions on the web page in real time and offer personalized recommendations to each customer based on their recent actions. For example, if a customer is browsing products in a specific category, the predictive system can display related products or content that helps them make a purchase decision. This real-time personalization improves the user experience and increases the likelihood of conversion, as the customer receives content tailored to their current interests.

Predictive analysis can also be applied to optimize the frequency and timing of email marketing campaigns. With machine learning models that analyze email open and click data, SMEs can identify the ideal times and frequency to send emails to each customer, increasing the likelihood that the customer will open the message and convert. For example, if a predictive model suggests that a customer segment tends to open emails on Tuesday mornings, the company can schedule its sends at that time to maximize open rates and campaign effectiveness.

Predictive analysis allows SMEs to optimize all aspects of their marketing strategy, from content personalization and segmentation to inventory management and advertising budget allocation. By using historical data and behavioral patterns, businesses can anticipate their customers' needs and create campaigns that respond to their interests at the right moment. This approach not only improves the effectiveness of campaigns but also strengthens the customer relationship, as it provides a relevant and personalized brand experience that increases customer satisfaction and loyalty to the brand.

- ## Examples of personalized marketing

Marketing personalization has significantly evolved in recent years, driven by advanced data analysis and precise customer segmentation. This ability to tailor messages, offers, and recommendations to each customer's needs and preferences is a powerful tool that allows SMEs to improve the relevance of their campaigns, strengthen customer relationships, and optimize profitability. Content personalization and product recommendations are two of the most effective strategies companies can implement to connect with their customers on a deeper level. By targeting each segment with specific messages and products, the company can better capture customer interest and increase the likelihood of conversion.

Personalized marketing is based on creating content that responds to the specific interests and needs of each segment. This personalization can be reflected in various customer touchpoints, such as emails, websites, and social media. Additionally, product recommendation is a key strategy within personalized marketing, as it allows you to suggest products or services that truly interest each customer based on their previous purchases or browsing patterns. Both strategies will be explored in detail below.

- ### Content personalization: Adapting emails and web pages to reflect the customer's interests

Personalizing the content that customers receive is essential for capturing their attention and encouraging interaction with the brand. One of the main channels where personalization has a noticeable impact is email. By tailoring messages to the specific interests and behaviors of each customer, the company can significantly increase the likelihood that the customer will open the email and make a conversion. Email personalization goes beyond simply including the recipient's name; it involves sending relevant content that truly adds value to the customer based on their interests, purchase history, and web behavior.

For example, if an SME detects that a group of customers shows interest in products from a specific category, such as technology, it can segment these customers and send them emails with relevant information about new tech products, discounts in that category, or practical tips related to the use of the products they have purchased. This personalization strategy ensures that the content is of interest to the recipient, which increases the likelihood that they will open the email, interact with the content, and ultimately make a purchase.

Content personalization also extends to websites, where it's possible to tailor the user experience based on their previous interactions and interests. For example, by using cookies and behavioral analysis, a company can identify which sections of the website are most relevant to each customer. With this information, the website can personalize the displayed content, highlighting products or services that match the user's preferences. To implement this type of personalization, SMEs can use content management systems (CMS) that allow for adaptive user experiences based on behavioral data. By personalizing the browsing experience, the company makes it easier for the customer to find what they're looking for, improving the user experience and increasing the likelihood of conversion.

Marketing automation tools like HubSpot or ActiveCampaign also offer advanced functionalities for content personalization in emails and web pages. These platforms allow SMEs to collect data on customer behavior and create segments based on specific interests. Then, by setting up automated workflows, the company can schedule the sending of personalized emails at key moments in the customer lifecycle, such as a welcome for new customers, product recommendations based on past purchases, or abandoned cart reminders. This automation capability allows SMEs to stay in constant contact with their customers, sending content that responds to their needs and interests at every moment.

Content personalization not only has a positive impact on conversion rates but also improves the customer's perception of the brand, as they receive messages that are relevant and useful. This helps strengthen the customer relationship, generating greater loyalty and increasing the likelihood of future purchases. By addressing each customer with content that responds to their preferences and behaviors, the company manages to differentiate itself from the competition and establish a meaningful connection with its audience.

- **Product recommendation based on segments: Personalized product suggestions based on previous purchases and browsing patterns**

Product recommendation is another key strategy in personalized marketing, as it allows companies to suggest products or services that genuinely interest each customer. The effectiveness of this strategy lies in analyzing behavioral data and past transactions, which helps identify purchasing patterns and specific preferences for each customer or group of customers. Based on this information, the company can offer personalized recommendations that align with each segment's interests, increasing the likelihood of purchase and enhancing the customer experience.

For an SME, implementing product recommendations based on segments is accessible using data analysis tools and ecommerce platforms that allow for personalized shopping experiences. For example, if an online fashion company sees that a segment of customers makes recurring purchases of seasonal clothing, it can schedule recommendations for new products in that category every time the customer visits the site. By showing products aligned with the customer's interests, the company maximizes the likelihood of a purchase and remains relevant to their needs.

An effective product recommendation strategy can also be based on analyzing browsing patterns on the web. By tracking customer interactions on the website, the company can identify which products have caught their interest and suggest similar or complementary products. For example, if a customer repeatedly visits the tech products section without making a purchase, the company can send them an email with product recommendations in that category, highlighting the benefits of each or even offering exclusive discounts to incentivize the purchase. This strategy allows the company to leverage every customer interaction with the brand, increasing conversion opportunities and improving the user experience.

E-commerce platforms like Shopify and WooCommerce offer product recommendation plugins that allow SMEs to set up recommendation systems in their online stores. These plugins analyze previous purchases and visits to specific products, generating real-time recommendations for each customer. For example, an online sports store could recommend complementary products like sportswear or training accessories to customers who have bought running shoes. This personalization in recommendations enhances the shopping experience and helps customers discover products of interest, thus increasing the average order value.

Product recommendations can also be personalized based on transactional data, such as purchase history and behavior in previous campaigns. By using machine learning techniques, SMEs can identify patterns in customer purchases and make recommendations based on products that other customers with a similar profile have bought. This approach, known as collaborative filtering, allows companies to leverage the knowledge generated by the behavior of their entire customer base, suggesting products that have been popular among customers with similar interests and preferences. This technique is especially useful in sectors like ecommerce and technology, where customers tend to explore products based on other users' recommendations.

Product recommendation based on segments also allows SMEs to maximize cross-selling and upselling opportunities. By knowing which products interest each segment, the company can suggest higher-value or complementary products that enhance the customer's shopping experience. For example, a customer who has purchased a laptop from an electronics store might receive recommendations for accessories like cases, portable chargers, or wireless mice. These recommendations not only increase the transaction value but also help the customer have a more complete user experience, improving their satisfaction and perception of the brand.

Tools like Dynamic Yield or RecoAI allow SMEs to implement product recommendations across multiple channels, such as websites, emails, and mobile apps. These platforms integrate behavioral and transactional data, enabling real-time personalized recommendations that adapt to each customer interaction with the brand. By using these tools, businesses can create a seamless and relevant shopping experience at every touchpoint, strengthening the customer relationship and increasing the likelihood of conversion at each stage of the purchase journey.

In short, both content personalization and product recommendation based on segments are key strategies that allow SMEs to improve the effectiveness of their marketing campaigns and optimize the customer experience. These strategies are based on advanced data analysis and the ability to segment customers according to their interests, behaviors, and specific needs. Implementing these tactics not only increases conversion opportunities but also helps strengthen customer loyalty and build long-term relationships that generate value for both the company and the customer.

7.4. Automated product and service recommendations

Automated product and service recommendations are an essential tool for SMEs looking to maximize sales and improve customer retention. Through recommendation systems, businesses can suggest relevant products and services based on customer behavior history, preferences, and purchases made by other customers with similar profiles. These systems analyze large volumes of data to identify interest patterns, allowing recommendations to be tailored to each customer in a personalized and real-time manner. This not only enhances the customer experience but also increases the likelihood of conversion, as customers find products that meet their needs more easily.

There are several recommendation methods, among which collaborative filtering and content-based filtering stand out. Collaborative filtering suggests products based on what other customers with similar interests have purchased, while content-based filtering focuses on the characteristics of the products the customer has viewed or bought. Both methods are effective and can be used in parallel to create a more comprehensive and accurate recommendation strategy.

For SMEs, recommendation systems can be implemented easily using accessible tools like Python and machine learning libraries, which allow for building a basic recommendation system without requiring extensive technical resources. Additionally, there are third-party APIs, like Algolia or RecoAI, that simplify the integration of recommendations into websites and apps, which is ideal for businesses looking for a quick and efficient solution. These platforms offer personalized recommendations based on real-time data, optimizing the customer experience in every interaction.

In addition to real-time implementations, automating recommendations on ecommerce platforms like Shopify or WooCommerce allows products to be suggested directly on the checkout page or in follow-up emails. This integration ensures that each customer receives suggestions for complementary products at the optimal moment, whether during the purchase process or in their inbox, improving the likelihood of making an additional purchase. Overall, recommendation systems represent an opportunity for SMEs to personalize their offering, build customer loyalty, and increase their revenue in an efficient and scalable way.

- ## Recommendation systems

Recommendation systems are a crucial tool in digital marketing and e-commerce, as they allow companies to offer personalized product and service suggestions for each customer, significantly improving the shopping experience. These systems analyze the customer's behavior history and purchase patterns of other users with similar profiles to identify relevant products that match their preferences and interests. Implementing automatic recommendations not only helps customers discover new products of interest but also increases opportunities for additional sales, the average order value, and long-term customer retention.

The most common methods in recommendation systems are collaborative filtering and content-based filtering. Both approaches leverage different types of data to generate relevant recommendations and are often used together to increase the accuracy and relevance of the suggestions. Collaborative filtering is based on the preferences and behaviors of other similar users, while content-based filtering focuses on the characteristics of the products a customer has shown interest in. The combination of these methods provides companies with a robust recommendation system that optimizes personalization, improves customer satisfaction, and ultimately drives sales.

- ### Collaborative Filtering: Recommendations based on the behaviors and preferences of similar users

Collaborative filtering is a recommendation technique that suggests products or services based on the behavior of other customers who share similar characteristics, preferences, or purchasing patterns. The idea behind this approach is that customers with similar interests and behaviors are likely to enjoy similar products. In the context of an online store, this method allows you to offer product recommendations that other customers with similar profiles have already purchased or rated positively. This technique is widely used on ecommerce platforms like Amazon or Netflix, where the system shows products or content based on what other similar users have bought or watched.

Collaborative filtering is implemented through algorithms that analyze large volumes of data to find patterns of similarity between users. There are two main types of collaborative filtering: user-based collaborative filtering and item-based collaborative filtering. In the first case, the system recommends products that other similar users have rated positively; in the second, it suggests products that share features with those the customer has already purchased. Both approaches aim to increase the relevance of recommendations and improve the user's shopping experience.

A practical example of how user-based collaborative filtering works in an online store would be the following: suppose a customer A has purchased gardening items, home tools, and plant accessories. If another customer B has shown a similar interest in gardening items and has purchased tools, the system will recommend products to B similar to those bought by A, such as plant accessories. This type of recommendation is effective because the system recognizes patterns in purchasing behavior and allows each customer to receive product suggestions that other users with similar interests have already acquired.

Item-based collaborative filtering, on the other hand, works differently. In this case, the system looks for products similar to those the customer has previously purchased, based on purchase history and the ratings the customer has given to specific products. In a music store, for example, if a customer has bought several alternative rock albums, the system can recommend other albums in that genre that have been well-rated by other customers who share their interests. This approach allows for recommendations that are precisely tailored to the customer's tastes, as it takes into account their individual preferences and compares them with the opinions and preferences of other users who have interacted with similar products.

The success of collaborative filtering lies in its ability to adapt to each customer's behavior and the purchasing patterns of the entire user community. The more information is collected about customer interactions and preferences, the more accurate the recommendations become, as the system has a larger dataset to identify similarities between users. E-commerce platforms can implement collaborative filtering using user-product matrices, where each cell represents an interaction between the user and the product, such as a purchase, a rating, or a visit. Machine learning algorithms like k-nearest neighbors or matrix factorization are used to analyze these matrices and find similarities between users and products, thus generating personalized recommendations.

One of the challenges of collaborative filtering is the cold start problem, which occurs when the system doesn't have enough data about a new customer or product. Without historical data or behavior patterns, the system struggles to offer accurate recommendations. To solve this problem, companies can combine collaborative filtering with content-based filtering or implement strategies that encourage new customers to interact with products through ratings or comments, thus providing the system with initial data to improve recommendation accuracy.

- **Content-Based Filtering: Recommendations based on product features**

Content-based filtering is another commonly used technique in recommendation systems, focusing on the characteristics of products that the customer has purchased or explored. Unlike collaborative filtering, which relies on the behavior of other users, content-based filtering analyzes the specific attributes of products, such as their category, brand, description, tags, and any other feature that allows for identifying similarities between products. The goal is to suggest products that share characteristics with those the customer has shown interest in before, which is especially useful when behavioral data from other users is limited or irrelevant to a particular customer.

Content-based filtering is effective when there is a large amount of descriptive data about the products, as it allows you to accurately identify the elements that might interest the customer. In a clothing store, for example, if a customer has shown interest in cotton t-shirts from a specific brand, the system could recommend other cotton t-shirts from the same brand or similar brands, as these products share relevant characteristics. This approach allows the customer to discover items that align with their preferences without relying on the interactions or preferences of other users.

To implement content-based filtering, companies use text processing algorithms such as TF-IDF or cosine similarity, which analyze product descriptions and measure similarity between them based on their attributes. These algorithms allow the system to identify which products are similar to those the customer has viewed or purchased, thus generating recommendations that directly respond to their interests. Additionally, content-based filtering is not limited to product recommendations; it can also be applied to other types of content, such as articles, videos, or services, which is useful for companies that want to personalize the customer experience across multiple channels and formats.

An example of content-based filtering in the context of an ecommerce would be an online bookstore offering book recommendations based on the genres and authors the customer has explored. If a customer has purchased several science fiction and fantasy books, the recommendation system can suggest other titles in those genres or by related authors, increasing the likelihood that the customer will find a book of interest. This approach is effective because it adapts to the customer's specific tastes based on their previous interactions, without relying on other users' purchase patterns.

Content-based filtering is especially useful in situations where behavior data from other users is scarce or not representative for a particular customer. This often happens on niche platforms or with highly specialized products, where customers may have unique interests not shared by many users. By focusing on product attributes, the system ensures that each recommendation aligns with the customer's individual preferences, improving the relevance and effectiveness of the recommendations.

Another advantage of content-based filtering is that it allows companies to maintain personalized recommendations in cold start situations, where customer or product behavior data is limited. By analyzing product characteristics instead of other users' behavior, the recommendation system can offer personalized suggestions from the start, improving the customer experience and facilitating their interaction with the brand.

Both recommendation methods—collaborative filtering and content-based filtering—offer distinct advantages and can be combined in a hybrid approach to improve the accuracy and relevance of recommendations. This hybrid approach allows you to leverage the best of both methods, generating recommendations that not only adapt to the specific interests of the customer but also consider the preferences of other users with similar profiles. The implementation of hybrid recommendation systems is a common practice in large ecommerce and streaming platforms like Amazon and Netflix, where personalization is key to retaining customers and increasing their loyalty to the brand.

In conclusion, recommendation systems based on collaborative filtering and content-based filtering are essential tools for SMEs to enhance the personalization of their customers' experience and optimize their marketing strategy. By offering recommendations that respond to each customer's interests and preferences, businesses not only increase conversion rates but also strengthen customer relationships and improve long-term loyalty.

- ## Simple implementation of a recommendation system with Python

Implementing a recommendation system with Python is an accessible and powerful strategy for SMEs that want to personalize their customers' experience on e-commerce platforms or mobile apps. Recommendation systems allow you to suggest relevant products or services to each user based on their behavior and preferences, increasing the likelihood of conversion and improving customer satisfaction. Using tools like Scikit-Learn and Pandas facilitates the creation of a basic recommendation system with collaborative filtering or content-based techniques, without the need for complex infrastructure. Additionally, third-party APIs like Algolia or RecoAI offer quick and efficient solutions for businesses that prefer an external integration instead of developing one from scratch.

For an SME, implementing a recommendation system with these tools allows not only to improve personalization in their sales channels but also to optimize resources and reach customers more strategically. Next, we will explore the implementation of a recommendation system with Python and the use of external APIs, detailing how to develop a basic recommendation system with Scikit-Learn and Pandas and how to integrate recommendation APIs like Algolia and RecoAI to achieve advanced personalization without the need for a robust technical team.

- ### Using Scikit-Learn to build a basic recommendation system

To begin, Scikit-Learn and Pandas are useful and accessible tools for creating a recommendation system based on collaborative or content filtering. Scikit-Learn is a machine learning library that includes supervised and unsupervised learning algorithms, while Pandas makes it easy to manipulate and analyze structured data, such as product data and customer preferences. To illustrate the process, we'll implement a simple recommendation system that can be used in an online store to recommend products to customers based on their purchase history and product similarity.

Let's say we have a dataset with two types of key information: customer purchase history and product characteristics. With this data, we can choose a collaborative filtering approach, where recommendations are based on customers' previous interactions with similar products, or a content-based filtering approach, where products are recommended based on their features. For this example, we'll build a content-based recommendation system that suggests products similar to those the customer has already viewed or purchased.

1. Data preparation: To implement this system, we need a dataset that includes the characteristics of each product (such as category, brand, and price) and the purchase history of customers. Below is an example of what the dataset might look like:

```python
import pandas as pd

# Datos de productos
productos = pd.DataFrame({
    'producto_id': [1, 2, 3, 4, 5],
    'categoria': ['tecnologia', 'tecnologia', 'ropa', 'ropa', 'hogar'],
    'marca': ['A', 'B', 'A', 'C', 'A'],
    'precio': [500, 700, 50, 45, 30]
})

# Datos de historial de compras (cliente_id, producto_id)
compras = pd.DataFrame({
    'cliente_id': [1, 1, 2, 2, 3],
    'producto_id': [1, 3, 2, 4, 5]
})
```

2. Preprocessing and transformation: To calculate the similarity between products, we will transform categorical features into numerical data. A common technique is to use the OneHotEncoder method from Scikit-Learn to convert variables like category and brand into binary variables representing each possible value. This will allow us to compare products based on these features.

```python
from sklearn.preprocessing import OneHotEncoder

# Aplicar OneHotEncoder a las caracteristicas categoricas
encoder = OneHotEncoder()
caracteristicas = encoder.fit_transform(productos[['categoria', 'marca']])
df_caracteristicas = pd.DataFrame(caracteristicas.toarray(), columns=encoder.get_feature_names_out())

# Combinar caracteristicas codificadas con el precio
productos_numerico = pd.concat([productos[['producto_id']], df_caracteristicas, productos[['precio']]], axis=1)
print(productos_numerico)
```

```
   producto_id  categoria_hogar  categoria_ropa  categoria_tecnologia  \
0            1              0.0             0.0                   1.0
1            2              0.0             0.0                   1.0
2            3              0.0             1.0                   0.0
3            4              0.0             1.0                   0.0
4            5              1.0             0.0                   0.0

   marca_A  marca_B  marca_C  precio
0      1.0      0.0      0.0     500
1      0.0      1.0      0.0     700
2      1.0      0.0      0.0      50
3      0.0      0.0      1.0      45
4      1.0      0.0      0.0      30
```

3. Calculating similarity between products: To recommend similar products, we need to compute a similarity matrix. Using cosine similarity, we can identify products that share similar features. This metric allows us to compare feature vectors and determine how similar they are to each other. Scikit-Learn offers functions like cosine_similarity to compute this similarity.

```
from sklearn.metrics.pairwise import cosine_similarity

# Cálculo de la matriz de similitud
similitud_productos = cosine_similarity(productos_numerico.drop('producto_id', axis=1))
print(similitud_productos)
[45]  ✓  0.0s

...   [[1.         0.99999682 0.99963623 0.99950254 0.99895333]
      [0.99999682 1.         0.9995982  0.9995045  0.9988887 ]
      [0.99963623 0.9995982  1.         0.99955102 0.99915708]
      [0.99950254 0.9995045  0.99955102 1.         0.99839782]
      [0.99895333 0.9988887  0.99915708 0.99839782 1.        ]]
```

4. Recomendation generation: With the similarity matrix, we can select the products most similar to those the customer has purchased. If a customer has bought a specific product, they will be recommended those products that have a high similarity to their purchase. To simplify, in this example, we will assume we recommend three similar products.

```
def recomendar_productos(producto_id, similitud_productos, productos, top_n=3):
    # Obtener índice del producto en la matriz de similitud
    indice_producto = productos[productos['producto_id'] == producto_id].index[0]
    # Obtener puntuaciones de similitud y seleccionar los productos más similares
    indices_similares = similitud_productos[indice_producto].argsort()[-top_n-1:-1][::-1]
    productos_recomendados = productos.iloc[indices_similares]
    return productos_recomendados

# Ejemplo de recomendación para un producto comprado
producto_recomendado = recomendar_productos(1, similitud_productos, productos)
print(producto_recomendado)
[46]  ✓  0.0s

...    producto_id  categoria  marca  precio
     1           2  tecnologia      B     700
     2           3       ropa      A      50
     3           4       ropa      C      45
```

This basic recommendation system uses feature similarity between products to offer personalized suggestions. It's a simple and effective approach that can be adapted to different types of product data, which is especially useful for SMEs looking to implement a recommendation system without complex infrastructure.

- **Using APIs for Recommendations: Integration with Algolia or RecoAl**

For SMEs that don't have a robust technical team or prefer a quick and scalable solution, third-party APIs offer an efficient alternative to implement recommendation systems without the need to develop the algorithm from scratch. Algolia and RecoAl are two popular platforms that offer recommendation systems that can be integrated via APIs into web or mobile applications. These tools allow companies to access advanced recommendation and data analysis algorithms without having to manage the infrastructure or data directly.

Algolia is a search and discovery platform that offers product recommendation features based on user behavior and product characteristics. Algolia allows you to integrate personalized recommendations into e-commerce sites, displaying relevant products according to search history, previous purchases, and user preferences. Algolia's API is highly customizable and allows you to adjust recommendations based on specific business metrics, such as relevance, popularity, or product conversion rates.

To integrate Algolia, companies need to create a product index on the platform and configure the recommendation rules. Here's an example of how to use the Algolia API in Python to get recommendations based on customer behavior:

1. Setting up Algolia: First, it's necessary to configure the product index and customer behavior data in the Algolia account.

2. Using the API for recommendations: Through the API, you can request recommendations from Algolia for a specific user. To perform this integration, you must first install the Algolia client in Python.

    `pip install algoliasearch`

3. Requesting recommendations with the API:

```python
from algoliasearch.search_client import SearchClient

# Configuración del cliente de Algolia
client = SearchClient.create('TU_APP_ID', 'TU_API_KEY')
index = client.init_index('nombre_del_indice')

# Obtener recomendaciones para un cliente específico
resultado = index.search('producto especifico', {
    'filters': 'categoria:tecnologia AND precio < 500'
})

# Mostrar recomendaciones
for hit in resultado['hits']:
    print(hit)
```

RecoAI is another platform that offers a recommendation service through an API, allowing SMEs to integrate machine learning-based recommendations into their ecommerce platforms or mobile applications. RecoAI allows personalization of recommendations through configurations that consider both customer behavior and product characteristics, generating real-time recommendations that optimize conversion.

For SMEs looking to use RecoAI, the integration is similar to Algolia. A product index is set up, and recommendation preferences are defined. The RecoAI API allows you to make recommendation requests based on each customer's browsing and purchase history, delivering a list of relevant products in seconds.

These recommendation systems via APIs offer a quick and scalable solution for SMEs that want to provide personalized recommendations without the need to develop and manage their own recommendation system. Integrating these APIs allows companies to offer a personalized shopping experience, making it easier for customers to find products of interest and improving customer retention and satisfaction.

Overall, both the use of Scikit-Learn and third-party APIs are viable options for SMEs to implement recommendation systems that improve personalization and optimize the customer experience. Depending on resources and specific needs, each company can choose the approach that best suits its business objectives and infrastructure.

- ## Real-time behavior-based recommendations

Implementing real-time behavior-based recommendations is an advanced strategy that allows SMEs to offer customers personalized products or services at the moment they interact with the platform, adapting suggestions based on their recent actions on the website or app. This real-time personalization is crucial in a competitive e-commerce environment, as it helps capture the customer's attention, making it easier for them to discover relevant products and improving their overall browsing experience. Two standout tools for achieving this kind of real-time implementation are Streamlit and Flask, which enable businesses to develop interactive and scalable applications without the need for complex infrastructure.

Streamlit and Flask are options that offer a combination of simplicity, speed, and flexibility, making it easy to create web applications that process and display dynamic recommendations. With these tools, a SME can implement a system that analyzes user behavior in real-time and displays recommendations based on previously viewed products, similar items, or items frequently purchased by other customers with a similar profile. By providing real-time recommendations, businesses can improve the user experience, increase the average order value, and foster customer loyalty.

Streamlit stands out for its ease of use and allows the creation of data and machine learning web applications with simple syntax, which is ideal for developers who want to prototype or develop interactive applications quickly. On the other hand, Flask is a Python microframework that enables the building of more customized and scalable web applications, which is useful for companies that want detailed control over the architecture of their recommendation system.

To implement real-time recommendations, it's important to have a system that captures user interactions, analyzes them immediately, and returns relevant products based on those interactions. This involves processing browsing data, viewed products, and any other signals of user interest to update recommendations in real-time, enabling a dynamic and personalized shopping experience.

- ### Implementing real-time recommendations with Streamlit

Streamlit allows you to create machine learning and data analysis applications with an interactive and attractive user interface. By focusing on visualization and interactivity, Streamlit makes it easy to integrate recommendation models that update in real-time in response to user actions, offering a rich user experience without requiring advanced knowledge in web development.

To implement a real-time recommendation system in Streamlit, the first step is to capture user interactions, such as the products they view, the categories they explore, or the searches they perform on the site. With this information, recommendations can be generated using collaborative filtering algorithms or content-based filtering, applying machine learning techniques that suggest relevant products based on the customer's previous interactions. Below is an example of how to structure a real-time recommendation application using Streamlit and a content similarity-based recommendation model.

1. Real-time interaction capture: Streamlit allows you to monitor user interactions through widgets like buttons, dropdowns, and text inputs, capturing actions easily and dynamically. For example, if a user views a specific product, we can store this information in a database or a temporary session variable, allowing the recommendation system to process it immediately and update the suggestions on screen.

2. Recommendation generation: Once user interaction is captured, the system can calculate real-time recommendations based on the available information. For this example, we will implement a simple content-based filtering model, which suggests products with similar features to those the user has recently explored. By using product feature data (such as category, brand, and price), the model can identify similarities and generate relevant recommendations.

3. Visualization of recommendations: Streamlit allows you to display updated recommendations in real-time using its intuitive API for visual interfaces. With elements like st.write() and st.image(), we can create a recommendations section that updates based on the user's recent interactions.

Here is an example of how to structure a basic Streamlit app for real-time recommendations.

```
import streamlit as st
import pandas as pd
from sklearn.metrics.pairwise import cosine_similarity
from sklearn.preprocessing import OneHotEncoder

# Ejemplo de dataset de productos
productos = pd.DataFrame({
    'producto_id': [1, 2, 3, 4, 5],
    'nombre': ['Laptop A', 'Laptop B', 'Camisa', 'Zapatos', 'Silla'],
    'categoria': ['tecnologia', 'tecnologia', 'ropa', 'ropa', 'hogar'],
    'marca': ['Marca1', 'Marca2', 'Marca1', 'Marca3', 'Marca1'],
    'precio': [500, 700, 50, 45, 30]
})

# OneHotEncoding para caracteristicas categóricas
encoder = OneHotEncoder()
caracteristicas = encoder.fit_transform(productos[['categoria', 'marca']])
productos_encoded = pd.DataFrame(caracteristicas.toarray(), columns=encoder.get_feature_names_out())
productos_encoded['precio'] = productos['precio']

# Calcular la matriz de similitud de productos
similitud_productos = cosine_similarity(productos_encoded)

# Función para recomendar productos similares
def recomendar_productos(producto_id, similitud_productos, productos, top_n=3):
    indice_producto = productos[productos['producto_id'] == producto_id].index[0]
    indices_similares = similitud_productos[indice_producto].argsort()[-top_n-1:-1][::-1]
    productos_recomendados = productos.iloc[indices_similares]
    return productos_recomendados

# Interfaz de usuario en Streamlit
st.title("Recomendaciones en tiempo real")
producto_seleccionado = st.selectbox("Selecciona un producto para ver recomendaciones", productos['nombre'])

if producto_seleccionado:
    producto_id = productos[productos['nombre'] == producto_seleccionado]['producto_id'].values[0]
    recomendaciones = recomendar_productos(producto_id, similitud_productos, productos)
    st.write("Productos recomendados:")
    for _, producto in recomendaciones.iterrows():
        st.write(f"- {producto['nombre']} (${producto['precio']})")
```

This example shows how to use Streamlit to offer real-time recommendations based on the product the customer selects. As the user interacts with the app, the recommendations are updated, providing a personalized and dynamic experience.

▪ **Implementation of real-time recommendations with Flask**

Flask, unlike Streamlit, is a web framework that offers greater control and flexibility over application development. This makes Flask an ideal choice for real-time recommendation systems that require advanced customization, as it allows for a more robust and controlled architecture for data interaction.

To implement real-time recommendations with Flask, the process involves developing endpoints that capture user interactions, process the data, and return personalized recommendations. Flask allows you to define routes and create REST APIs, which makes it easy to integrate with front-end applications or ecommerce systems in real time. Additionally, Flask is compatible with databases and other services, making it easier to handle large volumes of interaction data.

1. Data capture and user interactions: Just like in Streamlit, it's necessary to capture user interactions, such as viewed products or explored categories. However, in Flask, this data is stored in a database or in memory for later processing and analysis. Flask allows you to define specific routes to capture this information through POST requests, enabling real-time processing of interaction data.

2. Processing and generating recommendations: Once interaction data is captured, the system generates personalized recommendations for the user based on recent actions. Flask can use pre-trained machine learning models to make recommendations, applying collaborative filtering or content-based techniques based on the available data.

3. Real-time response: Flask allows returning recommendations to the front-end via JSON responses. This structure makes it easy for recommendations to be displayed in the user interface immediately, maintaining real-time interaction. The recommendations are updated based on user actions, improving the relevance of the suggestions and the overall shopping experience.

Next, a basic example of how to set up a recommendation system in Flask.

```
from flask import Flask, request, jsonify
import pandas as pd
from sklearn.metrics.pairwise import cosine_similarity
from sklearn.preprocessing import OneHotEncoder

app = Flask(__name__)

# Dataset y preprocesamiento
productos = pd.DataFrame({
    'producto_id': [1, 2, 3, 4, 5],
    'nombre': ['Laptop A', 'Laptop B', 'Camisa', 'Zapatos', 'Silla'],
    'categoria': ['tecnologia', 'tecnologia', 'ropa', 'ropa', 'hogar'],
    'marca': ['Marca1', 'Marca2', 'Marca1', 'Marca3', 'Marca1'],
    'precio': [500, 700, 50, 45, 30]
})

encoder = OneHotEncoder()
caracteristicas = encoder.fit_transform(productos[['categoria', 'marca']])
productos_encoded = pd.DataFrame(caracteristicas.toarray(), columns=encoder.get_feature_names_out())
productos_encoded['precio'] = productos['precio']
similitud_productos = cosine_similarity(productos_encoded)

# Función para generar recomendaciones
def recomendar_productos(producto_id, similitud_productos, productos, top_n=3):
    indice_producto = productos[productos['producto_id'] == producto_id].index[0]
    indices_similares = similitud_productos[indice_producto].argsort()[-top_n-1:-1][::-1]
    productos_recomendados = productos.iloc[indices_similares]
    return productos_recomendados

# Endpoint para recomendaciones en tiempo real
@app.route('/recomendaciones', methods=['POST'])
def obtener_recomendaciones():
    data = request.json
    producto_id = data['producto_id']
    recomendaciones = recomendar_productos(producto_id, similitud_productos, productos)
    resultados = recomendaciones.to_dict(orient='records')
    return jsonify(resultados)

if __name__ == '__main__':
    app.run(debug=True)
```

In this example, Flask provides an endpoint /recomendaciones that receives a product_id and returns similar products in JSON format. This approach allows the client interface to consume recommendations in real time, offering a personalized experience adapted to the user's recent interactions.

- **Automation of recommendations on ecommerce platforms**

Automating recommendations on ecommerce platforms is a fundamental strategy for SMEs to optimize personalization in their online stores. This strategy ensures that each customer receives product suggestions at the right time, both on the purchase page and in follow-up emails, which not only improves the user experience but also increases conversion rates and the average order value. Thanks to platforms like Shopify and WooCommerce, which offer advanced personalization tools and wide compatibility with recommendation systems, SMEs can implement automated recommendations without the need to develop a complex technical infrastructure.

The automation of recommendations uses machine learning algorithms to analyze customer behavior and offer personalized suggestions based on data such as purchase history, product visits, recent interactions, and browsing preferences. In an ecommerce environment, these recommendations can be implemented in various ways: on the product page, in the shopping cart section, and in follow-up emails. Each of these options presents an opportunity to influence customer purchasing decisions and maximize the profitability of each interaction.

For SMEs using ecommerce platforms like Shopify or WooCommerce, there are multiple ways to integrate automated recommendations, ranging from native apps on these platforms to external tools that sync via APIs. Below, the different options for automating recommendations and the benefits of each approach are explored in detail.

Shopify, a popular ecommerce platform, offers a range of apps and plugins specialized in automated recommendations. These apps integrate easily into Shopify stores and allow merchants to automatically suggest products based on a variety of criteria, such as product similarity, recent customer behavior, and other users' purchasing patterns. Shopify features apps like ReConvert Upsell & Cross Sell or Frequently Bought Together, which analyze customer data and recommend similar or complementary products. These plugins are designed to display suggested products at the most relevant moments, such as on the checkout page, when the customer has added an item to the cart, or at the end of a purchase, inviting them to explore additional products.

Integrating automated recommendations on the product page is one of the most effective techniques, as it allows you to suggest complementary products that increase the value of the purchase. For example, if a customer is viewing a specific product, such as a laptop, the recommendation system can suggest relevant accessories like cases, chargers, or external keyboards. This recommendation on the product page enhances the visibility of products the customer might need in combination with their initial purchase, creating an opportunity for cross-selling or upselling. For SMEs that want to customize this functionality without a complex infrastructure, Shopify offers apps like Personalized Recommendations, which use machine learning algorithms to analyze product features and customer behavior, providing recommendations dynamically and in real-time.

WooCommerce, which is an extension of WordPress and one of the most popular options for creating online stores, also provides options to automate product recommendations. WooCommerce allows SMEs to customize the shopping experience through product recommendation plugins that integrate easily and offer advanced personalization features. Product Recommendations is one of the most used plugins in WooCommerce, leveraging purchase history and customer behavior data to suggest relevant products on the product page, the cart page, and in follow-up emails. This plugin allows SMEs to set specific recommendation rules, such as recommending products from the same category or products that other customers bought together, and adjust them based on their business goals.

In addition to the options available directly on Shopify and WooCommerce, many SMEs choose to use third-party services that offer advanced recommendations through APIs. Platforms like RecoAI and Algolia Recommend allow the integration of advanced recommendation systems via APIs that synchronize in real-time with the online store. These solutions offer greater customization and flexibility in the development of recommendations, as the APIs can analyze large volumes of data and generate specific suggestions for each customer. Integrating a recommendation API allows SMEs to configure different customization rules, such as the frequency of recommendations, real-time updates of suggestions, and the personalization of recommendations based on customer response.

Follow-up email recommendations are also a key strategy in ecommerce, as they allow SMEs to continue interacting with the customer beyond the online store and increase the chances of conversion. For example, if a customer has abandoned a shopping cart, a reminder email that includes additional products or personalized promotions can motivate them to complete the purchase. Shopify and WooCommerce allow SMEs to set up follow-up emails that include product recommendations. Additionally, marketing automation platforms like Mailchimp or Klaviyo offer specific integrations with Shopify and WooCommerce, enabling personalized emails with product recommendations based on customer behavior and purchase history.

In Shopify, integrating automated recommendations into follow-up emails is easy thanks to the platform's compatibility with marketing automation tools. Apps like Klaviyo integrate with Shopify to send personalized emails, adjusting the suggested products based on the customer's behavior in the store. For example, if a customer has viewed a specific product but hasn't purchased it, the platform can send an email reminding them of the product, along with recommendations for similar or complementary products. This strategy not only increases the chances of conversion but also allows the company to maintain continuous communication with the customer, fostering loyalty and brand engagement.

The automation of recommendations on ecommerce platforms like Shopify and WooCommerce not only optimizes the sales process but also allows SMEs to save time and resources, as recommendations are generated automatically based on precise behavioral data. Automation tools allow large volumes of data to be analyzed efficiently and generate recommendations tailored to each customer, without the need for manual intervention. Moreover, the personalization of recommendations enhances the shopping experience, increases the average order value, and facilitates customer loyalty.

Another key functionality in automating recommendations is the ability to perform A/B tests to evaluate the effectiveness of different recommendation strategies. E-commerce platforms and recommendation API services allow A/B tests where different types of recommendations are shown to specific customer segments, evaluating which one generates better results in terms of conversion and additional sales. For example, an SME can test two different recommendation strategies on the product page, one with complementary products and another with products from the same category, and analyze which one is more effective for each type of customer. This analysis allows for adjusting recommendations based on results, maximizing their effectiveness and optimizing the return on investment for each recommendation campaign.

Automating recommendations in ecommerce also allows SMEs to implement hybrid recommendation systems that combine both collaborative filtering and content-based filtering. This strategy provides more accurate recommendations by analyzing both product features and the behavior of other customers with similar preferences. Advanced recommendation platforms like Algolia Recommend offer this hybrid capability, enabling SMEs to tailor their recommendations to the unique preferences of each customer. For example, an online store selling sports items can recommend products based on both the customer's interest profile and popular products among other customers who have purchased similar items. This combination improves the relevance of recommendations and increases the likelihood that the customer will discover products of interest.

Regarding technical integration, recommendation APIs allow SMEs to connect their ecommerce systems with external recommendation services simply and efficiently. This is particularly useful for companies without an in-house development team, as APIs usually come with detailed documentation and practical examples that simplify implementation. Additionally, recommendation APIs allow for advanced customization, which is ideal for SMEs that want to stand out in a competitive market and offer a unique user experience in their online store.

The automation of recommendations on ecommerce platforms like Shopify and WooCommerce provides SMEs with a powerful and accessible solution to optimize their personalization strategies and maximize the performance of every customer interaction. Whether through native apps on these platforms or by integrating advanced APIs, SMEs can offer recommendations that are tailored to their customers' interests and behaviors in real time, improving the relevance of each suggestion and strengthening customer relationships.

7.5. Psychographic Segmentation

Psychographic segmentation is an advanced marketing strategy that allows companies to classify their customers not just based on their actions, like purchases made or website visits, but also on their attitudes, interests, values, and lifestyles. Unlike demographic or geographic segmentation, which focuses on more static factors like age, gender, or location, psychographic segmentation delves into the more personal and motivational aspects that drive consumer behavior. This enables SMEs to better understand not only what a customer buys, but why they do it, providing key insights to design marketing strategies that align with the values and beliefs of each customer group.

For SMEs, psychographic segmentation can be especially useful when offering specialized products or services aimed at audiences with very specific interests. By understanding the internal motivations, desires, and values that guide their customers' purchasing decisions, businesses can tailor their messages and offers in a way that resonates authentically and personally. This personalization has the potential to build long-term relationships, increase customer loyalty, and improve the overall effectiveness of marketing campaigns. For example, an eco-friendly store might identify that a segment of its customers has a deep interest in environmental care and sustainability; knowing this information, the store can adjust its strategy to emphasize the positive impact of its products on the ecosystem, making the messages more persuasive and relevant to those customers.

Psychographic segmentation analyzes several key factors to create more homogeneous groups of customers in terms of their preferences and motivations. These factors typically include attitudes, interests, opinions, lifestyle, and values. These aspects are obtained through surveys, interviews, online behavior analysis, and data collected via interaction on social media or the company's website. Through data analysis techniques, SMEs can identify patterns in customer responses and establish psychographic segments that facilitate the personalization of messages and marketing campaigns. The advantage of this approach is that it provides a richer, more detailed view of the customer, allowing SMEs to design strategies that emotionally connect with their audience.

One of the key factors in psychographic segmentation is identifying the values and beliefs of customers. Values represent fundamental principles that guide people's lives and are reflected in their purchasing decisions. For example, some customers may value sustainability and respect for the environment, while others may prioritize innovation and advanced technology. By understanding these values, an SME can tailor its communication and positioning to align with the principles that are important to its customers. In the case of an organic products company, emphasizing the absence of pesticides and respect for the ecosystem in production can deeply resonate with customers who value sustainability and the well-being of the planet. On the other hand, a tech products company can focus on highlighting the innovation and efficiency of its products to connect with customers who value modernity and progress.

Psychographic segmentation also includes the interests and hobbies of customers, aspects that can greatly influence their purchasing preferences. For example, customers interested in outdoor sports might respond better to products that promote an active lifestyle, such as sportswear, hiking shoes, or camping equipment. An SME selling these products can use this information to develop campaigns that align with these interests, showing images and messages that reflect a passion for nature, adventure, and physical exercise. This strategy has the potential to capture customers' attention on an emotional and motivational level, improving the relevance and effectiveness of marketing campaigns. For a company dealing in cultural products, such as books or music, understanding customers' interests can lead to more accurate recommendations and promote authors, genres, or styles that match the preferences of each segment, increasing the likelihood of purchase and customer satisfaction.

Another fundamental component of psychographic segmentation is the customer's lifestyle, which ranges from their daily routine to their social activities, relationships, and aspirations. Customers with different lifestyles often have different needs and expectations regarding the products and services they consume. For example, a customer who leads an active life and exercises regularly may look for products that fit their lifestyle, such as nutritional supplements or sports equipment. On the other hand, a customer with a wellness-oriented lifestyle may be more interested in wellness products like essential oils, spa sessions, or meditation practices. SMEs that understand their customers' lifestyles can tailor their offerings and messaging so that each segment feels the company authentically meets their needs.

Personality is another important aspect of psychographic segmentation, and it can deeply influence buying preferences and how customers respond to marketing messages. A customer's personality can be classified into different types, such as extroverted, introverted, adventurous, cautious, among others. For example, a fashion company can segment its customers based on their personality, identifying those who seek to stand out and be original in their style, versus others who prefer more classic and discreet options. This segmentation allows the company to tailor its campaigns so they resonate with different personalities, using a bold and creative approach for more extroverted customers and a more elegant, timeless presentation for those who prefer a conservative style. This approach helps SMEs build a stronger emotional connection with each customer group, increasing the likelihood that messages will be well received and recommendations relevant.

In addition to psychological and social factors, goals and aspirations also play an important role in psychographic segmentation. Customers often have personal or professional goals that influence their purchasing decisions. For example, a person who aspires to improve their physical health may be interested in products that promote a healthy lifestyle, such as organic foods, exercise equipment, or vitamin supplements. An SME marketing these products can use psychographic segmentation to identify these customers and tailor their message to emphasize how their products help achieve a healthier, more active life. In contrast, a customer seeking professional success may be interested in productivity tools, online training, or the latest technology devices. By understanding these aspirations, companies can create campaigns that inspire customers and show them how their products can help them achieve their goals, thereby strengthening the emotional connection and improving brand perception.

Psychographic segmentation not only allows for personalized marketing messages, but it also facilitates the design of differentiated shopping experiences that meet the expectations of each customer segment. In an e-commerce context, this segmentation can be reflected in product organization, personalized recommendations, and campaign design. For example, an online store that understands its customers' interests and values can tailor the browsing experience to highlight products that match those specific interests. If the store identifies a group of customers who value exclusivity and luxury, it can offer them high-end products and a shopping process that conveys exclusivity, including details like personalized shipping or limited edition products. On the other hand, for customers who value sustainability, the store can highlight eco-friendly products and emphasize the brand's commitment to the environment, providing information on the positive impact of each purchase.

Regarding the collection of psychographic data, companies often use tools like surveys, interviews, and online behavior analysis to gather information about their customers' interests and values. Social media also offers a rich source of psychographic data, as it allows companies to observe customer interactions and topics of interest in real-time. Many SMEs leverage these platforms to interact directly with their audience and gain a better understanding of their motivations and preferences. Additionally, through text analysis and natural language processing, companies can identify recurring themes and patterns of interest in customer conversations and comments, gaining deeper insights into their attitudes and values.

Psychographic segmentation is especially valuable for SMEs wanting to build a lasting relationship with their customers and foster long-term loyalty. By aligning their marketing campaigns with the values and aspirations of each customer group, companies can create a sense of belonging and emotional connection that goes beyond a simple transaction. This emotional connection is a key factor in customer loyalty, as it fosters genuine commitment to the brand and increases the likelihood of repeat purchases. Additionally, when customers feel understood and valued, they are more likely to recommend the brand to family and friends, which positively impacts the company's reputation and facilitates the acquisition of new customers.

Finally, psychographic segmentation allows SMEs to stand out in a competitive market where personalization and message relevance are crucial factors for capturing customer attention. In an environment where consumers are constantly receiving marketing messages, those who perceive that a brand understands and responds to their specific needs and interests are more likely to engage and develop a loyal relationship. By implementing a psychographic segmentation strategy, SMEs can differentiate themselves from the competition, offering a personalized and differentiated customer experience that aligns with their clients' values and motivations, thereby strengthening their market position and increasing their customer retention capacity.

7.6. Geographic Segmentation

Geographic segmentation is an essential marketing strategy for SMEs that want to tailor their offers and campaigns based on their customers' location. This type of segmentation classifies customers according to their geographic location, such as country, region, city, or even neighborhood, allowing messages and offers to be adapted to the specific characteristics and needs of each area. For many local businesses or companies with limited geographic coverage, geographic segmentation is fundamental to maximizing the relevance of their campaigns and improving their connection with their audience, as it allows them to respond to the particularities of each market, such as cultural preferences, buying behaviors, and weather conditions.

Geographic segmentation offers a significant advantage for SMEs looking to optimize their resources and focus on customers with the highest conversion potential in specific areas. By targeting customers based on their location, businesses can tailor their campaigns to better meet the expectations and needs of each community. This is particularly useful for local businesses that rely on their physical proximity to customers to generate traffic and loyalty. Additionally, for services with geographic or delivery limitations, geographic segmentation helps improve efficiency by concentrating on areas where they can ensure an optimal customer experience. For example, a restaurant that only delivers to certain neighborhoods can limit its digital advertising to those same neighborhoods, optimizing its advertising budget and maximizing the effectiveness of its campaigns.

Geographic data allows for more precise offer personalization based on factors like weather conditions and local events. This is especially relevant for businesses whose products or services depend on the seasons or climate. For example, a clothing store can tailor its campaigns according to the weather conditions of each region, promoting coats and winter clothing in cold areas and summer clothes in warm climates. Similarly, local events like fairs, festivals, and celebrations provide opportunities to launch specific promotions that catch customers' attention in a culturally relevant context. A small business selling sports products could, for instance, promote personalized jerseys and items in cities hosting major sporting events, thereby achieving greater resonance with the interests of customers in that area.

Geolocation technology has transformed how SMEs can leverage geographic segmentation in their marketing strategies. With advanced tools, businesses can identify the exact location of their customers in real time, allowing them to display personalized offers and target proximity campaigns accurately. For example, by using geolocated ads on social media and search engines, SMEs can reach potential customers near their establishments, encouraging them to visit the store or take advantage of an offer at the right moment. Location-based ads are particularly effective for retail businesses, coffee shops, restaurants, and other shops that rely on foot traffic and proximity to attract customers.

In addition to geolocation technology, SMEs can also leverage digital platforms to segment their campaigns based on their customers' location. Advertising platforms like Google Ads and Facebook Ads allow businesses to target their ads to specific audiences based on location, selecting cities, regions, or even specific areas within a city. This is ideal for SMEs that want to maximize the impact of their marketing campaigns and reduce customer acquisition costs, as they can focus on areas where there is a higher likelihood of conversion. For example, a gardening services business could target its ads to residential neighborhoods with a high density of homes, where customers are more likely to need its services.

Geographic segmentation also allows SMEs to leverage cultural and regional differences in their marketing campaigns. Preferences and buying behaviors often vary from one region to another, and tailoring marketing messages to reflect these cultural differences can significantly improve the effectiveness of campaigns. For example, in some regions, consumers may prefer locally made products or those that reflect the area's culture and traditions, while in other areas, customers might value innovation or imported products more. By understanding these differences, an SME can adjust its messaging and position its products to resonate with the values and expectations of customers in each region, achieving a stronger connection and increasing the relevance of its offering.

Another advantage of geographic segmentation is the ability to conduct market tests in specific areas before launching a large-scale campaign. This is especially useful for SMEs that want to minimize risks and ensure their campaigns are well-received before investing in a broader rollout. For example, a company that wants to launch a new product can start by targeting its campaigns to a specific city or region, analyze customer response, and adjust the strategy based on the results. If the product is successful in that area, the company can extend the campaign to other regions with greater confidence in the effectiveness of its approach. This method not only optimizes the marketing budget but also provides valuable data on regional customer preferences.

Geographic segmentation in marketing emails is another effective practice for personalizing communication and enhancing the relevance of messages. SMEs can use the customer's location to send emails with offers and promotions tailored to the needs of each region, such as special discounts on seasonal products or local events. For example, an online sports store could send an email with winter sports equipment recommendations to its customers in cold areas, while suggesting outdoor and water sports products to those in warmer regions. By personalizing emails based on location, SMEs can improve open rates and the effectiveness of their email marketing campaigns, generating greater engagement and increasing conversion possibilities.

In the context of SMS marketing campaigns, geographic segmentation allows SMEs to send personalized messages to customers in specific areas, encouraging them to visit the physical store or take advantage of a limited-time promotion. This strategy is particularly useful for local businesses, which can direct their messages to customers nearby and create a sense of urgency that motivates visits. For example, a restaurant can send an SMS to regular customers in the neighborhood with a special offer during off-peak hours, thereby increasing traffic at strategic times and improving business profitability. The ability to reach customers at the right place and time makes location-based SMS marketing a highly effective tool for fostering customer interaction and loyalty.

For SMEs operating in multiple cities or regions, geographic segmentation facilitates inventory management and product supply based on demand in each area. By understanding customer preferences in each location, businesses can adjust their inventories to meet the specific demand of each region, avoiding issues of stock shortages or surpluses. For example, if a clothing retailer identifies that coats are more in demand in certain cold regions during winter, they can concentrate the inventory of those products in stores in those areas, maximizing availability and reducing transportation and storage costs. This approach not only optimizes logistics but also improves customer satisfaction by ensuring that the most popular products are available where they are needed.

The use of real-time location data is an advanced tool that allows SMEs to adjust their marketing strategies based on the customer's location at the precise moment. With geolocation technologies in mobile devices, businesses can detect their customers' location and send personalized offers in real-time, whether through push notifications, digital ads, or SMS messages. This strategy is especially effective for physical stores, which can attract customers nearby with last-minute offers or exclusive discounts. For example, a fashion store can send a push notification to customers in the vicinity, informing them about an in-store special sale or a promotion on seasonal products. This immediate response capability improves the likelihood of conversion and encourages in-store traffic.

Finally, geographic segmentation allows SMEs to optimize their advertising investment by focusing their resources on areas with the highest conversion potential. By concentrating on regions where the company has a larger customer base or where its products are in higher demand, SMEs can maximize the return on investment in their marketing campaigns. This is particularly important on digital advertising platforms like Google Ads and Facebook Ads, which allow targeting ads based on customer location. By limiting the geographic coverage of their campaigns, businesses can reduce advertising costs and improve campaign efficiency, achieving more effective results with a smaller budget. Additionally, this strategy enables SMEs to closely monitor customer responses in each area, providing valuable data to adjust future campaigns based on the results obtained.

In summary, geographic segmentation is a key tool for SMEs that want to personalize their offers and improve the effectiveness of their marketing campaigns. By adapting their messages and strategies based on the location of their customers, companies can increase the relevance of their campaigns, enhance their connection with the audience, and optimize their resources more efficiently.

- **Example of visualization by geographic segmentation**

A code and visualization example could be very useful to show how SMEs can apply geographic segmentation to analyze the distribution of their customers and adapt their marketing strategies. A practical case could consist of a fictional dataset containing customer locations (latitude and longitude) and their respective segmentation categories (e.g., 'Frequent', 'Occasional', and 'New').

With this dataset, we could visualize the geographic segmentation on a map, using Python tools like Folium to show the distribution of customers by region. This type of visualization helps identify areas with a high concentration of customers, making it easier to decide where to focus local marketing campaigns or specific promotions.

Here is the step-by-step code example, which includes data analysis, segmentation, and visualization on an interactive map.

- **Step 1: Data Preparation**

For this example, we created a fictional dataset of customers with information about their location (latitude and longitude) and their segmentation category.

```python
import pandas as pd

# Datos ficticios de clientes
data = {
    'Cliente': ['A', 'B', 'C', 'D', 'E', 'F', 'G', 'H', 'I', 'J'],
    'Latitud': [40.416775, 40.403482, 40.425563, 40.408463, 40.400722, 40.426332, 40.418506, 40.421278, 40.415178, 40.412345],
    'Longitud': [-3.703790, -3.699654, -3.711632, -3.700332, -3.707878, -3.703254, -3.703030, -3.702682, -3.712210, -3.701123],
    'Segmento': ['Frecuentes', 'Ocasionales', 'Frecuentes', 'Nuevos', 'Frecuentes', 'Ocasionales', 'Nuevos', 'Frecuentes', 'Ocasionales', 'Nuevos']
}

clientes_df = pd.DataFrame(data)
print(clientes_df)
```

```
✓ 2.6s

  Cliente   Latitud  Longitud     Segmento
0       A  40.416775 -3.703790   Frecuentes
1       B  40.403482 -3.699654  Ocasionales
2       C  40.425563 -3.711632   Frecuentes
3       D  40.408463 -3.700332       Nuevos
4       E  40.400722 -3.707878   Frecuentes
5       F  40.426332 -3.703254  Ocasionales
6       G  40.418506 -3.703030       Nuevos
7       H  40.421278 -3.702682   Frecuentes
8       I  40.415178 -3.712210  Ocasionales
9       J  40.412345 -3.701123       Nuevos
```

This basic dataset contains the coordinates of each customer and their segmentation category, which we will use to customize the map.

- **Step 2: Visualizing the geographical segmentation with Folium**

With Folium, we can create an interactive map that shows the location of each client, differentiating them according to their segmentation category. This type of map allows us to identify areas with a high concentration of clients and adapt marketing strategies according to the geographic distribution.

```
import folium
from folium.plugins import MarkerCluster

# Crear un mapa centrado en las coordenadas de los clientes
mapa_clientes = folium.Map(location=[40.416775, -3.703790], zoom_start=13)

# Crear un cluster para agrupar los puntos en el mapa
cluster = MarkerCluster().add_to(mapa_clientes)

# Diccionario para asignar colores a cada segmento
colores_segmento = {
    'Frecuentes': 'green',
    'Ocasionales': 'blue',
    'Nuevos': 'red'
}

# Añadir puntos de los clientes en el mapa
for idx, row in clientes_df.iterrows():
    folium.Marker(
        location=[row['Latitud'], row['Longitud']],
        popup=f"Cliente: {row['Cliente']}<br>Segmento: {row['Segmento']}",
        icon=folium.Icon(color=colores_segmento[row['Segmento']])
    ).add_to(cluster)

# Mostrar el mapa interactivo
mapa_clientes.save("mapa_clientes.html")
```

This code generates an HTML file with the interactive map. When you open it in the browser, you can see the location of each customer represented by a marker in a different color according to their segment: green for "Frequent" customers, blue for "Occasional," and red for "New." The MarkerCluster() function groups nearby points, making it easier to visualize when there is a high density of customers in the same area.

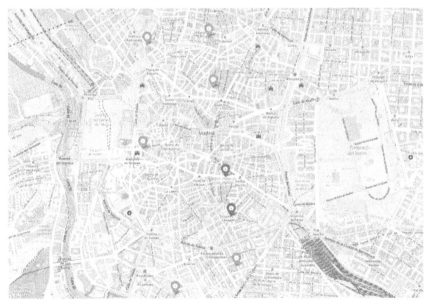

428

- **Step 3: Interpretation of the visualization**

With the generated map, we can perform a visual analysis of the distribution of customers based on their geographic segmentation. Some key points:

- Concentration of frequent customers: Areas with a high number of frequent customers can be strategic zones for promotions or events, as they reflect a loyal clientele. SMEs can use this data to plan retention campaigns or incentivize referrals in those areas.

- New and occasional customers: Areas where new and occasional customers predominate represent conversion opportunities. SMEs can focus on these zones for loyalty campaigns or upselling strategies, with the goal of turning these customers into frequent buyers.

- **Visualization extension**

To further enrich the analysis, we could use additional data, such as purchase history or visit frequency, and combine them with advanced segmentation tools in Python, like Scikit-Learn to apply clustering or psychographic segmentation in combination with geographic segmentation.

Chapter 8 - Advanced machine learning techniques for SMEs

8.1. Optimization algorithms: Demand forecasting and inventory turnover prediction

Optimization of operations is essential for SMEs to maximize their resources and offer quality service in competitive markets. In this context, optimization algorithms have become valuable tools for improving areas such as demand forecasting and inventory management. By predicting product demand and efficiently controlling inventory turnover, companies can avoid common problems like overstocking or running out of key products during peak demand, achieving greater operational efficiency and reducing unnecessary costs.

Demand prediction is a planning strategy that uses machine learning models to analyze historical sales data, seasonal patterns, promotional events, and other factors that influence consumer behavior. By anticipating product demand, SMEs can adjust their inventory levels and ensure optimal availability without overstocking or facing losses due to stockouts. Regression models and neural networks are two common approaches to demand prediction. Regression allows for identifying linear relationships between demand variables and external influences, while neural networks, particularly useful in complex data environments, offer advanced capabilities to capture non-linear demand patterns.

On the other hand, inventory turnover refers to how often a product is sold and replaced over a given period. Efficient turnover allows SMEs to better manage their stock, optimizing storage space and ensuring that high-demand products are available when customers need them. By implementing machine learning algorithms to analyze inventory turnover, companies can identify high and low turnover products, adjust their stock accordingly, and avoid both stockouts and overstocking. With dynamic inventory systems, machine learning algorithms enable continuous real-time adjustments, taking into account factors such as changes in demand and market conditions.

The use of time series in demand prediction and inventory turnover also plays an important role in optimizing operations. Time series models like ARIMA and Prophet capture patterns in the data over time and allow for predictions based on trends and seasonality. This is particularly useful for

SMEs that need to manage inventories that fluctuate based on seasonal events or growth trends.

Together, these optimization algorithms provide SMEs with a significant competitive advantage, allowing them to anticipate market needs, improve operational efficiency, and reduce costs in inventory management.

- ### Introduction to demand forecasting with machine learning

Demand prediction is a fundamental technique in inventory management and sales planning for SMEs, allowing them to forecast future product demand and adjust inventory based on these estimates. The ability to anticipate demand is essential to avoid overstock, which represents unnecessary storage costs, and stockouts, which can lead to lost sales and a potential decrease in customer satisfaction. In this context, machine learning becomes a powerful tool that allows the analysis of historical sales data, identification of seasonal patterns, evaluation of the impact of promotions, and consideration of other factors affecting demand. By doing so, SMEs can make accurate predictions and informed decisions to optimize their operations.

In demand prediction, regression models are one of the most widely used machine learning tools. These models allow you to identify relationships between a dependent variable, in this case, the demand for a product, and one or more independent variables, such as previous sales data, seasons, promotions, and any other relevant variables that may influence consumer behavior. Regression models include different variants, such as linear regression, polynomial regression, and random forest regression, which can be applied depending on the complexity of the dataset and the patterns you want to capture.

Linear regression is one of the simplest and most commonly used methods for demand prediction. This model assumes a linear relationship between the independent variables and the dependent variable, meaning that changes in the independent variables, such as the previous month's sales volume or the season of the year, are reflected in demand proportionally. This approach is suitable when demand shows a relatively constant trend or when analyzing factors that have a stable effect on demand. In an SME, for example, a linear regression model can be applied to predict sales of a basic product, such as a daily consumption food, where buying behavior is regular and predictable.

To train a linear regression model in the context of demand prediction, a historical dataset is used that includes both the demand variable and the relevant input variables. In Python, this can be easily implemented with libraries like Scikit-Learn, which allows you to fit the model with training data and evaluate its accuracy with test data. When implementing a linear regression model, it's important to preprocess the data and ensure the variables are normalized, which improves model performance and allows for a more accurate interpretation of the results. For example, a cleaning products company could use a linear regression model to forecast demand for its products based on factors such as the month, the number of promotions launched, and the amount of sales recorded in previous months.

Polynomial regression is an extension of linear regression that allows capturing non-linear relationships between independent variables and demand. This model is useful when there's a curved trend in the data, such as a progressive increase in demand during peak sales seasons. Polynomial regression provides a better fit for historical data and models demand variations more accurately. For an SME with seasonal products, like a clothing store that experiences significant demand increases during winter and summer, polynomial regression is particularly useful for capturing demand fluctuations more precisely. As with linear regression, polynomial regression is implemented in Scikit-Learn, and the model is trained and adjusted with historical demand data.

Another advanced approach to demand prediction is the use of regression with random forests. This model belongs to the family of ensemble algorithms and is based on building multiple decision trees, which together generate a more robust and accurate prediction. Regression with random forests is particularly effective when demand is influenced by multiple factors that interact in a complex and non-linear way. This model can handle large volumes of data and capture complex patterns without overfitting, making it an ideal choice for SMEs with detailed historical sales data that want more accurate predictions in complex contexts. A practical example would be a company that sells electronic products, where the demand for each product may depend on multiple factors, such as the season, the launch of new products, and special promotions. With regression with random forests, the company can more accurately predict sales based on all these variables.

For situations where data is more complex or when there are a large number of variables affecting demand, neural networks offer an advanced alternative in demand prediction. Neural networks are especially effective when the relationship between demand and input variables is non-linear and depends on multiple factors, such as weather, economic events, or changes in consumer behavior. Neural networks can process large volumes of data and discover patterns that are not evident through other regression models. This approach is useful for SMEs managing products with fluctuating demand, such as a store selling perishable foods where demand may depend on external factors like season, holidays, and weather.

Neural networks, and particularly deep neural networks, are capable of identifying patterns in historical data and making accurate real-time predictions. This is especially useful for ecommerce companies that need to adjust their inventory and logistics operations based on demand forecasts for each sales cycle. With Python libraries like TensorFlow and Keras, SMEs can implement neural networks to train demand prediction models, adjusting hyperparameters such as the number of hidden layers and nodes in each layer to optimize the model's accuracy.

In practice, a company can implement a neural network that integrates historical sales data, promotions information, weather, and other factors to forecast demand based on the time of year and purchasing patterns. This allows for more precise inventory adjustments and reduces the risk of product shortages or overstocking. An example could be a gardening supplies store that anticipates an increase in demand for certain products based on the weather and historical sales data. The neural network can forecast sales based on weather predictions and help the company prepare its inventory for the upcoming sales season.

Recurrent neural networks, such as LSTMs (Long Short-Term Memory), are an extension of neural networks designed specifically to handle sequential and temporal data. These networks can capture dependencies over time, which is ideal for demand forecasting in time series. LSTMs are useful for SMEs that want to improve the accuracy of their predictions by including the effect of the temporal sequence on demand. This allows businesses to identify patterns over weeks, months, or even years, and make inventory adjustments based on these trends. In a fresh food SME, for example, an LSTM can analyze the demand time series and predict consumption peaks based on historical data and overall demand trends, allowing for more precise and efficient inventory management.

The implementation of these models in the context of demand prediction requires a structured process, including data collection, preprocessing, training, and model evaluation. Historical sales data, seasonality patterns, promotions, and other relevant variables must be organized in a suitable format for model training. Additionally, thorough evaluation is essential to ensure the model's accuracy and its ability to generalize to new data. This evaluation is typically done using test data to verify that the model predicts demand accurately and consistently.

In addition, demand forecasting can benefit from the use of time series. These allow you to capture demand patterns over time and apply them to forecast sales evolution in future periods. Models like ARIMA and Prophet are common in time series forecasting and fit data with cyclical or trending patterns. Prophet, developed by Facebook, is especially useful for SMEs due to its ease of use and its ability to handle seasonality and outliers in the data. Time series offer a detailed view of demand behavior over time and allow you to adjust inventory and marketing strategies based on these patterns.

In conclusion, demand prediction through machine learning provides SMEs with advanced tools to adjust their inventory and improve sales planning. By implementing regression models, neural networks, and time series analysis, businesses can anticipate demand accurately and efficiently. These technologies allow SMEs to minimize storage costs, reduce the shortage of key products, and enhance customer satisfaction, creating a competitive advantage in a dynamic and demanding market environment.

- ### Inventory turnover with machine learning

Inventory turnover is a key aspect of efficient stock management, especially for SMEs looking to optimize their resources and minimize storage-related costs. Inventory turnover refers to how often a product is sold and replaced in the warehouse, and measuring this rate is essential to maintaining a balance between supply and demand. In this context, machine learning algorithms offer companies a powerful tool to predict inventory turnover, allowing them to adjust stock levels based on sales forecasts. This way, SMEs can make data-driven decisions to optimize storage space and ensure that high-demand products are always available for customers, avoiding both stockouts and excess inventory.

Inventory turnover has a direct impact on the efficiency of a company's operations. When a product's turnover is high, it means it sells frequently and must be quickly restocked to meet customer demand. Conversely, low turnover indicates that the product remains in inventory for long periods, which represents additional storage costs and a risk of obsolescence, especially in sectors where products lose value over time, like technology or fashion. For SMEs, which often have limited resources and storage space, optimizing inventory turnover is crucial to improving profitability and competitiveness in the market. This is where machine learning comes into play, offering advanced methods to analyze turnover patterns and make informed decisions about inventory management.

Product analysis based on high and low turnover is a central component of inventory management using machine learning. By classifying products according to their turnover, SMEs can prioritize restocking items with high and consistent demand while minimizing stock of low-turnover products that generate unnecessary storage costs. Machine learning algorithms, such as classification models and decision trees, can analyze large volumes of historical sales data to identify patterns in product turnover, classifying them into categories like high, medium, or low turnover. This classification allows SMEs to adjust their inventory strategy based on actual demand, allocating more resources to high-turnover products and freeing up space for items that need less restocking.

A clear example of how machine learning can help in inventory turnover analysis is the use of decision trees to classify products. Decision trees are classification models that work by splitting data into branches, based on decision rules that aim to maximize accuracy in product classification. This approach is particularly useful in inventory turnover as it allows for the analysis of factors like purchase frequency, sales volume, and seasonality for each product. By training a decision tree with historical sales data, an SME can identify specific patterns in product turnover and classify items based on their demand. This makes it easier to identify high-turnover products, which require frequent restocking, and low-turnover products, which can be stored in smaller quantities.

In addition to decision trees, clustering models are useful for identifying high and low turnover products. Clustering algorithms like k-means group products into categories based on their similarity in terms of turnover and other relevant factors. By applying k-means, SMEs can group their products into turnover clusters or segments, which makes inventory management easier by allocating resources according to the demand of each group. High turnover products will be grouped in a specific cluster, allowing the company to prioritize restocking and ensure availability. On the other hand, low turnover products are grouped in another cluster, helping the company reduce stock of these products and manage storage space more efficiently.

Another important aspect of inventory turnover is dynamic stock optimization, which involves automatically adjusting inventory quantities based on demand forecasts for each sales cycle. With a dynamic inventory system, SMEs can use machine learning algorithms that continuously monitor inventory and make real-time adjustments, ensuring the company always has the right amount of each product. Time series models, such as ARIMA or Prophet, allow for forecasting future product demand based on historical patterns and seasonal trends. By incorporating these forecasts into a dynamic inventory system, SMEs can proactively adjust stock levels, avoiding both overstocking and stockout issues.

Dynamic stock optimization offers a significant advantage for SMEs, as it allows for more flexible and adaptable inventory management. For example, a consumer goods company that experiences high seasonal demand during certain periods of the year can use a dynamic inventory system to adjust stock levels before the peak sales season begins, ensuring that products are available in the right quantities without overstocking. At the end of the season, the system can automatically reduce stock levels to avoid excess inventory, optimizing storage costs and improving operational efficiency.

Machine learning also allows for automating decision-making on inventory turnover and restocking by using predictive models that anticipate when a product will reach a critical stock level. Machine learning algorithms can analyze historical sales data and turnover rates to forecast when a product needs to be restocked, generating automatic alerts or even placing replenishment orders automatically. This approach is particularly useful for high-turnover products, where it is essential to avoid stockouts to prevent sales disruptions. In an SME dealing with perishable goods, for example, a predictive model can calculate the turnover rate of each product and forecast when restocking will be necessary, allowing the company to maintain a constant supply without incurring losses from products that have sat in storage for too long.

In practice, SMEs can implement dynamic stock optimization using Python tools and machine learning libraries like Scikit-Learn and TensorFlow. These libraries offer advanced models that allow companies to train machine learning algorithms with their sales and inventory data and develop a system that adjusts stock quantities based on demand forecasts. Additionally, cloud-based machine learning platforms like Google AI or AWS make it easier to implement real-time inventory prediction models, reducing the need for complex IT infrastructure and allowing SMEs to access advanced inventory optimization technologies.

The integration of dynamic inventory systems with machine learning also allows SMEs to respond to demand variations in real time, adjusting stock levels based on sudden changes in consumer behavior. For example, an electronics company launching an online promotional campaign can anticipate an increase in demand for certain products and adjust its inventory accordingly. Machine learning algorithms can analyze data in real time and detect demand spikes, allowing the company to increase stock levels before the products run out. This approach is ideal for companies that experience demand fluctuations due to promotions, seasonal events, or market changes.

For SMEs looking to implement a dynamic inventory system and optimize product turnover, it's essential to have up-to-date and accurate sales data, as well as a real-time inventory data collection system. The accuracy of inventory turnover predictions largely depends on data quality, so it's important for companies to record all relevant information about sales, returns, and product consumption. With precise and complete data, machine learning algorithms can make more reliable predictions and offer effective recommendations for inventory management.

Optimized inventory rotation with machine learning is a powerful strategy for SMEs looking to improve their competitiveness and increase the profitability of their operations. By forecasting product rotation and adjusting stock quantities based on demand forecasts, companies can minimize storage costs, reduce the risk of obsolescence, and ensure optimal product availability to meet customer demand. This strategy allows SMEs to flexibly adapt to market changes, offering a significant competitive advantage in a dynamic and constantly evolving business environment.

- **Use of time series**

Time series are a fundamental tool in demand forecasting because they allow you to analyze how certain data evolves over time and find patterns that help anticipate sales fluctuations. Demand forecasting based on time series enables the identification of trends, seasonality, and recurring cycles that influence product demand, which is especially valuable for SMEs looking to optimize their inventories and operations. Using time series models like ARIMA, Prophet, or LSTM allows companies to develop more precise demand projections tailored to their context, based on historical data and detecting patterns that go beyond mere data extrapolation. By understanding and anticipating these patterns, SMEs can better prepare for periods of high demand, plan their inventory more efficiently, and improve customer satisfaction by ensuring product availability at key times.

The ARIMA (Auto-Regressive Integrated Moving Average) model is one of the most commonly used traditional methods for forecasting time series and is especially effective in identifying and modeling linear and seasonal patterns in data. ARIMA is based on three main components: the autoregressive (AR) part, which models the dependency between current values and their past values; the moving average (MA) part, which captures the impact of fluctuations in the data; and the integration (I) part, which helps stabilize the time series when it's necessary to remove the trend. For an SME, ARIMA is a solid option when there is a substantial historical dataset available and short- to medium-term demand forecasts are needed. ARIMA is particularly useful in cases where demand shows clear seasonal patterns, such as the sale of Christmas products, where the model can identify the annual trend and predict the number of products needed to meet demand for the upcoming festive season.

To implement an ARIMA model, a preprocessing stage must first be conducted where historical data is transformed to remove any trend and seasonality components, ensuring the series is stationary. This step is crucial as the ARIMA model operates on stationary data, meaning the mean and variance of the series must remain constant over time. Once stationarity is achieved, the model is fitted using sales history, and the parameters are optimized, identified as (p, d, q), where p is the order of the autoregressive part, d is the degree of differencing to achieve stationarity, and q is the order of the moving average part. In practice, an SME can fit an ARIMA model to forecast demand for a specific product using historical sales data, anticipating fluctuations based on the time of year and thus optimizing inventory levels.

A modern and very popular alternative for time series forecasting is Prophet, an open-source tool developed by Facebook. Prophet is designed to handle time series with seasonal components, long-term trends, and anomalies or special events that can influence the data. This model is particularly useful for SMEs that want to make quick forecasts without the need for complex parameter tuning, as Prophet can automatically detect seasonal and trend components and is less sensitive to issues like outliers and data interruptions. Additionally, Prophet allows you to include extra information about special days, such as holidays or promotional events, making it easier to predict demand spikes during those days.

Prophet is ideal for SMEs that want a quick and accurate solution to forecast demand in sales cycles with seasonal patterns and regular fluctuations. Implementing Prophet is simple and requires few manual adjustments, making it accessible for companies with limited technical resources. In practice, an SME can use Prophet to predict product demand during key dates, such as Black Friday or the start of the summer season, allowing them to adjust their inventories to meet demand without overstocking or running out of products. For example, a sports goods company can use Prophet to forecast demand for certain items like swimsuits or camping gear in summer, ensuring they have the necessary quantity of these products to meet seasonal demand without ending up with excess inventory at the end of the season.

Prophet also allows the management of time series at different intervals and adjusts the analysis according to the characteristics of each series. This approach enables SMEs to use Prophet to forecast demand for multiple products in different periods, from monthly cycles to seasonal ones, adapting the forecasts to the nature of each product. One of the key advantages of Prophet is its ability to make predictions even when historical data has some gaps or discontinuities, which is often the case in SMEs that don't always have complete sales data. This allows companies to leverage Prophet even when the sales history is not entirely consistent, ensuring that the predictions are useful and aligned with the reality of each business.

The use of LSTM (Long Short-Term Memory) neural networks is another advanced option for time series forecasting when large volumes of data are available, and the goal is to capture complex nonlinear patterns. LSTMs are a variant of recurrent neural networks (RNNs) designed to process sequences of temporal data and long-term dependencies, making them ideal for time series with complex cycles and nonlinear variations. LSTMs are especially useful for SMEs that want to forecast demand in contexts where multiple interrelated factors affect sales, such as economic conditions, promotions, or competitor behavior.

LSTM neural networks are capable of analyzing and learning from long temporal sequences, retaining information from past events and using this information to make accurate predictions for the future. In the context of demand prediction, an LSTM network can analyze daily, weekly, or even annual sales patterns, taking into account additional factors such as weather, seasonal events, and ongoing promotions. For example, an SME in the fashion sector can use an LSTM network to forecast clothing demand according to seasonality, promotional events, and the evolution of purchasing trends over time. This allows them to adjust their inventory and tailor their offerings according to customer preferences in each season, optimizing both stock and customer satisfaction.

Training an LSTM network requires detailed historical data and, generally, a dataset large enough for the network to learn accurate patterns in sales data. Unlike ARIMA or Prophet, which focus on linear and seasonal patterns, LSTMs can capture complex nonlinear relationships in the data, which is especially useful for SMEs that want to incorporate additional variables affecting demand. LSTM networks are an advanced option that requires greater processing power and careful tuning of hyperparameters, such as the number of layers, memory size, and learning rate. However, LSTMs can significantly improve the accuracy of demand forecasts when you have a robust and well-structured database.

Data preprocessing is a crucial step in implementing time series models, whether using ARIMA, Prophet, or LSTM. In the case of ARIMA, it is essential for the time series to be stationary, so transformations like differencing or detrending are often necessary before fitting the model. With Prophet, preprocessing is simpler since this model automatically incorporates seasonality and trend components, but it's still recommended to clean the data and remove outliers that could affect prediction accuracy. For LSTM networks, preprocessing usually involves normalizing the data to improve model stability and performance during training.

The use of time series in demand forecasting gives SMEs a competitive advantage by providing precise and detailed information about demand fluctuations over time. By using models like ARIMA, Prophet, or LSTM, companies can anticipate periods of high demand, adjust their inventory levels, and plan marketing strategies based on sales patterns. This approach allows SMEs to optimize their inventory, reduce costs, and improve customer satisfaction by ensuring that products are available at key moments.

8.2. Identification of consumption patterns and stock control

The identification of consumption patterns and efficient stock control are essential pillars of inventory management for any SME. Through data analysis and the application of machine learning algorithms, it's possible to anticipate customer needs, predict demand, and adjust product stocks proactively. This not only improves responsiveness to market changes but also allows companies to optimize resources, reduce storage costs, and minimize the risk of stockouts or overstocking.

Consumption pattern analysis uses past purchase data to identify and classify customers based on their behavior, detecting which products have higher turnover and which require more or less frequent restocking. At the same time, stock control automation through algorithms allows continuous monitoring of inventory levels, generating alerts or even autonomously managing restocking orders. From classification techniques such as ABC analysis to advanced predictive models, these tools enable SMEs to have intelligent and automated control over their inventory, optimizing their responsiveness and reducing operational costs in stock management.

- **Analysis of consumption patterns**

Consumption pattern analysis has become a key tool for SMEs to understand customer behavior and optimize their inventory according to market demands. By using data and machine learning techniques, companies can identify consumption trends, predict which products will be in higher demand during certain periods, and consequently improve their stock management. With these techniques, SMEs can respond quickly to market changes, adjust their marketing strategies, and ensure that their products are available at the right time, avoiding both excess inventory and stockouts of key products.

The application of machine learning in the analysis of consumption patterns allows SMEs to observe specific buying patterns, identifying customer segments with similar characteristics and adapting their operations based on this data. Analyzing consumption patterns not only involves understanding customer purchasing behavior but also anticipating their needs, which provides a significant competitive advantage in an increasingly demanding and saturated market. One of the most effective ways to identify these patterns is through consumer behavior analysis, which classifies customers according to their purchase frequency, average order value, and preferred products. This type of analysis is primarily conducted using historical data, which is processed and analyzed with machine learning algorithms that detect patterns and predict future behaviors.

Consumer behavior analysis allows businesses to segment customers into groups based on their characteristics and purchasing patterns. By analyzing past purchase data, different consumer segments can be identified, enabling inventory strategies to be adjusted according to the needs of each group. For example, by analyzing purchase frequency, an SME can classify customers into segments such as frequent, occasional, or sporadic buyers. This type of classification allows the company to make informed decisions about which products to prioritize in inventory, focusing on those that are most popular among frequent customers. Additionally, by analyzing the average ticket, SMEs can distinguish between high-value customers, who tend to make larger purchases, and lower-value customers, who buy more affordable products or in smaller quantities. With this data, businesses can optimize their inventory, ensuring that the most demanded products by high-value customers are always available, and adjust their marketing strategies to attract more customers to these high-margin products.

Product preference analysis also plays a fundamental role in customer segmentation and inventory management. By studying the products preferred by customers, SMEs can identify which items generate the most interest and prioritize their restocking. This approach allows marketing campaigns and promotions to be adjusted, targeting the products that have the most acceptance among the public. For example, if a beauty products SME identifies that its customers show a preference for certain skincare products over makeup products, it can adjust its inventory and marketing strategy accordingly, focusing on promoting and ensuring the stock of skincare items. Customer segmentation based on behavior analysis is a powerful tool that allows SMEs to adapt their operations and improve inventory efficiency, optimizing their responsiveness and more accurately meeting their customers' needs.

To implement consumer behavior analysis, SMEs can use a variety of machine learning algorithms that process large volumes of data and extract relevant patterns in customer behavior. One of the most used methods to identify consumption patterns is k-means, a clustering algorithm that groups data into clusters based on their similarity. This algorithm is particularly useful for SMEs that want to segment their customers or products into categories based on purchasing behavior. K-means classifies customers or products into different clusters, each representing a segment with similar characteristics. For example, a food SME can use k-means to group its customers into clusters according to the type of products they tend to buy, their purchase frequency, and their average ticket. These clusters allow the company to personalize its marketing strategies and adjust its inventory according to the preferences and habits of each customer group.

To implement k-means in Python, SMEs can use machine learning libraries like Scikit-Learn, which makes it easy to fit the model and identify patterns in the data. The first step is to preprocess the data, which includes normalizing the variables so that all have a similar range and the algorithm works optimally. Once the data is prepared, the number of clusters or groups to be identified is selected, and the k-means algorithm classifies the data based on their characteristics. This segmentation allows SMEs to better understand their customers and make informed decisions about how to manage their inventory and marketing. For example, if the algorithm identifies a cluster of customers who frequently purchase premium products, the SME can ensure these products are always available and direct specific loyalty campaigns towards this high-value customer segment.

Another useful approach for analyzing consumption patterns is the use of decision trees. These models allow you to predict which products will be purchased based on certain variables, such as the time of year, active promotions, or customer profiles. Decision trees are especially useful for SMEs that want to understand how different factors influence the demand for their products and adjust their inventory accordingly. By implementing a decision tree, SMEs can analyze how certain events or characteristics affect their customers' purchasing behavior and predict which products will be in demand during different periods or under various conditions. For example, a clothing SME can use a decision tree to forecast the demand for certain items based on the season, ensuring they have enough stock of coats in winter and lighter clothing in summer.

The process of implementing a decision tree begins with collecting historical sales data and identifying the key variables that influence purchasing behavior. These variables can include factors such as seasonality, applied discounts, customer preferences, and any other relevant data. Once collected, the data is processed and used to train the decision tree model, which classifies observations based on the characteristics of each customer or product. This allows the SME to predict which products will be in higher demand under certain conditions and adjust their inventory strategies accordingly. Decision trees can also be used in combination with other machine learning algorithms to obtain more accurate predictions and improve customer segmentation.

Predictive models based on consumption patterns offer SMEs a significant advantage in terms of efficiency and profitability, as they allow them to anticipate market needs and proactively adjust their inventory. These models not only help predict which products will be in demand but also identify combinations of products that tend to be sold together, facilitating the creation of cross-selling or complementary sales strategies. For example, by analyzing consumption patterns, an electronics SME can identify that customers who buy mobile devices also tend to purchase accessories like headphones or chargers. With this information, the company can optimize its inventory of complementary products and create specific promotions to encourage the purchase of these items together.

In addition to consumer behavior analysis and clustering models, the use of association rules is also an effective technique for identifying consumption patterns. Association rules are particularly useful for uncovering relationships between products that are frequently bought together, allowing SMEs to make complementary product recommendations or design bundled promotions. This approach is commonly known as market basket analysis and helps identify products that are often purchased together. For example, a supermarket SME can use association rules to discover that customers who buy bread also tend to buy milk. With this information, the company can strategically place these products in the store or on their ecommerce platform, promoting cross-selling and optimizing their inventory strategy.

Implementing association rules and basket analysis requires a robust database that records all transactions made. Once the data is available, the association rules algorithm, such as the Apriori algorithm, is applied to analyze product combinations and extract relevant purchasing patterns.

This type of analysis allows SMEs to identify the most common product combinations and adjust their inventory based on these trends, ensuring that products that tend to sell together are available at the same time, thus improving the customer shopping experience.

Overall, the analysis of consumption patterns and the use of machine learning allow SMEs to optimize their inventory, personalize their marketing strategies, and improve customer satisfaction. Through customer segmentation, behavior analysis, and the identification of complementary products, SMEs can develop a comprehensive view of their customers' preferences and habits, making it easier to make informed decisions and adapt to market demands in real-time. The implementation of algorithms such as k-means, decision trees, and association rules provides companies with a deep understanding of consumption patterns, enabling them to respond quickly to market changes and optimize their inventory management according to customer preferences.

- ## Automation of stock control with machine learning

The automation of stock control through machine learning represents one of the most valuable applications for SMEs in optimizing their operations and improving the efficiency of their inventory processes. Thanks to machine learning algorithms, companies can manage their stock dynamically, adjusting product quantities based on demand fluctuations and turnover rates for each item. This automation not only reduces the manual effort required to monitor stock levels but also allows companies to anticipate product shortages and prevent unnecessary inventory buildup, thereby lowering storage costs and reducing the risk of obsolescence.

The automation of stock control begins with the continuous monitoring of inventory levels, a process carried out through sensors, inventory management systems (IMS), and algorithms that collect real-time data on the quantities of each product in the warehouse. This data is then analyzed by machine learning algorithms that detect consumption patterns and estimate future demand, generating automatic alerts when inventory levels fall below a set threshold. This threshold is determined based on product turnover, replenishment time, and demand variability, ensuring that the company has enough products to meet demand without overstocking. By implementing this type of automated control, SMEs can ensure their products are always available when customers need them, improving customer satisfaction and optimizing inventory management.

Stock depletion prediction is a key feature in inventory control automation, as it allows for accurate forecasts of when a product will run out and enables timely restocking orders. To achieve this, predictive models analyze the current demand for each product, its turnover rate, and other relevant factors such as seasonality and promotions. A predictive model can calculate how many days of inventory remain before stock runs out, giving the company enough time to restock the product without interruptions. In an SME dealing with high-turnover products, like a fresh food store, this prediction is particularly useful as it allows for just-in-time ordering to avoid waste of perishable goods and maximize food freshness.

Predictive models for stock depletion typically use regression algorithms to analyze demand trends for each product and calculate the probability of stockouts. For example, a linear regression model can predict daily demand for a product and project the date when current stock will run out based on the daily consumption rate. This approach is suitable for high-turnover products with stable demand. For products whose demand fluctuates due to seasonal factors or promotions, time series models like ARIMA or Prophet can be used, allowing for the capture of demand patterns over time and forecasting stock depletion based on these cycles. This type of prediction is particularly useful for SMEs dealing with seasonal products, such as a gardening store that experiences increased demand for certain products during spring and summer.

Predictive stock-out analysis not only generates automatic alerts, but it can also trigger automatic inventory replenishment in more advanced systems, sending purchase orders to suppliers when stock levels fall below a critical threshold. This process is known as automated replenishment and represents a major advantage for SMEs, as it allows inventory to be maintained at optimal levels without manual intervention. By using APIs, an SME's inventory systems can be directly connected to suppliers, facilitating the creation of replenishment orders based on the predictive model's forecasts. For example, in a retail company using an automated replenishment system, when a predictive model detects that sales of a product will increase in the coming week, the system can place an order with the supplier to ensure the product is available in inventory.

Another effective approach to efficient inventory management is the ABC analysis, a classification technique that organizes products based on their importance in the inventory and their sales volume. The ABC analysis classifies products into three categories: Category A, which represents the most important and highest value products; Category B, which includes moderately important products; and Category C, which contains the least important or lowest sales volume products. This classification allows SMEs to allocate resources more efficiently, focusing on maintaining optimal stock levels for Category A products, while managing Category B and C products with less demanding inventory policies.

The application of ABC analysis in stock control with machine learning involves using algorithms to classify products into three categories based on their sales patterns, profitability, and other relevant factors. By applying machine learning to ABC analysis, SMEs can optimize their resource allocation, ensuring that high-turnover and high-value products are always available, while low-turnover products are maintained in controlled quantities. For example, in an electronics store, ABC analysis might classify smartphones and laptops in category A due to their high demand and value, while accessories like cases or chargers might fall into category B or C. This allows the store to prioritize the restocking of main products and maintain adequate control of less important items in inventory.

The use of machine learning in ABC analysis offers the advantage of automatically updating classifications based on changes in demand, allowing SMEs to adjust their inventory policies in real time. This is particularly useful in dynamic markets where products can shift in importance based on market trends or promotional campaigns. By implementing a machine learning model in ABC analysis, SMEs can detect when a product in category B or C experiences an increase in demand and update its classification to category A. This way, the stock control system adapts to market conditions, ensuring that high-demand products are available at all times.

Automating inventory control with machine learning can also improve operational efficiency by reducing manual intervention and the risk of human error in stock management. In traditional inventory systems, employees have to constantly monitor stock levels, manually generate purchase orders, and adjust inventory based on sales and demand forecasts. With a machine learning-based automated system, all these tasks are managed autonomously, allowing the SME team to focus on higher-value activities like marketing strategy planning and enhancing customer experience. Inventory automation not only reduces the time and effort needed to manage stock, but also increases accuracy in demand forecasting and product replenishment, improving efficiency and reducing operational costs.

The automation of inventory control is complemented by the use of IoT (Internet of Things) sensors and real-time monitoring systems that collect data on stock levels and product movement in the warehouse. This data is integrated into the machine learning system, allowing the predictive model to be continuously updated based on actual demand and inventory status. In a food distribution SME, for example, sensors can monitor the quantity of each product in real-time, enabling the predictive system to detect when a product is about to run out and send an automatic alert for restocking. Additionally, IoT sensors can monitor storage conditions, such as temperature and humidity, which is crucial for perishable products that require constant quality control.

Automated inventory control allows SMEs to adopt a data-driven management approach, helping them make informed decisions and reduce inventory-related risks. For example, a clothing company can use an automated stock control system to manage its seasonal inventory, ensuring that the most in-demand products during the sales period are available in sufficient quantities and avoiding overstocking items that have lost popularity. This approach enables SMEs to tailor their inventory policies to the specific needs of each sales cycle, improving efficiency and increasing the profitability of their operations.

In summary, automating stock control through machine learning represents a significant competitive advantage for SMEs, as it allows for dynamic and adaptive inventory management, optimizing product availability and reducing costs associated with storage and restocking. By implementing techniques such as stock outage prediction and ABC analysis, companies can ensure that their inventory is aligned with market demands, improving their responsiveness and strengthening their position in an increasingly demanding market.

8.3. Machine learning for optimizing logistics routes

The optimization of logistics routes has become a priority for many SMEs looking to reduce transportation costs, improve delivery efficiency, and ultimately offer a faster and more effective service to their clients. In a context where expectations for speed and accuracy in delivery are increasingly high, the use of machine learning allows companies to make data-driven decisions, adapt to unforeseen variables, and optimize the logistics of their daily operations. By integrating advanced machine learning algorithms and optimization techniques, companies can adjust their routes to minimize time and costs, adapting in real-time to factors such as traffic, weather conditions, and demand patterns.

One of the key aspects of route optimization is the use of optimization algorithms, such as genetic algorithms or ant colony algorithms, which are capable of solving complex optimal route problems. These algorithms can analyze large volumes of data and find solutions that minimize transportation time and cost, resulting in more efficient logistics planning. Through predictive models, it is also possible to estimate delivery times with great precision, allowing SMEs to communicate the approximate delivery time to customers and improve the user experience.

Furthermore, route optimization with machine learning benefits from the use of geospatial data and real-time monitoring, which facilitates route planning based on the proximity of delivery or distribution points. Monitoring systems based on the Internet of Things (IoT) allow SMEs to continuously track deliveries and adjust routes in real time in case of unforeseen events, such as an accident or traffic congestion. In this way, logistics route optimization through machine learning provides SMEs with effective tools to improve their operational capacity and ensure a competitive and adaptive delivery service.

- **Optimizing Logistics Routes with Machine Learning**

Optimizing logistics routes with machine learning is one of the most effective solutions for SMEs to improve operational efficiency and significantly reduce transportation and logistics costs. Managing efficient routes has become a priority in many sectors due to the growing consumer demand for fast and accurate deliveries, as well as the need for companies to cut costs in transportation time, fuel consumption, and labor. With the support of machine learning algorithms, companies can analyze large volumes of data and find patterns or variables that affect the duration and cost of routes. This approach enables data-driven decision-making, leading to much more precise and effective route planning.

One of the biggest challenges in logistics is the traveling salesman problem, a classic optimization issue where the goal is to find the shortest or most efficient route that allows the carrier to cover multiple delivery points. To solve complex problems like this, machine learning offers advanced optimization algorithms capable of analyzing multiple variables and providing effective solutions tailored to each company's specific configuration. In particular, algorithms like genetic algorithms and the ant colony algorithm are powerful tools that help optimize logistics routes and, consequently, reduce delivery times and transportation costs.

Genetic algorithms are models inspired by the theory of biological evolution and work through a process of selection and recombination of possible solutions to find the optimal route. Starting with an initial "population" of possible routes, the algorithm evaluates each one based on criteria such as total distance traveled or journey cost. The most effective routes are selected for the next "generation," where they are recombined and mutated to generate new solutions. This process is repeated until the algorithm finds a solution that minimizes time and cost, providing an efficient route that helps the company reduce delivery time and transportation expenses.

For an SME, genetic algorithms are particularly useful because they allow complex routes to be managed much more effectively than traditional planning methods. Let's say, for example, that a food delivery SME has multiple orders in a high-traffic urban area. With a genetic algorithm, the company can analyze the different route combinations, taking into account variables such as the distance between delivery points, the time of day, and potential traffic jams. By applying this technique, the company optimizes route planning based on real traffic conditions, achieving faster and more efficient deliveries while optimizing the use of its vehicles and staff.

The ant colony algorithm is another optimization model inspired by nature, in this case, the behavior of ants when searching for food and mapping routes to their colony. This algorithm works by simulating the behavior of an ant colony that leaves pheromone trails on the shortest and most efficient routes to the goal. In the context of logistics optimization, the algorithm uses these principles to find the shortest or most efficient delivery routes, evaluating different paths and optimizing them based on the results obtained in each iteration. This technique is ideal for solving logistical problems that require optimal routes with multiple destinations and is especially useful for SMEs with complex urban delivery routes where there are many possible path combinations.

Ant Colony Optimization allows SMEs to improve logistics planning, as the model can adapt to real-time changes and select the most efficient route based on current conditions. In an e-commerce SME that handles home deliveries, the Ant Colony algorithm can be adjusted to minimize total distance and, consequently, reduce delivery time and fuel consumption. This not only increases efficiency but also enhances the customer experience by ensuring faster and more accurate deliveries. The savings in transportation costs and delivery times enable the company to improve profitability and offer more competitive prices.

In addition to optimization algorithms, machine learning allows for accurate delivery time predictions, which are essential for efficient planning and improving customer satisfaction. Delivery time prediction is based on predictive models that analyze historical data and real-time data on traffic, distances, weather conditions, and other factors affecting logistics. By having an accurate estimate of delivery times, SMEs can plan their routes more precisely and minimize delays. Moreover, these models allow companies to communicate an estimated delivery time to their customers, increasing satisfaction and trust in the service.

Predictive models for delivery times often use regression algorithms that analyze the relationship between variables affecting delivery duration. For example, a linear regression model can predict delivery time based on factors such as the distance between the warehouse and the destination, the time of day, and the presence of adverse weather conditions. In environments where traffic is a major factor, time series models or recurrent neural networks can be used to capture patterns over time and adjust predictions based on current conditions. This is especially useful for SMEs making deliveries in urban areas with high traffic congestion, where variations in delivery speed are significant.

Furthermore, neural networks and deep learning models can also help improve the accuracy of delivery time predictions. Neural networks can identify nonlinear and complex patterns in data, which is ideal for situations where multiple variables interact, such as traffic, weather, and operating schedules. These models allow for the analysis of large volumes of data and adapt predictions to changing conditions in real-time. For example, an SME delivering perishable goods can benefit from accurate delivery time predictions, as it can better plan its load distribution and ensure that products arrive in good condition, minimizing waste and guaranteeing customer satisfaction.

The implementation of route optimization and delivery time prediction in SMEs not only improves efficiency and reduces costs, but also provides an important competitive advantage by enhancing accuracy and reliability in logistics. Machine learning tools allow companies to adapt their routes in real time and make adjustments based on current conditions, which is crucial in sectors where punctuality and precision are essential for the customer experience. For example, in a fresh produce delivery company, route optimization ensures that deliveries arrive on time, preserving product freshness and increasing customer satisfaction. Additionally, by reducing transport times and fuel consumption, the company can minimize its carbon footprint and improve sustainability.

To implement these techniques, SMEs can rely on easily accessible machine learning tools, such as Scikit-Learn for data modeling and optimization algorithms, and geospatial analysis platforms like GeoPandas or Folium. These tools allow for the analysis of location data and proximity between delivery points, facilitating route optimization and logistics planning. With the support of geospatial data and real-time monitoring, SMEs can ensure that their delivery routes are as efficient as possible, adapting to the specific needs of each customer and optimizing their resources intelligently.

- **Predictive route analysis based on historical data**

Predictive route analysis based on historical data represents a significant advantage for SMEs looking to optimize their logistics operations, reduce transportation costs, and improve the efficiency of their product deliveries. By using historical data generated from previous routes and deliveries, companies can identify patterns that affect the time, efficiency, and profitability of their logistics operations. With these patterns and trends, businesses can predict and adjust their routes to anticipate external variables that complicate the process, such as peak-hour traffic, weather conditions, and unexpected events on the roads. The use of predictive models based on historical data allows SMEs to improve their strategic decisions and adjust their routes in real-time, maximizing the efficiency of each delivery while also enhancing customer satisfaction by ensuring greater accuracy in delivery times.

The first step in developing an effective predictive route analysis is to collect and store historical data from each delivery made by the company. This includes detailed information on departure and arrival times, the duration of each route segment, traffic conditions, and the specific locations of each delivery point. In many SMEs, this information can be obtained through GPS devices or tracking systems that monitor the real-time position and movement of vehicles. Historical delivery data allows you to observe fluctuations in transit times at different times of the day or week and detect seasonal patterns that can impact logistical efficiency. For example, routes in urban areas may experience congestion during peak hours and be much smoother during off-peak times, while delivery demand may increase over weekends or during high season periods.

Once enough historical data is available, SMEs can analyze this data to identify patterns and anomalies in delivery times and route durations. This initial analysis is essential to understand which factors most significantly impact the logistics of each delivery and how these factors vary across different periods or types of routes. By using machine learning algorithms, it is possible to analyze large volumes of data and find correlations between various variables affecting delivery time, such as traffic density, weather, or route length. At this stage, descriptive analysis is a key tool to observe the general characteristics of each route, such as average duration, waiting time at delivery points, and standard deviations. This data allows SMEs to adjust their expectations and plan more precise delivery times based on real information and historical patterns.

The next step in predictive route analysis is the implementation of machine learning models that can make predictions based on historical data and provide recommendations for route optimization. For this purpose, regression and time series models are very useful, as they can analyze trends over time and predict transit times based on factors like time of day, day of the week, and weather conditions. In SMEs, the linear regression model is one of the simplest and most effective techniques for predicting route duration based on continuous variables, such as distance and average traffic. However, in more complex logistics environments, advanced techniques like Recurrent Neural Networks (RNN) or Long Short-Term Memory (LSTM) can be used, which are capable of capturing complex relationships and non-linear patterns in temporal data.

One important aspect of predictive route analysis is identifying congestion points and problematic routes that could cause delivery delays.

Historical traffic and delivery data allow you to observe which sections of the route tend to be slower or where vehicles experience longer wait times. Through this analysis, SMEs can develop optimization strategies to avoid these sections during critical hours and thus improve the efficiency of their logistics operations. For example, if certain areas of the city are significantly congested in the mornings, the company can adjust its routes to avoid these areas at those times, redirecting vehicles to alternative routes that, although longer, result in faster delivery times due to lower traffic density.

In addition to avoiding congestion points, predictive route analysis also allows SMEs to optimize the distribution of their delivery points based on geographical proximity and accessibility. This is achieved through spatial optimization algorithms that group delivery points according to their proximity and minimize the total distance traveled. In this context, geospatial data is used to identify clusters of deliveries and plan routes where drivers can make multiple deliveries in a small area, thus reducing the total route time and transportation costs. This strategy is especially useful in densely populated urban areas, where travel times between different points can vary significantly depending on geographic location and local traffic.

To improve accuracy in route planning, SMEs can implement a delivery time prediction model that uses historical and real-time data to calculate the estimated time of arrival at each delivery point. This model can use real-time traffic information from sources like digital maps and monitoring systems to adjust delivery time predictions based on current conditions. The predictive delivery time model also takes into account weather variables, such as rain or snow, which can affect transit speed and cause delays on certain routes. With this predictive capability, SMEs can provide customers with more accurate estimated delivery times, thus improving customer satisfaction by meeting expectations and ensuring timely deliveries.

Another key aspect of predictive route analysis based on historical data is optimizing routes according to seasonal patterns or specific events that influence traffic and delivery demand. In certain sectors, such as e-commerce, peak periods like Black Friday or the end-of-year holidays generate an increase in delivery demand, which in turn increases congestion on logistical routes. By using historical data from previous seasons, SMEs can anticipate demand surges and adjust their routes and delivery times to adapt to these conditions. For example, a food delivery company might notice that during summer holidays, routes to certain tourist areas experience increased traffic and delivery times. With this information, the company can plan alternative routes or increase delivery frequency to avoid delays and meet customer demand.

Predictive route analysis also facilitates real-time alternative route planning, allowing SMEs to adapt to unforeseen situations like accidents or road closures that can affect delivery efficiency. Machine learning models that integrate real-time data can detect these events and suggest alternative routes to avoid problems on the roads. This is especially valuable in large cities and metropolitan areas, where traffic is highly variable, and issues on a route can cause significant delays. By having the ability to redirect their routes based on current conditions, SMEs improve their responsiveness to unexpected events and optimize the use of their vehicles and logistical resources.

The implementation of a predictive route analysis based on historical data also allows SMEs to identify opportunities for improvement in their operations and optimize their resource allocation. For example, by analyzing the performance of their logistics routes over time, an SME can detect patterns that suggest the need to adjust the number of vehicles or drivers assigned to certain routes based on demand and the average duration of each delivery. This allows the company to optimize the use of its human and material resources, minimizing costs and maximizing productivity. Additionally, the implementation of these models facilitates the integration of logistics planning with other areas of the company, such as inventory management and production planning, resulting in a more efficient and coordinated supply chain.

To carry out an effective predictive route analysis, SMEs can use accessible machine learning tools like Scikit-Learn and geospatial analysis platforms like GeoPandas, which facilitate the processing of geospatial data and the visualization of patterns in routes. These tools allow companies to analyze large volumes of historical data and generate accurate predictive models that optimize route planning based on the specific conditions of each geographic area. As machine learning models and historical data are integrated into logistical planning, SMEs can anticipate traffic challenges and improve their operational efficiency, achieving a more reliable and competitive delivery service.

- ## Use of Geospatial Data for Optimization

The use of geospatial data has become an essential tool for SMEs looking to optimize their logistics and distribution operations. By integrating location data and detailed maps with machine learning algorithms, companies can analyze and improve their routes, adjusting their delivery processes according to geographic and proximity needs. This not only reduces transportation costs and travel time but also contributes to greater customer satisfaction by enabling more precise and timely deliveries. For this type of optimization, tools like Folium and GeoPandas are fundamental resources, as they allow for the simple and effective visualization, analysis, and manipulation of geospatial data, facilitating adaptive and efficient route planning and execution.

The first step in implementing the use of geospatial data for route optimization is to collect detailed information on the locations of each delivery point, as well as the proximity of each customer or distribution area. This data is usually available in inventory management systems and customer databases, allowing SMEs to map their customers' locations and group delivery points based on geographic proximity. From this initial information, machine learning algorithms and geospatial analysis tools can determine the most effective routes for each set of deliveries. In this context, the proximity between customers and the distribution point is a key variable to minimize travel time and fuel consumption, thereby improving the company's profitability and efficiency.

Once the locations and proximity between delivery points have been identified, SMEs can use GeoPandas to perform a detailed analysis of these geospatial data. GeoPandas is a Python library that facilitates the manipulation of geographic data and allows for complex spatial operations, such as merging geographic data and creating catchment areas around delivery points. For example, an SME making deliveries in a city can use GeoPandas to create service areas around its distribution points, identifying customers within each area and grouping them based on their proximity to the nearest distribution point. This geographic segmentation allows for planning optimized delivery routes for each service area, reducing transportation time and costs and improving delivery punctuality.

Folium is another valuable tool in the process of optimizing logistics routes, as it allows for the creation of interactive maps and dynamic visualization of delivery routes. With Folium, SMEs can visually represent the locations of their delivery points and plot the optimized routes, making it easier to plan and execute deliveries. By visualizing the routes on an interactive map, the logistics team can identify potential problems or areas of congestion along the way and adjust the routes based on current traffic conditions. Additionally, Folium allows for real-time data integration, which is especially useful for SMEs that want to make adjustments to their delivery routes based on changes in traffic conditions or unforeseen events.

Geospatial data also allows SMEs to optimize their delivery routes by using clustering algorithms, which group delivery points based on proximity and reduce the total distance traveled. By applying a clustering algorithm like k-means, businesses can identify clusters or groups of customers located in the same geographic area and plan routes that cover each cluster efficiently. This approach is particularly useful in densely populated urban areas, where the proximity between delivery points allows for route optimization and reduced transportation times. In a food distribution SME, for example, using k-means to group delivery points based on their location can result in a shorter and faster delivery route, reducing transportation costs and improving the freshness of delivered products.

In addition to clustering algorithms, spatial optimization models allow SMEs to calculate the best route based on the distances between delivery points and the point of origin. These models analyze the map of possible route networks and select those that minimize total distance traveled and delivery time. With the support of geospatial data, companies can analyze the distribution of their customers and select routes that maximize the efficiency of each trip, taking into account factors such as traffic and the accessibility of each area. This type of optimization is especially useful in sectors where delivery speed is a crucial factor, such as perishable goods or those with high demand during certain seasons.

The use of geospatial data and machine learning tools also allows SMEs to improve route planning based on traffic conditions and other external factors that affect delivery times. For example, by integrating historical traffic data and real-time data, predictive models can adjust delivery routes according to current conditions, avoiding congested areas or routes with transit issues. This approach is especially valuable in metropolitan areas where traffic can vary significantly throughout the day. A company making deliveries in a large city, for instance, can use a geospatial optimization model to adjust its routes based on current conditions, choosing alternative routes during peak hours and minimizing delivery delays.

For SMEs operating in rural areas or regions with low population density, the use of geospatial data allows them to identify the best routes based on proximity between clients and available roads. Unlike urban areas, where there are multiple routes and transportation options, rural areas often have limited access and longer distances between delivery points. In this context, SMEs can use geospatial data to analyze the road network and select routes that minimize time and fuel consumption, ensuring that their vehicles cover the most deliveries in the shortest time possible.

The visualization of geospatial data is another important aspect of route optimization, as it allows the logistics team to see the distribution of their delivery points and evaluate the routes visually. With Folium and GeoPandas, SMEs can map their delivery points and plot optimized routes, which facilitates decision-making and helps identify potential problems or areas for improvement in logistics planning. The visualization of geospatial data allows for the observation of proximity between delivery points and assessment of the efficiency of the selected routes, which is especially useful in complex logistics operations with multiple delivery points spread over a wide geographic area.

In addition, geospatial data allows for proximity analysis between delivery points and distribution centers or warehouses, facilitating route planning based on the proximity to each distribution point. This approach is particularly useful for SMEs with multiple distribution centers that want to assign each delivery point to the nearest distribution center, thus optimizing logistics and reducing travel times. By calculating the distances between delivery points and distribution centers, companies can assign each delivery to the location that minimizes travel time and maximizes the efficiency of the logistics process.

Finally, using geospatial data for route optimization also allows SMEs to adapt to real-time changes and make adjustments to their routes based on unforeseen events. With the support of real-time visualization and monitoring tools like Folium and IoT sensors, companies can view the location of their vehicles on the map and adjust routes based on current traffic conditions, weather, and other external factors. This ability to adapt to changing conditions enables SMEs to improve efficiency and ensure on-time delivery, which is especially valuable in sectors where customer satisfaction heavily depends on delivery punctuality.

- ## Real-time monitoring of routes

Real-time monitoring of routes is an invaluable tool for SMEs looking to optimize their logistics operations, improve delivery efficiency, and reduce transportation costs. By integrating machine learning with IoT (Internet of Things) systems, companies can collect and analyze data on location, traffic, and environmental conditions in real time, allowing for route adjustments that ensure on-time delivery and minimize fuel consumption. In an environment where delays and traffic are common factors, the ability to monitor and adjust routes on the go provides a significant competitive advantage. This allows SMEs to respond quickly to unforeseen events, improving the customer experience and optimizing their logistics resources.

IoT systems are essential for real-time monitoring, as they enable the collection and transmission of data from delivery vehicles and other logistical units. These systems include GPS devices that record the vehicle's location, sensors that monitor the engine and fuel status, and environmental sensors that record weather or road conditions. All this information is transmitted to a centralized platform, where machine learning algorithms can analyze the data and provide valuable insights into the status of each delivery. This type of monitoring not only allows complete visibility of the location and progress of each vehicle but also facilitates route adjustments based on current conditions, optimizing both delivery time and fuel usage.

Machine learning combined with IoT enables the application of real-time learning techniques, which are essential for making adjustments to routes based on unexpected changes in traffic or road conditions. These techniques can detect patterns and make predictions about possible delays or issues on the routes, allowing the system to suggest alternative routes to the driver. For example, if an algorithm detects that traffic on a specific route has increased due to an accident, the system can redirect the driver to an alternative route that minimizes delivery time and avoids congestion. In this way, real-time learning allows SMEs to quickly adapt to changes in traffic conditions and improve the efficiency of their logistics operations.

One of the key benefits of real-time monitoring is the ability to reduce fuel consumption and transportation costs. Optimizing routes based on real-time traffic data helps avoid high congestion areas, which reduces the amount of time vehicles spend idling or moving at low speeds. This not only minimizes delivery times but also reduces fuel consumption and emissions of polluting gases. In an SME with a small fleet, these savings can make a significant difference in long-term operating costs, allowing the company to be more competitive and sustainable. Additionally, reducing fuel consumption has a positive impact on the company's carbon footprint, which is a relevant factor in today's business sustainability context.

The implementation of real-time learning techniques allows route monitoring systems to adapt and learn from continuously collected data. For example, by analyzing traffic patterns and delivery times at different hours of the day or days of the week, machine learning algorithms can make recommendations on the best times to schedule deliveries based on the route and location of each customer. This learning capability enables SMEs to plan their deliveries more efficiently, maximizing resource use and improving the customer experience. By incorporating this real-time data, companies can anticipate problems and adjust their logistics strategies to avoid delays and optimize the flow of their operations.

The use of IoT sensors also allows for detailed monitoring of vehicle conditions, which is essential for preventive maintenance and reducing costs associated with breakdowns or unexpected repairs. Sensors can detect engine problems, low fuel levels, or tire wear and transmit this information in real-time to the fleet management platform. This enables the logistics team to make informed decisions about each vehicle's maintenance and plan necessary repairs without interrupting delivery operations. In this way, real-time monitoring contributes to better fleet maintenance management, extending the vehicles' lifespan and minimizing repair costs.

In addition to operational benefits, real-time route monitoring also offers a significant advantage in terms of customer experience, as it allows SMEs to provide accurate and up-to-date information about the status of each delivery. By using delivery tracking apps, customers can see the real-time location of their products and receive accurate estimated arrival times. This not only improves customer satisfaction but also reduces the number of inquiries to the customer service team regarding delivery status. By keeping customers informed in real-time, SMEs can enhance the perception of their service and build greater trust in their brand.

The use of machine learning and IoT also enables the creation of automatic alert systems that notify the logistics team about critical events or conditions requiring immediate intervention. These systems can send alerts when a vehicle deviates from its planned route, when traffic significantly increases on a specific route, or when engine problems or other vehicle components are detected. This rapid response capability is essential to ensure that logistics operations remain in good condition and to avoid delays or delivery issues. In an SME that makes deliveries in a large metropolitan area, for example, automatic alerts allow the logistics team to take proactive measures to avoid problems and minimize the impact of unforeseen events on delivery efficiency.

The integration of real-time data with visualization tools, such as interactive maps and dashboards, makes it easier for the logistics team to monitor and make real-time decisions. Visualization tools allow you to see the location and status of each vehicle on a map in real time, which facilitates problem identification and more effective delivery coordination. In a logistics company using a centralized dashboard, the team can see the exact position of each vehicle, the estimated time of arrival at each delivery point, and any alerts related to traffic or vehicle status. This visibility allows for greater accuracy in decision-making and improves operational efficiency, as the team can intervene promptly and make route adjustments when necessary.

Another relevant aspect of real-time route monitoring is the ability to make proactive adjustments to route planning based on data collected during deliveries. Machine learning algorithms can analyze historical and real-time data to identify patterns that allow anticipation of common problems, such as high traffic congestion areas or poorly maintained road sections. This proactive approach ensures that route planning becomes increasingly accurate, as the system learns from each delivery and adjusts future routes based on the collected data. For an SME with complex logistics operations, this continuous learning capability represents a significant competitive advantage, as it allows for constant route optimization and ongoing improvement in delivery efficiency.

The combination of machine learning and IoT in real-time route monitoring also offers the possibility of improving the sustainability of logistics operations by reducing fuel consumption and minimizing the carbon footprint. By optimizing routes and reducing the time vehicles spend on the road, SMEs can decrease their fuel consumption and, in turn, reduce their emissions of polluting gases. This optimization not only has economic benefits for the company but also contributes to greater environmental sustainability, which is especially important in the current context of climate change and corporate social responsibility.

In short, real-time monitoring of routes through the integration of machine learning and IoT systems offers SMEs a series of significant benefits, from optimizing time and fuel consumption to improving customer experience and reducing operating costs. The ability to adjust routes on the fly and respond to unforeseen events allows SMEs to adapt to a dynamic and highly competitive logistics environment, achieving faster, more accurate, and efficient delivery service.

8.4. Dynamic pricing optimization with machine learning

Dynamic pricing optimization with machine learning has become a fundamental strategy for SMEs looking to maximize their revenue and profit margins in a highly competitive environment with constant changes in market demand. This dynamic pricing approach, where product or service prices are adjusted in real-time based on multiple factors, allows companies to quickly and efficiently adapt their prices, increasing their ability to respond to market conditions in real-time and optimize their sales. The key to success in dynamic pricing lies in the implementation of machine learning algorithms that continuously analyze variables such as demand, customer behavior, competitor prices, available inventory, and other contextual factors, enabling companies to calculate the optimal price at any given moment to maximize profitability.

The concept of dynamic pricing is not new; in fact, it is a strategy commonly used in industries such as aviation and tourism, where demand fluctuates significantly depending on the time of year, seat or room availability, and competitor behavior. However, the rise of e-commerce and access to advanced machine learning tools have made this strategy increasingly accessible for SMEs across various sectors, allowing them to leverage the benefits of real-time price adjustments. Machine learning algorithms enable the analysis of large volumes of historical and real-time data, identifying patterns in consumer behavior and demand, and making automatic decisions about the price of each product or service. In this way, SMEs can set prices that align with market realities at all times, maximizing both sales and profits.

To implement an effective dynamic pricing strategy, SMEs need to start by collecting detailed data on their sales, customer behavior, and competitor pricing. Sales data includes information on sales volume at different times of the day, week, or year, as well as the impact of specific events like discounts, promotions, or holidays. Analyzing this data allows businesses to understand how demand varies based on external factors and the company's own actions. Data on customer behavior, on the other hand, helps identify buying patterns and segment customers based on their preferences, willingness to pay, and response to price changes. Competitor pricing is also a key factor, as today's market is highly competitive, and consumers have easy access to price comparisons, meaning any price adjustment must consider competitors' pricing strategies to avoid losing sales.

Machine learning algorithms applied to dynamic pricing optimization can be classified into several categories, depending on their approach and the variables they analyze. One of the most common algorithms in pricing optimization is the multiple linear regression algorithm, which analyzes the relationship between price and several independent variables, such as demand, competition, and seasonal factors. This algorithm allows you to identify how each of these variables affects the optimal price and make real-time adjustments to maximize profit. For example, if demand increases during a competitor's promotion, the linear regression algorithm can adjust the price based on demand elasticity and inventory availability, achieving a balance between sales volume and profit margin.

Another approach to dynamic pricing optimization is the use of artificial neural networks, which are advanced machine learning models capable of identifying complex and non-linear patterns in the data. Neural networks are particularly useful in environments where multiple factors affect demand and where these factors interact in complex ways. Unlike regression models, which typically assume a linear relationship between variables, neural networks can capture more complex relationships and thus offer a more accurate prediction of the optimal price based on current market conditions. This approach is especially useful for SMEs selling products in highly competitive and volatile sectors, where changes in demand and customer behavior are frequent.

To improve the accuracy of machine learning models, SMEs can use supervised learning techniques and inferences based on historical data, which allow prices to be adjusted according to observed patterns from the past. In supervised learning, algorithms are trained using historical sales and competitor data, enabling the model to learn how different variables affect demand and profit margins. This way, the models can make predictions about the optimal price based on current conditions and adjust prices in real-time. For example, an ecommerce SME that sees an increase in demand during the year-end holidays can use a supervised learning model to adjust prices and maximize sales without sacrificing profit margins.

Another relevant factor in optimizing dynamic pricing is demand elasticity, which measures how sensitive consumers are to price changes. To calculate the optimal price, machine learning algorithms must consider how demand responds to price variations and adjust prices based on this sensitivity. For products with high demand elasticity, a small change in price can have a significant impact on sales volume, meaning the model must be particularly accurate in these cases to avoid revenue loss. For products with low elasticity, on the other hand, prices can be adjusted more flexibly without significantly affecting demand, allowing SMEs to maximize profit margins without worrying too much about the impact on sales.

The implementation of real-time dynamic pricing also allows SMEs to conduct A/B testing to evaluate the effectiveness of different pricing strategies based on specific variables. Through A/B testing, companies can compare the performance of different prices across distinct customer groups and analyze how each group responds to price changes. This strategy helps refine machine learning models and improve the accuracy of price predictions. For example, an SME can use A/B testing to analyze how different customer segments respond to a discount or price increase, and adjust their pricing strategy based on the test results. By combining dynamic pricing with A/B testing, SMEs can identify more effective pricing strategies for each customer group, thus improving both sales volume and profit margins.

In addition to product prices, dynamic pricing optimization can also be applied to services and subscriptions. In this case, machine learning algorithms analyze demand and customer behavior to adjust prices based on factors such as usage frequency, customer loyalty, and competition. For SMEs offering subscription services, using dynamic pricing allows them to adjust rates based on customer retention and satisfaction, ensuring prices remain competitive and attractive without sacrificing profitability. This approach is particularly useful in sectors where the value of the service varies depending on demand or where competitive conditions change rapidly, such as software or online entertainment services.

Machine learning models applied to dynamic pricing also allow for adjustments based on seasonal factors or specific events. For example, an SME can use historical data to identify seasonal demand patterns and adjust prices according to the trends of each season. In a clothing store, prices can be adjusted based on the time of year, while in an electronics store, prices can vary according to high-demand events like Black Friday or Cyber Monday. By anticipating these fluctuations and proactively adjusting prices, SMEs can maximize sales during peak demand periods and maintain a competitive pricing strategy throughout the rest of the year.

In addition to internal factors, dynamic pricing optimization must also consider external factors such as general economic conditions and industry trends. During times of economic crisis or recession, consumers tend to cut back on spending and look for lower prices, which means SMEs must adjust their prices to remain competitive and attract customers. On the other hand, in a high-demand context, prices can be increased to maximize profit margins without significantly affecting sales. Machine learning models can analyze these external factors and make pricing recommendations based on market conditions, allowing SMEs to adapt to economic changes and optimize their profitability.

In practice, the machine learning algorithms used for dynamic pricing can be implemented using accessible tools and libraries like Scikit-Learn for predictive modeling and Pandas for data manipulation. These tools allow SMEs to analyze large volumes of data, create price prediction models, and make real-time adjustments based on market conditions. The ease of access to these tools facilitates the implementation of dynamic pricing strategies, enabling businesses of all sizes to compete in an increasingly complex and globalized market.

In conclusion, optimizing dynamic pricing with machine learning is a powerful strategy for SMEs that want to maximize their revenues and profit margins in a highly competitive environment with constant changes in demand. By adjusting prices in real-time based on demand, competition, and other relevant factors, SMEs can respond quickly to market conditions and optimize their sales. This strategy requires the collection and analysis of detailed data on sales, customer behavior, and competition, as well as the implementation of machine learning algorithms that can calculate the optimal price at any given moment. By implementing dynamic pricing, SMEs not only improve their profitability but also strengthen their competitive position and ability to adapt to a dynamic and ever-changing market environment.

8.5. Sensitivity Analysis and Simulation

Sensitivity analysis and simulation are crucial tools for SMEs to foresee how changes in external factors, like market conditions or fuel prices, can impact key areas of their operations, especially logistics and inventory management. These approaches not only allow for more informed planning but also provide a proactive view that facilitates strategic decision-making in uncertain or volatile scenarios. Through simulations like Monte Carlo, SMEs can model different market conditions and assess the potential impact of these variables on their costs, delivery times, and stock needs, enhancing their ability to adapt to changing conditions and optimizing their supply chain.

Sensitivity analysis allows businesses to identify which variables have the greatest impact on their operational results and therefore require closer monitoring or control. Through this analysis, an SME can detect how changes in a particular variable, such as fuel prices, affect the total cost of transportation. By understanding the relationship between variables and outcomes, SMEs can develop strategies to reduce the impact of external changes and optimize their cost structure. This analysis is particularly relevant in the logistics and transportation sectors, where fuel accounts for a significant portion of operating expenses. For example, if the sensitivity analysis indicates that a 10% increase in fuel prices would raise logistics costs by 15%, the company can look for alternatives to reduce fuel consumption or plan more efficient routes that minimize distances traveled.

In the case of Monte Carlo simulation, this method allows SMEs to model diverse and complex scenarios where multiple variables are constantly interacting. By generating a large number of simulations or iterations, Monte Carlo provides a range of possible outcomes based on different input values and allows estimation of the probability of certain results occurring. In the context of logistics and stock control, Monte Carlo enables SMEs to anticipate fluctuations in product demand or the availability of materials and components, facilitating more precise and adaptive inventory management. This technique is particularly valuable for companies operating in environments where supply and demand can vary abruptly, such as seasonal markets or products with variable demand. By modeling these changes, SMEs can predict how many inventory units they will need based on different scenarios and adjust their stock levels accordingly.

To implement an effective sensitivity analysis, SMEs should start by identifying the critical variables that affect their operating and logistics costs. This can include fuel prices, labor costs, transportation time, and supplier availability, among other factors. Once these variables are identified, the next step is to analyze how changes in each of them affect the overall outcome, which allows the company to focus on the variables with the highest sensitivity and potential impact. For example, if an SME that makes deliveries to multiple locations finds that transportation time is highly sensitive to changes in traffic density, it can look for route optimization strategies or even reconsider delivery times to avoid peak congestion hours.

Sensitivity analysis is also useful for understanding how changes in product availability can affect stock levels and inventory needs. In times of high demand, such as during a product launch or high commercial activity periods, the availability of certain products can be uncertain. A sensitivity analysis allows you to assess the impact of potential supply delays or product shortages on the company's overall inventory. This way, the SME can better prepare for high-demand periods by adjusting stock levels or diversifying suppliers to mitigate the risk of shortages. For example, an electronics company can perform a sensitivity analysis to anticipate possible disruptions in the supply chain of critical components and adjust its inventory based on the likelihood of these disruptions.

Monte Carlo simulation, on the other hand, allows SMEs to generate multiple scenarios to evaluate the impact of different input values on logistics and inventory outcomes. The basis of Monte Carlo is the generation of probability distributions for each input variable, which allows for the modeling of multiple possible scenarios and obtaining a range of results that can be used for planning. For example, in the context of fuel prices, Monte Carlo simulation allows an SME to model different price scenarios and calculate how each possible price would affect the total transportation cost. From these scenarios, the company can develop a response strategy that considers a range of prices, improving its ability to adapt to market volatility.

Monte Carlo is also valuable in analyzing product demand and supply. By simulating different levels of demand and product availability, SMEs can anticipate periods of high demand or product shortages, allowing them to adjust their inventory and avoid overstock or stockouts. This technique is particularly useful in variable demand environments, such as consumer goods or seasonal products. By simulating multiple demand levels, the company can assess the probability that the current stock will be sufficient to meet demand in different scenarios, enabling more precise and efficient inventory management.

Sensitivity analysis and Monte Carlo simulation also allow SMEs to assess the impact of changes in economic conditions on their logistics operations. Factors such as inflation, interest rates, and exchange rates can affect transportation costs, product demand, and material availability. Through sensitivity analysis, the company can identify which macroeconomic variables are most relevant to its operating costs and evaluate how changes in these variables will impact profitability. For example, an SME that relies on international suppliers can use sensitivity analysis to assess how fluctuations in exchange rates affect the cost of its inputs and make informed decisions about pricing policies and import strategies.

In practice, SMEs can implement these methods using analytical and modeling tools that facilitate the calculation and interpretation of results. There are various software platforms that allow for Monte Carlo simulations and sensitivity analyses in an accessible way, such as Excel, Python with statistical analysis libraries, and specific simulation software. These tools enable companies to create customized models that reflect their operations and analyze how changes in key variables affect their results. By applying these methods, SMEs can improve their responsiveness to market changes and make informed decisions about their logistics, stock levels, and pricing policies.

For example, using Python, an SME can perform a Monte Carlo simulation to evaluate the impact of fuel prices on their transport costs. The simulation would generate multiple scenarios with different fuel price levels and calculate the total transport cost in each scenario, providing a probability distribution of transport costs based on fuel prices. This simulation facilitates a deeper understanding of risks and allows the company to plan its transport budget more accurately, anticipating the effects of possible fuel price fluctuations.

In addition, Monte Carlo simulation and sensitivity analysis can also be applied in supply chain planning, where delivery times and material availability can vary significantly. By simulating different delivery times and availability levels, SMEs can assess the impact of these changes on their inventory and their ability to meet demand. This assessment is especially valuable in situations where there are risks of delays or supply disruptions, such as during a health crisis or in times of high seasonal demand. By anticipating these changes, SMEs can adjust their orders and inventory to minimize the impact of delays and ensure the continuity of their operations.

Finally, the combination of sensitivity analysis and Monte Carlo simulation also allows SMEs to develop risk mitigation strategies that reduce the impact of market condition fluctuations. For example, if the sensitivity analysis reveals that the company is particularly vulnerable to changes in fuel prices, it can implement measures to reduce fuel consumption or consider alternative transportation options. Similarly, if the Monte Carlo simulation indicates a high risk of product shortages during certain times of the year, the company can increase its safety stock or diversify its supplier base to reduce dependence on a single supplier and improve its ability to handle supply chain disruptions.

In conclusion, sensitivity analysis and Monte Carlo simulation provide SMEs with advanced tools to understand and anticipate market changes and assess their impact on critical areas of logistics and inventory control.

8.6. Use of deep learning algorithms for advanced optimization

The use of deep learning algorithms for advanced optimization represents one of the most powerful tools for improving accuracy in demand forecasting and logistics planning, especially in contexts where available data is complex and presents non-linear relationships. Deep learning models, such as convolutional neural networks (CNN) and long short-term memory networks (LSTM), have proven particularly useful in these cases, allowing companies to identify patterns and trends in data that is difficult to interpret. The advantage of these architectures is their ability to process large volumes of information and extract complex patterns, which is invaluable for companies facing high demand volatility or multiple factors affecting their logistics operations.

To understand how deep learning algorithms can improve demand prediction optimization, it's important to highlight that consumer behavior and market trends often don't follow linear patterns. For example, demand for a product might depend on factors such as seasonality, marketing campaigns, competition, the global economy, and even unforeseen events like crises or pandemics. Traditional models, like linear regressions, are limited in their ability to interpret these factors as they tend to simplify the relationships between variables. However, deep learning offers the flexibility to build models that capture this complexity, allowing for more accurate predictions that are better aligned with real market conditions. For SMEs, which often face resource and planning constraints, this added precision can be key to managing inventory and logistics, reducing costs, and improving customer satisfaction.

Convolutional neural networks (CNNs) are known for their ability to analyze images, but they can also be adapted for processing complex tabular data and time series. In the context of demand forecasting, a CNN can be used to identify patterns in historical sales data in a more detailed way than traditional models. A CNN can detect specific patterns in time periods, such as seasonal trends or demand changes associated with external events. For example, in a clothing store, a CNN could detect increases in demand during sales seasons or holidays and adjust predictions based on these recurring events. This is particularly useful in the retail sector where demand can fluctuate based on multiple variables, and a CNN can identify patterns that repeat over different periods, providing companies with an accurate view of stock needs to anticipate demand.

Another type of network used in deep learning is the Long Short-Term Memory (LSTM) network, specifically designed for processing time series. LSTM networks can retain relevant information over long periods, which is crucial when working with sequential data like product demand over time. The structure of LSTM networks allows them to capture temporal dependencies and learn from long-term patterns, which is essential in sectors where demand is highly dependent on past events or prolonged economic cycles. In the context of an SME that needs to forecast demand to plan its inventory, an LSTM network can be trained to accurately predict future demand based on historical data, including variables such as previous sales, seasonal trends, and market fluctuations. This type of prediction is particularly valuable in companies that sell perishable or fast-moving products, as more accurate predictions help minimize the risk of overstock or stockouts.

In addition to demand prediction, deep learning algorithms are also effective in optimizing logistics routes, a critical aspect for companies with distribution and delivery operations. Logistics planning involves organizing multiple variables, such as delivery distances, transportation time, fuel consumption, and vehicle capacity constraints. Neural networks can process large volumes of traffic data, geospatial information, and time constraints, allowing them to identify optimal routes that minimize costs and delivery time. A deep learning model trained on historical route data and traffic conditions can predict the best route based on current conditions, adapting to unforeseen changes like traffic or weather. This approach not only allows SMEs to optimize their transportation costs but also improves delivery punctuality, which directly impacts customer satisfaction.

To implement deep learning algorithms in demand forecasting or logistics optimization, SMEs should start by collecting relevant data and building datasets to train the models. The necessary data may include historical sales, inventories, delivery times, purchasing patterns, and any other factors that influence demand or logistics planning. This data collection process is essential to ensure that the models have enough information to learn complex patterns and make accurate predictions. In many cases, companies can benefit from integrating their data systems with big data analytics platforms or IoT (Internet of Things) systems, which facilitate real-time data collection and allow for constant model updates.

Once the necessary data is available, the next step is to train the deep learning model to identify patterns and make predictions based on this data. For demand forecasting, the model can be trained using historical sales data and additional variables that influence demand, such as promotions, seasonality, and competitor pricing. For route optimization, the model can be trained on geospatial and traffic data to learn patterns in delivery times and suggest optimized routes based on current conditions. It's important for SMEs to invest time and resources in training and fine-tuning their deep learning models to achieve maximum performance and accuracy in predictions, as a poorly trained model or one that doesn't accurately reflect market conditions can lead to wrong decisions and unnecessary costs.

The implementation of deep learning models also involves evaluating and validating their accuracy. In the context of logistics planning, for example, a deep learning model that predicts the best route based on traffic data must be tested in real conditions to ensure its effectiveness. This validation process allows for the identification of potential errors or necessary adjustments in the model and ensures that the predictions are accurate and useful in the company's real context. In the case of demand forecasting, model validation involves comparing predictions with actual sales data and adjusting the model based on the results obtained. Validation is an ongoing process, as market conditions and customer behavior can change over time, and deep learning models must adapt to these new conditions to maintain their accuracy.

Another important aspect to consider when implementing deep learning algorithms is the interpretability and explainability of the models. Unlike traditional machine learning models, deep learning models can be difficult to interpret, which poses a challenge in terms of transparency and decision-making. In many SMEs, decision-makers do not necessarily have a deep understanding of deep learning, and it is important that the results and predictions are comprehensible and easy to interpret. To address this challenge, SMEs can use interpretability tools, such as variable importance visualization techniques or sensitivity analysis techniques, which allow them to understand how the model arrives at a prediction based on input variables. This way, company decision-makers can make model-based decisions with greater confidence and understand how changes in variables affect the outcomes.

Implementing deep learning algorithms for advanced optimization also requires a focus on scalability and the model's ability to be updated. As the company collects new data and market conditions change, deep learning models must be updated to reflect these new conditions. In some cases, this may involve retraining the model with more recent data, while in other cases, it may be necessary to adjust the model's parameters to adapt to changes in customer behavior or logistical conditions. This ability to update is essential to ensure that deep learning models maintain their accuracy and relevance over time, allowing SMEs to continuously optimize their operations and adapt to market changes.

Finally, it is important to consider that the implementation of deep learning in logistics optimization and demand forecasting requires infrastructure and technical resources. Unlike traditional machine learning models, deep learning algorithms usually require greater computational capacity, especially if complex architectures like deep neural networks or

LSTMs are used. SMEs can choose to implement their models on cloud infrastructures, which provide the necessary processing capacity without incurring hardware costs, or they can consider hybrid solutions that combine cloud processing with local processing to maximize efficiency and reduce costs.

In conclusion, the use of deep learning algorithms for advanced optimization represents a significant advantage for SMEs in demand prediction and logistics planning. By capturing complex and non-linear patterns in data, deep learning offers a highly accurate and adaptable approach to the needs of businesses facing volatile market conditions or operating in highly competitive sectors. From demand prediction based on seasonal factors and market events to route optimization using real-time traffic data, deep learning opens new opportunities for SMEs to maximize operational efficiency, reduce costs, and improve customer satisfaction.

Chapter 9 - BI Strategies for SMEs and Freelancers

9.1. Business intelligence strategies for SMEs: From data to action

In today's context, where competition is increasingly intense and market conditions change rapidly, having Business Intelligence (BI) strategies is no longer exclusive to large corporations. SMEs, which have traditionally had more limited access to advanced analysis tools, can now take advantage of accessible and effective BI solutions to transform their data into actionable insights that guide their business and strategic decisions. BI refers to the process of collecting, organizing, analyzing, and visualizing data so that companies can make decisions based on accurate and up-to-date information, thereby optimizing operations, improving customer experience, and increasing profitability.

A well-implemented BI strategy not only provides a deeper understanding of the company's internal and external data but also allows for trend forecasting and real-time decision adjustments. Collecting internal data (such as sales, customer behavior, and operational efficiency) and external data (such as market trends and competitor actions) enables SMEs to better understand their environment and adapt more swiftly. Contrary to what one might think, implementing a BI strategy doesn't necessarily require a large economic or technical investment. Today, there are tools like Google Sheets, SQL databases, and data visualization platforms like Power BI and Tableau that democratize access to BI and make it a reality for companies of all sizes.

The first step in a BI strategy is data collection and storage, a crucial phase that involves structuring and organizing information in formats that facilitate later analysis. For SMEs, this can be achieved with cost-effective yet efficient tools that ensure relevant data is centralized and easily accessible. Subsequently, the data must undergo a transformation and cleaning process to eliminate errors and standardize the information. This step is essential for obtaining accurate insights and can be largely automated using programming languages like Python and specific libraries for data processing, such as Pandas. Data transformation allows companies to identify patterns in the information, making it easier to obtain valuable insights that can influence key decisions, from marketing campaign planning to inventory optimization.

Once the data is prepared, the analysis and visualization phase turns the data into useful information. Data visualization tools allow SMEs to interpret large volumes of information easily, identifying trends and key metrics through graphs and visual dashboards. This not only makes data easier to understand for those without a technical background but also enables work teams to quickly detect opportunities and issues. In this sense, well-designed visualizations are essential for turning data into concrete actions, as they facilitate the interpretation of KPIs and the most relevant business metrics.

A key aspect of BI is identifying specific metrics or KPIs that allow companies to monitor the performance of their operations. In the case of SMEs, these KPIs often focus on areas like sales, marketing, customer retention, and operating costs, among others. Once KPIs are identified and established, constantly monitoring these indicators through BI tools helps the company evaluate its performance and adjust its strategies in real-time, maximizing effectiveness.

Finally, BI applications are not limited to generating performance reports; they also offer great potential for creating practical use cases where SMEs can use specific insights to optimize certain aspects of their business. These cases can include adjusting inventory based on demand forecasts, personalizing marketing campaigns according to customer behavior, or making price adjustments based on competition. In conclusion, a well-implemented BI strategy allows SMEs to move from reactive to proactive management, where decisions are based on accurate and up-to-date data, providing a significant competitive advantage in an increasingly dynamic and data-driven business environment.

- ### Definition of Business Intelligence (BI) for SMEs

The concept of Business Intelligence (BI) refers to the set of processes, tools, and technologies that enable the transformation of large amounts of data into useful and actionable information for decision-making in a company. BI encompasses all practices related to the systematic collection, storage, analysis, and visualization of data, with the aim of identifying patterns, trends, and insights that support strategic decisions. Historically, these analysis and visualization capabilities were limited to large corporations due to the infrastructure and technical resources required. However, today, BI tools have been democratized, making it possible for SMEs to implement business intelligence strategies to turn their data into key insights without the need for a large investment.

For an SME, access to BI represents a significant competitive advantage, as it allows them to analyze their performance in real-time, detect improvement opportunities, and respond more quickly to market changes. BI becomes a crucial tool because it enables these companies to leverage the data generated in every aspect of their operation, from sales and marketing to logistics and human resources management, thereby optimizing efficiency and improving decision-making at all levels. In an environment of constant competition and limited resources, the ability to make data-driven decisions allows SMEs to operate more strategically and effectively, with a more efficient use of resources.

The essence of BI lies in transforming data into understandable information, which can then be turned into action. In the context of SMEs, this means that the goal of BI is to extract valuable insights from data to improve daily or strategic decisions. A simple example is analyzing sales data to detect patterns in customer behavior, which can lead to decisions regarding inventory, pricing, and promotions. To achieve this transformation, BI relies on tools that allow the collection, storage, and analysis of large amounts of data in a centralized and accessible manner.

One of the barriers that SMEs have faced in adopting BI is the perception that this type of technology is expensive and requires experts for implementation. However, with the advancement of accessible tools, many of them free or low-cost, the BI implementation process has been significantly simplified. Today, tools like Google Sheets, SQL databases, and cloud services allow SMEs to efficiently organize their data and integrate it with other data sources to obtain a complete view of their operations. Similarly, data visualization platforms like Power BI, Tableau, and Google Data Studio have made it easier to access interactive charts and customized dashboards, enabling decision-makers in an SME to analyze information and extract insights without the need for advanced technical training.

The importance of BI for SMEs also lies in its ability to reduce risk and maximize profitability. As a company gains access to reliable and up-to-date data, it can make decisions with greater precision and less uncertainty. SMEs, which often do not have wide margins for error or the financial capacity to absorb large losses, particularly benefit from this real-time analysis capability, allowing them to quickly adjust their strategies when they detect opportunities or threats. For example, an SME can monitor the effectiveness of a digital marketing campaign in real time and modify it if it is not performing as expected, thus avoiding an unprofitable investment.

Another advantage of BI for SMEs is its ability to identify operational inefficiencies and areas for improvement. By analyzing their operational data, these companies can detect patterns that indicate inefficient processes, slow response times, or areas with high costs. This type of analysis can be crucial for implementing process improvements, optimizing resource allocation, and reducing operational costs. For example, an SME dedicated to manufacturing can use production data to identify bottlenecks in the supply chain or manufacturing process and take measures to resolve them, thereby improving productivity and responsiveness to demand.

To implement BI effectively, an SME must start by defining clear and specific objectives. This includes identifying which areas of the business will benefit most from data analysis and what key questions they expect BI to answer. For example, if the main goal is to improve sales, the company can focus on analyzing customer behavior, conversion rates, and the effectiveness of marketing campaigns. If, on the other hand, the goal is to optimize logistics, the company can concentrate on inventory turnover, delivery times, and the efficiency of distribution routes. By defining BI objectives, the SME can determine which data is necessary and how it should be structured to obtain the desired insights.

A fundamental aspect of a successful BI strategy is the quality and accuracy of the data. Collecting incorrect or incomplete data can lead to wrong conclusions and poor decisions. Therefore, it is important for SMEs to implement a data cleansing and validation process before analysis. This can include removing duplicates, standardizing formats, and correcting errors. Tools like Python and data processing libraries allow for much of this process to be automated, ensuring that the data is clean and ready for analysis.

Another key element in BI is the integration of different data sources. To get a complete view of operations, an SME might need data from multiple sources, such as physical store sales, e-commerce, customer service, and social media interactions. Integrating these data provides a holistic view that makes it easier to identify patterns and relationships that might not be apparent if the data were analyzed in isolation. Nowadays, there are solutions that allow you to connect and centralize various data sources into a single system, making it easier to analyze information from different channels and customer touchpoints.

The final phase in the BI process is data visualization and decision-making. The ability to transform data into visual graphs and tables makes information interpretation easier, allowing decision-makers to spot patterns and trends at a glance. Visualization tools like Power BI, Tableau, and Google Data Studio enable SMEs to create interactive charts and dashboards that update in real-time, providing a dynamic view of the company's status. These dashboards can be customized to display the most relevant key performance indicators (KPIs) for each area, allowing for constant and precise monitoring of the metrics that matter to each team.

An important aspect of BI is its practical application in business strategy. Through BI, an SME can identify customer behavior patterns and anticipate their needs. For example, by analyzing past purchase data, the company can predict which products will be in high demand during a specific season, thus adjusting their inventory and avoiding both stock shortages and excess unwanted products. This type of forecasting also allows SMEs to plan more effective marketing campaigns, targeting their efforts at customer segments most likely to make purchases, optimizing the marketing budget and increasing the profitability of each campaign.

Finally, BI also has valuable applications in managing the customer experience. By analyzing data from customer interactions, such as support queries or online reviews, an SME can identify areas for improvement in its service and pinpoint where customers are experiencing difficulties or dissatisfaction. This allows the company to adjust its service processes and enhance customer satisfaction, which contributes to greater loyalty and an improved company reputation.

In summary, BI is an essential tool for SMEs looking to improve their decision-making through data analysis. By transforming data into practical and accessible insights, businesses can adapt to a constantly changing environment, optimize their operations, and enhance customer relationships. Today's tools and technologies have democratized access to BI, allowing any company, regardless of size or budget, to implement a business intelligence strategy and leverage the value of their data to build a smarter and more competitive business.

- ## Key Components of a BI Strategy

An effective Business Intelligence (BI) strategy is based on several key components that help transform data into relevant and actionable information for decision-making. These components are essential for establishing a coherent workflow, where data is collected, organized, transformed, and analyzed systematically. For an SME, the correct implementation of these elements allows not only a better understanding of its operations and customer behavior but also greater agility in decision-making, based on reliable information.

The first component, data collection and storage, forms the foundation of any BI strategy, ensuring that the company has access to structured and quality data. The next step is data transformation, a process where errors are removed and data is adapted to facilitate analysis; in this phase, the use of programming tools and specialized libraries simplifies data cleaning and organization. Finally, analysis and visualization allow data to be presented clearly and visually, making it easier to interpret quickly and implement informed actions. These three components work together so that SMEs can maximize the value of their data and transform information into effective business strategies.

- ### Data collection and storage

The process of collecting and storing data is essential in a BI strategy, as it ensures that all relevant data for the company is accessible, organized, and stored in a structured manner. SMEs, like any other company, generate a large amount of data in their daily operations. This data comes from various sources, such as sales, social media interactions, customer behavior on the website, ecommerce transactions, inventory records, among others. For this data to be effectively analyzed and used, an appropriate and consistent storage structure is necessary to facilitate its access and manipulation.

One of the first steps in data collection is defining what information is relevant to the company's goals. This involves carefully selecting data sources and the types of information that will be collected. In an SME focused on retail, for example, sales data and in-store customer behavior can be essential, while in a service company, customer interaction and satisfaction might be priority areas. By defining these data objectives, the company can focus on collecting information that truly adds value and avoid storing unnecessary or redundant data.

Tools for data collection and storage have evolved, enabling SMEs to use simple and affordable options that don't require complex or expensive infrastructure. Google Sheets is an example of a free, easy-to-use tool that allows you to store and organize data in a structured way. While it's not ideal for large volumes of data, it's useful for small businesses starting to implement BI and needing an accessible system to store and manipulate basic sales, marketing, or customer information.

For companies that handle a larger volume of data or want more detailed control over their data structure and organization, SQL and NoSQL databases offer more robust options. SQL (Structured Query Language) is a standard language that allows managing relational databases, making it ideal for companies that need to store data in structured tables with clear relationships, such as sales transactions and product inventory. SQL databases like MySQL, PostgreSQL, and SQLite are easy to implement and offer advanced querying capabilities, allowing companies to extract specific information from large volumes of data. For example, an e-commerce company can store sales data in an SQL database and run queries to find out the best-selling products over a certain period.

On the other hand, NoSQL databases are a popular choice for storing data that doesn't have a defined structure or requires great flexibility. Unlike SQL databases, NoSQL databases like MongoDB and Firebase are designed to work with unstructured or semi-structured data, such as documents, JSON files, and large volumes of real-time data. This is particularly useful for SMEs that need to store data from multiple sources without a fixed structure, such as social media data, customer comments, or activity logs in a mobile app.

Data storage is not only limited to selecting an appropriate platform but also requires establishing an efficient data management system that allows for quick updates and access to information. In this context, cloud solutions like Google Cloud, Amazon Web Services (AWS), and Microsoft Azure have made scalable storage infrastructure more accessible for SMEs. These platforms allow companies to store their data securely and access it from any location, which is especially useful for businesses with remote teams or multiple physical locations. Additionally, cloud solutions offer scalability features that adapt to the company's growth needs, enabling increased storage and data processing capacity as the company generates more information.

In addition to storing data centrally, a good BI strategy requires integrating multiple data sources into a single platform. This means that data from different areas of the company (sales, inventory, marketing, etc.) must be connected and accessible so they can be analyzed together. Integrating data sources is essential to getting a holistic view of the company's operations, as it allows you to identify patterns and relationships that wouldn't be evident if the data were analyzed in isolation. Tools like Zapier or Integromat automate the transfer of data between applications, facilitating the consolidation of information into a centralized and accessible database for analysis.

In conclusion, data collection and storage form the foundation of an effective BI strategy for any SME. By clearly defining which data is relevant to their goals, selecting the right tools, and centralizing information in a structured and accessible system, SMEs can ensure their data is available and ready for analysis. A systematic approach to data collection and storage ensures that the company is prepared to leverage the value of information and make informed decisions based on reliable and up-to-date data.

- **Data Transformation**

Data transformation is one of the most crucial phases in a Business Intelligence (BI) strategy, as it ensures that the collected data is in a suitable format for analysis and decision-making. In this transformation process, the concept of ETL (Extract, Transform, Load) plays a fundamental role. ETL refers to the complete cycle where data is extracted from its original sources, transformed to meet quality standards, and loaded into a centralized system where it can be analyzed and used to generate valuable insights. This cycle ensures that the data reaching the BI system is accurate, consistent, and useful for the company's objectives. For SMEs, having a well-defined ETL strategy is essential to make the most of their data, optimizing accuracy and facilitating the integration of different information sources.

Data Extraction is the first step in this cycle. It involves identifying and extracting relevant data from various sources, which can include databases, spreadsheets, text files, ecommerce platforms, or CRMs, among others. In SMEs, it's common for data to be scattered across multiple formats and locations. For example, sales data may be on an ecommerce platform, customer records in a CRM, and marketing metrics in Google Analytics. ETL tools like Apache Nifi, Talend, or custom scripts in Python allow data extraction from multiple sources and prepare it for the next step. These tools automatically and continuously extract data, ensuring the information is always up to date.

Once extracted, the data goes through the Transformation phase, where it's cleaned, standardized, and adapted for effective analysis. During this phase, errors and outliers are removed, null values are handled, and units of measure and formats are standardized. For example, if a database has dates in the US format (MM/DD/YYYY) and another in the European format (DD/MM/YYYY), this field needs to be unified into a single format. Likewise, if there are errors or duplicate data, they are removed or corrected to avoid biases in the analysis. Data transformation not only increases analysis accuracy but also allows the integration of data from different sources into a coherent and unified set.

To carry out data transformation, Python and the Pandas library are fundamental tools, especially for SMEs looking for a cost-effective and highly customizable solution. Pandas is a library that allows you to manipulate and transform large volumes of data efficiently and easily. With Pandas, you can perform operations like data cleaning, handling null values, and converting data types quickly and scalably. For example, a company can use Pandas to remove rows containing incomplete data or to fill missing values with the mean or median of the dataset. These operations ensure that the data is clean and ready for analysis.

Another important aspect of data transformation is the creation of derived variables. This involves creating new columns or attributes in the dataset that provide additional and relevant information for analysis. For example, if an ecommerce company has sales data by date, they can create a column indicating the season of the year (spring, summer, etc.) or whether it is a holiday or weekend. These derived variables allow for more specific and detailed insights in the subsequent analysis. In this regard, Python and Pandas offer functionalities to create new variables easily and efficiently, which is essential for good data preparation.

Once the data has been transformed and meets the quality and format standards, it is then loaded into a centralized storage system, such as a data warehouse or a BI-supported database. This step ensures that the processed data is accessible to real-time analysis and visualization systems, allowing decision-makers to access reliable and up-to-date information. There are ETL tools that automate the loading process, connecting different data sources and automatically updating the central storage whenever changes occur in the source data.

- **Analysis and visualization of data**

Data analysis and visualization form the final phase in a BI strategy, where transformed data is presented in a visual and comprehensible manner so that decision-makers can easily interpret the information. This component is crucial as it allows the identification of patterns, trends, and relationships in the data that wouldn't be obvious at first glance. For an SME, the ability to visualize data clearly and accurately provides a competitive advantage by facilitating informed decision-making and identifying opportunities and problems in real-time.

Data visualization not only facilitates analysis but also improves the communication of insights between different teams and levels of the company. A well-designed dashboard allows managers, executives, and heads of sales, marketing, operations, and finance to monitor KPIs and key metrics in one place. Additionally, graphs and visualizations enable quick interpretation of the company's performance and data-driven decision-making without the need for advanced technical knowledge. In this sense, data visualization is a BI tool that makes information accessible to the entire organization, democratizing access to key insights for decision-making.

For data analysis and visualization, there are specialized tools that allow SMEs to create charts, dashboards, and interactive dashboards quickly and intuitively. Tableau and Power BI are two of the most popular data visualization platforms on the market, and both offer a wide variety of options for charts, tables, maps, and other visualizations that make data interpretation easier. Tableau allows users to create interactive dashboards and share them online or within the company, while Power BI offers advanced integrations with the Microsoft ecosystem and the ability to automatically update data from various sources, which is ideal for companies needing real-time reports.

For SMEs looking for a free and easy-to-implement solution, Google Data Studio is an excellent option, as it allows you to create dashboards connected to data sources like Google Sheets, Google Analytics, and SQL databases. Google Data Studio is particularly useful for companies that want a simple visualization tool without the need for a significant initial investment. The graphs and tables created in Google Data Studio can be easily shared, and the platform allows data to be updated in real-time, which is useful for tracking key metrics and creating custom reports.

In addition to commercial BI platforms, Python libraries like Plotly, Seaborn, and Matplotlib are powerful tools for creating customized and highly configurable visualizations. For SMEs that have already adopted Python as part of their BI workflow, these libraries allow for the programmatic generation of charts and dashboards, offering greater flexibility in design and customization. Plotly is particularly useful for creating interactive charts that can be integrated into web dashboards using the Dash tool, while Seaborn and Matplotlib are ideal for creating high-quality static visualizations for reports and presentations. These libraries also allow for the automation of chart creation and data updates, making it easier to maintain visual reports over time.

The choice of visualization tools will depend on the specific needs of the SME and the complexity of the data to be analyzed. However, regardless of the tool selected, it's important that the visualizations are clear and useful, presenting information in an intuitive and organized manner. Dashboards and charts should focus on the most relevant KPIs and metrics, avoiding information overload and prioritizing elements that allow users to make quick and informed decisions. A good visualization design simplifies data interpretation and guides the user towards the most important insights.

Furthermore, BI dashboards allow SMEs to implement a real-time monitoring system, making it easier to make operational and strategic decisions based on the company's current performance. For example, a retail company can use a sales dashboard to monitor product performance and adjust inventory strategies according to demand. Similarly, a service company can monitor customer satisfaction and conversion rates in real time, enabling marketing and customer service teams to respond quickly to any changes in consumer behavior.

In conclusion, data analysis and visualization are essential components of a BI strategy, allowing SMEs to turn data into useful and accessible information for all levels of the organization. Through visualization tools like Tableau, Power BI, Google Data Studio, and Python libraries, SMEs can create dashboards and interactive charts that make it easier to interpret key metrics and track business objectives. The ability to visualize data clearly and efficiently transforms analysis into an accessible and understandable resource, which improves the company's responsiveness and strengthens its competitiveness in the market.

- ## How to Transform Data into Business Decisions

Transforming data into effective business decisions is the core of any Business Intelligence (BI) strategy. In the context of an SME, this capability not only boosts competitiveness but also allows for informed decisions that maximize resources and optimize processes. The process of turning data into decisions involves several key steps, from identifying the fundamental metrics for the business to implementing real-time changes. Defining key metrics (or KPIs) is essential to establish a clear benchmark for performance, while practical cases demonstrate how these insights can be applied to achieve specific business objectives, such as improving customer retention, adjusting inventories, or personalizing marketing campaigns.

For many SMEs, the challenge lies in identifying which key performance indicators truly impact their business objectives. KPIs vary widely from one industry to another, and even within the same company, they can differ depending on the area of focus (sales, marketing, operations, etc.). However, by carefully selecting KPIs, an SME can concentrate on the metrics that will guide its growth and allow for real-time measurement of strategy effectiveness. This, combined with a data-driven decision-making approach, enables the company to move forward in alignment with its goals and quickly respond to changing market conditions.

Identifying the right Key Performance Indicators (KPIs) is essential to establish an effective BI system. KPIs are the metrics that reflect a company's performance in critical areas for its success and allow for the evaluation of whether the implemented strategies are achieving the desired objectives. For an SME, selecting the right KPIs involves a process of evaluation and prioritization based on specific business goals and needs.

A first step in defining KPIs is to clearly establish the business objectives of the company. If the main goal is to increase sales, the KPIs might include the number of transactions, the average sales value, and the customer conversion rate. If the focus is on improving customer retention, metrics like Customer Lifetime Value (CLV) and the retention rate would be priority KPIs. By defining these objectives, the SME can ensure that the selected KPIs are directly aligned with their strategic goals.

One of the most common KPIs in SMEs focused on commerce and product sales is the number of sales or revenue generated. This indicator provides an overview of the company's performance, but it should be complemented with other metrics for a more comprehensive understanding. The conversion rate, for example, measures the effectiveness of marketing campaigns and success in attracting customers. A high conversion rate indicates that the marketing strategy is generating a good return, while a low rate may suggest the need for adjustments in the communication strategy or product offerings.

Another key KPI for SMEs, especially those in ecommerce or digital services, is customer retention. This indicator measures the company's ability to keep its customers over time. Customer retention is critical, as a loyal customer tends to generate more revenue and is less costly to retain than acquiring a new one. In terms of BI, measuring customer retention allows the SME to assess the effectiveness of its loyalty programs and make adjustments to its customer service and service personalization strategies.

In addition to these specific KPIs, there are other relevant metrics for different sectors. In a retail store, inventory levels and product turnover are key indicators that allow you to assess efficiency in stock management. An optimized inventory reduces storage costs and improves product availability, ensuring that best-selling items are always in stock. On the other hand, in service companies, metrics like response time and customer satisfaction are essential for measuring service quality and improving the customer experience.

Segmenting KPIs according to different business areas also allows for more precise evaluation. For example, in the marketing area, KPIs like customer acquisition cost (CAC) and return on marketing investment (ROMI) are essential for analyzing the efficiency of advertising campaigns. These indicators enable the SME to adjust its marketing budget and optimize its campaigns, focusing on the channels and strategies that generate better performance. In the operations area, KPIs can include supply chain efficiency and delivery times, allowing the company to identify areas for improvement in its logistics processes and optimize inventory management.

Once the right KPIs have been defined, the next step is to set specific goals for each metric. For example, if an SME has a current conversion rate of 2%, it could set a goal to increase this rate to 3% in the next quarter. These goals should be measurable, achievable, and aligned with the company's resources and capabilities. Additionally, by setting clear targets, the company can evaluate the performance of its strategies continuously and make adjustments based on the results.

9.2. Implementation of dashboards and dynamic KPIs with Python and BI tools

The implementation of dashboards and dynamic KPIs is an essential tool for SMEs, facilitating real-time monitoring of business performance and allowing immediate adjustments based on data. Dashboards function as a visual 'control panel,' where graphs, indicators, and key metrics provide a comprehensive view of core areas such as sales, marketing, operations, and finance. For decision-makers, having a visual and understandable system in one place is invaluable, as it saves time, reduces complexity, and enables faster, more informed strategic decisions.

Dashboards are made up of intuitive visual elements that present KPIs (Key Performance Indicators) clearly and concisely, allowing for continuous monitoring. For SMEs, which typically operate with limited resources, the ability to react in a timely manner is a competitive advantage. This is especially relevant in sectors such as ecommerce or services, where immediate adjustment is crucial to respond to changes in customer behavior, product demand, or marketing metrics. A well-designed dashboard provides total and real-time visibility into the status of various business areas, becoming a tool that guides daily operations and allows for the immediate identification of improvement opportunities or critical areas.

In the market, there are multiple BI tools and technologies for creating dynamic dashboards that fit the needs and budgets of SMEs. Platforms like Streamlit and Dash by Plotly allow you to develop custom dashboards in Python, integrating real-time metrics interactively. These solutions are ideal for SMEs with internal technical expertise or those seeking advanced customization. Additionally, BI tools like Tableau, Power BI, and Google Data Studio offer powerful and accessible alternatives, enabling SMEs to create visual dashboards without programming, integrating various data sources, from Google Sheets to SQL databases or APIs.

One of the key aspects of implementing dashboards is the configuration of dynamic KPIs, as each sector and company has specific metrics that reflect their performance. These KPIs help SMEs focus their efforts on areas that directly impact their profitability, whether it's the conversion rate in an online store or the response time in a service company. Python offers excellent options to automate these KPIs, calculating and updating values in real-time with libraries like Pandas, and allowing them to be automatically reflected in the dashboards.

Finally, dashboards not only provide an overview of the business but can also be customized for each specific area. Customizing views for finance, marketing, operations, or human resources ensures that each team in the company focuses on the most relevant KPIs for their function, allowing for more precise and appropriate decisions. This implementation of dashboards and dynamic KPIs, using Python or BI tools, is a practical and effective strategy that strengthens informed decision-making, increasing the operational efficiency of SMEs and their ability to quickly adapt to market changes.

- **Introduction to Dashboards**

Dashboards have become an essential tool for data management and decision-making in SMEs. A dashboard, in Business Intelligence terms, is an interactive visual interface that allows real-time monitoring of the company's key metrics or KPIs (Key Performance Indicators), providing a comprehensive and detailed view of the performance across various areas such as sales, marketing, finance, inventory, and operations. This ability to centralize relevant information in one place not only simplifies analysis but also enables informed decision-making with speed and accuracy, a key advantage in today's dynamic and competitive environment.

The value of a dashboard for an SME lies in its ability to transform data into actionable insights. Companies, regardless of their size, collect a large amount of data from their operations daily, but this flow of information only has value when it is turned into useful knowledge for decision-making. A dashboard organizes and presents this data in a comprehensible way, using graphs, tables, and other visual elements, making analysis easier and allowing managers and executives to identify patterns, trends, and possible anomalies immediately.

One of the key aspects of dashboards is that they allow you to monitor the status of different KPIs in real time, eliminating the need to review multiple data sources or reports that may be outdated. For example, a well-configured dashboard allows an SME in the retail sector to see the inventory level of each product, the sales rate, and profit margins in real time, thereby adjusting sales or restocking strategies according to current needs.

Similarly, an SME operating in ecommerce can observe the performance of its digital marketing campaigns, monitoring data such as website traffic, conversion rate, and return on investment (ROI) for each campaign, thus optimizing resources and maximizing the impact of its advertising efforts.

For SMEs, the ability to integrate data from different functional areas into a single dashboard means that correlations and dependencies between KPIs can be observed. A manager can see how inventory relates to sales, how customer satisfaction affects conversion rates, or what impact delivery time has on repeat purchases. This ability to visualize the relationship between different metrics allows SMEs to better understand their business and make operational adjustments on the fly. For example, if a relationship is detected between decreased inventory in key products and a drop in conversion rates, the operations team can take immediate action to restock inventory and improve the customer experience, avoiding a potential loss of sales.

The customization of dashboards is also key in the implementation of Business Intelligence. A well-designed dashboard adapts to the specific needs of the company, allowing each business area to access the metrics it needs in the right format. A sales department, for example, may require a dashboard that shows the daily sales progress, the sales quota achieved compared to monthly targets, and the performance metrics of the sales team. On the other hand, the finance department might need a dashboard that displays revenue, costs, and profit margins, along with charts reflecting the historical evolution of each of these metrics. This customization allows each area of the company to access relevant and specific information, which maximizes efficiency in data analysis and enables more precise decision-making.

From a technical standpoint, dashboards offer the ability to automate data collection and processing. Tools like Python, using libraries such as Pandas, or BI platforms like Power BI and Tableau, allow you to set up an automatic data flow that updates in real-time or at a specified frequency. This means the data is always up-to-date, and dashboard users can rely on the metrics to reflect the current reality. This automation not only reduces the workload associated with report generation but also minimizes human errors and ensures that decisions are made based on accurate and timely information.

Another important advantage of dashboards is their ability to facilitate early detection of problems and opportunities. In an SME, any change in the market, customer demand, or operational efficiency can have a significant impact. A dashboard that updates in real time allows you to identify any deviation or trend change as soon as it occurs, which is especially useful in competitive or high-turnover environments. For example, a sudden change in sales conversion metrics may indicate a problem in the purchase process or in the performance of an advertising campaign, allowing the company to act quickly to resolve it. Likewise, an unexpected increase in traffic for a specific product could signal an opportunity to increase inventory for that item and capitalize on demand.

Dashboards also allow SMEs to set up custom alerts that automatically notify managers when a specific KPI exceeds or falls below a predefined threshold. This type of automatic notification is particularly useful for managing critical aspects such as inventory or customer satisfaction. For example, if the inventory level of a product drops to a critical level, the dashboard can send an alert to the operations team to place a restocking order in time. In this way, dashboards not only serve as a visualization tool but also become a proactive component in business management, alerting managers and preventing potential issues before they become obstacles.

The implementation of dashboards in an SME does not necessarily require a high level of investment in technology. Visualization and BI tools have evolved and become more accessible, meaning there are options that can be adapted to the needs and budget of any business. Platforms like Google Data Studio, Power BI, and Tableau offer solutions that allow SMEs to leverage their data without large investments in infrastructure or advanced technical skills. Additionally, code-based dashboards, such as those that can be developed in Python using Streamlit or Dash, offer almost unlimited flexibility and customization, adapting to any sector or type of business.

In summary, dashboards are a fundamental part of the Business Intelligence strategy for any SME. Their ability to centralize and visualize real-time data allows companies to manage their operations more efficiently and optimize their decision-making processes. Dashboards transform the continuous flow of data into clear and actionable insights, and thanks to their ability to adapt to the specific needs of each business, they have become indispensable tools for improving performance and ensuring a competitive advantage in today's market.

- ## Tools for building dynamic dashboards

The construction of dynamic dashboards with Python has transformed the ability of SMEs to monitor and analyze their data in real-time. Among the most notable tools for creating these information visualization systems are Streamlit and Dash, each offering different advantages that can be tailored to the specific needs of companies in terms of ease of use, customization, and functionality. Both platforms stand out for their flexibility and power, allowing SMEs to create visual interfaces that not only present the relevant KPIs and metrics but also integrate interactivity and real-time connection with various data sources. In a context where quick decisions are crucial, an updated and accessible dashboard is an essential tool to ensure that data guides business operations and strategy optimally.

Streamlit has established itself as one of the most accessible solutions for creating interactive dashboards without requiring deep knowledge of web development. Its simplicity allows users to focus on data analysis and information visualization without worrying about the backend structure, making it an ideal option for data developers who want to quickly implement functional and visual interfaces. On the other hand, Dash stands out for its flexibility and the extensive customization options it offers to developers, making it a robust choice for SMEs looking for a more advanced dashboard with specific functionalities and customized settings. Both tools have the potential to transform the way SMEs use their data, helping make information not only more accessible but also more useful for guiding strategic and operational decisions.

- ### Streamlit: Building interactive dashboards with simplicity and efficiency

Streamlit has quickly gained popularity due to its ease of use and minimalist approach to building interactive applications in Python. The tool allows data analysts and data scientists to develop functional dashboards in minutes, focusing on data logic and visualizations without the need for extensive web development. Streamlit uses an intuitive syntax, so users can create applications simply by following the Python programming flow, without worrying about creating interfaces or complex graphic elements.

The construction of a dashboard in Streamlit begins with installing the package and importing the library. Once installed, the developer can start the dashboard by simply running the command streamlit run file_name.py. This functionality is very helpful for data analysts who want to conduct quick tests and create prototypes without committing significant resources to development.

Streamlit allows users to easily add interactive elements, such as option selectors, sliders, and input boxes, which is ideal for adjusting filters and parameters in data analysis. This type of interaction is especially useful in a dashboard environment, as it allows the user to customize the visualization and analyze the data from different perspectives without having to modify the base code. For example, a retail company can use Streamlit to visualize daily sales, allowing the user to select specific dates or product categories through a dropdown menu. These interactive components enhance the user experience and allow for in-depth data exploration without requiring advanced technical knowledge.

In addition, Streamlit allows easy integration of charts from popular libraries like Matplotlib, Plotly, or Seaborn, which offers flexibility in creating custom visualizations that best represent the data in the specific business context. This is crucial for SMEs that want to highlight metrics such as sales, inventory, and performance indicators in a graphical format that facilitates visual interpretation. For example, an SME can create a bar chart to visualize the weekly evolution of sales, or a line graph to show trends over time. The integration of these libraries ensures that the dashboard maintains a professional visual quality, which is a fundamental aspect in data presentation for decision-making.

Another key feature of Streamlit is its ability to update data in real-time. By setting the data source to update periodically or through API requests, the dashboard in Streamlit can automatically reflect changes in the data without manual intervention. This allows SMEs to stay up-to-date with the latest metrics, such as available inventory, sales volume on a specific day, or the status of marketing campaigns. This type of real-time updating is crucial in fast-paced environments like ecommerce or retail, where the ability to make decisions based on current data can make a difference in profitability.

Streamlit's architecture is designed to optimize the workflow in Python, allowing users to make real-time adjustments to the code and see the changes immediately in the dashboard. This makes Streamlit ideal for creating dashboards that require quick tweaks, such as when the data analysis or marketing team needs to test different visualization configurations to identify patterns or correlations in business metrics. This agile development approach allows for a smooth and easy implementation of Streamlit in business environments, without the need for advanced infrastructure or front-end knowledge.

- **Dash (Plotly): Flexibility and advanced customization for business dashboards**

While Streamlit focuses on simplicity and quick deployment, Plotly's Dash is designed for those who seek a visualization platform with more advanced customization options. Dash combines Python with web development capabilities to create complex, highly interactive dashboards, ideal for SMEs that require detailed control over visual elements and dashboard interactivity.

Dash allows building interactive data visualization web applications using Python, HTML, and CSS, which provides a deeper level of customization. This means that developers can adjust not only the content of the dashboard but also its appearance and design, creating a more refined interface tailored to the specific needs of the company. This flexibility is especially useful for those SMEs that want to project a professional and differentiated image in their dashboards, or that need specific functionalities not available in other BI tools.

A key aspect of Dash is its ability to integrate real-time data and dynamically update dashboard components. This is particularly useful for monitoring KPIs that change quickly, such as marketing campaign performance or transaction volume in an online store. Dash allows you to set up callbacks in Python that activate when the user interacts with the dashboard or when the data changes. This makes it easy to create dashboards that respond to user input or real-time events, enhancing the user experience and providing a visualization environment that adapts to the changing needs of the business.

Dash offers advanced interactive components such as 3D charts, dynamic tables, and geographic maps, allowing SMEs to present their data in an intuitive and visually appealing way. For example, a logistics company can use interactive maps to track delivery routes and optimize route planning based on real-time traffic patterns. Similarly, a retail SME can use advanced bar and line charts to analyze sales trends of different product categories across various locations, adjusting their inventory and pricing decisions based on these insights.

Furthermore, Dash allows developers to connect the dashboard to different data sources using APIs, SQL databases, and CSV files, among other formats. This integration capability ensures that the metrics and KPIs displayed on the dashboard are always up-to-date and that the system can easily adapt to changes in the company's data infrastructure. The connection with APIs is particularly useful for SMEs that want to obtain external data, such as Google Analytics statistics, social media, or real-time financial data, which enhances the depth of analysis and provides a comprehensive view of the company's performance.

Another key benefit of Dash is its ability to be hosted on servers and accessed from web browsers, which allows you to share the dashboard with different team members or even external partners in a simple and secure way. This capability is especially valuable for SMEs with distributed teams or business partners who need access to updated information in real-time. By hosting the dashboard on a secure server, SMEs can ensure that data access is controlled and that only authorized users have access to sensitive business information.

The Dash community and extensive documentation are also beneficial for SME developers looking for a reliable and scalable BI solution. Backed by Plotly, Dash offers a range of additional tools and plugins that make it easy to customize and integrate new features. Moreover, the active community allows users to solve common problems, learn new techniques, and improve their development skills, which is an advantage for SMEs seeking to maximize the value of their investments in BI technology.

Both tools, Streamlit and Dash, offer robust and customizable options for creating dashboards in Python, but each is better suited to different needs. While Streamlit is ideal for quick and simple implementation, Dash provides a more advanced development platform that allows for the creation of complex, high-performance dashboards. The choice between the two tools will depend on the SME's priorities, its data structure, the specific goals of the dashboard, and the level of customization required. In any case, both options have the potential to transform how SMEs use their data for decision-making and operational management, providing a competitive advantage in an increasingly data-driven market.

- ## Integration with BI tools

The implementation of Business Intelligence (BI) tools has revolutionized how SMEs access, visualize, and use their data for decision-making. Among the most popular and accessible BI solutions for companies of all sizes are

Tableau, Power BI, and Google Data Studio, each with unique features and diverse integration capabilities that allow direct connection to various data sources. These BI tools not only simplify data management but also enable SMEs to create advanced dashboards that automatically update with the latest metrics and KPIs, providing a real-time view of business performance without requiring complex programming knowledge.

Tableau and Power BI are widely used visualization platforms in the BI field due to their flexibility and ability to integrate with various data sources, such as Google Sheets, SQL databases, and APIs. These tools allow businesses to access data directly and securely, facilitating the creation of dashboards that present relevant information in an intuitive and visually appealing way. Google Data Studio, on the other hand, is a free option developed by Google that allows the creation of dashboards directly connected to Google Sheets, Google Analytics, and other Google tools, making it ideal for SMEs seeking an efficient and low-cost BI solution. Below, we examine these tools and their implementation in creating dynamic dashboards and advanced visualization for SMEs.

- **Tableau and Power BI: Advanced Tools for Business Intelligence Dashboards**

Tableau and Power BI are BI tools that allow SMEs to create interactive and customized dashboards, capable of automatically updating with data from a variety of sources. Both platforms offer a range of advanced features, such as direct connectivity to databases and data analysis tools, enabling companies to visualize their metrics in real-time and perform a deep analysis of their performance.

Tableau is known for its advanced visual approach and ease of handling large volumes of data, making it a powerful tool for companies that need to visualize and analyze complex or massive data sets. Tableau allows users to connect their dashboard with multiple data sources, whether through SQL databases, Google Sheets, cloud services, or APIs. This integration capability ensures that data is always up-to-date, providing a real-time view of KPIs and key business metrics. Tableau is particularly useful for SMEs that manage large volumes of data or need to perform advanced analyses, as it allows the creation of complex and customized charts that help uncover hidden patterns and trends.

Furthermore, Tableau offers an intuitive drag-and-drop interface that allows users to build visualizations without needing advanced programming skills. However, to fully leverage Tableau's capabilities, it's advisable for users to understand the basics of data analysis and dashboard design, which will enable them to create more meaningful and effective visualizations. Tableau also offers a range of customization options, from interactive filters to advanced charts, allowing SMEs to tailor the dashboard to their specific needs and display only the most relevant metrics for each business area.

Power BI, on the other hand, is a tool developed by Microsoft that combines BI functionalities with native integration into the Microsoft ecosystem. This makes it an attractive option for SMEs already using tools like Excel, SharePoint, or Azure, as Power BI allows for seamless integration with these services. Like Tableau, Power BI allows connection with various data sources, including SQL databases, CSV files, Google Sheets, and third-party APIs. This integration capability is key for companies that want to centralize their data in one place, providing managers and department heads with a comprehensive and up-to-date view of the company's KPIs.

One of Power BI's standout features is its ability to work with large volumes of data, allowing businesses to analyze big data sets without compromising system performance. Power BI uses advanced compression technology, making it easy to analyze massive datasets without slowing down the system, which is especially useful for SMEs dealing with large volumes of sales, inventory, or digital marketing data. Additionally, Power BI offers data modeling and custom calculation functionalities, enabling users to create specific metrics that more accurately reflect the company's needs.

Both tools, Tableau and Power BI, allow automatic updates in dashboards, which is essential for real-time monitoring of KPIs. By using live connections to data sources, dashboards in Tableau and Power BI can always display the most current metrics, enabling SMEs to adjust their strategies based on up-to-date data. This real-time update capability is crucial for sectors like retail, logistics, and ecommerce, where changes in data can reflect customer demand or the performance of a marketing campaign.

- **Google Data Studio: A free option for creating interactive dashboards**

Google Data Studio is a free and accessible BI tool that allows SMEs to build interactive dashboards without additional costs. As part of the Google ecosystem, Data Studio offers direct integration with services like Google Sheets, Google Analytics, and BigQuery, making it easy to access key business data without complex setups. This tool is ideal for SMEs looking for a cost-effective but powerful BI solution, as it enables the creation of visual and dynamic dashboards with real-time data updates.

Data Studio's interface is intuitive and allows users to build visualizations using a 'drag and drop' method, which makes it easy to create charts and tables that present key metrics clearly and attractively. Additionally, Data Studio offers the ability to customize the design and appearance of dashboards, allowing SMEs to adapt the data visualization to their brand's image and style. Like Tableau and Power BI, Data Studio allows the creation of interactive filters, making it easier to explore data and analyze specific metrics according to current needs.

One of the benefits of Google Data Studio is its ability to connect directly with Google Sheets, a tool widely used by SMEs to store and manage data. This integration allows any changes made in a Google spreadsheet to be automatically reflected in the Data Studio dashboard, ensuring that the data presented in the dashboard is always up to date. Additionally, Data Studio integrates with Google Analytics, which is particularly useful for SMEs managing a website or online store who want to monitor traffic metrics, conversions, and user behavior in real time.

Data Studio also allows integration with external data sources through connectors, which expands the possibilities for data analysis and visualization for SMEs. There are native connectors for services like MySQL, PostgreSQL, and BigQuery, as well as third-party connectors that enable integration with APIs and external services like CRMs, ecommerce platforms, and digital marketing tools. This integration capability allows SMEs to consolidate data from different business areas into a single dashboard, providing a comprehensive view of the company's performance and facilitating informed decision-making.

A key feature of Google Data Studio is its ability to share dashboards easily, as it allows users to send links or access invitations to other team members or external collaborators. This is especially useful for SMEs that need different departments or business partners to have access to up-to-date information on business performance. Additionally, Data Studio allows you to set access permissions and restrictions, ensuring that only authorized users can view and edit the dashboard data, thus protecting the confidentiality of sensitive information.

The integration with Google Analytics is another significant advantage of Data Studio, as it allows SMEs to analyze the performance of their website or online store through customized visualizations. Data Studio dashboards can display metrics like web traffic, bounce rate, conversions, and user behavior on the site, which is essential for optimizing digital marketing strategies and improving customer experience. The ability to monitor these data in real-time enables SMEs to adjust their campaigns and strategies based on user behavior, thereby maximizing the impact of their marketing efforts.

In conclusion, Tableau, Power BI, and Google Data Studio all offer SMEs effective tools to build dynamic dashboards that enable advanced data visualization and analysis. While Tableau and Power BI stand out for their ability to handle large volumes of data and their extensive functionality, Google Data Studio is a free and accessible option that allows SMEs to create visual dashboards without a significant investment.

- **Setting Dynamic KPIs**

The configuration of dynamic KPIs (Key Performance Indicators) is an essential component of Business Intelligence (BI) strategies in any company, and it is especially valuable for SMEs looking to improve their efficiency and competitiveness in a constantly changing market. KPIs help companies focus their efforts on measurable and quantifiable metrics that reflect their performance in key areas such as sales, customer satisfaction, operational efficiency, and profitability. Instead of relying on traditional reports that can quickly become outdated, dynamic KPIs are integrated into real-time BI systems, allowing companies to monitor performance at all times and react swiftly to any deviation or change in market conditions.

For SMEs in different sectors, the initial challenge is often defining the KPIs that truly matter and contribute to achieving their strategic objectives. An online store, for example, can benefit from performance metrics such as conversion rate, average ticket size, and customer acquisition cost, while a service company might prioritize KPIs like response time and customer satisfaction index. These indicators not only measure current performance but also provide key insights for continuous improvement.

In the automation of KPIs with Python, metrics can be calculated and updated in real-time using libraries like Pandas. With these tools, companies can structure and analyze dynamic data that is immediately reflected in dashboards. This capability is essential for SMEs seeking efficiency, as it allows business leaders to quickly visualize the most relevant metrics and make informed decisions. Next, we will explore in depth how to select strategic KPIs and how to implement effective automation to keep these indicators updated in BI dashboards.

- **Defining relevant KPIs for SMEs**

The selection of relevant and strategic KPIs is the first step in setting up a dynamic BI system that functions as an effective decision-making tool. The choice of KPIs should be based on the specific business objectives of the company and the characteristics of the sector in which it operates. For an SME, choosing the wrong KPIs can lead to a misguided focus and the investment of resources in areas that do not add significant value to the business. The key is to identify those metrics that truly impact profitability, customer satisfaction, and long-term growth.

For an online store, KPIs can focus on aspects of the sales funnel and customer retention, as these factors have a direct impact on the profitability and growth of the business. One of the most common KPIs is the conversion rate, which measures the percentage of visitors who complete a purchase. This indicator is essential for understanding the effectiveness of the website and marketing campaigns in attracting and convincing potential customers. A low conversion rate may indicate problems in the purchase process or a lack of relevance in the campaigns, and can help guide improvements towards increasing conversions.

Another relevant KPI for an online store is the average ticket, which represents the average spend per transaction. A high average ticket can indicate a successful upselling or cross-selling strategy, while a low average ticket may suggest the need to review pricing or promotional strategies to encourage higher-value purchases. This metric allows the company to optimize its marketing campaigns and adjust its inventory based on customer preferences.

The customer acquisition cost (CAC) is another critical KPI in the online world, as it measures how much it costs to acquire a new customer through marketing and sales investments. This KPI is essential for ensuring the company's profitability, as if the CAC is too high compared to the customer's lifetime value (LTV), the company could be losing money on its acquisition efforts. This indicator allows evaluating the effectiveness of marketing campaigns and optimizing the budget allocated to customer acquisition.

For a service company, KPIs may be more focused on customer satisfaction and operational efficiency. Response time, for example, is a KPI that measures the average time it takes the company to respond to customer requests. In a sector where customer service is crucial, such as consulting or technical support, this KPI is essential to ensure that customers receive prompt and effective service. A fast response time can improve customer satisfaction and retention, while a slow response time can lead to frustration and a decrease in customer loyalty.

The Customer Satisfaction Index (CSAT) is another important KPI for service companies, as it measures the level of customer satisfaction with the products or services received. This indicator is vital for understanding customer perception and adjusting processes to improve the service experience. CSAT can be obtained through surveys and is reflected on a satisfaction scale that helps the company identify areas for improvement in customer service.

Once the relevant KPIs for the company have been defined, it is important to set up measurement systems that allow these indicators to be calculated automatically and accurately. This involves designing data capture and standardization processes that facilitate the generation of KPIs in a real-time BI dashboard. Data collection must be continuous and consistent to ensure that KPIs reflect the business reality at all times and enable agile, data-driven decision-making.

- **Automation of KPIs with Python**

Automating KPIs with Python is an efficient and cost-effective strategy for SMEs looking to implement a dynamic BI system without relying on expensive BI tools. Python offers a wide range of libraries and tools that make it easy to manipulate data and create automatic update processes for KPIs. By automating the calculation and updating of KPIs, companies can keep their dashboards in real-time and eliminate the need to manually update metrics, reducing errors and increasing efficiency.

One of the most widely used libraries in Python for KPI automation is Pandas, which allows for quick and efficient data manipulation and analysis. Pandas offers advanced functionalities for loading, cleaning, and transforming data, which is essential for obtaining accurate and consistent KPIs. Automating KPIs with Python starts with importing data from various sources, such as CSV files, SQL databases, or APIs. Once imported, the data can be cleaned and transformed using Pandas functions to ensure they are in the correct format for KPI calculation.

For example, to calculate the conversion rate of an online store, you can automate the process by dividing the number of sales by the total number of visitors over a given period. This calculation can be run periodically using a Python script that updates the dashboard each time new visit and sales data are recorded. Below is an example of Python code to calculate the conversion rate using Pandas:

```
import pandas as pd

# Datos de ejemplo
data = {
    'fecha': ['2023-01-01', '2023-01-02', '2023-01-03'],
    'visitas': [100, 150, 200],
    'ventas': [5, 10, 15]
}

# Creación del DataFrame
df = pd.DataFrame(data)

# Calcular la tasa de conversión
df['tasa_conversion'] = df['ventas'] / df['visitas'] * 100

# Visualización de resultados
print(df)
```

```
        fecha  visitas  ventas  tasa_conversion
0  2023-01-01      100       5         5.000000
1  2023-01-02      150      10         6.666667
2  2023-01-03      200      15         7.500000
```

This code calculates the conversion rate for each day based on visits and sales, updating the rate in real-time on a dashboard through a loop that refreshes the data as new records are received. Additionally, by integrating it into a real-time dashboard, the company can monitor the effectiveness of its marketing campaigns and optimize its strategy based on the results.

Another example of a KPI that can be automated with Python is the customer acquisition cost (CAC). To calculate this KPI, the total marketing expenditure is divided by the number of new customers acquired in a specific period. The Python script can update the CAC every time a new customer transaction is recorded or a marketing campaign investment is made, allowing the company to adjust its marketing budget accurately.

Beyond basic calculations, Python allows for the automation of KPI visualization in interactive dashboards using libraries like Plotly or Matplotlib, which is essential for providing a visual experience that makes data interpretation and decision-making easier. These libraries allow for the creation of customized charts, such as line, bar, and scatter plots, that show the evolution of KPIs in real-time and help company leaders identify key trends and patterns in business performance.

For service companies, automating the customer satisfaction index (CSAT) is essential for monitoring customer experience and responding proactively to customer needs. The CSAT can be calculated using surveys that collect customer satisfaction levels on a scale of 1 to 5, and Python can use this data to calculate the average satisfaction over a specific period. By integrating these results into a real-time dashboard, the company can see how customer satisfaction varies based on different factors, such as response time or service quality, and adjust its strategy to improve the customer experience.

In conclusion, setting up dynamic KPIs and automating them with Python is an accessible and powerful strategy for SMEs looking to optimize their performance and make data-driven decisions. From selecting strategic KPIs to implementing automated scripts that calculate and update metrics in real-time, KPI automation allows companies to simplify their monitoring process, improve efficiency, and react quickly to any changes in the business environment. By integrating KPIs into interactive and visually appealing dashboards, SMEs can turn their data into actionable insights that contribute to the long-term growth and sustainability of the business.

- **Customization of dashboards for different business areas**

Customizing dashboards for different business areas allows SMEs to tailor their Business Intelligence (BI) systems to the specific needs of each team, making it easier to monitor key performance indicators (KPIs) and improve decision-making in every department. As companies grow and face larger data volumes, the need for specialized dashboards for each area becomes crucial to optimize workflows, reduce response times, and increase overall efficiency. By creating dashboard views that reflect the specific priorities and challenges of finance, marketing, and operations, companies can centralize their data in a visually accessible and comprehensible system that promotes a data-driven culture.

For financial teams, customizing dashboards allows them to focus on essential KPIs for the company's sustainability and growth. Finance departments often need a clear view of profitability, profit margins, expenses, and cash flow. A financial dashboard designed specifically for this team should not only display basic accounting metrics but also include alerts for budget deviations, cash flow forecast reports, and real-time trend analysis. For example, using line or bar graphs, the finance team can track revenue trends over key periods and compare projected figures with actual ones.

Marketing departments, on the other hand, require a completely different perspective. A marketing dashboard must focus on metrics that reflect campaign success, customer acquisition efficiency, and user satisfaction. By integrating specific KPIs like return on ad spend (ROAS), conversion rate, and customer acquisition cost, the marketing team can monitor their advertising efforts in real time and adjust strategies on the fly. Additionally, data on social media engagement and website performance are essential for assessing brand perception and tailoring content based on audience preferences.

The operations area, on the other hand, benefits from a dashboard that focuses on the efficiency of production processes, inventory management, and logistical optimization. In this case, the key KPIs include inventory turnover rate, production cycle time, resource utilization, and delivery timelines. These indicators allow operations managers to observe patterns and adjust their production methods to reduce costs and improve service quality. Through a visually intuitive interface, the operations team can monitor production capacity in real-time, detect bottlenecks, and anticipate inventory needs based on projected demand.

Every functional area within the company has unique and specific needs when it comes to data visualization, and customized dashboards offer an effective solution by allowing each team direct access to the information that truly matters for their performance. The customization of dashboards enables each area of the company to focus its efforts on the critical points that affect their objectives, which facilitates the alignment of individual departmental strategies with the company's overall goals. A well-designed dashboard not only helps managers monitor and evaluate current performance but also provides a foundation for making strategic and tactical adjustments in real time.

For the creation of these customized dashboards, advanced BI tools are used to develop specific views for each area. These tools facilitate data integration from multiple sources, allowing the combination of sales, inventory, human resources, and marketing information into a single analysis platform. For the finance team, an ideal dashboard should include line charts to analyze revenue trends over time and bar charts showing the comparison of expenses versus budgets. Additionally, summary tables can be included to detail expense items by category and period, along with cash flow projections based on income and expense trends.

In the case of marketing dashboards, it's useful to include a combination of conversion charts, sales funnel analysis, and campaign reach metrics to provide the team with a detailed view of user interactions with the brand. Heat maps can be useful for analyzing visitor behavior on the website, allowing the marketing team to visualize which sections of the page attract the most attention. Additionally, a social media monitoring widget can be included to capture audience interaction and engagement in real time, allowing the team to assess brand perception and adjust content strategies based on audience reactions.

The dashboard for the operations team should include charts and visualizations that make it easier to track inventory and production at each stage. Control charts, such as Pareto diagrams, can be very useful for detecting recurring issues or identifying areas for improvement in production processes. Additionally, a summary table showing real-time inventory, along with alerts indicating low stock levels, allows operations managers to make quick decisions and avoid disruptions in the supply chain. To optimize logistics, a route map using geospatial data for delivery planning can provide a comprehensive view of transport routes and vehicle locations, helping to improve delivery times and reduce operational costs.

Another key aspect of personalized dashboards is the ability to provide real-time data and allow flexible configuration according to the needs of each department. Dashboards must be easily accessible and designed so that data updates continuously, providing users with an up-to-date view of their KPIs at all times. The ability to set personalized alerts is also an essential element, as it allows teams to receive instant notifications of significant data changes. For example, the finance team can receive an alert if expenses spike in a specific category or if anomalies are detected in revenue projections. Similarly, the marketing team can be alerted to a drop in conversion rates or social media engagement, enabling an immediate response.

Regarding the technology used to implement these dashboards, there are several options that allow you to customize data visualization for each business area. BI tools like Power BI, Tableau, Google Data Studio, and Plotly's Dash are excellent choices for creating highly configurable dashboards that offer flexibility and integration with various data sources. Power BI, for example, allows for advanced analysis and the creation of interactive charts with custom filters that make data navigation easier. Google Data Studio is an ideal tool for companies that want to easily integrate data from sources like Google Analytics and Google Ads, providing relevant data visualizations for marketing and sales teams.

In addition to choosing the right tools, creating a customized dashboard involves focusing on user experience and interface accessibility. An effective dashboard should be intuitive, allowing users to quickly find the information they need without requiring advanced technical skills. The structure of the dashboard must be clear and organized, with appropriate visualizations for each type of data and a color scheme that makes it easy to distinguish between different metrics. For the finance team, for example, it's essential that data related to income and expenses are easily accessible and that trends are displayed clearly and prominently. For the marketing team, conversion graphs and reach metrics should take center stage on the dashboard, with interaction charts and heat maps that help identify campaign performance.

Customizing dashboards also requires a stable connection to data sources to ensure that information is updated continuously and accurately. Real-time data integration is especially useful in environments where decisions need to be made quickly, such as in the case of an online store monitoring conversion rates and traffic in real-time during a sales campaign. By connecting the dashboard to cloud databases or APIs that provide real-time data, teams in each area can receive up-to-the-minute information and make timely decisions based on accurate data.

For SMEs, the ability to customize dashboards and have real-time data visualizations represents a significant competitive advantage. In a market environment where agility is key, having a clear and accessible view of KPIs allows companies to quickly adapt to market fluctuations and improve operational efficiency. Additionally, personalized dashboards foster collaboration between teams, as each area can focus on its own goals while sharing a common view of the data that impacts the business. The ability to set up specific dashboards for finance, marketing, and operations strengthens data-driven decision-making and allows SMEs to align their efforts with their growth and profitability objectives.

9.3. Real-time data-driven decision making

In today's context, the ability to make real-time data-driven decisions has become a crucial differentiator for businesses. For SMEs, this is even more relevant, as operating with limited resources makes efficiency and agility essential for success. Unlike traditional decision-making, where reports and analysis can take days or even weeks, a real-time approach allows companies to act immediately in response to market changes or customer behavior. This not only improves operational efficiency but also creates opportunities to maximize revenue, optimize resources, and enhance customer satisfaction.

Real-time decision-making allows SMEs to adapt to constantly changing market dynamics. For example, if a marketing campaign is not generating the expected results, an SME can immediately modify its approach, adjusting elements like content or targeting to maximize return on investment. This capability is especially useful in competitive and highly digital environments, where changes in demand or consumer trends can have a direct impact on profitability. In terms of inventory, real-time data can automatically alert the need to restock a high-demand product or adjust distribution based on emerging buying patterns.

Technologies for real-time data integration, such as APIs and data monitoring tools with Python, enable companies to connect their information systems into a single centralized platform. This integration allows data from Google Analytics, CRM, and ecommerce platforms to be updated in a data visualization dashboard, facilitating access to up-to-date information and avoiding reliance on outdated analysis reports. For SMEs managing marketing campaigns, inventories, or pricing, this continuous update allows them to make automatic adjustments based on predefined rules or specific notifications, enabling agile and optimized management of their operations.

In addition, automating real-time monitoring with libraries like Watchdog and Socket.io in Python allows changes to be detected and responded to immediately. These tools make it possible to implement instant notifications on a dashboard or send automatic alerts if significant data variations occur. This type of continuous monitoring not only increases response speed but also reduces the manual workload on teams, allowing them to focus on strategic tasks. For SMEs, this means better resource allocation and a more effective focus on value-added activities.

Real-time data-driven decision-making is a powerful strategy for enhancing the operational agility and competitiveness of SMEs, creating an environment where data is transformed into concrete and timely actions. This capability allows companies not only to react but also to anticipate and adapt their operations to maximize performance and respond effectively to market needs.

- ## Importance of Real-Time Decision Making

Real-time decision-making is a transformative resource for SMEs looking to optimize their processes and respond quickly to the changing dynamics of the market. In an increasingly competitive and technological business environment, the ability to react immediately to demand fluctuations, shifts in consumer trends, or price adjustments can be the factor that determines the success or failure of a strategy. For small and medium-sized enterprises, which often operate with limited resources, this type of operational agility provides a key competitive advantage, allowing them to improve efficiency and quickly adapt to new opportunities or challenges.

Real-time decision-making requires a solid data management structure that begins with the ability to constantly collect and update relevant information, such as marketing campaign performance, inventory levels, prices, and customer satisfaction. Current platforms and technologies allow data to be collected and analyzed instantly, making it easier for decision-makers to access relevant information at all times. With this up-to-date information, SMEs can make decisions based on accurate and current data, rather than relying on monthly reports or outdated analyses that can become irrelevant in a dynamic market.

One of the main benefits of this capability is the agility to respond to sudden changes in demand or consumer behavior. For example, during periods of high commercial activity, such as discount campaigns or seasonal events, SMEs with real-time information can adjust their inventories or modify their advertising campaigns on the fly, avoiding stockouts or resource waste. In a situation where a specific product is generating high demand, an SME can decide to reinforce the stock of this item and redirect its advertising budget towards those customer segments most likely to buy it. This agility to optimize inventory and marketing strategy in real-time reduces unnecessary costs and maximizes revenue.

Moreover, real-time decision-making has a direct impact on the operational efficiency of SMEs, optimizing every available resource. Instead of allocating staff or budget to areas that aren't generating the expected performance, companies can quickly analyze which processes are most effective and where improvements can be made. With real-time analytics tools, certain aspects of decision-making can be automated, so if an anomaly or deviation is detected in the data, the system sends an alert or even executes automatic actions. For example, if traffic in an online store suddenly increases, the system can trigger a high-demand alert, allowing inventory managers to make strategic decisions without delay.

To facilitate real-time decision-making, access to real-time data must be smooth and continuous, which involves using integrated analytics platforms that provide a consolidated view of all key business metrics. Many SMEs turn to customized dashboards, which centralize information from different areas (sales, marketing, inventory) in one place, making data access and understanding easier. Implementing these monitoring systems ensures that data is not only collected and stored but also constantly updated to reflect the current state of the business, eliminating the need to rely on static reports that can quickly become obsolete.

Agility in responding to unexpected events is another advantage of real-time decision-making. Imagine a situation where a supplier experiences a delay in delivering key materials or products. With a real-time monitoring system, company managers can be notified immediately, allowing them to quickly evaluate alternatives and take corrective action before the delay significantly impacts the company's operations. This responsiveness prevents issues from piling up and creates a more agile and efficient workflow, reducing downtime and improving customer satisfaction by ensuring that orders are fulfilled on time.

In the realm of digital marketing, real-time decision-making allows for adjusting campaigns based on their performance, which is especially useful on platforms that provide instant results, like social media or Google Ads. SMEs can continuously monitor the performance of their ads and make changes to content, targeting, or investment based on the results. If a campaign shows a low return on investment (ROI), those in charge can pause it and redirect the budget towards a more effective strategy, thus optimizing every euro invested. This real-time adjustment capability prevents the company from continuing to invest in ineffective strategies, allowing it to maximize the return on its advertising budget.

The optimization of real-time pricing is another area where SMEs can benefit by implementing decision-making systems based on current data. With dynamic pricing algorithms, companies can adjust prices based on factors like demand, competitor behavior, and market conditions. In the e-commerce sector, this strategy can be particularly effective, as it allows SMEs to attract more customers by offering competitive prices at key moments or taking advantage of demand increases to maximize revenue. For example, if a product shows an increase in demand, the dynamic pricing system could automatically adjust the price of this item to optimize profit margins, while for a product with low demand, the price could be adjusted to encourage sales.

Inventory management is another area where real-time decision-making can make a difference. A real-time connected inventory system allows the company to maintain optimal stock levels at all times, avoiding both shortages and excess products. By receiving instant data on the inventory level of each product, company managers can adjust their orders to suppliers more accurately, optimizing warehouse space and reducing storage costs. If a product sells quickly and stock decreases, the monitoring system can trigger an alert to notify managers to place a new order, preventing stockouts. This approach helps improve customer satisfaction by ensuring that products are available when the customer needs them and also maximizes revenue by avoiding lost sales due to out-of-stock items.

Real-time decision-making also has a positive impact on the customer experience. By having real-time information on user behavior and preferences, SMEs can personalize their offers and improve the customer experience. If it's detected that a customer has repeatedly visited a product on the website without making a purchase, the system can send a personalized offer to encourage conversion. This ability to react based on user interactions and offer a personalized experience not only improves the conversion rate but also increases customer loyalty, as they perceive a company that is proactive and focused on meeting their needs.

The use of machine learning and predictive algorithms in real-time decision-making is another powerful tool that SMEs can implement. Through predictive models, companies can anticipate demand and adjust their strategies before significant changes occur. For example, if the algorithm detects a rising trend in demand for a specific product, it can recommend an adjustment in production or inventory to meet that projected demand. In this sense, real-time decision-making is not only about responding to current events but also about forecasting and anticipating future needs, enabling more strategic and proactive management.

Finally, the cultural and organizational aspect of real-time decision-making is also essential. Implementing this approach requires the company to adopt a data-driven culture, where every team member understands the importance of using information as the basis for their daily decisions. This means SMEs must invest in training their employees to understand the benefits and possibilities of real-time data systems, so they can correctly interpret the information and use it effectively. When all levels of the organization participate in the data-driven decision-making process, the company as a whole becomes more agile, cohesive, and focused on achieving its strategic objectives.

In conclusion, real-time decision-making represents an invaluable opportunity for SMEs looking to improve their competitiveness and operational agility. By implementing real-time data systems, these businesses can reduce costs, optimize their operations, and increase customer satisfaction, making the most of every opportunity in a constantly changing market.

- **Real-time data integration with APIs**

The integration of real-time data through APIs is a key tool for SMEs to achieve a rapid and accurate response capacity in their decision-making processes. In an environment where customer needs and market conditions can change in a matter of hours or minutes, having up-to-date data allows SMEs to adjust their strategies in real time and maximize efficiency. APIs (Application Programming Interfaces) enable different applications and platforms to connect and exchange data automatically and continuously. Through these connections, SMEs can extract information from key platforms like Google Analytics, CRM systems, and ecommerce applications, and display this data on dashboards that update in real time. This infrastructure facilitates continuous monitoring of performance indicators, allowing decision-makers to act promptly in response to changes in critical business metrics.

Google Analytics is one of the most widely used platforms by SMEs for web traffic and customer behavior analysis. The Google Analytics API allows access to data on visits, interactions, and conversions on a webpage and transfers this information to a dashboard that updates in real-time. This is particularly useful in digital marketing campaigns, where understanding user behavior at each stage of the conversion funnel is crucial. If an SME sees a significant increase in traffic to a product page, it can adjust its marketing strategy to capitalize on this flow, whether by optimizing the page, launching a specific promotion, or reallocating its advertising budget to maximize the conversion of visitors into buyers. Integrating Google Analytics data through its API allows for continuous analysis available in real-time, without needing to download reports or wait for report generation.

In the context of customer relationship management, CRM (Customer Relationship Management) APIs allow SMEs to automatically extract and update customer data. CRM platforms like Salesforce or HubSpot store information about past interactions, purchase history, and customer preferences, which is invaluable for making strategic sales and marketing decisions. By connecting this data to a real-time dashboard, decision-makers can instantly see if a key customer has recently interacted with a marketing campaign, shown interest in a specific product, or raised a complaint or inquiry. With this information, the company can tailor its communication strategy or adjust the offer in real-time, achieving greater customer satisfaction and increasing the likelihood of conversion. CRM data integration also ensures that the sales team is always aware of any changes in customer behavior, optimizing the follow-up process and improving service quality.

For ecommerce companies, integrating APIs is essential to monitor customer activity on their sales platform and respond quickly to fluctuations in demand. Platforms like Shopify and WooCommerce have APIs that allow you to obtain data on inventory, the most visited products, and items in the shopping cart. This data is useful not only for managing inventory but also for improving the user experience. For example, if the system detects that a specific item is in high demand, the company can launch a special promotion or adjust the price to optimize profit margins. Additionally, with real-time API integration, SMEs can implement automatic alerts to be notified when a product's inventory is low, making it easier to plan and avoid lost sales due to stockouts.

The implementation of these real-time integrations can be complemented by using Python libraries like Watchdog and Socket.io, which facilitate continuous data monitoring and allow for automated actions based on specific changes in metrics. Watchdog is a Python library that monitors files and directories for changes, which is useful when the company needs to know instantly if a file or database has been modified. For example, in an inventory system connected to an online store, Watchdog can be configured to detect changes in the stock level of each product. If the inventory of an item falls below a critical level, Watchdog can trigger an alert for the purchasing team to place a reorder. Additionally, automatic actions can be programmed to make the order directly in the supplier's system, automating inventory management and ensuring that products are available to meet customer demand.

Socket.io, on the other hand, is a real-time communication tool that allows continuous and uninterrupted information exchange between the server and the client. This library is especially useful for applications that require constant and rapid updates, such as interactive dashboards where SMEs monitor performance indicators. With Socket.io, the server can send data to users as soon as there are changes in metrics, without the need for the user to manually refresh the page. This is particularly beneficial in contexts where quick decision-making is key. For example, in a digital marketing campaign, data on ad performance (such as clicks and conversions) can be sent in real-time to the dashboard via Socket.io, allowing the marketing team to make strategy adjustments based on current results.

The integration of APIs is also essential for automating data updates in dashboards, which facilitates real-time monitoring without the need for manual intervention. By automating these updates, those responsible for each area can access the most up-to-date information without delays, optimizing decision-making. In the context of a marketing campaign, for example, the team can instantly see if a strategy is working or if it needs adjustment, saving time and improving campaign efficiency. Similarly, in inventory management, changes in stock levels or demand for a specific product are immediately reflected in the dashboard, allowing for a quick response to market needs.

The implementation of API integration and real-time data monitoring tools also poses challenges, as SMEs need to manage large volumes of data and have a robust data infrastructure. However, these technologies are becoming increasingly accessible for small and medium-sized businesses, as many platforms offer simplified solutions for API connection and allow the integration of multiple data sources in one place. In many cases, CRM, ecommerce, and data analysis providers offer detailed documentation and tutorials to facilitate the setup of these integrations, enabling SMEs to implement real-time monitoring systems without the need for a large technical team.

The use of real-time data not only allows for efficient monitoring but also enhances the personalization of the customer experience by providing precise and up-to-date information about their preferences and needs. By combining data from different platforms through APIs, SMEs can gain a comprehensive view of each customer, enabling them to offer personalized recommendations, adjust offers, and improve customer service. This approach not only increases customer satisfaction but also boosts loyalty, as users perceive that the company understands and responds to their needs in real time.

On the other hand, the Python libraries used for data monitoring allow SMEs to manage and process this data efficiently. The combination of Python tools, such as Pandas for data manipulation and Matplotlib or Plotly for visualization, enables companies to analyze results in a single work environment and create customized visualizations that facilitate data interpretation. This is especially useful in sectors where consumer trends can change rapidly, such as retail or e-commerce. Through continuous monitoring, an SME can identify subtle changes in customer buying behavior, such as an increase in demand for certain products or a decrease in sales on specific days of the week, and adapt their strategies based on these patterns.

Real-time data integration also allows SMEs to generate automatic alerts that notify managers when there is a significant change in a key metric. For example, if the system detects that the conversion rate of an ad has fallen below a certain threshold, it can send an alert for the marketing team to review the campaign and make necessary adjustments. Similarly, in inventory management, an alert can be sent when a product's stock reaches a critical level, enabling the logistics team to take action to restock inventory in time and avoid lost sales. This ability to react to critical events in real-time optimizes resources and reduces the likelihood of errors, while improving the company's ability to adapt to market needs in an agile and efficient manner.

The integration of real-time data through APIs and the use of tools like Watchdog and Socket.io not only facilitates quick, data-driven decision-making but also allows SMEs to adopt a proactive, customer-oriented management approach. By having up-to-date data at all times, these companies can anticipate market demands, adjust their marketing strategies, and optimize operations to maximize profitability. Real-time monitoring tools also provide an additional layer of security and control over business processes, as they allow problems to be identified and corrected before they affect business performance. In a competitive environment, this ability to respond quickly and accurately is a key differentiator that can make the difference between a company that adapts to the market and one that falls behind.

Combined, the integration of APIs and Python libraries for real-time data monitoring provides a comprehensive and flexible solution for SMEs to manage their data efficiently and make the most of real-time information. The adoption of these technologies not only allows companies to adapt to market needs but also gives them a competitive advantage, enabling them to optimize resources, improve efficiency, and better satisfy their customers.

9.4. Historical data management for forecasting and long-term commercial strategies

Managing historical data is a fundamental tool for SMEs to build sustainable, fact-based business strategies, leveraging their own information to project the future and make informed decisions. The historical data accumulated over a company's daily operations contains valuable insights into consumption patterns, customer preferences, and sales trends. Analyzing this data allows companies to anticipate demand and optimize their internal processes, achieving a competitive advantage and reducing risks associated with assumption-based decisions. In this context, historical data becomes an asset that goes beyond its original value, serving as a foundation for developing short, medium, and long-term forecasts.

One of the most relevant uses of historical data in a business intelligence strategy is sales and demand forecasting. Through predictive models, such as time series, SMEs can anticipate the number of products needed at certain times of the year or predict the behavior of specific customer segments. This is especially valuable in industries with seasonal demand or where promotions and campaigns have a significant impact on sales volume. By using machine learning tools like ARIMA or Prophet, companies can obtain predictions based on previous data, allowing them to adjust their sales, marketing, and inventory strategies.

The integration of historical data into dashboards allows for a clear and accessible visualization of behavior patterns and trends, making it easier to compare current results with past performance. Dashboards, in addition to showing sales evolution, also help identify deviations from expected patterns and evaluate the effectiveness of commercial strategies. This visual approach to historical data makes the dashboard an essential tool for monitoring the financial and operational health of a company, allowing continuous adjustments to improve performance.

By analyzing historical data, SMEs can also develop long-term business strategies that optimize critical aspects like inventory and stock turnover. Thanks to the analysis of this data, companies can plan their orders based on specific patterns, avoiding unnecessary costs associated with overstock or product shortages during peak demand periods. This planning not only increases efficiency in inventory management but also improves the customer experience by ensuring product availability at key moments.

Finally, the use of prediction tools in Python makes it easier for SMEs to leverage their historical data without requiring advanced technical infrastructure. Libraries like Prophet and statsmodels offer accessible methods for analyzing and modeling historical data, allowing for accurate forecasts and contributing to the creation of data-driven business strategies, with tangible results and lasting benefits for the company.

• Use of Historical Data for Forecasting

For any business, historical data represents an invaluable source of information that allows you to detect behavior patterns and make well-founded forecasts. In the case of SMEs, access to this information provides a significant competitive advantage, as it enables them to react proactively to demand fluctuations, identify specific consumer behaviors, and adjust their operational strategies. Using historical data is not just about observing what happened in the past, but analyzing it to foresee the future with greater accuracy. By identifying patterns and planning based on facts, SMEs can avoid common problems like overstock or product shortages, optimize their sales force, and maximize the impact of their marketing campaigns.

Forecasting with historical data starts by identifying the key variables that affect the company's operations. These variables can range from sales volume to purchase frequency, transaction value, and other transactional data. For example, in a clothing store, sales may increase during certain seasons like Christmas or Black Friday, while in a service company, you might see a rise in customers during holiday periods. These demand cycles can be modeled and forecasted with statistical and machine learning tools. Time series models, such as ARIMA or Prophet, allow you to capture these patterns for more accurate projections.

- **Time series and predictions**

Time series analysis is a statistical methodology ideal for modeling and predicting data that depends on time. Time series are sequences of data ordered chronologically that are used to predict future values based on past values. In the context of SMEs, the use of time series models is especially useful for anticipating demand variations and adjusting operations based on these projections.

Among the most well-known time series models is ARIMA (AutoRegressive Integrated Moving Average), which combines three main components: the autoregressive model (AR), the integration (I), and the moving average (MA). Each component helps capture different aspects of the time series, such as the dependency between observations and long-term trends. ARIMA is widely used in the business world due to its ability to adapt to non-stationary data, which is common in businesses experiencing growth or decline in sales over time.

Implementing ARIMA in an SME is a relatively straightforward process that can be done using Python and libraries like statsmodels. Once implemented, the model can help predict future sales based on historical data. For example, a retail store that experiences sales increases during the summer and winter could use ARIMA to forecast sales volume in the months leading up to these seasons, thus adjusting inventory levels and optimizing its supply chain.

Another notable model for time series forecasting is Prophet, developed by Facebook. Prophet has become popular for its ease of use and its ability to handle data with trend and seasonality patterns. Prophet allows demand forecasting to be adjusted for specific phenomena, such as changes in consumer behavior during marketing campaigns or special events. Additionally, Prophet's simplicity makes it easy to implement, as it does not require complex optimization of initial parameters, and its performance is suitable for sales predictive analysis in an SME. By applying Prophet, a small business can create quick predictive models that are constantly updated based on new data, keeping forecasts aligned with market reality.

- ▪ Long-term trend analysis

Trend analysis is another key aspect of forecasting for SMEs, as it allows them to identify changes in demand and adjust business strategies proactively. By analyzing long-term trends, a company can determine whether a particular product shows sustained sales growth or if, on the contrary, its demand is decreasing. This type of analysis not only optimizes inventory and resources but also informs the possible need for product or service diversification.

A growth trend in product demand, for instance, might indicate the need to increase production capacity or establish contracts with new suppliers to avoid supply issues. On the other hand, if the trend shows a decline in sales, the company might reevaluate its marketing strategy or even consider reducing resources allocated to that product. This could involve reviewing advertising campaigns, seeking customer feedback to identify product issues, or exploring new ways to capture the attention of the target audience.

Current technology allows SMEs to conduct trend analysis in an accessible way through business intelligence platforms and data visualization tools. Programs like Tableau or Power BI are examples of solutions that enable companies to visualize the demand evolution of products, making trend recognition intuitive. Additionally, Python, through libraries such as Matplotlib and Seaborn, allows for the development of customized visualizations of trends, which is useful for making presentations to decision-makers or for incorporating results into business reports.

An important aspect of trend analysis is that it allows SMEs to identify changes in consumer behavior at both macro and micro levels. For example, if an SME operates in an industry subject to seasonal behavioral changes, historical data can show the ideal time to launch a promotional campaign or adjust product prices. This type of analysis can also reveal the evolution of customer perception regarding a product, highlighting the right moment to implement improvements or launch new versions of an existing product.

Long-term trend analysis also allows businesses to identify external factors that may affect demand. Factors such as the economic situation, changes in consumer habits, and new market trends can influence buying behavior and, consequently, impact the demand for specific products. SMEs that incorporate trend analysis into their forecasting strategy can make informed decisions that allow them to adapt to market conditions, thereby maximizing their long-term success opportunities.

- **Advantages of forecasting based on historical data**

SMEs that implement forecasting through historical data analysis gain significant benefits in various aspects of their operations. Forecasting helps reduce uncertainty and provides a solid foundation for strategic, operational, and financial decision-making. The main advantages include:

1. Inventory optimization: By knowing future demand, companies can adjust their inventory levels, thus avoiding the costs associated with overstock and stockouts. Forecasting helps maintain an adequate balance, reducing resource waste and improving efficiency in inventory management.

2. Adjustment of marketing strategies: With historical data, companies can design more effective marketing campaigns. By predicting periods of higher demand, SMEs can launch promotions at the right time, maximizing the impact of their campaigns.

3. Resource planning: Forecasting also allows companies to plan their human and financial resources efficiently. For example, if an increase in demand is anticipated, the company can hire additional staff or temporarily increase production capacity to meet market needs.

4. Improvement in supplier relationships: By knowing future demand, SMEs can establish more favorable agreements with their suppliers. This includes negotiations on prices, delivery times, and payment terms, optimizing the supply chain and improving the long-term business relationship.

5. Risk reduction: Forecasting based on historical data helps mitigate the risks associated with decision-making. By relying on reliable information about future demand, SMEs can reduce erroneous

decisions and improve their ability to adapt to unforeseen changes in the market.

- **Practical Implementation of Forecasting for SMEs**

Implementing a forecasting system based on historical data is a process that can be tailored to the reality of each SME, regardless of its size or budget. The first step is to collect and organize sales and demand data in a structure that allows for analysis. This includes recording relevant information such as the date of sale, the volume of products sold, the value of each transaction, the location of the sale, and any other variables that may influence demand.

Next, the company must select the forecasting model that best suits its needs. For SMEs, time series models like ARIMA and Prophet are accessible and effective options, as they adapt well to demand fluctuations and allow for short and long-term predictions. These models can be implemented on platforms like Python, using libraries such as statsmodels and Prophet, which offer simplified methods for model fitting and validation.

Once the forecasting model is implemented, the company must conduct tests and adjustments to ensure the predictions are accurate. This may involve tweaking the model's parameters or testing different input variables. Once the model is up and running, forecasts can be used to guide decision-making in various areas of the business, from inventory planning to marketing campaign design.

In addition, it is advisable for SMEs to integrate forecasts into their business intelligence systems and dashboards. This allows them to visualize predictions in real-time and make adjustments as needed. Integrating forecasting with current operational data facilitates the identification of behavioral patterns and improves the accuracy of business decisions.

- **Integration of historical data in dashboards**

Integrating historical data into dashboards allows SMEs to gain a strategic and detailed view of their performance over time, facilitating trend tracking and informed decision-making. This process involves accessing a large volume of past information, which can be presented in various visual formats so that managers in each area can understand the context and progress of their key metrics. Additionally, using historical data in dashboards allows for comparisons with current performance, enabling the identification of improvements or areas that require strategic adjustments. The design and updating of these dashboards is essential for transforming data into practical and actionable insights.

Historical data captures past customer behavior, sales, product performance, and other key aspects, providing a solid foundation for interpreting the present and predicting the future. For SMEs, which aim to optimize every resource, this information is particularly valuable as it allows them to precisely adjust their strategies and continuously improve. Integrating historical data into a dynamic dashboard also provides a clear and up-to-date view of growth patterns, which helps reduce uncertainty and base decisions on facts rather than assumptions.

The process of integrating historical data into dashboards involves several steps, from selecting and structuring the data to visualizing it on a platform that facilitates interpretation. For an SME, the goal is to ensure that each department has a tool that allows it to understand its own performance in the historical context and evaluate its current results based on expectations and goals. To this end, there are numerous tools that make it possible to collect, structure, and visualize data easily. Some of the most accessible and popular platforms include Tableau, Power BI, and Google Data Studio, which allow the creation of interactive dashboards that connect to various data sources.

One of the first steps in integrating historical data is to structure and clean the information. Many SMEs manage their sales, inventory, cost data, and other key metrics in separate systems or, in some cases, in spreadsheets that are not always up-to-date or standardized. For this reason, an effective integration process first involves organizing and cleaning the data so it can be efficiently connected to a dashboard. This requires transforming the information into a consistent format that allows for comparison between specific periods, and generally involves data normalization, removing duplicates, and identifying any potential inconsistencies.

The concept of trend visualization is central to using historical data in dashboards. By visualizing trends over time, an SME can observe recurring patterns, such as increased sales during peak seasons, a drop in demand during certain periods, or behavior changes related to specific marketing campaigns. Visualizing this data in dashboards can include line graphs to represent the evolution of a key metric, bar charts to compare performance across different periods, or scatter plots showing correlations between various variables. These types of graphs make it easier to identify patterns and, in many cases, detect subtle changes that, in the long run, can have a significant impact on the business's profitability.

A crucial aspect of implementing dashboards with historical data is the ability to automatically compare current performance with previous results. This not only facilitates progress monitoring but also allows for continuous evaluation of the impact of strategic decisions. By having a tool that enables the comparison of data from different years, months, or even days, those responsible for each area can make real-time adjustments to their strategies. For example, if the sales department observes a decrease in sales volume compared to the same period last year, they can investigate whether specific factors are affecting this behavior. Similarly, the marketing team can assess the effectiveness of a campaign by comparing the increase in current customers with those obtained in past campaigns.

To make comparisons between historical and current data, it is essential to have an interface that allows for the customization of filters and analysis periods. Dynamic dashboards offer this flexibility, which is particularly useful in environments where market conditions can change quickly. With filters that allow you to choose date ranges, segment data by region, or classify customers by value, the leaders of each area can focus on the aspects that truly impact their operations and adjust their strategies in a timely manner. For example, a dashboard that allows you to view performance by region can help identify growing markets, and in the case of a company operating in different regions, it will enable inventory and distribution decisions to be adapted to the demands of each specific market.

Real-time updates of historical data are another advantage offered by dashboard integration. Many BI platforms allow automatic connections with databases, meaning the data is continuously updated without manual intervention. This ensures that decision-makers are always viewing the most up-to-date information, which is particularly valuable in changing markets where old data quickly loses relevance. Continuous updates allow SMEs to observe not only historical performance but also how it evolves as market conditions change, providing a competitive edge by enabling quick reactions and precise adjustments.

In addition, dashboards that include historical data allow for the creation of projections and future scenarios based on patterns observed in the past.

Advanced BI tools enable the application of predictive techniques that use historical data to forecast future performance. This is especially useful in inventory management, where past purchasing patterns help predict future demand. Historical information provides a solid foundation for building predictive models that consider factors like seasonality or response to promotions, helping the company prepare its inventory in advance and reduce the risk of overproduction or stockouts.

The use of dashboards also facilitates the establishment of specific goals and objectives based on past performance. By having a clear view of previous results, SMEs can set realistic and measurable goals that align with their operational capacity and market context. A dashboard allows these objectives to be configured and progress to be monitored in a visual and clear way, motivating teams to achieve the set goals and quickly identifying any deviations that require strategic adjustments. For example, a sales target based on data from previous years becomes a concrete indicator that can be measured in real time, providing a sense of direction and control.

There are various data visualization tools that make it easy to use historical data in dashboards for SMEs. Platforms like Tableau, Power BI, and Google Data Studio offer pre-designed templates and customization options that adapt to different types of businesses. These tools are intuitive and allow you to connect various data sources, making it easy to integrate historical data in one place. Additionally, their ability to generate visual reports with a single click allows managers in each area to export the relevant information and share it with other teams or company management.

Another advantage of using historical data in dashboards is the ability to perform performance analysis by client. For SMEs looking to improve customer retention and increase customer lifetime value, integrating historical data into dashboards is crucial. By analyzing purchase frequency, spending volume, and other historical factors, the company can identify which clients generate the most value and create personalized strategies to retain them. This approach allows for tailored marketing campaigns for the most valuable customers, while also identifying patterns among clients who have decreased their purchase frequency, making it easier to implement reactivation campaigns.

As historical data accumulates over time, SMEs can use this information to perform profitability and return on investment analyses. Dashboards that integrate this information allow the calculation of returns on investments in different areas, such as marketing, product development, and geographic expansion. These analyses provide clear insights into which strategies are delivering the best results, enabling resources to be allocated to the areas offering the highest profitability. Additionally, in cases where results are less satisfactory, profitability analysis helps assess whether external factors have affected performance or if it's necessary to adjust the strategy to improve future outcomes.

The comparison of performance between specific periods is another key functionality of dashboards with historical data. Managers in each area can select periods of interest and see how their key metrics have evolved. This functionality allows for the evaluation of the effectiveness of implemented strategies and adjustments based on evidence. For example, an ecommerce company can compare this year's holiday campaign sales with those of previous years to assess whether its current strategy has been effective in attracting more customers and increasing revenue.

- **Long-term business strategies based on data**

The creation of long-term business strategies based on historical data is a powerful tool for SMEs, as it allows them to build an informed and forward-looking vision of operations and the market. Using historical data in strategic planning helps understand trends, seasonality, and behavior patterns that can influence the success of future business initiatives. By analyzing data, SMEs can not only prepare for anticipated events but also develop a more agile and effective response to unexpected changes. Planning based on historical data not only mitigates the risk associated with business decisions but also improves efficiency in resource allocation.

A strategy based on historical data requires a deep understanding of consumption patterns and customer behavior, as well as variability in inventory turnover. This way, SMEs can design marketing campaigns and adjust product offerings based on anticipated demand, ensuring the availability of the most relevant products at key times of the year and improving the customer experience. By having a solid foundation of historical data, the company can also reduce the impact of incorrect decisions by relying on objective projections that support each step of the strategy.

Strategic planning based on historical data allows SMEs to adopt a proactive rather than reactive approach. Historical data provides valuable context that helps businesses anticipate market trends and consumer behavior. For example, a fashion company that has analyzed past season sales data can predict which products will be in higher demand in the upcoming season and design its production and marketing strategy accordingly. This foresight not only improves the performance of commercial campaigns but also reduces costs associated with inventory and overproduction by enabling more accurate demand planning.

In terms of marketing campaign planning, historical data allows for the analysis of past campaign effectiveness and the optimization of future ones based on the results obtained. For example, if historical data reveals that certain promotions have positively impacted sales during the summer months, the company can adjust its seasonal marketing strategy to include similar campaigns in the future. Data also helps identify the most effective communication channels and adapt the campaign approach to capture the target audience's attention more efficiently. This way, the company maximizes the return on marketing investment by focusing resources on strategies that have proven to be most effective in the past.

Analyzing historical data is equally valuable when planning new product launches. Companies can use past sales data of similar products to forecast demand for new products and adjust their launch strategy. For example, a tech company planning to launch a new device model can analyze data from previous launches to identify periods of highest demand and the most effective sales channels. Additionally, historical data can reveal customer behavior patterns, such as a preference for buying during the initial days of a launch or a trend of waiting for discounts or promotions before making a purchase. This information allows for marketing campaigns to be planned in advance to maximize sales during peak demand periods.

Another fundamental application of historical data in long-term business strategies is inventory optimization. SMEs that analyze historical inventory turnover data can predict product demand during specific times of the year and adjust their stock levels accordingly. This reduces the risk of overstocking, which increases storage costs, and understocking, which can result in lost sales and a negative customer experience. Optimizing inventory based on historical data allows SMEs to maintain a balance between supply and demand, improving inventory management efficiency and increasing long-term profitability.

Forecasting inventory turnover is especially important for businesses that handle products with seasonal or time-limited demand. For example, a clothing store can anticipate increased demand for coats during the winter, or a sports equipment store can foresee higher demand for ski gear during snowy seasons. By predicting these demand fluctuations, the company can place advance orders and negotiate better prices with suppliers, reducing acquisition costs and improving profit margins. In this way, analyzing historical data not only improves inventory management but also optimizes costs and maximizes profitability.

In addition to inventory optimization, historical data can help identify opportunities to improve operational efficiency and reduce costs. By analyzing production, transportation, and storage data, companies can pinpoint areas where they can cut delivery times, enhance process efficiency, or reduce resource waste. For example, a food company can use historical sales and production data to adjust its supply chain and avoid waste of perishable products. This not only reduces costs but also improves the company's sustainability by minimizing the environmental impact of its operations.

Historical data is also useful for identifying customer behavior patterns and adjusting sales strategies based on these trends. For example, if the data reveals that customers tend to make more purchases during weekends or on certain days of the month, the company can adjust its sales and promotional strategies to capitalize on these opportunities. Similarly, historical data can reveal shifts in customer preferences, such as an increasing demand for eco-friendly products or a greater preference for online shopping. By identifying these trends, the company can adapt its offerings and marketing strategies to better meet customer needs and expectations.

Another important strategy that can benefit from using historical data is planning geographical expansion. Companies considering expanding into new markets can use historical data to analyze the performance of similar products in specific regions or countries and forecast potential success in new territories. For example, a fashion company can analyze sales data for its products in cities with similar demographic characteristics to predict the acceptance of its products in a new market. This information allows the company to make informed decisions about where and when to expand, minimizing the risks associated with expansion and maximizing growth opportunities.

Historical data analysis is also a valuable tool for identifying opportunities to improve services and products. For example, if historical data reveals that certain products have a high return rate or low customer satisfaction ratings, the company can investigate the reasons behind these results and make improvements in the product's quality or design. Likewise, historical data can reveal areas where the company could offer new services or products that complement its current offering and respond to the changing needs of customers. This ability to adapt to market demands and continuously improve is key to maintaining competitiveness and relevance in the market.

Regarding supplier relationship management, historical data provides a solid foundation for negotiating better terms and conditions. By analyzing past supplier performance in terms of delivery times, product quality, and contract compliance, the company can identify the most reliable suppliers and negotiate contracts that better fit its needs. For instance, if data reveals that a supplier has frequently delayed product deliveries during certain periods, the company can negotiate clauses that penalize these delays or seek alternatives that ensure greater supply stability.

Historical data also allows SMEs to assess the impact of technology investments and improve their infrastructure based on past results. For example, a company that has implemented a new inventory management system can analyze historical data to assess whether this investment has resulted in greater efficiency and cost reduction. Similarly, historical data allows for evaluating the effectiveness of infrastructure changes, such as expanding a production plant or implementing an automation system. This information is key for planning future investments and ensuring that resources are allocated effectively.

Finally, the use of historical data allows SMEs to set realistic performance goals and metrics that align with their operational capacity and growth objectives. By analyzing past performance and comparing it to current goals, the company can adjust its expectations and targets to be achievable and aligned with the market context. This realistic, data-driven approach enables SMEs to maintain a long-term strategic focus, avoiding both over-optimism and excessive pessimism. Additionally, historical data provides a benchmark against which the company can measure its progress and assess whether it is moving towards its goals or needs to make strategic adjustments.

In summary, the analysis of historical data and its integration into strategic planning allows SMEs to adopt an evidence-based approach to decision-making.

- **Prediction tools for SMEs**

To implement long-term forecasts, SMEs can leverage Python libraries specialized in time series analysis and statistical modeling, such as Prophet and statsmodels, robust tools that allow working with historical data effectively without the need for complex developments. These prediction approaches are especially useful for forecasting sales, managing seasonal demand, analyzing customer behavior, and adapting operational strategies. Prophet, developed by Meta, is ideal for time series with trends and seasonality, while statsmodels excels in the analysis of more structured data or in cases where more traditional statistical modeling is required.

By using Prophet, SMEs gain a powerful solution to break down time series data into clear, understandable components: trend, seasonality, and noise. This tool allows for customized forecast intervals and automatically and robustly handles outliers, trend changes, and seasonalities, even in scenarios where historical data does not follow strictly linear patterns. For example, a company can forecast future sales by analyzing historical data based on seasonal trends and demand during certain months of the year or purchase spikes around specific events.

As for statsmodels, its focus is more on econometric models and the creation of advanced regression models. For SMEs that handle data with regular patterns or want to understand how certain explanatory variables impact the outcome, statsmodels offers a range of robust options, such as the ARIMA model, which allows you to work with autocorrelated data. This is useful for identifying how product or service demand changes based on external variables or long-term patterns. For example, an SME in the retail sector experiencing demand spikes during holidays can use statsmodels to incorporate these factors into the model for a more accurate prediction, and thus anticipate these critical periods with an appropriate inventory or production strategy.

- **Implementation of Prophet for long-term forecasting**

To implement Prophet in time series analysis, three key steps must be followed: load the data, define the seasonality and trend parameters, and generate the model. Prophet handles data with annual, weekly, and daily seasonality well, and can also incorporate special days or relevant events. This capability is particularly valuable for businesses that see marked changes in demand during holiday periods, sales seasons, or special promotions.

A practical example of implementation with Prophet would be the analysis of seasonal demand in a retail store. The company can prepare its historical data in a date and value format, load the model, and allow Prophet to automatically identify the business's seasonal patterns. Additionally, by adding confidence intervals to the model, you can visualize not only the central forecast but also a range of possible variations, which is useful for assessing risk and preparing adequate inventories.

The Prophet model is built as follows:

```
from fbprophet import Prophet
import pandas as pd

# Cargar datos históricos de ventas
datos = pd.read_csv('ventas_historicas.csv')
datos.columns = ['ds', 'y']  # Prophet requiere estas etiquetas de columnas

# Inicializar el modelo y ajustar a los datos
modelo = Prophet(yearly_seasonality=True, weekly_seasonality=True, daily_seasonality=False)
modelo.fit(datos)

# Realizar predicciones a futuro
futuro = modelo.make_future_dataframe(periods=365)  # Predicciones para un año
pronostico = modelo.predict(futuro)

# Visualizar los resultados
modelo.plot(pronostico)
```

This script loads historical sales data, structures it in a format compatible with Prophet, and generates daily sales forecasts for the next year, displaying them in a graph. Prophet allows for manual adjustment of seasonality and trend variables according to the characteristics of the business and its market, providing flexibility to adapt to different consumption patterns. It's also possible to add additional factors such as specific events or promotions, which increases the accuracy of the forecasts in dynamic scenarios specific to each company.

- Implementation of statsmodels for econometric analysis

The statsmodels library provides a variety of advanced models that are useful for detailed and specific time series analysis, especially in contexts where the data shows autocorrelation or where complex econometric models are needed. One of the most used models is ARIMA (Autoregressive Integrated Moving Average), ideal for data that shows a stationary pattern with time autocorrelation.

For an SME, ARIMA is useful when analyzing sales, production, or customer behavior data that show regular patterns and you want to incorporate both the trend and the noise or variability over time. With statsmodels, a company can build models that include the influence of external factors, such as product launches or the impact of promotions, to obtain a prediction tailored to the specific market context.

The following shows how to implement an ARIMA model to make sales forecasts in Python using statsmodels:

```python
import pandas as pd
from statsmodels.tsa.arima.model import ARIMA
import matplotlib.pyplot as plt

# Cargar los datos de ventas históricas
datos = pd.read_csv('ventas_historicas.csv')
datos['Fecha'] = pd.to_datetime(datos['Fecha'])
datos.set_index('Fecha', inplace=True)

# Configurar el modelo ARIMA y ajustar los datos
modelo_arima = ARIMA(datos['Ventas'], order=(5,1,0))  # (p,d,q) donde p y q se ajustan
modelo_ajustado = modelo_arima.fit()

# Realizar predicciones
predicciones = modelo_ajustado.forecast(steps=12)  # Predecir los próximos 12 periodos (meses)

# Visualizar los resultados
plt.plot(datos['Ventas'], label='Ventas históricas')
plt.plot(predicciones, label='Predicción ARIMA', color='red')
plt.legend()
plt.show()
```

In this example, an ARIMA model with parameters (5,1,0) is used, fitting a model that integrates a combination of autoregression and moving average in a monthly sales time series. The parameters p, d, and q are selected based on autocorrelation analysis, which can be done with ACF (Autocorrelation Function) and PACF (Partial Autocorrelation Function) charts of the time series, available in statsmodels. This methodology allows the model to be adjusted to the characteristics of the time series and make predictions based on underlying patterns.

- **Comparison between Prophet and statsmodels for long-term forecasts**

Both tools, Prophet and statsmodels, are useful for making long-term predictions in SMEs, and the choice depends on the specific goals of the prediction and the structure of the historical data. Prophet is preferable for companies facing clear seasonal patterns and fluctuations around certain events, and when the model needs to automatically adjust for special days or abrupt changes in trend. In contrast, statsmodels is more suitable when a detailed econometric analysis is required and the data is structured without necessarily showing seasonality or requiring autoregressive modeling.

The combination of both tools can also be beneficial in projects where predictions need to be verified and validated using different methodological approaches. For example, a company could use Prophet to detect seasonality and statsmodels to model specific causal relationships in historical data. This integration enriches the decision-making process by providing multiple perspectives on the future behavior of critical variables such as product demand, projected sales, and consumer trends.

- **Practical implementation: Predicting sales of seasonal products**

Let's suppose that an SME dedicated to trading sports goods wants to forecast the demand for winter products like skis and thermal clothing. This company can use Prophet to adjust its prediction model considering the annual demand peaks that occur between October and February, and then use statsmodels to validate these predictions and identify possible correlations with additional factors, such as changes in the weather or sporting events.

With Prophet, the company can model annual seasonality and add exogenous variables that represent seasonal promotions or changes in economic conditions, increasing the accuracy of the forecast in the context of seasonal sales. By implementing this model, the company obtains a central forecast with confidence intervals that allow it to plan its inventories and anticipate adjustments in production or staffing during the high season.

In parallel, with statsmodels, the company can perform a detailed analysis to identify explanatory variables that influence winter product sales. This approach not only allows the company to anticipate demand but also to adjust its marketing and promotion strategy based on external conditions. For example, if the analysis of historical data shows a correlation between low temperatures and an increase in thermal clothing sales, the company can plan more effective advertising campaigns focused on geographic areas where a cold winter is expected.

- ▪ **Added value of predictions based on historical data for SMEs**

The use of forecasting tools in Python provides SMEs with a significant competitive advantage by reducing uncertainty and improving operational planning. By anticipating demand, adjusting inventories, and designing business strategies based on historical data, companies can optimize their resources and minimize the risks associated with demand variability. Integrating these models into dashboards allows executives to visualize projections and make strategic decisions in real time, increasing responsiveness and contributing to proactive and efficient management.

Data-driven predictions not only allow companies to optimize their purchasing and inventory decisions but also to set clear sales targets and evaluate performance against projected results. By implementing these predictive tools, SMEs gain not just an analytical tool but a solid foundation for long-term strategic decision-making based on rigorous analysis and the interpretation of trends and behavior patterns.

9.5. Use of data to improve customer experience

The use of data to improve the customer experience is a strategy that transforms the interaction and perceived value of a business. Today, SMEs have the ability to implement advanced real-time personalization techniques, tailoring their offers and communication to each customer's preferences thanks to the data collected from their interactions, both on the web and mobile apps. In the e-commerce sector, for example, data can dynamically change the product offer based on each visitor's behavior in real time, creating unique experiences and enhancing both satisfaction and conversions.

Data analysis allows SMEs to offer products and services in a much more precise way. Instead of presenting the same catalog to all users, the company can highlight products that truly respond to each customer's interests and behaviors. This personalization is especially powerful because it increases the relevance of each interaction and contributes to higher customer retention and loyalty, as well as a greater likelihood of repeat purchases.

One of the main elements of real-time personalization is the use of recommendation systems. Recommendation systems allow you to identify a user's preferences based on their browsing, purchase, and web interaction history, suggesting products similar to those they've previously viewed or that share characteristics with their profile. Using machine learning algorithms and predictive analysis techniques, the system can anticipate the customer's interests and suggest products they haven't yet explored, expanding their reach and relevance.

In the case of an online store, these systems allow the homepage and other key elements of the website to be adapted to highlight products that are likely to interest the visitor. For example, if a user has been browsing sports products, the system can modify the main page or store banners to feature sports products, offers in the same category, or recommendations of products that are often bought together with those the customer has viewed. This entire process is based on machine learning models and recommendation algorithms that dynamically adjust the site's interface to the customer's preferences in real-time.

Another effective use of data to improve the customer experience is analyzing their journey on the website, meaning the path they take from arriving at the site to deciding whether to make a purchase or leave the page. This analysis helps identify friction points or opportunities for improvement at each step of the purchase funnel, which is crucial for optimizing conversion. For example, if the data shows that many users abandon the page at the payment stage, the company can deduce that this part of the process could benefit from improvements, like simpler payment methods, free shipping, or clearer communication about costs. This information also allows the business to anticipate obstacles and offer help messages, guides, or recommendations that facilitate the customer's progress towards the final purchase.

In addition to optimizing the purchase journey, SMEs can also use data to perform dynamic segmentation based on real-time user behavior. This means that website visitors can be segmented based on their interactions, rather than relying solely on demographic or historical data. For example, a customer who frequently visits the site but hasn't made a purchase can receive special real-time promotions aimed at encouraging them to complete the transaction. This type of personalized segmentation not only increases the likelihood of conversion but also reduces the need to apply general discounts, as each user receives offers specifically aligned with their behavior patterns.

In the case of returning or loyal customers, data can help design a personalized shopping experience that takes into account their entire history with the company, including the categories of products they've purchased in the past, their purchase frequency, and personal preferences. With this information, SMEs can send regular recommendations or notifications about products that may interest the customer based on their previous purchases. This also allows for more precise and effective segmentation, where the company can identify customers who make regular purchases and send them specific reminders or incentives before their purchase cycle is complete.

Real-time personalization can also extend to customer service offerings. By analyzing data, the company can identify points where users may need additional support and offer proactive messages or real-time assistance. In an ecommerce site, for example, the system can detect if a customer has spent a long time on a specific product page without taking action and offer the option to chat live with an advisor to resolve any doubts they may have. This personalized attention increases the chances of conversion and improves the company's perception, as the customer feels they are receiving a service tailored to their needs.

The use of data in personalizing communication and marketing is equally effective. Instead of sending generalized email campaigns, SMEs can use behavioral information to segment campaigns based on each customer's individual preferences. For example, a customer who usually buys products on promotion or during specific sales events could receive personalized emails informing them of upcoming promotions or discounts in categories they are interested in. This strategy can also be applied to web notifications, SMS, or mobile apps, where personalized messages based on behavior are sent in real-time to users according to their previous actions or profile.

A method that is gaining popularity is the use of conversational artificial intelligence, such as chatbots and virtual assistants, to enhance the customer experience in real time. Data-driven chatbots allow SMEs to offer instant assistance 24/7, adapting to the specific needs of each customer based on their history and past inquiries. This type of tool is particularly useful in e-commerce, where customers may have questions about products, orders, or shipments and can receive a personalized response without waiting for a human agent. As automated systems, chatbots can serve multiple customers simultaneously, increasing efficiency and reducing wait times, which in turn improves customer satisfaction and strengthens their relationship with the company.

Real-time pricing adaptation is another form of data-driven personalization that is becoming increasingly relevant in the ecommerce sector. By analyzing factors such as demand, competition, and each customer's purchase history, SMEs can adjust their prices dynamically, offering special discounts or applying increases according to market conditions. This strategy allows for greater flexibility in pricing and ensures that customers receive offers that match their spending expectations. By applying machine learning models, prices can be optimized to maximize both sales and profitability, presenting an offer tailored to each user's profile in real time.

To implement these real-time personalization techniques, it is essential to have a robust data architecture that allows for the integration and analysis of data from different sources. Data analysis and machine learning tools like Python with libraries such as scikit-learn and TensorFlow, or visualization tools like Power BI or Google Data Studio, can process large volumes of data and provide real-time insights that translate into strategic decisions. Additionally, the ability to connect this data in real-time with the ecommerce system or CRM allows SMEs to adjust their offerings and communication based on current conditions, representing a key competitive advantage.

Data analysis also allows SMEs to implement experiments and A/B testing in real-time to identify which personalization strategies generate better results in terms of conversion, customer satisfaction, or retention. For example, you can test whether a product recommendation on the homepage or on the cart page is more effective in driving the final conversion. These experiments enable adjustments to strategies based on the data collected, continuously improving the customer experience and optimizing the effectiveness of each interaction.

Ultimately, using data to improve the customer experience translates into a significant advantage for SMEs, allowing them to offer a unique and personalized shopping experience. By identifying and adapting to each customer's specific interests, the company not only enhances its brand perception and increases customer satisfaction but also raises the likelihood of repeat purchases and loyalty.

Chapter 10 - Artificial Intelligence Solutions for SMEs

10.1. How can artificial intelligence improve sales and operational management?

Artificial Intelligence (AI) is transforming the way companies manage their sales and operations, providing SMEs with advanced tools to compete in an increasingly complex market. From predictive models that anticipate demand to the automation of operational processes, AI allows for the optimization of every aspect of the business in a way that, until recently, seemed accessible only to large corporations. Today, accessible platforms and tools have democratized AI technology, making it easier for small and medium-sized businesses to implement AI solutions without the need for large initial investments.

In sales, AI helps SMEs design strategies based on historical data, enabling the implementation of predictive models that anticipate demand fluctuations and allow for adjusting the product or service offering. This way, a company can foresee high and low seasons and proactively adapt its commercial strategies, ensuring inventory availability and avoiding lost sales due to stockouts. Additionally, through personalized recommendations, companies can offer customers specific products based on their past interests and behaviors, improving the shopping experience and increasing the likelihood of conversion and loyalty.

Another key area where AI can make a significant difference is in price optimization, through the implementation of dynamic pricing adjusted in real-time according to demand, competition, and purchasing patterns. These strategies allow SMEs to adjust their prices to maximize profits without alienating their customers, offering discounts or raising prices according to market conditions and current demand. In this sense, artificial intelligence provides valuable data to create a flexible pricing strategy that adapts to market changes.

On the other hand, in operational management, AI plays a crucial role in automating repetitive processes. Many operational tasks, such as data entry, inventory management, and information analysis, can be automated with AI, freeing up human resources to focus on strategic activities. In sectors like manufacturing or retail, inventory optimization and predictive maintenance are two areas of great impact, as they help avoid both overstock and stockouts of important products, while ensuring the uninterrupted operation of equipment and machinery. These types of applications not only improve efficiency and reduce costs but also enhance SMEs' responsiveness to any changes or needs that arise in the operational process.

The integration of artificial intelligence in sales and operations can radically transform how SMEs manage their resources, optimize sales, and strengthen customer relationships, becoming an indispensable tool in long-term growth and sustainability strategy.

- Improving Sales with AI

Artificial intelligence is redefining how SMEs can approach sales and customer management, allowing them to operate with precision, adaptability, and personalization. By integrating AI into their sales strategies, small and medium-sized businesses have access to advanced tools that, in addition to reducing costs, significantly improve the effectiveness of their commercial campaigns. These AI solutions are deployed in three key areas: predictive sales models, personalized recommendation systems, and dynamic pricing optimization. These approaches not only enhance the ability to anticipate demand but also provide customers with a personalized experience, thus increasing satisfaction and loyalty.

The use of predictive models for sales allows SMEs to forecast future demand more accurately, reducing uncertainty and optimizing resources. These techniques use machine learning to analyze historical sales data and anticipate consumption patterns. Predictive sales models can capture and process a variety of data, including seasonality, past promotions, advertising campaigns, and external factors such as the economic and social context. Additionally, through personalized recommendation systems, companies can enhance the shopping experience by offering customers products that, based on their history and preferences, are more likely to interest them. Finally, real-time price optimization, also known as dynamic pricing, allows for adjusting prices according to demand, inventory, competitor prices, and other factors in real time, thus maximizing profitability.

- Predictive models for sales

Sales forecasting is one of the most powerful approaches to improving the business efficiency of an SME, as it allows you to project future demand

and adjust resources accordingly. Machine learning models have become robust tools for predicting sales because they can identify complex patterns in historical data and make accurate predictions about market behavior. For an SME, using these models can mean the difference between having enough inventory during a high-demand season or suffering losses due to overproduction or stockouts.

One of the most common models for predicting sales is linear regression, which allows you to understand the relationship between different variables, such as price and demand. However, when aiming to capture more complex sales patterns, polynomial regression models or random forests can offer better results. These techniques can detect changes in sales trends caused by factors like seasonality, promotional events, or consumer behavior in the market. In particular, random forests are useful for SMEs that want to identify the most relevant factors affecting their sales, as the algorithm automatically selects the most significant patterns from a variety of data.

The implementation of predictive models in sales can also leverage advanced algorithms like neural networks, which detect complex patterns in large volumes of data. These techniques are highly valuable when SMEs have an extensive sales history and multiple variables influencing demand. Neural networks can analyze the combination of factors such as customer behavior, price variations, and the impact of marketing campaigns to make more accurate predictions. For example, in an e-commerce business, the model can capture how competitors' price fluctuations affect demand, allowing for adjustments in sales strategies based on the projections obtained.

In addition to mathematical and machine learning models, it is essential to establish a validation process for these models through techniques such as cross-validation or splitting data into training and test sets. This ensures that predictive models are accurate and can adapt to market changes. SMEs can make adjustments to their models based on performance, continuously optimizing predictions and data-driven decision-making.

- **Personalized recommendations**

Personalized recommendation systems are another standout application of AI in sales optimization. These systems allow an SME to suggest products or services to customers based on their purchase history, preferences, and the buying behaviors of similar customers. With personalized recommendations, a company can offer a more engaging and relevant shopping experience, increasing the chances of conversion and long-term customer retention.

Recommendation systems are generally divided into two main types: collaborative filtering and content-based filtering. Collaborative filtering uses the behavioral data of all users to find similarities and make recommendations. For example, if customer A and customer B have shown similar preferences in the past, the recommendation system will offer customer B products that customer A has purchased or rated positively. This method is especially effective when there is a large amount of user data available, as it allows the discovery of generalized behavioral patterns.

On the other hand, content-based filtering analyzes product characteristics and user preferences. This approach is useful for SMEs that want to recommend products similar to those a customer has purchased or viewed recently. By analyzing a customer's profile, the system can suggest products with similar features, maximizing the likelihood that the customer will find what they're looking for. This type of recommendation is particularly effective in sectors like fashion, electronics, and books, where product characteristics (size, color, author) play an important role in the purchasing decision.

The integration of these systems into ecommerce platforms has become an industry standard, thanks to tools and APIs that allow the implementation of recommendation systems without requiring advanced AI knowledge. For SMEs, this is an opportunity to improve the customer experience without a significant investment. Personalized recommendation systems can increase the average ticket by suggesting related or complementary products and enhance customer loyalty through a more satisfying shopping experience.

- **Dynamic price optimization**

Dynamic pricing optimization, or real-time pricing, is an advanced AI technique that allows prices of products or services to be adjusted based on multiple factors like demand, competition, and historical sales patterns. For an SME, this ability to adjust prices can make the difference between profitability and losing market opportunities. Thanks to machine learning algorithms, these factors can be continuously analyzed, enabling price adjustments to maximize profit or competitiveness.

Dynamic pricing systems are based on algorithms that evaluate inventory, competitor behavior, and customer willingness to pay in real time. These systems are particularly relevant in ecommerce, where demand can fluctuate significantly within hours or minutes. Predictive models used for price optimization often employ regression techniques or clustering algorithms that analyze optimal pricing patterns based on demand and available inventory. It is also common for these systems to integrate external data, such as the price of similar products on competitors' platforms or the impact of marketing campaigns, to make more precise adjustments.

AI allows prices to be adjusted automatically, raising prices when demand is high or when inventory is limited, and lowering them when there's overstock or competitors offer products at lower costs. This type of strategy allows SMEs to capture customers at the most opportune moments, ensuring competitiveness and maximizing margins. Additionally, dynamic pricing can be aimed not only at maximizing profits but also at improving the customer experience through promotions at key moments or personalized discounts based on the user's purchase history.

In addition to real-time price management, dynamic optimization systems also include price segmentation, where different prices are set for various customer segments based on their profile, purchase history, and willingness to pay. This strategy helps capture both price-sensitive customers through personalized offers and those willing to pay a premium for exclusive products or additional services.

The implementation of dynamic and segmented pricing allows SMEs to proactively adapt to demand, achieving greater competitiveness and optimizing their margins. In the current context, where competition and market volatility are constant, the ability to adjust prices in real-time is a key competitive advantage that enables a quick response to market fluctuations and maximizes profitability.

In conclusion, AI applications in sales improvement and price management open up a range of strategic possibilities for SMEs. By implementing predictive models, personalized recommendations, and dynamic pricing, small and medium-sized enterprises can optimize their resources, improve customer satisfaction, and increase their profit margins.

- ## Operational optimization with AI

Operational optimization is one of the most promising applications of artificial intelligence (AI) for SMEs, especially in a context where efficiency and competitiveness are essential for growth and market survival. AI enables companies to automate repetitive tasks, optimize inventory management, and anticipate machinery maintenance, freeing up resources and allowing for more precise and effective resource management. As AI advances, it becomes an accessible tool for SMEs, which can leverage its potential without the need for costly investments in technology or large development teams.

With operational optimization, SMEs can reduce costs, improve customer satisfaction, and make better use of human resources by spending less time on mechanical tasks and more on strategic activities. Automated processes help reduce human errors and increase the speed of response to operational needs. AI, in this sense, becomes a fundamental ally for increasing productivity, optimizing stock control, and improving the maintenance management of equipment or machinery in manufacturing and industrial companies.

- ### Automation of repetitive processes

The automation of repetitive processes is one of the most common applications of AI in operational optimization. Thanks to this technology, SMEs can free their staff from routine tasks that do not generate added value yet consume significant time and resources. This type of automation is achieved through the use of algorithms and machine learning systems that allow machines to perform processes autonomously, reducing errors and improving the speed of task execution.

One of the areas where automation of repetitive tasks has a significant impact is in data entry. Many companies still spend time manually recording information from their clients, orders, invoices, and other business documents. AI makes this process easier through optical character recognition (OCR), which allows for the automatic extraction and storage of data from physical or digital documents. For example, in a small financial services company, AI can automate the capture of information from contracts or receipts, storing this data in a management system that facilitates later consultation and analysis.

In addition to data entry, another area where AI can automate repetitive processes is in the analysis of large volumes of information. For example, machine learning algorithms can help a company identify patterns in sales data, allowing them to adjust their business strategies based on market trends. For a SME operating in a highly competitive environment, such as retail or online sales, having this type of real-time insight is a considerable advantage that improves responsiveness to changes in demand.

Inventory management can also benefit from automation, allowing companies to adjust stock automatically based on demand forecasts. By using AI systems, businesses can analyze sales and anticipate the volume of products needed for a specific season, avoiding overstock or shortages of key products. AI enables inventory systems to be constantly updated, syncing with sales and customer orders, which improves operational efficiency and reduces the risk of losses from unnecessarily stored products.

The automation of repetitive processes also includes managing communications. AI tools like chatbots allow for automating customer interactions on topics related to orders, returns, or FAQs. These types of applications have become an accessible solution for SMEs, as they don't require major developments and can be integrated into digital customer service platforms like social media, websites, or CRM systems.

- **Inventory Optimization**

Inventory management is a critical task for any business that handles physical products, as ineffective control can lead to significant losses, either from overstock or from lack of products at key moments. AI allows SMEs to optimize inventory control through predictive models that forecast product demand based on historical data and other relevant factors. This type of optimization not only improves supply chain efficiency but also reduces costs by minimizing the risk of waste or stockouts.

One of the most effective methods for managing inventory with AI is predictive analysis, which allows businesses to anticipate when and in what quantities certain products will be needed. Through machine learning algorithms, it's possible to analyze historical sales data, identify seasonality patterns, detect demand trends, and adjust inventory orders based on these projections. For example, a company that sells seasonal items like clothing or products for specific events can use AI to predict an increase in demand for certain products during festive periods, thus adjusting its inventory in advance and ensuring sufficient stock without incurring high storage costs.

Another application of AI in inventory management is the analysis of product turnover, which allows businesses to identify items with higher or lower movement within the inventory. This analysis helps classify products into categories based on their turnover speed, enabling SMEs to optimize storage space and prioritize restocking of high-demand products. By using clustering algorithms or classification techniques, companies can segment their inventory into specific groups (such as high-turnover products or low-demand items), making it easier to make informed decisions about stock management.

In addition to forecasting and inventory classification, AI enables the implementation of dynamic inventory systems. These systems automatically adjust the quantity of products based on real demand and predictions for the next sales cycle. For example, in an online store, AI systems can adjust inventory in real time, synchronizing stock with sales and generating alerts when a product is about to run out. This not only ensures that products are available for customers, but also minimizes the operational costs associated with manual inventory management.

AI can also optimize inventory management in complex environments where multiple storage locations are managed. In these cases, AI facilitates logistics planning, ensuring that each location has the necessary products to meet local demand. Through geospatial data analysis and optimization algorithms, SMEs can reduce delivery times, improve customer experience, and lower transportation costs.

- Predictive maintenance

Predictive maintenance is another area where AI has a significant impact on operational optimization, especially in the industrial and manufacturing sectors. Through machine learning techniques, predictive maintenance allows you to foresee when a machine failure is likely to occur, based on the analysis of historical performance data and other relevant variables. This not only prevents unexpected and costly downtime but also reduces maintenance costs by allowing interventions to be scheduled before major breakdowns occur.

Predictive maintenance uses a combination of sensors and AI algorithms that collect and analyze real-time data from machines. This data includes temperature, vibration, pressure, and other key indicators that reveal the state of the machinery. By identifying patterns in this data, AI can predict when a machine is at risk of failing, allowing the technical team to intervene in time and avoid a production interruption. This ability to anticipate problems reduces unplanned downtime, thereby optimizing productivity and improving operational efficiency.

In a manufacturing SME, for example, predictive maintenance can drastically reduce downtime and repair costs. By analyzing machine operation data, AI can detect signs of wear or imminent failure in specific components, allowing for preventive part replacement or adjustments. This strategy not only extends the equipment's lifespan but also enhances workplace safety by reducing the risk of accidents from mechanical failures.

Predictive maintenance can also be applied in environments where vehicles or transport fleets are used, such as logistics or distribution companies. In these cases, AI can analyze vehicle data, such as mileage, fuel consumption, and tire wear, to predict when maintenance is needed and optimize fleet usage. Scheduling maintenance based on the actual needs of each vehicle reduces operating costs, extends the lifespan of assets, and ensures efficient service for customers.

Regarding the implementation of predictive maintenance, there are multiple tools and platforms that allow SMEs to access these technologies without large initial investments. From IoT solutions that integrate sensors into machines to data analysis platforms using machine learning to identify patterns, predictive maintenance is within reach for companies of all sizes. Additionally, many of these platforms offer pay-as-you-go options, which allow SMEs to adjust the level of investment based on their operational needs.

In conclusion, operational optimization through artificial intelligence offers SMEs a series of competitive advantages, allowing them to reduce costs, improve efficiency, and free up human resources for more strategic tasks. AI has become an essential tool to automate repetitive processes, intelligently manage inventories, and predict machinery maintenance, providing greater responsiveness and adaptability in an ever-changing market.

10.2. Creation of chatbots and virtual assistants with AI for customer service

The creation of AI-based chatbots and virtual assistants has transformed the way businesses, including SMEs, manage customer service and user interactions. These systems are increasingly essential as they allow for personalized, fast, and efficient support without the need for large support teams or costly infrastructure. An AI chatbot can autonomously attend to customers, answering their questions and resolving common issues, while advanced virtual assistants can even guide customers through purchase processes and product recommendations, increasing the likelihood of conversion.

For SMEs, this technology represents an invaluable opportunity, as it offers continuous support (24/7) without the need to invest in additional staff, and it does so with a quality of interaction that constantly improves thanks to AI model learning. Chatbots, in particular, are a versatile and accessible tool, as they can be integrated into instant messaging platforms like WhatsApp, Facebook Messenger, or websites, allowing companies to reach their customers in the place and time they prefer. Moreover, with the advancement of AI and natural language processing (NLP), today's chatbots are capable of interpreting and responding in natural language, making interactions smooth and satisfactory for the customer.

There are numerous specialized platforms that facilitate the creation of chatbots for businesses of any size. Among the most popular are Google's Dialogflow, ManyChat, and Botpress, which allow the development of customized chatbots without requiring advanced programming knowledge. These platforms offer intuitive interfaces and powerful customization capabilities, making them ideal for SMEs looking to implement automated customer service solutions quickly. With these tools, it's possible to train the chatbot to answer frequently asked questions about products, services, or company policies, thus providing quick and consistent responses in interactions.

Another key capability that AI brings to chatbots is natural language processing (NLP), which allows them to understand the context and intent behind customer queries. By using libraries like spaCy or Hugging Face Transformers, you can create chatbots with advanced language comprehension capabilities, improving the accuracy and relevance of responses. This is especially useful for companies with complex customer service needs, as it enables the chatbot to distinguish between different types of queries and offer specific solutions, thus increasing user satisfaction.

Virtual assistants can play an even more active role in the buying process, assisting customers as they browse the website, suggesting products or services based on their preferences, and providing personalized support that encourages conversion. This function of virtual assistants turns AI into a strategic tool to improve not only customer service but also sales.

Ultimately, AI chatbots and virtual assistants allow SMEs to optimize customer service and strengthen their sales strategy. These tools are designed to be accessible, flexible, and effective, making them an attractive option for improving customer satisfaction while freeing up human resources for more strategically valuable tasks.

- ### Introduction to AI Chatbots

AI-based chatbots have become a powerful and increasingly accessible tool for SMEs looking to optimize customer service, provide quick and effective responses, and improve user experience without incurring high infrastructure costs. Essentially, an AI chatbot allows a company to automate much of the inquiries and information requests it receives daily, significantly reducing the workload of human staff and offering a smooth, 24/7 service experience. This ability to provide continuous and automated customer service is a remarkable competitive advantage, especially in an environment where customer expectations for speed and accessibility are ever-growing.

The implementation of an AI chatbot involves the use of algorithms that allow the machine to interpret user requests and access a knowledge base to provide coherent and relevant responses. A fundamental aspect of these chatbots is their ability to recognize patterns and learn from previous interactions, enabling them to progressively improve in terms of accuracy and efficiency. Thus, a chatbot not only acts as a static resource that automatically responds to predefined questions but also has the ability to adapt and refine its responses as it interacts with users. This adaptability is one of the differentiating elements that make AI-based chatbots more effective and realistic in their interactions, providing a more natural and personalized user experience.

For SMEs, implementing an AI chatbot represents an opportunity to offer customer service that rivals that of large companies, without the need to hire large teams or maintain an expensive call center. Cost reduction is undoubtedly one of the most evident benefits, as it allows the company to redirect financial and human resources to other strategic areas of the business. For example, a company with an efficient chatbot can maintain a small number of human agents who focus exclusively on resolving complex cases or performing higher-value tasks, while the chatbot automatically handles all the most common and repetitive requests, such as questions about return policies, order status, product specifications, or general inquiries about the company's services.

An AI chatbot is designed to handle multiple queries simultaneously, eliminating wait times for customers and improving their perception of the service. Unlike a human agent, who can handle only one or a few conversations at a time, a chatbot can manage hundreds or even thousands of interactions simultaneously. This scalability is crucial during periods of high demand, such as sales campaigns or holidays, when companies typically experience a significant increase in the number of inquiries and requests. By not being limited by time or workload, the AI chatbot ensures that every customer receives immediate attention, resulting in greater satisfaction and a more consistent user experience.

In addition to cost reduction and scalability, AI chatbots also offer the advantage of immediacy in response. The ability to respond instantly and accurately is especially relevant in an environment where customers expect quick answers and immediate solutions to their problems. AI allows the chatbot to quickly access stored information, such as product details, business hours, company policies, and other frequently asked questions, which facilitates providing accurate and fast responses. This response speed not only enhances the customer experience but also helps increase operational efficiency by resolving queries more quickly and effectively.

AI chatbots can also personalize their interactions, adjusting responses based on the context and the user's specific needs. For example, if a customer has recently made a purchase in the online store, the chatbot could recognize that transaction and provide specific information about the order status, shipping options, or return policies applicable to that product. This personalization capability is possible because AI chatbots can integrate with the company's internal systems, such as customer databases or inventory management platforms, allowing them to access relevant information in real-time and tailor responses based on each user's characteristics and preferences. As a result, the customer perceives more attentive service that is tailored to their needs, contributing to a stronger and more positive relationship with the company.

The process of configuring an AI chatbot usually involves defining a set of responses for common questions, known as 'intents.' These intents represent the different thematic areas that customers might inquire about and serve as the basic structure of the chatbot's knowledge. Based on these intents, the chatbot uses learning algorithms to identify the specific intent behind each question it receives and provide a coherent response. As the chatbot interacts with more users, its AI system processes and analyzes variations in queries, adjusting its responses to be more precise and relevant. In this way, the chatbot learns from each interaction and continuously improves its ability to respond correctly and promptly to customer questions.

Another advantage of AI chatbots for SMEs is their ability to collect and analyze data about customer interactions. By recording each query and response, the chatbot generates a significant amount of data that can be analyzed to gain valuable insights into customer interests, needs, and preferences. For example, by analyzing frequently asked questions, a company can identify demand patterns, areas for service improvement, or additional information needs that can be addressed on their website or other platforms. This data can also be useful for detecting recurring issues that customers experience with a specific product or service, allowing the company to make informed decisions to improve the quality of their offerings or adjust their business policies.

The ability to analyze interaction data also helps SMEs identify opportunities to improve their customer service processes. By identifying patterns and trends in customer queries, the support team can adjust the chatbot's predefined responses and enhance the interaction flow. This ensures that the chatbot remains relevant and effective over time, adapting to changes in customer needs and expectations. For example, if a chatbot detects that a significant number of customers are inquiring about a specific product during a marketing campaign, the company could adjust its inventory or focus on resolving recurring questions around that product, optimizing the customer experience in the process.

In addition, AI chatbots can also be used to improve customer retention and loyalty. By providing constant and high-quality service, chatbots help SMEs create a more pleasant and personalized user experience, which strengthens the long-term relationship with the customer. The ability to respond immediately to customer queries or issues reduces the likelihood of them becoming frustrated or dissatisfied with the service, which in turn increases the chances of the customer making a repeat purchase or recommending the service to others. In today's context, where customer loyalty is increasingly difficult to achieve, the ability to provide high-quality customer service through an AI chatbot represents an added value that can make a difference in terms of competitiveness.

Ultimately, implementing an AI chatbot allows SMEs not only to reduce costs and improve operational efficiency, but also to offer a level of service that can compete with large companies. AI has democratized access to advanced customer service tools, enabling small and medium-sized businesses to compete in terms of service quality without the need for large investments. A well-designed and configured AI chatbot not only acts as an automated point of contact but also contributes to the growth and strengthening of the brand by improving the customer experience and offering a closer, more efficient service. For SMEs, this technology represents a strategic investment that can make a significant difference in the customer relationship and their market positioning.

- **Accessible platforms for creating chatbots**

Platforms for creating chatbots have evolved rapidly in recent years, becoming increasingly accessible and affordable for businesses of all sizes, including SMEs and startups. Previously, developing a chatbot required advanced knowledge in programming and machine learning. However, today there are tools that allow companies to implement and customize chatbots without needing advanced technical training. This has been achieved thanks to platforms like Google's Dialogflow, ManyChat, and Botpress, which provide an intuitive interface and resources tailored for any user to build a functional and efficient chatbot.

Google's Dialogflow is one of the most comprehensive and popular platforms in the field of chatbots. This Google tool allows the design of chatbots capable of interpreting and processing natural language, enabling users to interact with chatbots in a more natural and fluid way. The most notable feature of Dialogflow is its ability to recognize and process intents.

In the context of a chatbot, an 'intent' represents the purpose or reason behind the user's question or message. Dialogflow allows the creation of multiple intents that reflect the most common inquiry topics, such as questions about opening hours, order statuses, or return policies. Additionally, Dialogflow includes an intuitive graphical interface for defining these intents, making it easy for businesses to configure the chatbot according to their specific needs without the need for coding.

To set up a chatbot in Dialogflow, you first define a set of training phrases corresponding to each intent. These phrases are examples of how users might formulate a query or question about a particular topic. Dialogflow uses these training phrases to automatically identify patterns and synonyms in the language, allowing the chatbot to respond to a variety of queries that refer to the same intent. By using natural language processing algorithms, Dialogflow can improve its accuracy and responsiveness as it interacts with more users. Additionally, Dialogflow allows you to integrate the chatbot into different messaging platforms such as WhatsApp, Facebook Messenger, and websites, expanding the chatbot's reach and accessibility.

On the other hand, ManyChat is a widely used platform for creating chatbots focused on instant messaging, particularly on Facebook Messenger. ManyChat stands out for its simplicity and focus on conversational marketing, making it an ideal tool for businesses looking to promote products, run marketing campaigns, or attract customers through personalized and automated messages. Unlike other platforms, ManyChat does not focus on intent recognition or natural language processing; instead, it allows for the configuration of predefined conversation flows where users select options or follow a guided sequence of responses. This flow structure makes configuration easy and allows chatbots to maintain control of the conversation, guiding the user through a predetermined path that answers their questions in a sequential and organized manner.

One of the main advantages of ManyChat is its ease of integrating marketing automation tools. For example, you can connect the ManyChat bot with email lists, CRMs, or customer management systems, allowing for a personalized experience where the bot can remember specific details about the customer and tailor its responses based on this information. Many companies use ManyChat to send welcome messages, promote new products, or automatically answer frequently asked questions, which reduces the load on the customer support team and improves the user experience. Like Dialogflow, ManyChat allows the integration of the bot into various platforms and communication channels, although its main focus is Facebook Messenger.

Botpress is another standout option in chatbot development, especially for companies looking for an open-source solution. Unlike Dialogflow and ManyChat, which are cloud-based services, Botpress is an open-source platform that allows companies to host the chatbot on their own infrastructure, offering greater flexibility and control over the tool's customization and security. Being an open-source solution, Botpress is highly customizable, allowing developers to modify the code and adapt it to the specific needs of the company. This is especially useful for businesses that require deeper integration or want to maintain full control over the data collected by the chatbots.

Botpress uses a modular structure that makes it easy to integrate different functionalities. Some modules allow you to add natural language processing features, while others enable the creation of complex conversation flows or integration with databases and APIs. Like Dialogflow, Botpress allows you to define intents and entities so that the chatbot can interpret the context of the conversation and respond appropriately. However, due to its open-source nature, Botpress is a more advanced option that may require some technical expertise to fully configure and customize. Nevertheless, this platform provides an excellent option for companies looking to build a robust and adaptable chatbot, especially in environments where data privacy and security are a priority.

Each of these platforms offers unique advantages and is geared towards different types of businesses and needs. For an SME, choosing a platform will depend on several factors, including the complexity of the chatbot they want to implement, the level of customization required, and the available budget. Dialogflow is an excellent option for companies looking for a chatbot with advanced natural language processing capabilities, while ManyChat is ideal for social media marketing campaigns and for those who want a quick setup without technical complexity. On the other hand, Botpress is the right choice for companies that require full control and detailed customization, especially in environments where data security is a major concern.

These platforms also offer great flexibility regarding the channels where the chatbot can operate. Both Dialogflow and ManyChat and Botpress can integrate with a variety of channels, allowing companies to provide a consistent customer service experience across multiple platforms. This is especially relevant in an environment where customers interact with companies through various touchpoints, from social media to messaging apps and websites. The ability to integrate the chatbot across all these channels ensures that customers receive the same quality of service regardless of the medium they use to contact the company. Additionally, the platforms allow for the implementation of real-time automated responses, ensuring that customers get an immediate reply regardless of the time or volume of inquiries, which is a key competitive advantage.

Another important feature of these platforms is their ability to record and analyze customer interaction data. Dialogflow, ManyChat, and Botpress allow companies to collect data on the most frequent queries, common intents, and areas of customer interest. This data is extremely valuable as it enables the company to identify patterns in customer behavior and tailor their marketing and service strategies accordingly. For example, if it's detected that many customers are inquiring about the availability of a particular product, the company can decide to strengthen the promotion of that product or adjust their inventory to meet demand. This way, the chatbot not only acts as a virtual assistant but also becomes an analytical tool that provides actionable insights to improve decision-making.

Finally, these platforms also offer options to customize the appearance and tone of the chatbot's responses, allowing SMEs to adapt the chatbot's interaction style to their brand identity. This is particularly important for creating a user experience that is consistent and reflects the company's values. Good customization can make the chatbot feel friendlier and more accessible, improving the customer's perception of the company and strengthening their relationship with the brand.

• Use of NLP (Natural Language Processing)

Natural Language Processing (NLP) is essential for the development of advanced chatbots that can understand and respond to customer queries in a precise and natural way. Unlike basic chatbots that rely on predefined responses and specific keywords, chatbots with NLP capabilities have a deeper understanding of words, phrases, and the context of a conversation, allowing them to interact with users more intelligently and flexibly. For SMEs, a chatbot with natural language processing can significantly improve the customer service experience by providing accurate and quick responses, answering complex questions, and understanding the intent behind queries, resulting in more satisfying interactions for users.

The use of NLP in chatbots focuses on two main aspects: Natural Language Understanding (NLU) and Natural Language Generation (NLG). Natural Language Understanding focuses on interpreting and analyzing the user's input text to identify the query's intent and extract key entities, while Natural Language Generation is used to produce coherent and natural responses that meet the user's needs. In the context of chatbots, NLU is particularly relevant because it allows the chatbot to correctly interpret the intent of a question or comment and determine the most appropriate response.

- **NLP and Intent Understanding in Chatbots**

One of the biggest challenges when developing a chatbot with NLP is correctly identifying the user's intent, a process that is done through intent classification. Every user query has an underlying intent, whether it's asking a question, requesting information, or expressing a complaint. To handle this, supervised classification models can be used, trained with labeled examples of common intents. This way, the model can generalize and predict the intent in future queries.

Libraries like spaCy and Hugging Face Transformers have greatly facilitated the implementation of these capabilities in Python. spaCy, for example, is an optimized library for natural language processing that allows you to perform tasks like tokenization, syntactic analysis, and named entity recognition quickly and accurately. spaCy models can be trained and adapted to different types of language and themes, which is useful for companies that need to tailor the chatbot to the specific language of their sector or customers.

In the case of Hugging Face Transformers, this library provides access to advanced NLP models based on deep neural networks, such as BERT (Bidirectional Encoder Representations from Transformers) and GPT (Generative Pre-trained Transformer). These models have been trained with large volumes of data and have an advanced understanding of language, allowing them to identify complex intentions and respond to questions that may require some context. For SMEs, using a pre-trained model from Hugging Face Transformers can be an efficient way to implement a sophisticated chatbot without the need to train a model from scratch.

- ### Using spaCy for entity recognition and tokenization

In the context of a chatbot, named entity recognition is a key functionality, as it allows the identification and extraction of specific data within user queries. For example, if a customer asks, "What is the shipping cost to Madrid?", a chatbot with entity recognition capabilities can identify "Madrid" as a location and "shipping cost" as an intent. This identification enables the chatbot to provide an accurate response instead of a generic one. spaCy is highly efficient in these tasks, as it allows the training of custom models that can recognize specific entities relevant to the company, such as product names, geographical locations, or industry-specific terms.

Tokenization is another fundamental process in NLP and involves dividing a sentence or text into smaller units called tokens, which can be words, phrases, or individual characters. spaCy makes this tokenization process easier and provides a structured analysis of tokens, such as the type of word (noun, verb, adjective, etc.) and its relationship with other words in the sentence. This allows for a more detailed interpretation and enables developers to configure responses that depend on the grammatical or semantic context of the query.

A practical example of how spaCy can be implemented in a chatbot would be for an SME in the retail sector, where the customer service chatbot can interpret queries like "I want to buy a blue T-shirt in size M." With spaCy, the chatbot can identify "T-shirt" as a product, "blue" as a color, and "size M" as a specific feature, which allows the system to provide direct and relevant responses, guiding the customer to products that match their description.

- ### Implementation of Transformers for Advanced Chatbots

The Hugging Face Transformers library allows you to implement advanced NLP models that understand the context of conversations more deeply. Unlike other NLP models that analyze words sequentially, Transformers process information in parallel and consider both forward and backward context in a sentence. This results in a better understanding of complex and ambiguous phrases, as the model has a complete view of the sentence at once.

For a chatbot that handles detailed or highly complex queries, Hugging Face models like BERT or GPT-3 can be very effective. These models allow for responses with a high degree of accuracy and can adapt to a variety of topics and contexts. For example, a chatbot implemented in an electronics store using GPT-3 could answer questions like "What are the differences between model A and model B in terms of resolution and storage?" This type of question involves comparing specific features and requires the chatbot to understand the relationship between the mentioned elements.

Moreover, Hugging Face provides tools to fine-tune pre-trained models, allowing businesses to adapt these models to their specific needs. With a small amount of additional training data, Transformer models can be specialized to answer questions related to products, services, or company policies. This means that an SME could adapt a Transformer model so that the chatbot better understands queries related to their products, using specific vocabulary and responding according to the information available in their database.

- **NLP in generating coherent and natural responses**

The ability of advanced chatbots to generate natural responses is one of the greatest benefits of implementing NLP in their systems. Language generation models like GPT-3 use a Transformer-based structure to generate text that mimics human language, producing responses that are not only correct from an informational standpoint but also natural and fluid in their expression. This enhances the user experience, as the responses are friendlier and more approachable, rather than appearing as automated replies.

For an SME, this ability to generate responses can be especially useful in sectors where customer interaction plays a crucial role in the overall brand experience. For example, a small business in the tourism services sector could use a chatbot with language generation capabilities to respond to inquiries about tourist destinations, travel packages, or accommodation recommendations in a way that feels natural and personalized. The chatbot can generate responses like, "If you're looking for a relaxing experience, we recommend visiting our travel packages to Mallorca during the off-season. Would you like more information about the activities available at that time of year?" which provides a more complete and engaging user experience.

- **Advantages of NLP in Adapting the Chatbot to Different Contexts**

Natural language processing also allows chatbots to be more adaptive, meaning they can adjust their responses based on the context of the conversation. This is particularly important in cases where an initial user query is followed by additional questions that depend on the previous answer. For example, if a customer asks the chatbot about the availability of a product and then follows up with a question about the estimated delivery time, a chatbot with advanced NLP capabilities can remember the context of the conversation and provide a coherent response without the user needing to repeat their initial question.

The use of NLP allows chatbots to be more sensitive to these types of situations, as they can identify changes in topic, respond to follow-up questions, and adjust their tone based on the flow of the conversation. This is crucial in complex or long interactions, where the user might need detailed information about various aspects of a product or service. Thanks to this adaptability, the chatbot can act as a personal assistant guiding the customer through the conversation, thereby improving the user experience.

- **Optimization of the customer experience through NLP**

Finally, implementing NLP in chatbots allows companies to collect data on user queries and use this information to optimize the customer experience. By analyzing interactions with the chatbot, an SME can identify patterns and trends in queries, allowing them to adjust the chatbot's responses and improve accuracy over time. For example, if interaction analysis reveals that many users are asking about international shipping, the company can optimize the chatbot to provide detailed answers on this topic, thereby reducing the number of repetitive queries.

Furthermore, NLP allows feedback mechanisms to be incorporated into the chatbot, so users can indicate whether a response was helpful or if they need more assistance. With this feedback, SMEs can continue to improve the chatbot's effectiveness by adjusting responses and adapting the NLP model to provide a more precise service aligned with customer needs.

In conclusion, natural language processing is a key tool for creating chatbots that offer a highly satisfying customer service experience, tailored to the needs and expectations of users. Thanks to libraries like spaCy and Hugging Face Transformers, SMEs can implement advanced chatbots without needing to build complex models from scratch, benefiting from NLP advancements to deliver personalized, accurate, and natural interactions.

- ## Customer service automation

The automation of customer service is one of the most relevant uses of chatbots in the business environment, especially for small and medium-sized enterprises (SMEs) looking to improve efficiency and reduce costs without sacrificing service quality. By implementing chatbots, businesses can automate a large volume of repetitive and simple queries, allowing them to redirect human resources towards more complex tasks or personalized attention in specific situations. This enables customer service teams to work more efficiently and optimally, as repetitive interactions that usually demand much of their time are automatically managed by the chatbot system.

- ### Frequent queries resolution

One of the greatest benefits of using chatbots in customer service is the ability to automate the resolution of frequent queries. These queries often cover recurring topics that customers need to resolve quickly, such as the status of an order, product exchange options, return policies, stock availability, or shipping procedures. These topics, while essential for customer satisfaction, don't usually require human intervention to be resolved, as the responses are mostly standard and based on established procedures. Thanks to chatbots, up to 80% of these queries can be managed without human intervention, significantly reducing the workload in customer service departments.

Chatbots can be programmed to recognize specific patterns in customer questions and respond immediately with the appropriate information. For example, when faced with a question like 'Where is my order?', the chatbot can access the shipping database, check the delivery status, and provide an updated response in a matter of seconds. This not only speeds up the customer response but also reduces wait times, improving the overall user experience. Moreover, in a market where immediacy is key to customer satisfaction, this automation becomes a competitive advantage for the company.

The resolution of frequent queries through chatbots not only improves customer satisfaction but also optimizes the company's internal resources. By reducing the number of queries that require human attention, the need for a large customer service team is minimized, allowing companies to save on operating costs. This is especially beneficial for SMEs, as they can compete with larger companies in terms of service quality without the need for large investments in staff or infrastructure. Chatbots can offer a consistent and efficient experience, removing much of the administrative burden from customer service agents and allowing them to focus on more complex and specific queries.

- **Multichannel support**

In the digital era, customers expect to interact with businesses through multiple channels and have a consistent experience on each of them. This means that customer service must be available on various platforms, such as websites, mobile apps, WhatsApp, Facebook Messenger, Instagram, and other social networks. The integration of chatbots across multiple channels becomes an effective solution for SMEs, as it allows them to provide a seamless, omnichannel customer service experience without needing to maintain specialized teams for each platform.

A multichannel chatbot can adapt to the environment of each channel, adjusting the tone and style of responses according to the platform's context and the customer's profile. For instance, on WhatsApp, messages tend to be more informal and brief, while on a corporate website they can be a bit more formal and extensive. An advanced chatbot can automatically adjust to these differences, providing a personalized and consistent experience that enhances customer satisfaction and reinforces the brand image.

In addition to adapting to the style of each channel, multichannel chatbots allow for centralized information and a unified customer experience. This means a customer can start a query on the company's website, continue it on WhatsApp, and finish it on Instagram without the chatbot losing track of the conversation or repeating the same information. This continuity is essential for ensuring an uninterrupted user experience and makes the process easier for the customer, who doesn't need to explain their issue on each new channel or platform. The ability of chatbots to retain the context of the conversation across all communication channels also allows for greater personalization in responses and faster replies to inquiries.

To implement a multichannel chatbot, companies typically integrate the chatbot into a Customer Relationship Management (CRM) platform, where interaction data is centralized. This allows the chatbot to access real-time customer information, including purchase history, previous inquiries, and any other relevant interactions, enriching the responses and enabling greater personalization. This type of integration is especially useful for order tracking and providing information on company policies, current promotions, and any other data the customer has previously inquired about. Additionally, a multichannel-capable chatbot can actively track inquiries to ensure all questions receive an appropriate response, and if the customer needs further assistance, it can transfer the conversation to a human agent.

- Practical example of a multichannel Chatbot

To better understand the functioning and benefits of a multichannel chatbot, let's consider the example of an SME in the e-commerce sector that sells fashion products. In this case, the company could implement a chatbot available on its website, WhatsApp Business account, and Facebook page. Suppose a customer visits the company's website to check the status of an order. By interacting with the chatbot, the customer receives the requested information but later needs to make another inquiry about the return process and decides to send a message from their WhatsApp account. The WhatsApp chatbot picks up the query from where it was left on the website, providing the customer with detailed information about the return process.

Since the chatbot is connected to the company's database and has access to all relevant information, it can manage this interaction seamlessly. Furthermore, if the customer needs to make an additional inquiry on Facebook about products in stock, the chatbot on that platform will have access to previous interactions and can respond consistently and in context. This seamless, multichannel experience is key to improving customer satisfaction, as they receive quick and effective answers without needing to start a new conversation on each channel. Additionally, the company saves time and resources, as the chatbot can manage these inquiries autonomously without human intervention.

- Benefits of multichannel automation for SMEs

Multichannel customer service automation offers multiple benefits for SMEs, especially in terms of efficiency, reach, and service quality. By implementing a chatbot that operates on various platforms, companies can extend their presence on the most popular communication channels without the need to manage each one individually. This allows an SME to be available for its customers on their preferred channels, ensuring that each interaction is handled consistently and professionally.

The time savings are another important benefit. Thanks to chatbots, the customer service team doesn't need to respond to every inquiry in person; they only need to step in for complex situations or cases that require a personalized solution. The time saved by human agents from not having to answer frequent and repetitive questions can be invested in improving the service or in value-added activities, such as managing special claims or supervising critical interactions. Additionally, chatbots allow for continuous support 24 hours a day, 7 days a week, ensuring that customer inquiries are addressed even outside of business hours. This ability to provide uninterrupted customer service increases customer satisfaction and enhances the brand's perception.

From a customer experience perspective, multichannel support enables quick and personalized interaction, strengthening the relationship between the customer and the company. By responding effectively and consistently across multiple channels, the customer perceives a high-quality service that is consistent at every touchpoint with the brand. Additionally, access to the customer's historical information allows the chatbot to offer product or service recommendations, which in turn encourages cross-selling and improves customer retention.

- **Integration with internal systems and continuous improvement**

For a chatbot to function efficiently in a multichannel environment, it is crucial that it is integrated with the company's internal systems. This means it must have access to product databases, inventory management systems, and CRM platforms, allowing it to provide up-to-date responses based on real data. This integration is especially important for companies that handle large volumes of information or depend on frequent updates, such as ecommerce businesses. Through these integrations, the chatbot can access and update information in real-time, ensuring that responses are always accurate and relevant.

On the other hand, continuous improvement is a fundamental aspect of automating customer service. AI-based chatbots learn from each interaction, which means they can adapt and improve over time. This allows the chatbot to become increasingly accurate and efficient in resolving queries, and to offer more personalized and relevant responses based on previous interactions.

- ## Virtual assistants for sales

Virtual sales assistants have emerged as a powerful tool that not only simplifies the buying experience but also increases the likelihood of conversion, allowing companies to offer a personalized and proactive experience. These assistants, unlike basic customer service chatbots, are specifically designed to guide the user throughout their buying journey, providing recommendations, resolving specific questions about products and services, and even facilitating transactions.

The added value of virtual assistants lies in their ability to personalize interactions based on the customer's needs, behaviors, and preferences. Through artificial intelligence algorithms, these assistants can analyze patterns in the customer's purchasing behavior, visit history, and previous interactions with the company to offer a tailored experience. This personalization is essential in the modern shopping experience, where customers value relevant recommendations and support throughout the selection process.

- ### Functionality and Role of Virtual Assistants in Sales

The main goal of the virtual assistant in sales is not only to answer questions but also to make recommendations and anticipate the customer's needs, guiding them throughout the purchasing process. Artificial intelligence technology enables these assistants to suggest products or services based on customer preferences, purchase history, and consumption trends. They can also provide detailed product information, answer complex questions, and manage all types of transactions, such as order processing and payment management.

The role of these assistants is not limited to answering questions: they go a step further by generating specific recommendations. For example, in a clothing ecommerce, a virtual assistant could recommend a combination of garments based on the customer's initial selection, suggesting accessories or styles they might like. Similarly, in an electronics store, an assistant can suggest complementary accessories, such as cases or chargers, based on the device the customer is purchasing. This type of recommendation increases the chances of cross-selling and up-selling, maximizing the value of each transaction.

An essential feature in the functionality of virtual assistants for sales is their ability to manage and anticipate the question-and-answer process throughout the buying journey. By answering common questions such as product features, shipping options, delivery times, or return policies, the assistant allows the customer to move forward quickly without needing to consult other sources. This helps reduce abandonment rates, as doubts that could halt the buying process are resolved immediately, eliminating friction in the customer journey.

- **Personalization in the shopping experience**

Personalization is a key element that virtual assistants bring to the shopping experience. As customers interact with the assistant, it can adjust its communication style and recommendations based on the customer's profile. This ability to adapt recommendations in real-time makes the interaction more relevant and engaging for the user, creating a stronger connection with the brand and generating a shopping experience that the customer perceives as tailor-made.

To achieve effective personalization, virtual assistants rely on machine learning algorithms that analyze user behavior on the website, their search patterns, and previous purchases. For example, a customer who has been browsing tech products will receive recommendations aligned with their interests, while someone who has frequently visited the home products section will get suggestions tailored to that category. This personalization can help increase conversion in an ecommerce, as a customer who feels understood and supported in their needs is more likely to complete their purchase.

In addition, virtual assistants can integrate additional information from multiple data sources, such as the CRM or the company's social networks, enriching the knowledge about the customer and enabling even more precise personalization. The ability to integrate this data quickly and efficiently allows the assistant to build a comprehensive picture of the customer, tailoring each recommendation and suggestion to their specific preferences. This ability to adjust the experience based on customer interaction strengthens loyalty and promotes a long-term relationship with the brand.

- **Increase in conversion probability**

The role of virtual assistants in sales conversion is fundamental. Thanks to their ability to guide the customer, make recommendations, and resolve doubts in real time, these assistants reduce shopping cart abandonment and accelerate the decision-making process. Customers who receive precise guidance during their shopping experience tend to feel more confident and satisfied with their decisions, which translates into a higher conversion rate.

The virtual assistant can also identify when a customer is undecided or has doubts about a specific product and provide additional information to help them make a decision. This ability to detect and respond to signals of indecision is key to reducing the likelihood of cart abandonment. By providing additional information about product features, other users' reviews, or the benefits of the purchase, the assistant can directly influence the customer's final decision.

Moreover, virtual assistants are designed to maximize the average ticket of each transaction through upselling and cross-selling techniques. For example, if a customer is buying an electronic device, the assistant can suggest complementary accessories, extended warranties, or additional services that enhance their experience with the product. These data-driven recommendations not only increase the value of each sale but also improve the shopping experience by offering relevant solutions that complement the customer's original purchase.

- Optimization of the purchasing process

One of the main advantages of virtual sales assistants is their ability to optimize the buying process. By reducing the number of steps needed to complete a transaction, virtual assistants make it easier for the customer to finish the purchase in less time and without interruptions. These assistants are designed to help the customer navigate quickly and efficiently, resulting in a smoother and more satisfying shopping experience.

Virtual assistants can also use reminder and follow-up techniques to reduce shopping cart abandonment. For example, if a customer has added products to the cart but hasn't completed the purchase, the assistant can send personalized reminders, even offering discounts or additional incentives to motivate the completion of the transaction. This technique is particularly effective in ecommerce, where cart abandonment is a recurring issue that impacts the store's conversion rate.

Another important aspect of optimizing the purchasing process is the ability of virtual assistants to simplify the payment process. Often, customers abandon their purchases during checkout due to the complexity or number of steps required. By integrating the virtual assistant into the payment system, it is possible to guide the customer through each step and resolve any issues that may arise, reducing the likelihood of abandonment at this critical stage.

- **Post-sale follow-up and customer loyalty**

The role of the virtual assistant does not end once the transaction is completed. In fact, post-sale follow-up is one of the key functions of these assistants, and it's essential for strengthening the customer relationship. Once the customer has made a purchase, the virtual assistant can continue to engage by offering additional support, answering product-related questions, and managing order tracking. This level of support enhances the customer's perception and increases the likelihood of repeat purchases in the future.

The virtual assistant can also provide recommendations for related products based on the purchase made, encouraging repeat sales and strengthening customer loyalty. For example, a customer who has purchased an appliance can receive recommendations for accessories, maintenance products, or extended warranties. This approach not only generates additional revenue for the company but also enhances the customer experience by offering options that complement their purchase.

In addition, virtual assistants can gather information about the customer experience after the purchase, allowing the company to make improvements in its processes and products. This feedback becomes a valuable resource for adjusting sales strategies and further personalizing the customer experience in future interactions.

- **Practical example of a virtual assistant for sales in an Ecommerce SME**

To illustrate the impact of a virtual sales assistant in an SME, let's consider an e-commerce store that sells technology products. The company implements a virtual assistant on its website to help customers at every step of the buying process, from product search to checkout. A potential customer arrives at the website and starts looking for a laptop. The virtual assistant guides them through the available options, shows comparisons between different models, and provides information on compatible accessories like cases and chargers.

When the customer selects a specific model, the assistant provides information about the warranty, return policies, and shipping options, eliminating any doubts that could hinder the purchase. Once the customer decides to complete the purchase, the assistant guides them through the payment process, ensuring everything is clear and simple. Additionally, the assistant suggests a warranty extension service, increasing the value of the transaction.

Days after the purchase, the virtual assistant contacts the customer to ensure they are satisfied with their purchase and offers recommendations for other related products that may interest them, such as additional accessories for the laptop or external storage devices. This post-sale follow-up strengthens the relationship between the customer and the brand, increasing the likelihood that the customer will make future purchases.

- **Future of Virtual Assistants in Digital Sales**

Advancements in artificial intelligence and machine learning are constantly improving the capabilities of virtual sales assistants. In the future, these assistants will be increasingly able to understand and anticipate customer needs with greater accuracy, providing even more personalized and relevant recommendations. Moreover, with the development of technologies like natural language processing and voice recognition, virtual assistants will become more intuitive and natural in their interactions, offering a user experience similar to that of interacting with a human sales advisor.

Companies that adopt this technology will be better positioned to compete in a market where personalization and customer service efficiency are key success factors. Virtual sales assistants not only enhance the shopping experience but also optimize the company's operational efficiency by automating repetitive tasks, reducing cart abandonment, and maximizing the value of each transaction.

10.3. Sentiment analysis on social networks and review platforms

Sentiment analysis on social media and review platforms is an increasingly valuable tool for SMEs, as it allows them to understand how customers perceive their brand or products in real-time. In a digital market where consumers express their opinions immediately and publicly, the ability to identify opinion patterns can make a significant difference in a company's strategy. Through natural language processing (NLP) techniques and artificial intelligence algorithms, sentiment analysis allows companies to classify user comments into positive, negative, or neutral categories, providing a clear perspective on the overall sentiment of their audience.

For SMEs, this type of analysis represents a competitive advantage by offering valuable insights without requiring large investments. Knowing the opinion of customers through their comments on social media or reviews on platforms like Google Reviews or Trustpilot allows companies to adjust their marketing strategies, improve their product offerings, and act quickly in the event of a reputation crisis. Speed in decision-making is crucial; a company that can identify and respond to negative perceptions in real-time has a greater chance of mitigating its impact and protecting its brand image.

The applications of sentiment analysis range from monitoring social media to managing online reputation. In social media, where comments can be extensive and varied, AI helps process large volumes of text quickly, identifying trends in audience perception. This analysis can uncover areas for improvement or recognize successes in marketing strategy, which is essential for building a stronger connection with the target audience. On review platforms, where feedback is often more direct and detailed, sentiment analysis helps SMEs identify specific aspects of their products or services that customers value or find unsatisfactory.

To implement this type of analysis, SMEs can use Python libraries such as VADER or advanced sentiment analysis APIs provided by services like Google Cloud Natural Language or IBM Watson. These tools, although different in complexity and precision, offer scalable options for companies of various sizes. Additionally, real-time monitoring through platforms like Hootsuite or Brandwatch allows for immediate reactions to critical or highly relevant mentions. Together, these tools and technologies enable SMEs to turn customer feedback into strategic decisions, improving both customer satisfaction and market competitiveness.

- **Importance of sentiment analysis for SMEs**

Sentiment analysis has emerged as a powerful tool for SMEs to understand how customers perceive their brands, products, or services. In the digital age, consumer interaction with companies has multiplied across different platforms, and the way customers express their opinions has radically changed. Today, comments and reviews are public and accessible in real-time, creating both opportunities and challenges for businesses. Through sentiment analysis, SMEs can monitor and classify these opinions into positive, negative, or neutral categories, allowing them to gain valuable insights that support strategic decision-making.

One of the most significant advantages of sentiment analysis for SMEs is that it allows them to continuously evaluate how their products or services are perceived without having to wait long periods for traditional surveys or market research. This represents a substantial shift in adaptability, especially in markets where trends can change rapidly. The ability to obtain immediate feedback from customers gives companies a deeper understanding of their expectations and experiences. Instead of reacting to negative situations with improvised measures, sentiment analysis enables companies to detect recurring patterns and respond proactively by adjusting marketing strategies, improving products or services, or anticipating potential crises.

A key aspect of sentiment analysis for SMEs is the accessibility they now have to conduct this type of analysis without incurring high costs. Previously, this kind of technology was only available to large corporations, but today there are multiple tools and platforms that allow small businesses to implement sentiment analysis models easily. Open-source libraries like VADER or TextBlob, as well as APIs from providers like Google Cloud Natural Language or IBM Watson, make it possible to perform real-time, large-scale opinion analysis. This democratized access allows SMEs to compete on the same playing field as large companies, gaining valuable insights without a prohibitive cost.

Another way in which sentiment analysis adds value to SMEs is by allowing them to adjust their marketing strategies in an informed manner. The insights gained through this technique help identify which marketing messages resonate best with customers and which generate a negative perception. For example, if a recent social media campaign has generated negative comments, the company can quickly detect this and adjust its message before a negative perception consolidates among its customers. Additionally, sentiment analysis allows for identifying areas for improvement in products or services, which is crucial for SMEs that want to remain competitive in crowded sectors. When customers share their experiences on social media or review platforms, they do so directly and honestly, providing the company with valuable data on what works and what needs adjustment.

Sentiment analysis also allows SMEs to respond quickly and effectively to potential reputation crises. In today's environment, a negative comment can go viral in minutes, and companies need to act fast to contain the impact. A sentiment analysis system can alert the company when negative mentions reach a critical threshold, allowing them to respond immediately with personalized and effective solutions. This quick response not only minimizes damage to the company's reputation but also shows customers that their opinions are valued and that the company is committed to delivering a quality experience. By intervening promptly, SMEs can prevent negative comments from escalating into a larger crisis.

In addition to managing potential crises, sentiment analysis allows SMEs to strengthen their relationship with customers through a more customer-focused approach. By better understanding their audience's expectations and needs, SMEs can tailor their strategies and improve customer satisfaction, which is essential for fostering brand loyalty. For example, by identifying positive patterns in customer feedback about certain products or features, companies can highlight those points in their communication and further enhance what customers already value. Similarly, when negative patterns are detected about a specific aspect, the company can take action to rectify it and show customers that their feedback is valued and their satisfaction is a priority.

Sentiment analysis is also a valuable tool for innovation. By having a clear understanding of what truly matters to customers, SMEs can develop new products or adjust existing ones to better align with market demands. This information becomes a guide for decision-making involving resource allocation and long-term strategy development. SMEs that regularly apply sentiment analysis can observe how customer opinions evolve over time and anticipate future trends, strengthening their market position.

The flexibility of sentiment analysis makes it an adaptable tool for multiple channels. SMEs can implement it on social media, review platforms, their own websites, and any other channel where customers interact with the brand. Each of these channels offers unique insights; while social media can provide a general view of audience sentiment about a specific campaign or event, review platforms offer more detailed opinions about individual products or services. By integrating the insights obtained from all channels, SMEs achieve a 360-degree view of their brand perception, allowing them to make more precise and effective adjustments in every area of their operation.

Furthermore, sentiment analysis can complement other data analysis tools already implemented in an SME, creating a more robust business intelligence strategy. For example, by combining sentiment insights with sales data or user behavior on the website, the company gains a complete perspective of the performance of its strategies and can correlate changes in sales with changes in customer perception. This synergy between sentiment analysis and other data analyses provides a significant advantage in decision-making, allowing the company to react with agility and precision.

Sentiment analysis is also particularly valuable in sectors where the customer experience is crucial, such as retail, hospitality, and ecommerce. In these sectors, customer perceptions and experiences directly influence sales and retention. SMEs can use sentiment analysis to quickly identify aspects of their customer experience that need attention, such as service, the purchasing process, or product quality, allowing them to make targeted improvements that have a direct impact on customer satisfaction and loyalty.

Finally, sentiment analysis allows SMEs to constantly measure the impact of their strategies over time. As new products, campaigns, or policies are implemented, the company can monitor how customer perception changes and adjust its efforts accordingly. This ability to measure audience perception in real-time makes sentiment analysis an essential tool for maintaining relevance and competitiveness in an ever-changing market. By leveraging data from opinions and comments, SMEs not only gain a better understanding of their customers, but also strengthen their ability to respond quickly and accurately to market needs.

- ## Applications of Sentiment Analysis

Sentiment analysis has gained significant importance for SMEs, allowing them to monitor public perception of their brand and products on social media and review platforms. This tool offers the possibility to capture real-time customer sentiment, as more and more people turn to these channels to express opinions, suggestions, criticisms, or experiences. Through advanced natural language processing (NLP) and machine learning techniques, companies can detect patterns of satisfaction or dissatisfaction and use these insights to improve their offerings, adjust marketing campaigns, and manage their reputation.

One of the most important applications of sentiment analysis is monitoring social media, which has become a key space for direct communication between companies and consumers. Social media offers a constant flow of real-time information where customers can express their opinions about a company or product instantly. By applying AI to the analysis of comments and posts on networks like Twitter, Facebook, or Instagram, SMEs can early identify potential perception problems, recurring dissatisfaction patterns, or mentions that represent opportunities for improvement. For example, if a company launches a new marketing campaign, sentiment analysis can quickly show how it is being received, allowing for immediate adjustments or responses if necessary.

To implement sentiment analysis on social media, SMEs can use specialized tools or APIs that capture and analyze comments, hashtags, and mentions on these platforms. The use of machine learning and text processing techniques allows for the automatic classification of comments into positive, negative, or neutral categories, and then groups them to understand the most recurring themes. A food company, for example, can use this analysis to detect whether a new campaign about the sustainability of its products is generating positive responses or facing specific backlash, such as criticism related to the authenticity of its sustainable practices. Monitoring social media with AI not only enables the company to respond to potential image crises but also to adapt its messages to better align with customer concerns.

Sentiment analysis also allows for the detection and management of online reputation on review platforms, a channel that is increasingly decisive in consumer decision-making. Reviews on sites like Google Reviews, Yelp, or Trustpilot are consulted by thousands of people and concretely reflect customer experiences and opinions. For an SME, an accumulation of negative reviews can be a significant barrier in the process of acquiring new clients, as the company's digital reputation becomes a decisive factor when consumers choose their products or services.

Sentiment analysis on review platforms allows SMEs to address negative feedback in a timely manner, as they can accurately identify the most common criticisms and take specific actions. If, for example, an online electronics store sees in the reviews that customers often complain about the delivery service, they can take steps with their logistics operator to improve delivery times or communication about order status. Similarly, positive reviews can be used to identify strengths in the offering that should be highlighted in future marketing campaigns. For SMEs, managing these reviews and using sentiment analysis to extract specific insights is an effective way to adjust their strategy proactively.

In the realm of online reputation management, sentiment analysis provides a key advantage: preventive control. By analyzing customer comments and reviews, a company can anticipate major issues and prevent negative perceptions from spreading and affecting the brand's image. Furthermore, this analysis helps improve the customer experience by quickly identifying pain points or recurring complaints, allowing the company to make changes that reflect attention and respect for consumer opinions.

On the other hand, sentiment analysis on social media and review platforms is a useful tool for comparing yourself to the competition. SMEs can use it to analyze not only their own mentions but also those of other companies in the same sector, identifying the strengths and weaknesses of the competition. This allows them to detect opportunities for improvement in their own service or adjust their strategy based on customer preferences. A restaurant that notices, for example, that customers of a competitor complain about the lack of vegetarian options on the menu can consider adding such dishes to their own offerings. This type of strategic analysis not only improves the company's position but also allows it to respond to the needs of a customer segment looking for certain features in their consumption options.

The impact of sentiment analysis extends to increasing customer loyalty. By proactively responding to customer feedback and criticism, SMEs can strengthen their relationship with customers and show that they value their opinions. This direct and active connection with customers is an important factor for retention. An effective response to a negative review or a corrective action based on customer feedback generates a positive perception of the brand and a sense of commitment and empathy. This helps build a loyal and satisfied customer base that recognizes the company not only listens but acts on their feedback.

In terms of tools and techniques for conducting sentiment analysis, SMEs have a wide range of options. They can use cloud service APIs, such as Google Cloud Natural Language API, to analyze large volumes of text with quick and accessible implementation. These tools allow companies to process mentions and reviews automatically, classifying the overall sentiment and providing useful metrics like average sentiment score. This type of solution is especially useful for companies without their own technical team, as the initial setup and integration of these APIs are relatively simple.

Another popular option is social media monitoring platforms like Hootsuite or Sprout Social, which allow SMEs to track their mentions and reviews in real time, with built-in sentiment analysis. These platforms show the general sentiment of mentions, enabling the company to quickly identify if there is a shift in brand perception and make informed decisions. They also allow for grouping comments into categories, identifying recurring themes, and seeing the evolution of sentiment over time. This continuous monitoring capability helps SMEs create a dynamic communication strategy that effectively responds to changes in customer sentiment.

In short, sentiment analysis allows SMEs to transform customer comments and opinions into a tool for continuous improvement. In addition to immediate applications for managing reputation, the information obtained can be used to enhance product development, service quality, and customer communication.

- **Tools for sentiment analysis**

Sentiment analysis, essential for understanding customer perceptions, can be approached using various tools, especially with Python libraries and sentiment analysis APIs. These solutions allow SMEs to automate the analysis of customer comments on social media and review platforms, making it easier to quickly categorize opinions into positive, negative, or neutral. To implement this, you can choose either tools developed in Python or cloud-based natural language processing (NLP) services. Next, we'll explore each of these alternatives, discussing their features, configurations, and benefits for sentiment analysis in the context of SMEs.

One of the most recognized libraries in Python for sentiment analysis is VADER (Valence Aware Dictionary and Sentiment Reasoner), specifically designed to evaluate sentiments in short texts like tweets, reviews, or comments. This tool is based on a pre-classified dictionary of terms combined with grammar rules that identify the intensity of sentiment in the text, such as the use of adverbs and punctuation. Unlike other analysis approaches, which may require extensive model training or complex preprocessing, VADER stands out for its simplicity and accuracy in analyzing user emotions in natural language.

To get started with VADER, the first step is to install the nltk library, which includes VADER among its resources. After installation, you load the analyzer and use it for text analysis with just a few lines of code. Below is a basic example of its implementation:

```
import nltk
from nltk.sentiment.vader import SentimentIntensityAnalyzer

# Descargar VADER en nltk
nltk.download('vader_lexicon')

# Crear un analizador de sentimientos
sia = SentimentIntensityAnalyzer()

# Analizar el sentimiento de un texto
texto = "Excelente servicio y productos de alta calidad. ¡Muy satisfecho!"
resultado = sia.polarity_scores(texto)
print(resultado)
```

```
[1]   ✓ 5.1s

...   {'neg': 0.0, 'neu': 1.0, 'pos': 0.0, 'compound': 0.0}
      [nltk_data] Downloading package vader_lexicon to
      [nltk_data]     ...AppData\Roaming\nltk_data...
      [nltk_data]   Package vader_lexicon is already up-to-date!
```

The result of this analysis is a score that indicates the intensity of sentiment in the categories of negative, neutral, and positive, along with an overall score (compound). This compound score allows you to determine the predominant tone of the text; for example, a positive compound value indicates an overall positive sentiment. This approach is useful for classifying comments or reviews on e-commerce platforms or social media, providing SMEs with a quick overview of customer feedback.

Another commonly used library for sentiment analysis in Python is TextBlob, which performs sentiment analysis using a polarity and subjectivity approach. TextBlob provides easy access to language processing tools and is ideal for applications where analysis doesn't require extremely high precision but does need quick implementation. To use TextBlob, you first install it and then create a TextBlob object that analyzes the sentiment of a sentence or paragraph.

```
from textblob import TextBlob

# Análisis de un texto con TextBlob
texto = "Los precios son elevados, pero la calidad es excelente."
blob = TextBlob(texto)

# Obtener polaridad (sentimiento general) y subjetividad
print("Polaridad:", blob.sentiment.polarity)  # Valor entre -1 (negativo) y 1 (positivo)
print("Subjetividad:", blob.sentiment.subjectivity)  # Valor entre 0 (objetivo) y 1 (subjetivo)
[1]  ✓ 0.1s

...  Polaridad: 0.0
     Subjetividad: 0.0
```

TextBlob provides two metrics: polarity, which identifies whether the comment is positive or negative, and subjectivity, which measures the degree to which the text reflects a subjective opinion or an objective observation. This allows SMEs to analyze reviews in more detail, detecting not only the sentiment orientation but also the intensity of the opinion.

For SMEs that prefer to use scalable and low-maintenance solutions, cloud platform sentiment analysis APIs are an excellent choice. These APIs allow for complex analysis without the need to train or maintain NLP models. Some of the most used APIs include Google Cloud Natural Language API and IBM Watson Natural Language Understanding.

Google Cloud Natural Language API allows for precise sentiment analysis by applying advanced machine learning across different languages. Additionally, this API includes other NLP functionalities like content classification and entity analysis, providing a complete context of customer comments. To start using Google Cloud Natural Language API, you need to create a project in Google Cloud and enable the API. Then, by using the google-cloud-language library in Python, you can analyze the sentiment of a text as follows:

```
from google.cloud import language_v1
from google.cloud.language_v1 import enums

# Crear cliente para la API
client = language_v1.LanguageServiceClient()

# Definir el texto a analizar
texto = "El servicio fue rápido y el producto es excelente."

# Crear el tipo de contenido a analizar
document = language_v1.Document(content=texto, type=enums.Document.Type.PLAIN_TEXT)

# Realizar análisis de sentimientos
sentiment = client.analyze_sentiment(document=document).document_sentiment

# Imprimir los resultados
print("Puntuación:", sentiment.score)
print("Magnitud:", sentiment.magnitude)
]
```

The API returns two important values: the score (sentiment score), which reflects the overall tone of the text on a scale from -1 to 1, and the magnitude (sentiment magnitude), which represents the intensity of the sentiment. This data provides a complete view of the customer's tone, allowing SMEs to identify comments with a high emotional load that may require a timely response.

IBM Watson Natural Language Understanding is another popular option, known for its advanced sentiment analysis capabilities and its adaptability for businesses of any size. IBM Watson offers a flexible API that not only analyzes sentiment but also extracts entities and concepts, providing additional context to the comments analyzed. The following code demonstrates how to perform sentiment analysis using IBM Watson:

```
from ibm_watson import NaturalLanguageUnderstandingV1
from ibm_watson.natural_language_understanding_v1 import Features, SentimentOptions
from ibm_cloud_sdk_core.authenticators import IAMAuthenticator

# Configuración de la API
authenticator = IAMAuthenticator('API_KEY')
natural_language_understanding = NaturalLanguageUnderstandingV1(
    version='2022-04-07',
    authenticator=authenticator
)
natural_language_understanding.set_service_url('URL_IBM_WATSON')

# Definir el texto a analizar
texto = "Estoy muy descontento con el producto, no cumplió con mis expectativas."

# Análisis de sentimientos
response = natural_language_understanding.analyze(
    text=texto,
    features=Features(sentiment=SentimentOptions(targets=[texto]))).get_result()

# Imprimir resultados
print("Sentimiento general:", response['sentiment']['document']['label'])
print("Puntuación de sentimiento:", response['sentiment']['document']['score'])
```

Watson classifies sentiment as positive, negative, or neutral and provides a score that helps understand the intensity. Its customization capabilities allow it to analyze comments based on specific topics, such as customer service or product quality, which is useful for SMEs that want to get detailed insights into different aspects of their operations.

Both APIs, Google's and IBM's, are powerful options for SMEs that want to implement sentiment analysis without the need for maintaining their own models, making them ideal for companies that need to scale their sentiment analysis capabilities without dedicated data science teams. By using these cloud solutions, SMEs can leverage advanced NLP models without worrying about technical infrastructure or model maintenance, since cloud platforms continuously update their services to improve accuracy and performance.

Cloud-based APIs also offer the advantage of processing large volumes of data in real-time, which is essential for businesses with a high influx of comments and reviews. For example, in the case of an online store that receives hundreds of opinions daily, the API can analyze the data of each review and generate insights instantly, providing the company with a constant perspective on how customer perception is evolving. This real-time analysis allows for timely reactions to negative feedback and helps identify emerging trends, such as growing interest in a specific product or concern over a common issue among customers.

Another important benefit of these APIs is the ability to easily integrate with other business platforms and tools. Both Google Cloud and IBM Watson offer connections and SDKs that adapt to different management systems and CRM platforms like Salesforce or HubSpot. This integration facilitates the automated analysis of customer messages in CRM and their classification into specific categories, allowing sales and customer service teams to prioritize the most relevant interactions. For example, a comment classified as negative could trigger an automatic alert for the support team, while a positive comment could be recorded as a loyalty opportunity.

When comparing the use of Python libraries like VADER and TextBlob with Google Cloud and Watson APIs, libraries are generally recommended for small or experimental projects, while APIs are better for companies with larger data volumes and scalability requirements. Although VADER and TextBlob are free and easy to implement, their scope is limited in terms of precision and adaptability for languages other than English or Spanish. On the other hand, cloud-based sentiment analysis APIs have multilingual coverage and can interpret complex nuances in texts, including irony, sarcasm, and double meanings, which is crucial in contexts like social media where informal and colloquial language is common.

Choosing the right tool depends on the context and the company's needs. If the SME requires a one-time analysis and has a technical team that can manage Python configurations, VADER or TextBlob are very useful and cost-effective options. On the other hand, for SMEs looking for continuous real-time monitoring without constant intervention, Google or IBM APIs are much more robust and recommended options.

In the end, using these sentiment analysis tools allows companies to take a proactive approach to managing their reputation. For example, by using automated sentiment analysis on social media and review platforms, a company can anticipate common customer issues or concerns. If negative comments related to a specific product increase, the company can adjust its marketing campaigns, modify its messages, or even reformulate its offering before the negative perception significantly affects sales.

In addition, sentiment analysis can strengthen customer loyalty by allowing the company to automatically identify its most fervent advocates. Customers who consistently leave positive reviews or express satisfaction on social media can be rewarded through loyalty programs, exclusive discounts, or mentions in advertising campaigns, thus increasing the likelihood that they will continue to buy and recommend the brand to other consumers.

Finally, it is important to keep in mind that sentiment analysis, although powerful, is not infallible. There are inherent technical limitations, especially when it comes to interpreting sarcasm or figurative language, and sometimes the systems can misclassify the tone of a message. To overcome this challenge, it is advisable for SMEs to combine automated analysis with manual review in more complex or ambiguous cases, thus ensuring accurate interpretation and an appropriate response.

In conclusion, both Python libraries and cloud APIs offer a wide range of options for SMEs to implement sentiment analysis according to their specific needs and technical resources. Whether through customized solutions or scalable analysis services, using sentiment analysis represents a strategic step forward to improve customer relationships, optimize brand perception, and foster a trusting relationship with the customer base.

- ## Real-time brand mention monitoring

Real-time brand mention monitoring is a fundamental practice for any SME seeking a continuous and accurate view of how it is perceived in the market. Constant analysis of mentions and comments allows companies to respond promptly to critical situations, optimize their positioning, and strengthen their connection with customers. This practice has become a necessity in the digital age, where consumers interact and express their opinions actively on social media, review platforms, and other online channels.

To implement effective real-time monitoring, SMEs can turn to various specialized tools such as Hootsuite and Brandwatch, which offer a detailed view of mentions and allow for comprehensive reputation management. These tools have positioned themselves as industry leaders due to their ability to collect data from multiple online sources and present information in visual dashboards, where the marketing or customer service team can analyze the flow of comments, mentions, and reviews. This approach allows for the identification of patterns in a visual way, facilitating decision-making in specific situations. Additionally, by integrating sentiment analysis, these tools provide an even more complete view of the tone of conversations around the brand.

The advantage of using Hootsuite and Brandwatch lies in their ability to integrate multiple platforms and communication channels into a single monitoring system. These solutions allow SMEs to track mentions on social networks like Twitter, Instagram, and Facebook, as well as on blogs, forums, and other relevant websites. In the case of Hootsuite, the tool also offers integration with messaging platforms like WhatsApp or Messenger, allowing businesses to monitor direct interactions with customers and respond quickly to inquiries or concerns. Brandwatch, on the other hand, is known for its ability to perform an exhaustive analysis of social networks and other online media, extracting detailed insights about trends, the most used keywords related to the brand, and overall perception.

The sentiment analysis features of these tools are essential for providing an accurate perspective on public opinion around the brand. Sentiment analysis allows SMEs to understand not just how many mentions their brand receives, but also whether those mentions are positive, negative, or neutral. For example, a spike in negative mentions could indicate a potential problem or a developing crisis, while an increase in positive mentions might signal the success of a recent campaign or a favorable change in brand perception. This ability to identify the emotional tone in mentions allows companies to anticipate possible issues before they escalate into crises, thus providing a significant competitive advantage.

Another advantage of real-time monitoring is the ability to perform comparative analysis with the competition. Many brand monitoring tools, including Hootsuite and Brandwatch, allow you to analyze your brand's performance compared to direct competitors. This helps SMEs assess whether their brand position is strong and identify areas for improvement. For example, if customers praise a competitor for fast delivery or service quality, the SME can pinpoint these areas for improvement and adjust their operational or marketing strategies to stay competitive. The ability to compare also allows companies to better understand industry trends and changes in consumer expectations.

Moreover, these tools allow for the automation of alerts and notifications when there are significant changes in mentions or the tone of conversations. This is especially useful for SMEs that may not have a team dedicated exclusively to monitoring. Real-time alerts ensure that the marketing or customer service team is immediately informed if there's a spike in negative mentions or if a specific keyword starts appearing frequently. This automatic alert function ensures that no relevant comment or mention goes unnoticed, allowing SMEs to react quickly to changes in the digital environment.

For example, if a brand receives repetitive comments about a specific product, the tool can send an alert so the team can review the feedback and determine if there's an issue with the product or if it's a trend in user perception. The company can then act to resolve any issues proactively, such as updating the information on the website, publishing a statement, or, if necessary, making adjustments to the product offering.

For SMEs, real-time mention monitoring is not only useful in crisis management but also in identifying opportunities to engage with the audience. By observing positive mentions, the company can respond directly to customers to thank them for their support, which helps strengthen loyalty and commitment to the brand. Additionally, monitoring allows the identification of brand advocates, those customers who frequently express positive comments or recommend the brand on social media. Building relationships with these advocates can help the SME increase its visibility and improve brand perception.

Real-time monitoring also allows companies to be more reactive in their marketing strategies. For example, if a marketing campaign is getting a positive response on social media, the company can decide to expand the campaign or replicate it across other channels. Similarly, if a negative reception is observed, the company can quickly adjust the message or stop the campaign to prevent the negative impact from spreading.

Integrating this monitoring data into the daily workflow is essential to getting the most out of real-time sentiment analysis tools. Many platforms allow data exports and generate custom reports that facilitate internal analysis. At the end of the day or the week, the marketing team can review these reports to better understand trends and adjust their strategy based on customer feedback and overall perception.

The ability to combine mention monitoring with additional data, such as sales metrics or advertising campaign performance, provides a holistic view of the business and allows SMEs to make adjustments across all areas. For example, by observing a correlation between positive comments and increased product sales, the marketing team can focus their efforts on promoting that product more intensively. On the other hand, if negative mentions are linked to a drop in sales, the company can take corrective measures more quickly and efficiently.

Finally, real-time brand mention monitoring is a powerful tool that helps SMEs adapt to the dynamic environment of the digital market. As consumer expectations and industry trends constantly change, having a tool that allows you to monitor and analyze the general sentiment of the public gives companies the ability to maintain relevance and competitiveness in their sector. For SMEs, this quick reaction capability translates into greater control over their reputation, a better relationship with their customers, and an advantage over competitors who are not using these technologies efficiently.

10.4. AI for advanced customer segmentation

Artificial intelligence offers SMEs an unprecedented opportunity to perform advanced customer segmentation, going far beyond traditional demographic-based segmentation. By using AI to analyze and classify customers, businesses can identify behavior patterns, consumption habits, and specific preferences that allow them to tailor marketing strategies to a much higher level of personalization than conventional segmentation. This means that SMEs can engage more effectively with each segment of their audience, optimizing their marketing efforts and boosting conversion rates, customer retention, and loyalty.

AI applied to advanced segmentation uses machine learning, data analysis, natural language processing, and predictive models to identify groups of customers with similar interests and behaviors. This segmentation goes beyond age, gender, or location and explores interaction patterns, the frequency and type of products purchased, preferred communication channels, and even emotional responses to the brand. Thanks to these techniques, SMEs can create advertising campaigns, messages, and promotions tailored to each segment, maximizing the relevance and impact of their marketing strategies.

Instead of limiting itself to categorizing customers into broad general groups, AI allows for division into highly specific subgroups. For example, a company selling sportswear can discover through AI that some of its customers value the functionality and durability of the products, while others prioritize fashion trends and design. With this advanced segmentation, the company can develop marketing strategies that highlight the specific features each customer segment values, increasing the likelihood that each group will identify with the brand and make a purchase.

A popular technique in advanced segmentation with AI is customer clustering using unsupervised algorithms, such as the k-means algorithm. This type of algorithm identifies natural groupings within the data, forming clusters that share similar characteristics without needing to specify which attributes to look for. For example, an e-commerce company could use k-means to segment customers based on their purchasing patterns: those who regularly buy high-end items, those who frequently purchase discounted products, or those who make occasional purchases of products from different categories. These groups can then receive targeted marketing campaigns, enhancing the relevance of the content and, consequently, the results of each campaign.

Another key aspect of AI in advanced segmentation is the analysis of transactional and behavioral data. Transactions provide information on what customers buy, how often, and in what quantities. By applying machine learning models, SMEs can uncover hidden patterns in this data, such as the propensity of certain customers to buy specific products at certain times of the year or the average time between purchases. For example, in a grocery store, AI could identify customers who buy organic products in large quantities at the beginning of the month and generate a specific discount campaign for them at that time, thus increasing the likelihood of conversion.

AI can also identify behavioral patterns in each customer's buying journey. This is particularly useful in digital environments, where every action taken by the customer (clicks, time on page, interaction with content) becomes valuable data that AI can analyze to determine which products generate the most interest, how often customers visit before making a purchase, or what type of advertising messages elicit the greatest response. Using these insights, an online store can develop personalized strategies, such as product recommendations based on browsing behavior, or send personalized reminders to users who have shown interest in specific products but haven't completed the purchase.

Natural Language Processing (NLP) is another crucial tool in advanced customer segmentation using AI. NLP allows SMEs to analyze customer texts and comments to capture their opinions, emotions, and expectations. Through techniques like sentiment analysis, a company can classify comments into positive, negative, or neutral sentiment categories. This allows them to identify, for example, customers who are satisfied with product quality but express dissatisfaction with shipping times. With this information, the company can tailor its communication to specifically address these groups and their concerns, thereby improving brand perception.

In addition, predictive segmentation analysis using AI allows businesses to anticipate changes in customer behavior and adjust marketing strategies accordingly. Predictive models based on machine learning can detect consumption trends from historical data, enabling SMEs to foresee how customers are likely to react to new marketing campaigns, product launches, or price changes. For example, if a model predicts that a group of customers is more likely to make impulse purchases during end-of-season discount campaigns, the company can send them personalized notifications during those days, thus increasing the campaign's effectiveness.

Advanced segmentation through AI also allows SMEs to tailor the customer experience in real-time. In digital environments, AI models can analyze customer behavior in real-time to adjust the browsing experience and product recommendations according to each user's current interests. For instance, a customer browsing a sports product section might automatically receive suggestions for other similar products or active promotions in that category, increasing the likelihood of purchase and enhancing the customer experience.

The use of AI in advanced customer segmentation also opens the door to automating marketing campaigns. With detailed and well-defined segments, SMEs can set up automated campaigns that run based on customer actions or predefined conditions. For example, if a customer abandons their shopping cart on an ecommerce site, the system can automatically trigger a reminder email with a specific discount, encouraging the customer to complete their purchase. This type of AI-based campaign increases marketing efficiency as it allows the company to respond automatically to customer actions at the right time with a personalized message.

Furthermore, advanced segmentation with AI allows SMEs to conduct a deeper analysis of the customer lifecycle. Using machine learning techniques, it is possible to analyze the likelihood of a customer making a repeat purchase or abandoning the brand after a certain interaction. This enables the company to classify customers according to their retention potential and develop personalized strategies to retain the most valuable customers or try to win back those who have stopped engaging with the brand. In this sense, AI not only facilitates segmentation based on current characteristics but also provides a long-term view, where customers are classified based on their value and the effort the company should invest in retaining them.

An effective advanced segmentation strategy using AI requires proper data integration. SMEs must ensure that relevant data is available and organized in an accessible way for AI models. This involves integrating data sources such as sales records, social media interactions, website visits, satisfaction surveys, and other relevant data into a single system. Business intelligence solutions and customer relationship management (CRM) systems can facilitate this integration, allowing AI to access a complete and consistent data set. This data integration is crucial for segmentation to be accurate and relevant, as it enables AI models to consider multiple factors and generate truly useful customer groups for decision-making.

AI-generated segment visualizations are also important for marketing managers to understand and apply insights effectively. Visualization tools allow each segment and its main characteristics to be displayed in charts or diagrams, which simplifies analysis and strategic decision-making. For example, a marketing team could visualize how customer segments have evolved over time or how certain behaviors correlate with higher spending on specific products. By visualizing these insights, marketing managers can make informed adjustments and focus their resources on the segments with the greatest potential.

For SMEs, using AI in advanced customer segmentation is an investment that offers a significant return in terms of campaign efficiency and effectiveness. By focusing on the segments with the highest potential and personalizing each message, companies can maximize the value of their marketing resources and achieve tangible results. Moreover, with a more detailed understanding of their customers, SMEs can build stronger, long-lasting relationships, increasing both customer loyalty and overall satisfaction with the brand.

10.5. Automation of marketing with AI

The automation of marketing through artificial intelligence has become a powerful and accessible tool for SMEs to maximize their resources and optimize the effectiveness of their campaigns without the need for large marketing teams or extensive investments. In an environment where digital competition is increasingly fierce, the ability to dynamically adjust marketing strategies in real-time, based on accurate data and predictive analysis, allows companies not only to adapt but also to stay ahead of consumer trends and behaviors. By incorporating AI into marketing automation, SMEs can execute complex and personalized campaigns that continuously optimize their results based on performance and data obtained, without constant manual intervention.

The automation of marketing with AI works by combining advanced techniques in machine learning, data analysis, and real-time optimization. Instead of marketing teams having to oversee every change or constantly make decisions about adjusting ads, budgets, or messages, AI takes control of these elements, optimizing them based on user behavior and campaign objectives. Tools like Adext AI and Albert AI have positioned themselves as robust solutions for SMEs looking to implement automated marketing campaigns. These platforms can manage multiple channels simultaneously, optimize ad spending, and personalize ads for different customer segments, increasing the chances of success for each campaign while minimizing the human effort required.

One of the key aspects of automating marketing with AI is optimizing the budget in real-time. AI-based tools continuously monitor ad performance and automatically adjust budget allocation to the channels or ads that are generating the best results. Instead of distributing the budget in a fixed manner or based on ad-hoc human decisions, AI analyzes response patterns, user interactions, and real-time conversions to focus resources on the campaign elements with the highest return. This way, an SME can ensure that every euro invested in marketing is directed towards the most profitable strategy, reducing waste and increasing the return on advertising investment.

Another advantage of automating marketing with AI is the creation of content and personalization based on each customer's interests. Through the analysis of behavioral data and interaction history, AI can determine which type of content is most appealing to each customer segment and tailor ads or messages accordingly. For example, if a customer shows particular interest in specific products or a category of services, the AI system can generate personalized ads or recommendations that highlight those products or categories, increasing the likelihood of conversion. This level of personalization would be nearly impossible to implement manually, but with AI, SMEs can offer each customer a personalized and relevant experience, improving the brand relationship and increasing the likelihood of a purchase.

Dynamic audience segmentation is another key aspect of marketing automation with AI. As customers interact with the brand, AI can adjust segments based on behavior and updated data. This means that if a customer who usually makes low-value purchases starts showing interest in high-end products, AI can automatically reclassify them into a premium customer segment, allowing the marketing strategy to be adjusted for them in real time. Dynamic segmentation enables SMEs to quickly react to changes in customer behavior and adapt campaigns without human intervention. This way, marketing efforts are always aligned with the current profile and status of each customer, increasing the relevance and effectiveness of every interaction.

Regarding automation tools, Adext AI and Albert AI are standout examples that have simplified the implementation of AI in digital marketing campaigns for SMEs. Adext AI focuses on optimizing ads on platforms like Google Ads and Facebook Ads, automatically adjusting ads and budget to achieve maximum performance. It uses machine learning to analyze the results of each campaign and redistribute the budget towards the most effective ads. This tool also identifies and expands audience segments that show a higher response, adapting ad content to increase the conversion rate in those specific groups.

On the other hand, Albert AI has positioned itself as a complete solution for the comprehensive management of campaigns across multiple channels. Its system can analyze large volumes of data, optimize the budget, adjust content, and generate new ads in real-time. Albert AI uses machine learning algorithms to learn and predict which types of ads will be most effective for each customer group, optimizing the strategy and adapting to market trends without manual intervention. This tool is particularly useful for SMEs looking for a system that manages the entire lifecycle of their digital marketing campaigns, from ad creation and personalization to budget distribution and optimization based on results.

AI-based email automation platforms can identify the best times to send emails, the type of content that interests each customer the most, and the ideal sending frequency to maximize response. Instead of sending mass emails, SMEs can implement personalized and automated email campaigns that align with each recipient's individual preferences. Additionally, AI allows for detailed tracking of each customer's response, adjusting future communications based on the results obtained. This increases open and click-through rates while reducing the likelihood of emails being marked as spam.

Dynamic remarketing is another powerful resource that AI offers for marketing automation. Through this technique, AI systems can identify customers who have shown interest in specific products but haven't completed the purchase, and send them personalized ads reminding them of those products. This type of remarketing is especially effective in ecommerce, where many users browse and explore products without necessarily buying them on their first visit. By reminding them of the products they were interested in, AI increases the likelihood of conversion and keeps the brand in the customer's mind. Additionally, dynamic remarketing can include additional recommendations based on products similar or complementary to those the customer initially viewed, encouraging the purchase of additional products.

The automation of ad creation is another area where AI can make a big difference in marketing efficiency for SMEs. Through content generation techniques, AI can create multiple versions of ads, each with slight variations in text, images, or calls to action. These versions can be automatically tested through A/B testing to identify which ones work best for each customer segment. Once AI identifies the most effective ads, resources are focused on those optimized versions, maximizing results without requiring constant supervision from the marketing team.

In addition to optimizing and personalizing campaigns, AI allows for the analysis and prediction of consumer trends. By analyzing historical data and current user behavior, AI systems can identify patterns and anticipate future buying trends. This predictive capability is especially useful for SMEs, as it allows them to anticipate changes in demand and adjust their campaigns and strategies before they happen. For example, an online store can foresee an increase in demand for certain products due to seasonality or past campaigns, and AI can adjust ads and budgets to maximize the impact of campaigns during these high-demand periods.

Real-time analysis of campaigns is another significant advantage of AI-driven marketing automation. AI-based platforms can continuously monitor campaign performance across all channels and automatically adjust elements that are not working as expected. This means that if a social media ad is not generating the desired response, the AI can pause it, optimize it, or redirect the budget to more effective ads. This real-time analysis and adjustment capability minimizes resource waste and ensures that every marketing action is aligned with campaign goals at all times.

Finally, measuring results is an essential aspect of any marketing campaign, and AI facilitates this process by analyzing large volumes of data and generating detailed reports on the performance of each campaign. AI not only measures conventional KPIs (key performance indicators) such as ROI or conversion rate but also identifies patterns in the results that may go unnoticed with traditional methods. For example, AI analysis can reveal that certain types of ads perform better at a specific time of day or that certain messages generate more interactions on certain devices. These insights allow SMEs to continuously refine their marketing strategies and base decisions on accurate data.

AI-driven marketing automation offers SMEs a comprehensive solution that not only simplifies the management of complex campaigns but also enables a level of personalization and efficiency that is impossible to achieve through manual methods. By adopting these tools, companies can maximize the impact of their marketing efforts, optimize resource use, and remain competitive in an ever-evolving digital market.

10.6. Image recognition with AI for ecommerce

Image recognition with artificial intelligence has revolutionized ecommerce by opening new possibilities for product categorization and enhancing the customer experience through advanced visual searches. For SMEs operating in this field, adopting these technologies can be a significant differentiator, improving precision and efficiency in inventory management while making product searches easier for users. AI allows for the automatic analysis and categorization of large volumes of product images, eliminating the need for manual tagging. Moreover, advanced visual recognition models can help SMEs offer search features that allow customers to find products by uploading an image or photo, without needing to know the exact name of the item.

One of the most relevant applications of image recognition in ecommerce is the automatic categorization of products. With computer vision algorithms, systems can recognize specific visual features in each product image and classify them into categories accurately. This is especially useful in sectors with wide product ranges, such as fashion or accessories. For example, an online clothing store can use AI to automatically distinguish between shirts, pants, dresses, or jackets in its catalogs, reducing the time and errors associated with manual tagging. Accuracy in categorization is essential not only to improve user navigation but also to ensure that products are presented appropriately on the website and in internal search results, thus optimizing the shopping experience.

AI also facilitates the creation of automatic tags and descriptions based on visual information. Algorithms can detect details such as color, style, or material type, generating useful product tags for the end user. Thus, a customer searching for a "brown leather jacket" can find the desired product more easily, even if it is not tagged with those exact words, as the AI system visually recognizes the features and labels the product accordingly. This type of automated categorization not only reduces the time spent on inventory management but also improves product visibility in both external and internal search engines, increasing the likelihood of conversion.

Another significant advantage that image recognition with AI brings to SMEs in ecommerce is visual search. This technology allows customers to find similar products by uploading an image to the ecommerce platform. The image recognition algorithms analyze the photo and present a selection of products that resemble the item shown. Visual search is particularly appealing to customers who don't have a precise description of what they are looking for, or those interested in products of a specific style they've seen elsewhere or on social media. When implemented correctly, this functionality offers a more intuitive and personalized shopping experience, eliminating the need for textual searches and improving site usability.

Convolutional Neural Networks (CNNs) are the key underlying technology in image recognition for ecommerce. These networks are designed to mimic the functioning of the human visual system, breaking images into smaller parts and analyzing each of these fragments to detect complex visual patterns. CNNs can differentiate shapes, textures, colors, and other specific details, making them an ideal tool for product recognition and categorization. By training these networks with large amounts of labeled images, SMEs can develop highly accurate recognition models that can classify and categorize products quickly and efficiently. These models can also adapt and improve over time through continuous learning, allowing the system to stay up-to-date even when product styles evolve.

In addition to visual search, AI-powered image recognition allows for the detection of similar products based on the visual characteristics of other items in the catalog. This translates into a significant improvement in recommendation strategies, as it allows for suggesting alternative or complementary products based on their appearance. For example, a customer viewing a leather handbag can receive recommendations for other similar models or accessories that match the selected bag's style. These types of visual recommendations not only personalize the shopping experience but can also increase the average ticket by encouraging the purchase of additional products. For SMEs, this capability is particularly valuable, as the AI system identifies relationships between products that might go unnoticed using traditional recommendation methods based solely on purchase history.

Another valuable function of image recognition is the automatic determination of image quality. For an online store, the visual quality of photographs is essential as it directly affects the product's perception and the likelihood of purchase. AI models can evaluate the quality of each image uploaded to the platform, identifying common issues such as low resolution, poor lighting, or incorrect framing. This analysis allows SMEs to maintain a quality standard in their product catalog, ensuring that the images presented to customers are clear and attractive. Consistency in visual quality not only improves the overall appearance of the website but also helps build a professional and trustworthy brand image.

Image recognition systems can also assist in detecting fraud or counterfeits. In sectors like fashion, counterfeit products are a recurring problem that affects brand perception and customer satisfaction. AI can identify specific patterns and details of original products and compare them with items uploaded by sellers or suppliers. If the system detects significant discrepancies that could indicate a counterfeit, it can flag the product for further review. For SMEs operating in marketplaces or collaborating with various suppliers, this technology provides an additional layer of security, protecting their reputation and ensuring the authenticity of the products they offer to customers.

Implementing image recognition in ecommerce also contributes to the analysis of visual trends. AI allows SMEs to analyze which types of products or styles are most popular at a given time, based on user interaction data and analysis of images viewed or searched on the platform. With this information, companies can adjust their marketing strategies and product selection to align with current trends, maximizing sales opportunities. For example, if the system detects an increase in searches for clothing of a certain color or style, the SME can adjust its inventory or highlight related products on the main page to capture customer interest.

In addition, AI image recognition can be integrated into logistics and inventory control. By using cameras and computer vision systems, SMEs can monitor stock in real time and obtain precise information on the location and quantity of each product in their warehouses. This facilitates inventory control and allows for better replenishment planning. For instance, by performing a visual scan of the shelves, AI systems can alert inventory managers when a product is about to run out or when there are discrepancies between physical stock and inventory records. This level of control helps avoid overstock or stockouts, which in turn improves operational efficiency and reduces costs.

Reverse image search is another innovative application that SMEs can implement on their ecommerce platforms. This feature allows users to find similar products on other websites or social media and then search for those same products in the SME's online store, increasing conversion possibilities. For example, a customer who sees a product on social media can capture an image and search for it directly on the SME's site, removing friction from the buying process. Reverse image search turns visual inspiration into a direct purchase, capturing the customer's attention at the moment of highest interest.

The advances in deep learning have made image recognition technologies increasingly accurate and accessible for SMEs. With pre-trained models and cloud services like Google Cloud Vision, Microsoft Azure Computer Vision, and AWS Rekognition, companies can implement these functionalities without needing extensive hardware resources or specialized technical staff. These services allow SMEs to perform real-time image recognition and scale their use according to demand. Additionally, they offer customization options, enabling businesses to tailor the models to their specific needs.

Finally, image recognition also helps improve accessibility on ecommerce websites. AI can automatically generate image descriptions that make navigation easier for visually impaired users who rely on screen readers to access visual information. This functionality not only expands the potential customer base but also contributes to inclusion and corporate social responsibility by making ecommerce accessible for everyone.

10.7. Use of AI for competitor analysis

The competitive analysis with artificial intelligence is an increasingly accessible strategic tool for SMEs looking to improve their market position. Thanks to AI, it's possible to collect and analyze large amounts of data in real-time, allowing constant monitoring of competitors' activities, including their pricing strategies, promotions, and marketing tactics. Instead of relying on infrequent manual analyses, SMEs can implement AI systems that continuously monitor these factors and generate alerts or response recommendations to significant changes in competitors' tactics.

One of the most important aspects where AI can assist SMEs is in analyzing competitor prices. With web scraping tools and machine learning models, businesses can monitor the prices of specific products on their competitors' websites and automatically detect price changes. This information is especially valuable for adjusting prices in real time and ensuring that the company's products remain competitive in the market. By analyzing price change patterns in the competition, AI can also help predict discount strategies or promotions that might arise during specific periods, such as sales seasons or special events. This allows SMEs to respond quickly by implementing similar discounts or promotions and avoiding customer loss due to lack of price competitiveness.

In addition to prices, AI allows the analysis of competitors' digital marketing strategies. Specialized AI tools can monitor advertising and social media campaigns of other companies, detecting changes in ads, types of content shared, platforms used, and key messages. This analysis enables SMEs to identify which strategies are producing good results in the sector and adjust their own approach accordingly. For example, if a company notices that a competitor has launched a campaign with a new message or approach on social media, they can adjust their posts to follow that trend or differentiate from it, depending on their business objectives.

AI also enables a deep analysis of competitors' web traffic data. Using machine learning techniques and advanced web analytics tools, SMEs can estimate the amount of traffic their competitors' pages receive, as well as user dwell time, traffic sources, and visitor behavior on the website. This allows them to identify patterns in the competitors' customer acquisition and retention strategies. With this data, an SME can adjust its own website and content strategy to capture more organic traffic or improve conversion rates by emulating the successful tactics of their competitors.

Another significant advantage of using AI in competitor analysis is the ability to predict market behavior patterns. By applying machine learning algorithms to competitor data, SMEs can anticipate strategic moves such as new product launches or geographic expansions. Predictive models can be based on variables like the history of product launches, the frequency of marketing campaigns, or changes in pricing structures. This way, SMEs can prepare in advance and seize opportunities or mitigate risks arising from these moves.

Competitor reputation analysis is another important area where AI plays a crucial role. SMEs can use sentiment analysis on social media and review platforms to understand how customers perceive their competitors. This includes detecting criticism, praise, and recurring themes in consumer comments about competitors' products or services. If an SME notices that customers are dissatisfied with a particular aspect of a competitor's product, they can exploit this weakness and stand out with a campaign that addresses precisely that point. On the other hand, if there are features highly valued by customers in competitors' products, the company can consider integrating or improving these features in its own offering.

Automating the analysis of news and trends about the competition is another relevant aspect. AI can constantly monitor news sites, industry blogs, and social media to identify any mentions of competitors or detect trending topics that may impact the market. Using natural language processing (NLP), AI can classify and analyze large volumes of text, summarizing the most important mentions and detecting key events that may require a quick response. For example, if a competing company announces a strategic alliance or a new investment, AI can alert the SME, allowing them to use this information to adjust their strategy and strengthen their competitiveness.

Tracking competitors' products in ecommerce is another interesting application for AI. Through automated tracking systems, SMEs can monitor the inventory and availability of their competitors' products on various sales platforms. This is useful for anticipating competitors' moves during high-demand seasons. If the system detects that a competitor has run out of stock on a popular product, the SME could increase the visibility of that same product on their platform, taking advantage of the lack of availability in the market to attract those consumers.

AI tools can also help SMEs understand and anticipate competitors' promotional campaigns. By analyzing competitors' behavior during holidays, seasonal sales, and other special events, AI can predict when competitors are most likely to launch offers and how they performed in previous campaigns. This allows the SME to plan its promotion schedule and align with industry trends, even boosting offers when competitors are less active. This facilitates strategic planning that maximizes the impact of marketing and sales campaigns.

Keyword analysis and competitor SEO is another area where AI offers advantages. SEO analysis tools can identify the most used keywords by competitors and analyze how they are positioned in search results. AI helps interpret this data and propose adjustments in keywords, content, or link-building strategies for the SME to improve its ranking in relevant searches. This is essential for capturing web traffic organically and optimizing SEO investment.

SMEs can also benefit from analyzing competitors' points of sale and distribution channels using AI. By studying where and how competitors are distributing their products, an SME can identify opportunities to diversify its channels or strengthen those that are performing best. AI allows companies to collect and analyze data from multiple sources, such as sales reports, social media mentions, or inventory analysis, to better understand the competition's distribution strategy and respond proactively.

In competitive analysis, speed and accuracy are two critical factors, and this is where AI truly shows its value. Instead of conducting sporadic and manually updated reports, AI enables a constant flow of data and real-time analysis, giving SMEs the agility needed to quickly adapt to market changes. The responsiveness offered by AI is especially valuable in dynamic and highly competitive sectors, where the ability to react quickly can make the difference between gaining or losing market share.

For SMEs, adapting these AI tools to their needs and budget is a key aspect. AI technology has been democratized in recent years, with platforms and tools offering accessible and scalable solutions, allowing small businesses to access advanced competitive analysis capabilities without incurring large investments. Additionally, many of these tools offer flexible subscription plans or pay-as-you-go options, enabling SMEs to adjust their costs based on their needs and resources.

The use of AI for competitor analysis also makes it easier to identify competitive advantages. Algorithms can detect areas where the SME excels compared to the competition, which can be used to develop marketing campaigns that highlight these strengths. For example, if an SME offers better delivery times than its competitors, this advantage can be emphasized in its communication strategy, maximizing the positive perception among its customers.

To implement AI in competitive analysis effectively, it is essential for the SME to have clarity about the objectives of its competitive monitoring and the type of data it wants to collect and analyze. This allows the company to choose the right tools and train AI models according to the specific priorities of the business. A well-defined strategy in competitive analysis helps avoid collecting irrelevant data and focuses resources on the insights that have a real impact on decision-making.

Lastly, AI enables cross-competitive analysis by combining information from various sources, providing a more comprehensive view of the competitive landscape.

Epilogue

At this point, we have walked together through a journey that highlights the power of data in politics. I have shared with you tools, methods, and strategies that can revolutionize the way you make decisions, from process automation to the ability to anticipate problems before they arise. But there's something I want to make very clear: the tools, by themselves, are not everything. They are just that, tools. Without the right human touch, without the correct interpretation, and without the experience to back them up, they will not make a difference.

In the book, almost always in a theoretical way, I've been showing you the things that could be done, and I assure you that the possibilities are much broader. Developing each of the initiatives mentioned in these pages would probably have required a book for each one. So don't hesitate to call me or ask about any topic that caught your attention. I'll be happy to talk with you. There's so much that can be done, and this book is just the beginning.

If there's one thing I've learned in my career, it's that while data science and artificial intelligence are changing the rules of the game, the value of people remains irreplaceable. You can have access to the most advanced algorithms, you can automate every aspect of your management, but in the end, it's you or your team who must make the decisions. And that's where the real value comes in: those who know how to handle these tools and, above all, how to interpret the data so that they truly tell a story. Because data without interpretation is just numbers, cold and impersonal. It's the person behind them who gives them meaning, who connects them with reality and human needs.

And this is where I want to pause. While I've shown you how you can start working with data on your own, I'm aware that time is a limited resource, especially in the political world. If you don't have the time to train or delve into these topics, you can always rely on an expert. But not just any expert: someone who knows the world of politics, who understands its nuances, its timing, its urgencies. It's not just about knowing data, but knowing how to communicate that data, how to turn it into messages that truly reach citizens, and how to devise effective strategies.

I'm telling you clearly: surrounding yourself with people who master both data and the political environment will be your competitive advantage. It's very easy to fall into the temptation of hiring theorists who, although brilliant in their field, are unaware of the complexities of daily political life. Don't underestimate the importance of working with people who understand how offices work, how public opinion shifts, and what a politician needs to survive in an often hostile environment. The leap you'll make will be incredible if you have a team that knows how to balance data and political strategy effectively.

And I'll tell you something else: you have no excuses. Either you start working, training, and developing what you've learned in this book, or you send me an email or call me, and together we'll start planning your victory in the next elections. Because, in the end, it all comes down to this: Are you willing to take the step? If you wait for others to do it for you, if you let time pass without seizing the opportunity you have in your hands today, you'll be the one left behind.

This book has aimed to show you that, although technological tools are impressive, the real value lies in people. People who know how to interpret that data, who can translate it into concrete decisions, and who have the ability to lead with intelligence in an environment where knowledge and experience still matter. Training and knowledge are not abstract concepts. They are what will set you apart, what will allow you to make a difference compared to others who see data as just a passing trend or another accessory.

If I've learned anything, it's that politics is an art. An art that combines the tangible, like data and technology, with the intangible, like leadership ability, empathy, and strategic vision. We cannot think that technology, no matter how advanced, will replace these human factors. On the contrary, the key is knowing how to integrate them. Politics will remain, at its core, a human domain. And the politicians who know how to unite these two dimensions— technology and humanity—will be the ones who lead the change in the coming years.

So, once again, I ask you: Are you ready to take that step? Data is the future of politics, but its power will depend on the hands that manage it. You have the key to lead that change. Don't wait for others to do it for you. Take control, form your team, learn or let them help you, but don't get left behind. The future is waiting for you, and data will be your best ally if you know how to use it wisely.

ABOUT ME

I'm Rubén Maestre, and I like technology, artificial intelligence, and data science—areas I've been interested in and developing for some time now. I can say that I have training in Python, data science and analysis, communication, and digital marketing. I also hold an MBA in Sport Management, focusing on sports club management and event organization.

I have worked for years developing this knowledge across a wide range of sectors, almost always with the aim of helping SMEs and freelancers achieve their goals, whether in communication, digital marketing, and lately, optimizing their processes, improving efficiency, and making better decisions to achieve them. And I also have some time to do personal projects of all kinds, trying to step out of my comfort zone and continue discovering new ideas, technologies, or tools.

I started, so to speak, in the world of sports, in sports management both in the office and on the field, where I undoubtedly learned key skills such as teamwork, project leadership, and people management, as well as the effort and sacrifice needed to achieve set goals. These have helped me a lot in the next steps I took toward the working world, especially in SMEs and freelancers, helping companies in various sectors grow and overcome challenges, which have been many, I assure you.

Lately, I've been involved in data science projects, business development, and AI training for major organizations, like ITERH (Technological Institute of Energy and Water Resources), an exciting project where I have the CEO's trust to develop advanced tools in data analysis, visualizations, and predictive models to create products and analyses at ITERH, while also exploring LLM models that I'm very excited about. Additionally, my extensive experience in digital marketing and communication has allowed me to create many strategies to support and boost sales, improving ROI for SMEs and freelancers. That's why this book on data is very focused on SMEs and freelancers, with special attention to sales.

In addition to my business experience, as I mentioned earlier, I always find time for personal projects. I have that Mediterranean entrepreneurial mindset that honestly gives me more headaches than joy, but that's how we are in Elche. I have projects underway like PcFutsal.es, a futsal manager, and Coast to Coast, an interactive experience based on a trip I took across the United States, with the idea of innovating and exploring new ideas outside traditional frameworks. I also have my own fashion brand, #SUPERCLAW, where I experiment with marketing strategies and business management.

I could tell you much more about a thousand battles, but I understand this book is about data and technology, and you'll want to know more about things in that field. Well, for example, I've worked on a project analyzing large volumes of data with the U.S. airport punctuality project or an NBA analysis, both using Streamlit to create interactive interfaces. I also have a huge database with Spanish football data. All of this has helped me gain new knowledge and develop skills in different industries, from sports to artificial intelligence.

And now, in the present... I'm back to being self-employed in Spain. They say that man is the only creature that trips over the same stone twice, and I think this will be the 4th or 5th time... The idea is to help SMEs and freelancers access data science and analytics, promoting these technologies to improve efficiency in their businesses. My vision is clear: to bring technology closer to those who think it's out of reach, making it accessible, understandable, and above all, useful for small businesses. So if you have any questions, contact me. I'm sure I can help, and as I say, you'll come for the price and stay for the service.

From a young age, politics has always been a world that interested me. I've participated in different associative projects, both at university and in other areas of my life, and eventually, I ended up joining one political party and then another. I believe that in Spain, we lack political culture, more people willing to get involved, and a civil society that works to attract the best towards politics and public management. I've always thought we need more people who want to contribute their experience and fewer who are solely driven by personal interests. We need more people who understand what politics is and what it can do for citizens, and fewer fanatics or radicals from political parties or those interested in enriching themselves through politics. Maybe I'm a dreamer, but if this book can help generate that change, if it encourages someone else to get involved and work towards a more honest and efficient politics, then it will have been something great.

In addition to all this, and just in case you're looking for me out there, I've worked in various media outlets, writing articles, directing radio programs like 'Crucemos el Rubicón' on Radio Intereconomía. I've managed media outlets and created content on platforms like YouTube or Podcasts. This has taught me the importance of proper communication and improved my ability to convey information appropriately through the right channels.

With this unique blend of experience in data science, artificial intelligence, communication, and digital marketing, not to mention my training and many years in sports, I continue to seek new challenges, always with the goal of helping companies reach their full potential through the use of technology and data analysis. I invite you to connect, whether through social media, email (data@rubenmaestre.com), or my website: www.rubenmaestre.com, or any other means. It doesn't have to be for me to sell you anything. We can chat with no obligation, see synergies, collaborate on projects, embark on an adventure... really, talk to me. I'll be waiting. And well, thank you very much for purchasing this book. I hope it has been useful to you. And hopefully, it won't be the last one...

www.ingramcontent.com/pod-product-compliance
Lightning Source LLC
LaVergne TN
LVHW022332060326
832902LV00022B/3990

END